HOUSEHOLD INVENTORIES OF
HELMINGHAM HALL
1597–1741

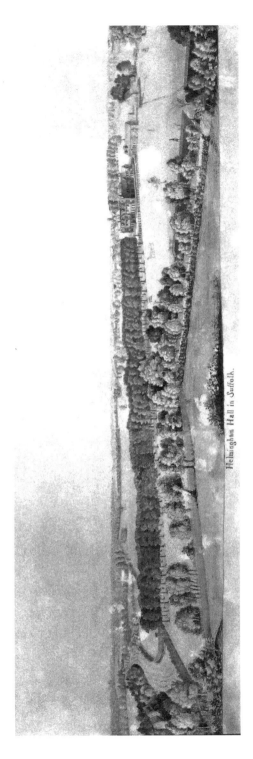

Helmingham **Hall** in Suffolk.

Helmingham Hall from the south-east. Unattributed and undated, but estimated to be between 1741 and 1783. The 1741 inventory refers to only one 'lay pond' whereas two are visible in the foreground and on Joseph Hodskinson's map of 1783 (SRS, 15 (1972), sheet VIII). See Plate 17 for an enlarged detail of the house and outbuildings. At Helmingham Hall, reproduced by kind permission of the Lord Tollemache

HOUSEHOLD INVENTORIES
OF HELMINGHAM HALL
1597–1741

Edited by
MOIRA COLEMAN

General Editor
VICTOR GRAY

The Boydell Press

Suffolk Records Society
VOLUME LXI

A Suffolk Records Society publication
First published 2018
The Boydell Press, Woodbridge

ISBN   978-1-78327-274-7

Issued to subscribing members for the year 2017–2018

The Boydell Press is an imprint of Boydell & Brewer Ltd
PO Box 9, Woodbridge, Suffolk IP12 3DF, UK
and of Boydell & Brewer Inc.
668 Mt Hope Avenue, Rochester, NY 14620–2731, USA
website: www.boydellandbrewer.com

The publisher has no responsibility for the continued existence or accuracy of
URLs for external or third-party internet websites referred to in this book, and
does not guarantee that any content on such websites is, or will remain, accurate
or appropriate

A catalogue record for this book is available
from the British Library

This publication is printed on acid-free paper
Printed and bound in Great Britain by TJ International Ltd, Padstow

CONTENTS

List of illustrations   viii

Foreword   x

Acknowledgements   xi

Abbreviations   xii

Introduction   xv

Editorial methods   xxxvii

THE HOUSEHOLD INVENTORIES OF HELMINGHAM HALL

     29 September 1597   3

     October 1626   45

     January 1707/08 [1708]   110

     22 October 1741   132

Appendix A: The development of Helmingham Hall, 1597–1741   153

Appendix B: The Tollemache family at Fakenham Magna,
     c. 1622–1665   190

Glossary and index of household goods   214

Bibliography   330

Index of people and places   337

The Suffolk Records Society   343

ILLUSTRATIONS

Colour plates between pages 122 and 123
I   Catherine Tollemache, wife of Lionel Tollemache, later 1st baronet
II   Sir Lionel Tollemache, 2nd baronet
III   Four young ladies: the first four children of Sir Lionel Tollemache, 2nd baronet
IV   Lionel Tollemache, 4th baronet and 3rd Earl of Dysart
V   Lionel Tollemache, 5th baronet and 4th Earl of Dysart
VI   Detail of 1729 survey of the Helmingham Estate by Richard Tollemache

Genealogical Table   *page* xiv

Black-and-white illustrations
Frontispiece: Helmingham Hall from the south-east. Unattributed and undated, but estimated to be between 1741 and 1783

Plates
1   Letter from Thomas Brereton to the Earl of Dysart, 22 December 1720, incorporating a sketch-plan of Helmingham Hall   xxxi
2   Detail from the 1597 household inventory of Helmingham Hall   4
3   Detail from the 1626 household inventory of Helmingham Hall   90
4   Detail from the 1708 household inventory of Helmingham Hall   129
5   Detail from the opening of the 1741 household inventory of Helmingham Hall   133
6   Helmingham Hall, south elevation   154
7   Helmingham Hall, north elevation   154
8   Helmingham Hall, west elevation   155
9   Helmingham Hall, east elevation   155
10   Ground floor plan of Helmingham Hall by J.C. Dennish of Ipswich, 1950s   156
11   The courtyard of Helmingham Hall, looking north   157
12   Speculative ground floor layout of Helmingham Hall in 1597   158
13   Access points and external features of Helmingham Hall identified in the 1626 inventory   159
14   Detail from the 1729 survey of the Helmingham estate by Richard Tollemache   160
15   Speculative ground floor layout of Helmingham Hall in 1708   161
16   Speculative ground floor layout of Helmingham Hall in 1741   162
17   Speculative guide and key to the 1741 layout of Helmingham Hall, viewed from south-east   163
18   Comparison of the 1720 sketch by Thomas Brereton with the 1950s plan by J.C. Dennish   187
19   'Lugdons', Fakenham Magna, site plan, 1622   192

20 'Lugdons', Fakenham Magna, detail of the house from the plan of
    1622   193
21 Site plan of 'Lands of Calabors, of late Ballards', Fakenham Magna,
    1622   195
22 Sketch of the Catherine wheel swan-mark appended to an agreement
    of 9 April 1634   202

The editor and publishers are grateful to all the institutions and persons listed for permission to reproduce the materials in which they hold copyright. Every effort has been made to trace the copyright holders; apologies are offered for any omission, and the publishers will be pleased to add any necessary acknowledgement in subsequent editions.

FOREWORD

It never ceases to amaze me that Helmingham Hall has stood virtually unchanged since the Tollemache family moved here in 1480, and completed their new home in 1510 – the year Henry VIII came to the throne. It began as a Tudor moated home, and with a number of changes over the centuries it continues to be just that today. We still pull up the drawbridge every night and lower it each morning.

It has taken an immense amount of time and hard work to piece together the details of not just one, but four inventories covering the history of Helmingham Hall over a period of 150 years from 1597 to 1741 and five generations of the Tollemache family. To read the Introduction is by itself a fascinating and illuminating history of the family, of the problems with which each generation had to contend, and how and when they lived their everyday lives.

As a result, with the able assistance of retired county archivist Victor Gray, now honorary archivist at Helmingham, Moira Coleman has produced a fascinating study of what the succeeding generations of the family had in their rooms and how they used them. She has in many ways brought them back to life. For some reason, between 1622 and 1665, two generations of Sir Lyonel Tollemache and their wives moved out of Helmingham to a more modest home called Lugdons in Fakenham Magna between Woolpit and Euston.

We may never know the reasons for this move – perhaps it was ill health, perhaps their wives thought Helmingham Hall was too cold, perhaps rebuilding was in progress. Indeed the story of Fakenham Magna has always been a mystery to the present day family and it is with grateful thanks to Moira Coleman that we now know so much more about this period before the family returned to Helmingham. It is my hope that the work by Moira Coleman shown in the following pages will help future generations, not only of the family, but also future archivists and historians, through the detail and light shed on this story of long ago.

The Lord Tollemache
Helmingham

ACKNOWLEDGEMENTS

A debt of gratitude is due foremost and principally to the Lord Tollemache for permitting access to his home and the Tollemache family archive at Helmingham Hall over many years and with unfailing encouragement and enthusiasm. I am indebted also to Victor Gray not only for his professional expertise as Lord Tollemache's honorary archivist at Helmingham Hall but also for his patience and support extended in the role of general editor of this volume. Notable discoveries were made and shared generously by him as a result of his own research, particularly relating to the life of the 4th Earl of Dysart, and are acknowledged individually throughout this volume. I am grateful to Sir Lyonel Tollemache for allowing publication of material transcribed from Tollemache family papers held in the Buckminster Park Archive. The late Dr John Blatchly, MBE, was a generous scholar, ever willing to respond and correspond about Helmingham Hall, its contents and its people, and did so over many years. The help of academics, archivists and curators was sought, and their time has been given generously, particularly in answering the many queries that arose during compilation of the glossary and index of household goods, and particular thanks are due to Peter Brears, Clare Browne, Bethan Holdridge, Nick Humphrey, Simon Swynfen Jervis, Dr Charles Kightly, Sarah Medlam, Susan P. Mee and Maria Singer. In Suffolk, much support was given by Stephen Podd, who drew often and willingly on his detailed knowledge of Helmingham and its environs, sharing queries with other historians, including Edward Martin, and widening the pool of knowledge and enthusiasm for Helmingham that has contributed to this volume. Thanks are due also to staff at the Suffolk Record Offices in Bury St Edmunds and Ipswich, to contributors to the finished illustrations, Mike Durrant and Peter Farmer, and to the National Trust for permission to reproduce portraits held in their collections at Ham House. Responsibility for errors and omissions, whether inadvertently in these acknowledgements or elsewhere in this volume, rests with me.

Moira Coleman
April 2017

ABBREVIATIONS

BPA	Tollemache family papers in the Buckminster Park Archive
Coleman	Coleman, Moira, *Fruitful Endeavours: the 16th-century household secrets of Catherine Tollemache at Helmingham Hall* (Andover, 2012)
Edwards	Edwards, R. (ed.), *The Dictionary of English Furniture*, revised edition, 3 volumes (Woodbridge, 1986)
Halliwell	Halliwell, J.O., *Dictionary of Archaisms and Provincialisms*, 2 volumes (London, 1872)
Ham House	Rowell C. (ed.), *Ham House: 400 years of collecting and patronage* (Yale, 2013)
Helmingham Archive	Archives of the Tollemache family at Helmingham
Kerridge	Kerridge, E., *Textile Manufactures in Early Modern England* (Manchester, 1985)
Lawson	Lawson, Jane A., *The Elizabethan New Year's Gift Exchanges 1559–1603* (Oxford, 2013)
NRO	Norfolk Record Office, Norwich
ODNB	*Oxford Dictionary of National Biography* Online
OED	*Oxford English Dictionary* Online
Oswald	Oswald, A., 'Helmingham Hall, Suffolk' Parts 1–5, *Country Life* 9 August–4 October 1956
PSIA(H)	*Proceedings of the Suffolk Institute of Archaeology (and History)*
Smythe	George Smythe's household accounts for Lionel Tollemache, 1587–9 (SRO(I), HD 1538/253/165)
SRO(B)	Suffolk Record Office, Bury St Edmunds
SRO(I)	Suffolk Record Office, Ipswich
SRS	Suffolk Records Society
Suffolk probate index (Ipswich)	Grimwade, M.E. (compiler), Serjeant, W.R. and R.K. (eds), *Index of the Probate Records of the Court of the Archdeacon of Suffolk 1444–1700*, Volume I (1979) and Volume II (1980), The British Record Society
Suffolk probate index (Sudbury)	Grimwade, M.E. (compiler), Serjeant, W.R. and R.K. (eds), *Index of the Probate Records of the Court of the Archdeacon of Sudbury, 1354–1700*, 2 volumes, The British Record Society, 1984
TNA	The National Archives, Kew
Tollemache 1949	Tollemache, E.D.H., *The Tollemaches of Helmingham and Ham* (Ipswich, 1949)
Yaxley	Yaxley, D., *A Researcher's Glossary: of words found in historical documents of East Anglia* (Dereham, 2003)

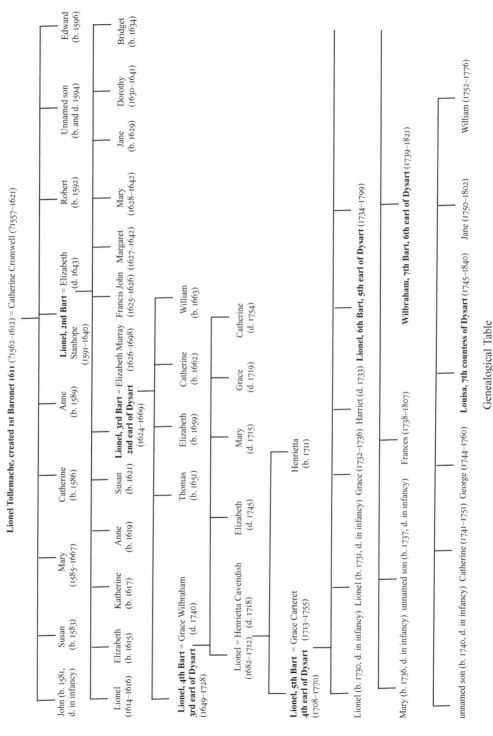

Lionel Tollemache, created 1st Baronet 1611 (?1562–1612) = Catherine Cromwell (?1557–1621)

John (b. 1581, d. in infancy) | Susan (b. 1583) | Mary (1585–1667) | Catherine (b. 1586) | Anne (b. 1589) | **Lionel, 2nd Bart** = Elizabeth Stanhope (1591–1640) | Robert (b. 1592) | Unnamed son (b. and d. 1594) | Edward (b. 1596)

Lionel (1614–1616) | Elizabeth (b. 1615) | Katherine (b. 1617) | Anne (b. 1619) | Susan (b. 1621) | **Lionel, 3rd Bart** = Elizabeth Murray **2nd earl of Dysart** (1626–1698) (1624–1669) | Francis John (1625–1626) (1627–1642) | Margaret (1627–1642) | Mary (1628–1642) | Jane (b. 1629) | Dorothy (1630–1641) | Bridget (b. 1634)

Thomas (b. 1651) | Elizabeth (b. 1659) | Catherine (b. 1662) | William (b. 1663)

Elizabeth (d. 1745) | Mary (d. 1715) | Grace (d. 1719) | Catherine (d. 1754)

Lionel, 4th Bart = Grace Wilbraham **3rd earl of Dysart** (d. 1740) (1649–1728)

Lionel = Henrietta Cavendish (1682–1712) (d. 1718)

Henrietta (b. 1711)

Lionel, 5th Bart = Grace Carteret **4th earl of Dysart** (1713–1755) (1708–1770)

Lionel (b. 1730, d. in infancy) | Lionel (b. 1731, d. in infancy) | Grace (1732–1736) | Harriet (d. 1733) | **Lionel, 6th Bart, 5th earl of Dysart** (1734–1799)

Mary (b. 1736, d. in infancy) | unnamed son (b. 1737, d. in infancy) | Frances (1738–1807) | **Wilbraham, 7th Bart, 6th earl of Dysart** (1739–1821)

unnamed son (b. 1740, d. in infancy) | Catherine (1741–1751) | George (1744–1760) | **Louisa, 7th countess of Dysart** (1745–1840) | Jane (1750–1802) | William (1752–1776)

Genealogical Table

INTRODUCTION

The transition of sixteenth-century Helmingham Hall, and the elevation of its family from the status of gentry to earls within the span of 150 years, is the context for transcription of this sequence of Helmingham's four household inventories dated 1597, 1626, 1708 and 1741. The documents remain in the house, which is the private residence of the Lord Tollemache, Timothy, 5th Baron Tollemache, KCVO, and reflect the family's elevation between 1612 and 1655 from gentlemen to baronets and baronets to earls. The inventories begin when Helmingham Hall was the sole seat of Lionel Tollemache Esq., created 1st baronet in 1611.[1] By 1741, it was one of several seats at the disposal of Sir Lionel's ancestors, by now Earls of Dysart. The conjunction of a Suffolk house more than five centuries old, occupied by a noble descendant of its founding family and home to its archives is notable enough; but the survival of a sequence of four household inventories is uncommon by any standards, adding value to the record and to its merit for publication by Suffolk Records Society.

The Tollemache family, their archives and principal properties, 1597–1741

The Tollemache family archive at Helmingham Hall includes a bound volume containing two household inventories.[2] The first is dated 29 September 1597; but the second is recorded only as October 1626, with a sizeable space left between the month and the year for a date that was never recorded.[3] The volume measures 29.5 cm x 20 cm and is bound in vellum. Inscriptions on the front and rear covers are too faint to be legible. Both inventories are recorded on paper which varies in quality and thickness and is in fair condition overall. All 164 pages are numbered faintly in pencil in a later hand. The 1597 inventory comprises the first 105 pages, incorporating numerous annotations, some of them dated, extending the record to 1609. Annotations include periodic summaries of linen and plate as well as comments on condition or amendments to descriptions of items. Few entries are illegible, but fading of the ink is more pronounced on some folios than others. Most pages are inscribed on *recto* sides only, but annotations are added on *verso* sides. In some instances, the imprint of *verso* additions is clearly visible on *recto* sides. The 1626 inventory comprises the remaining fifty-nine pages of the bound volume.[4] More pages are inscribed on both sides than in the earlier inventory, the writing is crowded on each page and overall there are many deletions, insertions, comments and emendations, some of which are dated, extending the record to 1633. Generally, there is less evidence of fading in the 1626 inventory than in the 1597 one. Partial transcriptions of these two inventories were made in the nineteenth century; these

---

1 The circumstances of Sir Lionel's elevation are discussed later in this section.
2 Helmingham Archive, T/Hel/9/1/1.
3 Reasons are suggested in Appendix A, where the complex route taken by the compiler of the 1626 inventory is followed and examined.
4 T/Hel/9/1/1.

were copied verbatim and published in the twentieth century.[5] This Suffolk Records Society volume offers the first complete transcription of the originals of both.

In 1597, when the first of these inventories was compiled, Helmingham Hall was occupied by Lionel Tollemache, gentleman, JP and sheriff of Suffolk under Elizabeth I.[6] Anecdotal comments and discrete lists of linen and plate were added, some of them in Lionel's own hand, between 1604 and 1609. In 1612 he was elevated to a baronetcy by James I, but died within the year.[7] In the same year, his heir, Sir Lionel, 2nd baronet, married Elizabeth Stanhope, daughter of John, 1st Baron Stanhope of Harrington (Northamptonshire).[8] The Stanhope family lived in London and it is clear from anecdotal comments in the 1626 inventory that Sir Lionel and Lady Elizabeth Tollemache also maintained a London house.[9] A decade later, in 1622, Sir Lionel, whose hand and personal comments proliferate in the extensive 1626 inventory, acquired a second Suffolk property known as 'Lugdons', at Fakenham Magna,[10] some four miles south-east of Thetford and eight miles north-east of Bury St Edmunds. The 1626 inventory incorporates details of the numerous items removed from Helmingham to Fakenham Magna between 1626 and 1633. For this reason and because Fakenham Magna was home to two generations of the family, Appendix B introduces additional records with a focus on the family's forty-year commitment to their home in this west Suffolk parish between 1622 and 1665.

The second baronet died in 1640 and the title passed to his son, also Lionel. With the marriage in 1648 of Sir Lionel, 3rd baronet, to Elizabeth Murray came Ham House, Richmond (Surrey).[11] Elizabeth's father, Sir William Murray, 1st Earl of Dysart, was a staunch royalist, and by the time of his daughter's marriage he was living in exile, first in France and then in Antwerp, where he died in 1655.[12] His title passed to his daughter; and when Elizabeth became Countess of Dysart in her own right, her husband, Sir Lionel Tollemache, 3rd baronet, adopted the title of 2nd Earl of Dysart.[13] In 1655 a household inventory of the contents of Ham House was compiled for the 2nd Earl, providing a record of the family's possessions during the interregnum, a period during which there is no surviving inventory for Helmingham

5   The Helmingham Archive contains handwritten transcriptions of parts of the first fifteen pages of the 1597 and the first eight pages of the 1626 household inventories, both dated to 1912 and attributed to Mary, Lady Tollemache (T/Hel/9/1/2 and 9/1/3 respectively). Both were acknowledged when reproduced by Nicolas Barker in *Two East Anglian Picture Books* for the Roxburghe Club in 1988. In 2012 selected extracts were transcribed from the original 1597 inventory and reproduced in Coleman, *Fruitful Endeavours*, pp. 93–100.

6   SRO(I) HD 1538/253/151, Letters Patent of Queen Elizabeth I, appointing Lionel Tollemache as sheriff of Suffolk, 16 November 1592. He served in the role again in 1609, in the time of James I (see footnote 58 below).

7   SRO(I) FB46/D1/I, Helmingham parish register.

8   The marriage was recorded on 16 December 1612: City of Westminster Archives Centre, St Martin-in-the-Fields parish register, 19 January 1551–31 October 1619.

9   See 1626 Transcription: 26.536, 26.1200.

10 1622 is the date of the earliest record of Lugdons in the Helmingham Archive, T/Hel/24/6, a collection of documents discussed in Appendix B.

11 Ham House was retained by the Tollemache family until 1949, when it passed into the care of the National Trust.

12 Tollemache, 1949.

13 William Murray died during the interregnum and although Elizabeth Murray succeeded to his title in 1655, she sought, and was granted, a new patent of nobility in 1670, confirming the patent of 3 August 1643 by which her late father had been created 1st Earl of Dysart and Lord Huntingtower (Tollemache, 1949).

Hall.[14] The evidence offered in Appendix B suggests that the family spent less time at Helmingham during this period, favouring occupation of Fakenham Magna and Ham House.[15] The 2nd earl died in 1669, four years after the family relinquished their Fakenham Magna property.[16] Some time after 1675, his heir, 4th baronet and 3rd Earl of Dysart, purchased the Northamptonshire property Harrington from the Stanhopes following the death without issue of Charles, 2nd Baron Stanhope.[17]

The impact of the earldom upon the contents and arrangement of Helmingham Hall is evident from the two eighteenth-century household inventories in the Helmingham Archive. Sir Lionel Tollemache, 4th baronet and 3rd Earl of Dysart, compiled the record dated January 1708.[18] The stitched but unbound document (titled on the reverse) comprises twelve folios, written closely on both sides of the paper and legible bar minor instances of bleeding of the ink and damage to unprotected upper and lower edges of some pages. Folio numbers are not inscribed but have been inserted as editorial descriptions in the transcription. The 3rd earl died in 1727 but because his son had predeceased him, his titles and properties at Helmingham, Ham, Harrington (Northamptonshire), London,[19] and Woodhey (Cheshire) passed to his grandson, Lionel, Lord Huntingtower.[20] Woodhey had come to the family through inheritance by the 3rd earl's wife, Grace, née Wilbraham.[21]

The 3rd earl's grandson, Sir Lionel, 5th baronet and 4th Earl of Dysart, was responsible for the inventory of 22 October 1741.[22] This is the grandest of the sequence, recorded in a red morocco-bound ledger with a gilt-ruled border and centrally placed coronet above the letter T on the front cover, and with marbled end papers. The volume cover, which measures 31 cm x 19.5 cm, has ensured that the thirteen white paper pages are undamaged. The record, which opens with a title page, is inscribed throughout on *recto* sides. The cursive hand is clear and legible, and the record concludes with 'Finis'. Folio numbers are not inscribed but have been inserted as editorial descriptions in the transcription.

The 1708 and 1741 inventories make it possible to see how far the interior décor and contents of Helmingham had changed since 1626 in the hands of successive

---

14 Described by the National Trust as 'c. 1655' (*Ham House*, p. 434), this household inventory is the earliest that survives for Ham House, which suggests that Sir Lionel Tollemache, 3rd baronet, instigated at Ham the pattern of recording household goods already well established in his Helmingham household. The 1655 household inventory listed the contents of the house immediately following the death of his wife's father.

15 Elizabeth, Countess of Dysart, remarried within months of her husband's death, becoming the second wife of John Maitland, then Earl but later Duke of Lauderdale. The Lauderdales invested heavily in the remodelling and interior embellishment of Ham House until the Duke's death in 1682. Their collections are the principal subject of the National Trust's publication, *Ham House* (2013). That volume includes also transcriptions of seven household inventories for Ham House dating from 1655 to 1844, two of which were compiled by the Tollemache family, the 2nd Earl of Dysart in 1655 and the 3rd earl in 1728.

16 The evidence for this date is discussed in the conclusion to Appendix B.

17 In 1745, the 4th earl had Harrington Hall demolished.

18 T/Hel(S)/9/1/5.

19 In 1720 the property was described as 'the Corner-House out of Marlborough-St. into Poland-St., London'; see footnote 90 below.

20 The affairs of the 4th earl, and in particular how they were affected by the demise of his father, Lord Huntingtower, are discussed later in this introduction.

21 The Woodhey house was demolished by the 5th Earl of Dysart (6th baronet); Peckforton Castle was built on the estate between 1844 and 1852 by John, 1st Baron Tollemache (Tollemache, 1949, pp. 115; 164).

22 T/Hel(S)/9/1/1.

earls of Dysart. In both inventories, the contents of the hall reflect its new role as a rural ancestral seat, coloured by a growing taste for antiquarianism. An appetite for art, quickened by visits to Europe, is evident in the display of portraits, prints, perspective views of European cities and the heads of their past rulers and leaders. Contemporary taste for social commentary emerges, too, with a collection of Hogarth prints. At a more basic level, by 1741 washing the laundry is no longer a task undertaken at the hall, only the less demanding tasks involved in its finishing and storage.[23]

The four inventories provide a domestic context for the changes that influenced the Tollemache family's life in this 150-year period and offer a rich resource for social and domestic historians. From an editorial point of view, this richness warranted emphasis and to be made as accessible as a non-digital resource could reasonably allow. As a result, each element of a detailed description is captured by cross-referencing in the combined glossary and index of household goods. Every transcription entry is given a number prefaced by a date code related to the inventory: 97 for 1597, 26 for 1626, 08 for 1708 and 41 for 1741. In the glossary each numerical reference enables pinpoint retrieval of the item in its transcription. As a result, each sequence of dates shows at a glance when a household item fell out of use, came into use or, alternatively, when their names came to mean something entirely different.[24] Extensive cross-referencing ensures that particularly rich descriptions, such as that of a pair of mouse-dun velvet hangers, embroidered with silver, are acknowledged and readily discoverable.[25] The four inventories offered also an opportunity to identify changes to the building, and the evidence is presented in Appendix A, supported by plans and illustrations. Commentary throughout the 1626 inventory justified a closer look at the family's forty years in their second Suffolk home at Fakenham Magna, which is the subject of Appendix B. Beyond all of this, the documents have added significance because household inventories are rare in comparison with probate inventories; and not least because Helmingham has four of them.

Household inventories, probate inventories and hybrids

Beyond their individual and cumulative historical value outlined above, each of the Helmingham Hall quartet raises fundamental questions. Generally, do they confirm what distinguishes a household inventory from a probate inventory? Specifically,

---

[23] Later evidence records a payment of 'Goody Curtice's bill for washing our linnen at Helmingham from Christmas to the 20th January', amounting to 19s. 6d., paid on 22 January 1750 (BPA Volume 932).

[24] The inspiration for this method comes from the work of Jane A. Lawson in *The Elizabethan New Year's Gift Exchanges* (2013). Lawson's cross-referencing system enables her reader to search for and find every attribute of the gifts given and received by Elizabeth I. Gifts are indexed not only by the name of each item, but by its material, colour, design, maker and donor. As a result, searching the book offers the reader all the benefits and richness of the printed page combined with the efficient tools of a digital word search. It was solely as a result of Lawson's cross-referencing that invaluable information was gleaned regarding the silver gifts attributed to Queen Elizabeth I recorded in the 1597 Helmingham household inventory, whose likely provenance is discussed in footnotes 91–92 to the 1597 Transcription.

[25] In this case, as well as appearing alphabetically under 'h' for hangers, which are defined, each attribute of 26.874 is indexed under *colours*, *embroidery* and *textiles* respectively.

how does each define the 'household'? Finally, a question that should be asked of any household inventory, why was each compiled, and why now?

Many thousands of inventories have been transcribed and published. A catalogue and bibliography, which does not distinguish between household and probate sources, was compiled by Simon Swynfen Jervis for the Furniture History Society in 2010.[26] The volume lists 12,316 published inventories dating from 1078 to 1864. In 2012, a supplementary list notes a further 442 records.[27] Since then, new research, including this volume, has undoubtedly increased that combined total of 12,758. A recent example is the 'Inventory of the contents of Coldham Hall, 1737', transcribed in Suffolk Records Society's Volume LIX (2016).[28] The Coldham Hall record, ostensibly a household inventory, is atypical because its compiler, the widowed Elizabeth Rookwood, assigns monetary values to her possessions. Values are something rarely seen in a household inventory except by way of a discrete addendum relating to a work of art, for example, as is the case at Ham House in 1683.[29] Some of Elizabeth Rookwood's valuations were based on what she had paid for items, confirming that she maintained her expenditure records assiduously, a discipline that is recognisable in the eighteenth-century archives of the Tollemache family as later extracts will show, although this did not extend to recording values in their household inventories.

The distinction between household and probate inventories is clear: the primary purpose of a probate inventory was to record the assessed value of a deceased person's estate, and its compilation was a statutory requirement.[30] In direct contrast, household inventories of the periods covered here were compiled only at the behest of the householder.[31] The task would not be taken lightly because the records were time consuming and labour intensive to produce, as footnotes to the Helmingham Hall transcriptions and further analysis in Appendix A will reveal. Unlike the probate inventory, the purpose of a household inventory was not to ascribe monetary values to items but to record their location; what else they record is idiosyncratic: at Helmingham this varies from the highly detailed, room-by-room description of contents (material, design, colour, construction, age and condition) to the economical listing of items within a group of rooms or connected spaces. Unlike the probate inventory, which was intended to be valid at a fixed point in time, the household inventory could continue in use as a working document, recording the outcome of periodic stock-checks and amendments until superseded by a new version. At Helmingham, the earliest inventory is dated 9 September 1597 but has additions and annotations dated to 1609. The next is dated October 1626 but detailed annotations, many of which are dated, and a complex coded system of cross-check marks show that this

---

26 *British and Irish Inventories: A List and Bibliography of Published Transcriptions of Secular Inventories* (2010).

27 *Addenda and Corrigenda to British and Irish Inventories* (2012).

28 Francis Young, ed., *Rookwood Family Papers, 1606–1761*.

29 Not ascribed to a valuer, this is a list of 191 pictures, described as 'An estimate of the pictures in Ham House', *c.* 1683, bound with a volume containing the Lauderdale Whitehall Lodgings and reproduced in *Ham House* (2013), pp. 463–5.

30 The National Archives website (accessed July 2016) summarises the responsibility: 'Up to 1782 every executor or administrator was required to send the registry of the court an inventory of the deceased's goods. The inventory itemised the estate held by the deceased, including: leases; chattels; debts owed and owing; cash; crops; stocks; slaves. Real estate (land) was not normally included in estimates and totals.'

31 As distinct from the preparation of later inventories of household contents compiled to satisfy insurance providers.

was a working document until at least 1633. The third inventory, 'taken in January 1707/8'[32] (1708), and the fourth one, dated 22nd October 1741, are self-contained, each revealing little or no evidence of subsequent checking.

The Helmingham household inventories vary considerably in the amount of detail they provide. The 1626 record is expansive, including anecdotal comments that succeed in providing insight into the process of compilation and add immediacy to the record. For example, when an item is not where it should be in 1626, as in the case of some long ladders which belong in 'the barne', then an answer is provided, from which we learn coincidentally that 'hewing' of trees is taking place near the church and that is where the long ladders can be found.[33] Similarly, there are some half-inch planks missing from the Millhouse Chamber, but all is well: they were lent by the bailiff for Catchpole's wedding.[34] The variations between the inventories raise a further question: how does each compiler interpret the extent of the household? Given that the primary task of a household inventory is to list all portable (not integral) items by their location in the house, then definition of the term 'household' should be unproblematic, but the Helmingham Hall documents suggest otherwise. Each of the four describes structures within and beyond the moated hall, but the extent of what they describe is significantly different at each date. Taken at face value, the 'household' of 1597 apparently burgeoned from sixty-three named spaces, rooms or structures to 128 in 1626, when every conceivable working space, from the pigeon house to the slaughterhouse, is recorded. There is little doubt that both existed in 1597 because payments for the repair of both were noted in by Helmingham's household steward, George Smythe, between 1587 and 1589.[35] As a result some caution was needed when estimating the extent of Helmingham Hall and its household offices at any date other than 1626, and the speculative layouts of the house offered in Appendix A reflect this.

When it comes to defining household property as distinct from the family's personal possessions, the inventories are revealing, if confusing. In 1597 the detailed and colourful contents of the 'Wardrobe' are listed under the name of each family member (including six of the seven children). However, there is not a ruff, cuff or undershirt to be found. This stands in stark contrast to the intimate detail of these items listed in the 1629 probate inventory of Arthur Coke of Bramfield, near Yoxford.[36] Does this mean that in 1597 outerwear, in particular, at Helmingham Hall is deemed to belong not to individuals but to the household? The 1626 record is different again, its inventory of the wardrobe offering no names of wearers and listing only a variety of clothes related to mourning. However, this did confirm storage at Helmingham Hall in readiness for use by the family, now more frequently at Fakenham Magna, whenever they returned to Helmingham for a family burial. In 1708 the wardrobes are locked up and inaccessible and in 1741 they are no longer listed.

---

32 Prior to 1752, each new year commenced on 25 March (Lady Day); the presentation of the date in this inventory confirms that the compilation was completed in January 1708.

33 1626 Transcription, 26.1407

34 1626 Transcription, 26.1365.

35 SRO(I), George Smythes' household accounts for Lionel Tollemache, 1587–89: HD 1538/253/165. Abbreviated throughout as Smythe.

36 F. W. Steer, 'The inventory of Arthur Coke of Bramfield, 1629', *PSIA* 25, Part 3 (1951), pp. 264–87.

Ironically, given the comments above, resident staff at Helmingham Hall in 1626 leave no doubt about what belonged to 'the household' and what did not, and their challenges are recorded.[37] This suggests the extent of the task for an inventory compiler, because either the 'owner' of the items challenged must have been present when the list was being made or, alternatively, the list had to be shared, whether in writing or by reading aloud, to any member of staff occupying a recorded room. Given that there is capacity for at least twenty residential staff in the 1626 house, the implications are clear. More constraints and limitations are revealed in Appendix A which traces and suggests reasons for the compiler's tortuous route. Limited light beyond the daylight hours, supplied only by portable lamps or candles, was an impediment to both identifying and writing, let alone the arduous task of naming, counting and recording every item in a house with more than sixty separate rooms and additional outbuildings, some of them beyond the moat. The number of entries alone gives some idea of the scale of the task, particularly bearing in mind that an entry in the transcription sometimes describes composite items, each of whose material, design, construction or colour will be noted. There are 1,216 entries in the 1597 inventory, rising to 1,549 in 1626. Uniquely, the 1708 inventory includes the dimensions of many of the items recorded in its 704 entries, from dessert glasses to bedsteads; and in 1741 there are a comparatively modest 622 entries. What is certain is that the dates noted in the heading of each inventory (noted only by the name of the month in 1626 and 1708) represent the end of a task that may have taken days or even weeks to complete.

A subsidiary question raised by the inventories relates to the notion of what is 'portable'. Features integral to the structure, including chimneys, hearths and ovens, are not listed but their presence can be recognised from the implements associated with them, such as andirons, brushes and tongs, all evidence of a fireplace. Paradoxically, locks are considered portable and Appendix A explores the emphatic approach to household security that is evident in the 1626 inventory, from the interior of the hall to the park gates.

Unlike a probate inventory, whose purpose is obvious, every household inventory poses a fundamental question: given the lack of a legal imperative, and bearing in mind the investment of time and effort demanded by its production, why was such a record compiled, and, more importantly, why now?[38] At Helmingham, this question must be answered four times. In each case, the production of a household inventory coincided with events that were of significance to the resident family.

The 1597 Inventory

The 1597 inventory reveals the extensive resources required to sustain the Helmingham household, comprising the family of nine, their twenty or so resident staff and periodic guests. Running the hall was tantamount to running a small hotel, but in this case the hotel reared, produced and processed many of its commodities on site. All this needed organisation and management, and the role of the mistress of the house at the time, Catherine Tollemache, is clarified by reference to contemporary

---

37 See footnotes 60, 105 and 106 to the 1626 transcription.
38 The most predictable reason is that a family was preparing for a protracted absence, effectively mothballing one property before moving to another. In the latter situation, a family would take linen and plate with them, but otherwise all else remained in situ and portable goods were listed room by room in the household inventory.

domestic records. Appendix A analyses how the household inventory reveals the character of the house and evidence of modest changes to its layout, some of them structural. The disruption caused by building work explains the purpose of the document's compilation. At such times, belongings were packed and protected for temporary storage and often moved from room to room as work progressed, so it was important to keep track of items in readiness for their reinstatement.[39] But, in turn, what prompted building work at this time?

The year 1597 marked a watershed for the family and it is no coincidence that the portrait of Catherine Tollemache, illustrated in Plate I, was painted in the same year that the hall was being modernised. December 1596 marked the end of a long period of inherited financial responsibility, so there was, at last, capacity to spend money on the family home. The last of Lionel and Catherine Tollemache's seven surviving children was born in 1596; importantly, the last three were sons.[40] The task faced by Lionel Tollemache now was to secure the future responsibly for his heir, a matter in which his widowed mother and her family could claim considerable experience. To provide a context for his life in 1597, a retrospective view is essential.

Lionel Tollemache was between thirteen and fourteen years of age when his father died, aged thirty, on 18 December 1575.[41] A pressing need, addressed in the last ten days of his father's life, was to secure a future for Lionel's young mother, thirty-year-old Susan (née Jermyn), who, otherwise, would have been left without the means of adequate financial support. Hasty though the arrangements had to be in terms of the time available, their planning was meticulous: first, the dying man entered into a legal agreement with his in-laws; second, he made and signed his will, the conditions of which were subject entirely to the terms of that legal agreement. Under the agreement, dated 2 December 1575,[42] the Jermyns pledged to provide an income for Susan Tollemache in widowhood and for the rest of her natural life and to clear outstanding debts accrued by her husband.[43] In return, the Jermyns were to enjoy the income of 400 acres of the Manor of Framsden for a period of 21 years from December 1575 at a token rent of 12d. per annum. The subsequent will, dated 18 December 1575, was conditional upon the agreement, freeing the estate of a burden of debt which would almost certainly have forced the sale of Helmingham Hall. The loss of some £150 per annum[44] was the price the heir had to pay for a previous generation's profligacy, but he would not face this constraint alone.

In addition to assuring Susan Tollemache's financial future, her family found one of their own through whom to secure and increase her status: on 18 February 1576, barely two months after the death of her Tollemache husband, she was married to

---

39 The frequent moving of items will be obvious from the 1626 household inventory.

40 Baptismal records in the Helmingham parish register are dated 1 August 1591 for Lionel, 1 December 1592 for Robert and 9 June 1596 for Edward.

41 SRO(I), FB46/D1/I, Helmingham parish register.

42 SRO(I), HD 1538/253/155.

43 Lionel's father appears to be held responsible for an ill-considered gamble which saw the family lose the best part of their estate at Bentley, south of Ipswich, an act which angered his own father (d. 1572) so greatly that the vituperative terms of the father's will (TNA, PROB 11/54) leave no doubt about his disappointment in his heir and his concern for his infant grandson. In the event, the son survived his disappointed father by only three years, leaving a thirty-year-old widow and their thirteen- or fourteen-year-old son, head of household at the time of the 1597 inventory. History would repeat itself in events that triggered compilation of the 1708 inventory.

44 The value is estimated on the basis of rents recorded for 400 acres of the Manor of Framsden Hall in 1612–13. By crude estimation, £150 is worth over £22,000 at 2005 values based on the National Archives currency converter.

her second cousin, William Spring, a union which soon conferred additional status: between 5 and 9 August 1578, while at Bury St Edmunds, Elizabeth I knighted both Robert Jermyn, Susan's brother, and her husband, William Spring, then sheriff of Suffolk, a role bearing responsibility for the onerous task of preparing the county for the royal progress.[45] For Sir William's stepson, young Lionel Tollemache, a noble union was on the cards, too; the sooner he married, the sooner he would take responsibility for his inheritance. At the age of eighteen years he travelled to North Elmham in Norfolk, where he was married on 18 February 1580 to Catherine, daughter of Henry, 2nd Lord Cromwell (and great-granddaughter of Thomas Cromwell). Apart from her noble background, Catherine brought with her the advantage of maturity: at twenty-three she was five years older than Lionel and barely twelve years younger than his mother.[46]

Catherine Tollemache proved to be scholarly, charitable, medically skilled and actively involved in the management of the household and its resources.[47] All Lionel Tollemache needed now was the assurance of a male heir. Within the first year of their marriage, he and his wife appear again in the parish records of North Elmham, where they bury an infant son, John.[48] No record has been found of intervening baptisms or burials, but the next piece of evidence suggests that Catherine was moved to Pakenham, home of her mother-in-law, Lady Susan Spring, for the birth of Susan, the first of four consecutive daughters.[49]

Lionel's future, it seems, was overseen by strong women: his mother expresses her deeply held beliefs about the value of a strict moral code and religious observance in a no-nonsense letter written to Lionel while he was on active service at Tilbury Camp in 1588. Lady Susan vilifies the Spanish and the threat of Catholicism they carry across the seas with them, warning her son that the consequences of being a morally weak man or, worse, an inadequate soldier, are dire.[50] Her letter ends on a conciliatory note with news of her eldest granddaughter, Susan; and other evidence confirms that Susan was housed with Lionel's mother at the time, reinforcing a strong bond doubtless forged at Pakenham with the child's birth.[51]

By the time Lionel Tollemache marched to Tilbury Camp in 1588 to face the Spanish on land with (reportedly) more than four thousand Suffolk men under the leadership of his stepfather, Sir William Spring, he still had no male heir.[52] It would be 1591 before a jubilant entry in the Helmingham parish register confirmed that a son was born to Catherine and Lionel Tollemache at 'duodecim nocte', midnight,

---

[45] Colourful contemporary descriptions of the entry into Suffolk, attributed to the chronicler, Thomas Churchyard, speak of Spring at the county boundary accompanied by a welcoming party comprising 'two hundred young gentlemen cladde all in white velvet and three hundred of the graver sort apparrelled in blacke velvet coates and faire chaynes ... with fifteen hundred serving men more on horsebacke ... ' (quoted in Z. Dovey, *An Elizabethan Progress* (Stroud, 1996), p. 40).

[46] There may well have been financial advantages, too, but no marriage agreement has been found to confirm this.

[47] Coleman.

[48] A.J. Legge, *The Ancient Register of North Elmham, 1538–1631*, p. 80.

[49] In SRO(B), FL614/4 the Pakenham parish register records that 'Mistress [Miss] Susan Talmage' was baptised there on18 September 1583.

[50] T/Hel/1/1, letter dated 10 August 1588 from Lady Susan Spring to her son.

[51] SRO(I) HD 1538/253/165, George Smythe's household accounts for Lionel Tollemache, 1587–89, which record payment, some time between 6 and 20 June 1588, to one of the household staff who was sent 'to Pakenham to measure Mistress Susyan [sic] for her gown'.

[52] Anon., *History of the Spanish Armada* ... , p. 15.

on 1 August 1591, and baptised Lionel on 15 August.[53] Two more sons were to follow, Robert in 1592 (the year in which Elizabeth I appointed Lionel as sheriff of Suffolk) and Edward, their final child, in 1596; there was a loss between them, another son, unnamed when he was buried at Helmingham on 24 April 1594, and therefore probably stillborn.[54]

The inventory of 1597 records Helmingham at the point when Lionel Tollemache was free of the twenty-one-year burden he carried as a consequence of the loss of income from the Framsden estate. Furthermore, he had an heir in whose future to invest with confidence. It is little wonder that this same year saw the painting of his wife's portrait, nor that the couple took the opportunity to give some attention to their home. The inventory records the addition of a new parlour, changes to the main hall, rearrangement of 'old' rooms and working spaces put to new uses (all summarised in Appendix A). Even so, the lessons of good household economy were not abandoned: despite the sumptuous clothes in Lionel's wardrobe, the provision of the new parlour, acquisition of an up-to-the-minute board game, some new furniture (for staff as well as the family rooms) and seats with cloth-of-gold coverings, there are records of sheets 'made at Helmingham' in 1596 and 1597, and in the latter year eleven pairs of old linen sheets 'lengthened' by taking the best of what remained from two pairs to prolong their lives.[55]

Features of the 1597 household inventory illuminate its role as muniment, forming part of the documentary evidence of the family's entitlements. In particular, additions and annotations reveal the editing, and later the hand, of Lionel Tollemache. There is a total deletion of the first version of the list of 'Plate, silver and gilt' and its replacement with another, still in the handwriting of the compiler, recording donors' names as evidence of provenance for specific pieces. This list was updated on 16 February 1604 but written in the hand of Lionel Tollemache, who claims some pieces recognisable from the earlier list as gifts from Elizabeth I (who had died eleven months earlier, on 24 March 1603). Verifying these claims to royal provenance led to the discovery that although some items may well have been royal gifts, they were not made directly to the Tollemache family.[56] A further version of the list was updated to 2 May 1608 and is, again, written in Lionel Tollemache's own hand. This notes that ten items were purchased new in 1609 (97.1215). In addition, when recording pieces recognisable from both earlier versions, Lionel Tollemache notes his judgement of 'not prized' for certain items or, more likely, their donors, one of whom was his wife's late brother, Edward, 3rd Lord Cromwell, who had died in Ireland in 1607, disgraced and deeply in debt.[57] The timing of Lionel Tollemache's comments (1604–1609) is significant, coinciding with the period when his affairs were undoubtedly under scrutiny: in 1609, under James I, he was once again appointed as sheriff of Suffolk.[58] Simultaneously, and more importantly, his name had been proposed for the title of baronet.[59] The title was new, instigated by James I

---

[53] SRO(I), FB46/D1/I, Helmingham parish register.
[54] SRO(I), FB46/D1/I, Helmingham parish register.
[55] The 1597 transcription includes discrete inventories of linens rich with anecdotal comments about their source, condition and storage: see 97.970–97.1089.
[56] See 1597 transcription, footnotes 91–92.
[57] Further details are provided in footnote 96 to the 1597 Transcription.
[58] Alfred Suckling, 'High Sheriffs from 1576 to 1845', *History and Antiquities of the County of Suffolk*, Volume 1 (Ipswich, 1846), pp. xlii–xlviii.
[59] E.D.H. Tollemache, in *The Tollemaches of Helmingham and Ham* (p. 46), cites a letter (undated), to Lionel Tollemache from William Strode, who signed himself 'Your assured loving cosn'. Strode

with the aim of raising money for the settlement of Ireland. The king would offer the dignity of a baronetcy to two hundred gentlemen of good birth, with a clear estate of £1,000 per annum, on condition that each should pay into the King's Exchequer a sum equivalent to three years' pay for thirty soldiers at a rate of 8d. per day per man (£1,095).[60] The year of 1611–12 proved momentous for the Tollemache family: on 22 May 1611, Lionel Tollemache was elevated to the hereditary title of baronet.[61] At a further ceremony, on 24 May 1612, he was created a knight bachelor on account of his being a baronet not previously honoured with a knighthood;[62] but he did not live to enjoy his newly acquired honours, for Sir Lionel Tollemache died on 5 September 1612 and was buried at Helmingham the same day.[63]

By the time the 1626 household inventory was compiled, Helmingham Hall was no longer the sole residence of a recently created knight and baronet but one of three properties available to his son and heir, Lionel Tollemache, 2nd baronet. Viewed in retrospect, the family arrangements made in 1575 had laid the ground for a pattern of fruitful marital unions supported by aspirational planning and management designed to sustain successive generations.

The 1626 Inventory

In comparison with the view of life at Helmingham Hall in 1597, when the majority of the house was dedicated to self-sufficiency, the 1626 inventory reveals that Sir Lionel Tollemache, 2nd baronet (Plate II), introduced luxurious goods and a measure of increased comfort to the house. Simultaneously, the inventory confirms that he spent seven years removing items from Helmingham to equip a second Suffolk home at Fakenham Magna, an acquisition that may have resulted from his wife's family connections.[64]

On 16 December 1612, barely a fortnight after his father's death, Sir Lionel Tollemache, 2nd baronet, married Elizabeth Stanhope, daughter of John, 1st Baron Stanhope of Harrington, Northamptonshire, at the church of St Martin in the Fields in the parish of Westminster, Middlesex.[65] Lady Elizabeth gave birth to a son, baptised, predictably, Lionel, at St Martin-in-the-Fields on 2 March 1614; but he died in childhood and was buried at Helmingham on 28 September 1616.[66] The heir to Helmingham was another Lionel, baptised on 25 April 1624, not at Helmingham nor even in London, where by now Sir Lionel and Lady Elizabeth had a town house, but at Fakenham Magna in Suffolk.[67] Events in the years between 1616 and 1624

---

confirmed that Lionel's name had been put forward (by Lord Northampton) as one of twenty-two sealed submissions of support for prospective baronetcies but advised that 'The patents are not as yet delivered to any, for I doe learn that the prties must cumm upp to give security for the payment of the two other payments'. From this, it can be deduced that Sir Lionel was required to pay the second and third of three instalments in excess of £330 each. A subsequent letter from Strode, also undated, claims that only eighteen of the twenty-two had been selected.

60 G.E. Cokayne, *Complete Baronetage* (1906, reprinted 1982).
61 T/Hel(S)/2/2, Letters patent creating Lionel Tollemache a baronet, 22 May 9, Jas. I (1611).
62 William A. Shaw, ed., *The Knights of England*, Vol. II, Central Chancery of the Orders of Knighthood (London, 1906), p. 151.
63 SRO(I), FB46/D1/1, Helmingham parish register.
64 All removals are itemised in Appendix B.
65 City of Westminster Archives Centre, St Martin-in-the-Fields parish register, 19 January 1551–31 October 1619.
66 SRO(I), FB46/D1/I, Helmingham parish register.
67 SRO(B), FL569/4, Fakenham Magna parish register.

involved more losses, and in 1621 Sir Lionel and Lady Elizabeth Tollemache were confronted with three family deaths. Lady Elizabeth's father, Lord Stanhope, died on 9 March 1621. Less than three weeks later, Sir Lionel's mother, Dame Catherine Tollemache, died and was buried at Helmingham on Lady Day, 25 March 1621. Lord Stanhope's seat was Harrington in Northamptonshire, but his preference for London is made clear in his will.[68] At the end of this year, on 20 December 1621, Lady Elizabeth's uncle, Sir Michael Stanhope, died and Sir Lionel was one of the executors of his will.[69] It was after these events that Sir Lionel acquired the Fakenham Magna property but the decision seems not to have been related directly to bequests. Despite references to 'the Stanhope Heiress', Lord Stanhope left to 'my welbeloved daughter My Lady Tallemache a peece of plate to the value of ten pounds or thereabouts'.[70] As for Dame Catherine Tollemache, to each of her three sons and three of her four daughters (and to her cousin, Anne Cromwell) she bequeathed 'a pece of gould of two and twentye shillinges, to make eache of them a ringe of gould with a deathes head ingraven', nothing more.[71] Beyond this gift, Sir Lionel was not favoured: Dame Catherine appointed her eldest daughter and first-born child, Susan (the widowed Dame D'Oyly) as her executrix and principal beneficiary.[72]

As in 1597, there was some lessening of financial responsibility following the death of a parent. Since 1613, Sir Lionel had been paying to his mother, Dame Catherine, a rent of £324 per annum for 800 acres of her 1200-acre dower property, the manor of Framsden.[73] Under the conditions of her jointure and dower, stipulated in her husband's will, Dame Catherine had the right to hold Framsden, and any income she could derive from it, only during her natural lifetime: it was not hers to bequeath.[74] Upon her death, the property reverted to her husband's male

---

[68] TNA, PROB/11/137. Lord Stanhope died in 1621; despite references to the 'Stanhope Heiress' (Tollemache 1949), Lord Stanhope's will confirms only this modest gift of silver to his daughter. According to the Royal Commission on Historic Monuments in England (RCHME) (*Northamptonshire*, vol. II, pp. 73–9, Harrington Hall descended to Lord Stanhope's son, Charles (this is confirmed in by Lord Stanhope's will), who died in 1675 without issue (by which time his sister, Lady Elizabeth Tollemache, had died also). The RCHME commentary adds: 'The subsequent history of the manor is not clear and there are discrepancies in the published accounts, but it seems to have been acquired by marriage by Lord Tollemache later third Earl of Dysart, in the late 17th century and remained with that family for some time.' The timing of the acquisition, if not the means, seems to be supported by references to Harrington in the Helmingham Archive, the earliest of which is dated 1680 (T/Hel/3/33), in the time of the 3rd Earl of Dysart.

[69] T/Hel/3/27. Sir Lionel Tollemache and Thomas Cornwallis, Esq. were joint executors.

[70] TNA, PROB/11/137, Will of John, Lord Stanhope, Baron of Harrington, 1621.

[71] T/Hel(S)/3/116, Will of Catherine Tollemache, dated 19 March 1621.

[72] Dame Catherine Tollemache, declaring herself to be 'of Ipswich … sycke in bodye but of good and perfect remembrance', died on 24 March and her funeral took place at St Mary's church, Helmingham, the next day, appropriately Lady Day, and the first day of the new year according to the church's calendar. The wording of her will and the nature of her bequests combine to suggest that she was not only of perfect mind but also of a very strong mind. The deeply religious overtones of the will are not unusual for the time; but Dame Catherine's reluctance to mention Helmingham, referring throughout to 'the parryshe where I shall depart this lyfe' but never giving it a name, appears to be deliberate. The extent of her estate, and its whereabouts in Ipswich, remain unidentified.

[73] SRO(I), HD 1538/228/1–19 (19), Indenture: Dame Katherine Tallemache to her son, Lionel, 2nd Baronet, 1613.

[74] TNA, PROB 11/120, Will of Sir Lionel Tollemache, Baronet, 1613. Under the terms of his will, Dame Catherine was excluded from enjoying any benefit relating to timber, or timber-bearing lands lying within the extensive manor of Framsden. The 2nd baronet's accounts (T/Hel/21/1) confirm this

heirs, who would continue to bequeath it as dower for their widows for several generations more. However, as was the case for Sir Lionel's late father, the land provided a fruitful source of flexible collateral, a benefit for which he had to pay during his mother's lifetime. Dame Catherine's death therefore signalled the end of rental payments and the anticipation of rental income from the Manor of Framsden. For Sir Lionel, these were contributory factors in the timing of building work at Helmingham; but reasons for the acquisition of Fakenham Magna, and for production of the 1626 household inventory, may be more deeply embedded in personal family circumstances.

Sir Lionel and Lady Elizabeth had four daughters by 1621,[75] but the continuing lack of an heir after nine years of marriage must have been of concern. The decision to move to Fakenham Magna suggests a deliberate break with the old order, made easier, perhaps, after the death of Dame Catherine. Sir Lionel's youngest brother, Edward, was still resident at Helmingham Hall at this time, where a room is named as his in the 1626 inventory.[76] Edward, born in 1596, unmarried, and twenty-five years old by the time his mother died in 1621, was, by 1653, an inmate of Bethlem Hospital, although neither the circumstances nor the date of his committal can be confirmed.[77] It is possible that after Sir Lionel and Lady Elizabeth moved to Fakenham, Edward continued to live at Helmingham Hall, where staff could support his needs. Speculation aside, it is noticeable that after the move to Fakenham seven more children were to be born and baptised there, including the long-awaited heir, Lionel, in April 1624. A further son, Francis John, was baptised in September 1625 but did not survive beyond infancy and was buried at Fakenham on 21 October 1626. The short space of time between the child's birth and death may explain the unfinished heading of the Helmingham household inventory, in which the day of the compilation was never recorded but a distinct space was left between the month and the year: 'October 1626'. After the birth and loss of Francis, five more baptisms are recorded in the Fakenham Magna parish register: Margaret, 20 March 1627; Mary, 8 August 1628; Jane, 30 September 1629; Dorothy, 14 December 1630; and the couple's last child, Bridget, on 3 July 1634. In all, four of their children were buried at Fakenham in their parents' lifetime. Some of the surviving daughters were married and had their own children baptised in the parish church there.[78]

Sir Lionel appears to have acquired the property known as 'Lugdons' in or about 1622. The earliest references to it in the Helmingham Archive include a sketch of the house and its immediately surrounding lands and a separate, detailed survey of the

---

with a record of timber cut at Bentley and sold to his mother (presumably because she was living in Ipswich).

75 Elizabeth (b. 1615), Katherine (b. 1617), Anne (b. 1619) and Susan (b. 1621), illustrated in Plate III. All four were named beneficiaries in the will of Thomas Harvy of Cretingham, 3 January 1622/3, each to receive a 'spur royal' (a gold noble). The Helmingham Archive (T/Hel/21/1) confirms that Harvy collected rents in Cretingham on behalf of Sir Lionel, described in his will as 'master Sir Lionel Tallemach' (clearly, his master) to whom he bequeathed a 'bay horse colt of 2 years old' (Wills of the Archdeaconry of Suffolk, 1620–1624, edited by Marion E. Allen, SRS, 31, 1988, p. 225, no. 406).

76 Based on the room described in the 1626 inventory as 'Mr Edward Tollemache's Room', which was in or near the clock tower.

77 BPA volume 873, 'Symon Neale his accompt to the honorable Lyonell Tollemache' (8 Sept. 1653–8 Sept. 1656): 'The Stewards of Bethlem Hospital for Mr Edward Tollemache his Mich. Quarter 1653: £3 18s. 0d.'.

78 SRO(B), FL569/4, Fakenham Magna parish register.

manor of Fakenham Magna, both dated 1622:[79] all are discussed and illustrated in Appendix B. What led to the choice of a family house in the same county as Helmingham and barely thirty miles distant is unclear; but a link with Lady Elizabeth's cousin, Bridget Stanhope, is worthy of consideration. Bridget was the daughter of Sir Michael Stanhope, of Sudbourne. Sir Michael died in 1622 and Sir Lionel Tollemache was one of the executors of his will.[80] Bridget was some seven or eight years old when her father died and it was not uncommon at the time for betrothals to be arranged well in advance, the marriage to follow with the onset of puberty. This is likely to have been the case with Bridget, who, in 1630, at the age of about fifteen years, was married to George Feilding (from November 1622, Earl of Desmond). As one of her father's executors, Sir Lionel would have had first-hand knowledge of any arrangements concerning Bridget. It is feasible that the two women, Lady Elizabeth Tollemache and her young cousin, Bridget Feilding, contrived to live in close proximity to one another in marriage but this is tenuous: what is clear is that the Earl of Desmond occupied Euston Hall between 1630 and 1655, and that his lands adjoined Sir Lionel's property at Fakenham Magna. Furthermore, the 2nd baronet's successor, Sir Lionel Tollemache, 3rd baronet and later 2nd Earl of Dysart, had an ongoing relationship with the Earl of Desmond, sharing a gardener and acquiring additional land from him, as Appendix B will show.

Whatever the catalyst governing the choice of Fakenham Magna, there is no doubt that the 1626 household inventory records the systematic removal of items for the next seven years from Helmingham to the Fakenham house (all are listed in Appendix B). Nonetheless, the inventory simultaneously reveals the addition to Helmingham Hall of a two-storey wing with cellars and significant changes to the internal layout of the house, discussed in Appendix A, confirming that this was a period of change, not of abandonment. Having a second property meant that Sir Lionel and Lady Elizabeth could live in comfort, free from the inevitable disruption caused by building work at Helmingham Hall. In his role as vice admiral of Suffolk, Sir Lionel was called upon regularly to be at Ipswich, only some ten miles away from Helmingham; and it was at Helmingham Hall that he died on 6 September 1640.

Eight years later, the son for whom the 2nd baronet and his wife had waited so long, now Sir Lionel, 3rd baronet, would continue in the tradition of marrying well. In 1648 his union with Elizabeth Murray, who became Countess of Dysart in her own right, enriched the Tollemache family with Ham House, Richmond (Surrey), and ennobled them further when Sir Lionel adopted the title of 2nd Earl of Dysart.[81] Fakenham Magna, as Appendix B will show, continued to be the focus of family life for two more generations; but Helmingham and its estate continued to sustain the family, surviving the Civil War and the interregnum to take on a new significance for the son who would become 3rd Earl of Dysart, born in 1649 and compiler of the 1708 inventory for Helmingham Hall.

---

[79] T/Hel/24/6.
[80] T/Hel/3/27: Sir Lionel Tollemache and Thomas Cornwallis, Esq. were joint executors.
[81] See footnote 13 above.

The 1708 Inventory

This inventory reflects post-Restoration England through the cosmopolitan and urbane tastes of the 3rd Earl of Dysart (Plate IV), propelling Helmingham Hall into an age that is a world apart from the one recorded in the 1626 inventory. The 1708 compiler records that 'My Lord' occupies not the parlour of his predecessors but an 'appartment' in which he 'lodges'. The hall has become the 'Great Hall' and its walls (and those of the 'Great Staircase' described with it) are covered with over fifty pictures, some of them family portraits still in place today, others popular and of their time, including one described as '1 large picture of a cookshop': the cookshop was still considered in France to be a questionable venue for gentlemen and aristocrats, but one which was increasingly acceptable in England.[82] A tea-pot with a gilded handle, a chocolate mill and chocolate pot make an appearance, all designed specifically for the making of beverages unknown at Helmingham at the time of the 1626 inventory. Kitchen implements are purpose-designed, such as a tin apple roaster, a screw-press for almonds and a 'round fish slice'. Delftware, made fashionable only recently, provides a range of dishes. Whilst mahogany is undoubtedly dominant, walnut and marble appear more frequently in descriptions of furniture and decorative items, with oval emerging as a new and recurrent form. Smaller items are 'japanned', fashionably lacquered. Looking-glasses and table-forks, both abhorred as things of the devil in the previous century, are now socially acceptable, in place and in use at Helmingham Hall. Practically devoid of glassware in 1626, Helmingham now lists a large stock ranging from wine glasses, syllabub dishes, glasses for sweetmeats and others for jellies, through to bottles in which to keep leeches.[83]

The 1708 inventory leaves no doubt that Helmingham Hall now reflects its status as the country seat of the 3rd Earl of Dysart. His principal seat in 1708 is Ham House, Richmond (Surrey). Already handsome when occupied by the 2nd earl, it was made more splendid in the late seventeenth century by the attentions of his mother and her second husband, the Duke of Lauderdale.[84] In 1708, Helmingham has taken on something of the sophistication of Ham House but human frailties are as common as ever and it is these that identify why the 1708 inventory was compiled. In circumstances bearing unfortunate similarities to those faced 150 years earlier by the grandfather of the 1st baronet, his descendant, now the 4th baronet and 3rd Earl of Dysart, would face the death of his son in 1712 at the age of thirty leaving a widow, an infant son and considerable debts.[85] Both grandson and debts would become lifetime responsibilities for the 3rd earl, whose title passed to his grandson, Lionel, in 1727. The 3rd earl was acutely aware of his son's impecunious state when the 1708 household inventory was compiled in January of that year, barely four months before the birth of his grandson and eventual heir, who was born on 1 July. The two events are undoubtedly linked by the earl's desire to prepare for an uncertain future that was unimaginable and undetectable from a reading of the household inventory alone.

---

[82] 1708 Transcription, see 08.118 and footnote 9.

[83] See glossary and index of household goods for definitions and histories of all items mentioned.

[84] The Lauderdale collections of fine art and furniture are the principal topic of *Ham House*, emerging in essays related to acquisitions made over a period of 400 years; for context, see 'The Duke and Duchess of Lauderdale as Collectors and Patrons' on pp. 116–35.

[85] The debts, discussed later in this section, are enumerated in the 3rd earl's extensive will (TNA/PROB 11/613/273).

A programme of financial preparation followed the compilation of the household inventory in January 1708. In the next month, February, the earl agreed with a London shipwright, Richard Burchett, to sell to him a total of 1061 'standing timber oakes' from Helmingham, spread over four years, Burchett agreeing to take a quarter of the agreed timber per annum. The deal is formalised in an indenture dated 31 May 1708, confirming that Burchett will pay 'Six and Fifty Shillings of lawfull money of Great Britain' per load for a total of 5000 loads, a load stipulated as 'forty foot guirt measure' (40 cubic feet).[86] In total, the sale was worth £14,000. Burchett agreed to make an advance payment of £500 and further payments of £500 at intervals, subject to his taking timber to that value. The language of the agreement is eloquent about the process: 'The said Earl of Dysart doth further promise and agree that during the said term of four years the said Richard Burchett and his or their servants workmen and labourers, with carts, wains, carriages, working tools and implements shall have free and quiet liberty of ingress, egress and regress in by and through all usual and reasonable or most common waies or passages made or to be made during the said time to hew, cutt out, dig saw pits, saw, convert and have, take or carry away to and for their own use all the said timber oakes.' The carrying away would have been by horse and cart to Woodbridge or, more likely, the larger port at Ipswich and from there by sea to London. Burchett's conditions stipulated that he would not remove anything less than 'six inches square at the top': all else, including bark stripped from the large trees and their undersized tops, would be left for the estate staff to collect, utilise, store or dispose of during the next four years. The environs of the hall must have looked ravaged by the end of it, for the areas described as 'the Old and the Newe Parks' alone yielded 400 of the 1061 oaks, the remaining 661 felled where they stood on seven other nominated sites.[87]

The four-year agreement with Burchett proved to be timely, for the earl's son, Lord Huntingtower, died in July 1712. In 1709 the extent of his debt was suggested by the terms of a mortgage, redeemable by a payment of £12,000, for which numerous manors forming part of the income generation from the family estates in Suffolk, Cheshire and Northamptonshire were pledged as security.[88] The 3rd Earl of Dysart's own highly complex will, dated 1723, refers to the debt and the means by which he attempted to protect his grandson from any further liabilities.[89] However,

---

[86] T/Hel/22/5.

[87] T/Hel/22/5: the sites (with the number of trees to be taken from each) were named as: John Caddow's meadow (328); John Friend's ground (40); Wm. Wood's field (61); Francis Newson's (11); Bullitoft's Ground (19); [illeg.] (142); Pages Ground (55). Burchett agreed also to take any other oaks of not less than 30 feet 'guirt measure' to make up the agreed total of 5000 loads.

[88] T/Hel/123/9, 15 March 1709, and T/Hel/123/10, 16 March 1709, recite the terms of the mortgage raised by Lionel, Lord Huntingtower and his wife, Henrietta, to cover debts already accrued by them, and paid by John Ward of Hackney (Middlesex). For £100, and an annuity of £400 payable to Lord Huntingtower and his wife, during the lives of his parents, the Earl and Countess of Dysart, and payment of Lord Huntingtower's debts by John Ward, Lord Huntingtower offered as security all the family estates in Suffolk, Northamptonshire and Cheshire that are named in the 3rd earl's will and are cited in the section on the 1741 inventory. The mortgage was redeemable by payment of £12,000 to John Ward one year after the death of the Earl or Countess of Dysart. Lord Huntingtower died in 1712 and the full extent of his debts, and the impact they had upon his father, the 3rd Earl of Dysart, and his son, who became the 4th Earl of Dysart, are exposed in the 1741 commentary.

[89] TNA, PROB 11/613. Will (and codicils) dated 13 March 1723. Probate granted 8 February 1727. The extensive and complex will is discussed in more detail in the next section of this introduction, when its terms were enacted following the 3rd earl's death in 1727, and help to explain the timing of the 1741 inventory.

the 4th earl was still embroiled in the aftermath arising from his late father's debt in 1741, as discussion of the 1741 inventory will reveal. In the meantime, between the sale of the Helmingham oaks and the 3rd earl's own death in February 1728, he looked to an investment in the future, one that would mature well beyond his own span, with plans to replant oaks to replace those felled in 1708.

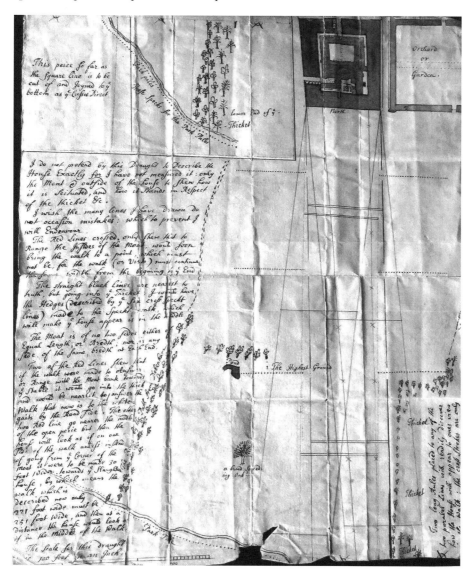

Plate 1. Letter dated 22 December 1720 to the 3rd Earl of Dysart from Thomas Brereton, in support of a proposal for a new planting of oaks in the park north of the hall. Brereton's sketch of the moated house, top right of his letter, has provided the source for creation of the plans used elsewhere in this volume. Helmingham Archive, T/Hel/1/64, reproduced by kind permission of the Lord Tollemache

In 1720, by which time the 3rd Earl of Dysart was 71 years old, his steward, Thomas Brereton, surveyed the Park lying to the north of Helmingham Hall with tree-planting in mind. Brereton produced not only measured plans for an avenue of oak trees but a sketch-plan of the hall itself, both incorporated in a letter dated 22 December 1720 (reproduced in Plate 1) and addressed to the Earl of Dysart at his London home.[90] Without his sketch and comments, it would be impossible to interpret the complex arrangement on the north side of Helmingham Hall at the dates of the three household inventories. However, more importantly, Brereton's letter expresses a paradigm of the eighteenth-century philosophy of landscape improvement: that it was both acceptable and desirable to achieve a picture-worthy feature (a 'visto' as Brereton puts it) that is also productive. In this case, Brereton explained, with drawings of the sight-lines of the intended avenue from the hall, that the moat was not square, nor was the house. Accordingly, he proposed that the new avenue be planted at an angle so that it appears straight when viewed from the house but economically incorporates the proposed new planting into existing groups of trees. His justification for this last is that the purpose of the scheme is 'chiefly to raise timber'. He concludes his proposal with the heartening news that 'I have agreed with three more labourers to do this, the ditching only reserving to myself, the starting of the work and sowing the akerns which we shall begin soon after Christmas if the weather continue open, else as the season shall allow'.

The metaphor is inescapable: the sowing of the acorns in 1720 is the 3rd earl's investment in his heir's future (and beyond). The 3rd Earl of Dysart died in February 1727. Records maintained by his heir show that Sir Lionel Tollemache, 4th Earl of Dysart, not only inherited the title and estate from his grandfather, but shared also his meticulous approach to recording income and expenditure. The 4th earl's attention to detail was well founded: although the 1741 household inventory and supporting material provides ample evidence that he committed himself and his resources to the enhancement of Helmingham Hall, his responsibilities extended also to resolving the ever-deepening problems arising from his late father's debts.

The 1741 Inventory

Plate V is a portrait of the 4th earl believed to have been painted in 1730, the year after his marriage to Grace Carteret in July 1729 and two years after he had inherited his grandfather's title. He is wearing the robes of a peer and the earl's coronet is on the console table beside him. Whilst Appendix A shows how he expended time, money, energy and enthusiasm on improving both the hall and the grounds at Helmingham, there is another narrative to counter this view of an untroubled, privileged existence. The entry below is taken from one of the 4th earl's 'Receipt books', which recorded income and expenditure randomly, not always distinguishing whether the sums related to Helmingham, Ham, Charing Cross or Harrington. However, there is no doubt that the poignant entry below related to an event at Helmingham:[91]

11 November 1730: [received by John Peck]

---

[90] T/Hel/1/64: the letter was addressed to 'The Rt. Hon. Earl of Dysart at The Corner-House out of Marlborough-St. into Poland-St., London'.

[91] From BPA volume 926 (1729–1755): 'Receipt book of the Earl of Dysart recording payments for personal, household and estate expenses at Helmingham, Ham House, Charing Cross and Harrington.'

Two & twenty shillings for tolling the bell two & twenty hours at depositing the body of His Honr's Son, Lord Huntingtower.

In common with the experience shared by three generations of his ancestors, the 4th earl and his wife had lost their first-born son and heir within the first year of their marriage. The loss was to be one of many: Grace, Countess of Dysart, died in 1755, at the age of 42, having borne fifteen children in twenty-six years of marriage.[92] This was not the only echo of ancestral burdens: by 1741, when the household inventory for Helmingham Hall was compiled, the 4th earl was actively involved in resolving the problems caused by the debts of his late father, Lord Huntingtower, who had died almost thirty years earlier. Despite the best efforts of the 3rd earl to protect his grandson, the debt faced by the 4th earl in 1741 stood at more than twice the sum mentioned in his grandfather's will.

The will of the 3rd Earl of Dysart is lengthy, extending to eighteen pages of repetitive legal clauses designed to ensure the security of the title through the male line in the event that his grandson should either die before succeeding to the title, or fail to produce a male heir.[93] In summary, the 3rd earl's bequests made provision for the following:

that his grandson, Lionel, Lord Huntingtower, at the age of 21 or upon his marriage, whichever was the earlier, was to ratify all the bequests set out in the will. Some of these related to income from manors and lands to be held in trust for him by his grandmother, the Countess of Dysart, income to which he would not be entitled until he reached the age of twnty-four (or until he married, if earlier);

that the burden of debt accrued by the 3rd earl's late son, Lord Huntingtower, had been discharged 'by several great payments that I have made' to John Ward; and that the £12,000 security held by Ward, his late son's principal creditor, was, therefore, due to the estate and should be released as agreed, with interest, within one year of the 3rd earl's death;[94]

notwithstanding the above, the complex clause ends with the proviso: 'but my will and mind is that the same shall not be assigned over upon such payment lest by such assignments some other debts of my said deceased son should be brought upon the said estate and the estate of my said grandson should be made lyable to the same'.

The 3rd earl's affection and concern for his widow emerge in the clause stating that if she so requested '3 fatt bucks and 3 fatt does' should be presented to her annually from the Parks at Helmingham, or £40 in lieu.

The dowager Countess of Dysart made her own will in 1732, appointing four executors including her two surviving daughters, named now as the Lady Elizabeth Cotton, wife of Sir Robert Salisbury Cotton, and Lady Katherine, Marchioness of Carnarvon, widow of John, late Marquis of Carnarvon. To Elizabeth, she left all her diamonds, rings, pearls and jewels; to the widowed Lady Katherine, she left all her interest in a leasehold property described as 'my dwellinghouse set on the south side of Grosvenor Street in the parish of St George, Hanover Square' and all its contents. She died on 26 April 1740 and was buried at Helmingham on 2 May, where her

---

[92] Of these, five sons and three daughters survived into maturity. Following the death of the 4th earl in 1770, the titles of 5th and 6th Earl of Dysart passed, respectively, to Lionel (1734–1799) and then his brother, Wilbraham Tollemache (1739–1821).

[93] TNA, PROB 11/613. Probate copy, 8 February 1727 (citing codicils dated 13 March 1723).

[94] This contradicts the terms of the mortgage, cited in footnote 88 above, in which it was agreed that the mortgage could be redeemed at any time by a payment to Ward of £12,000, and suggests, or confirms, that the 3rd earl felt that he had more than adequately paid Ward off.

wish was to be 'laid in the vault with my late husband … and my mind and will is that the same [the ceremony] be with privacy but decent'.[95] Modest cash bequests were detailed, including £50 to set up two monuments in Helmingham church in memory of her deceased daughters, the Lady Mary and Lady Grace Tollemache. A thoughtful gift of £100 was bequeathed to 'the Minister, Churchwardens and Overseers of the Poor of the parish of Harrington'. This sum was to be expended on 'the purchase of lands, tenements and hereditaments … and the rents, profits and proceeds thereof yearly and for every year for ever to pay, apply and dispose of for the putting forth of a poor child of the said parish'. The child's 'apprentice, nomination and appointment' was to be overseen by the minister, etc. and 'two or three of the principal inhabitants of the parish'. All of the 'plate, silver and gold or silver gilt which belongs to me shall, immediately after my decease, be weighed and valued by two goldsmiths and equally divided' between her two daughters, who were to hold it on trust for their children. In the event that there were no children, then the plate was to go to her grandson, Sir Lionel, 4th earl. Anything else owned but not already bequeathed was to be sold by her executors and the proceeds to be divided between her daughters and their children.

In theory, the death of his grandmother gave the 4th earl unrestricted access to the family properties which had, until then, sustained her; but the evidence suggests otherwise. In spite of the 3rd earl's wishes and his carefully orchestrated will, the debts of the late Lord Huntingtower persisted, and his grandson was liable for more than twice the £12,000 originally mentioned. By 1741, the 4th earl was forced to raise a mortgage of £26,000.[96] This is confirmed in the Helmingham Archive by a lease and release of a mortgage dated 4 and 5 March 1741. The documents recite, at great length, the complicated transactions and situations arising from the problems of the late Lord Huntingtower (whose widow, Henrietta, the 4th earl's mother, was still living, and to whom almost £6,000 of the money was due). Further, the documents confirm the wish of the 4th Earl of Dysart to raise funds to clear all his obligations arising from his late father's debts. Security for the mortgage was, once again, those manors belonging to the family estates in Suffolk, Cheshire and Northamptonshire, as described in his grandfather's will: 'all that the Manor of Harrington in the County of Northampton and all those the manors of Helmingham Crooks in Helmingham and Bockinghall in the County of Suffolk and all those mannors or ffarms of Woodley Beach in Eilston Bernihall [?], Aperham, Wardle, Wetnall Abbots ffee in Nantwich in the County of Chester and all his Lordships messuages, tenements and hereditaments in the Countyes of Northampton, Suffolk and Chester'.[97] In addition, under the terms of an agreement made on 6 March between Samuel Child of Lincolns Inn, Esq. and the 4th Earl of Dysart it was agreed that as long as the 4th earl paid interest at 4 per cent on the mortgage debt of £26,000, Samuel Childs would not call in the capital.[98] Four per cent of £26,000 amounts to £1,040 per annum.[99]

It was in the context of these events that a household inventory for Helmingham Hall was compiled on 22 October 1741. Six months earlier, an amendment to the Ham House household inventory of 1728 was made immediately following the

---

95 TNA, PROB 11/702. Will dated 25 May 1732, proved 13 May 1740.
96 Equivalent to approximately £2,223,540 at 2005 values, according to TNA currency converter.
97 T/Hel/123/15, 16: Lease and release of mortgage, 4, 5 March 1741.
98 T/Hel/123/17.
99 Almost £90,000 per annum at 2005 values, according to TNA currency converter.

death of the Dowager Countess of Dysart. This appears as an insertion, dated 17 April 1741, appended to the inventory of the Duchess's goods, compiled at Ham in 1728 following the death of her husband, the 3rd earl.[100] In 1728 the contents of the Ham House greenhouse had been recorded as 19 lemon trees, 101 orange trees, 40 cherry trees, 25 oleanders, 7 myrtles, 1 Spanish jasmine, 35 bay trees. This record was updated on 17 April 1741, noting 13 lemons, 94 oranges, 5 'momenplena',[101] 22 oleanders, 7 myrtles. The 35 bay trees and 40 cherry trees listed in 1728 are not mentioned, but it is likely that the stock of both had been moved outdoors by 17 April 1741, whereas in 1728, when the inventory was dated 2 February, they would still have needed the protection of the greenhouse. The amendment suggests what was to come next at Helmingham, where the gardens and grounds were the subject of the 4th earl's ongoing attention in parallel with repairs to the hall and other estate properties, gathering pace in the 1750s and 1760s. However, the 1741 inventory shows that he had already altered the layout of the interior of Helmingham Hall, changes that are explored in Appendix A, but a glimpse of his activity is offered below, extracted from his 'Receipt book' of 1729–55, to close this introduction on a note of optimism:

14 June 1736 [sic]	Trees and seeds sent to his Lordships Seats of Helmingham and Ham, also for extra works more than keeping the Garden [paid to Thomas Greening]	150	0	0
20 January 1737	Received of the Right Hon'ble. The Earle of Dysart by the Hands of Richd. Tallmache the Sum of Ninety pounds and fourteen shillings being in full for a new Bell & running five other Bells as also for Clappers and Brasses and all other demands.	90	14	0

I do hereby promise that in case the Tenor Bell at Helmingham in the County of Suff. Lately by me Run, shall not be approved on by The Said Earle of Dysart, that then in such case I will Run the Same again and make it to His Lordship's satisfaction gratis.[102]

---

[100] The transcription in *Ham House*, p. 468, suggests that the list is headed an 'auct' of the contents of the greenhouse in 1741, but an 'acct' (account) seems more likely.

[101] Based on John Harvey's *Early Gardening Catalogues*, 1972, these were probably 'Amomum Plinii', otherwise known as *Solanum pseudocapsicum*, Winter or Jerusalem Cherry, grown for its scarlet berries.

[102] Inscribed in the receipt book (BPA vol. 946) by the payee. Unnamed here, it is likely to have been Thomas Lester, whose comment appears against a payment a decade later in the same receipt book, recorded on 4 March 1747: 'The balance of a bill for new casting a Tenor bell weight 15 cwt 2 qtrs & 9 lb at 6d per hund [cwt.] & new running, £1. 4s 0d and in exchange for an old tenor bell weighing 12 cwt 2 qtrs & 9 lb at Helmingham Church which said sum is in full of all demands whatsoever by me, Thos Lester'. The *Victoria History of the County of Middlesex*, vol. 2, pp. 165–8 (accessed via British History Online), describes the industry of bell-founders locally, noting that Thomas Lester was foreman to Richard Phelps, who died in 1738, bequeathing his business and the lease of his foundry to Lester. It was Lester who moved the business from Essex Street to 32 and 34, Whitechapel Road. He died in 1769. Commissioned by the 6th Earl of Dysart in 1815 to commemorate the Battle of Waterloo, a new peal of eight bells, cast by Thomas Mears, of the Whitechapel foundry, was presented to St Mary's church, Helmingham, in 1816. (http://www.suffolkbells.org.uk/ helminghambellshistory.php). By the early years of the 21st century, a weakened timber bell frame caused the bells to remain silent for some years until fund-raising enabled the construction of a new metal frame. The 'Waterloo bells' were heard again following a service of rededication on 15 October 2011. Contractors for the renovation work were, appropriately, the Whitechapel Bell Foundry.

| 16 August 1738 | A bill of carriage for goods to and from London beginning January the 31st 1738 and ending June the 13th 1738 | 63 | 8 | 7 |
| 2 May 1739 | For three chimney pieces set up at Helmingham & for other work done at Ham [Henry Cheere] | 136 | 19 | 0 |

There are marble chimney pieces at Helmingham Hall now, believed to date from the time of the 4th Earl of Dysart; and on 15 October 2011 St Mary's church celebrated the restoration of its full peal of bells, which had not been rung since 2001. In 1766, beyond the scope of this work, the earl employed a gardener at Helmingham to bring the grounds up to scratch, promising to pay for new glass for the frames and new trees for the plantations. The rest was up to William Dimmock, imported from Twickenham, who was paid £52 10s. 0d. per annum to ensure that the best produce of its kind was raised in season in the kitchen garden for the earl's table, that all the walks around the moat (and, indeed, beyond, in the park) were well mown, that the plantations in the park were maintained; and, not least, that the flower beds were well filled and tended. Today, that tradition endures and Helmingham's gardens and grounds are of national importance.[103] Of the contents described in the four inventories, little remains in the hall now; but the bones of the house occupied by the families of the 1st baronet in 1597, the 2nd baronet in 1626, the 3rd Earl of Dysart in 1708 and, most especially, the 4th earl in 1741, are still recognisable.

---

103 Historic England Grade I Listing for the Park and Gardens, reference 1000270.

EDITORIAL METHODS

A key to features unique to the original document is provided at the beginning of each transcription but the following conventions are adopted throughout:

Insertions in the original documents are shown as: \ ... /

Deletions which can be read are shown as: < ... >

Illegible words are indicated by: [*illeg.*] or where words or phrases are made illegible or missing due to damage: [*damaged*]

Where uncertainty exists about a word or number, it is prefaced by [*?*]

Original spelling has been retained, with the following exceptions: j has replaced i and v has replaced u where modern usage demands them; the archaic letter thorn (þ, later written as y) has been expanded to 'th'. Obvious abbreviations have been extended without comment.

Forenames and surnames have not been modernised.

Suspensions and contractions used in the original documents have been extended in square brackets, apart from those that are readily understood (such as 'Item' and 'Mr'). Ampersand (&) has not been extended to 'and'. No attempt has been made to retain superscript minimalisations such as 'xxx^{tie}' (thirty).

Punctuation has been amended only to aid the reader, but never where it might impose a questionable reading. Final punctuation marks, including full stop (.) and forward slash mark (/) have been excluded for inventory entries but retained otherwise. The use of capital letters has been modernised and minimised.

Numbers, weights and measures used in the original documents are retained here and no attempt has been made to correct arithmetical errors. In sums of money the abbreviation 'li.' has been modernised as '£', but the abbreviations 's.' or ('sh.') and 'd.' have been retained.

The original layout of the documents has not been retained and a number has been added to each transcription entry. The numbering sequence begins anew at '1' for each inventory, prefaced by a two-digit date code related to the date of that inventory: 97 for 1597, 26 for 1626, 08 for 1708 and 41 for 1741. This simplifies cross-referencing throughout the volume and enables pinpoint retrieval of items catalogued in the comprehensive glossary and index of household goods. This system avoids the need for repetitive footnotes and definitions in the transcriptions of the 4091 entries, many of them describing composite items.

THE HOUSEHOLD INVENTORIES
OF HELMINGHAM HALL
1597, 1626, 1708 AND 1741

Helmingham Hall Archives

THE 1597 HOUSEHOLD INVENTORY

Helmingham Hall Archive T/Hel/9/1/1

Helmingham Hall
An inventorie taken there the 29 of September 1597[1]

[1] In the Hall
97.1	Imprimis ij long tables
97.2	vj forms
97.3	j livery cupboard
97.4	ij benches
97.5	ij candle plates of brasse
97.6	iij lavure staves
97.7	j cornet staff
97.8	j dragge
97.9	j flew
97.10	j casting nett
97.11	ij cunnye hayes
97.12	ij drawing lines
97.13	j lyned hawkes pearke
97.14	j payer of low yron cobyrons

[2]
97.15	\<vjj> \vj/ joyned stolles bought since of wainscot
97.16	iiij wallnuttree formes bought since this inventory was made ij formes for the new window be somewhat longer than the other ij, whch be for the longer table; ij of them bought in the year 1597 the other ij in the year 1598 and the vi joyned stolles was bought in the year 1597. L.[2]

[3] In the Parlour[3]
97.17	Imprimis j long table
97.18	j squeare table
97.19	ij long livrye cupboards
97.20	v formes

---

1   The record includes notes of acquisitions made between 1605 and 1608. Numbers in **bold** represent folio numbers appended to the top right-hand corner of the inventory pages at a later date. Household goods are defined in the glossary.

2   'L' is Lionel Tollemache (later 1st baronet), who annotates the inventory elsewhere.

3   With the extensive lists of household linen listed from 97.970 to 97.1090, there is a reference to cloths 'for her Parlour' (97.1008), referring to Catherine (née Cromwell), Lionel Tollemache's wife. See also footnote 5 below.

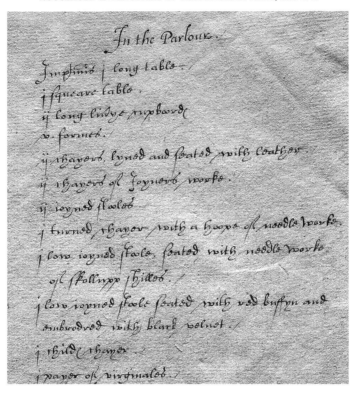

Plate 2. Detail from 1597 inventory, f. 3, 'In the Parlour', noting the 'goose game' and a pair of virginals, the only musical instrument then recorded. Helmingham Archive, T/Hel/9/1/1, reproduced by kind permission of the Lord Tollemache

97.21	ij chayers, joyned and seated with leather
97.22	ij chayers of joyners worke
97.23	ij joyned stooles
97.24	j turned chayer with a hoope of needleworke
97.25	j low joyned stoole, seated with needleworke of skallupp shilles
97.26	j low joyned stoole seated with red buffyn and embrodred with black velvet
97.27	j childs chayer
97.28	j payer of virginales
97.29	j payer of tables
97.30	j table with the goose game[4]

---

[4] Reference to the 'goose game' in September 1597 is notable, because this was a newly created game, according to Halliwell (1872, Volume 1, p. 410): 'On the Stationers' registers, 16th June, 1597, was licensed, "The newe and most pleasant game of the goose" '. Volume 2 of Ogilvie's *Imperial Dictionary of the English Language* (1855) provides a detailed definition (p. 410): 'A game of chance formerly common in England. It was played on a card divided into small compartments numbered from 1 to 62, arranged in a spiral figure around a central open space, on which, at the beginning

97.31   ij scutchions of armes in frames
97.32   j longe carpet of turkey worke
97.33   j cubboord cloth of greene
97.34   j dosen of cushens of turkey worke
97.35   j other cushen somewhat bigger, of tapistry
97.36   iij hangings of arras
97.37   j payer of brasen cobyrons
97.38   j payer of tonges
97.39   j payer of bellowes
         The following five entries have been deleted as a block:[5]
97.40   <j box of wayneskott
97.41   ij payer of boules
97.42   j partradge nett
97.43   j dagger, ij knyves, and a bodkinge, in a scabbard of watchet velvet
97.44   j hawkes glove>

[5] In the Buttry[6]
97.45   Imprimis j cupboord with iij lockes & iij keyes[7]
97.46   j bread binne with a partition
97.47   j old chiste
97.48   j keeler
97.49   j joyned table
97.50   j plancke used for a table
97.51   ij covering baskets
97.52   iij shelves
97.53   ij dosen and one table rings
97.54   ij voyder knyves
97.55   j litle joyned stoole
97.56   j chipping knyfe
97.57   j drinking bottell in forme of a dagg
97.58   ij great black jackes
97.59   j great bearded stone jugge
97.60   j lesser bearded stone jugge
97.61   v lesser black jackes
97.62   v candlestickes

---

of the game, the stakes were laid, and during the game any forfeits paid. It was played by two or more persons with two dice, and the numbers that turned up to each designated the number of the compartment on which he might place his mark or counter. It was called the *game of goose* because at every fourth and fifth compartment in succession a goose was depicted on the card, and, if the throw of the dice carried the counter of the player on a goose, he might move forward double the actual number thrown.'

5   Speculatively, the block deletion (97.40–44) of sporting and hunting items, and the presence in 'her Parlour' (see footnote 3) of embroidered furniture, a child's chair, a modern game and a musical instrument marks the influence of Catherine Tollemache. By now, Lionel's wife was well established in the ancestral home, having spent 17 years at Helmingham.

6   The buttery housed drinking vessels and some plates and dishes and presented food ready for service ('plating up' today), whether to diners seated at tables in the adjacent hall or in the first-floor dining chamber. See Appendix A for discussion of how and when the buttery was resited subsequently.

7   This triple-locked cupboard almost certainly housed silver and silver-gilt drinking vessels belonging to the family's collection of plate, detailed at 97.1091–1216. A similar cupboard can be found in the household steward's storehouse (see footnote 11 below).

97.63   vij dosen trenchers
97.64   vi basons, iiij sausers
97.65   j voyder
97.66   ij dosen fruite trenchers

[7] In the Beere Seller[8]
97.67   Imprimis xxx hogsheads
97.68   viij beere stales
97.69   ij keelers

In the wine Seller
97.70   j funnell
97.71   Imprimis j great broad binne, with ij leedes
97.72   j little table
97.73   j hogshead of claret wine
97.74   iij emptie hoggsheads
97.75   ij small vessels with vineger
97.76   j glasse bottle covred with leather
97.77   j other wicker bottle of glasse
97.78   ij small barrels, the one ollyves the other with capers[9]
97.79   j gallypott with capers

[9] In Smyth[e] his storehouse[10]
97.80   Imprimis j cupbord with iij lockes & iij keyes[11]
97.81   Item 1 keepe
97.82   ij coffers
97.83   j hamper
97.84   iiij torches
97.85   j shelfe
97.86   j fyre forke
97.87   j oyle bottle
97.88   ij great peawter [sic] pottes
97.89   j wine pott of pewter
97.90   j great bearded stone jugge
97.91   i lesser stone jugge

---

8   In the next generation, storage for beer was greatly enlarged, as was the capacity for brewing it in a newly equipped brewhouse: see 1626 inventory, in particular footnote 92.

9   This is the only inventory to refer to supplies of olives and capers, and confirms the family's continuing taste for sophisticated imports, evident a decade earlier. George Smythe's household accounts of 1587–89 record payment of 2s. for '3 pintes of oliffes and a pot to bring them in'. This was less than six weeks before Lionel Tollemache rode to Tilbury Camp with more than four thousand other Suffolk men prepared to face the threat of invasion by the Spanish. Hostilities had an impact on the family's purchase of luxury goods that year, the quantity halving in comparison with 1587 (Coleman, pp. 37–8).

10   By 1597, George Smythe had been Tollemache's household steward for at least ten years, confirmed by the survival of his weekly accounts for Helmingham Hall, covering the period 1587–89. Items in his storehouse are sufficient to serve the entire household, including staff, with valuable items kept under lock and key (see next footnote).

11   See footnote 7 above regarding a similarly well-secured cupboard in the buttery. This one is likely to have held silver and silver-gilt dishes and plates for service to diners, detailed below in the inventories of plate (97.1091–1216).

97.92   iij new candlestickes of brasse
97.93   j brasen chaffing dishe
97.94   v chargers
97.95   iiij dosen and j new great platters
97.96   iiij dosen and v middle platters
97.97   xj great dishes
97.98   iij dosen middle dishes
97.99   ij dosen and iiij small dishes
97.100 j dosen sallet dishes
97.101 iij dosen sausers
97.102 j dosen of sausers with eares
97.103 ix porringers
97.104 xv pie plates
97.105 ij pewter saltes with covers
97.106 v weightes of lead, conteyning xlb & an halfe
97.107 xviij great old platters
97.108 viij middle platters
97.109 xvj old peeces of pewter to be exchanged
97.110 ij old basons, & j old chamber pott to be exchanged
97.111 ij yron candleplates
97.112 ix old candlestickes to be exchanged

[11] In the kitchin
97.113 Imprimis iiij dresser bords
97.114 Item ij shelves
97.115 j scalding board
97.116 ij brasen boylers
97.117 ij kettles of brasse
97.118 j great brasse pott
97.119 j posnet
97.120 v dreeping pannes
97.121 j chaffer
97.122 iiij yron rackes
97.123 iij tramells
97.124 xiij speets
97.125 j trevet
97.126 ij payer of pot hookes
97.127 j fyre forke
97.128 j beef forke
97.129 j yron peele
97.130 j yron chaffing dishe
97.131 j skommer
97.132 j payer of musterd quearnes
97.133 j yron ladle
97.134 j clyver
97.135 j shreading knife
97.136 ij chopping knyves
97.137 j bread grate
97.138 j pestle and morter of woode
97.139 j salt box

97.140 j vineger bottle
97.141 j turnespeet wheele
97.142 j pepper box
97.143 Item ij gridyrons
97.144 j old baking panne
97.145 j frying panne
97.146 iij payles
97.147 j washing keeler
97.148 j yron to lay before the fyer
97.149 j bowle
97.150 x deepe platters
97.151 iiij broad verged platters
97.152 v old fleet platters
97.153 iij broad verged dishes
97.154 xj great dishes
97.155 xv middle dishes
97.156 xv small dishes
97.157 porringers viij
97.158 xij new sausers
97.159 v pie plats
97.160 ij chargers
97.161 j pewter cullender

[15] In the Pastrey[12]
97.162 Imprimis j cupboord with locke & key[13]
97.163 ij molding boords
97.164 v shelves
97.165 j old brasse panne
97.166 v pipkins
97.167 j flower keeler
97.168 v trayes
97.169 iiij crankes for speets
97.170 j boule

---

12 This room, despite the presence of cranks for spits, was not equipped with a fire. Its separation
from the kitchen ensured a cooler environment well suited to the making of pastes, which embraced
not only flour-based mixtures familiar as pastry but confections generally. The terms 'pastry' and
'pastry chef' are still in use today to describe the art of confectionery and its practitioners. Contemporary evidence from Catherine Tollemache's surviving recipes confirms that pastes of fruit and
sugar, or almonds and sugar, required deft handling and long periods of protracted drying, sometimes extending to days (Coleman, pp. 90–114). The pastry is described in 1626 and 1708 but is not
mentioned in the 1741 inventory.

13 On 27 October 1588, Smythe records payment of 3s. 6d. 'for making my mistresses cubbard and for
the locke', almost certainly referring to this cupboard, since the pastry was the domain of Catherine
Tollemache. Anything under lock and key and accessible only to her, including the moulds and decorative stamps she specifies in her recipes for fruit and almond confections, would not be recorded in
the 1597 inventory; but the 1626 inventory does record a 'carved cake print', consigned to storage
with other superannuated items in the wardrobe (26.766).

In the Larder[14]
    97.171 Imprimis j salting trowgh
    97.172 iij plankes
    97.173 j chopping blocke
    97.174 iiij bryne tubbes
    97.175 j lard tubbe
    97.176 j shelfe
    97.177 iiij leading weits conteyning together 86 lb
    97.178 j larde pott of earth
    97.179 xxxv yron spurkets

[17] In the husbandmens hall[15]
    97.180 Imprimis j long table
    97.181 Item j long forme
    97.182 j benche
    97.183 j short forme
    97.184 ij small shelves
    97.185 j bell
    97.186 j batfouling nett

In the vergis house[16]
    97.187 Imprimis ij hogsheads
    97.188 ij barrels
    97.189 j halfe barrell
    97.190 j herring barrell
    97.191 j barrell with bay salte
    97.192 j tubb with bay salte
    97.193 j old payer of mustard quearnes

[19] In the inner Dairie[17]

---

[14] The distinction between a larder and a lard house (see footnote 19 below) is usually explained as the first being for 'dry' tasks, principally for storage of meat, and the second for 'wet' tasks. However, the 1597 inventory is not that clear cut. More than a storage area, the larder was equipped for the processes of jointing, salting and curing pork meats for supplies of ham and bacon. Pork fat, rendered and clarified to become lard, was stored here also.

[15] Throughout the 1597 and 1626 inventories (and, indeed, in George Smythe's household accounts), staff are referred to collectively as 'husbandmen', never 'servants', a word that is used in both the 1708 and 1741 documents. However, by 1626 the husbandmen's hall appears to be out of use and its site used for other functions (see footnote 101 to 1626 inventory).

[16] Verjuice is the juice of unripe crab apples (or grapes, although there is no evidence of these in the inventories). The fruit was stamped, not pressed, confirmed by the lack of a press here. Given the seasonal nature of the task, the verjuice house was a useful additional storage space for most of the year, a role evident from the list of its contents. The barrels of bay salt and the herring barrel indicate that this role included the salting of fresh herrings. Smythe's accounts from a decade earlier show that although some were purchased 'red' (soaked in brine, strung up and smoked), and some 'white' (can mean fresh but also salted), there were also large purchases of fresh herring that coincided with the purchase of barrels of bay salt, evidence that the fish were home-salted at Helmingham. In the period from 14 February to 19 December 1587, for example, the accounts record the purchase of 8 cades of 'herrings' but only 2 of 'white' and none of red until March 1588. The 1626 inventory is the only one of the four to identify a 'fish chamber' (see 1626 inventory, footnote 117).

[17] The inner dairy reveals the means of production of large quantities of cheese, some of it the soft and sophisticated 'angelot' cheese, referred to in the inventories variously as angelet and angellica, for

97.194 Imprimis j double cheese presse
97.195 Item j cheese tray
97.196 j cheese boorde
97.197 iiij shelves
97.198 j milk tubbe
97.199 j milke cowle
97.200 ij churnes
97.201 xxvj milk boules
97.202 ij churnes
97.203 xxxvj milk boules
97.204 ij whey boules
97.205 j butter keeler
97.206 j butter boule
97.207 iij milk keelers
97.208 j clensing boule
97.209 vj great cheese fatts
97.210 xij copper cheese fatts
97.211 ij printing cheese breeds
97.212 ij playne cheese breeds
97.213 ix smaller cheese breeds
97.214 iij creame ferkins
97.215 j maw ferkin
97.216 j ote meal ferkin
97.217 j pint
97.218 ij angelet fatts
97.219 j pudding panne
97.220 ij payer of milke tonges
97.221 j lanterne
97.222 j hearing temes
97.223 iij fleting dishes
97.224 ij maw potts
97.225 vi milke pannes
97.226 \viij newe mylke bowelles of the traye fashion/ [*in another hand*]

[21] In the outwarde Dairie[18]
97.227 Imprimis iij formes
97.228 Item j shelfe
97.229 j quaile cage
97.230 iij great brasse kettles
97.231 ij dying pannes
97.232 j washing tubbe
97.233 j bucking tubb
97.234 iiij cowles
97.235 ij whey keelers

---

which there were two dedicated vats and nine 'breeds' (breads), the lids used to press these smaller cheeses. For discussion of angelot cheese see footnote 20 below.

[18] Despite its name, which persists in the 1626 record (see footnote 104 to 1626 inventory), the contents suggest strongly that the outer dairy functioned partly as a storage space but principally as a laundry. It is not until 1708 that a laundry is identified by name.

97.236 j washing keeler
97.237 j little keeler
97.238 ij trevets
97.239 j tramwell
97.240 j fyer panne
97.241 j payer of tonges
97.242 j payer of bellowes
97.243 j rostyron
97.244 xiiij payles
97.245 j stone jugge

In the Lard house[19]
97.246 Imprimis ij shelves
97.247 Item j long stoole
97.248 j carte stuffe ferkin
97.249 xi earthen \pots/ with stuffe
97.250 j chopping boord
97.251 j chopping knyfe
97.252 j towe combe
97.253 ij yarne reeles

[23] In the Cheese Chamber[20]
97.254 Imprimis iiij cheese boords
97.255 j hanging shelfe
97.256 j cheese caske
97.257 ij sowse tubbes

In the Bultinge house[21]
97.258 Imprimis j bulting hutch
97.259 j minging trough
97.260 iiij great tubbes
97.261 j minging boule

---

19 See also footnote 14 above, relating to the larder. Despite the presence of the chopping board and knife, the lard house appears to be largely redundant as the site of preparatory or 'wet' tasks relating to processing joints of pork. The presence of the pots of 'stuff', in this case cart grease, is a hint that the clarification of pork fat might have taken place here, although there is no evidence of the boilers or other vessels for heating it. Storage of the tow comb and yarn reels suggests that the fibres of flax or hemp might have been prepared here in readiness for weaving. See also 97.1016 for evidence of linen produced at Helmingham from home-made yarn.

20 Cheese made in the dairy needed to be ripened and stored in a separate space offering an ambient temperature. Apart from the hard cheeses emerging from the press, the soft 'angelot' or angelet cheeses were stored here, too, but they demanded different handling, apparent from the 'sowse tubs' and the 'cheese caske'. Angelot cheeses made in the 'angelet' vats (97.218) demanded regular washing in salted water during ripening (in this context, the souse, or brine, in the tubs, 97.257) and could be stored in brine once ripe (in the cheese cask, 97.256).

21 The flour resulting from grain milled in the hall's millhouse (97.288–291 and footnote 24) was bolted and refined through sieving here prior to use. In 1626 this space is described as the 'meale howse' and graduated sieves are described explicitly. In 1597 the qualities of coarseness and fineness are undoubtedly possible, given the presence of seven different sieves, four of them described as 'bultelles', which are cloths. The 'minging' or mixing of dough began here, too, before it was carried to the next space described in the inventory, the bakehouse.

97.262 iij sives
97.263 j little keeler
97.264 iiij bultelles
97.265 j skeppe
97.266 j shelfe

In the Back house[22]
97.267 Imprimis j mulding boord
97.268 ij other boords
97.269 j forme
97.270 j yron peele
97.271 iij oven leeds

[25] In the Brew House[23]
97.272 Imprimis j copper
97.273 Item j meesh fatt
97.274 j wort fatt
97.275 j yeild fatt
97.276 j cooler
97.277 ij tubbes
97.278 j hogshead
97.279 xij keelers
97.280 ij cowles
97.281 j trough
97.282 j jett
97.283 j sholve
97.284 ij kovres
97.285 j candle plate
97.286 j stuke
97.287 iiij payles

---

22 Bakehouse. Next door to the bulting house, where flour was graded and dough mixed intially, this is where bread was 'moulded', kneaded and formed into loaves, and baked for the household, which, at this date, comprised some thirty people including the resident staff. The fire-heated oven itself is not described since it was an integral part of the structure, but the 'leeds' or lids which closed it are listed because they are portable. The space is equipped simply with boards, flat surfaces on which to knead and form the bread, and an iron peel, the long-handled, flat, spade-like implement used to place the dough in the oven and withdraw it when cooked. Bread-baking would have begun with the coarser household loaves which demanded the highest temperature; then 'manchet', the finer, whiter bread formed into large rolls, baked at a cooler temperature. Some of Catherine Tollemache's recipes for sweetmeats and fruits refer to the relative temperatures (hot, warm) offered by the bread oven whereas marchpane needs the oven to be 'as hot as you would have it for manchet' (Coleman, p. 107).

23 At a time when only spring water was fit to drink and hot beverages were unknown, beer was consumed daily and in large quantities. Both the bakehouse and the brewhouse relied upon supplies of yeast, so their proximity to one another was logical. The 1597 brewhouse is equipped with one copper, for boiling the malted barley in water, and three vats and a cooler to accommodate subsequent stages of the brewing process. The 1587–89 household accounts confirm that the household purchased supplies of hops and that the quantities increased significantly from 25 lbs in 1587 to 46 lbs in 1588 (Coleman, p. 35).

In the Mill House[24]
97.288 Imprimis j horse mill furnished, wth ij payer of stones
97.289 Item j payer of worne stones
97.290 ij collers and ij payer of trayse
97.291 j fanne

[27] In the foules house[25]
97.292 Imprimis ij coopes
97.293 Item j trough
97.294 iij vergis hogsheads
97.295 j runlet
97.296 j oate tubbe
97.297 j other old tubb
97.298 ij vergis trowghes
97.299 ij meale tubbes

In the inner foules house
97.300 Imprimis j trowgh
97.301 Item j boule
97.302 ij lockes and ij keyes

In the yarde[26]
97.303 Imprimis j grindstone with an yron cranke
97.304 j cutting hooke
97.305 j rake for the mote

---

24 Smythe's accounts record payments for 'betyng' (beating) the mill four times in 1587 and once in 1588 (Coleman, p. 14). Beating refers to the re-dressing of millstones, a specialist task which Helmingham's domestic miller was clearly unable to undertake. The Helmingham payments are not all legible, but range from 6d to 20d. Yaxley (2003, p. 10) gives references from 1536 for 'betyng the mill', and from 1647 for 'beating on the stones of the horse mill'. Between the two, evidence from James E. Thorold Rogers, *History of Agriculture and Prices in England*, VI (1887, p. 692), records that in 1610 a 'chief miller, which can expertly beat, lay, grind and govern his mill' was paid 46s. per annum, whereas a 'common miller, which cannot beat and lay, but grind only' was paid 31s. 8d. per annum. Domestic and tenant mills were common at this time because by 1600 over half of Suffolk's manorial mills had fallen out of use. Mark Bailey provides a range of evidence for this in *Medieval Suffolk* (2007, pp. 198, 233–4), citing the drastic loss of population due to the Black Death and, subsequently, an equally drastic reduction in the cultivation of arable land. Until the 18th century, horsemills, like the one at Helmingham, were employed by those who could afford them (and handmills otherwise). The two sets of stones recorded here are described in more detail in the 1626 inventory (26.1352–1354), which offers the last detailed view of the mill's contents. In compiling this footnote, I am indebted to Stephen Podd and Tim Booth for sharing their expertise on mills and milling.
25 A decade earlier, Smythe's accounts confirm that the hall was by no means self-sufficient in eggs, with payments made regularly between February and November in 1587 and 1588 to 'Mother Joon', although the record is silent on quantities (Coleman, pp. 28–9, 34). In the same period, numerous purchases of chickens, ducks and geese were made. The 1626 inventory description of the 'poultery howse' (26.1276–1290) suggests a capacity significantly greater than that of the 1597 fowls' houses.
26 The yard offers evidence of outdoor maintenance, with a cutting hook, the means of sharpening it, and a rake to remove detritus from the moat.

In the stilling yarde[27]

97.306 Item iij boords
97.307 j shelfe
97.308 ij runlets
97.309 j brasse pott
97.310 j pestle and a mortar
97.311 vi stilles with their furniture
97.312 j lymbeck
97.313 j stone pott, typt with silver and gilt
97.314 j other pott typt with silver

[28] *The reverse of folio 27 presents the first of several discrete summaries added to the 1597 inventory. The first entry is not deleted but is repeated on the following line in a manner which sets the pattern for presentation of all following entries.*

A note of the whole sume of the fetherbeds bolsters blankets and coverletts as be sett downe in this booke 29 of September anno dni 1597[28]

97.315 Imprimis of dounebedds – 5
97.316 Imprimis of doune bedds ffyve – v
97.317 Item of ffetherbedds Thirtie thre – xxxiij
97.318 Item of downe bolsters ffyve – v
97.319 Item of ffetherbolsters Thirty one – xxxj
97.320 Item of doune pillowes tenn – x
97.321 Item of fether pillowes seaventeene – xvij

---

27 Known in other households (see below) as the stillhouse, the Helmingham 'yard' suggests an area not fully enclosed and suggests a significant scope and scale of activity in 1597 (sustained in 1626, see footnote 110 to the 1626 inventory. Here there are 'six stills and their furniture', a high number for a gentry household in comparison with the five stills recorded at the larger Hengrave Hall (Suffolk), home to Sir Thomas Kytson in 1603. Hengrave's nether and upper stillhouses (Gage, 1822, pp. 36–7) also embrace some culinary and confectionery-making activities which are carried out elsewhere at Helmingham (in the bakehouse and pastry, in particular). The 1597 stilling yard characterises the influence of Catherine Tollemache. Here she extracted essential oils and waters from combinations of home-grown plant material and combined them with exotic imported gums and resins. Her recipes record a wide range of uses such as the 16th-century equivalent of air fresheners (perfumes burned over charcoal), 'washing balls', perfumed soaps for personal use, and a moth-deterrent described as 'a sweete muske to ley emongst cloathes, woollen or linen … not offending the head' (Coleman, pp. 117–41). Contemporary household evidence shows that the work was seasonally taxing, dominated by the availability of raw materials, particularly when it came to the making of rose-water, a widely used ingredient in culinary and medical recipes recorded by Catherine Tollemache. In the three-week period from 26 June to 17 July 1587, Smythe's accounts record five separate purchases of 'roses' amounting to a total of 10,500 (never less than a thousand at a time) at an average cost of 1s. per thousand. Prices fluctuated little, reflecting a modest advantage to bulk buying. In 1588 the weather wreaked havoc with roses, bringing them into bloom earlier and in greater numbers, but curtailing the supply rapidly. Smythe had to cram his purchases of 11,600 flowers, and Catherine her 'stilling' activities, into just 8 days.

28 Updated commentary on items as diverse as the family's valuable plate and its growing stock of household linen is unique to the 1597 inventory. Here, the cumulative summary of bedding was confirmation of the items recorded individually throughout the document and is a sign of careful management and close scrutiny; both characteristics recognisable in Catherine Tollemache (see Coleman, pp. 147–9). The numbers are a stark reminder of the workload and responsibilities of the household in her time, noting a total of 44 beds. There must have been some uncertainty, or perhaps exhaustion, on the part of the recorder, who entered down beds twice (97.315 and 316), inserting the total number in words in the second entry and using that presentation as the pattern for the remainder of the list, but neglecting to delete the first entry.

97.322 Item of blanketts thirtie ffyve payer – xxxv payer
97.323 Item of ffustin blanketts one payre – j payre
97.324 Item of coverletts thirty nyne – xxxix
97.325 Item one greene Irish rugg – j
97.326 Item of fflock bedds six – vj
97.327 Item of fflock bolsters six – vj

[29] In the Dyning Chamber[29]
97.328 Imprimis j squear table
97.329 Item j livry cupboard
97.330 ii joyned formes seated with Candish his stuffe being cloth of gould & fringe with yealow and carnation silke[30]
97.331 j dosen stooles of joyners worke seated with red & yellow caffa, the fringe red & grene silke and covered with buckram covers
97.332 ij lowe joyned stooles, seated with straw couler taffatie [taffeta], imbrodered with watchit velvet, & fringe of the same couler
97.333 iij low joyned stooles, seated with needle work, whereof ii are wrought with oaking leaves, & the other j with pease flowers
97.334 j little chayer seated and backed with turkey worke with armes
97.335 j joyned chayer seated & backed with white caffa & imbroydred with silke of diverse collrs
97.336 j joyned chayer seated and backed with yellow satten, cutt, & striped with silver
97.337 j other chayer seated and backed with blewe velvet, and imbroydred with crimson satten
97.338 j long carpet of turkey worke
97.339 j squear carpet of turkey worke wrought with armes
97.340 j longe carpet and a cupboard cloth of copper gold dornex of diverse coulers
97.341 j dosen of cushions of turkey worke wrought with armes
97.342 iiij newe hangings of arras
97.343 ij other hangings of arras
97.344 j window cloth of arras

[31] In the best Chamber
97.345 Imprimis j posted beddsted
97.346 Item j matt
97.347 j downe bedd
97.348 j downe bolster

---

[29] The room's importance is reflected in the descriptions of sumptuous textiles and design details, all of which are explored in the glossary, and the rare evidence, at this date, of window coverings. Food served at the square table must have been half-cold by the time it had been carried from the kitchen to the buttery, where it was 'plated up' and then carried up the staircase to the dining chamber.

[30] Diarmaid McCulloch suggests that 'Candish' was Thomas Cavendish, and his 'stuff' some of the goods he sold on return in 1588 from one of his voyages. Cavendish, born in 1560 at Trimley St Martin, was a maritime adventurer and navigator, and was said to have been the third person to circumnavigate the globe. Reputedly, when he returned to Plymouth in 1588, his ship's topmast was covered with cloth of gold and its sails and crew's clothing were made of silk damask seized from one of the many Spanish galleons he pillaged (*ODNB*). His surplus hoard is almost certainly the source of the cloth of gold gracing Helmingham's forms in 1597.

97.349 ij downe pillows
97.350 ij fustine blankets
97.351 j coverlet of arras
97.352 j tester, head peece, & valance of grene taffatye embrodred with silver
    & silke of diverse coulers fringed with greene silke & silver
97.353 v grene taffaty curtaines
97.354 j chayer seated and backed with grene velvet
97.355 ij low stooles seated with grene velvit
97.356 v hangings of arras
97.357 j cupboord cloth of turkey worke with armes
97.358 j livery cupboard
97.359 j cushen cloth forme
97.360 j payer of tonges
97.361 j payer of cobyrons
97.362 j fyer panne
97.363 j chamber pott

In the inner Chamber to the same[31]
97.364 Imprimis j posted bedsted
97.365 j tester of red & watchet say
97.366 j matt
97.367 j bolster
97.368 ij wolling blankets
97.369 j cov[e]ring

[33] In the Corner Chamber
97.370 Imprimis j carved bedstead
97.371 j tester and head peece of yealow damaske embrodred with purple
    velvet, with armes the vallence fringed with purple & yealow silke
    fringe
97.372 vj curtaines of yealow purple [*sic*] silke
97.373 j matt
97.374 j downe bedd
97.375 j downe boulster
97.376 ij downe pillowes
97.377 ij wolling blankets
97.378 j coverlet of dornex of diverse coulers
97.379 j whit twilt
97.380 vj peeces of old red & yeallow say
97.381 j hangings and ij peeces of Arras
97.382 j greene cupboord cloth embrodred with velvet of diverse coullers
97.383 j livry cupboord
97.384 j cushen cloth stoole
97.385 j chayer & ij stooles imbrodred with black velvet uppon red cloth
97.386 j fyre panne

---

[31] 'Inner' chambers to the principal rooms throughout Helmingham Hall at this date are most likely to be occupied by staff, perhaps on a temporary basis. This one, in common with others at this time, is unheated and furnished simply.

97.387 j payer of tonges
97.388 j payer of cobbyrons
97.389 j chamber pott

In the Closset to the same Chamber
97.390 Imprimis ij peeces of red and yealow say
97.391 ij old window clothes
97.392 j bed matt

[35] In the middle Chamber
97.393 Imprimis j posted bedstedd
97.394 j matt
97.395 j fether bedd
97.396 j boulster
97.397 ij downe pillowes
97.398 j payer of wolling blankets
97.399 j coverlet wrought with buckes in redd & yealow < darnex> \of wollen worren/
97.400 j tester and valence of cloth of silver & black velvet, fringed with black silke and silver
97.401 iij curtaines of black and whit sasenet
97.402 j chayer seated and backed with red buffon and embrodred with black velvet
97.403 j old cushen of satten of bridges
97.404 j livery cubborde
97.405 j cupbord cloth of greene \cloth/
97.406 j window curtaine of red and grene say
97.407 iiij hangings of redd and greene saie
97.408 j payer of tonges
97.409 j payer of cobyrons
97.410 j fyre panne
97.411 j chamber pott

In the two bedd Chamber
97.412 Item ij posted beddstedds
97.413 ij matts
97.414 ij feather bedds
97.415 ij boulsters
97.416 j payer of wolling blankets
97.417 ij cov'rings of wolling redd & blew

[37] In the greene Chamber[32]
97.418 Imprimis j field bedstedd
97.419 j matt
97.420 j downe bedd

---

[32] The name is ironic, given the range of colours mentioned in this room; however, it may have once accommodated furniture and furnishings now occupying the 'Best chamber' (97.345–363). The colour green is comparatively unusual for furnishings in the 1597 house but less so in 1626, when this room's name persists (1626 Inventory, footnote 44).

97.421 j downe boulster
97.422 ij downe pillowes
97.423 ij wolling blankets
97.424 j cov'rlet of wolling red and grene, wrought with birds & buckes
97.425 j tester of red say imbrodred with yealow twist and cloth of silver, and
       fringed with grene <and yeallow> crewell fringe
97.426 iij curtaines of red say
97.427 iiij hangings of dornex black and white
97.428 ij window clothes, and j cubbord cloth of the same
97.429 j chayer seated and backed with tufte taffaty black and purple
97.430 j window cushen and ij other cushens of blew and yealow coope worke
97.431 j cushen cloth stoole
97.432 j liv'ry cupboord
97.433 j payer of andirons
97.434 j fyre panne
97.435 j payer of tonges
97.436 j chamber pott

In the inner Chamber to the same
97.437 Imprimis j posted bedsted
97.438 j matt
97.439 j fether bedd
97.440 j boulster
97.441 j blanket
97.442 j cov'rlet of wolling [woollen] redd and blew
97.443 j linnin teaster

[39] In my M[aste]r: his Chamber[33]
97.444 Imprimis j field bedstedd
97.445 Item j matt
97.446 j fetherbedd
97.447 j boulster
97.448 j payer of wolling blankets
97.449 j wolling cov'rlet of red and blew
97.450 j tester of red say, hanged with belles
97.451 v curtaines of red say
97.452 j low bedsted
97.453 j payer of cobyrons
97.454 j matt
97.455 j payer of tonges
97.456 j fetherbedd

---

[33] This is the only one of the four inventories to suggest that no separate room is set aside for the mistress of the house. Footnote 44 identifies what may well be a separate ground-floor room for Lionel Tollemache, perhaps replacing one previously allocated to 'men' (discussed in footnote 42) but neither is named for him specifically. In 1597 the shared marital chamber offers two beds (one of them 'low' which may be for the occasional use of staff) and locked chests and trunks, three of which contain the highest qualities of household linen. See Appendix A for further discussion of the evolving provision and purpose of rooms allocated to Sir Lionel and Lady Elizabeth Tollemache in 1626, and to the earls of Dysart and their wives in 1708 and 1741.

97.457 j payer of bellowes
97.458 j boulster
97.459 j fyre panne
97.460 xij pillowes
97.461 ij cushens
97.462 ij wolling blankets
97.463 iij chamber potts
97.464 j cov'rlet of wolling red and grene
97.465 j grene Irish rugge
97.466 j cannapie of yellow sattan & black tufte taffatie
97.467 j lyvery table
97.468 j cushen cloth cupboord
97.469 ij ioyned chayers
97.470 j turned chayer
97.471 j grene chist wth ij lockes & ij keyes bounde with yron
97.472 j black leather chist bound with yron, with ij lockes and ij keyes
97.473 j black leather chist with a lock and a key and iij drawers
97.474 j flat black leather chest bound with yron with a lock and a key
97.475 j little coffer inlayd with armes, wth lock and key
97.476 j little truncke cov[e]red with seales skinnes with a lock and a key
97.477 j broad box with a lock and key
97.478 j cupboord cloth of blew and grene dornex

[41] In the Nurserie[34]
97.479 Imprimis j posted bedstedd
97.480 Item j matt
97.481 j fether bedd
97.482 j boulster
97.483 j payer of wolling [woollen] blankets
97.484 j cov'rlet of dornex of diverse coullers
97.485 j tester of course linnin
97.486 ij low bedstedds
97.487 ij matts
97.488 ij fether beds
97.489 ij payer of wolling blankets
97.490 ij cov'rlets of dornex of diverse coullers
97.491 j little cupboord with a lock & key
97.492 j black leather chist bound with yron
97.493 j longe shelfe
97.494 j truncke with a locke and key
97.495 j little box with lock and key
97.496 j chamber pott

In Mistris Ciscelies Chamber[35]
97.497 Imprimis ij posted bedstedds

---

[34] By 1597 Lionel and Catherine Tollemache's family of seven children was complete: their four daughters ranged in age from 8 to 14 years, and their three sons from 15 months to 6 years. The infant's clothes are not listed.
[35] Mistress Cicely was the children's nurse.

97.498 Item ij matts
97.499 j downe bedd
97.500 j joyned keepe
97.501 j downe boulster
97.502 j lit[t]le shelfe
97.503 j fetherbedd
97.504 j candle sticke
97.505 j boulster
97.506 ij payer of wolling blankets
97.507 j pillow
97.508 ij cov'rlets of dornex of div'rse coulers
97.509 ij testers whereof the one buckrum, th'other linnin
97.510 ij trunkes with either of them a locke & key
97.511 j little flat coffer, cov'red with leather, wth lock & a key
97.512 j long chist with locke and key
97.513 ij other plain chistes, with eyther a lock & key

[43] In the maides Chamber[36]
97.514 Imprimis j trundle bedstedd
97.515 Item j matt
97.516 j fether bedd
97.517 j boulster
97.518 j payer of wolling blankets
97.519 j red wolling cov'rlet
97.520 j tester of red and grene buckrum
97.521 j great truncke with locke and key

In the working Chamber[37]
97.522 Imprimis great coffer for spice
97.523 Item j little cupboard
97.524 j trunke with locke and key
97.525 ij little tables
97.526 j carpet of dornex
97.527 j chayer with an embrodred backe

---

[36] Given her room's proximity to both the marital chamber and the nursery, the maid probably served the family's personal needs and supported Mistress Cicely in caring for the children. Notwithstanding the provision of a tester over her bed, and of a high-status feather-filled mattress, the bedstead itself is a 'trundle', implying that it was low enough to be pushed under another bed and readily portable.

[37] This designation is unique to the 1597 inventory. Here, positioned within easy reach of the marital chamber, the nursery, the nurse's and maid's chambers, such a room would have enabled Catherine Tollemache to create medical remedies whether for the household or the community beyond it. Her memorial in St Mary's church, Helmingham, honours her for 'her pitie towards the poore and her charitie in releeving 'through her skill & singular experience in chirurgery the sick and sore wounded'. In the working chamber, 'great coffer for spice', and the 'great' pestle and mortar offered most of what she would require; her concession to comfort was a chair with an embroidered back. Notably, the locked trunk here (97.524), unlike those in the marital chamber and other rooms, does not contain linen. The likelihood is that it contains substances potentially rarer or more toxic than those that might be accessible to trusted staff and stored in the apparently unsecured 'great coffer for spice'. A commonplace book contains medical notes in her own hand and recipes contributed to her. These specify a wide range of exotic and expensive ingredients ranging from myrrh to gold (Coleman, pp. 41–57).

97.528 j cushen
97.529 j great pestle and mortar

[45] In the Drying Chamber[38]
97.530 Imprimis j smoothing table upon trestles
97.531 j red chist bound with yron, wth a pad lock
97.532 j great truncke with ij lockes and j key
97.533 j black chist bound with yron
97.534 j lesser trunke with lock and key
97.535 j long chist
97.536 ij other longe chistes wth eyther a lock and key
97.537 j joyned chist with lock and key
97.538 j other chist with a lock and key
97.539 j shipp chist bound with yron
97.540 iij other old chistes
97.541 j frying panne
97.542 j candle coffer
97.543 j great hamper
97.544 j close stoole
97.545 j great brasse pott
97.546 j middle brasse pott
97.547 ij lesser brasse potts
97.548 j linnin flasket

In the Soope [Soap] house[39]
97.549 Imprimis xiij pewter candlesticks
97.550 Item iij chamber potts
97.551 ij copper chaffers
97.552 iij skillets
97.553 ij perfuming pannes
97.554 j lanthorne

---

38 The drying chamber is where laundry can be aired, smoothed (ironed) and stored. However, the 1597 inventory, although explicit about the smoothing table and trunks for storage, makes no mention of an iron but includes a 'frying panne'. The pan, if preheated by filling with hot coals or embers, would retain a clean base suitable for sliding back and forth across laundry: this is the only plausible evidence for ironing in the entire inventory. In 1626 and 1708, a similar room exists but in 1741 drying tasks take place in the laundry (see footnote 41 to the 1741 inventory).

39 Like the working chamber (see footnote 37), the soap house is listed only in the 1597 inventory and, like the stilling yard, reflects some of the activities of Catherine Tollemache (see footnote 27 above). Essential oils and perfumed waters created in the stilling yard were used here, behind a locked door (97.564), in the making of soaps and other deodorising agents for use in the household. Arguably, given the presence of 13 pewter candlesticks and a linen wheel, candle making also took place here; and the household accounts from a decade earlier show no purchases of candles between 1587 and 1589 but plenty of rushes. Rushes, dipped in tallow or oil, would have been evil-smelling but were used commonly for torches. However, the general evidence of refinement at Helmingham suggests that candles were more likely to have been of beeswax. Both the accounts and this inventory (97.570) show that bees were kept at Helmingham and it is probable that the household used its own beeswax for high-quality candle making. The wax was first melted and strained and allowed to dry and bleach in strips. When ready for use, the strips were heated. Above the pan of hot wax, wicks were hung in loops and the pewter ladle (97.560) was used to ladle wax over them. The wicks were probably of hemp or flax, their threads spun on the linen wheel (97.555), a small wheel designed for the purpose. In 1708 there was a 'candle chamber' (see footnote 37 to the 1708 inventory).

97.555 j linnin wheele
97.556 ij soope boxes
97.557 ij still pannes
97.558 ij pewter cullenders
97.559 j brasen pestle and morter
97.560 j ladle of pewter
97.561 j pan for a close stoole
97.562 j payer of wafer yrons
97.563 j payer of bellowes
97.564 j lock upon the doore with a key

[47] In the Gallerye[40]
97.565 Imprimis j litle trunke with lock and key, wherein is a black horsemans armor
97.566 j trunke chest with lock and key
97.567 j long table with trestles

In the old Chamber[41]
97.568 Imprimis iij cloose stooles, with iij pannes
97.569 j linnin presse
97.570 iij bees skeps

In the old mans Parlor[42]
97.571 Imprimis j posted bedstedd
97.572 j matt
97.573 j fetherbedd
97.574 j boulster
97.575 j payer of pillowes
97.576 j payer of wolling blankets
97.577 j cov'rlet of wolling, red and blew
97.578 j tester and vallence of black velvet, and ashe coullered damaske, with fring[e] of the same couller
97.579 iij curtaines of blew and red say
97.580 v hangings of blew and yellow say
97.581 j liv'ry table
97.582 j cupboord cloth of arras
97.583 j joyned chayer

---

40 It is probable that the black horseman's armour in the trunk (97.565) was treasured as a reminder of Lionel Tollemache's safe return from Tilbury, and England's perceived success, following the failed attempt at invasion by the Spanish in 1588 (see also footnote 52). This space is recognisable in the 1626 inventory as the 'brushing gallery', and retains the trunk with its significant contents (26.579). Items impossible to launder could be brushed clean here before being carried up the stairway leading from the gallery and returned to storage on the floor above, where both the wardrobe and armoury were located in 1597. See also footnote 49 to the 1626 inventory and footnote 35 to the 1741 inventory for later manifestations of the gallery.

41 The odd assortment of contents suggests that the 'old chamber' is now a storage area, probably on the ground floor because of the presence of bee skeps.

42 Given the descriptions that follow, this appears to be on the ground floor and, as with the previous chamber, is a room, speculatively once set aside for the use of a man or men, that has been put to a new use.

97.584 j turned chayer
97.585 ij window clothes of blew and yellow say
97.586 j payer of cobyrons
97.587 j chamber pott
97.588 j fyre panne
97.589 j payer of tonges

[49] In the inner Chamber to the old mans Parlo'r
97.590 Imprimis j postedd bedsted
97.591 j matt
97.592 j fetherbedd
97.593 j boulster
97.594 j blanket
97.595 j cov'rlet of dornex
97.596 ij payer of andyrons
97.597 j payer of tonges

In the Chamber going into the garden[43]
97.598 Imprimis j short framed table
97.599 j old payer of virginalles
97.600 j yron to set before the fyer in the night
In the entery
97.601 Imprimis j joyned forme
97.602 ij joyned stooles
97.603 ij childrens chayers

[51] In the old Parlour[44]
97.604 Imprimis j posted bedstedd
97.605 Item j matt
97.606 j downe bedd
97.607 j downe boulster
97.608 ij downe pillowes
97.609 j payer of wolling [woollen] blankets
97.610 j cov'rlet of dornex of div'rse coullers
97.611 j tester and vallence of coope worke, red and yellow, the fringe red and
            yellow crewell
97.612 v curtaines of red and yellow say
97.613 v hangings of dornex, black and yellow
97.614 j liv'ry cupboard
97.615 j cupboord cloth of black and white dornex
97.616 j great red chist with locke and key
97.617 j danske chist, inlayd, with lock and key
97.618 j chayer seated and backed with grene satten of bridges & embrodred

---

43 This, and the 'entery' following, suggest a room on the ground floor.
44 This room has been adapted from its old use as a parlour to offer a comfortably equipped sleeping
    chamber for someone of high status, judging by the descriptions of furniture and furnishings, and
    the benefit of a fireplace. The presence of a longbow and a shaft, which might have historical signifi-
    cance, and, indeed, the locked chests, suggest that this room, could, perhaps, be a ground-floor
    chamber reserved for the use of Lionel Tollemache.

with armes of crimson velvet
97.619 j joyned chayer
97.620 j turned chayer
97.621 j screene turned, with buckrum etc.
97.622 j fyre panne
97.623 j payer of tonges
97.624 j payer of andyrons
97.625 j chamber pott
97.626 j long bow
97.627 j shafte

[53] In the gatehouse Chamber
97.628 Imprimis j field bedsted
97.629 j matt
97.630 j fether bedd
97.631 j boulster
97.632 j pillow
97.633 ij wolling blankets
97.634 j wolling cov'rlet red and blew
97.635 j tester and valence of grene buffen, fringed with grene crewell
97.636 v curtaines of grene buffen
97.637 v hangings of a cloth of a mixt couler
97.638 j liv'ry cupboard
97.639 j cupboord cloth of greene
97.640 j fyre panne
97.641 j chayer of joyned worke
97.642 j old cushen of grene sattan of bridges
97.643 j payer of tonges
97.644 j payer of cobyrons
97.645 j chamber pott

In the inner Chamber to the same
97.646 Imprimis j plaine bedsted
97.647 j matt
97.648 j fether bedd
97.649 j boulster
97.650 j payer of blankets
97.651 j cov'rlet of black and whit wollinge [woollen]

[55] In the three bedd Chamber
97.652 Imprimis iij posted bedsteds
97.653 jj matts
97.654 iiij fetherbedds
97.655 j flock bedd, and j flock boulster
97.656 iij wolling blankets
97.657 iiij boulsters of feathers
97.658 iij wolling \coverletes/ blankets black and white
97.659 j candle plate

In the kitcheners Chamber[45]

97.660 Imprimis ij borded bedstedds
97.661 ij flock beds
97.662 ij boulsters
97.663 j blanket linsie wolsie
97.664 ij whit wolling blankets
97.665 j cov'rlet of listes
97.666 j shelfe
97.667 j candle plate

In Mr Bell his Chamber[46]

97.668 Imprimis j posted bedstedd
97.669 j matt
97.670 j fetherbedd and boulster
97.671 j pillow
97.672 ij payer of wolling blankets
97.673 j cov'rlet of wolling red and blew
97.674 j turned chayer
97.675 j tester of sackin of birdes eyes
97.676 vj hangings of dornex grene and blew
97.677 ij cushions of tapstrey

[47] In Lyonell Wieth his Chamber[47]

97.678 Imprimis j posted bedsted
97.679 j matt
97.680 j fetherbedd
97.681 j boulster
97.682 ij wolling blankets
97.683 j cov'relet of red cloth
97.684 j shelfe

In Baytons Chamber[48]

97.685 Imprimis j posted bedsted with a joyned tester
97.686 j matt
97.687 j fetherbedd
97.688 j bolster

---

[45] The kitchener was answerable to the cook (whose own chamber is described later) and there were probably more than one kitchener: certainly the room is equipped with two beds (mattresses) with flock fillings, the lowest quality, of which there were few at Helmingham in 1597.

[46] Mr Bell appears to have some status, judging by the fact that although his room has no fireplace, it does have wall hangings.

[47] Lionel Wyeth is mentioned as an employee of the estate in the 2nd baronet's accounts (T/Hel/21/1). The surname recurs later in this inventory in relation to linen purchased from the wife of Robert 'Wieth' (97.1037).

[48] Bayton occupies a simply furnished, unheated room but his role is uncertain. He is neither cook nor butler because there are chambers allocated to the holders of both roles, and, despite recurrence in the 1626 inventory, the surname appears in neither Suffolk probate index for Ipswich or Sudbury. It is feasible that Bayton was the 'cater', a peripatetic role dedicated to acquiring, in particular, perishable goods on behalf of the household. Smythe's accounts do not name the 'cater' but confirm that expenses incurred on his travels, mostly related to his horse, were paid by the household (Coleman, pp. 25–6).

97.689 j payer of wolling blankets
97.690 j cov'rlet of wolling black and white
97.691 j turned chayer
97.692 ij bordes joyned together

In the Butlers Chamber
97.693 Imprimis ij new liv'ry bedstedds
97.694 ij matts
97.695 ij fetherbedds
97.696 ij boulsters
97.697 j blanket of wolling
97.698 ij red wolling cov'rlets
97.699 j cov'rlet of old tapstrey

[59] In George Smith his Chamber[49]
97.700 Imprimis j posted bedsted
97.701 j matt
97.702 j fetherbedd
97.703 j bolster
97.704 j payer of wolling blankets
97.705 j cov'rlet of red cloth
97.706 j old chist
97.707 j turned chayer
97.708 j hand gunne
97.709 j payer of tonges
97.710 j short table upon trestles

In the Husbandmens Chamber[50]
97.711 Imprimis j posted bedsted
97.712 ij borded bedstedds
97.713 j matt
97.714 iij flock bedds, and iij flock boulsters
97.715 ij payer of wolling blankets
97.716 j red cov'rlet of cloth
97.717 j cov'rlet of red and yellow dornex

In the Porters Lodge
97.718 Imprimis j new liv'ry bedsted
97.719 j matt
97.720 j fether bedd and ij boulsters
97.721 j payer of wolling blankets

---

[49] As household steward, George Smythe holds a position of responsibility within a strict hierarchy of household staff. His room is notable for including a handgun which is listed as part of the household goods. The pair of tongs suggests a fireplace. See also footnote 10 regarding Smythe's longevity in his role.

[50] As noted elsewhere, it is not until 1708 that the term 'servants' is used in the inventories; until then, 'husbandmen' denotes unnamed but essential staff, at least some of whom are resident in the house. The husbandmen's chamber, like that of the kitchener's, is equipped with flock mattresses, the lowest quality of filling.

97.722 j cov'rlet of dornex red and yealow
97.723 ij payer of trestles wth bords upon them
97.724 j little forme
97.725 iij shelves

In the Cookes Chamber
97.726 Imprimis j plaine bedsted
97.727 j matt
97.728 j fether bedd and boulster
97.729 j payer of wolling blankets
97.730 j cov'rlet of red cloth
97.731 j old chest bound with yron
97.732 j turned chayer

In the Chamber over the brewhouse[51]
97.733 Imprimis j table uppon trestles
97.734 Item j shelfe

In the lit[t]le Chamber next to the same
97.735 Imprimis j plaine bedsted
97.736 j matt
97.737 j fetherbed and boulster
97.738 j peece of a wolling blanket
97.739 j red cov'rlet of cloth
97.740 j old cov'rlet of tapstrey
97.741 j little shelfe

In the Stable Chamber
97.742 Imprimis j plaine bedsted
97.743 j matt
97.744 j fetherbedd
97.745 j bolster
97.746 j payer of wolling blankets
97.747 j cov'rlet of dornex of div'rse coulers
97.748 j old chist
97.749 j short board uppon trestles

[63] In the Armorie[52]
97.750 Imprimis j black horsemans armour complete with a placket, edged with black velvet & silver lace
97.751 j other black horsemans armour complet[e]

---

[51] The brewhouse is described earlier. See footnote 23.
[52] The 'old' contents of the 1597 armoury confirm that little was discarded. A gentleman of Lionel Tollemache's status was required by statute to provide and maintain armour and weapons not only for himself but as a contribution to the Elizabethan militia, the expectations being based on his net worth, whether in land or goods (Boynton, 1971, p. 299, summarising rates between 1558 and 1621). The private effort and resources required to uphold the country's defences are evident not only from the 1597 inventory but also from Smythe's household accounts of a decade earlier. In 1587, payments to the armourer amounted to 5s. 3d. for his visits in April and November; between 4 April and 24 August 1588, the total rose to 19s. 10d. In addition to paying for his expertise (between 4s. and 5s.

97.752 ij whit horsemans armour complet[e]
97.753 j other whit horsemans armour wanting a vest
97.754 ij black corselets complet[e]
97.755 vi whit corselets complet[e]
97.756 vij almon ryvets
97.757 ij petronelles with cases and eyther of them, a horning flaske, and a mowld
97.758 j copper petronell with a case
97.759 j brasing pistall with a horning flaske, and string of crimson silke
97.760 j cast of pistales with fyre cockes, and a payer of mowldes
97.761 j other cast of pistales, inlayd with bone
97.762 j other cast of pistales whereof the one is inlayd with bone
97.763 j arming sword and dagger, gilt
97.764 j rapier with a gilded hilte
97.765 vi swords
97.766 iij rapiers
97.767 viij daggers
97.768 ix old fences
97.769 j partisine
97.770 iiij halberds
97.771 vi black billes
97.772 xvi javelins
97.773 ij pickes
97.774 iij old callin barrels
97.775 j brasen pictur which cam out of a grave stone[53]
97.776 xij old flaskes
97.777 j old copper panne
97.778 j old hamper

[65] In the wardrobe[54]
97.779 Imprimis iij fether beds

6d. per visit), purchases included supplies for his use: sand and oil with which to scour and polish the armour; thread, fustian and buckram to repair leather items; and new copper rivets and studs for what were almost certainly the flexible suits of armour known as almain rivets (see glossary). Footnote 40, above, suggests the significance of the suit of armour stored not in the armoury but in a chest in the gallery on the floor below (97.565); the Introduction summarises a letter written to Lionel Tollemache by his mother, addressed to him at Tilbury Camp and dated 10 August. By then he had heard Elizabeth I deliver her rousing 'heart and stomach of a king' address; and by then the danger of invasion had been averted.

53 This sounds to be a brass removed from a tomb or memorial: it was still in the armoury in 1626 (see 26.753).

54 The wardrobe record, extending to ten full folios, permits an intimate view of the Tollemache family as it will never be seen again in its household inventories, with clothes organised by wearer, including six of Lionel and Catherine Tollemache's seven children. The descriptions begin with items of needlework and furnishings in storage before listing accessories and high-status saddlery, and the apparel clearly belonging to Lionel Tollemache, who emerges as a fashionable and well-dressed gentleman now much in the public eye. By letters patent of Elizabeth I (SRO(I), HD1538/134/8), he was appointed a justice of the peace in April 1586. The task brought him into regular contact with his counterparts in the leading families of Suffolk, demanding travel back and forth across Suffolk in all seasons and weathers (MacCulloch, *Suffolk and the Tudors*, Oxford, 1986, pp. 36–7); and he had to be dressed for the part. The gown worn by Catherine Tollemache in her 1597 portrait (Plate I) reflects the comparative simplicity and modesty of her own wardrobe and, notably, her name is not ascribed to

97.780 Item ij boulsters
97.781 j coverlet of dornex of diverse coullers
97.782 iij payer of blanckets of wolling
97.783 j other old wolling blanket < of w >
97.784 j carpet for a long table of tapstrey
97.785 j cubboord cloth of tapestrey
97.786 j window cushen of needle worke wrought with slippes of silke of
    diverse coullers corded with a backe of grene velvet
97.787 j other cushen of cremson <velvet> damaske embrodred with cloth of tissue,
    and the back of red say
97.788 j other cushen of cloth of tissue, crimson and gold, with a backe of
    crimson damaske
97.789 ij cushens of <damaske> mockadow embrodred with black velvett & blew
    twist, the back sides of black tuft taffatie
97.790 j squear cloth of grene
97.791 iij cushens of gold arras, wrought with black moores
97.792 iij cushens of tapestrey, wrought with lyllies, rosses, and vyolets
97.793 iij cushens of tapestrey, wrought with pumgranets
97.794 j litle cushen cloth of cloth of gold, with a pillow of satten of bridges
97.795 Dublets and hoose
97.796 j whit satten dublet
97.797 j payer of hose of purple velvet layd with gold and silver lace, wane wise
    j black satten dublet pinked
97.798 j payer of black satten hoose layd with a small black silke lace upon the
    panes and cannons

[67] In the wardrobe
97.799 Item j black satten dublet & hose with a broad black silke lace in spaces
97.800 j jerkin of cloth with gold and silver buttons and loops
97.801 j dublet and hose of black satten, layde with a curled silke lace right
    downe
97.802 j black satten dublet cut, & hose, the panes layd with curled lace
97.803 j dublet and hoose of black taffaty cutt
97.804 j dublet of ashe coullered taffety stryped and cutt
97.805 j payer of hose of ashe coullered velvet, the panes layd with gold lace
97.806 j dublet of filbierd coullered taffatie cut
97.807 j payer of russet coullered velvet hose, the panes layd with silver & gold
    lace
97.808 j canvise dublet, with a payer of hose of wrought velvet, of corket red
97.809 j dublet and hose of cammell heare growgraine
97.810 j whit fusten dublet
97.811 ij fusten dublets of clay couller
97.812 ij payer of cloth hose
97.813 j greene satten dublet, with ij arming points of black silke and silver,
    with great silver tagges

---

the stock of gowns, vastguards and kirtles listed, but can be inferred. Smythe's accounts for 1587–89
show that small items such as stockings for the children and sleeves for Catherine Tollemache were
made locally. Catherine Tollemache's strong opinions regarding the cut of her sleeves are revealed
in an obsequious letter from her London tailor, Roger Jones, written in 1605 (Coleman, pp. 131–3).

97.814 j lace of black silke and silver
97.815 j payer of russet velvet hose, the panes of russet silke and <silver> gold
lace
97.816 j dublet and hoose of browne saking
97.817 j old payer of russet velvet hose
97.818 j old payer of black satten hose layd with black lace
97.819 viij yellow silke points with silver taggs whereof j wanteth a tagge

[69] In the wardrobe
Silke stockings
97.820 iij payer of black
97.821 ij payer of watchet
97.822 j payer of carnation
97.823 j payer of greene
97.824 j payer of a filbird color

Worsted stockings
97.825 ij payer of a mixed couller whit & grene
97.826 j payer mixed watchet and greene
97.827 j payer mixed watchet & yellow
97.828 ij payer mixed whit and yellow
97.829 jj payer mixed sea grene & white
97.830 j payer of sea grene
97.831 j payer of a flame couller
97.832 j payer of a popping Jaye grene
97.833 j payer of blacke

Boote hoose
97.834 j payer of carsey of a sand couller
97.835 iij payer of grene knytt hose

Gloves
97.836 iiij payer of playne gloves sweete, whereof ij payer layd with silver lace
97.837 j payer of tande sheepes lether

Garters
97.838 j payer of black cipris
97.839 j payer of grene cipris
97.840 j payer of french garters of flame couller
97.841 j payer of duckes meat couller

[71] In the wardrobe
Hatts
97.842 iij black felt hatts, whereof one lyned with velvet, with one of them a
black silke cipris
97.843 j other black silke cipris
97.844 ij girdles and hangers of needle worke of silver and gold, whereof the one
is lyned with orring tawney velvet, & the other with grene velvet
97.845 j girdle and hangers of silver, lyned with ashe coullered velvet
97.846 j silvered rapier & ij silvered daggards

97.847   j gilt dag[g]er
97.848   j black rapier & a payer of hangers of black silke, &c
97.849   j hawking bagg
97.850   j string with tassels of silver, for a dagger
97.851   j string of black silke, for a dagger
97.852   j payer of damasked spurres
97.853   j payer of black spurres
97.854   ij payer of new Spanish leather shooes
97.855   ij payer of old Spanish leather shooes
97.856   ij payer of black velvet pantafles
97.857   j payer of tawney Spanish leather pantafles
97.858   j payer of Spanish leather pumpes
97.859   j black velvet cloke lyned with shagg
97.860   j Dutch black velvet cloake with sleeves, layd with a broad black silke
        lace
97.861   j black velvet jumpe, layd with a broad silver lace
97.862   j horsemans coate of black velvet, layd with black silke and gold lace,
        and black silke and gold buttons, lyned with yellow taffaty
97.863   j taffaty cloke layd with black silke lace
97.864   j plaine black taffatie cloke

[73] In the wardrobe
97.865   j cloake of French grene cloth, layd with a brode gold lace, lyned
        throughout with velvet
97.866   j cloke of Valentia blew cloth, bound with a gold and silver lace
97.867   j cote of black velvet, layd with a plaine silke lace
97.868   j foot cloth of black cloth, layd with a velvet billament lace
97.869   j privie dublet of buffe
97.870   j cornet of black and whit damaske
97.871   j cloake of purple cloth bound about with a silver and gold lace
97.872   j black cloth cloke, layd with a black silke lace
97.873   j riding cloke of russet cloth, lyned with grene bayes
97.874   j morning cloake
97.875   j beaver hatt with a gold bande

    Saddels with their furnitur[e]
97.876   j saddle corded with black velvet & fringed with black silke & silver
        fring[e]: and a cover of black leather
97.877   j headstall, raynes, breast plate, quirace and a quirace lace, all suitable
        to the crimson saddle, having upon them xiiij tassels & ij buttons &c

[75] In the wardrobe
97.878   j padd saddle of spanish leather garded with black velvet, with a payer of
        stirripps of copper
97.879   j furnitur of black leather studded, belonging to the same saddle
97.880   j steele saddle corded with buffe leather
97.881   iij other saddles, corded with buffe, having to each of them a payer of
        stirripps & iij girts also iij quiraces & iij quirace laces of black and white
        crewel
97.882   iij payer of stirripps & stirripp leathers

97.883 ij close stooles, with their pannes

Gownes[55]
97.884 j gowne of black velvet with hanging sleeves
97.885 j plaine gowne of black velvet bound about with a black lace
97.886 j old black velvet gowne
97.887 j tuft taffaty gowne bound about with a curled gold lace
97.888 j old tuft taffatie gowne black and purple
97.889 j cloth gowne of silke russet, layd with gold <lace> buttons & bound
       about with gold lace
97.890 j morning gowne with a curtle & stummacher

    Vastguards, Curtles, and Sleeves
97.891 j black satten vastgard printed & cutt, with stumacher and sleeves
97.892 j ashe coullered vastgard of satten, cut and bound about with a parchment
       lace of gold
97.893 j old black satten curtle cut
97.894 j heaire couller satten curtell with a stumacher cutt

[77] In the wardrobe
97.895 j black velvet curtle cut and lyned with gold chamblet
97.896 j curtle of cloth of silver
97.897 j whit satten curtle cut upon crimson with sleeves of the same
97.898 j old black velvet curtle, layd with a broad gold lace
97.899 j cornation velvet curtle, layd with a broad silver lace
97.900 j old vastgard of black tuft taffaty
97.901 iiij payer of vardingall sleeves
97.902 j payer of sleeves & stummacher of ollyve couller taffaty, lyned with
       sasenet of fylbirde couller
97.903 j payer of sleeves and stummacher of a chestnutt couller, lyned with a sea-
       water greene sarsnett
97.904 j payer of black velvet sleeves, cut and drawen out with lawne
97.905 ij payer of sleves & ij stummachers of whit tuft sacking
97.906 ij breeds of black velvet

    Petty coots
97.907 j petty coote of sea water grene damaske embreodred with black velvet,
       and twist of silver
97.908 j old peach couller petty cote garded with black velvet
97.909 j cloke, a safegard [*sic*] & hood of purple cloth layd with gold bow
       buttons
97.910 j whit satten cloke layd with a broad silver lace
97.911 j whit taffaty cloke bound with a whit[e] silk lace
97.912 j black tuft taffaty cloke furred

---

[55] Although not headed with her name, the descriptions that follow relate to the apparel of Catherine
Tollemache. The list is modest in comparison with that relating to her husband, but see footnote 54
above, particularly in relation to her opinions about sleeves.

[79] In the wardrobe

    Silk stockings

97.913 j payer of peach couller silke stockings

97.914 j payer of watchet silke stockings

97.915 j payer of black velvet pantaffels

97.916 j coullered hatt with a gold bande

97.917 ij brushes

    Gownes of M[ist]r[es]s Susans[56]

97.918 j ash couller damaske gowne with hanging sleves, bound about with a parchment lace of silver

97.919 j whit[e] callasina gowne bound about with a parchment lace of silver

97.920 j old gowne of cloth of sand couller with hanging sleeves, bound about with a silver lace

97.921 j morning gowne

97.922 j payer of grene taffaty sleves & stomacher drawen out with whit sasenet

97.923 j payer of whit[e] taffaty sleves, drawne out with whit <taffaty> sasenet

    Apparell of Mistris Maries[57]

97.924 j grene damaske gowne layd with silver lace

97.925 j grene gowne of French say, bound about with lace of seawater grene silk & silver

97.926 j payer of seawater grene taffaty sleeves

97.927 j morning gowne

97.928 j pettiecote of carnation & whit striped stuffe, buffen

[81]   Apparell of mrs [Mistress] Catherines[58]

97.929 j grene gowne of French say, bound about with lace of seawater grene silke & silver

97.930 j payer of seawater grene taffaty sleeves

97.931 j morning gowne

97.932 j petty coate of carnation & whit striped buffen

    Apparell of Mistris Annes[59]

97.933 j grene gowne of French say, bound about with lace of seawater \grene/ silke and silver

97.934 j payer of sea water grene taffaty sleves

---

[56] Listed in order of age, the inventory describes the apparel of six of the Tollemache family's seven children, beginning with Susan, who was about 14 years of age in 1597. Susan was named for Lionel's mother, now Lady Susan Spring, and her clothes are distinctive in comparison with those of her three younger sisters.

[57] The apparel of Mary, just 12 years old at the time of this inventory, and her two younger sisters aged 11 and almost 8 are broadly similar. Baptised at Helmingham on 6 July 1585, Mary was named for Catherine Tollemache's mother, Lady Cromwell (née Mary Paulet, daughter of the Marquis of Winchester), wife of Henry, 2nd Lord Cromwell.

[58] Catherine, named for her mother, was baptised at Helmingham on 7 August 1586, barely a year after her elder sister, and was therefore 11 years old at the time of the inventory.

[59] Anne, the last of the four daughters, was baptised at Helmingham on 9 November 1589.

97.935 j morning gowne
97.936 j petty coote of cornation & whit striped buffen

Apparell of M[aste]r Lionell's[60]

97.937 j black dublet and hoose of searge
97.938 j morning cloake
97.939 j black hatt
97.940 j coullered hatt
97.941 j dublet of tuft canvise
97.942 j whit canvise dublet
97.943 j girdle

Aparell of M[aste]r Roberts[61]

97.944 j grene damaske coote
97.945 j hatt

[83] In the wardrobe[62]

97.946 j truncke wherein is iij payer of old hangers and iij girdels of gold lace
97.947 ij payer of boote hoose topps layd with silver lace
97.948 Also certaine old gold buttons & gold lace &c
97.949 xiij trunkes
97.950 ij great chistes
97.951 ij chayers of Joyners, & j of turned
97.952 iiij bedd lynes
97.953 ij plankes upon iij trestles
97.954 j old planke uppon trestles
97.955 j counter table
97.956 j carpet frame
97.957 j hunters horne typt with silver
97.958 j port mantue
97.959 ij payer of old spurres
97.960 j old velvet girdle

In the Chamber next the wardrobes[63]

97.961 ij old grene carpets
97.962 j old chist bound with yron
97.963 j other old chist
97.964 j trunke
97.965 iiij matts
97.966 j cradle of wickers

---

60 Lionel and Catherine Tollemache's first son and fifth surviving child was born on 1 August 1591 and baptised Lionel on 15 August at Helmingham. Barely 6 years old at the time of the inventory, he is equipped, nonetheless, to participate in the solemn ceremony of mourning, a role that would be expected of him as part of his responsibilities as the son and heir apparent. He inherited Helmingham in 1613, at the age of 22, and it will be his hand that is seen prominently in the 1626 inventory.

61 Robert, not quite 5 years old, was second son and sixth surviving child of the family. He was baptised at Helmingham on 1 December 1592.

62 Although there was another son born to the family, baptised Edward at Helmingham on 9 June 1596, nothing is recorded in the 1597 wardrobe for him because he was only 15 months old. Edward was still resident at Helmingham in his thirties: see footnote 30 to the 1626 inventory.

63 This room in the roof void is used for storage of old and infrequently used items.

97.967 j site saddle
97.968 j pillion
97.969 j old gowne of ash couller bayes with sea grene and gold buttons

[84]   linin bought xvijth of August 1605[64]
bought of Bullok[65]

97.970	Item x payer of holland shetes	x
97.971	Item v payer of pillowbers	v
97.972	Item vi towells of diaper	vi
97.973	<all these bought of Bullock>	
97.974	Item iiij dozzen of diapur napkins	

from Cropton
97.975 Item viij towells of hemping cloth
97.976 Item iij dozzen of hemping napkins
97.977 all of [?Cropton] yearne[66]

linin bought this year
1606

bought of Bullok[67]
97.978 Item iiij dozzen of diapur napkins
97.979 Item vi diapur towels

bought [of] Sherwode[68]
97.980 Item j damask taboll cloth longe
97.981 Item j towel
97.982 Item j dozzen of damask napkins

linin bought this year[69]
1607

97.983	Item of shetes such as I lye in[70]	xx payer
97.984	Item pillowberes to them	iiij payer
97.985	Item pillowberes to them more	xx payer

---

64 This is the first of ten folios of discrete summaries of linen, recording stocks and their storage and purchases between 1605 and 1609. The layout of the first table seems to have been an experiment in providing a numerical cross-check, sometimes adopted in other tables of annual purchases, but not always.

65 Here, the supplier in 1605 was Bullok, perhaps a descendant or kinsman of the Ipswich mercer, William Bullok[e], who died in 1551 (Suffolk probate index, Ipswich). The household returns to Bullok for other high-quality items in 1606.

66 The comment that these items of linen were all of Cropton's yarn suggests that he was spinner, weaver and supplier.

67 See footnote 65 above.

68 There are Sherwode wills showing the name at nearby Syleham and Hoxne (Suffolk probate index (Ipswich)).

69 If 1607 is a record of purchases, as opposed to stock, no suppliers' names are provided; however, it is apparent that whilst previous years replenished table linen, 1607 is dedicated to the purchase of new bed linen.

70 The 'I' is tantalisingly inexplicable because the quality of the 'shetes such as I lye in' is not defined; however, there is a hint in the record of a solitary pair of 'fine' pillowbeers which suggests that the previous items were less than fine. On that basis, 'I' may be a senior member of the household, responsible for compiling (or dictating) these lists of linen, rather than a member of the family.

97.986	Item one payer of fine pillowberes	j payer
97.987	Item of tabell napkins xij dozzen and iij	xij dozen

[85] In the black leather chiste
in my M[aste]r his Chamber

97.988 Linnen[71]

97.989 ffirst j payer of fyne holland sheets of ij breads & iij yards & iij quarters longe

97.990 j other payer of fyne holland sheets of iij breds the length iij yards

97.991 j other payer of fyne holland of ij breeds & a halfe; the length iij yards

97.992 j other payer of fyne holland of iij breeds, the length iij yards & half a quarter

97.993 j other payer of fyne holland of iij breads, the length iij yards & halfe a qr

97.994 j other payer of fyne holland sheets of iij breds the length iij yards & half a qr

97.995 j other payer of fyne holland without any seame, the length iij yards & a half

97.996 j other payer of fyne holland of iij breads & a half, the length iij yards & a qr

97.997 j other payer of fyne holland of ij breeds, the length iij yards & a qr

97.998 j other payer of fyne holland of ij breeds the length iij yards & a qr

97.999 j other payer of ij breeds <& a halfe>, the length iij yards & \an half/ <a quarter>

97.1000 j other payer of fyne holland of ij breeds the length ij yards & <a> halfe a qr

97.1001 j other payer of fyne holland of ij breeds the length ij yards & iij qrs

97.1002 j other payer of fyne holland of ij breeds the length ij yards iij qr

97.1003 j other of 2 brede & a half, the length 3 yards half a qr

97.1004 Holland sheets somewhat courser

97.1005 j payer of ij breeds, the length iij yards & a half

97.1006 j other payer of ij breds, the length iij yards & a qr

97.1007 j other payer of ij breds, the length iij yards & a half

[86] linin bought
1608[72]

97.1008	Item of bord clothes for her parlor vj	vj
97.1009	Item of new square clothes iij[73]	iij
97.1010	Item of new square clothes more iij	iij
97.1011	Item new oyster towells of this year 1608 and 1607[74]	xij

---

71 'Linnen' is used here to distinguish it from lower-quality items (also of linen) listed from 97.1004. See further the types of linen in the glossary.

72 1608 is a year for replenishing table linen, some of it destined for 'her parlour', which is a telling reference to the influence of Catherine Tollemache, or, perhaps, an oblique reference to a room reserved for her use. Stolton (97.1012) is, presumably, a supplier. The name does not recur.

73 There is a square table in the first-floor dining chamber (97.328) to accommodate the square cloths noted here and in the entry following.

74 Oysters were cheap and plentiful: in 1587, Smythe paid 3d. per hundred, rising to 4d. per hundred in 1588, quantities warranting the 'towels' to protect diners who enjoyed them a decade later. The 1626

97.1012	Stolton	
97.1013	Item new X[*sic*] hall bord clothes	iij

linin bought 1609[75]

97.1014	<Item j longe tabill cloth for the parlor	j>
97.1015	Item ij short tabell clothes for the parlor	ij
	Item vj cubbord clothes of the sam[e]	vj
97.1016	Item iiij bord clothes for the parlor of Cropton and of ouer home-made yearne[76]	iiij
97.1017	Item v more towells of Cropton againe	v
97.1018	Item xl payers of hemping shetes of viijd and xd yerd	xl
97.1019	Item hall bord clothes vj	vj
97.1020	Item dresser clothes vj	vj

[87]

97.1021 Sheets bought of Mrs ?Sherman 3 payer, whereof:
97.1022 j payer of ij breeds, the length iij yards, wanting half a quarter
97.1023 j other payer without a seame, the length iij yards and a qr
97.1024 j other payer of fyner sheets of ij breeds, thee length ij yards, a qr, and half
97.1025 j payer of fyne holland sheets of iij breds, whereof the one is iiij yards long & a half, the other iij yards and iij qr

In the blacke chest bound wth yron in the drying chamber[77]
97.1026 Bought of Bridgman
97.1027 vii payer of ordinary sheets of ij breeds & a half, the length three yards and a half
97.1028 v payer of pillowbeeres
97.1029 Bought of Sickelmer
97.1030 iiij payer of ordinary holland sheets of ij breeds and a half, the length iij yards iij qrs
97.1031 iij payer of holland pillowbeeres
97.1032 iij payer of old holland sheets of ij breeds, the length iij yards and a qr

in a chist in Mrs Cisselies chamb[e]r
97.1033 More of pillowbeeres xxxvij payer, & j odd one

[89] In the great trunke with 2 lockes and a key, in the drying chamber[78]
97.1034 Bought of Buckenham[79]

---

inventory describes an oyster table (26.21) and a set of oyster knives in a case (26.1030).
[75] This year sees the purchase of both table and bed linen. The costs per yard (8d. and 10d.) suggest two of 'hempen' sheets, the lowest quality, probably for staff beds.
[76] Was 'ouer home-made yearne' used for all four of these cloths, all woven, perhaps, by Cropton? The yarn would have been spun from home-grown hemp or flax.
[77] This, unlike most chests in the drying chamber (see 97.530–48), had no lock.
[78] As might be expected of a chest in the room where linen was smoothed, pressed and aired, a large stock was held here.
[79] The name Buckenham may well refer to the ancestors of a family of linen weavers at South Lopham, on the Suffolk–Norfolk border, some 25 miles from Helmingham, where hemp had been grown for centuries and weaving became concentrated in the two villages of North and South Lopham. By the 19th century the family of Buckenham had developed a reputation for producing high-quality linens

97.1035   j payer of new hemping sheets of ij breeds, the length iij yards and a
          quarter
97.1036   xxvj payer of old sheets
97.1037   Bought of Robert Wieth his wife[80]
97.1038   j payer of flaxen sheets of ij breeds & a halfe, the length iij yards &
          halfe a qr
97.1039   vj bord clothes for the hall

In a lesser trunke with lock and key, in the drying chamber
97.1040   xix payer of old sheets whereof xi payer are lengthened[81]
97.1041   vi payer of overworne sheets

In the red chist bound with yron in the drying chamber
97.1042   Made in the yeare, 1596[82]
97.1043   xxij payer of servingmens sheets, of ij breeds the length ij yards and
          a quar
97.1044   xx payer of other sheets, and j odd sheet

In an old chist in the drying chamber
97.1045   Made at Helmingham this present year, 1597[83]
97.1046   xij payer of new course hemping sheets of ij breeds, the length ij
          yards and iij qr
97.1047   x payer of new hemping sheets somewhat courser of the length and
          bredth of the former xij

[91] In a joyned chist with lock and key, in the drying chamber
97.1048   Napery[84]
97.1049   v squear clothes   }
97.1050   iij carving clothes   }
97.1051   xv cupboord clothes   }
97.1052   ix towels   }

---

for a high-status clientele. In 1837, the first year of Queen Victoria's reign, Thomas Buckenham of
North Lopham gained a coveted Royal Warrant to supply diaper and huckaback tablecloths to the
new monarch. Their production survived into the 20th century, ending with a three-day sale of looms
and linen in November 1925. A stained-glass window in the Lady chapel of South Lopham church
(dedicated to St Nicholas but, as the result of an error in an historical guide, known since 1829 as St
Andrew's), commemorates Louisa Buckenham (d. 8 May 1878) with images from the biblical story
of Dorcas. A central panel shows linen made by Dorcas being given to St Peter, while surrounding
panels include images of plants, including flax.

80   As noted in footnote 47, the name of Wyeth, or Wieth, recurs in the Helmingham Archive. Suffolk
     wills include one Robert Wyeth of Monk Soham (d. 1622) (Suffolk probate index (Ipswich)). Monk
     Soham lands formed part of the Helmingham manorial holdings, making it likely that Robert's
     unnamed wife wove linen from locally grown flax.
81   An example of household economy at Helmingham.
82   Sheets made in 1596 are noted irrespective of whether applying to all 42 pairs of sheets or only the
     first 22 pairs. The year prior to the compilation of the inventory was clearly notable for replenishing
     the stock of bed linen for the 'servingmen' resident at Helmingham Hall.
83   Replenishment of the stock of coarse bed linen continues apace in the inventory of 1597 with the
     acquisition of a further 22 pairs of sheets.
84   The record moves from a calendar of repair and replenishment to one of storage of table linen, or
     napery, but continues to refer to suppliers of new items while not ascribing dates.

97.1053	ix dosen napkins whereof ij dosen are overworne	} of hempinge cloth
97.1054	viij rubbers	}
97.1055	v hall table clothes	}
97.1056	iij husbandmens clothes	}
97.1057	iiij dresser clothes	}
97.1058	x new dyaper towels	
97.1059	iiij carving clothes, bought of Danby	

In the greene chist in my m[aste]r his chamber

97.1060	xiiij boord clothes, whereof one is finer than the rest	}
97.1061	ij cupboord clothes	}
97.1062	vi short bord clothes	}
97.1063	iiij other short boord clothes whereof one is fyner than the rest	} of holland
97.1064	v carving clothes	}
97.1065	ix flaxen cupboord clothes	}

In a trunk in the maids chamber

97.1066	x dosen and x napkins of Holland
97.1067	ix dosen of browne napkins
97.1068	j dosen of napkins wrought with a blew chevern
97.1069	viij towels
97.1070	iiij dresser clothes

[93] In the black leather chist with a lock and a key, in my m[aste]r his chamber

97.1071	iij long boord clothes	}
97.1072	ij cupboord clothes	} of dyaper
97.1073	j towel	}
97.1074	ij dosen and xi napkins	}
97.1075	Bought of Mr Sherman	
97.1076	ij boord clothes	}
97.1077	j towel	} of dyaper
97.1078	ij dosen napkins	}
97.1079	iiij cupboord clothes	}
97.1080	iiij towels	} of new dyaper
97.1081	iiij dosen & v napkins	}
97.1082	iiij long clothes	}
97.1083	ij cupboord clothes	}
97.1084	j carving cloth	} of damaske
97.1085	ij towels	}
97.1086	ij dosen & xi napkins	}
97.1087	j long boord cloth	}
97.1088	j cuppoord cloth	} of new damaske
97.1089	j carving cloth	}
97.1090	Also in this chist is the needleworke bedd	

*Folio **95** has been crossed through in its entirety with 'X'. The second version appears on Folio **97**, where descriptions are informed by additional details of donors and recipients.*

97.1091   **[95]** *Plate*[85]
97.1092   j bason and eawer, with armes, duble gilte
97.1093   j other bason and eawer, with armes, parcell gilt
97.1094   j other bason and ewer
97.1095   iij standing cuppes, with covers double gilt
97.1096   ij tankerds with covers, double gilte
97.1097   ij potts with eares & covers double gilte, whereof j hath armes
97.1098   iij broad boules parcell gilt
97.1099   j gilt boule with a cover
97.1100   ij broad silver boules
97.1101   iij silver boules, and j cover
97.1102   iij lesser boules
97.1103   ij broad boules
97.1104   j salt double gilt, with a cover with armes
97.1105   j squear salt double gilt
97.1106   j other salt double gilt
97.1107   j other salt with a cover
97.1108   j other gilt salt
97.1109   j litle bell salt double gilt with a cover
97.1110   j potion peece, with an eare
97.1111   j porringer with an eare
97.1112   vi fruite plats
97.1113   ij spoones duble gilt
97.1114   vi appostle spoones
97.1115   j dosen spoones with knoppes
97.1116   j dosen playne silver spoones
97.1117   viij other silver spoones

[97] Plate, Silver and gilte[86]
97.1118   j bason and eawer double gilt, with armes
97.1119   j other bason & eawer with armes, prle gilt
97.1120   j great high standing cupp double gilt, given to Mr Lyonell at his christning, by my La: Springe his godmother & grandmother[87]
97.1121   j cupp double gilt, in fashion of a nutt, with a wrethen stalke, given to
Mr Lyonell at his christning by his godfather Sir Robert Wingfield[88]

---

85   The deleted list, 97.1091–1117, can be compared with the one following.
86   Written in the same hand as the deleted list, but probably dictated and incorporating numerous amendments relating to design and provenance.
87   Lionel, Lionel and Catherine Tollemache's first son and heir. His 'godmother and grandmother', Susan, described as 'My La[dy] Springe', married her second cousin, William Spring, following the untimely death of her Tollemache husband in 1575 (see Introduction).
88   This second christening gift to young Lionel Tollemache came from his godfather, Sir Robert Wingfield (who died in 1596, a year before the inventory was compiled). One of Sir Robert's daughters (a Mistress Warner) is noted as a goddaugher in the 1572 will of Lionel Tollemache (young Lionel's great grandfather). Sir Robert is mentioned also as a beneficiary in the will of young Lionel's grand-father, the unfortunate Lionel who died at the age of 35 on 18 December 1575. He bequeathed to Sir Robert Wingfield (and to 15 other beneficiaries) 'one gold ring waying 20 shillings'. Sir Robert lived not far from Helmingham, at Letheringham Hall, and his second wife, Bridget, was Sir William Spring's sister. As Bridget Spring, she compiled a manuscript of medical remedies, both procedures and medicines, including 'my brother Sprynges medycyne for Burnynge or Scaldynnge' which

97.1122   j cupp duble gilt, in fashion of a peare with a wild man clyming upp thee stalke, given to Mr Edward at his christning by his godfather & unkell Lord Edward Cromwell[89]

97.1123   ij tankerds double gilt, with covres & eares which my mr bought him self

97.1124   j pott double gilt with eares & a cover with armes

97.1125   j pott somewhat lesser, double gilt with eares and a man upon the cover

97.1126   iij broad boules parcell gilt, with one covr unto them prcell gilt¶ [sic]

97.1127   iij silvr boules & j covr

97.1128   j gilt boule with a cover ¶[sic]

97.1129   iij lesser boules

97.1130   ij broad silver boules for creame

97.1131   j squear salt double gilt with a covr with <u>armes</u> \a man in the toppe/

97.1132   ij highe salts double gilt, with j covr with armes

97.1133   j litle bell salt double gilt, of Mr Lyonells

97.1134   j gilt salt with a cover \rownde/

97.1135   j other salt with a cover \gilte through't/

97.1136   ij great spoones double gilt with knopps

97.1137   j dosen of silver spoones with gilt knopes

97.1138   j dosen of new playne silver spoones

97.1139   vj appostle spoones

97.1140   viij silver spoones

97.1141   vi fruit plats of silver, with armes

97.1142   j potion peece of silver

97.1143   j porringer of silver with an eare

97.1144   j suger box of silver with armes

[99] An inventorie taken the xvjth of februarie 1604[90]
Plate silver and gilte

97.1145   j bason and eawer percell gillte with armes

97.1146   j bason and eawer plaine with armes

97.1147   j bason and eawerr newe bought of plaine silver rownde with armes graven on them bothe

97.1148   ij heigh standinge pottes wrought dubblle gillte with armes graven on them bothe

97.1149   j heigh standinge cupe dubble gilte with a cover and a man in the tope

---

involved the application of crushed onion to the affected place. Bridget married Sir Robert Wingfield in 1580 (the year in which Catherine Cromwell married Lionel Tollemache), but predeceased her husband, dying in 1590. Given her physical proximity to Helmingham for ten years, and her close link to the Tollemache family, she may well have been a source of advice and influence for Catherine Tollemache in her own medical work. Indeed, another of Bridget Spring's medical recipes comes from the Marquess of Winchester, Catherine's maternal grandmother. This, 'for the meseles and pockes to brynge them fourthe' advocates boiling figs in a pint of stale ale until reduced by half and then adding a little English saffron (see J. Spring, 'Medical Recipe Book of the Spring Family', *Suffolk Review*, 38, 2002, pp. 1–14).

89   The donor described as Lord Edward Cromwell is Catherine Tollemache's brother, who inherited the title of 3rd Lord Cromwell on the death of their father in November 1592. See footnote 96 below for the fate of this gift and its donor.

90   This update to the 1597 inventory of plate, dated 16 February 1604, is undoubtedly written by Lionel Tollemache himself, using the possessive 'my' to refer to members of his family. In comparison with the handwriting of the compiler of the inventory, the head of household's hand is challenging, as are some of his claims and comments, described in the footnotes following.

	given to Lionell by my mother
97.1150	j other heigh standinge cupe rounde dubblle gilte with a cover and a man in the tope given to lionell
97.1151	j other gilte cupe given to Edwarde with a cover and a man in the tope [*sic*] huntinge the stalke
97.1152	ij dubble gilte pottes with covers the one with armes the other with a man in the tope
97.1153	ij dublle gilte tankards with covers
97.1154	j dublle gilte boulle with a cover, geven by Quene Elisabeth[91]
97.1155	iij brode percell gilte boulles with one cover with armes in the tope X \exchanged for the thre heigh standinge cupes newe bought the 27 April 1608/
97.1156	j other gilte boulle with a cover and a ringe in the tope
97.1157	iij plaine silver boulles with a cover
97.1158	iij plaine lesser silver boulles
97.1159	ij plaine brode silver bowles for creame
97.1160	j dubble bell salte dubble gilte with armes wrought, geven by Quene Elizabethe[92]
97.1161	ij high saltes dubble gilte with armes and armes in the tops
97.1162	j square dublle gilte salte with armes and a man in the tope
97.1163	j other ronde salte plaine dublle gilte with armes
97.1164	j littell bell salte dublle gilte with armes
97.1165	ij dubble gilte spones with L and T
97.1166	j dosen spones with gilte knopes with L and T
97.1167	j dosen spones with rownde gilte knopes
97.1168	j dosen of plaine silver spones
97.1169	vj spones with apostelles, it is hoolph a dosen ?[*illeg.*]

---

91 No gift from the Queen is identified in the list of 1597 and Elizabeth I died on 24 March 1603, eleven months before this inventory of plate was compiled. Every gift she made and received during her long reign was recorded, whether presented during the New Year gift exchange or as 'free' gifts, those that were personal, celebrating events such as the christenings of children of members of the royal court. Neither the rolls recording New Year's Gift Exchanges from 1559 to 1603 nor those of all the 'free' gifts made by the Queen reveals any to a member of either the Tollemache or Spring families (nor the Jermyns, Lady Spring's family). However, a regular recipient of gifts of silver from the Queen was Mary, Baroness Cromwell, Catherine Tollemache's late mother, who died on 10 October 1592, and it is possible that she was the original recipient of this bowl. Interrogation of the Elizabethan gift rolls confirms that gifts were exchanged between the Queen and Lady Cromwell every year between 1567 and 1585 (see Lawson, p. 638 for summary of references to Mary Cromwell, née Paulet), and the Queen's gifts to Lady Cromwell are always silver, made by one of the royal goldsmiths. Two are cups, one is a bowl, one a tankard and one a plate. Of these, a contender for the item listed at 97.1154 is the Queen's gift to Lady Cromwell in 1576 (Lawson, 2013, item 76.292, p. 198) of a gilt bowl with a cover, weighing 12¼ ounces, made by Affabel Partridge.

92 As confirmed in the previous footnote, there is no evidence for this being a gift from the Queen directly to the family, nor identifiably one given by her to Lady Cromwell. The Queen did, however exchange gifts with Henry Cromwell (1537–1604), knighted in 1564, and his wife, Joan, who died in 1584. Sir Henry was a first cousin once removed to Catherine Tollemache's late father, Henry, 2nd Lord Cromwell. This is a tenuous link and an unlikely route; but Sir Henry received numerous gifts of silver from the Queen almost every year between 1565 and 1603, and his wife between 1571 and 1584 (Lawson, 2013, p. 638). Most items are not described, and of those that are, none is described as a salt.

[100] An inventorie taken of it the
xvith of Februarie 1604[93]

Plate

97.1170	j silver suger boxxe with armes graven on the cover
97.1171	j silver chafin[g] dishe with armes graven uppon the side of it
97.1172	iiij silver candellstickes with armes graven on them all
97.1173	vj sillver plates, with Joyces cote on his, graven on the side of them all[94]
97.1174	j silver porringer \exchanged the 27 of Aprill 1608/ \with a cover now/
97.1175	j silver potion pece with armes graven on the sides
97.1176	j gallie pote tipped and footted with silver
97.1177	ij littell plaine silver spones to take onto suger

[101] An Inventory taken the Second daye of
Maye in anno domini 1608 viz ...

Plate silver and guilt

97.1178	Imprimis	j bassoon and eawer parcell guilt with armes
97.1179		j bassoon and eawer plaine with armes
97.1180		j bassoon and eawer new bought of plaine silver rounde with armes graven on them both
97.1181		ij highe standinge potts wrought dubble guilt with armes graven on them bothe
97.1182		j heighe standinge cupe dubble guilt wth a cover and a man in the tope given to Lionell by my mother
97.1183	\not prized/	j other heighe standinge cupe rownde dubble guilt with a cover and a man in the tope given to Lionell[95]
97.1184	\not prized/	j other guilt cupe given to Edward with a cover and a man houldinge the stalke[96]
97.1185		ij dubble guilt potts wth covers the one wth armes the

---

93 The inventory dated 16 February 1604 lists the family's existing items (notably those engraved with arms) as well as what appear to be some newly acquired pieces added as late as 1609 (even though the list is headed 1608). The link with ancestry is important to Lionel Tollemache, for it was around this time that his name was first proposed for a baronetcy. Now, anxious to pursue his route to a new title offered by the new king, James I, Lionel Tollemache takes every opportunity to stake and document his claim, not least through his record of plate.

94 'Joyce's cote' refers to the arms of the Joyce family, who held Creke Hall and its lands at Helmingham until union through marriage with the Tollemache family.

95 The great high-standing cup, whose design and provenance are described in detail at 97.1121, was the christening gift of Sir Robert Wingfield to Lionel's son. Why was the silver-gilt cup 'not prized'? Was the design, with its 'man in the top' considered old fashioned? This seems unlikely, given that the preceding item, a christening gift to young Lionel from 'my mother', is of the same design. Was the comment made as a result of some unease about the donor, as in the item following?

96 The item, described fulsomely at 97.1122 as a christening gift to son Edward from Catherine's brother, Edward, 3rd Lord Cromwell, is relegated to one line and treated to the dismissive marginal comment 'not prized'. This almost certainly reflects an opinion about the (recently deceased) donor rather than about the gift. Edward, 3rd Lord Cromwell, had died the year before, 1607, in reduced circumstances. In 1592 Edward Cromwell succeeded to the title on the death of his father but was plagued by a legacy of expensive and protracted legal disputes and worse. Faced with charges of high treason, he was imprisoned in the Tower of London in 1601. He submitted to the Queen's mercy, was pardoned and fined £6,000. Lord Cromwell was restored to favour by James I, but continued financial difficulties forced him to quit England for the prospect of advancement through military service in Ireland. His Leicestershire manors (as well as his horses and carriage) were seized to pay his creditors, and in September 1605 he exchanged lands in England for the barony of Lecale in Co. Down. His time in Ireland was short lived: he died at Lecale in September 1607 (*ODNB*).

	other with a man in the tope
97.1186	ij dubble guilt tankards wth covers
97.1187	j dubble guilt boule with a covr given by Quen Elizabeth[97]
97.1188	j heighe standing \dubble/ guilt cupe wth a \heighe/ cover to it, and armes, wth the thre leved grese new bought
97.1189	j other heighe standinge cupe dubble guilt wth armes \ engraven wth cheane worke/ new bought wthout a covr
97.1190	j other heighe standinge cupe wthout a cover dubble built, with armes ingraven upon it wth rosse slippes wrought uppon it new bought
97.1191	j other guilt boule wth a cover & a ringe in the tope
97.1192	iij plaine silver boulles wth a cover
97.1193	iij plaine lesser silver boulles
97.1194	j other heighe standinge cupe \dubbell gillt/ of skollope shills with arms and with a cover to it with a heigh top

[102] Plate

97.1195	ij plaine brode silver boulls for creame
97.1196	j dubble bell sault dubble guilt wth a cover wrought given by Quen Elizabethe[98]
97.1197	ij heighe saults, dubble guilt wth a covr and armes in the tope
97.1198	j square dubble guilt sault wth a cover and a man in the tope
97.1199	j other heighe sault dubble guilt wrought with a cover
97.1200	j other rownd sault plaine dubble guilt with a cover
97.1201	j littell bell sault dubble guilt wth a cover
97.1202	j plaine littell silver sault wth a cover
97.1203	ij dubble guilt spones wth L and T
97.1204	j duzen <guilt> spones wth guilt knopes with L and T
97.1205	j duzen spones wth rounde guilt knopes
97.1206	j duzen spones plaine
97.1207	vj \v/ appostells spones
97.1208	j suger silver boxe wth armes graven on the cover \& a spone/
97.1209	j silver chaffyne dyshe wth armes graven uppon the syde of it
97.1210	vj silver platts wth Joyces cote graven on them all uppon the syde of them[99]
97.1211	j silver porringer wth a cover & armes graven
97.1212	j silver potion pece wth armes graven on the side
97.1213	j gallie pote tipped & futted wth silver
97.1214	ij plaine littell silverr spones to take out suger
97.1215	x peces of silver plate beinge of v severall stiles bought in Ao 1609
97.1216	a broade plaine silver salte

---

97 This is the item identified first in the 1604 list of plate (97.1154), the provenance of which is suggested in footnote 91 above.

98 See footnote 92 above.

99 See footnote 94 above.

THE 1626 HOUSEHOLD INVENTORY

Helmingham Hall Archive T/Hel/9/1/1

The following are marginal marks confirming a post–1626 check. Sometimes more than one mark is made, suggesting checks were made at different dates:

+
O
Ø
Θ
o
₀
⊗
X *or* x

qr *or* qur	Indicates a query; sometimes clarified by additional information
r	Uncertain. May be a variant of 'rem'
rem	Remaining, sometimes qualified by a number of items
W, w *or* want	Taken to mean 'wanting', sometimes clarified by additional information

[105][1]

An inventory taken att Hellmyngham halle the [blank][2] of October 1626: of all suche householde stuffe as was there remaynenge the daie & yeare abovesaide[3]

In the halle

26.1	+	Imprimis one longe <slideboard> table & frame wth a cover & boxe for peces to restt in
26.2	+	Item one other table fframe wth twoe leaves to be drawne out
26.3	+	Item one liverye cupborde wth one settle joyned to the walle
26.4	+	Item vi joyned formes
26.5		Item twoe joyned benches wth twoe newe peces of seelinge
26.6		<one cobiron & one iron forke for the fire>

---

[1] T/Hel/9/1/1 contains the 1597 and 1626 household inventories bound together. Folio numbering for 1597 ended with 103; two folios were numbered but left blank and 1626 commences on 105.

[2] An obvious gap was left for the date. For discussion of this, and of the building layout suggested by the 1626 inventory perambulation route, see Appendix A.

[3] Dated annotations confirm that the document was amended until at least 1633.

26.7	<W>	Item one otter fflewe + \sent to ffakenham/[4]
26.8	+	Item two brasseinge candleplates whereof one with twoe sockets
26.9	+	Item one cuppborde of waynescott joyned like seelenge under neath the halle windowe
26.10	Things to be sente to ffakenham	Item one bundle of things packed up in a dornex coverlitt wth a peece of a coutche chaire
26.11	+	Item one haukes pearke
26.12	+	Item X javelings fringed & armed wth blacke & white towards the topps
26.13	+	Item one staffe for the annciente
26.14	+	Item 4 horsemens staves whereof two with heads & two without
26.15	+	Item one bell hangeinge in an Iron frame
26.16	+	Item one iron dogge in the chimnye & a great iron fireforke
26.17	+	Item ii staggs heads: & viij bucks heads

In the halfe pace betwene the halle & the celler for stronge beere[5]

26.18	+	Item twoe joyned formes one wth a broaken foote
26.19	+	Item one haukes pearke
26.20	+	Item one iron spurkitt

In the halfe pace nexte the parlour doore

26.21	+	Item one fouldenge table for oysters wth an olde foldinge frame thereunto
26.22	removed to Ffakenham or some other place[6]	Item one peece of joyned worke like a deske to sett a booke or a lookinge glasse against it
26.23	+	Item one brassinge candle plate
26.24	+	Item twoe broade peeces of iron wth twoe feete apeece to sett before the prlor fire when it is raked upp
26.25	+	Item one wicker skreene & frame
26.26	+	Item one peece of waynescott to sett before the prlor chimnye in smmr
26.27	+	Item one thinge made for to rubbe the prlor wthall
26.28	+	Item one locke & kie unto the doore in the back yarde[7]

---

4   The first of many references to items removed from Helmingham Hall to the recently acquired property known as 'Lugdons' at Fakenham Magna, discussed in Appendix B, where all removed items are listed.

5   The 1626 inventory is unique in using this description: a halfpace denotes a step, a change in level. The cellars, expanded since 1597, are visited later (26.1035–1055).

6   See comments in list of items removed (or not found) in Appendix B.

7   See Appendix A for discussion of security, an overriding concern in 1626.

[106] In the parl[ou]r

26.29	+	Item one locke & kye to the doore
26.30	+	Item one longe table & frame wth twoe draweinge leaves
26.31	+	Item one shorter table & frame wth 2 draweinge leaves
26.32		Item one <fouldeinge> table \with 2 fouldinge leaves one longer than the other/ wth a Dutch frame of wallnuttree
26.33		Item one other 8ft. square fouldeinge table & frame
26.34	+	Item one liverie cupborde wth twoe settles \& twoe drawers/ one above the other
26.35	rem[?ains]	Item twoe longe ould fashioned joyned formes
26.36	i want[ing]	Item foure other joyned formes of wallnutt tree whereof twoe longer & two shorter + 2[8]
26.37	rem	Item ij joyned stooles the leafe of one broaken
26.38	rem	Item 4 \blacke/ leather backed chaires doone wth broad yellowe nailes whereof 2 greater & <one> \2/ lesser
26.39		Item one little chaire seated & backed wth turkye worke
26.40		Item one lowe stoole covered wth nedleworke fringed
26.41		Item one coutche chaire nothinge in it but a canvas bottom
26.42	Thinges appointed to be sente unto	{<Item one other fouldinge table wth a turned pillar & a crosse foote to beare it up beinge to fasten against a wall
26.43	ffakenham[9]	{Item twoe boxes one greater & thother lesser>
26.44	+	Item one great boxe in the windowe nexte the courte yarde[10] wth locke & kye used for to putt wrytings in
26.45		Item one little blacke leather boxe
26.46	1+[11]	Item twoe verie faire large mapps of the worlde in frames[12]
26.47		Item one lesser mappe
26.48	+	Item two large peeces of arras hangeings fastened to the wall in twoe severall places
26.49	rem	Item ffoure turkye worke carpetts wrought in diverse colours whereof one, verie large & greate, thother three lesser

---

8   The annotation '+2' to the right of the entry suggests that on a subsequent check only two of the four forms were located.

9   See list of removals in Appendix B.

10   See Appendix A and Plate 13, where the inner courtyard is marked as '1'.

11   The purpose of the numeral '1' is uncertain but it may indicate that only one map was located at the time of the check.

12   Sir Lionel Tollemache, 2nd baronet, had a liking for maps, clocks and mathematical instruments (see footnote 14 below regarding sundials), and his portrait (Plate II) shows him standing beside a table bearing either a clock or other instrument.

26.50	+	Item one verie large fire pann, tongs & 2 greate andirons \& paire of bellows/
26.51	+	Item one paire of candle snuffers of brasse
26.52	w	Item one arrowe with a forked heade \qr/ and one forked heade for an arrowe
26.53	+	Item twoe eskutcheons of armes in the chimnye-peece
26.54	qr	In the windowe next the courte yarde[13] 2 peecs of small brasse cutt for dialls, & a brassinge gnomon or corke to sett in the middle of the diall[14]
26.55	+	Item 2 iron spurkitts
26.56		Item one paire of scales to waighe outlandishe goolde with a boxe of waights
26.57	+	Item one paire of tables inlaide wth bone to playe att chess wth a broaken joint wth xxvj or xxviijt white & blacke table men[15]

[107] In the newe chamber nexte the great parl'r commonlie called my Maisters Chamber[16]

26.58		Item twoe locks & kyes to the 2 firste doores
26.59		Item the chamber hanged rounde wth greene & yellowe dornixe
26.60		Item twoe curteyns for the windowes of the same dornixe with ringles & 2 curteyne rodds
26.61		Item one newe square table to open wyth lock & kye
26.62	+	Item one liverie cupborde
26.63	+	Item one coutch frame borded in the bottom
26.64	r	Item one paire of tables with xxix table men
26.65		Item one greate paire of brasse cobirons: wth fire panne & tongs with brasse heads

---

13 This may or may not be the same window as the one described in 26.44.

14 There are several descriptions of dials in this inventory (see glossary, **dial**). It is possible that this sundial was designed for indoor use. Later examples are described in Joseph Moxon's *Mechanick Exercises or the Doctrine of Handy Works*, published posthumously (London, 1703). In his day, Moxon was famed for his skills as a maker of terrestrial and celestial globes, mathematical instruments, maps and charts. He was a Fellow of the Royal Society and hydrographer to the King (Charles II), a position he held at the time of his death in 1691. When his 'Exercises' were issued posthumously in book form, the publishers chose to add over forty pages of Moxon's 'Mechanick Dyalling: showing how to draw a true Sun-Dyal on any given Plane, however Scituated … ' (pp. 307–52). Moxon leads the 'mechanick' through a series of exercises in measuring and drawing dials on both vertical and horizontal planes; but bearing in mind where the components of this dial are recorded at Helmingham, it is quite probable that it was intended to be used inside the parlour. Moxon's final section (pp. 342–52) is entitled 'To make a Dyal on the Ceiling of a Room, where the Direct Beams of the Sun never come', which seems entirely appropriate for the location of the 1626 parlour, whose 'window next the courtyard' was on the ground floor and faced East, with limited enjoyment of the 'direct beams of the sun'.

15 Although other gaming tables, games and 'tablemen' are mentioned in all four inventories, this is the only document to mention chess.

16 This is evidence of a 'new' room or suite of ground-floor rooms (discussed further in Appendix A) dedicated to Sir Lionel's use. The phrase 'first two doors', each with locks and keys, suggests a linking space, perhaps dictated by the depth of a back-to-back chimney flue.

26.66		w	One leadeinge staffe for a capteyne guilt, the heade broaken off
26.67		w	One other leadeinge staffe of brazell wth twoe tassells wth silver collers & the topp tipped wth silver with a greene buckerum cover
26.68		w	Item one musket rest with tassells the topp tipped with silver
26.69	Carried to <Hellmingham> \Faknam/ +		Item one inlaide chiste for wryghteings
26.70		+	Item one square boxe guilded & painted
26.71		+	Item one other lyttle square boxe <guilded and> painted
26.72		+	Item one other ovall fashioned boxe \guilded/ <painted>
26.73		w	Item one rapire & punniarde wth guilt inlaide hilte a blacke velvette scabberde to the punnyarde
26.74		+	Item one shorte sworde wth a crosse hilte guilt wth a russett scabberde & knyfe in yt
26.75		+	Item one velvett scabberde for a shorte sworde
26.76			Item twoe iron spurketts
26.77		w	Item one paire of bellowes
26.78			Item one paire of iron doggs for the brasse andirons
26.79			Item one other paire of smalle lowe andirons
26.80		w	Item one whales bone rodd

In the clossett of the wright hand comeinge in att the doore[17]

26.81			Item one locke & kye to the doore
26.82			Item one presse wth drawers for wrightings
26.83		r	Item one inlaide chiste wth locke & kye
26.84			Item one liverie table
26.85		r	Item one cabbinett wth drawers locke & kye upon a trestle
26.86			Item one joyned cofer wth locke & kye
26.87	Carried to <Hellmyngham> \Faknam/ r		Item one large blacke leather truncke locke & kye
26.88		r	Item one seales skynne truncke wth locke & kye
26.89		r	Item one other lesser blacke leather truncke locke & kye
26.90		r	Item diverse small things: as boxes, gunns, crosse bowe cases, quailes netts, hampers horse bits & bosses, a tressell & blacke leather pattent boxe

---

[17] This and the closet following are sizeable spaces and appear to be part of the suite of rooms for Sir Lionel, as do the closets on either side of the chimney.

[108] In the next clossett upon the right hande[18]

26.91   Item one locke & kye to the doore
26.92   Item one cuppborde for wrightenges with darnex central partitions
26.93   Item one iron scuppett
26.94   Item the romphe mattedd

In the clossett upon the right hande of the chimnye[19]

26.95   Item one locke & kye to the doore
26.96   Item the chamber hanged rounde wth verders beinge wryt in number twoe windowe peeces of the same twoe longe windowe curteynes of the same with curteyne rodds & ringles
26.97   Item one partition curteyne of the same wth ringles & curteyne rodd
26.98   Item one newe square table & frame
26.99   Item one deske to wright upon
26.100   Item one joyned stoole
26.101   Item one frame wth XX pictures
26.102   Item one joyned frame wth foure shelves to sett books upon
26.103   Item the romphe matted
26.104   Item a womans picture in a frame
26.105   Item twoe shelves one upon bracketts
26.106   Item one brasse spurkett

In the clossett upon the lefte hande of the chimnye[20]

26.107   Item one fouldeinge screene of buckerum wth a wooden frame
26.108   Item one wooden frame to sett a picture upon when yt is a lyminge
26.109   Item a plate of leade wth diverse boxes & other small odd things

Folios 109 and 110 are blank.

[111] In the chamber opposite to the Parlor doore[21]

26.110   Item one locke & kye to the doore
26.111   Item one postead beddsteade \<matted & corded>/ the heade carved & inlaide with guilte/ knobbs upon the teasterne
26.112   Item 5 greene saie curtens wth ringles, & 3 curten rodds
26.113   Item one <ffeather> \downe/ bedd, & ffeather, boulster, one <ffeather> \downe/ pillowe, 2 \newe/ <yellowe> Irishe blankitts, one yellow & soote coloured darnixe coverlitt with a matt, & corde
26.114   Item the chamber hanged rounde wth old blewe & yellowe <lynsiye>

---

18   This closet has floor coverings, notable for Helmingham, even at this date. The use of 'romphe' (26.94) to describe rooms or spaces is unique to this inventory.

19   For a closet, or inner chamber, this is an impressive space with floor coverings, window curtains and tapestry hangings around the walls. Here are shelves for books, a table and a writing desk, suggestive of a private study area, perhaps the precursor to a library. There is no room designated as a library in the Helmingham household inventories until 1741.

20   This closet, in which no window is mentioned, appears to be set aside for painting or, at least, for storing items relating to painting. See glossary, **limn**.

21   This room 'opposite the Parlour door' is on the ground floor, has a fireplace and is equipped as a bedroom. Some of the contents are dated and there is confusion about the fillings of the bed (mattress), bolster and pillow. There is a curtain rod over the window but apparently no curtains: this looks to be a room in transition.

\saye/ hangeings
26.115 Item one liverie table wth a old greene carpett
26.116 Item one greate turned chaire
26.117 Item twoe old fashioned formes
26.118 Item a ffirepan & tongs & twoe andirons
26.119 Item one curteyne rodd over the windowe

In the Musique Parlor[22]

26.120		Item a locke & kye unto the doore
26.121		Item two greate leather backed & seated chaires printed done wth yellowe nayles
26.122		Item one old fashioned chaire, backed & seated wth greene coloured stuffe being much worne
26.123		Item one paire of virginalls locked upp
26.124		Item one small treble organ
26.125	W+	Item att the further ende of the saide organ nexte unto the clossett one large peece of cloathe whereon pte of a picture is begun to be limned
26.126		Item twoe sentchings of armes over the portall of the doore in a fframe eache of them
26.127	X	Item twoe lowe cobbirons
26.128		Item one greene windowe curten of coton & curten rodd
26.129	Carried to Fakenham	Item one pewter standishe wth the appurtenancs

In the clossett
26.130 Item one lock & kye to the doore
26.131 Item iiij lute cases & 2 sittern cases all wth locks in the heads but no kyes
26.132 Item small shelves 6

In the other clossett
26.133 Item 2 borded cases for instruments

[112] The great staires goinge unto the Dyneinge Chamber[23]
26.134 Item upon the firste landeinge place one old fashioned joyned stoole
26.135 Item one picture of a dogge hanginge against the walls
26.136 Item one brassinge candleplate att the heade of the staires

---

22 It is likely that the 1626 Music Parlour emerged from the spaces occupied in 1597 by the Parlour and the 'Chamber going into the garden' and is sited in the west range. The room's designation is unique to the 1626 inventory adding to the view of cultured pursuits now enjoyed by the Tollemache family when resident at Helmingham Hall. The range of musical instruments in this room and its two 'closets' is extensive in comparison with those identified in 1597, which recorded only two pairs of virginals, one of them described as 'old'.

23 This locates the Dining Chamber on the first floor, a fact that had to be assumed in 1597, and suggests a staircase rising in two flights with 'the first landing place' from which 'My Lord's Chamber' is accessed.

In the chamber called my lords chamber[24]

26.137			{Item one locke & kye to the door
26.138	All these things in the greate newe matted		{Item one turned posted bedstead matt & corde the bedsteade of wallnuttree wth teasterne & vallence of ashe coloured tobyne & goulde the vallence fringed
26.139	chamber		{Item one greeneishe coloured cover for the teastern of the bedd of buckerum
26.140			{Item one doune bedd & doune boulster
26.141			{Item towe doune pillowes
26.142			{Item twoe Spanishe wollen blanketts
26.143			{Item one greene rugge
26.144	In the best chamber		{Item a hollande wool twilte
26.145	All these		{Item 8t guilte knobbs for the teasterne
26.146	things in the		{Item v: curteynes of ashe coloured taffata laced
26.147	said greate		{Item iij curteyne rodds
26.148	chamber		{Item one counterpointe of ashe coloured taffata laced wth orreinge tauneye and ashe coloured lace suitable to the curteynes & lyned with ashe coloured bayes
26.149			Item vi bedd staves
26.150			Item one chamber pott
26.151			Item foure peeces of tapestrye hangeings
26.152			Item one chimnye peece of tapestrye
26.153			Item one mappe in a frame hanged for a chimnye peece
26.154			Item one peece of blacke & white darnixe upon the <lefte> ryght hand comeinge in att the door
26.155		r	Item 2 greene saie curtens for the windowes & curteyne rodds one of the curteynes reacheth to the plancher
26.156		r	Item twoe windowe cushions of Irishe stiche on the one side & ashe coloured taffata on the other side laced wth orrenge tauneye & ashe coloured lace fringed rounde, & packed up wth the curteynes of the bed in an olde sheete
26.157		r	Item one liverie cupborde
26.158		r	Item one cupborde cloathe of turkye worke

---

[24] As with the spaces dedicated to Sir Lionel Tollemache on the ground floor, his first-floor chamber comprises a suite of interconnected rooms, one of them equipped with a fireplace. Although there are a framed map designed for a chimney piece and plenty of chairs and other seating, the main chamber of the suite is in the process of being re-equipped and significant items of furniture, particularly the bedstead, are being dispersed, some to 'the greate new matted chamber' and some to the 'best' chamber, which prove to be one and the same room (26.223–255).

[113] In my lo: chamber still

26.159	r	Item one highe chaire of Irishe stiche fringed & a cover to it of buckerum
26.160	r	Item one lowe chaire of Irishe stiche wrought wth silke fringed wth a cover of buckerum
26.161		Item two highe stooles of Irishe stiche fringed wth buckerum covers
26.162		Item twoe lowe stooles wrought wth Irishe stiche fringed wth buckerum covers
26.163	r	Item <twoe> a foote stoole of Irishe stiche <wrought with silke and crewell> fringed, wth a buckerum cover
26.164	r	Item a paire of cobbirons \dubble/ knobbed wth brasse
26.165	r	Item firesholve & tongs suyteable
26.166	r	Item one paire of bellowes
26.167		Item the chamber matted

In the inwarde chamber

26.168 Item one liverie beddsteade matt & corde
26.169 Item one feather bedd & feather boulster
26.170 Item one paire of wollen blankitts
26.171 Item one darnixe coverlitt
26.172 Item a locke unto the doore, wthout a kye

In the clossett

26.173 Item one closse stoole & pan

In the chamber at the greate staires heade

26.174 Item a locke & kye to the chamber doore
26.175 Item the chamber hanged rounde wth darnixe greene & yellowe
26.176 Item one greene saie windowe curteyne & curteyne rodd
26.177 Item one posted beddsteade coloured blewe; with vallence & teasterne imbroydered upon purple saie wth slipps & fringed
26.178 Item vi guilte knobbs
26.179 Item one doune bedd, & 2 doune pillowes
26.180 Item one feather boulster
26.181 Item twoe Spanishe wollen blankitts
26.182 Item one greene rugge
26.183 Item v taffata curtens white & redd
26.184 Item iij curten rodds
26.185 Item a matt & corde
26.186 Item one liverie table
26.187 Item a greene cloath cupbord cloath

[114] In the former Chamber

26.188 Item one greate chaire of the Irishe stich <illeg.> wth a buckerum cover over it
26.189 Item iij lowe stooles of Irishe stiche wth covers of saie
26.190 Item one paire of lowe andirons

26.191   Item fire sholve tongs & bellowes
26.192   Item the chamber matted
26.193   Item one chamber pott

In the dyneinge chamber[25]

26.194	Item one locke & kye to the doore
26.195	Item one longe table & frame wth twoe draweinge leaves
26.196	Item one shorter table & frame wth 2 draweing leaves
26.197	Item one liverie cupborde
26.198	Item twoe formes seated wth cloathe of golde, wth covers of yellow buckerum
26.199	Item one dosen of highe stooles seated wth redd & yellowe silke stuffe wth fringe, & cases to them of buckerum
26.200	Item one little stoole & twoe little chaires seated with crimson satten, imbroydered wth blacke vellvett & fringed, wth cases to them of buck erum
26.201	Item one greate chaire of white taffata imbroydered & fringed beinge much worne
26.202	Item one greate chair of goolde chamlitt imbroy dered wth purple velvitt wth a buckerum cover; & fringed
26.203	Item two turkye worke carpetts wrought wth slipps the one verie longe & thother shorter wth the borders wrought like pomegranets
26.204	Item vi turkye work cushions that came out of the parlour
26.205	Item ij longe windowe cushions of crimson velvett wth crimson tassells & fringed & lyned wth stripett satten packed up in pte of an old sheete
26.206	Item one great chaire of blewe velvett imbroydered wth crimson satten wth a case of buckerum and fringed
26.207	Item two little stooles corded wth cloathe of silver beinge white & fringed
26.208	Item one highe chaire corded wth crimson velvett
26.209	Item one foote stoole of crimson velvett.
26.210	Item two highe stooles of crimson velvett
26.211	Item twoe lowe stooles of crimson velvett, all the

---

[25] As in 1597, the dining chamber is, at first sight, furnished sumptuously. Indeed, some of the decorative items are recognisable from the earlier inventory, particularly the forms seated with cloth of gold (see 1597 transcription, 97.330). With two tables, both with 'drawing leaves' by which they can be extended, and an assortment of seating, the 1626 room looks to be capable of accommodating some thirty diners in comfort. However, there are signs of movement or dispersal of items: the long window cushions of crimson velvet are 'packed up in part of an old sheet'; whilst six turkey-work cushions had come out of the parlour.

			whole sute of crimson velvet fringed & covered wth buckerum cases, lined wth paper
26.212	All this sute removed unto ffakenham		Item twoe Irishe stiched chaires wth armes fringed & covered of buckerum to them the one greate & thother lesser
26.213			Item one other highe chaire of Irishe stitche wthout armes
26.214			Item one lowe chaire of Irishe stiche
26.215			Item xii high stooles seated wth Irishe stich
26.216			Item iiij lowe stooles seated wth Irishe stiche, all the wholl suite of Irishe stiche fringed & corded wth buckerum cases of greene lyned wth pap[er]

[115] In the foresaide dineinge chamber

26.217			Item iiij curteynes of greene saie in the windowes hangeinge open wth ii curteyne rodds
26.218			Item a little footestoole
26.219		w	Item a paire of bellowes
26.220			Item a paire of cobirons firesholve, & tongs playne
26.221		W	Item a bristle brushe wth a wooden handle
26.222			< Item one lowe blacke leather chaire>

In the beste chamber nexte the great chamber[26]

26.223		Item ii locks & one kye unto the ij doores
26.224		Item v peeces of tapestrye hangeings lyned wth canvas in stripes
26.225		Item twoe windowe peeces of tapestrie
26.226		Item twoe greene windowe curteynes of saie & curteyne rodds
26.227		{Item one newe fielde bedsteade all varnished blacke, wth vallence, teasterne, & heade peece of blacke velvett imbroydered wth silke slipps, the toppe of the teasterne of buckerum lined wth sarsinet
26.228	Nowe in the wardrape	{Item viijt guilte knobbes & feathers belongeinge to the bedd beinge of diverse coloures & nowe in the wardrape
26.229		{Item v: curteynes of changeable taffata of purple & greene wth ringles to them & 3 curteyne rodds

---

26 The 1626 'best' chamber, in common with other rooms, is clearly in the throes of change. The 'new' field bedstead, exotic with its black varnished framework, canopy and headboard of black velvet embroidered with silk panels, most likely of flowers and plants ('slips'), its gilt knobs and feathers, is currently in storage in the wardrobe (which is in the roof void), whilst the mattress, bolster, pillows and blankets are 'in my lord's chamber' (where, as mentioned earlier, there is no bed). Is the black field bedstead coming from or going to the 'best' chamber? Or is it heading for 'my lord's chamber'? Is this 'best chamber' destined to become 'the black velvett room and closetts' in 1708? (See 1708 transcription, 08.401–08.429).

26.230	In my lord's chamber		{Item one doune bedd & doune boulster
26.231			{Item twoe downe pillowes
26.232			{Item twoe fusten blanketts
26.233			Item one white rugge
26.234			Item one matt & corde
26.235	In the wardrape		{Item one counterpointe of changeable taffata of purple & greene lyned wth greene bayes
26.236		r	Item one chamber pott
26.237			Item iiij beddstaves
26.238			Item one liverie table or cupborde
26.239		r	Item one greene cupborde cloath imbroydered wth velvett
26.240	In my maisters clossett		{Item one other cupborde cloath of turky worke of slipps
26.241			Item one cusheinge cloathe stoole
26.242		r	Item one greate chaire backed & seated wth black velvett imbroidered wth slipps & fringed
26.243		r	Item one lowe chaire of blacke velvett suitable to the former
26.244		r	Item ij lowe stooles & one footestoole suitable to the chaires the bedd chaires & stooles wth cases of greene buckerum lyned wth pap[er]

[116] In the beste chamber[27]

26.245		r	Item one other chaire seated wth tente stiche wth a buckerum cover
26.246		r	Item tywoe longe windowe cushions of blacke velvett imbroydered with silk slips & fringed, lyned wth tamye, & ashe coloured tobyne
26.247			Item one square table & a turkyeworke carpett being ye second table and second carpet
26.248			Item one greate mappe in a frame hangeinge over the chimnye
26.249			Item < greate andirons all but the feete of brasse> \one paire of small brasse andirons/ with covers of heare coloured cotton
26.250			Item one fire panne & tongs all of brasse
26.251		r	Item a paire of bellowes
26.252			Item the rompht matted

---

[27] This is an abbreviated heading and continues the detailed description of the 'best chamber next to the great chamber' begun on the previous folio. Here are the windows and fireplace, the small inner room and closet which together comprise a suite of 'best' rooms. The only item which goes from here to Fakenham Magna is a black leather trunk without a lock. One description is particularly notable in 26.247, identifying the square table and its cover (the turkey-work carpet) as being 'the second table and second carpet'. Both items recognisable from the 1597 inventory (97.328 and 97.339 respectively), these were removed from the dining chamber. Still good enough for use in the 'best' chamber, they are now 'second', demoted from the dining chamber with the introduction of its two drawleaf tables (26.195 and 26.196).

26.253	removed to Fakenham		Item one blacke leather truncke wthout a locke
26.254			In the clossett
26.255			Item one closse stoole & pann

In the Inwarde Chamber

26.256		r	Item one liverie bedsteade matted & corded
26.257		r	Item the teasterne & headpeece of redd & blewe saie fringed
26.258		r	Item one feather bedd & ffeather boulster
26.259			Item one paire of \newe/ wollen blanketts
26.260		r	Item one coverlitt of diverse coloures
26.261			Item three hangeings of Eyrelonde
26.262			Item one old fashioned joyned stoole

In the chamber att the Clocke staires over againste Mr Edw: Tallemaches[28]

26.263	All these things except the	{Item one posted bedsteade matt & corde with a teasterne of olde diamonde wrought stuffe
26.264	bedsteade matte	{Item one ffeather bedd & boulster
26.265	corde & teastern	{Item ij olde blanketts
26.266	removed into Balls his chamber for feare of the ratts	{Item one olde redd coveringe, all wth beddinge come out of the brewehouse chamber
26.267		Item a furr table upon tressells
26.268		Item one iiij footed stoole
26.269		Item one greate wooden chiste like a church chiste
26.270		Item one Iron candle plate
26.271		Item a locke & kye unto the doore

Over the clocke staires[29]

26.272	Item one greate clocke wth ij great leaden waights & lynes unto the same
26.273	Item one bell belonginge unto the clocke hangeinge in a frame over it in the toppe of the howse
26.274	Item one locke & kye to the clockehowse doore

[117] In Mr Edward's chamber[30]

| 26.275 | Item one posted bedsteade, matt & corde |

---

28 This and the two following descriptions relate the clock tower and the stairs leading to it with Mr Edward's chamber. Appendix A presents evidence of its likely location and concludes that it was detached from the main house or, at the very least, not accessible from within the house. The marginal note about the removal of items because of potential damage from rats is a stark reminder of the realities of life in a moated Tudor house. This infested chamber is simply furnished, in direct contrast to the rooms described previously. Although mentioned in the annotation, a chamber ascribed to Balls is not listed in the inventory but is probably a staff chamber in the east range.

29 The clock and its bell 'at the topp of the howse' is mentioned for the first time in this 1626 inventory. However, Smythe's household accounts record the purchases in 1587 and 1588 of a stroke line and a watch line for the clock, which suggests an instrument similar to the one described here.

30 Edward Tollemache was the youngest brother of Sir Lionel, 2nd baronet. Baptised on 9 June 1596, and now 30 years old, he was the only one of Sir Lionel (1st baronet) and Lady Catherine Tollemache's

26.276   Item the teasterne & vallence of cope work
26.277   Item a feather bedd & feather boulster
26.278   Item ij pillowes one downe & the other fine feathers
26.279   Item ij whitt wollen blanketts
26.280   Item a darnixe covringe
26.281   Item the chamber hanged rounde wth white & blacke darnixe
26.282   Item one liverie table
26.283   Item one joyned stoole
26.284   Item ij lowe cobirons
26.285   Item fire sholve & tonges
26.286   Item a locke & kye to the doore

In the newe chamber[31]

26.287		Item ij doores unto the chamber wth locks & kyes
26.288		Item vi peeces of tapesterie hangeings three peeces of them suited & one peece properlie a windowe peece
26.289		Item 2 windowe curteynes of greene cotton & 2 curten rodds
26.290		Item a longe picture for a chimnye peece in a fframe
26.291	Removed unto the yellow taffata chamber	{Item one posted bedsteade wth teasterne vallence & headpeece of greene taffata imbroydered with armes, the vallence wth a verie deepe stile & silver fringe & covered with 3 peeces of lynnen cloath
26.292		{Item v greene taffata curteynes wth ringles
26.293		Item 3 curteyne rodds
26.294		Item a large doune bed & doune boulster & twoe doune pillowes
26.295		Item a matt & corde
26.296		Item a hollonde wool twilte
26.297	r	Item a paire of Spanishe blanketts
26.298		Item a greene rugge
26.299		Item a greene taffata counterpoint lyned wth Jane fusten
26.300		Item iiij bedstaves
26.301		Item a chamber pott
26.302		Item one backed chaire of greene vellvett fringe & ij lowe stooles of greene velvett suitable

[118] In the newe chamber still

26.303		Item one liverie cupborde wth a carpett of turky worke

---

seven children to remain unmarried and to be resident still at Helmingham. The room allocated to him in 1626 is sparse: it has a fireplace but apparently no coverings to the window nor on the floor, although it has wall hangings. See Introduction, footnote 77, for evidence of Edward Tollemache's residence at Bethlem Hospital in 1653.

31 Marginal notes in the inventory suggest that its contents are in transition, suggesting that this is a recently 'new' space with the benefit of its floor being 'matted' (26.308).

26.304			Item one square table wth a carpett of turkye woorke
26.305	Nowe in the crymson taffata chamber		Item one cusheinge cloathe stoole
26.306			Item a paire of cob irons dubble knobbed wth brasse & the fire pann & tongs wth brasse knobbs
26.307			Item a paire of bellowes
26.308			Item the chamber matted

In the clossett

26.309 Item one closse stoole & panne
26.310 Item one greate firepan wth a cover full of hooles

In the inward chamber

26.311 Item one halfe headed beddsteade matted & corded
26.312 Item one feather bedd & feather boulster
26.313 Item one paire of wollen blankitts newe
26.314 Item one yellowe rugge
26.315 Item one cannoppie of Eyrelonde with vallence fringed wth iij curteynes to the same
26.316 Item one old fashioned joyned stoole

In the crimson taffata chamber

26.317			Item one locke & kye to the doore
26.318			Item one posted bedsteade matt & corde
26.319		r	Item vj guilte knobbs, v crimson taffata curteyns & iij curteyne rodds
26.320			Item the teasterne & vallence of crimson taffata fringed & covered wth twoe peeces of lynnen cloath
26.321			Item one flocke bedd
26.322			Item one fusten ticked downe bedd
26.323			Item one doune boulster & ij doune pillowes
26.324			Item one paire of Spanish blanketts
26.325			Item one crimson rugge & crimson taffata counter point lined wth jane fustine
26.326			Item iij newe peeces of tapestrie hangeings & one olde peece under the windowe
26.327			Item one greene saie windowe curten & curten rodd
26.328			Item one great chaire of crimson velvett fringed & twoe lowe stooles of crimson velvett suitable corded with an old linnen cloath
26.329		r	Item one lowe stoole of needleworke
26.330			Item one liverie cupborde
26.331			Item one turkye worke cupborde cloathe
26.332			Item iiij bedstaves
26.333		r	Item one chamber pott
26.334			Item ij lowe andirons firesholve & tongs
26.335		r	a paire of bellowes, nowe in the dairie

[119] In the clossett

26.336   Item one olde closse stoole & pan

In the inwarde chamber

26.337   Item one locke but noe kie unto the doore
26.338   Item one half headed beddsteade matt & corde
26.339   Item one feather bedd & boulster
26.340   Item one paire of wollen blankitts
26.341   Item one coverlitt red & yellowe
26.342   Item one olde fashioned joyned stoole

In the yellowe taffata chamber[32]

26.343   Item one locke & kye to the doore
26.344   Item iiij peeces of tapestrie hangeings unsuited
26.345   Item one greene saie windowe curteyne & curteyne rodd
26.346   Item one peece of redd & blewe saie under the windowe
26.347   Item one posted beddsteade carved with matt & corde
26.348   Item the teasterne of yellowe imbroydered wth purple velvett & vallence suytable with fringe & the headpeece with armes
26.349   Item v curteynes of yellowe sarsnett & iij curteyne rodds
26.350   Item one doune bedd & boulster wth fusten ticks
26.351   Item ij doune pillowes
26.352   Item ij Spanishe blankitts
26.353   Item one yellowe rugge
26.354   Item iiij bedstaves
26.355   Item one chamber pott
26.356   Item one liverie cupborde
26.357   Item one cupborde cloath of turkye worke
26.358   Item one greate chaire of yellowe satten striped wth silver & fringed
26.359   Item ij lowe stooles of yellowe satten imbroydered wth watchett velvett fringed
26.360   Item one cushion cloath stoole
26.361   Item one paire of cobirons fire pane & tongs
26.362   Item one paire of bellowes

In the clossett

26.363   Item one closse stoole & pann

In the inwarde chamber

26.364   Item one halfe headed bedsteade matt & corde
26.365   Item one feather bedd & feather boulster
26.366   Item a paire of wollen blankitts
26.367   Item one coverlitt of yellowe greene & blewe darnix
26.368   Item one old fashioned joyned stoole

[120] In the gatehouse chamber

---

[32]   The contents of this room match closely those in the room described in 1597 as the 'Corner Chamber' (97.370-389).

26.369		Item one locke & kye unto the doore
26.370	Removed unto the wardrape	{Item one posted bested carved wth matt & corde {Item the teasterne vallence & heade peece of <white> \blewe & yellowe/ striped stuffe fringed & viiijt painted knobbs blacke & white
26.371	The curteynes in ye wardrape	Item v blewe & yellowe saie curteynes & 3 curteyne rodds
26.372	In the chamber	{Item one featherbedd & feather boulster
26.373	called ye	{Item ij doune pillowes
26.374	Steward's	{Item a paire of Spanishe blankitts
26.375	chamber	{Item one redd rugge
26.376	one peece wanting	Item xij peeces of verders hangeings whereof one for a chimnye peece & iij for windowe curteynes & 2 curteyne rodds
26.377		Item one peece of tapestrie hangeinge under the windowe nexte the inwarde courte yarde [33]
26.378	r	Item one chamber pott
26.379	want j	Item ij bedstaves
26.380	In the wardrape is the carpett +	Item one liverie cupborde wth a redd bayes carpett
26.381	w	Item one olde fashioned joyned stoole
26.382	w	Item one other joyned stoole
26.383		Item a paire of andirons, fire sholve & tongs
26.384		Item the chamber matted

In the inwarde chamber

26.385		Item the doore goeinge towards the inwarde chamber wth a locke but noe kye
26.386		Item the doore unto the inwarde chamber a locke wthout a boult & kye
26.387		Item one lowe bedsteade wth a matt at the heade
26.388	In the Nurserye	{Item one featherbedd & boulster
26.389		{Item a paire of wollen blankitts
26.390		{Item a blewe coverlitt
26.391		Item a matt & corde

In the garrett over the yellowe taffata chamber [*Blank*]

[121] In Mr Johnsons chamber[34]

26.392	Item one posted bedsteade matt & corde with a teasterne of a steyneinge cloath
26.393	Item one feather bedd & ij feather boulsters
26.394	Item twoe blankitts
26.395	Item one burde eyed coverlitt
26.396	Item one plancke for a table upon ij tressells

---

[33] In 1626 the room appears to extend from front to back of the south range, with windows on both sides, the one on the north facing the inner courtyard.

[34] This marks the beginning of a sequence of rooms for named staff.

26.397   Item one locke & kye to the chamber doore
26.398   <one lute [illeg.] case>

In the clossitt
26.399   Item a peece of a deale plancke fastened unto the wall to wright upon
26.400   Item one little shelfe under the same
26.401   Item iiij other little deale shelves
26.402   Item one trestle wth ij feete
26.403   Item a locke & kye to the clossett doore

In Mr Riseings chamber[35]
26.404   Item one <halfe headeded [sic]> \liverye/ bedstead ij matts \one matt
         wanting/ & one corde
26.405   Item one <downe> \feather/ pillowe
26.406   Item ij wollen blankitts
26.407   Item one birde eyede coverlitt
26.408   Item one square table & frame
26.409   Item one joyned stoole
26.410   Item one olde fashioned wooden chaire
26.411   Item iij shelves one above another
26.412   Item one olde trunke fashioned chist bounde wth Iron
26.413   Item one holberds heade the iron worke
26.414   Item one locke & kye unto the doore
26.415   Item one paire of small tonges
26.416   Item one redd & greene windowe curteyne without ringles or curteyn
         rodd

In the Brewehowse chamber
26.417   Item one locke & kye unto the doore

[122] In the chamber att the staires foote nexte the brewehowse called Seamans
chamber[36]

26.418		Item a locke & kye unto the doore
26.419		Item a carved bedsteade wth an inlaide headepeece matt & corde
26.420	w	{Item the teasterne vallence & v curteynes of greene <tammy> \satten/
26.421		{Item iij curteyne rodds
26.422		{Item <viij yellow> \v guilte/ knobbs
26.423		Item one fether bedd & boulster
26.424		Item a paire of wollen blanketts

35 The use of 'Mr Riseing' in this entry suggests a member of staff to whom others were answerable.
    Variants of this name recurred in the late 16th and early 17th-century wills listed in the Suffolk
    probate index (Ipswich); all but one were in the vicinities of Beccles and Lowestoft. The exception
    was a William Rysyng at Kettleburgh, not far from Helmingham, who died in 1607.
36 This heading locates the stairs, another chamber and the brewhouse, all suggesting that the east range
    was not accessible directly from the south range. A will is recorded in the Suffolk probate index
    (Ipswich) for a Robert Seaman of Helmingham who died in 1617; the 'Mr Seaman' noted here may
    be a descendant or kinsman.

26.425		Item a coverlitt wroughte in checkerworke of divers coloures
26.426		Item one liverie table
26.427		Item one wooden joyned chaire
26.428	w	Item one other turned chaire verie olde broken
26.429		<Item one joyned stoole>
26.430	w	Item one olde closse stoole & panne
26.431		Item a paire of olde <broaken> \bowed/ lowe cobirons
26.432		Item a paire of tonges & < broaken> firepan \wanting/
26.433	w	Item one green saie curteyne with ringles & curteyne rodd
26.434		Item one chamber pott

In the chamber under the gatehouse called the porters chamber

26.435 Item one liverie bedsteade matt & corde
26.436 Item one featherbedd & feather boulster
26.437 Item one paire of russett blankitts
26.438 Item one coverlitt of lists
26.439 Item one olde chiste
26.440 Item one shelfe
26.441 Item one locke & kye to the doore
26.442 Item one Iron candleplate
26.443 Item 3 paire of <fowles> bowles 4 are paired & 2 are not

[123] In the chamber called Mr Robert Tallemache his chamber[37]

26.444		Item one locke & kye to the doore
26.445		Item the chamber hanged rounde with darnixe and a curteyne to the windowe of darnixe & a curteyne rodd
26.446		Item one carved bedsteade matt & corde wth an inlaide headpeece
26.447		Item the teasterne & vallence of watchett coloured saie hanged wth guilte knobbs like buttens, & drapings wth tassells on the ends, besides viiijt greater guilt knobbs all wanting
26.448		Item v watchet saie curteynes & ringles, wth iij curteyne rodds
26.449		Item one ffeather bedd & doune boulster
26.450		Item \twoe/ <feather pillows & one> doune pillowe
26.451		Item a paire of Irishe blankitts
26.452		Item one blewe rugge
26.453	w	Item j beddstaffe

---

37 This refers to Robert (baptised at Helmingham on 1 December 1592), the 2nd baronet's younger brother. Unlike their brother Edward's chamber (26.275–286), this is a comfortable suite adorned with three pictures. However, according to the inscription on his mother's memorial (1620/21) in St Mary's church, Helmingham, Robert was married by then to Dorothy Lane, of Staffordshire. The name of this room suggests this, since it is 'called Mr Robert Tallemache his chamber'. Contents of the room are being dispersed: 25.457 confirms that the livery table (essential for dressing) has been moved to the Steward's chamber, which is the next room to be described.

26.454		Item one chaire imbroydered upon tamiye \buffine/ <[illeg.]> with blacke vellvett in flowers
26.455	w	Item one greate waynescott chaire, & one lesser
26.456	w	Item iij joyned stooles
26.457		Item one liverie table <removed into the stewards chamber>
26.458		Item one seagreene carpett of cloath wth the heade lefte upon it
26.459		Item a paire of lowe andirons
26.460		Item a fire sholve & tongs
26.461	w	a paire of bellowes
26.462	w	Item iij small pictures
26.463		Item one little shelfe upon bracketts

In the closset
26.464 Item one little table & frame
26.465 Item 4 little shelves
26.466 Item a casement curteyne with ringles & one curteyne rodd
26.467 Item one locke & kye unto the doore, the kye broaken

In the inwarde chamber
26.468 Item one featherbedd & boulster
26.469 Item twoe white wollen blankitts
26.470 Item a coverlitt of listes
26.471 Item one \peece of/ matt upon the ground

[124] In the Stewards Chamber[38]
26.472 Item a locke & kye to the doore
26.473 Item one highe posted beddsteade matt & corde
26.474 Item the teasterne of black velvett & white \damaske/ <velvet>, the headpeece of blewe lynnen cloath, iij blewe & redd saie curteynes & iij curten rodds
26.475 Item one featherbedd & boulster & feather pillowe
26.476 Item ij white blankitts
26.477 Item a coverlitt of blewe & redd
26.478 Item one liverie table
26.479 Item a weynescott chaire
26.480 <Item a liverie table that came out of Mr Roberts chamber>
26.481 Item 3 cobirons whereof one broaken
26.482 Item iij shelves one above another
26.483 Item one ffirepann: & one curteyne rodd in the windowe

In the clossett
26.484 Item one plancke fastned against the wall to wright upon
26.485 Item a peece of old darnixe upon the same

---

[38] This is taken to be the household steward, presumably George Smythe's successor. As befits a member of staff holding senior responsibility, the chamber has a fireplace, a canopied bed and the potential for a curtain at the window (there is a rod but no covering is mentioned). The livery table moved from Mr Robert's chamber is noted here, but the comment is not dated.

26.486   Item one joyned stoole
26.487   Item twoe shelves
26.488   Item one springe locke & kye to the doore

In the corner chamber or gable end[39]

All things removed.

26.489   {Item a locke & kye to the doore
26.490   {Item iij posted bedsteads matts & cordes
26.491   {Item one featherbedd & feather boulster
26.492   {Item twoe white wollen blankitts <& a coverlett of
          lists of greene & yellow>
26.493   {Item one darnix covringe lyned wth another old
          one < yt is in the gable & there are things packed
          up in it to sende to ffakenham>
26.494   {Item iij flocke bedds & flocke boulsters
26.495   {Item a greye blankitt
26.496   {Item a verie olde blewe & tauny covrlitt \worne
          up/
26.497   {Item ij other halfe headed bedsteads wch came of
          the brewehowse chamber wth feete & sides
26.498   {Item one heade of a posted bedd
26.499   {Item one broaken trundle bedd feete & studs
26.500   {Item a tailers shoppborde

In the enterie betwene the corner chamber & Nunns chamber[40]

26.501   {Item one longe forme wth foure feete
26.502   All things   {Item one old trunke fashioned chist wthout a
         removed   bottom
26.503   {Item one locke & kye unto the doore gooinge into
                          the apricocke yarde
26.504   {Item 2 small troughes
26.505   {Item 3 owd bords

[125] In John Nunns chamber[41]

26.506   Item a locke & kye to the doore
26.507   Item one liverie bedstead matt & corde wth 2 bords

---

39 A few items are packed ready for transport to Fakenham but everything else has been moved from
    the space, reinforcing the view of disruption already noted in other rooms. There is, in the Wardrobe
    (26.886), an entry for a 'square table or a counter' which could be synonymous with the 'tailers
    shoppborde' (26.500).

40 Like the preceding 'corner' chamber, every item has been cleared from this room. An 'enterie'
    suggests a ground-floor access and this is confirmed by the reference to the lockable door (26.503)
    leading to the 'Apricocke Yard', an outdoor space suitably sheltered and probably surrounded by
    walls against which the apricots were trained and from which they would enjoy stored heat. See Plate
    13, which suggests a location at 'h' for the apricot yard and at 'i' for the entry itself.

41 John Nunn has responsibilities relating to the park, and later entries (26.712–714) place him at a
    'house' there, in addition to this chamber: perhaps his occupation of one or the other was dictated by
    the seasonal demands of the park. Certainly, the items other than furniture which are listed here, in
    what appears to be a ground-floor room, all relate to tasks and activities related to the park, including
    the crossbow, bolts and arrows for hunting (26.516 and 26.517), nets for trapping hawks (26.513),
    and a hook to use when climbing trees (26.518).

		about the bedd
26.508		Item one feather bedd & feather boulster & a flocke boulster
26.509		Item twoe white wollen blankitts
26.510		Item one coverlitt of lists yellowe & greene
26.511	w	Item 2 lowe stooles one wth 3 feete & thother wth foure feete
26.512		Item one joyned stoole of an old fashion
26.513		Item one window leafe & vj wryenetts to take younge hawkes in
26.514		Item a table sett upon pinns fastned unto the wall against the windowe
26.515		Item a wooden racke wth an iron pinne & ij hooks to bende a bowe to putt on the string
26.516	w	Item 4 gaffle bowes wth nutts & vj benders, one bowe in a case, one shoulder knyfe
26.517	w	Item a case wth iij boults with iron heads & iij arrowes one wth a forked heade
26.518	w	Item one climbeinge hooke

In Baitons chamber[42]

26.519		Item a locke & kye to the doore
26.520		Item one posted beddstead wth a joyned teasterne matt & cord
26.521		Item one feather bedd & feather boulster & feather pillowe
26.522		Item twoe white wollen blankitts
26.523		Item a coverlitt of lists
26.524		Item one half headed bedstead matt & corde
26.525		Item one featherbedd & feather boulster
26.526		Item one flocke bedd & flocke boulster
26.527		Item twoe white wollen blankitts
26.528		Item one coverlitt of lists
26.529		Item a turned chaire
26.530		Item an olde table
26.531	w	Item an olde cofer wthout a lidd or cover
26.532	w	Item a shutt for a windowe
26.533		{Item one other ffeather bedd & ffeather boulster: 2
	r	blankitts white wollen and a coverlitt of listes
26.534		{Item one flocke boulster

In the husbandmans chamber[43]

26.535		<Item a locke & kye to the chamber doore>

---

[42] There was a chamber for Baiton, or Bayton, in the 1597 inventory and the same bedstead appears in it now. Later in the inventory, the name is presented as 'Baighton' (see marginal annotation to entries 26.712–714). See comments at footnote 56 to the 1597 inventory relating to Bayton's potential role.

[43] As with other rooms, items are being removed and the reuse of a bed-cord (redeployed to tie up a table) is a reminder that not only did the family have Fakenham but also a London property. The removal of the husbandmen's bedding is another sign that changes were taking place.

26.536	The corde taken of to corde up a table sente up to my la[dy's] chamber to London		Item one halfe headed bedesteade matt & corde
26.537		x	Item one flocke bedd & feather boulster
26.538		x	Item one white blankitt & a coverlitt of lists of greene & yellowe
26.539			Item one other half headed beddsteade matt & corde
26.540		x	Item twoe olde flocke bedds & ij flocke boulsters
26.541			All the bedds blankitts & covrlits removed unto the gable end chamber Item one white blankitt & a coverlitt of lists of greene & yellowe
26.542			Item one other halfe headed beddstead with a borded bottom
26.543			Item twoe shelves, & one other deale shelfe upon the ground
26.544			Item one foure footed little forme
26.545			Item twoe iron candleplats
26.546			Item a wooden shackle wth an iron pinne

[126] In the greene chamber[44]

26.547		o	Item one locke & kye to the doore
26.548	nowe in the wardrape	o	Item the chamber hanged rounde wth hangeings & windowe curteynes of Eyrelonde ij curteyne rodds in the windowes
26.549	nowe in my la: chamber The curtens removed into my la: chamber wth the teastern & vallence & knobbs & curteyne rodds o		Item one fielde bedsteade matted & corded wth teasterne & vallence & v: curteynes of yellowe saie & iij curteyne rodds
26.550		o	Item viij.t guilte knobbs wth bells & buttons about the vallence
26.551		o	Item one feather bedd & feather boulster
26.552	<In the		Item one doune pillowe & one feather pillowe
26.553	nurserye>	o	one paire of <wollen> \Irishe/ blankitts
26.554			Item one coverrlitt of greene & red wollen
26.555	the teastern		Item one other fielde bedsteade inlaide matted &

---

44 The 'green' chamber is clearly another room in transition, leading to confusion on the part of the compiler, who deletes mention of the Nursery twice and amends details of the bed and bolster fillings several times. This could, however, be a sign of exhaustion.

	vallence curteyns & curteyne rodds & knobbs in my la: chamber	o	corded with teasterne vallence & \v/ curteynes of redd saie wth iij curteyne rodds & viij guilt knobbs
26.556	\<In the nurserye>		Item one \<feather>\<doune> \doune/ bedd & \<doune> \<feather> \doune/ boulster [sic]
26.557	\<In the nurserye>		{Item one feather pillowe & one doune pillowe, one paire of Spanishe blankitts
26.558		o	Item one covrlitt of wollen of divers coloures
26.559		o	Item iiij bedd staves
26.560	one of them in \<Baightons> \Seamans/ chamber qur: where is thother pott		{Item ij chamber potts
26.561		o	Item one liverie table
26.562	In my lady's chamber		Item one cupborde cloath of blewe cloath
			Item twoe greate weynescott chaires
		o	Item one cushion of rede & blewe stuff
26.563	Removed to ffakenham		Item one lowe stoole corded wth blacke velvett
26.564	one of the cobirons broaken sithence [since] Nunn hadd them[45] o		Item one paire of lowe cobbirons, fire sholve & tongs
26.565	o		Item one paire of bellowes

In the inwarde chamber

26.566		o	Item one locke & kye to the doore
26.567			Item one posted beddstead wth ij matts & a corde
26.568		w	Item one broaken trundle beddstead
26.569		w	Item one old backed chaire wth an old seate corded wth leather
26.570		w	Item one other turned chaire broaken
26.571			Item one little shelfe
26.572	Belonginge to the stable		Item one ffeather bed & feather boulster 2 blankitts & a coverlet of lists that came of the stable

---

[45] This undated annotation does not reveal when the cobirons found their way into Nunn's possession, nor why: there is no fireplace recognisable in the descriptions of either his chamber (26.506–518, above) or his chamber 'in the Park' (26.712–714 below).

chamber   chamber since the Inventorie was made[46]

In the chamber comeinge up the backe staires to goe unto the haukes mew[47]

26.573	w	Item one locke & kye to the staires heade doore
26.574	w	Item one trundle beddstead & one of the shoes broaken
26.575	w	Item the feet & twoe shoes for another bedd
26.576		Item one shelfe

In the hawkes mewe[48]

26.577   <Item one clever to chopp hawkes meat>

[127] In the brusheinge gallerie[49]

26.578   Item one longe table upon twoe trestells

26.579   Item iij trunkes locked upp: in one of them a horsemans armour furnished in blacke cotton cases

26.580   Item att the Armorye staire foote one greate chist locked upp

26.581   Item a locke & kye unto the doore goeinge from the brusheinge gallerie unto the greate staires heade

26.582   Item one weynescott screen wth a broken foote goinge upp towards the Armory

In the corner underneath the wardrape staires

26.583   Item one closse stoolle & panne

26.584   Item the cannopie frame belongeinge unto the bedd in my la chamber & iij curteyne rodds

26.585   Item one locke & kye unto the doore there hence unto the brusheinge gallerie

In my ladies chamber[50]

| 26.586 | | Item a locke & kye to the portall doore |
| 26.587 | r | Item one painted beddsteadde heade, the postes & |

---

[46] This suggests that the shifting of items (and possibly occupants) from one chamber to another was ongoing, even though there is no date to confirm when the move of items between this rom and the stable chamber occurred.

[47] The chamber described in these entries is less important than the other pieces of information contained in the heading: there is a 'back' staircase and it leads to a hawks' mew.

[48] See Appendix A for discussion of the location of the hawks' mew. Despite the lack of a similar description in the 1597 inventory, the 1587–89 household accounts provided confirmation that hawks' meat was being purchased even then; see glossary, **hawk**.

[49] This space was described as the 'gallery' in the 1597 inventory (see 1597 transcription, 97.565–567). Its function is clarified now as a brushing gallery, a space in which to brush clean soiled items of apparel or equipment prior to their return to the wardrobe or the armoury, both housed in the roof void above, access to which is described in the entries. The locked trunk containing the horseman's armour was there in 1597 (97.565) and is clearly an item of continuing significance to the family. In 1708 there is no mention of a gallery but in 1741 it re-emerges as the 'Long Gallery', a description discussed in the Introduction and in footnote 35 to the 1741 transcription.

[50] Lady Elizabeth Tollemache, née Stanhope, wife of Sir Lionel. At the time when this 1626 inventory was being compiled, Lady Elizabeth was undoubtedly at Fakenham Magna. Her infant son, Francis John, born in September 1625, was buried at Fakenham Magna on 21 October 1626 (SRO (B) FL569).

			pillows & fframe above in the wardrape where the saddles are
26.588		r	Item a matt & corde
26.589			Item a downe bedd & boulster
26.590			Item ij downe pillowes
26.591		r	Item ij white wollene blanketts
26.592		r	Item one white hollande wolle twilte
26.593	A cushion of redd and blewe stuff which came out of the greene chamber sent to ffakenham[51]		Item vj beddstaves Item one chamber pott
26.594		r	Item one pewter peece
26.595			Item one bedd stoole & panne
26.596			Item one coutch chaire of stammell wth watchet lace & fringe suitable
26.597			{Item one greate longe cushion of stammell laced & fringed wth foure greate tassells att eache corner one, <in colour> suitable, to the coutch trimminge
26.598	removed to ffakenham		{Item ij lesser <scarlett> \stammell/ cushions suitable to the coutch \trimming/
26.599			{Item the coutch & cushions \covrd/ <\corded/> [sic] with cases of buckerum
26.600			{Item one stammell cannopie laced & fringed wth whatchett coloured lace & fringe
26.601			{Item the vallence iiij curteynes of stammell coloured cloathe whereof twoe greater & ij lesser wth heade peece all suitable to the topp, beinge all packed uppon a <peece of> darnix cupborde \ cloathe/
26.602			Item iij great blacke leather trunkes
26.603		r	Item one great danske chist
26.604		r	Item one little viij.t square table \of wallnuttree/ wth an inlaide border and a scutcheon in the midest, standinge upon one piller wth a foote made triangle wise
26.605		r	Item one liverie table
26.606			Item one other little cupborde table wth a locke & kye

---

[51] This, and the frequent deletions and insertions to numerous entries, suggest that the compiler was under pressure, perhaps cold or exhausted. Alternatively, the compiler was working from, but unable to correctly interpret, a record drafted by someone else, and was prompted to correct entries subsequently, most likely by Lady Elizabeth, who would have been most familiar with every detail of the items being moved to Fakenham Magna at her direction.

[128] In my ladies chamber still[52]

26.607		r	Item one little lowe stoole of <tent> \broad/ stiche
26.608		r	Item one great greene saie windowe curten & <one> \twoe/ lesser wth <twoe> \three/ curteyne rodds
26.609			<Item one little brasse diall in the windowe>
26.610	Removed to ffakenham nowe Carver hathe it to mende	r	Item one little clocke & larm:[53]
26.611		r	Item two small pictures hangeinge in frames
26.612		r	Item one other picture wthout a frame
26.613		r	Item one square borde planed verie smooth wth a stringe \used/ for a boxe
26.614			Item a paire of cobirons, fire sholve & tongs
26.615		w	Item a paire of bellowes
26.616			Item one longe curteyne rodd wth a hooke to beare it up in the midste

In the maids chamber next my ladies

26.617 Item one posted bedsteade wthout a teasterne matted & corded
26.618 Item one featherbedd & feather boulster
26.619 Item twoe white wollen blankitts
26.620 Item one covrlett of lists
26.621 Item one olde posted bedsted wth a teaster of painted cloathe matt & corde
26.622 Item ij feather bedds & ij feather boulsters <whereof one bed boulster, one covrlitt of lists & ij blanketts came of the brewhouse chamber>
26.623 Item iiij blankitts
26.624 Item ij coverlitts one of lists & thother of byrde worke
26.625 Item one greate chiste
26.626 Item ij truncks
26.627 Item one shelve upon pinnes
26.628 Item a iiijor square boxe wthout a cover

In the nurserie chamber[54]

26.629		Item ij posted bedsteads matts & cords wth paynted teasters & headepeeces & a peece of redd saie between the side of ye head & the wall

---

52 The corrections to entries 26.607–609 may have been dictated or drafted by someone with an intimate knowledge of detail (such as the type of stitching on the low stool, for example) but rather less about the location of items. See 26.54 for the little brass dial entered and summarily deleted at 26.609.

53 The annotation to this reference reveals that this early example of a clock with an alarm had gone to Fakenham Magna where 'Carver' had it to mend. See glossary, **clock**. Carver is a recurrent name in the 1587–89 household accounts of George Smythe and is paid for tasks ranging from carriage, running errands and, as here, repairs.

54 The contents of the nursery chamber suggest a space no longer in active use, filled with broken, old or 'very old' items. See Appendix B for discussion of the family's increasing use of Fakenham Magna as their home. The comment in entry 26.636 relating to the 'wall that is nexte the moate' is a tentative suggestion that this room is on the ground floor.

26.630		Item ij feather bedds & ij feather boulsters
26.631		Item iij paire of white wollen blankitts
26.632		Item one wollen coverlitt yellowe coloure
26.633		Item one other coverlitt redd coloure
26.634	w	Item more one other covrlitt of blacke & redd
26.635		Item more one other covrlitt of watchett & tunye iiijer in all
26.636		Item one peece of dubble darnixe betwene the bedd & the wall that is nexte the moate
26.637	r	Item one old feather cushion corded wth twill

[129] In the Nursery still

26.638		Item one settle for a bedd
26.639		Item twoe longe tables one upon a frame & thother fastened with pinnes to the wall & one square table wth a broken frame
26.640		Item one little table wth a cupborde in it
26.641		Item one olde leather trunke
26.642		Item one childs chaire verie old
26.643	w	Item one olde boxe wthout a cover
26.644		Item ij peeces of darnex hangeinge crosse the middle of the chamber nayled to a crosse beame
26.645	w	Item iij bowles
26.646		Item one weynscott cupborde for a chimnye peece
26.647		Item one paire of highe irone andirons
26.648		Item one paire of bellowes
26.649		Item a paire of tongs

In the dairie maids chamberr att the old staire heade

26.650	Item a locke & kye to the staire foot doore
26.651	Item one halfe headed beddsteade matt & corde
26.652	Item one feather bedd & feather boulster
26.653	Item one paire of wollen blankitts
26.654	Item one darnixe covrlitt of blewe & greene
26.655	<Item one blacke leather trunke>
26.656	Item one longe table upon iiij^or feete wth ij leaves upon joinds att eache end to be turned upp
26.657	Item one candleplate
26.658	Item one lowe forme upon iiij^or feete
26.659	Item one deale boxe wthout a cover

In the chamber betwene the maids chamber & dryeinge chamber[55]

---

[55] This room appears to be a storage area, despite the presence of two beds. The missing key is an item that recurs throughout the 1626 inventory, notably on doors to communication spaces and access points to staff chambers, doubtless partly to limit the opportunities for illicit dalliance between male and female staff. However, access through so many locked doors must, at times, have been a time-consuming and even a fraught occupation, particularly if trying to find an escape route from a fire, for example. See Appendix A for discussion of site access and security emphasised by the 1626 inventory.

26.660		Item one locke to the doore wthout a kye
26.661		Item one halfe headed beddsteade wth sides & feete
26.662		Item one trundle beddsteade
26.663		Item one wicker skepp to putt soulde lynnen into
26.664		Item one old chist wth a cover bound wth iron one lesser wth a cover one other wthout a covr wherein netts are
26.665		Item an olde coatch
26.666		Item a nedleworke frame
26.667		Item a carpett frame
26.668		Item an old borde
26.669	So far +	Item an old closse stoole wthout a pann

[130] In the dryeinge chamber[56]

26.670 Item one locke & kye to the doore
26.671 Item one longe table upon tressells
26.672 Item one other plancke for a table upon tressells
26.673 Item one greate redd chyste bounde wth iron
26.674 Item one great trunke wth lynnen that my la: keepe the kye herselfe
26.675 Item other truncks some of them verie olde} v in all
26.676 Item one other greate wooden chiste
26.677 Item one olde wicker baskitt to putt lynnen in
26.678 Item twoe other wicker baskitts to carrie lynnen in one newe & thother old
26.679 Item one presse for lynnen
26.680 Item one sufferinge presse to drye lynnen on
26.681 Item one playne wooden stoole wth feett iiij[or]
26.682 Item one carpett frame wherein is a peece begun to be wrought corded wth a peece of lynnen cloath[57]
26.683 Item ij heareinge lynes
26.684 Item one olde hamper
26.685 Item iij wooden hoopes

In the gromes chamber[58]

26.686	These things	Item one liverie bedstead matt & corde
26.687	removed into	{Item one ffeather bedd & feather boulster
26.688	the inward	{Item ij wollen blankitts
26.689	chamber ovr	{Item one covrlitt of lists

---

56 Some of the contents of the drying chamber are recognisable from the 1597 inventory (97.530–548). Notably, this room contains the only reference to linen storage in this inventory (26.674) but, because the trunk is locked, the contents cannot be described. It is likely that the family took their linens with them to Fakenham Magna and that the locked supply remaining at Helmingham represents only a proportion of the household stock. Linens are listed extensively in 1597 (with updated inventories to 1609), their summaries listed from 97.970 to 97.1089, in 1708 (08.667–08.683) and in 1741 (41.428–41.449 and 41.459).

57 The 'carpet frame' holds a piece of needlework in progress, the canvas secured to the frame with linen cloth. Carpet, at this date, continued to refer to coverings for the surfaces of furniture rather than floors. See also glossary, **carpet**.

58 The groom's chamber looks to have been cleared and its contents moved to a chamber over the 'inward dairy'.

26.690   the dairie   Item one shelfe

[131] In Humferyes chamber[59]

26.691		Item one locke & kye to the doore
26.692		Item one liverie beddsteade matt & corde
26.693		Item one featherbedd & ij feather boulsters the tike of the one made of an olde sacke
26.694	+	Item a paire of white wollen blankitts
26.695	+	Item one olde coverlitt of listes
26.696		Item iiij shelves
26.697		Item one meddowe rake worne up
26.698	W+	Item one fouleinge peece to shoote haukes meate
26.699	+	Item one sythe wth sythe staffe & forke to mowe the walkes withalle
26.700	+	Item one other cockeinge peece
26.701	want i	Item ij greate iron trapps
26.702		Item one brasse chaffer belongeinge to the kitchen
26.703	w +	Item one cockeinge nett wth a canvis case, belongeinge to the wardrape
26.704	w +	Item one cockeinge cloathe
26.705	+	one olde conye haye \carried to ffakenham/ [*added in a different hand*]
26.706		Item vj paire of flatt bowles
26.707		Item one slurr bowe & bender
26.708	w +	one paire of clymeinge hookes
26.709	w +	one paelinge wimble Humferie chalenge it as the gift of Edmund Boore[60]
26.710		Item two little hatchetts twoe olde hooke
26.711		Item one little olde blacke jacke

In John Nunn's chamber in the p[a]rke[61]

26.712	Nowe in	Item one featherbedd & boulster of feathers
26.713	Baightons	Item ij white wollen blankitts
26.714	chamber	Item one coverlitt of lists

---

59   It would be uncharacteristic for this inventory to record a given name, rather than a surname, but Stephen Podd, who has examined the locality closely over many years, advises that this 'Humfereye' is most likely to be Humphrey Moore. The list of contents leaves no doubt about the scope of his responsibilities in and about the grounds. Read in conjunction with the rooms immediately following, Humfery occupies a building in the Park.

60   This is an outright challenge: the compiler has no alternative but to record Humfery's assertion that the paling wimble (an augur used to create holes in which to insert wooden posts for the park pale, or protective fencing) belongs to him and is not household property. Furthermore, Humfery can justify his claim with his evidence that the paling wimble was a gift from Edmund Boore. The initial 'B' is indisputable, but Stephen Podd believes this to be an error in the record, and that the giver was Edmund Moore, who was responsible previously for the care of the park. If this is so, then the inventory compiler was unaware of the facts, perhaps because of unfamiliarity with Helmingham and its families. He was, at least, willing to record the challenge.

61   This second entry recording John Nunn places his chamber firmly 'in the parke', although its contents (no bedstead, merely coverings) have been moved. As noted previously, a park house might have been occupied on a seasonal basis, as both Nunn and 'Humfery' have chambers there.

[132] In the middle chamber att Humferies howse[62]
26.715 Item one locke & kye unto the doore
26.716 Item one little foure footed stoole

In the garrett there[63]

| 26.717 | | Item one locke & kye unto the doore |
| 26.718 | w | one longe narrowe borded boxe |

[133] The Armory[64]

26.719		Item one locke & kye to the doore
26.720		Item v horsemens armes wth headpeeces & ga[u]ntlets[65]
26.721		Item viij olde corslitt foote armes
26.722		Item vij olde fashioned foote armes used in the time when they hadd arrowes
26.723		Item ij carbynes for horsemen wth powder flaske & cases the stocke of the one broaken
26.724		Item one carbyne wth an inlaide stocke & frenche locke wth a powder flaske & case to it
26.725		Item one caliver wth an inlaide stocke wth a flaske touche boxe, and a case to putt it into
26.726		Item ij petronells wth frenche lockes & inlaide stockes and cases to them
26.727		Item one petronell wth an inlaide stocke & Englishe fire locke and one other wth a plaine stocke & frenche locke wth ij cases for them joyned together, and a powder flaske
26.728		Item ij daggs wth ij Englishe fire locks and twoe cases for them joyned together
26.729		{Item one longe French pettronell wth a French locke and a case to put it into
	w	{Item one longe Frenche petronell stocke wth a frenche locke & a case unto it the barrell taken out; both these laste were fechte lately from Carvers[66]
26.730		Item one orrenge taunye coton case for the beste

---

62 The heading asserts that this chamber is in 'Humfery's howse', which appears to be uninhabited, or at least, not equipped for occupation.

63 The presence of a garrett suggests a two-storey building in the park. Both the garrett and the chamber below it are equipped with locks and keys.

64 The perambulation route has returned from the environs of the park and is now in the armoury housed in the roof void of Helmingham Hall, accessed by stairs from the brushing gallery in the south range, as described in entries 26.578–585. Obsolescence is evident from the terms used in entries 26.721 and 26.722; some of the firearms listed in 1597 are identifiable in 1626, but now there are more, including carbines and calivers with inlaid stocks, and 'daggs' (pistols). See glossary, **gun**, where each is described.

65 The suits appear to be additional to those listed in 1597 (97.750–756).

66 The bracketing together of the items marked as 'w' indicates that at least one item has been with 'Carver', whose name was mentioned earlier in relation to a clock sent to him for repair (see 26.610).

75

horse armes wth ij other orrenge tammy cotton cases for the gantelett gloves[67]

26.731   Item one other orrenge taunye cotton bagge wherein is a steele bresteplate suitable to the beste horse armes

26.732   Item iij olde bullett baggs & girdles to them[68]

26.733   w   Item one other olde bullett bagge wth bulletts in it

26.734   Item ij olde gunnes wth matche locks

26.735   Item ij rapiers wth scabberds

26.736   want i   Item ix swords viij wth crosse hilts all wth scabberds but one

26.737   Item viij daggards wth scabberds & one wthout

26.738   Item ix coats of male

26.739   Item x halberde bills one wthout a staffe

26.740   Item one great longe javelinge

26.741   Item xvi olde javelings

26.742   Item ij pikes wth heads

26.743   Item ij horsemens staves wthout heads

26.744   Item vij pike staves wthout heads

[134] In the Armorie still

26.745   Item xj cappes for heade peeces

26.746   Item xxi olde arrowes moste of them wthout heads

26.747   Item one greate buffe leather saddle wth stiropes & stirope leathers

26.748   Item ij docks for lighte horsses & ij croppers

26.749   Item xxx posts to hange armr upon[69]

26.750   Item one stoole wth a raile over it to sett saddles upon

26.751   Item one iij footed trestle

26.752   Item one olde greate chiste & cover

26.753   Item one longe brasse picture[70]

26.754   Item one olde brasse panne to sett cooles or ashes in

[135] In the old wardrape[71]

26.755   Ø   Item a locke & kye to the staire foote doore

26.756   Ø   Item one greate loome with diverse prclls of wooleworke unto the same belongeinge

26.757   Ø   Item iij hampers wth covers

---

67   This and the following entry describe 'best' horse arms, carefully stored in cotton bags to prevent excessive tarnishing: the items are pieces of armour for horsemen.

68   Entries 26.732 to 26.744, where this folio ends, detail items that can be identified in 1597, largely the bladed weapons used by foot-soldiers. The 'coats of male' noted in entry 26.738 almost certainly include the seven coats of flexible body armour identified as almain rivets in 1597 (97.756). See also glossary, **armour** and **gun**.

69   The 30 posts enabled large items of body armour to be supported.

70   The 'long brass picture' remains in the armoury where it was identified in 1597 (97.775).

71   The wardrobe, described as a continuous space in 1597, is now presented in 1626 as consisting of 'old' and 'new' sections. What is immediately apparent is that the door to the staircase (from the brushing gallery) is locked but the inference is that the 'old' wardrobe space is then open to access directly from the stairs. The second obvious feature is that with the exception of a 'new' cobweb brush (26.785), many items described in the old wardrobe are, indeed, old.

26.758		Ø	Item a little hande lome to worke thrumes on or fringe
26.759		Ø	Item one other hande lome to worke Irish on
26.760			Item one little boxe wth a worne smale staye in the drawer
26.761		Ø	Item a paire of great blads to winde silke or crewel
26.762		Ø	Item twoe twisterers wth iron wheeles for silke or crewell
26.763		Ø	Item ij olde turned chaires
26.764		Ø	Item one screene of wicker wth a piller to sett it up; the piller wthout a foote
26.765			Item one \old/ wicker cradle
26.766		Ø	Item one carved cake print
26.767		Ø	Item one olde thinge wth hoopes sometimes a chaire to sitt in a stove or whotthouse
26.768		Ø	Item twoe greate chists one hooped wth iron
26.769		Ø	Item 4 railes for a bedds heade & v curteyne rodds, twoe longe & <iii> <j> jj these rodds shorter
26.770			Item iij olde closse stooles \decayed/ [*in another hand*]
26.771		Ø	Item iiij old closse stoole pannes \now 3/ [*in another hand*]
26.772			Item a warmeing pann
26.773			<Item iij peecs of old darnix blacke & white>
26.774	carried to ffakenham		Item <*illeg.*> \ij greate/ hangeinges of saie greene & red \old/ [*in another hand*]
26.775			Item one other olde peece of saie, blewe & redd
26.776			Item an olde flocke bedd tike
26.777			Item one wrought old headpeece for a bedd
26.778		Ø	<Item a peece of a blacke velvett saddle cloathe>
26.779			Item one old fashon bagge sometimes used to carrie a cloake in
26.780	the one used to peece bedds wthall Ø		Item ij olde sackeinge pillowe cases
26.781			Item one olde peece of sackeinge
26.782			Item a hempeinge roope acrosse the chamber whereon many of these foresaide thinges doth hange
26.783		Ø	Item iiij iron screwes for a bedd wth iij iron crankes to turne in the screwes & v wooden turned knobbs for a bedd
26.784		Ø	Item one great doore & one lesser wth a [h]aspe
26.785			Item one copwebb brushe newe

[136] In the newe wardrape[72]

26.786	Ø	Item one locke & kye to the doore
26.787	Ø	Item a longe leafe of a table cutt asunder in the midest sett upon iij trestles
26.788	Ø	Item one coverlitt wrought in flowers of redd & watchet the groundeworke yellowe
26.789	At Faknam	Item one olde greye sumpter cloath imbroydered wth a red & yellowe cloath wth armes & with a broade lace
26.790	Ø	Item one olde white cloathe ground laced wth redd bayes
26.791	These hangeings are sett downe	{Item one greate peece of tapestrie hangeinges yned in pte with peeces of white koord canvis in a chist comp. story of … [*illeg.*]
26.792	twice; both heere & in the yellowe taffatie chamber[73]	{Item iij other peeces of tapestrie hangeings; or rather carpetts
26.793		Item one olde turkye worke carpett
26.794		Item one mallett & a wrinche for to corde a bedd
26.795	September 1633 App[ar]ell/ it was brought to Fakham and afterwards as I remember, made into chaires and stooles[74]	Item one darke <sea greene> \French greene/ cloathe cloake wthout cape or lyneinge
26.796	Ø	Item ij peeces of blacke taffata beinge sometimes the lyneinge for a cloake pincked
26.797	Ø	Item one other taffatie lyneinge for a cloake of a <horse flesh> \taunye/ coloure pincked
26.798	Ø	Item a dublett & hoose of blacke satten cutt imbroydered wth silver droppings wth a blacke silke & silver galowne lace, and xv silk & silver points upon the peece \now 14/ [*in another hand*]

---

72 The 'new' wardrobe is secured by a locked door. This suggests that it is part of a separate area of the roof void, not merely a section of the 'old' wardrobe, which appears to be accessed directly from the stairs. The contents of the new wardrobe from 26.798 to 26.807 and 26.811 to 26.814 are items of apparel associated with the ceremony of mourning. It seems likely that these were maintained at Helmingham for family funerals, irrespective of whether the family was resident here or at Fakenham Magna.

73 This undated comment relating to the bracketed items of tapestry is clear evidence of a careful cross-check; the four pieces are listed in the yellow taffeta chamber as 'unsuited' (26.344).

74 This dated comment is notable, both for the evidence it provides of recycling a cloak, and for its use of 'I' in the annotation. September 1633 confirms that the 1626 document was used and re-used for at least seven years after compilation, with the location of every item important enough to warrant scrutiny.

At this point in folio 136, a note [transcribed separately below] has been pinned to the left-hand edge of the page in such a way that it can be turned back to reveal the remainder of the entries:

26.799	Ø	Item a purple coloured cut satten dublett trimed wth ij silke & goolde laces in eache seame
26.800	Ø	Item a blacke cloathe cloake trimed wth ij satten smalle \laces/ & bone buttons & lyned wth velvett blacke
26.801	Ø	Item one other blacke cloath cloake bordered & lyned wth blacke printed velvett & turned wth iij greate blacke broade laces
26.802		Item one brantched blacke damask gowne wth ij broade silke & goolde laces, lyned wth velvett blacke \at ffakenham/
26.803	Ø	Item one blacke silke shagge lyneinge for a cloake
26.804		Item one <russett> \blacke/ taffata cloake lyned wth the same
26.805		Item one other <russett > \blacke/ taffata cloake lyned wth the same & laced in squares with 2 & 2 tufted laces blacke
26.806	Ø	Item a blacke satten jackett laced worne thicke wth broade silver & golde laces & lyned wth blacke <russett> taffata
26.807	Ø	Item a horsemans coate of blacke vellvett wth hangeinge sleeves lyned wth yellow taffata & laced wth gold lace

Note appended (pinned) to Folio 136

Thinges broughte from Hellmyngham to ffakenham
Auguste the 7th 1629[75]

26.808	Item one blacke taffata cloake laced wth blacke purle lace and lyned wth taffita
26.809	Item one russett taffita cloake lined wth russett taffita sarsnett
26.810	Item one frenche greene cloath cloak wthout cape or lyneinge

[137] In the wardrap still

26.811	Ø	Item one blacke cloath cloake unlined wth xiiij black laces
26.812	Ø	Item one blacke velvett cloake wthout a cape or lyneinge wth xii broade russett silke laces
26.813	Ø	Item one lyneinge for a cloake of blacke taffata pincked
26.814		Item one blacke cloath cloake bordered & lined wth blacke shagge baies
26.815	Ø	Item one broade peece of blacke buckerum to packe up these foresaide things

---

[75] This note, identifying items removed to Fakenham, is dated four years before the annotation discussed above, but refers to the same cloak.

26.816	Ø	Item xiiijteen turkye worke cushions wth armes[76]
26.817	packed up to be sent unto ffakenham	{Item vi cushenings of arras iii of them wth pome-granetts & thother wth a roose[77]
26.818	all at Faknam	Item iiij other great cushions of arras worke all of them wth golde[78]
26.819	now at Faknam	Item one smalle \long/ cushion imbroydered
26.820	now at Faknam	Item one other \little long/ cushion case, of brantched velvet unfilled
26.821	now at Faknam	Item one longe cushion of white taffata imbroidered gingerlyne velvett & backed wth orrenge tammy & purple taffata
26.822	now at Faknam	Item one other longe cushion of yellowe damaske imbroidered wth purple velvett, backed wth silke chamlitt <&> \in/ divers colours
26.823	Ø	Item one white woole cradle twilte
26.824		Item iiij brushes of lists
26.825	Ø	Item one damaske bearinge cloathe <taunye>\of crimson/ coloured imbroidered wth blacke velvett a blacke fringe & lyned with scarlett bayes
26.826	Ø	Item one peece of taunye baies
26.827	one given to William Nunn	Item iij olde blacke beaver hatts
26.828	Ø	Item iij redd cloath horsemans coats laced wth white lace & lyned wth white lynnen cloath
26.829	Ø	Item iiij redd cloathe honnces for coatche horsses turned wth yellowe lace & fringe & lyned twoe of them wth buckerum & thother twoe wth course canvis
26.830	Ø	Item iij peeces of blacke cloath thone greater & thother less
26.831	Ø	Item one newe blacke foote cloath imbroidered wth blacke velvette fringed aboute, & hanged wth blacke silke tassells lyned wth buckerum
26.832	Ø	Item one other blacke foote cloath wth iij velvett laces lyned wth buckerum

Between folios 136 and 137, bound into the spine of the volume, the following note is written on one side of a tiny fragment of paper:

26.833 2 carpetts of tapestry whereof one shorter used for a cubbard cloth the other longer for a table cloth brought to Faknam the 13 of ... [*missing*]

---

[76] The fourteen turkey-work cushions now consigned to storage are almost certainly the same as twelve of turkey work and two of tapestry recorded in the 1597 Parlour inventory (97.34 and 97.35). Perhaps the fact that they bear coats of arms dictated their retention at the ancestral seat of Helmingham, unlike the decorative cushions earmarked for use at Fakenham (see footnote following).

[77] The designs are recognisable in the 1597 inventory of the Wardrobe, where they were described as three 'wrought with lyllies, rosses and vyolets' (97.792) and three 'wrought with pumgranets' (97.793).

[78] Speculatively, the use of gold identifies these four cushions are those described separately in 1597 (see 97.788 and 97.791).

[138] In the wardrape still

26.834	Ø	Item one blacke morneinge hoode
26.835	Ø	Item the lyneinge of a dublitt of white taffata sarsnet, in pt
26.836	Ø	Item iiij peeces of ashe coloured tobyne
26.837	Ø	Item a tauny taffata lyneinge of a dublit
26.838	Ø	Item one peece of cloath of <goulde> \silver/
26.839	Ø	Item one little bundle of blacke lace wch sometimes came of a cloake
26.840	Ø	Item v yellowe silke points wth sillver taggs, one tagg wanting
26.841	Ø	Item iii \blacke/ silke & silver laces wth iiij silver taggs
26.842	Ø	Item one peece of brantched blacke velvett
26.843		Item one peece of tauny diamond velvett
26.844	Ø	Item one bundle of blacke & white silke lace
26.845	Ø	Item ii paire of blacke velvett slippers
26.846	Ø	Item iij olde striped curtens \2/ wth ringles
26.847	Ø	Item ii ffusten blankitts old
26.848		<Item one paire of green & oliefe coloured drawers to weare over britches>
26.849	Ø	Item one little peece of redd shagged baies
26.850	Ø	Item iiij peeces of greene coton
26.851		Item one peece of orrenge taunye stuffe
26.852	Ø	Item ii olde bodies for chilldrenes gownes of rede bayes laced
26.853	Ø	Item one old hollande woll twilte for a bedd
26.854	Ø	Item a paire of lynnen bootehoose the topp of the one wth vi broade goold laces
26.855	Ø	Item viiijt great knobbs & ffeathers belonginge to the beste chamber bedd
26.856	Ø	Item ij bunches of broade blacke russett lace
26.857		Item one buntche of taunye & popinejaye greene lace
26.858	Ø	Item coloures \for an armour/ of black & white damaske wth a rede crosse and a blacke & white fringe
26.859	now at Faknam in the best chamberr bought thether against my daughter Allingtons lying in of her firste child[79]	Item ij great peeces of birde worke \curteynes/ wth ringles used in my la: chamber

---

[79] Elizabeth, daughter of Sir Lionel and Lady Elizabeth Tollemache, married William Allington, Esq. (later Lord Allington) in the parish church at Fakenham Magna on 20 February 1631 (SRO (B) FL

26.860		Item one liverye cupborde cloath of greene belongeinge unto the dairie chamber
26.861	Ø	Item iij curteynes of taunye \or redd/ saie wth ringles
26.862	Given to Peirson	\<Item one paire of lynnen boote hose toppd wth blacke silke lace\>
26.863	Ø	Item ij blacke cloath capes for cloakes
26.864	Ø	Item goolde hatbonds
26.865		Item a buntch of rust coloured galowne lace
26.866		Item one cloath of gold coller for a dublett wth \ij / satten laces

[139] In the wardrap still

26.867	Ø	Item j paire of golde hangers & girdle imbroidered upon satten & lyned wth greene velvett
26.868	Ø	Item one paire of girdle & hangers laced wth gold twiste fringed wth greene & layed wth leather
26.869	Ø	Item one paire of girdle & hangers imbroidered wth silver & lyned wth blacke velvett
26.870	Ø	Item one paire of girdle & hangers imbroidered wth black silke upon cloath of goold wth blacke fringe & lyned wth blacke velvett
26.871	Ø	Item ij blacke imbroydered girdles wth blacke fringe & lyned wth black velvett
26.872	Ø	Item one paire of playne silke grograinte hangers lyned wth blacke velvett
26.873	Ø	Item one paire of hangers of Spanish leather hangers wth blacke fringe
26.874	Ø	Item one paire of hangers imbroydered wth silver upon mouse dunn velvett & lyned wth velvett
26.875	Given to Peirson	\<Item one paire of goold hangers lyned wth crimson velvett\>
26.876		Item one other paire of hangers imbroidered wth goold lyned wth mouse dunn velvett; Mr Jermy hadd the girdle
26.877	One given to the ffrenchman Ø	Item vij white satten pickeadillies
26.878	Ø	Item one peece of deroye coloured cloathe
26.879	Ø	Item one pennye stonne hoode for a horsemans headpeece laced with greene lace
26.880	Ø	Item iij deroye coloured paire of bootehoose topps three of cloathe & one of bayes one paire wth a broade lace
26.881	Ø	Item v daggards iij wth guilt handles & ij wthout
26.882	Ø	Item iij swords one wth a guilt pummell & thother inlaid

---

569) and a son of the couple was baptised there on 11 April 1633, although whether or not he was their first child is uncertain. The use of 'my daughter' in the annotation confirms, once again, the hand and direct involvement of Sir Lionel or Lady Elizabeth.

26.883	Ø	Item ij greate wooden chists wth locks wthout kyes
26.884	Ø	Item xi \rndabout 10/ trunks x wth locks & ij that hath kyes in them some greater & some lesser[80]
26.885	Ø	Item v hampers iiij wth lidds & j wthout, noted but j
26.886	Ø	Item one square table or a counter
26.887	Ø	Item one shelfe upon pinns in the walle
26.888	They were brought to Faknam, as I remember, and made into curtaines to part the great parlor[81]	Item viij^t peeces of greene & yellowe darnixe some greater & some lesser wch came out of my maisters seconde clossett upon the right hande goinge in out of the great parlr
26.889		\Item one little bundle of tammy liste which came from Humfery his brother/
26.890		Item 4 peeces of blacke & white darnixe wch came out of the old wardrape
26.891		Item one hamper wch came out of the old wardrape nowe wth papers

[140] In the chamber att the further ende of the wardrape

26.892	Ø	Item one locke & kye to the doore
26.893	Ø	Item ij tables upon iiij tressells one to worke on[82]
26.894	Ø	Item the painted posts pillers & railes belongeinge unto the bedd in my Ladies chamber, <the head> topp railes[83]
26.895	Ø	Item one paire of <olde> virginalls made like a harpe
26.896	Ø	Item one olde waynescott chaire
26.897		Item twoe armed chaires wthout seats & backs
26.898	Ø	Item twoe feather cusshions old; one of blewe & yellowe stuff & thother of redd & blewe stuff
26.899	Ø	Item ij formes for saddles
26.900	Ø	Item one old chist
26.901	Ø	Item ij olde trunkes \Ø nowe but j/
26.902	Ø	Item one topp or cover for a chariott
26.903	Ø	Item one great plancke
26.904	Ø	Item one great iron cobbiron
26.905	Saddles	Item ij crimson velvett scotch saddles old imbroy-dered & laced wth tufts

---

80 A rare example of the compiler being unable or unwilling to count the trunks, which suggests that they were piled together or were otherwise inaccessible for close inspection.

81 'I' is, once again, either Sir Lionel or Lady Elizabeth recalling the re-use of these textiles. Bearing in mind that this folio is still recording the contents of the new wardrobe, then the textiles had already been removed from 'my maisters seconde clossett'.

82 The working table may well have been for use in this space when preparing items for use or attending to them afterwards, since not all are old or superannuated.

83 See 26.587 for the site of these items prior to their removal to this space, described then as the 'wardrape where the saddles are'.

26.906		Item one great crimson velvett saddle wth silver traise fringed, wth a cover of blacke leather
26.907	Ø	Item one great taunye velvett saddle imbroydered & laced wth broade silke golde lace wth a reddishe leather cover lined wth yellow coton
26.908	< Ø>	Item one greate blacke velvett saddle laced verie thicke wth blacke silke lace, wth a blacke leather cover lyned wth blacke coton
26.909	Ø	Item one other greate russett leather saddle wth a paire of french stirropes & stirope leathers
26.910	Ø	Item a scotche saddle covered wth white leather
26.911	Ø	Item one other greate blacke leather saddle wth a seat of blacke velvett & a yellowe brasse pommell
26.912	Ø	Item one russett leather saddle stitched wth watchet t silke wth a russett leather cover
26.913	Ø	Item one other great buffe leather saddle wth stiropes & stirop leathers
26.914	Ø	Item ij great stirropes wthout leathers
26.915	Ø	Item ij peeces of blacke buckerum to cover the saddles
26.916	Ø	Item the headstall reaynes brestplat & docke coverd wth blacke vellvett wth silk & silver tassells belongeinge unto the <last foote cloath> blacke velvett saddle trimmed wth silver

[141]

26.917	the docke wantinge Ø	Item one other headestall & reanes breastplat <& docke;> covered wth crimson velvett
26.918	Ø	Item one crop trappers & brestplate covered wth blacke velvett & studded wth brasse
26.919	Ø	Item one headstalle & reaynes wth a silke false reayne crope & trappers covered wth blacke velvett wth blacke fringe beinge pte of the furni-ture belongeinge unto a woomans saddle
26.920	Ø	Item one headestsall raines crop & bresteplate covered wth blacke cloath beinge pt of the furni-ture belongeinge unto \a mourner/ < a wooman's saddle allsoe>
26.921	Ø	Item ij other olde reaynes & ij headestalles corded wth blacke vellvett
26.922	Ø	Item one blacke leather suite of headestall reaynes brestplat & croper, studded in a yellowe buck-erum bagge
26.923	Ø	Item in a yellowe coton bagge all the furniture belonginge unto the taunye velvett saddle imbroy-dered & wth goold lace
26.924	Ø	Item in the same coton bagge all the furniture (except the bitt) belongeinge unto the blacke velvett saddle, the bitt was in the storehowse next the hall & is now amonges the rest of the things

26.925	qur	Item iij peeces of sackeinge
26.926	Ø	Item v blacke velvett scabberds for daggards
26.927		<Item iiij daggardes scabberds of velvett blacke>
26.928	Ø	Item <twoe> \one/ velvett scabberdes for swords blacke
26.929	Ø	Item one leather scabberde for a sworde
26.930	Ø	Item vij false leather sworde scabberds
26.931	qur	Item one case for a sworde hilte of blacke leather lined wth yelloe coton
26.932	qur	Item one small picture in a frame
26.933		Item one great bitt wth yellowe bosses
26.934		Item one other great bitt wth blacke bosses formerlie mentioned to be in the stoorehowse
26.935	Ø	Item one poste pillion \of Spanish leather/ stitched wth watchet & orrenge coloured silke made for the scotch saddle corded wth white leather

[142] In the stoorehowse next the hall

26.936	o	Item one locke & kye unto the doore
26.937	o	Item a cupborde wth twoe locks & ij kyes[84]
26.938	o	Item a keepe wth a locke but noe kye
26.939	o	Item one greate trunke fashioned chist wth a locke but noe kye
26.940	o	Item one longe chiste wth a locke & kye
26.941	o	Item a little square table
26.942	o	Item a hamper of broaken candlesticks & other \old/ things
26.943	o	Item ij shelves & one hangeinge shelfe } iij in all
26.944	o	Item one greate stonne jugge wth a broaken mouth & ij small juggs
26.945	o	Item one other greate jugge & vj middle juggs all of them cwart
26.946	o	Item one greate glasse bottle covered wth leather
26.947	o	Item iij wicker bottles, & one earthen vinegar bottle
26.948	ij screwes of iron belongenge to the coutch bedd in the Prlr[85]	
26.949	o	Item one greate iron trappe wth a springe
26.950	o	Item twoe leaden waights
26.951	o	Item one olde paire of broaken tables wth some tablemen

---

[84] This double-locked cupboard may contain valuable items of plate, inaccessible and therefore unrecorded.

[85] This entry, although not recorded as an insertion, occupied the margin.

26.952		o	Item a lynnen bagge wth a paire of boules wch came out of the prlor
26.953		o	Item xxiiij dosen & ix of newe trenchers[86]
26.954		o	Item iiij dosen & vi of fruite trenchers of sevrall sorts
26.955		o	Item one greate breade grate & cover
26.956		o	Item one wooden boxe to putt redd leade in
26.957		o	Item one paire of wooden scales
26.958		o	Item one wyer byrde cage
26.959		o	Item viij iron barrs
26.960		o	Item one paire of broade dryeinge irons to drye hearbs for medicyne; a j rounde paire for cakes
26.961		o	Item the heade of a javelinge
26.962		o	Item one turned wooden spurkett
26.963		o	Item twoe fruite frailes
26.964		o	Item one olde fryeinge pann
26.965	Brasse	o	{Item vi peeces of brasse ingraven whereof one like a harpe
26.966		o	{Item one brasseinge candleplate
26.967		o	{Item one brasseinge chafeing dishe
26.968		o	{Item one little brasseinge chaffer
26.969		o	{Item one brasseinge bakeinge pann wth a brasse cover wth three feete & ij eares
26.970		o	{Item one little skillett wth the iron frame to yt
26.971		o	{Item one little brasseinge skimmer
26.972		o	{Item one broade brasse pan
26.973		o	{Item one brasse cullender, wch latelie came out of the armorie chamber

[143] *A note is pinned to this page and is transcribed separately below*

26.974	Pewter	+	Item ij greate pewter fflaggons
26.975		+	Item one wyne pott wth a cover & a spoute
26.976		+	Item nyne pewter candlesticks whereof one wth a man supportinge twoe socketts
26.977		+	Item one little salt saller for the halle
26.978		+	Item one other greate stubbe salt wth a cover the middle pte loste
26.979		+	Item twoe broade basons & ewers suyteable
26.980		+	Item iiij dosen & a halfe of silver fashioned pewter of vij severall sorts one lesse than others vi of eache sorte, & tenn sa[u]cers
26.981		+	Item the next sorte of pewter of the biggest boyle meat dyshes xxiij whereof one of them a peece broaken out & another of them cracked
26.982		+	Item of the next sorte unto the biggeste xiiij x

---

86 The document clearly records this amount of 'newe' trenchers but 24 dozen and 9 (297) seems an improbably high number. The entry following records 4 dozen and 6 (54) fruit trenchers and this is credible. Speculatively, the previous entry may be read as 20 and 4 dozen and 9, which would amount to 77 trenchers.

26.983	+	Item of the middle sorte – vj x
26.984	+	Item of another lesser sorte vj x
26.985	+	Item of sallett dishes – iiij x
26.986	+	Item of pottengers – vij x
26.987	+	Item an other sorte of peweter somewhat older than the former whereof; of the biggeste sorte – viij^t; v: of them crackt
26.988	+	Item of the next sorte – xijijj [sic]
26.989	+	Item of the nexte sorte – ix
26.990	+	Item of another <middle> \lesser/ sorte – xviij
26.991	+	Item of sa[u]cers – ix
26.992	2 [sic] +	Item iiij voyders whereof ij greater & ij lesser
26.993	+	Item iiij deepe boile meate dyshes, whereof one newe x
26.994	+	Item vjj greate olde boyle meate dishes whereof iiij crackt
26.995	+	Item viij other dishes some greater & some lesser of sevrall sorts all in pte molten with vergis except one
26.996	+	Item one cullender
26.997	+	Item one little newe rounde bason without any inke or stampe
26.998	+	Item iij olde basons & ij ewers, the cover of the one broaken of
26.999	+	Item xxj pye plates whereof ij longe & xix rounde x
26.1000	+	Item xv: peecs of old pewter not fitt for use
26.1001	+	Item iij barrell locks wth kyes, & one howse locke wth a kye
26.1002	+	Item one locke for a cofer wthout a kye
26.1003		Item iij prke gate locks wthout kyes
26.1004		Item one little fleshe hooke

Note pinned to folio 143, written in another hand:
  Brought from Hellmingham the 1 of October 1630[87]

26.1005 42 dishes of sillver fashion, of 7 severall sortes, ther being 6 dishes of every sorte, 10 sillver fashion sausers and 9 sillver fashion round plates, of 3 severall sortes \and 1 long venison plate/

26.1006 1 great iron trevit

26.1007 2 \<new>/ kellers of the newer sorte, wch Harlings wife, used in the dayry

[144] In the panterye[88]
26.1008	o	Item a locke & kye to the doore

---

87 Given its proximity to the list of pewter items, these 'sillver fashion' pieces, removed to Fakenham on 1 October 1630, are unlikely to be of silver, of which nothing is mentioned in the 1626 record. It seems probable that the collection of family plate had already found its way to Fakenham prior to September 1626.

88 There was no pantry described in the 1597 inventory but a comment in entry 26.1019, below, identifies the space in 1626.

26.1009		o	Item one cupborde wth iij lockes the kyes lost, one of the cupbord dores broaken of the yemmers[89]
26.1010		o	Item one broade binge wth ij locks bute one kye thother loste
26.1011		o	Item one killer to <wash glasses in> to sett boane in
26.1012		o	Item one joyned table & one table against the walle
26.1013		o	Item ij foure footed formes
26.1014	Removed unto the prlor nowe in the wardrape		Item iij greene cloath carpetts belongeinge to the prlor j long & ij shorter
26.1015		o	Item vj shelves upon bracketts
26.1016		o	Item xxxiijor [?34] wicker rings for the table
26.1017		o	Item a square borde & stonne to presse the lyninge
26.1018			Item 10 halle trenchers nowe in the dairie
26.1019		o	Item the panterye dore att the seller staire heade one locke to the same but noe kye[90]
26.1020			Item one kape for breade
26.1021			Item one knyfe to scrape trenchers wthall

In the inwarde panterye[91]

26.1022		o	Item one locke & kye to the doore
26.1023		o	Item ij coveringe baskitts one old & thother newer
26.1024		o	Item <3> j white stone jugge <the one crackt>
26.1025		o	Item <xiij> \x/ black jacks 1 great & thother lesser
26.1026		o	Item iij beere glasses & j wyne glasse ij of them broaken footed iii vyneger crewetts, j of them crackt
26.1027		o	Item iij voyder knives
26.1028		o	Item <one> wooden bottles iij
26.1029		o	Item iij cases for knives ij wth covers
26.1030		o	Item iiij oyster knyves in a case
26.1031		o	Item an iron sockett belongeinge to the seller to sett a candle in
26.1032	Sent to ffakenham wth horse bitts		Item a wicker hamper wth a cover
26.1033		o	Item one broade shelfe & iiij other
26.1034			Item xxxviijt white & blacke tablemen

---

[89] This is more than likely one of the two triple-locked cupboards designed to securely hold the family's plate when described in 1597, but redundant in 1626 now that there is apparently no plate to protect at Helmingham Hall. The cupboard described here is missing its keys and one of the doors is broken off the 'yemmers' (see glossary, **jemmer hengell**).

[90] The cellar stairhead mentioned here helps to identify the location of the pantry and to confirm ground-floor changes that had occurred between 1597 and 1626.

[91] The 'inward pantry', like the pantry, is a designation new since 1597, and created from the areas described then as the Buttery and Smyth[e]'s Storehouse.

[145] In the newe seller[92]

26.1035		Item one locke & kye att the staire heade doore going into the still yarde
26.1036		Item one pumpe & praytree wth a leadeinge sisterne
26.1037		Item one brasseinge cocke
26.1038		Item one killer wth feete to washe glasses in
26.1039		Item one latch killer
26.1040		Item ix beere stalls
26.1041		Item one tilter
26.1042		Item one shorte iiij footed forme

In the stronge beere seller

26.1043		Item a locke & kye to the doore next the hall
26.1044		Item iij beere stalls
26.1045		Item one tilter
26.1046		Item a leafe to one of the seller windowes[93]
26.1047		Item one latche killer

In the wyne seller[94]

26.1048		Item a locke & kye to the doore
26.1049		Item one greate candle chiste
26.1050		Item one table upon ij tressells
26.1051		Item one wyne stalle
26.1052		Item one great glasse bottle
26.1053		Item vj wicker bottles
26.1054	X	Item xxxix storringe wyne bottles
26.1055		Item one old wyne caske the heade out

[146] *A note is pinned to this page and is transcribed separately below*

In the kitchen[95]

26.1056	+	one locke & kye to the doore +
26.1057	+	Item twoe dresser bords +
26.1058	+	Item one scaldeynge borde +
26.1059		{Item ij brasse boylers nowe in the dairie
26.1060		{Item one greate brasse boyler sometimes used to make doggs meate nowe in the scullerye
26.1061		{Item iiij brasse kettles one little olde one & one of the other the bayle broaken of sometimes
	Brasse	belongeinge to the bakeinge howse

---

92 In 1597, Helmingham recorded two cellars, one for beer and one for wine. In contrast, this 'new' cellar is one of two dedicated to beer and a third one for wine.

93 The leaf (shutter) to 'one of the cellar windows' confirms that at least one of the cellars is partially above ground level. Plate 11 (p. 157), a 2016 view from within the inner courtyard, shows demi-lune glazing to the cellars.

94 The wine cellar, in common with the new cellar and the strong beer cellar, is secured by a locked door. Gone are the 30 hogsheads recorded in 1597 (97.67) and in their place are 39 'wine storing bottles', but in all likelihood the wine cellar occupies the same location as it did then.

95 The original kitchen (of *c.* 1510) would have been detached from the main house to reduce the risk of fire damage. The kitchen was subsequently linked to the house as the building was gradually extended; but its location at the coolest, north-east corner of the moated site is unlikely to have changed.

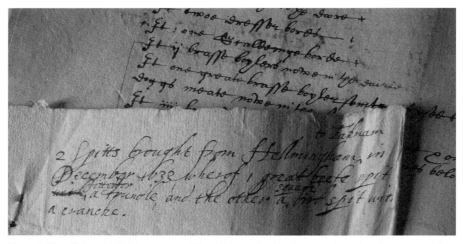

Plate 3. Detail from 1626 inventory of the kitchen, f. 146, showing the pinned note recording two spits brought from Helmingham to Fakenham in December 1633. The great spit for beef and the square spit for birds were removed in time for festivities to be celebrated at the Fakenham house. Helmingham Archive, T/Hel/9/1/1, reproduced by kind permission of the Lord Tollemache

26.1062		{Item one greate brasse pott }
26.1063		{Item iij middle brasse potts } v in all
26.1064		{Item one little brasse potte }
26.1065		Item ij paire of pott hookes
26.1066	o i	Item vij speets iij wth trundles for the wheele
26.1067	o i least	Item iiij crancks to turne speets wthall
26.1068	o i least	Item iiij latche panns, & one other little latch pann
26.1069	o j paire +	Item ij paire of iron racks
26.1070	o j middle	Item iiij skilletts ii greatter & ii lesser
26.1071	o +	Item iij trammells in the chimnye hangeinge upon a great iron barr
26.1072		Item one great trevett nowe in the scullerie
26.1073		Item iij small trevetts
26.1074	o +	Item one fire forke wth a sockett & a staffe too yt
26.1075	o +	Item one iron poole
26.1076	o	Item one paire of musterde quearnes
26.1077	o	Item one \iron/ cle[a]ver <wth a wooden handle>
26.1078		Item one shreddinge knyfe \nowe in the dairie/
26.1079		Item one breade grate the cover wantinge
26.1080	o	Item one salte boxe
26.1081	o +	Item one turnespeete wheele & ij lynes
26.1082		Item ij rostinge irons \nowe in the scullerie/
26.1083	the old freepan wanting +	Item ij freeinge pans \one in the dairie and the other beinge a verie olde one in the pasterie/
26.1084	o +	Item one iron to laie before the fire
26.1085	o 2 +	Item ij irons before the range, & one peece of an other the peece carried up into the fyshe chamber & laid amongst the old iron

26.1086	o +	Item one shorte forme to sitt upon
26.1087	o +	Item one peece of iron for the turne speet wheele

Note, in different hand, pinned to folio 146

26.1088   2 spitts brought from Hellmingham to Faknam in December 1633, whereof j great beefe spit fitted for a trundle, and the other a square bird spit with a crancke.[96]

[147]

26.1089	Brasse	Item one brasse skimmer & one brasse ladle nowe in the dairie
26.1090		Item one bastengge ladle
26.1091		Item one beefe forke
26.1092	+	Item one brasse morter & iron pestle
26.1093		Item one woodeinge mortar & ii wooden pestells nowe in the scullerie
26.1094	+	Item one choppinge blocke nowe in the dairie
26.1095		Item one brasse candleplate
26.1096	o +	Item iij shelves to sett brasse upon
26.1097	o +	Item iiij other shelves
26.1098		Item one neats tree to hange up a bullocke upon belongeinge to the slaughter howse
26.1099		Item one boxe to putt pricks in
26.1100	o +	Item a brasseinge cocke

In the pasterie[97]

26.1101	o +	Item a locke & kye unto the doore
26.1102	o +	Item ij little locks & kyes to a spice cupbord in the wall[98]
26.1103	o +	Item ij mouldeinge bords
26.1104		Item ij wooden peeles
26.1105	o	Item one forme wth iiij feete
26.1106	o +	Item ij shelves
26.1107		Item one old fryeinge pan noted in the kitchinge
26.1108	o	Item one chiste for spicerye wch was inventoried in the dairie[99]

In the scullerie[100]

26.1109	+	Item a locke & kye unto the doore
26.1110	+	Item one olde chiste

---

[96] December 1633 is the latest date mentioned, confirming that this inventory was a working document for at least seven years after its compilation. See Plate 3.

[97] The role of the Pastry is unchanged since recorded in 1597.

[98] The secure cupboard, now designated for spice, was noted in 1597 (97.162), although now it appears to have gained another lock and key.

[99] The spice chest has been moved back and forth between the Pastry and the 'Middle' Dairy, its progress recorded in the annotation to 26.1225.

[100] The scullery, like the pantry and inward pantry, is a designation new since 1597; in large establishments it was the area dedicated to the care of plates, dishes and kitchen utensils; the contents here do permit scouring, and perhaps the brick and chalk beaten with the mallet was used as a scouring powder.

26.1111	+	Item a place like a shelfe to scoure on
26.1112	+	Item iij shelves
26.1113		Item one lowe stoole wth iiij feete
26.1114		Item one wooden mallett to beate bricke & chalke

In the husbandman's halle

26.1115	o	Item ij pillers whereon a table did lie, it is att fakenham the table \made a pasterie borde/[101]
26.1116		Item one longe forme wth iiij feete
26.1117		Item one shelfe

[148] In the vergis howse

26.1118	o	Item one verges stall, & a hoggshead of verges nighe full
26.1119	o	Item one tilter
26.1120		Item a bottom stone for a payre of musterde quearnes
26.1121	o	Item a locke & kye to the doore

In the larder

26.1122	o	Item one locke & kye to the doore
26.1123	o	Item one saulteinge troughe & cover
26.1124	o	Item ij plancks to laie meate one
26.1125	o	Item one chopping blocke with 4 feete
26.1126	x	Item twoe brine tubbs
26.1127	o	Item one sault tubb wth a cover that came out of the verges house
26.1128	o	Item ij little shelves & one hangeinge shelfe
26.1129	o	Item v leadeinge waights (viz) one quarter of a <hound> \pound/, a 7 pounde, iiij lb, iij lb & ij lb[102]
26.1130	o	Item one paire of wooden scales & beams hangeinge wthout the doore wch came out of the fysh chamber
26.1131	o	Item one butchers axe
26.1132	o	Item ij bings [bins] to putt sault in
26.1133	o	Item iij earthen potts
26.1134	o	Item one hooke of iron to hange upon a paiere of

---

[101] The entire entry relating to this demounted and reused long table is written in the same hand, including the insertion regarding its new function at Fakenham as a pastry board. This suggests that the entry was recorded in September 1626 and that the husbandmen's hall was already out of use at that date, as its sparse contents suggest.

[102] The 1597 inventory of the larder records clearly four lead weights, not defined individually, amounting to 86 lbs (see 97.177); however, the 1626 attempt at describing five weights individually is curious: the deletion of 'hound' and replacement with 'pound' is, at first sight, a clear-cut case of human error; but was the compiler about to write 'hundredweight' and changed his mind? One quarter of a hundredweight, amounting to 28 lbs, would be more credible than a quarter of a pound (especially for weighing quantities of lard); but even if that was the intention, the compiler did not make this clear with a further amendment. The figure '7' is very clearly written and cannot be mistaken for anything else but is an uncharacteristic presentation. Speculatively, there was a shift in thought and expression from hundredweights and stones (7 lbs is half a stone) to pounds and a reversion to the more usual roman numerals to describe the other weights descending in sequence. The five weights would then amount to 44 lbs.

		scales to waighe a quarter of beefe or the like
26.1135	o	Item ij whaie killers wch came out of the middle dairie whereof one decayed in part
26.1136	o	Item one olde heareinge milke clense which came out of the milke dairie

In the rompthe betwene the old hall & larder [103]

26.1137	o	Item one locke & kye unto the doore
26.1138	o	Item one lowe foure footed forme to kill & dresse swyne upon

[149] In the outward dairie[104]

26.1139	⊗	Item twoe doores wth locks & kyes
26.1140	⊗	Item one table upon two pillers
26.1141	⊗	Item one cupborde wth iij feete wch came out of the Stillyard
26.1142	o	Item one greate kettle called a boyler to skald milke bowles in
26.1143	O i of them lesser	Item ij lesser brasse kettles & one little one wch came out of the bakeinge house sometimes used there
26.1144		Item one copper kettle
26.1145		Item one brasse skimmer wth a wooden handle
26.1146		Item one roste iron
26.1147	+o	Item one trevett
26.1148	+	Item ij hakes hangeinge upon a shorte iron barr
26.1149	The bellowes Balls claime to be his[105]o	Item j firesholve & tonges & a paire of bellowes wch came out of Mr Robts chamber[106]
26.1150	Ø	Item a paire of longe shanked andirons
26.1151	Ø	Item one brasse water cocke
26.1152	Broaken	Item one little stone jugge wch came out of the inward panterie
26.1153	Ø	Item one lowe bentche to sett brasse on
26.1154	Ø	Item one forme wth iiij feete
26.1155		Item one lesser forme stoole wch came out of the husbandmans chamber
26.1156	Ø	Item one lowe foure footed stoole for the buckeinge tubb

---

[103] 'Rompthe' here seems to denote the spaces that have emerged as the result of changes to the building layout. See also footnote 18.

[104] As in 1597, the function of the outer dairy embraces laundry tasks. However, what becomes more apparent here is the evidence of access to some means of heating water, as essential for cleaning dairy utensils as for laundry.

[105] Despite this being the second direct mention of 'Balls', the first alluding to items removed to his chamber (see footnote 28 above), there is no room in this inventory that is identifiably his. His challenge is noted. See footnote following.

[106] The contents of the room previously occupied by Mr Robert Tollemache are being dispersed: here are the tools required to maintain and clean the fire in the outer dairy, which governs its ability to provide heat for boiling water. Again there is a challenge to household ownership, duly noted, from Balls, who maintains that the bellows are his.

26.1157	+	Item one little iiij footed stoole wch came out of the barne
26.1158	Ø	Item one thicke shorte plancke wth feet to laie lynnen on
26.1159	o	Item one greate buckeing tubbe
26.1160	o	Item one lesser buckeinge tubbe
26.1161	o i lesser	Item one greate rinseinge tubbe; & one lesser
26.1162	o	Item one buckeinge killer
26.1163	o	Item one washeinge killer wth iij feete
26.1164	o °	Item one swill cowle & coulestaffe
26.1165	o °	Item one masheinge tubb: wch came out of the brewehowse used there for a worte tubb
26.1166	o °	Item ij killers to coole worte wthall wch came oute of the brewehowse
26.1167	o °	Item one newe breweinge stoole for the masheinge tubb to stande upon
26.1168	o °	Item one tapp staffe & a newe wicker wiltche
26.1169	o °	Item one clenseinge seeve for worte newlie bottomed
26.1170	o	Item <one> old cheese table wch came oute of the middle dairie used for a worte tubb
26.1171	Ø	Item ij shelves
26.1172	Ø	Item one washeinge blocke
26.1173	Ø	Item one heareinge lyne hangeinge crosse the dairie

[150] In the inward dairie[107]

26.1174	⊗	Item one locke & kye to the doore
26.1175	⊗	Item iiij shelves
26.1176	⊗	Item one forme & one broade stoole
26.1177	⊗	Item one milke cowle & cowle staffe
26.1178	⊗	Item iij olde churnes from shed
26.1179	o	Item one barrell churne from shed made in Ao: i6i7
26.1180	Brasse o	Item one broade milke pann
26.1181	⊗ 15	Item milk boules fitt for use} xv: nyne other somewhat decayed in all xxiiij
26.1182	⊗ 5i [sic]	Item vi milke killers
26.1183	o +	Item one butter killer & one milke killer bothe upon feete
26.1184	i o 7	Item viiijt great cheese fatts <one> \2 paste use
26.1185	i <07> <08>	Item xj smaller cheese fattes & ij littler one full of hooles in the bottom
26.1186	o	Item one angellica fatt
26.1187	o	Item one printeinge breade
26.1188	0 4 °	Item iiij small cheese breads

---

[107] The inward dairy is one of two rooms (the middle dairy follows) containing all that could be expected of a well-equipped domestic regime in which milk from the household herd of cows was processed into cream, butter and cheese. See glossary entries for **butter**, **cheese**, **cream**, **maw**, **milk** and **whey** for definitions and descriptions of the equipment allocated to each process as described throughout the four inventories.

26.1189	0 4 °	Item iiij \great/ cheese breads whereof one that was printed nowe turned playne
26.1190	°	Item one other great cheese breade not fitt for use
26.1191	+ °	Item one suyett pot
26.1192	⊗ 2	Item ij creame ferkins
26.1193	⊗ °	Item one newe ferkyn to putt in mawes
26.1194	⊗	Item one oatemeale ferkyne
26.1195	⊗ <2>	Item ij paire of milke tonges
26.1196	o <2> \i/	Item iiij fleeteinge dishes whereof ij decayed
26.1197	o 1 °	Item ij butter pints one newe
26.1198	o +	Item one churne dishe
26.1199		Item xviij cakes of dere suett
26.1200		Item one little rounde hooped boxe wthout a cover to send morning milk cheese to ffakenham or London[108]
26.1201	Brasse { °	Item one greate brasse kettle the baile broaken of
26.1202	{ 01	Item one great broade brasse panne
26.1203	{ 02	Item twoe middle brasse panns
26.1204	{0j °	Item one other broade brasse pann fleeter & lesser than the former
26.1205	{	Item one little brasse pann wth an iron baile
26.1206	o	Item v little earthen curde cullenders
26.1207	o	Item one olde trafeinge dishe to clense milke wthall

[151] In the middle dairie

26.1208	⊗	Item one newe locke & kye to the doore
26.1209	⊗	Item one olde coule with saulte
26.1210	⊗	Item one newe dubble cheese presse wth beetle & wedges for one; & iron pins for bothe
26.1211	⊗	Item one greate salteinge traye for cheese
26.1212	⊗	Item one hangeinge shelfe
26.1213	⊗	Item iij other shelves
26.1214	o	Item one milke tubb latelie renewed
26.1215	⊗	Item one killer used for wennell calves mawe & whaye killer
26.1216	o	Item vi milkeinge pailes, iiij of them newe
26.1217	o	Item one swill paile
26.1218	⊗2	Item iiij deepe cupps
26.1219	⊗	Item one old ferkyn wth white sault
26.1220	o	Item one choppinge blocke
26.1221	⊗	Item one mawe pott
26.1222	⊗	Item one stoole to laie the cheese tubb on

---

108 This revealing annotation confirms that whether or not Helmingham Hall was occupied, its function as the family's supplier of produce is undoubted, with the finest cheese, that made from the first or 'morning' milking, being transported both to Fakenham and London. Accounts relating to work at the Fakenham Magna property in 1622–23 (cited in Appendix B) confirm that a new dairy was being added, and it may be that the family relied upon Helmingham, particularly for cheese, until the work at Fakenham Magna was complete.

26.1223	⊗	Item one sowse tubb nowe used for a pouldering tubb
26.1224 Brasse		{ Item one old frye pann to frye pryt in
		{ Item one skillett in a frame:
26.1225 removed unto the pasterie againe	o	Item one chiste that came out of the pasterie wth locke & kye used there for spicerie, & nowe to putt in candle
26.1226	o	Item one longe stoole, and a knyfe to dresse sowse
26.1227	o	Item one verges bottle belongeinge to the kitchen
26.1228	o	Item one stonne vyneger bottle
26.1229	⊗	Item one newe heareinge milke clense
26.1230 Pewter		{Item iij dishes of a middle sorte of pewter old, for boilemeat
removed unto the stoorehowse		{ Item ij lesser dishes
		{ Item ij sallett dishes
		{ Item iij butter dishes
		{ Item one sacer, & a small salte saller
26.1231		Item one cleaver wth a wooden handle belongeinge to the larder
26.1232		Item one wyer candlesticke
26.1233	⊗ o j 2	Item ix newe dairie cloathes; & iij old} xiij [sic] in all wth ij churne cloathes
26.1234	o	Item ij puddinge baggs

In the cheese chamber

12.1235	o	Item one locke & kye to the doore
12.1236	o	Item ix bords to laie cheeses on; uppon xi tressells
12.1237		Item an olde traye to putt ffennell seede in
12.1238		Item vi earthen potts iiij wth boores grease one with bacon grease & one wth capons grease

In that wch was the greasehowse nowe a butterie[109]

26.1239	o	Item one locke & kye to the doore
26.1240		Item ij shelves one lyeinge upon an other
26.1241	o	Item j newe beere stalle
26.1242	o	Item iij newe ferkyns
26.1243		Item one runlitt, wch came out of the wyne seller
26.1244		Item one longe stoole

[152] In the still yarde

26.1245	o	Item vi leaden stills over one furnace[110]
26.1246	o	Item vi pewter covers unto the same some greater and some lesser
26.1247	o	Item one little brasseinge water cocke & iron doore

---

[109] The 'greasehouse' is almost certainly the 1597 'lard house', described in footnote 19 to the 1597 transcription. Then, as now, it is a space described next to the cheese chamber.

[110] The detailed description of the six stills over a furnace confirms that the scope and scale of distillation activities recognisable at Helmingham Hall in 1597 is sustained in 1626 (see footnote 27 to 1597 transcription for details).

		[inserted] to the furnace mouthe
26.1248	o	Item one table fastened upon ij bearers between twoe posts & the wall
26.1249	o	Item iiij shelves to sett glasses upon
26.1250	o	Item one greate chiste wth a cover to putt ashes in
26.1251		Item one old brasse panne for cooles or ashes
26.1252	o	Item iij postes wth a heareing lyne to hange lynnen upon[111]
26.1253	o	Item one grindeinge stonne & crancke of iron wth a frame to hange it in a troughe

In the bakeinge howse

26.1254	o o	Item one locke & kye to the doore
26.1255	o o	Item one mouldeinge borde
26.1256	o o	Item one other borde to sett breade one when yt is drawne out of the oven
26.1257	o	Item one bracke for breade
26.1258		Item one flower killer
26.1259		Item one little hearinge yeist clense
26.1260		Item one salte boxe
26.1261	o i	Item ij wicker skeppes the one to carrie bread in & thother a meale skepp
26.1262	o o	Item one iron peele & iron coole rake
26.1263	o	Item one iron trevett
26.1264		Item one olde hamper
26.1265		Item one kouleinge peene
26.1266		Item ij wooden oven leeds

[153] In the meale howse[112]

26.1267	o o	Item one locke & kie to the doore
26.1268	o o	Item one boulteinge hutch
26.1269	o	Item one broade sifteinge killer
26.1270	o o	Item one deepe plancke mingeinge hutch[113]
26.1271	o	Item ij meale tubbes of olde hoggsheads & one branne tubb
26.1272	o	Item one flower bowle
26.1273	o	Item one meale seeve
26.1274	o	Item ij boutells one finer & thother coursser
26.1275	o	Item one dowe scrape[114]

In the poultery howse

26.1276	o	Item one locke & kie to the doare

---

[111] The heat of the furnace was clearly put to good use for drying linen on this hair line.

[112] This was described as the 'bultinge' (bolting) house in 1597 when it housed the same functions of sieving, grading and dough-making.

[113] The minging, or mixing, hutch was present in 1597 and confirms that the purpose of the mealhouse extended then, as in 1626, to the initial preparation of dough, further confirmed below.

[114] The 'dowe' scrape confirms that dough has been formed here in readiness for the completion of bread-making in the bakehouse.

26.1277	o	Item ij greate coopes wth borded backes, the one wth iiij particons and thother wth iij p'rticons wth ij old plancks upon them, wch covereth them in parte
26.1278	o	Item one lesser coope wth a borded backe & bottome wth a borded cover & water trough the coope wth iij particons
26.1279	o	Item one other longe coope wth a borded topp & backe, railed in the botton, wth xiiij borded particons
26.1280	o	Item one water troughe unto the same
26.1281	o	Item one other middle coope wth a borded cover open att the backe to sett againste a walle wth staves in the bottom & covered in parte with a borde for the foules to stande upon wth iij particons and wth a water troughe unto the same
26.1282	o	Item one other lowe borded coope, back, tope, & botton, the bottom wth hooles in it behinde; wth xiij boarded particons
26.1283	o	Item one chickeinge coope wth a borded topp, & backe, staved in the botton wth ij borded particons, & with a troughe to give them meat in
26.1284	o	Item one other little lowe chickeinge coope open at the back wth a borded toppe & bottom, the bottom sawne wth open spaces behinde, this coope lieth upon the topp of one of the greate ones
26.1285	o	Item ij old hearinge barrells one wth a cover to putt fowles meate in
26.1286	o	Item one olde little traye to mynge capons meat in
26.1287	o	Item an old troughe
26.1288	o	Item an olde forme wth feett
26.1289	o	Item an irone spade wth a socket & handle to yt to make cleane the coopes
26.1290	o	Item a mucke skeppe

[154] In the brewehowse[115]

26.1291	o	Item one locke & kye unto the doore
26.1292	o	Item one greate brasse copper, wth iii bords to lay over it
26.1293	o	Item one greate mashe fatt wth a false bottom & wth a penn staffe, stuke & underbecke
26.1294	o	Item one greate guile fat
26.1295	o	Item one greate newe worte tubb, & twoe lesser worte tubbs; the bigger of these twoe lesser tubbs nowe used by the dairie maide for a masheing tubb

---

[115] In order to keep the two beer cellars well stocked, the 1626 brewhouse has been re-equipped with three new wort tubs (the old ones put to use elsewhere, as described in 26.1295). See glossary, **brewing**, for a detailed explanation of the process revealed by these and other entries in the four inventories.

26.1296	o	Item twoe stirrers for the mashe fatte
26.1297	o	Item one greate cooler
26.1298	o	Item one dalle, & ij jetts i wth a bearer to sett under the dale to guide the beer into ye hoggsheads
26.1299	o	Item ij shorte dales used when they clensed into cowles for to save beere from spillinge betwene the fatt & the cowle
26.1300	o	Item one gatherrer
26.1301	o	Item ij roopes wth eyes & coule staves to them to carrie beere uppon; and an iron sporkett to hange them on
26.1302	o	Item ij halfe rounde stooles to stande upon to strike of worte
26.1303	o	Item one other lowe forme wth feet
26.1304	o	Item one other lowe foure footed stoole
26.1305	o	Item ij hopp skepps the one verie old & other newer
26.1306	o	Item one olde ferkyne to putt hopps in
26.1307	o	Item ij tunnels to clense wthall with iron spouts
26.1308	o	Item iiij beere stalls
26.1309	o	Item xxxijj [sic] hoggsheads whereof one came out of the verges howse, one out of the stronge beere seller, & one out of the wyne seller[116]
26.1310	o	Item vj killers whereof ij used by the dairie maide for worte killers
26.1311	o	Item one brasseinge water cocke
26.1312	o	Item one pumpe & iron prayetree in the back yarde wth a dale to bringe the water into the copper

[155] In the ffishe chamber[117]

26.1313	o	Item one locke & kye to the doore
26.1314	o	Item an olde chiste wth a cover to putt lynge in
26.1315 Sent to ffakenham		Item an olde hoggsheade used to putt hoppes in
26.1316	o	Item xxxjtie [sic] staves for the sides & botton[m] of an olde worte tubbe that came out of the brewehowse & vi hoopes that doth belonge unto the same
26.1317	o	Item an olde paire of musterde quearnes stoones
26.1318	o	Item ij old hakes
26.1319	o	Item ij iron bonds for great kettles wth bailes
26.1320	o	Item one great iron bonde wth ij handles for a cauldron
26.1321	o	Item one olde iron bonde for the topp of a brasse pann wth ij eares
26.1322	o	Item one iron bonde for a kettle wth one ringle

---

[116] Although only three are noted here as removals from other rooms, the hogsheads may well include thirty previously housed in the 1597 beer cellar (97.67).

[117] This designation confirms that there was, at least in 1626, an area dedicated to the storage of salted and cured fish (see 1597 transcription, footnote 16). However, it is also apparent from the list of contents in 1626 that the fish chamber provides storage for superannuated household goods.

26.1323	o	Item an olde bindeinge for a kettle wth\out/ a baile
26.1324	o	Item in an wooden borde moulde to runn sheete leade in – divers parcells of old iron manye of them fitt for present uses
26.1325	o	Item ij olde iron foorestoole pillars & a ?rawe piller for a carte
26.1326	x	Item iij old herringe barrells
26.1327		Item iij other olde barrells
26.1328	o	Item olde stocke lockes wthout kyes – xix
26.1329	o	Item one iron for a dunge crome
26.1330	o	Item one posted beddsteade wth sides & feete
26.1331	o	Item one other posted bedsteade sometimes corded wth girth webbe
26.1332	o	Item ij old turned postes for the feete of a bedd
26.1333	o	Item one greate longe iron to sett before the fire
26.1334	o	Item one iron printed; to sett at a chimnyes stocke
26.1335	o	Item iij peeces of pipes of leade
26.1336	o	Item one stone to grinde coloures of leade upon[118]
26.1337	o	Item one rounde boxe with a cover wth vij hollowe leads to putt coloures in for a lymner[119]
26.1338	o	Item one pruneinge knyfe for a garden
26.1339	o	Item one verrie olde closse stoole panne
26.1340	o	Item an olde brasseinge bottom of a still, & one old brasse candle plate
26.1341	o	Item an olde baskitt to carrie chickeings upon a horse
26.1342	o	Item twoe barrells sometimes used to carrie fyshe in
26.1343	o	Item vij other old feather tubbs
26.1344	o	Item one old borded chiste wthout a cover
26.1345	o	Item one old doure

[156] *Presumed to be a continuation, or an update, of the Fish Chamber contents, lacking any marginal 'stock-check' marks.*

26.1346		Item an old paile wherein are the leads of an olde casteing nett
26.1347		Item one verie old flewe wth leads & corkes
26.1348		Item iiij longe pitchforks
26.1349		Item j meddowe rake & 2 rakes heads
26.1350		Item iiij javellinge rakes

[157] In the mill howse[120]

26.1351	Θ	Item one locke & kye to the doore
26.1352	Θ	Item one horse mill compleate
26.1353	Θ	Item one paire of stones for harde corne

---

[118] This and the entry following are explored in the glossary for **limn**.

[119] This is a paintbox: see footnote above.

[120] The millhouse is mentioned, but its contents not listed, in 1708, and not listed at all in 1741. These 1626 entries therefore provide the last clear view of its equipment and capacity, detailed in the 1597 transcription, footnote 24.

26.1354	Θ	Item one other for mault wth hoppers & all things thereunto belonginge
26.1355	Θ	Item ij meale hutches & one scuppett to gather up the meale with a board for one t'ovor [one to the other]
26.1356	Θ	Item one paire of traises & leather coller wch came oute of the stables
26.1357	Θ	Item one olde weynescott chaire broaken in part
26.1358	Θ	Item of bricke & tile bords 89 which came from the kelne
26.1359	Θ	Item twoe peeces of a broaken millstonn
26.1360	Θ	Item ij tressells used att the tile kilne[121]
26.1361	Θ	Item j ffann
26.1362	Θ	Item one paire horse blindells

< In the Spanyells Kennell>[122]

In the Millhowse Chamber

26.1363	o	Item one locke & kye to the doore
26.1364 3 sent to ffakenham		Item of elmeinge borde wch came from the brick kilne xxij
26.1365		Item ij halfe inche bords nowe at Catchpooles of 12 foot apeece le\n/tt by the Bailive att his weddinge[123]

In the Spanyells Kennell

| 26.1366 | Θ | Item a locke & kye to the doore |
| 26.1367 | Θ | Item ij borded benches for doggs to lye upon |

In the Stable

26.1368	o	Item one locke & kye to one of the doores, & one wooden longer crosse barre unto the other doore, & ij chaines on the out side one for eache doore, to be locked crosse the doore
26.1369	o	Item one longe racke wth a borde in the toppe & one longe manger
26.1370	+	Item v borded p'rticons for the horsses
26.1371	+	Item v woden baile trees hanged for particons one nowe downe
26.1372	o	Item ij standers for to sett candles on & one iron sockett
26.1373	o	Item one bentch to sett saddles uppon
26.1374	o	Item one foure footed forme
26.1375	o	Item one pitcheforke
26.1376	o	Item one olde wooden scuppett

---

[121] Presumably synonymous with the brick kiln (see footnote 150 below).

[122] The kennels are described below.

[123] This comment offers a rare glimpse of social life, in this case Catchpole's wedding, where a pair of 12-foot-long boards, probably laid over trestles to create a table, would have ensured that plenty of people could join the celebration. The Suffolk probate index (Ipswich) lists numerous Catchpoles in the vicinity, including a Katherine Catchpole of Helmingham, who died in 1628.

26.1377	°	Item one hand mucke barrowe
26.1378	+	Item ij pailes
26.1379	+ °	Item ij backs of coatch harnis nothinge good butt the buckles
26.1380	°	Item one ffrench curriscombe & ma\i/ne combe

[158] In the Saddle howse

26.1381	°	Item one locke & kye to the doore
26.1382	°	Item one oate chiste wth ij locks & kyes
26.1383	°	Item one greate saddle chiste
26.1384	+	Item one liverie saddle wth stirropes stirope leathers & an old bridle
26.1385	°	Item ij little oate seeves; & an old halfe pecke
26.1386	+ °	Item one newe post pillion to ride upon
26.1387	+ °	Item one paire of blindles
26.1388	+	One wateringe snarfle
26.1389	°	One headstall roope & chaine to lead a horse to water
26.1390	+ °	Item one leaden boxe & cover for oyntment
26.1391	+	Item one horne to give a horse drinke in

In the stable chamber

26.1392	Θ	Item one locke & kye to the doore
26.1393	Θ	Item one corne screene
26.1394	Θ	Item one seeve
26.1395	Θ	Item ij corne scuppetts & one other broaken one \ nowe 2 broaken & j newe/
26.1396	Θ	Item an old tubb wth an old coatch bedd in it
26.1397	Θ	Item iij sawne peeces for coatch pales
26.1398	Θ	<Item one corne screene>
26.1399	Θ	Item j fann j bushill \newe & one old/ 1 pecke & 1 halfe pecke

Item [*sic*] voance roof over the stable chamber[124]

26.1400	Θ	Item one locke & kye to the doore
26.1401	Θ	Item one oate chiste wth a cover made of an old hoggshead
26.1402	Θ	Item iij old buffe saddles the pomells taken out
26.1403		Item 4 sawne peeces for coatch pooles

In the Barne for corne[125]

26.1404		Item one newe fanne & one bushill
26.1405		Item one longe ladder & one shorte
26.1406	Θ	Item a locke & kye unto eache doore one lost, the corne barn both [illeg.]

---

[124] Halliwell (p. 907) defines 'vance roof' as a garrett.

[125] Confirmation, lacking from the 1597 record, of a storage barn for corn destined for grinding at the on-site mill.

Ladders shorte & longe[126]

26.1407		Item ij one shorte one nowe in the Coatchhowse stable one other longe ladder nowe at the hewings by the churche bothe those aforesaid named to be in the barne[127]
26.1408		Item one longe ladder nowe att Mr Morris his howse named to be in the woorke howse[128]
26.1409	Ɵ stett	Item one other verie longe ladder nowe att Downe-ings named to be over the cartehowse placed[129]
26.1410		Item one other longe ladder wth deale sties in the inward courteyard[130]
26.1411		Item one other for the gardiners use[131]

[159] Coatche howse[132]

26.1412	Ɵ	Item one olde coatche \noe wheeles/ wth iiij wheeles
26.1413	Ɵ	Item ij tumberelles, one wth shodd wheeles & the other wth shodd wheeles \broaken/
26.1414	Ɵ	Item one iron boult & batten to the doore

In the coatche howse stable

26.1415	Ɵ	Item one locke & kye to the doore
26.1416	Ɵ	Item one kaske wth a borde in the toppe
26.1417	Ɵ	Item one manger

In the Croft stable

26.1418	Ɵ	Item a locke but no kye to the doore
26.1419	Ɵ	Item one racke \old/ & manger \old/

In the husbandmans stable[133]

26.1420		Item one locke & kye unto the doore
26.1421		Item one racke & manger
26.1422	o j	Item ij cartt saddles

---

[126] The check on the whereabouts of ladders is unique to this inventory and reveals useful valuable information.

[127] The 'hewings by the churche' confirm that either tree-pruning or tree-felling is in progress near the church.

[128] The identity of Mr Morris (the 'Mr' suggests a person of some status) and the whereabouts of his house were not pursued: the name is uncommon in the Suffolk probate index (Ipswich) and no Morris (or variant) relates to Helmingham or nearby: but the comment about the long ladder suggests that Mr Morris's house is nearby and is unequivocal about the storage place of the ladder when it returns.

[129] The Suffolk probate index (Ipswich) lists an Abiall Downing(e), yeoman, at Framsden (d. 1660), and the inventory comment, coupled with that noted above, suggests that work was being carried out to the roofs or upper parts of Helmingham estate properties, as suggested by this 'very long' ladder.

[130] A long ladder currently in the inner courtyard suggests work to the upper part of the walls or roof of Helmingham Hall.

[131] The 1626 inventory is the only one of the four to specify contents of the gardens at Helmingham or, as in this case, implements being used there. A 'gardner's chamber', presumed to be for the gardener, is mentioned in the 1741 inventory (see footnote 41 thereto).

[132] The image conveyed by this brief description of the coach house suggests redundancy; if the family were already resident at Fakenham Magna, their coach would have been with them.

[133] Judging by the marginal comments noting items removed to Fakenham, draught-horses are in use both there and at Helmingham.

26.1423	o j	Item ij paire of hande traise
26.1424		Item one other newe paire wthout seales
26.1425	o j	Item iij old carte roopes
26.1426	o j	Item ij paire of fill bells
26.1427	o j	Item ij paire of shacke traise
	one sent to fakenham	
26.1428		Item ij dudfen halters
26.1429		Item one open halter
26.1430	one sent to fakenham 03	Item 5 horse collers in prt leather
26.1431		Item iiij[or] paire of ploughe traysses whereof one used att the mill
26.1432		Item one old hauser roope wth an iron hooke
26.1433		Item one seed skeppe

[160] In the husbandman's storehowse[134]

26.1434	Ө	Item one locke & kye to the doore
26.1435	Ө	Item ij ploughe sheares & plough coulters
26.1436	Ө	Item one old iron beame for skailles & ballans to them
26.1437	o	Item one iron balance wthout a beame
26.1438	Ө	Item one dunge crome
26.1439	Ө	Item a <crapple> cradle rave for a carte
26.1440	Ө	Item v: hookes for <crapple> cradle raves
26.1441	o	Item one iron boulte for a paire of trayses
26.1442		Item ij pullies & iij iron trundles \j now: & j iron peen/
26.1443	o	Item iij sheepes brandes \2 nowe/
26.1444		Item iij ploughe eares of severall fashions
26.1445	o	Item one iron piller for the foorestooles of a carte
26.1446	Ө	Item one whipple tree one ? ... ste hook & a chaine
26.1447	Ө	Item one greate fire pann
26.1448	Ө	Item a crosse peece of woode to winde or scrue about a roope in a paire of traices, called a barrell
26.1449	Ө	Item <one> \2/ carte saddle trees
26.1450	Ө	Item ij longe hagge sawes
26.1451		Item the tines of a springe trapp to ketch mowles
26.1452	Ө	Item ij greate chayunes to drawe timber wthall \prt want./
26.1453	Ө	Item vi carte strakes \nowe 5/
26.1454	Ө	Item ij great jemmer hengells, & one ky[e] belongeinge to the hengell of some great doore
26.1455	Ө	Item the toppe ende of a speete racke

---

[134] The sequence of stable and storehouse both designated as 'husbandmen's' offers a view of arable and animal husbandry undertaken to supply the household. By the time of the subsequent and undated checks, some items, or parts of them, have gone since they were recorded in 1626, but the means of branding sheep, ploughing, cultivation, haymaking and maintenance of woodland and parkland are still in evidence.

26.1456	Ꝋ	Item one greate ploughe chayne
26.1457	Ꝋ	Item \1/ ij foote chaines that gooeth next the ploughes eare & a beareing chaine
26.1458	Ꝋ	Item one carpenders Adds
26.1459	Ꝋ	Item one shave & hande sawe
26.1460	Ꝋ	Item one olde spade & scuppett
26.1461	Ꝋ	Item one other broaken scuppett, the iron worke good still
26.1462	Ꝋ	Item one greate stocke locke the kye wanteinge
26.1463	Ꝋ	Item one cuttinge spade for haye
26.1464		Item one hatchett & hooke
26.1465	°	Item one iron hammer; & <one> \2/ iron wedges
26.1466	Ꝋ	Item vij old irons for casements
26.1467	Ꝋ	Item viij hoopes for carte naves
26.1468		Item one peece of a great iron chayne wth nyne linkes
26.1469		Item vij great horse coller bells
26.1470	Ꝋ	Item one trough & one shelfe & certeyne tile pins

[161] Item [sic] in the worke howse

26.1471	Ꝋ	Item one locke & kye to the doore \the locke broakenge/
26.1472	Ꝋ	Item ij benches to worke one
26.1473		Item xxiii bunches of sapp lathe & one of hazle lathe
26.1474		Item one shorte thicke plancke
26.1475	Ꝋ	Item one troughe to stampe crabbes in
26.1476	Ꝋ	one wooden verges streyner
26.1477	Ꝋ	Item 4 peeces of sawne elmeing timber
26.1478	Ꝋ	Item 1 trundled shodd
26.1479	Ꝋ	Item one old paire of shodd wheeles
26.1480	Ꝋ	Item one paire of old large broaken harrowes, & one old plough
26.1481		Item one paire of drafts for a coatch

In the slaughterhowse[135]

26.1482	Ꝋ	Item one locke & kye to the doore
26.1483	Ꝋ	Item ij planke posts soe called wth hooles to hange up a bulloce upon wth one greate iron ringle to the one of them
26.1484		Item one puntche to undersett a beast when it is a fleainge
26.1485		Item one iron crooke wth a handle
26.1486		Item one iron jabbinge pricke
26.1487		Item one roope to drawe in a bullocke

---

135 Although few of the service buildings needed to support the household at Helmingham Hall were described in its 1597 inventory, there was certainly a slaughterhouse on site then. Smythe's household accounts record payment of 3d. for mending the lock on the slaughterhouse door in November 1588 and, more importantly, the income received from the sale of hides, money which went directly into the household funds. Between April 1587 and 31 March 1589 the household steward sold a total of 16 hides, mostly to 'Lacy', receiving a consistent sum of 10s. 6d. each.

26.1488	Ө	Item ij neats trees, & one other wth an iron to hange a sheepe or calfe while they fleae it
26.1489		Item one bludd paile
26.1490	Ө	Item one bludd boule in the grounde
26.1491	Ө	Item one barrowe to laie neats sowses upon

In the cart howse

26.1492	o j	Item ij carts the one borded in \the/ booth \sides/, thother open wth ij paire of wheeles shodde wth iron & ij carte ladders wth redgwithes & wombroopes
26.1493		Item one drugge wheele bounde wth iron, the fellowe to it wantinge
26.1494		Item one drafte for a coatch when the horse goeth lengthwise
26.1495		Item <ij> \a/ paire of olde wheeles bounde wth iron
26.1496		Item one olde paire of greate harrowes
26.1497		Item one old ploughe wth an iron eare & foote chaine
26.1498		Item iij longe elmeing planks wch nowe belongeinge unto the slideinge table att ffakenham

[162] In the puets howse[136]

26.1499	Ø	Item one locke & kye to the doore
26.1500		Item an old troughe & an olde traye
26.1501		Item one borded broade old chiste standeinge before the doore with a cover the sides & bottom lyned wth leade used to water fishe in
26.1502		Item v boards nailed over heade to cover it wthall and one ovis borde lyeing upon them

In the swill howse

26.1503	o	Item a locke but noe kye unto the doore
26.1504		Item one woode sesterne in the ground to putt hoggs meate in
26.1505	o	Item one wooden jett

Hoggstroughes

| 26.1506 | o jj | Item iiij hoggstroughes one next the swill howse, one in the boores stye, one in the yard next the Boores stye, & one in the hoggscoate next the Boores stye |
| 26.1507 | | Item in the boores steye one great doore with hooks \ij in the husbandmans stable/ |

---

[136] Puets are peewits, lapwing, kept for household consumption. Although the peewits' house is not mentioned in the 1597 inventory, Smythe's household accounts of 1587–89 confirm that they were kept at Helmingham then, recording payments of 14s. for 'two dosen puets' in June 1588 and 3d. for 'keping of the puets' the following month. By 1626, however, despite the lock and key to the door, the old fish tank, trough and tray suggest that the peewits may no longer inhabit their house.

In the pumpe howse[137]

26.1508		Item one locke & \noe/ kye to the doore
26.1509	Θ	Item one leaden pumpe & long iron praytree
26.1510	Θ	Item one great leaden sesterne

In the inwarde courteyarde[138]

26.1511	Θ	Item one great longe barre reaching from the wall unto one of the leaves of the \<illeg.\> gate wth an iron locke & kye[139]
26.1512	Θ	Item one other longe barre for the other side of the greate gate[140]
26.1513	Θ	Item one locke & kye unto the wickett gate wth a chayne of iron to barr crosse the same[141]

Item [sic] the backe bridge yarde next the dayrye[142]

26.1514	Θ	Item a locke & kye unto the gate
26.1515	Θ	Item one greate crosse barre reacheinge from the walle unto the gate
26.1516	Θ	Item one brasseinge water cocke
26.1517	Θ	Item one little doggs kennell in the wall wth ij doores \j door want./

In the back yarde betwene the moate & the kitchen[143]

26.1518	Θ	Item one locke & kye to the doore
26.1519	o	Item ij old hutches to keepe firritts in
26.1520	o	Item one old pitchforke

[163] In the outwarde courte[144]

26.1521		Item ij formes wth feete for benches in the Arbor
26.1522		Item one stonne rowler wth an iron in eache end and a wooden frame to drawe it by
26.1523		Item one wooden rowler wth an iron in eache end and a crosse iron wth a sockett to rowle it withall

---

[137] This sounds to be a substantial housing for the pump. See 26.1312, which mentions water being pumped to the brewhouse from the back yard; and Plate 13 (p. 159), where 'c' identifies the yard.

[138] See Plate 13 where 'l' identifies the inner courtyard.

[139] The illegible word is probably 'great' as this would concur with all other references to this principal gate marking entry to Helmingham Hall from the south, identified by 'm' on Plate 13.

[140] Clearly there was a bar to fit across each half of the great gate. Plate 13, supported by Appendix A, identifies the yards and gates mentioned throughout this 1626 inventory, in which security is mentioned frequently.

[141] The 'wicket gate' described here survives today within the 'great gate'.

[142] Thought to be synonymous with the 'back yard', identified on Plate 13 as 'c'.

[143] Identified on Plate 13 as 'e'.

[144] Although its appearance may well have altered since 1626, Plate 14 (a small detail from the 1729 survey of the Helmingham Estate by Richard Tollemache, of which Plate VI shows a larger section) clearly shows the outward, or outer, court (identified by 'a'). The frontispiece illustration (post-dating Plate VI) shows that the principle of an outer court persisted, although the brick walls suggested in Plate 14 have been replaced with post-and-rail fencing.

In the long walke betwene the garden and the moate[145]

26.1524	o	Item one wooden rowler wth an iron in eache end & a crosse barre wth a sockett & a staffe to rowle it withall
26.1525	o	Item one turned poste wth a faire brasse diall upon it

In the garden[146]

26.1526	Item one locke & kye to the doore
26.1527	Item one spade
26.1528	Item one iron rake
26.1529	Item one iron howe
26.1530	Item a paire of garden sheires
26.1531	Item one wheelebarrowe
26.1532	Item one sithe newe to mowe the walks
26.1533	Item one stonne rowler wth <a stonne> an iron in each ende & a fframe to rowle it withall
26.1534	Item <one> twoe brasse water potts one greater & one lesser
26.1535	Item one bentch to sitt upon wth a backe

In the moate

26.1536	Item one old boate \1 new boate/

In the ffeasant yarde[147]

26.1537	Item one springe locke & kye unto the doore
26.1538	Item one little brasse diall upon a poste
26.1539	Item a tubb to putt feasants meat in & a borde to cover it
26.1540	Item one paile & ij little leaden panns to sett water in

In the dovehouse[148]

26.1541	Item one locke & kye to the doore
26.1542	Item one table to give the pigeons meat uppon

[164] In the stable yardes[149]

26.1543	Item m bricke
26.1544	Item m square tile
26.1545	Item m roof tile
26.1546	Item m halfe rounds

---

[145] Identified on Plate 14 (p. 160) as 'b', and is a feature recognisable today as a grass causeway separating the moated house from its separately moated gardens to the west, also clearly visible in Plate 14.

[146] The locked door (26.1526) to the 1626 garden is suggested by the gate visible at 'c' on Plate 14.

[147] The entry at 26.1538 suggests some ornamentation.

[148] Not mentioned in the 1597 inventory, as discussed in the introduction.

[149] The quantities of bricks and tiles here and at the brick kiln (see footnote following) are expressed as 'm', an estimate indicative of 'thousands' of items. Assuming that the stable yards were immediately east of the moated house, the quantities give some indication of work in progress, particularly to roofs.

Att the bricke kelne[150]
26.1547	Item m bricke
26.1548	Item m tile
26.1549	Item m pavements

---

[150] This is the only one of the four inventories to make mention of the brick kiln; the confirmation that there are thousands of bricks, tiles and pavements in stock here and in the stable yards may have been confirmation that the household had earmarked them for building works in progress. A brick kiln was still in operation in the 20th century, located north of the park (close to the site occupied now by North Park Farm, TM18463 58550).

THE 1708 HOUSEHOLD INVENTORY

Helmingham Hall Archive T/Hel(S)/9/1/5

**An Inventory of all the
Household Goods in Helmingham Hall in
Suffolke taken in January 1707 [1708][1]**

[1] In the Kitchen[2]

08.1	1 long grate with 5 forbarrs and 2 barrs at the bottom
08.2	1 pair of cheeks
08.3	2 ffenders
08.4	1 pair of cobirons
08.5	4 racks one being a smooth one
08.6	3 hayles
08.7	1 doggs wheele
08.8	2 pair of pott hookes
08.9	1 old ffire shovle, poker and sifter
08.10	1 old iron jack
08.11	4 brass pottage potts
08.12	2 tin boylers & 1 small boyler, this & one of the other are in iron frames
08.13	1 old kettle
08.14	6 spitts
08.15	3 triangle trevetts
08.16	2 dreeping pans
08.17	1 quart skellett
08.18	1 pinte skellett
08.19	1 ffish stueing pan and cover
08.20	2 sauce pans
08.21	1 flatt sauce pan (or preserveing pan)
08.22	1 tin cover for pewter dishes
08.23	2 brass pailes
08.24	1 wooden paile with an iron hoop
08.25	1 brass basting ladle
08.26	1 egg slice
08.27	1 fflesh fork
08.28	1 brass sconce
08.29	4 dressers, one with a drawer
08.30	1 keller
08.31	1 long fform

---

[1] The document title is displayed on its reverse (folio 12 of 12).

[2] The perambulation followed by the compiler of this inventory is unlike either of its predecessors, both of which set out from the hall. See Appendix A for discussion of routes.

08.32	1 lether chaire			
08.33	2 griddirons			
08.34	3 brass pottlids			
08.35	1 drudgeing-box			
08.36	1 wooden handle bowle			
08.37	1 old stewing boyler and cover			
08.38	1 stock lock			
08.39	2 spitt chaines			

08.40	Old Pewter[3]	1 dish about	26 inches diameter	
08.41		8 dishes about	22	
08.42		2 dishes about	20½	
08.43		4 about	17	
08.44		2 about	16½	
08.45		1 deep one about	13½	
08.46		4 about	13½	
08.47		1 about	12	
08.48		4 intermesses about	12½	
08.49		1 pye plate	17	
08.50		1 pye plate	14½	
08.51		1 salver	17	
08.52		1 salver	09	
08.53		2 dishes about	18½	
08.54		21 pottage plates		
08.55		35 other plates		

08.56	New Pewter	1 dish about	19	These cyphered
08.57		8 dishes about	16½	[with]
08.58		8 dishes about	12	Earls corronetts[4]
08.59		11 plates		
08.60		48 plates not cyphered		

08.61	Other Pewter	2 flaggons, each holding about a gallon
08.62		1 pinte pott
08.63		1 halfe pinte cupp
08.64		2 square salts
08.65		1 high round salt
08.66		1 little saucer
08.67		1 pair of high candlesticks
08.68		2 chamber potts
08.69		1 bedd pann

---

[3] The record of dimensions in this inventory is exemplary. The pewter dishes are the first of many items whose measurements are recorded.

[4] From 25 March 1669 Sir Lionel Tollemache, 4th baronet and 3rd Earl of Dysart (30 January 1649–23 February 1728).

[2] In the Passage, Scullery, Pastry, Bakehouse and Bolting roome[5]

08.70	2 iron barrs for a long grate
08.71	1 large salt tubb
08.72	1 brass morter and an iron pestell
08.73	1 iron frying pann
08.74	1 iron peele
08.75	1 wooden pye peele
08.76	4 brass pattepans with 3 bottoms
08.77	6 tin pattepanns with 3 bottoms
08.78	1 round bakeing pann 13 inches wide with a bottom
08.79	1 bottom of another panne something larger
08.80	2 rowling pinns
08.81	2 fflower ffirkens
08.82	1 two eared tubb
08.83	1 dough scraper
08.84	1 lawne scieve
08.85	1 kneading bowle
08.86	2 large tubs
08.87	1 sifting keller
08.88	1 small old keller
08.89	1 large kneading keller
08.90	1 meall scuppett
08.91	1 bolting hutch
08.92	1 fflower bingg [flour bin]
08.93	3 dressers
08.94	1 old stoole
08.95	1 old broaken lether chaire
08.96	3 stock locks

In the Servants Hall, Store clossett and Passage[6]

08.97	1 long table with double leafe; each 23 foot long and 2 foot 8 inches wide[7]
08.98	2 long fforms, one 10 foot the other 7 foot & ½ in length
08.99	1 mustard querns
08.100	1 dresser
08.101	1 round brass stue ffish-pann
08.102	1 brass cullender
08.103	1 round brass ffish slice, nigh 16 inches wide
08.104	1 gallon skellett
08.105	2 three pint skelletts
08.106	1 sauce-pann
08.107	1 tin droping baster
08.108	1 lether jack

---

5 The grouping together of rooms and summarising of their contents is a characteristic of this inventory, making it impossible to ascribe items to individual spaces.

6 As noted in footnote 5, individual items cannot be ascribed to each of the spaces grouped together in the heading. but see footnote 7.

7 There is no doubt that the dimensions of this table place it in the servants' hall, where it has the capacity to accommodate a large number of staff.

08.109 1 lether bottle
08.110 1 earthen-pott of about the size of halfe a pail-full
08.111 1 round brass bakeing-pan 15 inches wide with bottom above mencioned
08.112 2 old tin covers for dishes
08.113 1 iron triangle trevett
08.114 1 pair of brass scales
08.115 1 box with 13 particions
08.116 1 old hutch
08.117 3 stock locks

In the Great Hall, and Staire-case[8]

08.118 1 large picture of a cooks-shop in a black frame[9]
08.119 2 pictures at full length of a gentleman and lady in mourning: in black & gilded frames[10]
08.120 1 young gentlemans picture at full length in a black and gilded fframe
08.121 1 picture of 4 young ladyes, hand in hand[11]
08.122 4 pictures to the knees
08.123 8 pictures to the waste
08.124 12 ceesars heads, about 26 inches 21 inches wide within the fframes[12]
08.125 8 other heads about the same size
08.126 29 other lesser pictures of heads about a foot or 18 inches square
08.127 1 large pair of cob-irons
08.128 6 brass ovall sconces
08.129 11 halfe pikes[13]
08.130 1 ovall table about 5 foot in length
08.131 1 iron plate lock with brass screws
08.132 1 curtain-rodd
08.133 1 little cedar table 2 foot and 2 foot and halfe

[3] In the Housekeepers Store roome[14]

08.134 1 press cupboard

---

8 The designation 'Great Hall' appears for the first time, described as the 'Hall' in 1597 and 1626.

9 By the late Restoration period, cookshops had acquired a reputation for being the fast-food outlets of their day. A contemporary account of the English cookshop exists, written by Monsieur Henri Misson, who travelled throughout England in the 1690s. His work was translated into English by John Ozell as *Memoirs and Observations [of Monsieur Henri Misson] in his Travels over England* (London, 1719). Misson says (p. 146): 'A Frenchman of any distinction would think it a great scandal in France to be seen to eat in such a place; and indeed custom will not allow it there; but in England they laugh at such niceties ... here a Gentleman of 1500 livres a Year enters a Cook's shop without fear of being at all despised for it and there dines for his shilling to his heart's content. I have often eat in that manner with a Gentleman of my acquaintance that is very rich, and was a Member of the House of Commons.'

10 These pictures are of Sir Lionel Tollemache, 2nd baronet, and his wife, Lady Elizabeth (née Stanhope), who were responsible for the 1626 inventory. Their portraits remain in the hall. See Plate II for portrait of Sir Lionel.

11 This painting, illustrated in Plate III, survives in the hall. The four young ladies, one of whom is in a cradle, were the first four daughters of Sir Lionel (2nd baronet, d. 1640). See caption to Plate III for detail; see also footnote 75 to Introduction.

12 This and the following two entries amount to a total of 49 'heads'.

13 In the 1626 inventory, despite the increasing use of firearms by then, pikes were still useable weapons and stored securely in the armoury (26.742–744), whereas the half pikes displayed now are redundant, albeit decorative.

08.135 1 large chest
08.136 1 screw-press for almonds
08.137 1 foursquare jappan voider
08.138 1 eight square jappan voyder
08.139 1 white marble morter 11 inches and ½ diameter within and 6 inches
          and ½ deep
08.140 1 wooden pestell
08.141 1 bale for a pail
08.142 4 old boxes – viz't: one of wainscott, three of deal
08.143 1 old lawne scieve
08.144 1 old tin tunnel
08.145 1 little old tin cullender
08.146 2 old broaken brass candlesticks
08.147 2 earthen potts each holding about a pailfull
08.148 2 lesser earthen potts
08.149 1 gallon pitcher
08.150 1 three pinte pitcher
08.151 1 white cracked sillibub-pott with a cover
08.152 9 wooden square trenchers
08.153 3 steele cross-bowes
08.154 1 broaken cross-bow
08.155 1 pair of gaffles
08.156 1 barrell of lamblack
08.157 1 pinte chocolet pott
08.158 1 chocalat mill
08.159 2 curtain rods
08.160 1 old pair of tongues
08.161 1 small tin pasty-pan
08.162 2 old tin watering-potts
08.163 1 round hard brush
08.164 1 high stove
08.165 1 kettle belonging to it
08.166 1 brass two eared boyeling pann of about a gallon
08.167 1 preserveing-pan of about 3 pintes
08.168 1 saucepan with three ffeet
08.169 1 brass sconce and 1 old weather glass
08.170 1 picture of King Charles the first and his two sons
08.171 1 tin apple roaster
08.172 3 escuchions
08.173 1 hair cydar bagg
08.174 5 high square glass bottles and 1 round one like those they keep leeches
          in, etc.
08.175 Delf:ware etc. 3 deep basons about 8 inches diameter
08.176   2 plaine and 3 firbelowed dishes about 10
08.177   5 dishes matched about 8
08.178   2 blue shallow dishes something wider
08.179   2 pritty plates   }
08.180   3 plates of another sort } about 8 inches and ½
08.181   9 plates of another sort }

08.182		4 basons about 6 inches diameter 3 whereof are broaken edged
08.183		2 tea dishes[15]
08.184		2 blue ovall potts for potted meat: 5 inches long and 4 wide
08.185	Glasses	5 basons about 7 inches and ½ diameter
08.186		3 basons about 4½
08.187		5 dishes about 4½
08.188		4 flatt dishes about 5½
08.189		6 firbelowed dishes about 4
08.190		2 saucers about 5¾
08.191		6 glasses one inch high from about 5½ inches diameter to 3½
08.192		3 about 3 inches high to keep sweetmeats in
08.193		4 wrought glasses for jellies about 3 inches high
08.194		8 plaine ones for jelleys something lower
08.195		7 more for jelly's about 2 inches high
08.196		1 salver one inch and ½ high and 3 and ½ diameter
08.197		6 tumblers about 3 inches diameter
08.198		1 sweetmeat glass fitt for the salver
08.199		3 little dishes about 3 inches diameter
08.200		1 cruett
08.201		13 whip sillybubb glasses, whereof 4 are crackt
08.202		2 white earthen basons
08.203		2 white earthen chamber potts
08.204	Panns for	17 small round ones taper
08.205	Cakes	6 straight ones round
08.206		6 ovall ones
08.207		6 four square
08.208		6 three square
08.209	Pattepanns	1 ovall about 9 inches long
08.210		1 ovall shorter
08.211		1 ffirbelowed without a bottom
08.212		1 butter scraper of bone
08.213		1 des[s]ert pewter basket
08.214		1 pewter still
08.215		1 stock lock

[4] In the Parlour, drawing-room, and two rooms over against them, etc.[16]

08.216	1 ovall table about 4 foot 8 inches in length
08.217	1 white marble table 5 foot long and 2 foot 5 inches wide square[17]
08.218	1 white marble cistern, ovall 3 foott 4 inches long within and 6 inches deep

---

15 Tea was first sold in England in 1658 (Colquhoun (2007), Taste, p.148). Tea dishes were the precursor to teacups, similar in appearance to deep saucers. For definition of **delftware** and index of other items related to **tea** see glossary.

16 The parlour recalls designations in the preceding inventories; but the drawing room is new since 1626.

17 This is the first mention at Helmingham of marble as a decorative material, used here for a table, and in the entry following for a cistern.

08.219 1 spring clock
08.220 12 cane chaires
08.221 3 pair of dogs[18]
08.222 2 harth brushes
08.223 3 pair of bellows
08.224 1 fire-shovell
08.225 1 pair of tongs
08.226 4 curtain rods
08.227 2 iron plate locks
08.228 6 brass plate locks
08.229 1 brown china tea-pott, with a guilded handle[19]
08.230 1 blue china bason
08.231 1 green china tea dish[20]
08.232 1 tumbler glass[21]
08.233 2 rummer glasses
08.234 3 covers for glasses
08.235 4 cruetts
08.236 5 small wine glasses
08.237 2 high narrow wine glasses
08.238 2 wine glasses the same shape but flourished
08.239 1 hammer
08.240 1 high glass to keep leeches in etc.[22]
08.241 3 pieces of Portugall platt about 8 foot and ½ wide and in all about 24 foot long[23]
08.242 1 piece of rush matt about 14 inches wide and 12 foot long
08.243 1 straw bed
08.244 1 old map of Italy
08.245 1 wallnutetree table with a drawer
08.246 1 pair of walnuttree stands
08.247 1 lookinglass about 25 inches one way and 20 the other in a walnuttree frame
08.248 1 cedar close-stool box with a crimson velvett seate[24]
08.249 6 elboe}   scarlett damask chaires
08.250 6 other}
08.251 6 elboe chaires of blue damask

---

[18] From this and entries 08.222 to 08.225 inclusive, it can be assumed that, between them, these rooms have at least three fireplaces. See Appendix A for discussion of how these spaces were altered in 1741.

[19] See footnote 15 above.

[20] See footnote 15 regarding tea dishes.

[21] Glass is mentioned throughout this inventory and marks a significant change at Helmingham Hall, where previously only bottles were of glass.

[22] This is the first mention of leeches being kept ready for use at the Hall, although there is evidence that this mode of treatment was already favoured by the 2nd baronet, whose accounts (T/Hel/21/1) mention payment for bleeding.

[23] This and the entry following confirm that floor coverings were made of plaited, as well as woven materials, in this case of rushes.

[24] Sophistication is evident in the description of this enclosed chamber-pot (*OED* does not confirm use of the term 'commode', in this context, until 1851). Positioned within easy reach of the reception suite, the close stool is elevated from the necessary to the elegantly desirable with its cedar case and velvet seat.

08.252　2 square stooles with buff coulored velvett seates

In the Three roomes beyond the drawing roome
08.253　1 lifting up table about 3 foot 8 inches square: with particions under it
08.254　1 cross foulding frame for a table
08.254　3 deall dores (two painted white)
08.256　severall pieces of old wainscott and lumber

In the roome where Mr Bockenham lay[25]
08.257　The walls all covered with speckled sey except the chimney-end and behinde the bed
08.258　1 bedstead about 8 foot to the top of the knops
08.259　4 curtains of purple cloth, laced with a whitish silk lace: double valance laced with the same and whitish silk ffringe: the beds-head, teaster, counterpane and cover for a table, of the same
08.260　1 old sey window curtain
08.261　4 curtain rods
08.262　1 old bed next the coards
08.263　1 ffether bed
08.264　1 bolster
08.265　1 pillow
08.266　3 blanketts
08.267　1 table about 3 foot 2 inches long and 2 foot wide
08.268　1 pair of round stands
08.269　1 elboe }　　chaires covered and laced as the curtains etc.
08.270　2 other }
08.271　1 elboe chair covered with a clouded sey
08.272　1 joynt stool with a lether cushion seate
08.273　1 pair of andirons}　　with brass knops
08.274　1 pair of tongs }
08.275　1 old pair of bellows

In the next room and clossetts
08.276　The walls all covered with a speckled sey[26]
08.277　1 bedsted about 6 foot high

---

[25] The late occupant was the Revd Anthony Bokenham, rector of Helmingham until 1689 when his refusal to conform to the taking of oaths to King William and Queen Mary forced him to resign the rectory (Acorn Archive, 'A Life of Dr Humphrey Prideaux', transcribed by Raymond Forward, accessed via ancestry.com). Bokenham appears to have acted as the 3rd earl's estate steward and it is likely that the room was set aside for his occupation when he was at the Hall in this capacity. An undated letter from him to the earl, concerned with a range of estate matters, survives in the Helmingham Archive (T/Hel/26/11). Whilst still in post as rector at Helmingham in February 1686, Bokenham officiated at the marriage of his only daughter, Bridget, to Humphrey Prideaux (appointed dean of Norwich Cathedral in 1681). Bridget predeceased her father in 1700, but in 1694 she gave birth to a son, Edmund (d. 1745), who became well known for his topographical drawings, including a set recording the formal gardens at Euston Hall exactly as they were described by John Evelyn in his diary entry for 10 September 1677. Bokenham died in 1704, by which time he was almost 90 years old. The 1708 inventory designation as the room 'where Mr Bockenham lay' suggests that it has not been reallocated since his death.

[26] See glossary, **wall coverings**, for other examples and confirmation that these were removable, portable and distinct from hangings.

08.278 1 matt next the coards
08.279 1 ffeather bed
08.280 1 bolster
08.281 2 blanketts
08.282 1 green rug
08.283 4 old blue sey curtains with scoloped vallance etc.
08.284 1 old map of Europe
08.285 1 map of part of Scotland
08.286 1 pair of cobirons
08.287 1 table about 3 foot square
08.288 2 elboe }   old chaires
08.289 2 other }
08.290 3 old stooles with cushion seates
08.291 5 peeces of pavement of unpolished white marble that will be about 15 inches square of superficiall measure each[27]

In the room next the Brewhouse

08.292 1 half headed coarded bedstead
08.293 1 flock bed
08.294 1 fflock bolster
08.295 1 bed matt
08.296 1 coverlit
08.297 2 cobirons one higher than the other
08.298 2 wooden chaires

[5] In the Brewhouse

08.299 1 copper about 6 foot 9 inches diameter and 2 foot 6 inches deep
08.300 1 boarded cover to the copper
08.301 1 mashing-fatt widest at the bottom 3 foot deep and 5 foot and ½ wide at the top
08.302 1 cooler 12 foot long 6 foot wide and 12 inches deep
08.303 1 working ffatt widest at the bottom 3 foot deep and 7 foot wide at the top
08.304 1 tub widest at the top being 3 feet and ½ there and 2 foot 6 inches deep
08.305 1 trough (under the mashing fatt) 7 foot long, 19 inches and ½ deep and the same wide
08.306 1 trough to lye from the copper to the mashing fatt 6 foot long
08.307 1 trough to reach from the copper to the cooler 9 foot 6 inches long
08.308 1 wicker thing to stand up in the mashing fatt 3 foot 3 inches high
08.309 2 things to stirr the malt about in the mashing fatt
08.310 1 baskett to stop the hopps from running into the liquor in the cooler
08.311 1 ladeing scoop
08.312 1 thing to shift about the yeast in the working fats
08.313 3 benches
08.314 1 cole rake

---

[27] Although apparently not yet in use, these pieces of unpolished white marble 'pavement' have the potential to create a small decorative area (forming part of a hearth, for example) measuring 15 by 75 inches.

08.315 1 ffire fork
08.316 1 flatt trough for the liquor to run in from the pump to the copper 3 foot
        and ½ long

In the Hen-house
08.317 6 coopes being round the room

In the Laundry, Cheesehouse, Dairy and Larder
08.318 1 oak table 3 foot broad: the frame 7 foot and ½ long: the leafe in 3 parts
        in all 14 foot long
08.319 1 ash table leafe (8 foot long: 2 foot 10 inches wide) upon two tressles
08.320 1 square elm table 4 foot and ½ long and 2 foot wide
08.321 1 joynt stoole table about 21 inches square
08.322 1 washing block upon four ffeet
08.323 1 lether chair
08.324 1 lether stoole
08.325 2 hailes
08.326 1 pair of cobirons
08.327 1 large fire fork
08.328 1 brass kettle houlding 3 or 4 pailes full
08.329 1 horss to hang linen upon
08.330 4 smoothing hand irons
08.331 1 clapper for napkins
08.332 1 short spit
08.333 1 brass sconce
08.334 1 pair of high brass candlesticks
08.335 1 brass warming-pan with a wooden handle
08.336 1 copper pott holding about a quart to heat trimming water in
08.337 1 shreading knife
08.338 1 copper holding about 18 pailes full with a cover
08.339 1 cheese press with two screws
08.340 2 large bucking-tubs
08.341 1 salting trey
08.342 2 cheese fatts
08.343 2 cheese-breds
08.344 1 butter keller
08.345 1 milk trey
08.346 1 large kettle for dogs meat
08.347 1 kettle holding about 2 pails full
08.348 1 brass ffrying-pan
08.349 1 pair of garden sheers
08.350 2 marking irons of L & T
08.351 1 large }   basketts to carry clothes in
08.352 2 small}
08.353 1 long salting trough
08.354 2 round powdering-tubs with covers
08.355 2 dressers
08.356 1 chopping-block
08.357 2 cleivers
08.358 2 bowles to put cold meat in

08.359 1 kettle holding about a pail and halfe
08.360 1 wooden beam and scales
08.361 1 64 pounds }
08.362 2 28 pounds }   leaden weights
08.363 1 33 pounds }
08.364 1 7 pounds   }
08.365 2 hanging shelves

[6] In the Pantries

08.366 1 press cupboard
08.367 2 tables each about 4 foot and ½ long and 2 foot wide
08.368 5 leather chaires
08.369 2 lether stooles
08.370 1 tin sconce
08.371 1 bell to ring in hands
08.372 1 perewig block
08.373 4 turkey work cushions
08.374 1 wicker voider
08.375 1 ale stoole
08.376 1 halfe barrell
08.377 1 bread rasp
08.378 10 white hafted knives[28]
08.379 12 white hafted fforkes[29]
08.380 2 silver salt sellers[30]
08.381 9 silver spoones
08.382 1 two quart stone gotch
08.383 1 one quart stone mugg
08.384 2 water bottles
08.385 6 old fashioned cruets
08.386 1 large water glass
08.387 5 beer glasses
08.388 6 wine glasses

Second Story[31]

In the Gate:house Chamber[32]

08.389 11 peeces of fflowery hangings, about 8 foot deep and 6 foot wide each
08.390 1 bedstead about 8 foot high, the sides of the teaster and vallance of
        raised silk embroidrey, with green and blue woosted ffringe
08.391 5 speckled woosted and linen curtains, no curtain rods

---

[28] See glossary, **knife**, for comment on the appearance of knives as part of the household, and see
footnote 29 regarding forks. White-hafted suggests bone handles.

[29] This is the first appearance of table forks in the Helmingham inventories. See glossary, **fork** and its
introduction to the English dining table in the 17th century.

[30] The salt cellars and spoons listed next are the only items of silver recorded in this inventory.

[31] This is the first of the Helmingham inventories to confirm rooms by floor level.

[32] In contrast to the opening description of this inventory, which began at the kitchen, the perambulation
of the first floor begins in the centre of the south range with the gatehouse chamber. Although the
chamber sounds to be decorated and furnished sumptuously with its '11 flowery hangings', there is
no mention of tools for a fireplace, although one was clearly evident both in 1597 and 1626.

08.392 1 ffether bed
08.393 1 ffether bolster
08.394 1 bed-matt
08.395 1 blankett lined with peeces of the same of the hangings, etc.
08.396 1 coverlit matching the hangings of the room
08.397 1 chair the arms covered with crimson velvett: the seat of ticking stuffed
with ffeathers: with red silk ffringe
08.398 1 arm wooden chair carved and inlaid
08.399 2 buffett stooles with stuffed seats
08.400 1 long round trunk lined

In the Black velvett room and clossetts

08.401 3 peeces of tapestry hangings about 10 foot deep viz't:
16 foot and ½
12 foot   wide
9 foot
08.402 1 bedstead about 9 foot high, the head and sides of the teaster and
vallance of black velvett embroidered; and yellow, white and green
silk ffringe
08.403 5 curtains 6 foot long of green silk yard and ⅛ wide there being 7
bredths
08.404 7 plumes of particoloured ffeathers upon the beds:top
08.405 2 ffether beds
08.406 2 bolsters
08.407 2 pillows
08.408 4 blanketts
08.409 2 bed:matts
08.410 4 curtain rods
08.411 1 silk embroidered quilt 2 yards ¾ wide, and 2 yards and ½ long with a
small blue and white silk ffringe round it
08.412 1 halfe headed bedstead
08.413 1 green silk quilt lined with green bayes 3 yards ¾ long and 3 yards ⅛
wide
08.414 1 elboe chair of black velvet wrought like the beds:head, etc.
08.415 1 chair with fine turkey work (or tapestry) seat
08.416 1 chaire the seat and back of course turkey-work
08.417 1 foulding stoole with stuffed seat
08.418 1 oak table 3 foot 4 inches long, and 2 foot 5 inches wide
08.419 1 red jappaned square stand with ledges round the top
08.420 1 green cloth table carpett yard and three quarters long, and yard and
half wide, with a wrought flowered border of 3 inches wide round it
08.421 1 red cloth carpett about a yard square with 18 narrow yellow footings
and a yellow woosted ffringe round it
08.422 1 high oak table 4 foot long and 21 inches wide
08.423 2 window curtains of speckled green linsea woolsea
08.424 1 pair of dogs with brass knops
08.425 1 pair of tongs with a brass top
08.426 1 pair of English black jappaned bellows
08.427 1 harth brush
08.428 1 turkey wrought cushion

08.429   1 Indian brush for hangings

[7] In the Chamber over the roome where Mr Bockenham lay[33]

08.430   The walls about 9 foot high covered with 5 peices of tapestry, none
being over the chimney, nor behind the beds:head

08.431   1 bedstead about 7 foot high the outside of the teaster and valance of
scarlet silk with a scarlet silk fringe 4 inches deep and a small fringe
on the seames of the same-coloured silk

08.432   6 curtains of ell wide scarlet searge, each one bredth about 5 foot deep

08.433   1 ffether bed

08.434   1 ffether bolster

08.435   1 bed-matt

08.436   1 blankett

08.437   1 yellow linsey woolsey coverlit

08.438   4 curtain rods

08.439   1 oak table 4 foot 8 inches long and 2 foot 2 inches wide

08.440   1 wainscott table of three heights about 4 foot long and 19 inches wide

08.441   1 bench 6 foot long with a stuffed seat and yellow silk fringe about 2
inches deep round it

08.442   1 turkey work cushion

08.443   1 pair of cobirons

In the Red Chamber and clossets[34]

08.444   5 pieces of tapestry hangings about 10 foot deep viz't:
16 foot
13 foot
12 foot   wide
10 foot
8 foot

08.445   1 bedstead about 9 foot high

08.446   1 half headed bedstead

08.447   4 curtains: duble top vallance: bottom vallance: the beds-head: and large
counterpane: all of red cloth laced round and at about a foots distance
lenthwaies with a blue silk lace: and the top vallance both without and
within hath a blue silk fringe about 8 inches deep, and the curtains
are lined with a bloom coloured silk

08.448   3 ffether-beds

08.449   2 ffether bolsters

08.450   3 pillowes

08.451   1 oak table 4 foot long and 2 foot wide

08.452   1 table carpet 5 foot long and 3 foot and ½ wide of red silk damask: one
side and each end bordered 3 inches with black cut velvet and red
twist

---

[33]   See footnote 25 above regarding the Revd Anthony Bokenham.

[34]   The description of the chamber and its closets confirms the pattern of three interconnecting spaces
recognisable from several suites described in the 1626 inventory. The description of the ten-foot-high
hangings, whose widths amount to 59 feet, the fireplace and the 'locking' cedar close stool (08.462)
confirm that this room is furnished for a person of high status.

Plate I. Catherine Tollemache, née Cromwell, wife of Lionel Tollemache, later 1st baronet, a portrait attributed to Robert Peake the Elder, c. 1597 at Helmingham Hall. Photograph reproduced by kind permission of the Lord Tollemache

Plate II. Sir Lionel Tollemache, 2nd baronet, c. 1612–1621 at Helmingham Hall. Reproduced by kind permission of the Lord Tollemache. Photograph by Mike Durrant

Plate III. Described in the 1708 inventory as 'four young ladies, hand-in-hand', the first four children of Sir Lionel Tollemache, 2nd baronet, painted c. 1621. From left to right: Elizabeth, b. 1615, Katherine, b. 1615, Anne, b. 1617, Susan, b. 1619 and, in the cradle, Susan, b. 1621. Details superimposed at the top left-hand corner of the painting are misleading because they refer not to the 2nd baronet but to his father (whose first surviving children were also daughters). The citation summarises events of significance in the 1st baronet's life, including his two appointments as sheriff of Suffolk, the first under Elizabeth I (1592) and the second under James I (1609); his elevation to a baronetcy by James I (1611); and the date of his death (1612). At Helmingham Hall. Reproduced by kind permission of the Lord Tollemache. Photograph by Mike Durrant

Tollemache Earl of Dysart born 1648.
Son of y Duchess of Lauderdale

Plate IV (opposite). Lionel Tollemache, 3rd Earl of Dysart. Attributed in the National Trust collections as 'An Unknown Gentleman, called Lionel Tollemache, 3rd Earl of Dysart (1649–1727)' by Sir Peter Lely c. 1660, although the young man looks to be more mature than this date suggests and shows him, perhaps, closer to 1669, when his father, the 2nd earl, died. The portrait is inscribed, top right, with the legend: 'Tollemache, Earl of Dysart, born 1648, Son of the Duchess of Lauderdale'. This refers to the widowed Countess of Dysart's remarriage, in 1672, to John Maitland, Duke of Lauderdale. Ham House, copyright The National Trust

Plate V (opposite). Lionel Tollemache, 4th Earl of Dysart. Attributed in the National Trust collections as 'Lionel Tollemache, 4th Earl of Dysart (1708–1770) by John Vanderbank the younger'. Formerly Lord Huntingtower, Lionel Tollemache inherited the title from his grandfather, the 3rd Earl of Dysart (see Plate IV), in 1727. In this painting of c. 1730 he wears the robes of peerage and his earl's coronet is visible on the console table beside him. His grandfather used the coronet as the basis for a topiary design which is visible in Thomas Brereton's 1720 sketch and discussed in Appendix A. The 4th earl was responsible for wide-ranging enhancements to Helmingham, discussed in Appendix A. Ham House, copyright The National Trust

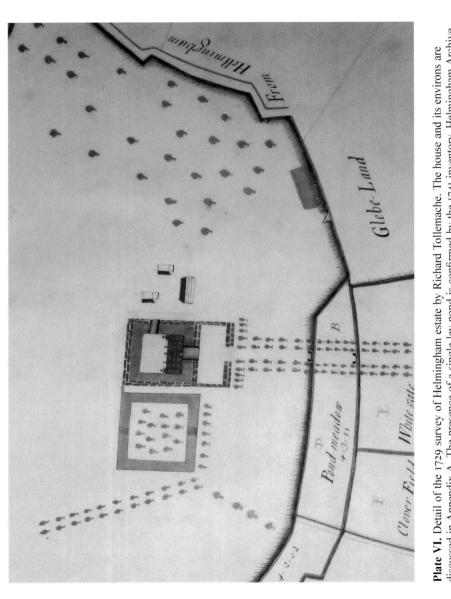

Plate VI. Detail of the 1729 survey of Helmingham estate by Richard Tollemache. The house and its environs are discussed in Appendix A. The presence of a single ley pond is confirmed by the 1741 inventory. Helmingham Archive, T/Hel(S)/27/4, reproduced by kind permission of the Lord Tollemache

08.453 2 under quilts

08.454 2 bed-matts

08.455 3 window curtains about 3 yards long: in all 7 bredths of yard wide red serge

08.456 5 curtain-rods

08.457 6 chaires the backs and seats of red cloth: with a blue silk lace roud and brass nails

08.458 2 square stooles matching the chaires

08.459 2 square stooles covered with red cloth and a small fringe and brass nails round

08.460 1 oak table of 2 heights about 4 feet and ½ long, and 25 inches wide

08.461 1 joynt stoole

08.462 1 locking cedar close-stool box with brass rings: a cedar boarded seat and a pewter pan in it

08.463 1 pair of andirons 2 foot and ½ high cased with brass

08.464 1 plaine pair of bellows

In the Chamber and clossets over the drawing roome

08.465 5 peeces of tapestry hangings about 9 foot deep viz't:
8 foot wide devided
13 foot
12 foot   wide
12 foot
10 feet and ½

08.466 1 turkey work carpet over the chimney about 2 yards ¾ long and one yard ¾ wide

08.467 1 turkey work carpet about 5 yards and ½ long and 2 yards ¾ wide under the bed

08.468 1 bedstead about 9 foot high: the 4 curtains: double vallance at top and lower vallance: the bedshead: and teaster all of red cloth, the outside vallance and curtains adorned with scarlett silk loops, and narrow scarlett footings, and the fringe to the top vallanc[e]d without and within 9 inches deep of scarlett silk: and the curtains lined with red silk

08.469 1 bedsted about 2 yards and ½ high: the head: tester: and vallance of yellow silk damask wrought with purple velvet and gimp: with a blue and yellow silk ffringe about 9 inches deep upon the vallance

08.470 4 curtains of blue and yellow serge paned in breadths about 9 inches wide

08.471 2 ffetherbeds

08.472 2 under quilts

08.473 2 bed-matts

08.474 3 bolsters

08.475 3 pillows

08.476 1 red silk quilt about 9 foot ½ one way and 11 foot and ½ the other

08.477 2 window curtains of yard wide white callico stript: about 8 foot long: in all 7 bredths

08.478 9 curtain rods

08.479 The coverlit of the bed and \covering of the/ walls in the inner room are of speckled green linsey woolsey

08.480 9 chaires the seats and backs covered with red cloth: and a small fringe and brass nails round
08.481 1 walnuttree table with a drawer
08.482 1 pair of eight square walnuttree stands
08.483 1 black harth brush
08.484 3 small pair of bellows
08.485 2 high square stooles with stuffed seats
08.486 1 chest 4 foot 8 inches long
08.487 4 gilded clawes for beds feet
08.488 1 picture of a head in and [sic] ovall frame carved and gilded
08.489 1 picture to the waste in a plain oak moulding frame
08.490 1 clothes brush: the top covered with yellow mohaire
08.491 1 pole to smooth a bed withall
08.492 1 pair of andirons with brass knops
08.493 1 brass fire shovell: 1 pair of brass tongs

[8] In the Dineing roome[35]

08.494 5 pieces of tapestry hangings about 10 foot deep: viz't:
16 foot and ½
14: and ½
12: and ½   wide
10 foote
8 foote
08.495 5 chaires the seats and backs of crimson velvett
08.496 6 square } stooles covered also with crimson velvett: the chaires and stooles with narrow fringe on the seams: and fringe about 9 inches deep round the lowest edges: the ffringe is of crimson silk
08.497 6 longish}
08.498 1 pair of tables with 24 men
08.499 1 fore-glass for a charriott
08.500 1 other pair of tables with 2 dice boxes and [?] men
08.501 1 iron plate lock with brass ornaments

In the Appartment my Lord Lodges in[36]

08.502 5 pieces of Scotch-plad hangings 2 yards and ½ deep: viz't:
13 foot and ½
5: and ½
5 foot
4 foot
2 foote
08.503 3 pieces of tapestry hangings: each about 12 foot ½ wide and 8 foot and

---

35 The height of the dining room is at least 10 ft and the combined width of its tapestry hangings amounts to over 60 ft but it appears to have no dining table and no fireplace, although the next room includes two pairs of bellows, one of which might belong here.
36 The earl's apartment, embellished with 'Scotch-plad', is over 9 ft 6 ins in height and appears to be a single room equipped for sleep, writing and conversation, with seating for up to twelve people on chairs and a couch. Three pieces of furniture are described as 'eight square' (octagonal), a shape fashionable at the time. The dimensions of the calico curtains (08.524–525), supported by five curtain rods, suggests four windows of equal width and one narrower window.

½ deep

08.504 1 bedstead about 9 foot 6 inches high

08.505 6 curtains and the outside vallance at top and bottom of Scotts-plad, and set round with a \narrow/ blue and white silk fringe as are the hangings. The curtains lined with yellow silk, and the upper out-side vallance are bordered with yellow silk and black fflowers scoloped: and a blue and white knotted silk fringe about 3 inches deep

08.506 4 pieces of black flowered yellow silk about a quarter of a yard wide and the length of the curtains sett round with a blue and white fringe at the two hind corners of the bed. The beds-head: teaster and inside vallance are yellow silk quilt with a yellow silk fringe 5 inches deep upon the vallans.

08.507 1 ffether bed

08.508 1 bolster

08.509 1 pillow

08.510 1 under quilt

08.511 3 blanketts

08.512 1 yellow silk quilt (upon the bed) about 3 yards square with a yellow silk ffringe about 2 inches deep on each side and at the feet

08.513 8 chaires the backs and seats covered with Scotch-plad and a small blue and white silk ffringe round

08.514 1 chair the seat and back covered with clouded silk: and a fringe about 2 inches deep round it

08.515 1 long couch covered with flowered crimson velvett

08.516 1 cross framed stoole covered with flowered crimson velvet

08.517 1 Turkey work cushion

08.518 1 oak table 3 foot long and 23 inches wide

08.519 1 eight square table about 2 foot 4 inches over

08.520 1 eight square stand about 14 inches over: and a lether cover to it

08.521 1 writing stand eight square about 2 foot over with the Tollemaches arms inlayed in the middle

08.522 1 case for a childs knife: ffork: and spoon

08.523 1 table lookinglass about 22 inches one way and 9 the other within the frame

08.524 1 window curtain about 3 yards long: of 3 bredths of yard and ⅛ wide white calico

08.525 1 other window curtain of the same calico 3 bredths about 2 yards and ½ long

08.526 5 curtain:rods

08.527 1 close stool box covered with Kidermister stuff with yellow bayes seat and a pewter pan

08.528 1 pair of dogs

08.529 1 pair of tongs

08.530 1 fireshovell

08.531 2 pair of bellows

08.532 3 iron plate locks with brass ornaments

In the Passages

08.533 1 double leafed table 7 foot 4 inches long and 3 foot wide

08.534 1 square table 3 foot 10 inches long and 2 foot and ½ wide

08.535 2 large chests
08.536 1 chest without a bottom
08.537 3 large trunks
08.538 1 childs chare with carved frame and cane seat and back
08.539 1 long curtain rod with the frame of a bed: and headboard vallans boards
        etc.

[9] In the Chambers the Young Lady's Lay in and clossetts etc

08.540 2 coarded bedsteds about 8 foot and ½ high with blue and white
        Kiddermister-stuff curtains : heads: teasters: and counterpanes: and
        instead of vallans a white and red tufted cotton fringe set on scolloped
08.541 1 coarded bedsted about 8 feet and ½ high with white dimoty curtains
        and head
08.542 1 coarded bedstead about 7 foot high: The teaster: head: and vallans of
        green silk with raised work of coats of arms etc: and a green silk
        fringe about 6 inches deep on the vallans
08.543 5 yellow sey curtains
08.544 4 curtain-rods
08.545 1 long curtain-rod quite cross the roome
08.546 6 ffether beds
08.547 4 fether bolsters
08.548 6 pillows
08.549 4 bed-matts
08.550 7 blanketts
08.551 1 yellow rug
08.552 1 Cypress chest 6 foot long
08.553 1 chest of drawers
08.554 1 small table cupboard
08.555 6 cane chairs
08.556 1 pair of dogs
08.557 1 table lookinglass: 11 inches and ½ and 9 inches and ½ within the
        frame
08.558 1 small brass sun-dyall
08.559 1 press cupboard
08.560 2 oak tables 3 foot 1 inch long and 2 foot 1 inch wide
08.561 1 arms chair of speckled stuff
08.562 2 backed stooles } The seats of crimson satten flowered with black
08.563 1 square stoole   }   velvett and gold coloured gimp
08.564 1 little oak table about 3 foot long and 15 inches broad
08.565 2 small draughts in oak frames about a foot the longest way
08.566 4 large Turkey, or Morocco cushions
08.567 2 childs clothes basketts about 22 inches long and 16 inches wide
08.568 1 vinegar rundlett
08.569 1 little bell
08.570 2 square stooles covered with red cloth and flowered with yellow gimp
        etc.
08.571 2 square stooles covered with clouded stuff
08.572 1 small trunk about a foot long
08.573 1 round topt trunk about 2 foot 7 inches long
08.574 1 press cupboard with 3 small cubords on the top of it

08.575 1 table 4 foot 3 inches long and 20 inches broad with 2 cubords in it
08.576 1 draught of part of the celestiall clobe [sic] in an oaken frame
08.577 1 chair covered with clouded linsey Woolsey
08.578 1 stoole about a foot broad and 6 foot long with a stuffed lether seat: with a gold colour silk fringe 2 inches deep round it
08.579 1 square stoole the seat covered with a hair colour damask and a mixt silk fringe 2 inches deep round it
08.580 1 lucit to weave narrow fringe in etc.
08.581 2 round topt trunk 3 foot 10 inches long with severall iron hoops
08.582 2 things to sett trunks or boxes upon

In the Candle:Chamber[37]

08.583 1 large trunk four foot long
08.584 1 trunk 22 inches long with iron hoops
08.585 1 childs cane chaire
08.586 5 lether bags (about the size of common cushions) full of ffethers
08.587 1 peece of a lead pipe about 2 foot long
08.588 1 childs going cart
08.589 1 brass warming-pan
08.590 5 fuddling-glasses
08.591 1 dice box for a pair of tables
08.592 1 iron plate-lock no key
08.593 1 deal box with 12 particions in it
08.594 2 winces for bed-screws
08.595 3 screws for bed-posts
08.596 4 deal boxes and other lumbar

[10] In the Chamber over the Kitchen[38]

08.597 2 bedsteads 6 foot 8 inches high with speckled green and yellow linsey-woolsea curtains tacked to the sides and feet
08.598 2 ffetherbeds
08.599 2 bolsters
08.600 1 large pillow
08.601 1 blankett
08.602 2 peices of hanging 3 yards long and 2 yards wide for coverlits
08.603 1 large chest 5 foot 9 inches long and 2 foot 3 inches wide
08.604 1 high oak table about 4 foot 7 inches long and 2 foot 4 inches wide
08.605 1 chest 4 foot and half long
08.606 3 square stooles with stuft seates
08.607 1 cane chaire
08.608 1 other chair and stoole without seats
08.609 1 Turkey work cushion
08.610 1 low bench about 5 foot long – or a step to set by a bed side
08.611 1 map of Suffolk in an oaken frame

---

[37] The name of this room is reminiscent of the soap house, a designation unique to 1597, where candles were made (see footnote 39 to 1597 inventory).
[38] There is no evidence of a fireplace, but the room would have enjoyed some warmth from the chimney flue rising from the kitchen.

In the Passages & Drying-Room, &c.

08.612 2 trestles with a table leafe upon them about 16 foot long & 3 foot & half broad

08.613 1 large trunk 4 foot & half long, ribbed with iron, having in it blue flocks

08.614 1 large wooden trunk with netts in it

08.615 1 table about 6 foot long and 2 foot broad

08.616 2 double leafed tables about 4 foot 7 inches long & 3 foot 10 inches broad each

08.617 1 table that the ends draw out about 3 foot broad & the full length 14 foot

08.618 1 livery table about 5 foot long & 20 inches broad, with other lumbar

In the Chamber over the Laundry[39]

08.619 1 pair of cobirons

08.620 1 lether chaire

08.621 1 little stoole with a stuft seat

08.622 1 pair of tongs

08.623 1 small pair of bellows

In the Chamber over the Dairy

08.624 1 bushell

08.625 1 seed-mande

08.626 1 brass-barrelled gun

08.627 1 long gun

08.628 4 pistells

In the Passage over the Pantries and chest there

08.629 Turkey-work carpetts:
1 about 8 foot long and 6 foot wide
1 about 6 foot long and 4 foot and half wide
1 about 16 foot long and 7 foot wide
1 about 8 foot 4 inches square
1 about 17 foot and half long and 8 foot wide

08.630 Tapestry hangings:
1 peice about 5 foot square
1 peice about 11 foot deep and 4 foot and half wide

08.631 6 backs and 6 seats of blue damask covers of chaires with yellow and black silk tufted fringe

08.632 2 peices of paned hangings of scarlett damask and sky coloured mohaire: 2 yards long and 1/8 deep, one peice about 7 yards and half wide, the other about 3 yards and half wide, both set round with a narrow scarlet and white silk fringe

08.633 2 window curtains of stript ¾ and 1/8 of a yard wide muslyn together 6 bredths, about 3 yards long

---

39 This chamber appears to have a fireplace, judging by the presence of cobirons, tongs and bellows. This would have shared the flue rising from the laundry below, where water was heated in the copper.

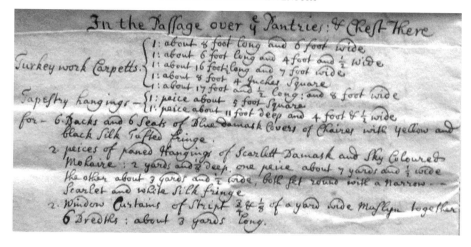

Plate 4. Detail from 1708 inventory, f. 10, illustrating a range of measurements, a feature unique to this document, with descriptions of textiles and their colours. Helmingham Archive, reproduced by kind permission of the Lord Tollemache

In the Roomes over the Brewhouse & Woodroom, &c.

08.634   2 frames of tables with some other lumbar

In the Mens Garrett and Wardrope over the Hall &c., the other Wardropes being locked up[40]

08.635   3 half-headed bedsteads
08.636   1 half of a foulding eight square table about 3 foot over
08.637   1 table 4 foot 9 inches long and 2 foot and half wide
08.638   1 table 7 foot and half long and 3 foot 9 inches wide
08.639   1 dresser about 8 foot long upon two tressles
08.640   2 large chests with musicall instruments in them
08.641   3 other chests
08.642   9 trunks
08.643   1 harpsicorde
08.644   5 troupers saddles
08.645   1 moulding for a mantletree 7 foot 9 inches long
08.646   4 peices of carved moulding for an ovall panell over a chimney
08.647   Severall peices of old hangings and other lumbar

[11] In the Cellers[41]

08.648   8 long ale-stooles
08.649   8 butts
08.650   17 hogsheads
08.651   2 high kellers

---

[40] The inference is that there is a room above the great hall, confirming that it was not open to the rafters in 1708.

[41] This discrete heading confirms that perambulation of the ground and first floors of the main house is complete.

08.652   34 tubbs
08.653   2 wooden tunnels
08.654   1 mallett
08.655   1 brass cock
08.656   3 tapps
08.657   1 pump with a lead cistern
08.658   1 prickle full of empty flasks
08.659   \16: doz. and/ 3 bottles of strong beer
08.660   \2: doz. and/ 4 bottles with hogshead beer
08.661   2 bottles with clarrett wyne
08.662   \17 doz. and/ 3 empty bottles
08.663   36 pinte bottles
08.664   6 pinte bottles with some sort of stilled waters

In the clock-house and rooms about it[42]

08.665   1 large pendulum clock with large lead weights and all other things
thereto belonging
08.666   1 lather of 16 staves

linen[43]

08.867   7 dimoty counterpanes
08.868   1 damask towel
08.869   \11 doz. and/ 8 diaper napkins
08.870   2 muslyn window curtains
08.871   10 table clothes   }
08.872   11 doz. and 8 napkins   }   Diaper
08.873   1 towell   }
08.874   4 table clothes   }   Huckoback
08.675   45 napkins   }
08.676   31 pair of sheets and one odd one
08.677   17 pillowbiers
08.678   12 towells
08.679   2 round towels
08.680   2 walletts
08.681   7 Hall table clothes
08.682   2 callico table clothes
08.683   1 trunk of linen locked up

---

42 This discrete heading suggests an area detached from the main house.
43 If this is an inventory of the entire household stock of linen, including items in use, it would not
allow for more than about ten beds to be in use regularly. However, more linen may be stored in
the locked trunk (08.683). There appears to be a sizeable stock of table linen. The lack of a table in
the description of the first floor dining chamber may indicate that the great hall is now the focus of
dining, supported by the mention of '7 hall table cloths' in this linen inventory.

08.684   **Nothing in the Mill house Except the Mill etc.**[44]

In the Stables and over them[45]

08.685   2 oat bings
08.686   1 iron shovel
08.687   4 pitch-forks
08.688   1 corn-skreen
08.689   2 halfe headed bedsteads
08.690   2 old fashioned tables
08.691   1 arm chaire
08.692   1 joynt stoole
08.693   1 half bushell measure and a peck together
08.694   1 scieve
08.695   1 hand-barrow

In the yards, Coach-house, etc.

08.696   1 waggon
08.697   2 carts
08.698   1 tumbrell
08.699   1 slead
08.700   5 ladders
08.701   1 charriot lined with grey cloth
08.702   2 pair of trace
08.703   1 dudfin
08.704   3 collers

---

[44] The 1597 and 1626 inventories confirmed that the mill was driven by a horse. A two-storey building would have been required to accommodate this and, given the sequence in this inventory of mill-house, stables, yards and coach-house, etc., the likelihood is that it stood on a site beyond the moat to the east, as indicated by 'd' on Plate 14 on page 160.

[45] Saddles and items of harness are conspicuous by their absence throughout this inventory but some may have been inaccessible because they were stored in the locked wardrobes.

THE 1741 HOUSEHOLD INVENTORY

Helmingham Hall Archive T/Hel(S)/9/1/1

Note that in the original document entries are presented as continuous text, the items being defined by initial capital letters and separated by commas. To preserve the referencing system adopted for this volume, entries are presented on separate lines in this transcription.

[1] An inventory of Helmingham Hall &c.

[2] An inventory of the goods & furniture &c. in and about Helmingham Hall, taken October 22nd 1741[1]

First Floor[2]

No. 1[3]

My Lord's Dressing Room[4]

41.1	A walnuttree bureau, with a scrutore and glass doors
41.2	1 Dutch boat in a glass frame
41.3	2 telescopes
41.4	2 square mahogany tables with drawers
41.5	A small dressing glass
41.6	1 spring clock by Graham[5]
41.7	1 pendulum clock by Gray[6]
41.8	2 mahogany stands
41.9	2 red velvet stools
41.10	2 blue stools
41.11	2 blue damask chairs
41.12	2 pair of blue watered stuff window curtains
41.13	1 portrait in a black frame and gilded border, 2 in miniature in gilded frames
41.14	1 large landscape over the chimney in black frame and gilded border, 2 others in gilded frames over the doors

---

[1] Given its extent, it is unlikely that this inventory was taken in a single day.
[2] Describes the ground floor.
[3] The numbering of each description may have been a way of measuring the task (and perhaps sharing it between staff); alternatively, the numbers may have been related to a schedule or a plan, but none has been found to confirm this.
[4] The room that is described next is called the library and closet, presenting a view of a ground-floor suite of rooms dedicated as much to the 4th earl's pursuit of his studious interests as to the business of dressing. This inventory is unique in designating a room (and items) dedicated to dressing.
[5] George Graham, 1673–1751 (*ODNB*). See glossary, **clock**.
[6] Benjamin Gray, 1676–1764 (*ODNB*). See glossary, **clock**.

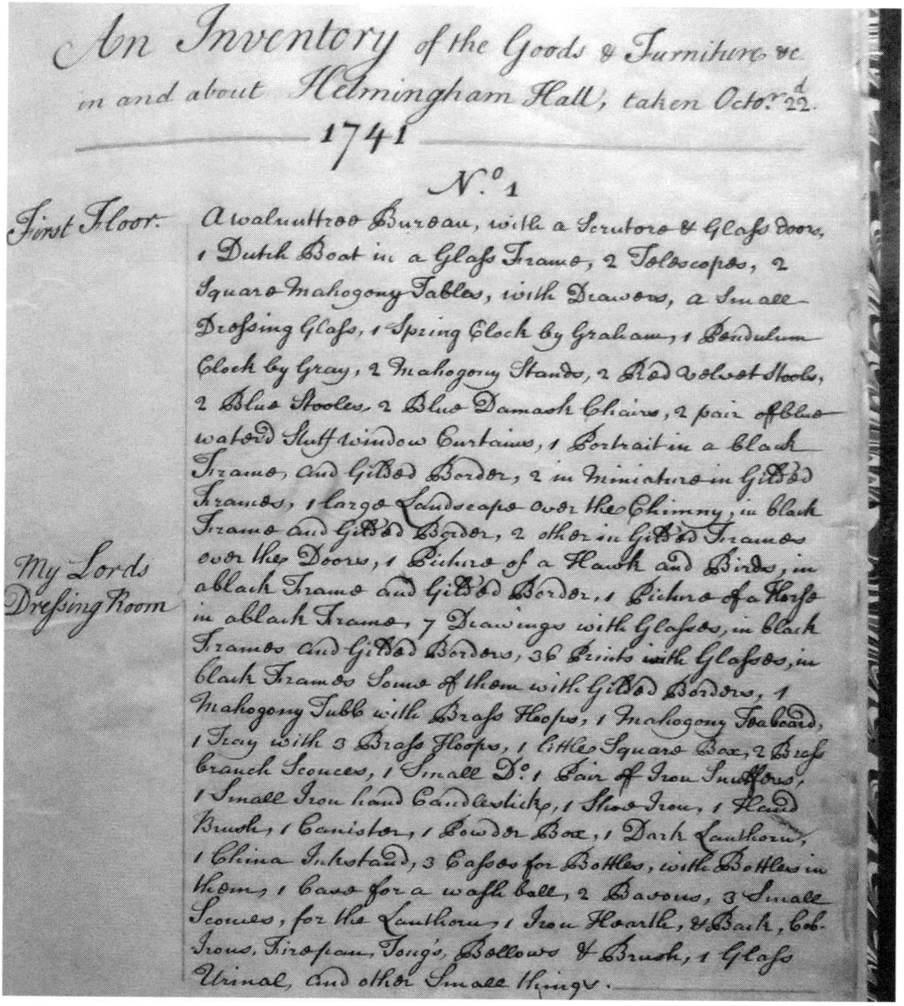

Plate 5. Detail from the 1741 inventory, f. 2, rich with detail of furniture, clocks and pictures in newly created rooms dedicated to the use of the 4th Earl of Dysart. An area reserved for the intimate routines related to dressing at Helmingham Hall is introduced for the first time in this inventory. Helmingham Archive, reproduced by kind permission of the Lord Tollemache

41.15	1 picture of a hawk and birds in a black frame and gilded border
41.16	1 picture of a horse in a black frame
41.17	7 drawings with glasses in black frames and gilded borders
41.18	36 prints with glasses in black frames, some of them with gilded borders
41.19	1 mahogany tub with brass hoops
41.20	1 mahogany teaboard
41.21	1 tray with 3 brass hoops
41.22	1 little square box
41.23	2 brass branch sconces, 1 small ditto

41.24	1 pair iron snuffers
41.25	1 small iron hand candlestick
41.26	1 shoe iron
41.27	1 hand brush
41.28	1 canister
41.29	1 powder box
41.30	1 dark lanthorn
41.31	1 china inkstand
41.32	3 cases for bottles, with bottles in them
41.33	1 case for a wash ball
41.34	2 basons
41.35	3 small sconces for the lanthorn
41.36	1 iron hearth and back
41.37	Cob-irons
41.38	Firepan
41.39	Tongs, bellows and brush
41.40	1 glass urinal and other small things

No. 2

In the Library and closet, exclusive of books[7]

41.41	1 mahogany writing desk covered with green cloth
41.42	2 red velvet stools
41.43	1 leather couch
41.44	2 globes with leather cases
41.45	1 mahogany reading desk
41.46	1 mahogany stand
41.47	1 old step ladder
41.48	1 mahogany close stool
41.49	1 Japan'd cistern
41.50	6 pistols
41.51	2 leather powder flasks and 1 pouch
41.52	6 couplings for hounds
41.53	1 gun-case
41.54	1 horn powder flask
41.55	1 iron hearth and back
41.56	Cobirons
41.57	Tongs
41.58	Firepan
41.59	Bellows & brush
41.60	6 brass-cased locks[8]

---

[7] This is the first household inventory to designate a room as a library at Helmingham Hall (this is not the library's first home: see Appendix A), but a personal collection of books was well-established at Helmingham by now. In his will the 4th earl's grandfather expressed his wish that his library and books should remain with the house to be enjoyed by whoever held the freehold of the property (TNA, PROB 11/613). As the 1741 description confirms, the books themselves were not considered household property. The bookcases were not mentioned because they were integral to the structure.

[8] As noted in earlier inventories, locks were considered portable. Locks are noted less frequently in this inventory and 'brass-cased' is a description unique to this document. The assumption here is that these are fitted to doors, or to the locks on either side of one door. Locks of any description are conspicuous by their absence from the 1708 inventory (and, indeed, in both Tollemache inventories

[3] No. 3

Gateway Room

41.61	1 large mahogany chest with a leather cover
41.62	1 chest cased with iron, and stand
41.63	1 round mahogany table
41.64	1 blue damask couch with bed and bolster
41.65	8 blue damask chairs
41.66	4 curtains and valence
41.67	2 landscape pieces in gilded frames
41.68	5 portraits, 3 of them in gilded and 2 in black frames
41.69	1 picture in a gilded frame over the chimney
41.70	1 iron hearth and back, with cobirons, firepan, tongs, bellows and brush
41.71	2 brass-cased locks

No. 4

Courtoy's Room

41.72	1 bed and bedstead, flowered stuff curtains and valence, with window curtains of the same
41.73	1 mattress
41.74	3 blankets
41.75	1 flowered quilt
41.76	1 bolster, 1 pillow
41.77	1 square table
41.78	1 writing desk
41.79	1 oval table
41.80	1 armed chair
41.81	Cobirons, firepan and tongs

No. 5

Tallemach's Room[9]

41.82	1 bed and bedstead, purple cloth curtains and valence, laced
41.83	1 mattress
41.84	3 blankets
41.85	1 bolster and pillow
41.86	1 old window curtain
41.87	3 chairs
41.88	1 old candle stand
41.89	Firepan, cobirons, tongs, bellows & brush

---

for Ham House, dated 1655 and 1728 (*Ham House*, pp. 434–6 and 465–8 respectively). However, the 1741 record is similar to the 1626 inventory in which locks are mentioned throughout and ascribed to doors and items of furniture. By 1741 the decorative value of locks was well established. In 'Under lock and key' (*Country Life*, 27 April 2016, p. 89) Matthew Dennison describes how 'the best examples of English lock smithing combine outstanding metalwork with technical ingenuity and decorative flair'.

9   Richard Tollemache, who acted as the 4th earl's steward, and was responsible for the 1729 survey of the Helmingham Estate, details of which are illustrated in Plates VI and 14 (page 160). This room would have been set aside for his occasional use when he needed to stay at the hall.

No. 6

In the long Drawing Room[10]

41.90	1 fine, large, inlaid table with a green cloth cover
41.91	2 large red tabby couches
41.92	10 chairs covered with red watered stuff
41.93	3 pair of red tabby window curtains and valence, lined with ditto
41.94	1 large carpet
41.95	1 printed firescreen
41.96	1 portrait in miniature of My Lord on copper, in a gilt frame
41.97	20 Italian prints with glasses in black frames
41.98	1 iron stove and back, firepan, poker, bellows and brush
41.99	3 brass-cased locks

No. 7

Little Stuc[c]o Room

41.100	1 mahogany card table with a green cloth cover
41.101	1 square Japan'd tea table and handboard
41.102	1 mahogany stand
41.103	8 blue and white china coffee cups
41.104	7 cups and saucers, tea and cream pot, with sugar dish and bason of the same
41.105	1 flowered callicoe cover to the table
41.106	1 pair of red watered stuff curtains
41.107	1 printed fire screen
41.108	6 black leather chairs
41.109	8 portraits, 17 ditto in miniature [f. 4] in black frames and gilded borders
41.110	8 prints of the cartoons, with glasses and black frames
41.111	6 prints of Hogarth's 'Harlot's Progress' with glasses, in black frames and gilded borders
41.112	1 iron hearth and back, with cobirons, tongs, firepan, bellows and brush
41.113	In the closet, 1 iron hearth and cobirons
41.114	3 brass-cased locks

No. 8

Passage and new staircase[11]

41.115	1 large mahogany oval table, 1 small ditto
41.116	2 red velvet armed chairs
41.117	1 glass lantern with a mahogany frame
41.118	1 portrait in a black frame and gilded border
41.119	2 large maps on rollers

---

10   This room resulted from the conversion of what had been two rooms.

11   In December 1744, Joshua Kirby, described as 'the Ipswich painter', was paid £10 3s. 0d. for accumulated accounts related to 'painting the three new rooms and staircase' (BPA volume 927). See footnotes 37 and 39 for identification of these new rooms. See Appendix A for location of this staircase and other 'new' features mentioned in the 1741 inventory. Long delays between the submission of accounts and their payment make it likely that Kirby's 1744 payment relates to this new staircase. See also footnote 35 below for later work at Helmingham Hall undertaken by Joshua Kirby (son of John Kirby, author of *The Suffolk Traveller*, 1735).

41.120 8 perspective views of cities and 18 other prints, all in black frames
41.121 1 brass-cased lock

No. 9
Old Drawing Room next the Parlour[12]
41.122 1 large leather screen gilt and painted
41.123 1 Indian fire-screen
41.124 2 pair of red watered stuff curtains & valence
41.125 12 chairs
41.126 2 portraits in black frames and gilded borders
41.127 1 iron hearth and back, with cobirons, firepan, bellows and brush
41.128 2 brass-cased locks
41.129 The room hang'd with red silk damask and white tabby

No. 10
Parlour[13]
41.130 1 fine inlaid table with a green cloth cover
41.131 1 square mahogany table
41.132 1 white marble table on a carv'd frame
41.133 1 white marble cistern
41.134 1 mahogany dumb waiter
41.135 12 black leather chairs
41.136 3 pair of red watered stuff window curtains & valence
41.137 1 leather screen, gilt and painted
41.138 1 Indian fire-screen
41.139 9 portraits in black frames and gilt borders
41.140 2 Italian prints with glasses and black frames
41.141 22 prints of Don Quixote, with glasses and black frames
41.142 Hogarth's 'Rake's Progress', 8 prints, with glasses, black frames and gilded borders
41.143 3 other prints by Hogarth, with glasses, black frames and gilded borders
41.144 1 plan of Suffolk Estate on rolls
41.145 1 iron hearth and back, with cobirons, firepan, tongs, bellows and brush
41.146 1 oyl cloth for the floor
41.147 2 brass cased locks

[5] No. 11
Great staircase, upper and lower landings with passage next the Parlour[14]
41.148 2 portraits
41.149 1 large mezzo tinto print of the Emperor of Germany
41.150 2 of the Virgin Mary
41.151 7 maps, &c. on rolls
41.152 9 prospects of the city and great church of Milan, in black frames
41.153 2 small portrait prints, 1 of them in a gilt, the other in a black frame

---

12 Note the use of 'old', which continues to suggest rooms on the west side of the house.
13 Heated and equipped for dining for up to twelve people. There is no longer a dining chamber on the first floor, nor is any room designated as a dining room in this inventory.
14 In 1708 the great hall and staircase were described together; ostensibly, this is the same staircase, its location discussed in Appendix A.

41.154   1 large map with the heads of the Kings of England, on rolls

41.155   2 views and 1 plan of Greenwich Hospitall

41.156   27 maps, plans and perspective views of various places, all in black frames

41.157   1 glass lantern with a mahogany frame

41.158   1 square mahogany table

41.159   2 oaken oval tables

No. 12

First room next the Parlour

41.160   1 couch, 6 chairs, hangings, window curtains & valence, all red damask

41.161   1 Japan'd and gilt tea table, on which are 6 cups and sawcers, 3 coffee cups, 1 tea and cream pot, 1 bason, 3 large sawcers, all enammeld china, overall a flowered callicoe cover

41.162   1 oval portrait with a gilt frame

41.163   4 portraits, 2 of them in miniature with black frames and gilt borders

41.164   1 iron hearth and back, with cobirons, firepan, tongs and bellows

41.165   2 brass-cased locks

No. 13

Second room next the Parlour

41.166   1 red coach-head-bed, curtains, valence, head and top, counterpain, hangings, window curtains and valence, 2 arm'd chairs, 6 other chairs, all red damask, the bed curtains lined with red silk

41.167   2 mattresses

41.168   3 blankets

41.169   1 white Holland quilt

41.170   1 bolster

41.171   2 pillows

41.172   1 large walnuttree cabinet, 1 small ditto

41.173   1 square mahogany table with a drawer, and a large dressing-glass

41.174   1 portrait of My Lord in a gilt frame and glass before it

41.175   2 portraits in miniature, black frames and gilded borders

41.176   1 iron hearth and back, cobirons, firepan, tongs, bellows & brush

41.177   In the closet, a back-gammon table, with a rattling boxe and 3 dies

41.178   1 brass-cas'd lock

No. 14

Great Hall

41.179   1 long oaken table[15]

41.180   6 Windsor chairs

41.181   1 large glass lantern

41.182   1 large kitchin piece painted[16]

---

[15] A long table but only six Windsor chairs: presumably seating had to be carried from elsewhere if large numbers of diners were to be seated or, perhaps, new furniture was awaited; by now, dining for up to twelve people is catered for in the parlour (see footnote 13, above). In 1708, the great hall also lacked seating, perhaps an indication of its emerging role as an entrance space rather than a dining space.

[16] This may be the painting of the cookshop mentioned in the 1708 inventory (08.118).

41.183 2 large portraits at full length, 2 other of a smaller size, 2 other historical pieces, 1 portrait on horseback, all in black frames with gilded borders
41.184 1 large pastoral piece and 2 portraits in gilded frames
41.185 2 large cobirons
41.186 4 small bells
41.187 1 brass-cased lock
41.188 48 leather buckets[17]

[6] No. 15

Butlers Pantrey [sic]
41.189 1 deal dresser
41.190 4 shelves
41.191 3 drawers with locks, in one of which are 2 silver salts, 1 silver punch ladle
41.192 1 deal press in which is 1 large mahogany tray
41.193 1 small waiter, with vinagar cruit & pepper caster
41.194 3 wine glasses
41.195 6 brass sconces
41.196 1 double iron plate rack
41.197 1 knife basket, with 11 ivory hafted knives and forks
41.198 1 square red cloth stool
41.199 1 iron lock[18]

No. 16

New Room next the Pantery [sic][19]
41.200 1 new deal dresser with 3 drawers
41.201 1 new press, in which is 1 large china dish, 4 of a smaller size, 3 china plates, with glass belonging to the desert, which I cannot particularize,[20] 1 earthen jarr with sweetmeats
41.202 1 Japan'd lock[21]

No. 17

Kitchen
41.203 4 copper & 3 brass stew pans
41.204 3 copper & 2 brass sauce pans
41.205 5 copper stew pots with covers & bailes
41.206 1 copper fish kettle and cover, &c.
41.207 1 copper baking pan, 4 ditto, 2 of them without bottoms
41.208 1 large copper cistern
41.209 2 copper flaggons, a large one & a small one
41.210 2 copper coffee and 1 chocolate pot, and mill

---

[17] Fire buckets.
[18] Not brass-cased, as in the residential rooms, but iron. See also footnote 21.
[19] See Appendix A for discussion of 'new' rooms and spaces mentioned in the 1741 inventory. See also footnotes 37 and 39 below, regarding the decoration of 'three new rooms' by Joshua Kirby, of which this is one.
[20] Presumably because the item (perhaps a set) to which this belongs cannot be located.
[21] The door to this new, utilitarian space is equipped with a 'Japan'd' lock, a finish achieved by lacquering or coating with shellac, as distinct from the unadorned 'iron' lock at 41.199.

41.211	4 copper tea kettles and lamp
41.212	1 copper knife tray
41.213	1 copper skillet
41.214	1 large brass strainer
41.215	3 iron chopping knives
41.216	1 large brass pan and skimmer
41.217	1 large tin sconce
41.218	3 larke spits and 3 iron skewers
41.219	3 brass basting ladles
41.220	1 pair of iron tongs
41.221	1 pair of flesh forkes
41.222	1 copper warming pan
41.223	1 large grater
41.224	1 copper kitchen and furniture[22]
41.225	2 brass slices
41.226	7 hand & 5 stand brass candlesticks, 4 iron ones
41.227	2 large cobirons, 2 small ditto
41.228	1 lamp to a tea kettle
41.229	1 brass sawce boat
41.230	25 pattypans
41.231	1 copper plate basket
41.232	1 horn, 1 wooden salt cellar
41.233	3 round, 2 long pewter salts
41.234	26 great and small pewter dishes
41.235	10 soop-plates [soup plates]
41.236	31 best plates, 31 ordinary ditto
41.237	2 pewter rings to set dishes on[23]
41.238	Old pewter not fit for use, being 6 plates & 4 dishes
41.239	1 copper, 1 brass boyler
41.240	1 iron pot
41.241	1 copper as it hang
41.242	5 large iron spits
41.243	2 grid irons
41.244	1 dripping pan, 1 iron stand for ditto
41.245	3 iron stands for the stoves
41.246	1 brass pestle and mortar
41.247	1 marble mortar and wooden pestles
41.248	1 iron oven lid
41.249	3 haiks
41.250	2 iron dogs
41.251	1 iron trivet
41.252	**[f. 7]** An [sic] fender
41.253	1 iron grate with 7 bars and 2 cheeks
41.254	1 smoak [sic] jack and chain for the spit
41.255	Tongs, firepan, poker and salamander

---

22 See potential definitions of **kitchen** in the glossary.

23 Earlier versions included some made of wicker: for definition, and the importance of their first mention at Helmingham Hall in 1597, see glossary, **table rings**.

41.256   1 pair of cobirons
41.257   1 wooden reflector
41.258   1 plate rack
41.259   1 hand-bell for dinner
41.260   1 large dresser and forme

No. 18

Servants Hall[24]
41.261   1 long table on trusses
41.262   1 old square table with a drawer
41.263   1 coffee mill
41.264   1 hatchment
41.265   1 pail with iron hoops
41.266   1 pewter cullender
41.267   1 iron lock

No. 19

Flower room & Bake-House[25]
41.268   1 tin spice box
41.269   1 flower [flour] tub
41.270   1 hanging shelf
41.271   2 sieves
41.272   1 old cubbard
41.273   1 flower [flour] hutch
41.274   1 dough kellar [keeler]
41.275   1 square table
41.276   1 iron oven lid, with a peal & rake
41.277   2 bread raspers

No. 20

Brew House[26]
41.278   1 large copper as it hang, with an iron door to the furnace, 1 copper cock
        to the copper
41.279   2 pumps, 1 from the moat, the other from the under deck[27]
41.280   1 large tub and under deck
41.281   2 large brewing tubbs[28]
41.282   3 large coolers
41.283   3 troughs
41.284   1 hop sieve
41.285   2 iron prongs
41.286   2 step ladders and some other small things

---

[24] The designation suggests a communal room but there appears to be no seating. The term 'servants' (rather than the earlier 'husbandmen') was used first in the 1708 inventory.

[25] Flour room, described in earlier inventories as the bolting house, where sieving and grading of flour took place and, as here, the preliminary mixing of dough.

[26] Appendix A discusses the evidence suggesting that the brewhouse has been moved to a new site since 1708.

[27] Described in earlier inventories as 'underbeck', defined in the glossary under **brewing.**

[28] See Appendix A for evidence of purchases of new brewing equipment.

No. 21

Back-House and next the Dairy
41.287 2 coppers as they hang
41.288 1 leaden pump
41.289 2 wash kellars
41.290 1 stand kellar
41.291 1 trough
41.292 1 butter kellar
41.293 1 churn with 2 winches
41.294 1 cheese tub
41.295 5 milking pails with iron hoops
41.296 4 cheese fats & 2 cheese breeds
41.297 1 cheese press[29]
41.298 1 leaden salting tray

No. 22

Dairy
41.299 2 milk trays
41.300 12 kellars
41.301 2 earthen pots
41.302 2 cream cups
41.303 1 milk sieve
41.304 1 pair of cheese tongs

No. 23

Steward's Room[30]
41.305 1 large wainscot press
41.306 1 old oaken cubboard, 1 small ditto
41.307 1 large square table
41.308 4 joynt stooles
41.309 4 chairs
41.310 1 box iron
41.311 1 old keep
41.312 1 pepper box
41.313 1 dredging box
41.314 1 mustard pot
41.315 1 salt box
41.316 29 black hafted knives and 50 forks
41.317 1 sugar greater [grater]
41.318 2 haiks
41.319 1 gridiron
41.320 1 firegrate in which are 6 barrs in an iron frame, 2 iron cheeks to ditto, 1 fender, 1 firepan, a pair of tongs, and a poker
41.321 2 pails with iron hoops

---

[29] The press and other items attest to the making of cheese but there is no mention of the cheese chamber, where the cheeses were left to ripen, described in the three earlier inventories.
[30] In this case the household steward (referred to as the 'housekeeper' in the 1708 inventory).

[8] No. 24

Dry Larder

41.322	2 candle hutches
41.323	1 deal box
41.324	7 punch bowls
41.325	10 glasse salts
41.326	4 wine glasses
41.327	4 stone jars
41.328	5 glass jars

No. 25

Wet Larder

41.329	1 salting tray
41.330	1 chopping block
41.331	1 chopping knife
41.332	1 ax[e]
41.333	1 powdering tubb
41.334	9 earthen jars
41.335	2 hanging shelves with iron hooks
41.336	2 iron beams and wooden scales, 7 leaden weights, 3 of them of 56 pound each, 1 of 28 pound, 1 of 14 pound, 1 of 7 pound, 1 of 3 pound, 1 half pound and 1 2-pound brass weight

No. 26

Small beer and ale cellar[31]

41.337	1 leaden pump
41.338	1 filtring stone
41.339	1 cowl & stafe
41.340	4 ale stools
41.341	2 pipes with iron hoops
41.342	1 hogshead stand
41.343	7 hogsheads
41.344	2 large tubbs, 1 small ditto
41.345	3 beer kellars
41.346	6 pipes
41.347	3 hogsheads, 1 half ditto
41.348	1 cowl
41.349	1 tunnell
41.350	3 ale stools
41.354	1 tilter
41.352	3 wine bings lock'd up

No. 27

Old beer & wine cellar[32]

41.353	3 pipes, 2 hogsheads and 3 ale stools

---

[31] Small beer (weak beer) and ale, unlikely to have been kept for long periods. This space also stores wine. See 41.352 and glossary, **bin**.

[32] Note the use of 'old': there is no mention of a new cellar, although one was specified in 1626 when three cellars were defined.

Second Floor[33]

No. 28

Lady's dressing room

41.354	1 square table with a drawer, 1 dressing glass on ditto
41.355	6 chairs lined with green damask
41.356	2 pair of green damask window curtains
41.357	2 mahogany tables, 1 square, the other round
41.358	1 fire screen
41.359	1 iron hearth and back, with cobirons, firepan, tongs, bellows and brush
41.360	1 carpet
41.361	1 close stool
41.362	1 small print with a glass and gilded frame
41.363	4 prints with glasses, black frames and gilded borders
41.364	8 Dutch & 8 French prints in black frames

No. 29

Lord & Lady's Bed-Chamber

41.365	1 green damask coach head bed
41.366	Counterpain, valence, curtains to bed and windows, hangings, 6 chairs, 1 great easey ditto, all green damask, the bed curtains lined with green silk
41.367	2 mattresses
41.368	4 blankets
41.369	1 white holland quilt
41.370	2 small pillows
41.371	1 mahogany night table
41.372	1 square mahogany table with a drawer
41.373	1 walnuttreee cabinet
41.374	1 portrait in a black frame and gilded borders
41.375	1 iron hearth and back, with cobirons, firepan, tongs, bellows & brush
41.376	1 brass cased lock

[9] No. 30

Back stairs and Gallery[34]

41.377	8 Dutch landscapes
41.378	2 perspective views of citys
41.379	7 prints, framed & with glasses and black frames
41.380	1 brass cased lock

No. 31

Long Gallery[35]

---

33 First floor.
34 See footnote 35 regarding the 'gallery'.
35 This is a corridor serving at least five bedrooms. In 1597 the same space can be identified, then described as gallery, and in 1626 as brushing gallery. By 1708 only first-floor passages are mentioned and there is no mention of any 'gallery'. The attribution of 'long gallery', like 'great hall', suggests an appetite for antiquarianism. The designation seems to have persisted for at least another sixteen years, confirmed by an account paid on 19 February 1757 'to Kirby House Painter and Company

41.381 32 perspective views of cities, 5 plans of Ham House, 1 Dutch plan of Zurich, all in black frames

41.382 2 mahogany glass lanterns

41.383 1 long matt

No. 32

1st room in Gallery

41.384 1 small field bed with green curtains and quilts

41.385 3 blankets

41.386 1 bolster

41.387 Green damask hangings and window curtains

41.388 2 small square stools, lined with green damask

41.389 2 black leather chairs

41.390 1 small oaken table

41.391 1 portrait in a black frame

41.392 1 iron hearth and back, with cobiron, firepan, tongs & brush

41.393 1 brass cased lock

No. 33

2nd room in Gallery

41.394 1 green damask tent bed

41.395 Curtains to bed & windows with counterpain, valence, &c. of the same

41.396 1 mattress

41.397 3 blankets

41.398 1 white holland quilt

41.399 1 bolster and small pillow

41.400 1 small field bed with white dimity curtains

41.401 3 blankets and red coverlet

41.402 1 bolster & 1 pillow

41.403 1 square table with a drawer and dressing glass

41.404 1 bureau

41.405 5 black leather chairs

41.406 1 red velvet stool

---

the sum of Thirteen Pounds in full of their Bill and all demands for fetching out & painting the Tollemache Pedigree, shield & Arms with Helmets, mantlings, Crest & other decorations which are over the Chimnies in two of the Rooms in the long Gallery at Helmingham.' (I am indebted to my editor, Victor Gray, for bringing this to my attention.) Kirby and Company was the Ipswich partnership between Joshua Kirby and Andrew Baldry, herald painter. Of the five numbered rooms off the gallery described in the 1741 inventory, all have fireplaces so it is impossible to know which two were 'fetched out & [newly?] painted' by Joshua Kirby sixteen years later. But the discovery goes some way to answering the questions raised by Arthur Oswald, expressed in his *Country Life* article of 4 October 1956, p. 714: 'These paintings raise a problem of dating, for while the heraldry appears to have been done in the 19th century, the design of the tree (it is a pear tree, to judge by the fruit) looks much earlier, and the 18th-century cornice stops short on either side of the painting as though intentionally to avoid interference with it. The latest marriage commemorated on the impaled shields is that of the fourth Lionel Tollemache, first baronet (died 1612), and Katherine Cromwell, but the large shield in the middle is heraldically meaningless ... The explanation may be that the trees were painted in the early part of the 17th century and had become rather dilapidated by 1800, and that either then or in 1841 the heraldry was re-painted, partly from guess-work.' Prior to his 'fetching-out' of the 'pedigree', Kirby had been employed thirteen years earlier at the Hall in his capacity as house-painter: see footnote 11 above.

41.407 1 portrait of My Lord in miniature done on copper in a gilt frame
41.408 14 Italian prints with glasses in black frames
41.409 1 iron hearth and back, with cobirons, firepan, tongs, bellows and brush
41.410 1 close stool
41.411 1 brass cased lock

No. 34

3rd room in Gallery
41.412 1 yellow camblet tent bed, with window curtains, bed curtains, valence,
        counterpain and hangings of the room all yellow camblet
41.413 1 mattress
41.414 3 blankets
41.415 1 flowered quilt
41.416 1 bolster
41.417 1 little pillow
41.418 1 square mahogany table with a drawer
41.419 1 small square table
41.420 5 black leather chairs
41.421 2 portraits, 1 of them in miniature, both in black frames
41.422 1 iron hearth and back, with cobirons, firepan, tongs and bellows
41.423 1 brass cased lock

[10] No. 35

4th room in Gallery
41.424 1 bed with green water'd stuff curtains, valence &c. with window
        curtains of the same
41.425 1 mattress
41.426 3 blankets, a bolster and pillow
41.427 1 flowered counterpain
41.428 2 trunks and 1 chest in which are the following linnen:-
41.429   6 pair of holland sheets
41.430   5 pair of flaxen
41.431   2 pair of Irish cloth
41.432   7 large damask cloths, 7 small ditto
41.433   4 dozen of damask napkins
41.434   14 fine diaper cloths
41.435   10 dozen of diaper napkins
41.436   18 long napkins
41.437   1 long cloth
41.438   27 co[a]rse napkins
41.439   12 little table cloths
41.440   4 new holland pillowbeers, 3 old ones
41.441   3 dimity covers for beds, 4 dimity curtains for ditto
41.442   4 pillowbeers marked D, 3 very old ones
41.443   6 green and white pieces for curtains for beds
41.444 In the great chest:-
41.445   12 hock-a-back table cloth for the Stewards Room
41.446   5 breakfast cloths for ditto
41.447   8 table cloths & 8 towels for the Servants Hall
41.448   14 pair of ordinary sheets for servants

41.449   6 pair of a better sort for ditto
41.450   2 square tables, 1 of them with a drawer
41.451   1 green stoole
41.452   3 red chairs
41.453   1 still and iron chafing dish
41.454   The room and closet hang'd with tapestry
41.455   1 old screen
41.456   Cobirons, fender, tongs, firepan, bellows and brush
41.457   A parcell of jelly glasses in the closet
41.458   1 old brass lock
41.459   \14 diaper towels forgot in the linnen/[36]

No. 36

5th room in Gallery
41.460   1 great leather trunk
41.461   2 old octagon stand tables
41.462   1 old keep
41.463   1 small red leather trunk
41.464   2 red velvet chairs
41.465   1 deal box, in which is Lord Huntingtower's bridle, sad[d]le and furniture
41.466   2 red pistol cases
41.467   Yellow damask window curtains and hangings
41.468   2 cobirons, 1 firepan
41.469   A long high square table, on which are 40 small prints with glasses and
            black frame
41.470   1 old looking glass
41.471   Kirby's Survey of Suffolk in a black frame, with some small trifling
            things in the closet, as canisters, &c.
41.472   1 Japan'd lock

No. 37

New Bill[i]ard room[37]
41.473   1 black velvet couch with 2 cushions finely wrought, all on a carv'd
            frame
41.474   1 large mahogany reading stand
41.475   1 square mahogany table with drawers
41.476   [f. 11] 1 spinnet
41.477   2 black leather arm'd chairs
41.478   3 large portraits, 1 small ditto, 1 fruit piece, all in black frames and
            gilded borders
41.479   1 iron hearth and back, with firepan and tongs
41.480   2 brass cased locks

No. 38

Little room hang'd with red paper

---

[36] A rare example of an error, recognised and corrected by the compiler of this inventory.
[37] Noticeably lacking a billiard table, although one remains in the old billiard room (41.512). See
      glossary, **billiards**, for detailed definition of the game in the eighteenth century and Appendix A for
      discussion of new rooms and their locations.

41.481 Exclusive of books and what is in the closet, which is lock up [sic]
41.482 6 guns
41.483 1 print intitled the Scotch peers protest, &c. with their coat of arms[38]
41.484 1 brass firepan
41.485 2 brass cased locks

No. 39

Clock Room
41.486 1 deal dresser with 6 drawers
41.487 83 wine and beer glasses
41.488 6 rummers and 19 water glasses
41.489 12 glass sawcers
41.490 2 large flowered glass muggs, 6 small ditto, 11 plain ditto
41.491 2 large decanters, 4 quart ditto, 2 pint ditto
41.492 127 china plates
41.493 15 large and small china dishes
41.494 1 large china punch bowl
41.495 1 old square red stool
41.496 2 genealogical rolls in cases
41.497 1 map of England on rolls
41.498 In the closet 1 eight-day turret clock, with a bell & stone dial plate
41.499 2 iron locks

No. 40

Red Room
41.500 1 bed
41.501 1 mattress
41.502 3 blankets
41.503 1 flower'd quilt
41.504 1 bolster and small pillow
41.505 Red cloth curtains and valence, lin'd with red silk
41.506 5 red cloth chairs
41.507 2 window curtains of red stuff
41.508 1 large, long square chest, in which are 6 green water'd stuff window curtains, 1 old green cushion, 3 guns, 1 halbert, 2 fishing rods, 1 small stand
41.509 The room lined with tapestry
41.510 2 iron cas'd locks
41.511 Note the closet out of the Red Room is not particularized

No. 41

Old Bill[i]ard Room
41.512 1 bill[i]ard table lin'd with green cloth (sticks &c in the closet adjoyning to the Red Room)
41.513 1 couch

---

[38] This print may relate to events spearheaded and later recorded by John Dalrymple, 2nd Earl of Stair (1673–1747), who co-ordinated a campaign to elect opposition peers at the general election of 1734 (*ODNB*).

41.514 9 chairs, 1 arm'd ditto, all red silk damask
41.515 3 red velvet chairs
41.516 4 mahogany stands for candles, 2 Japan'd ditto
41.517 The room hang'd with tapestry
41.518 1 iron hearth and back
41.519 Cobirons, firepan, tongs & bellows
41.520 1 large long chest
41.521 1 brass cased lock

No. 42

Chamber next [the] staircase
41.522 6 arm'd chairs, cover'd with blue silk damask
41.523 2 blue water'd stuff curtains and valence to window
41.524 The chamber hang'd with tapestry
41.525 1 brass cased lock

[12] No. 43

Further chamber
41.526 1 bed, with curtains, valence & counterpain, blue camblet
41.527 1 mattress
41.528 3 blankets
41.529 1 flower'd quilt
41.530 1 bolster & little pillow
41.531 1 square mahogany table with a drawer
41.532 1 walnuttree chest of drawers with a leafe to let down like a table
41.533 1 pair of blue camblet window curtains and valence
41.534 6 walnuttree chairs
41.535 1 portrait in a black frame and gilded borders
41.536 4 hunting prints in black frames
41.537 1 screen covered with maps
41.538 1 iron hearth and back with cobirons, firepan, tongs, bellows and brushes
41.539 2 brass cased locks
41.540 The room hang'd with tapestry
41.541 In the closet adjoyning, a round close stool

No. 44

New square room next the Nursery[39]
41.542 1 portrait in an oval frame, gilt
41.543 2 Japan'd locks, and in the passage leading to 4 ditto [sic]

No. 45

Nursery
41.544 1 bed with plad curtains and valence, lin'd with yellow silk, at the head
and top of the bed and valence within side, yellow silk quilted
41.545 1 mattress
41.546 3 blankets

---

[39] See Appendix A for discussion of rooms described as new in the 1741 inventory; see also footnote
11 above.

41.547   1 flower'd quilt
41.548   A bolster and pillow
41.549   1 chest of drawers
41.550   2 square tables, one of which with a drawer
41.551   1 red velvet stool, 2 red cloth ditto
41.552   1 little square stool
41.553   3 children's chairs
41.554   1 pair of white window curtains and valence
41.555   1 large print concerning Charles the 1st in a black frame
41.556   1 iron fender, cobirons, firepan, tongs, bellows & brush

No. 46

Left hand of nursery
41.557   2 beds on 1 bedstead, with old silk valence
41.558   3 blankets
41.559   1 bolster and pillow
41.560   1 old bedstead
41.561   1 hutch
41.562   A little close stool and cribb

No. 47

Right hand of nursery
41.563   1 bed and bedstead with green stuff curtains
41.564   3 blankets
41.565   1 green coverlet
41.566   1 bolster
41.567   Green stuff window curtains, arm'd chair and cushion
41.568   1 red cloth chair, 1 wicker ditto

No. 48

Chamber over the Stewards Room
41.569   1 bed and bedstead with red cloth curtains, lac'd and fringed
41.570   3 blankets
41.571   A flower'd quilt
41.572   1 bolster
41.573   2 window curtains of green cloth
41.574   5 red cloth chairs, 2 blue cloth ditto
41.575   1 old chest
41.576   In the chimney 1 iron back

No. 49

Chamber over Back-house[40]
41.577   2 beds and bedsteads, with green water'd stuff curtains
41.578   6 blankets
41.579   1 striped coverlet
41.580   2 bolsters
41.581   1 old leather stool

---

[40] Confirmation that some outbuildings were two storeys.

[13] No. 50

Gardners[41] Chamber

41.582	1 bed and bedstead with old red stuff curtains
41.583	3 blankets
41.584	1 old coverlet
41.585	1 bolster
41.586	1 square table
41.587	1 chair
41.588	1 large chest of drawers

No. 51

Laundry[42]

41.589	1 large deal dresser with 12 drawers
41.590	2 linnen horses
41.591	1 long table
41.592	5 old chairs
41.593	1 iron grate with 5 barrs and iron cheeks, 1 iron fender, shovel, tongs and poker
41.594	1 copper sawcepan for starch
41.595	4 smoothing irons
41.596	1 ironing cloth

No. 52

Footman's Room next the Court Yard

41.597	1 bed and bedstead, with blue water'd stuff curtains and valence
41.598	2 blankets
41.599	1 carpet coverlet
41.600	1 bolster
41.601	2 chairs
41.602	In the closet adjoyning, 1 deal cubboard

No. 53

Next the moat

41.603	1 bed and bedstead, with blue water'd stuff curtains and valence
41.604	2 blankets
41.605	1 carpet coverlet & a bolster
41.606	1 old stool and table with a drawer
41.607	1 wig block

No. 54

Stable chamber

41.608	3 beds and bedsteads
41.609	3 blankets
41.610	1 bolster

---

41 This may be a surname, but more likely refers to a chamber for the gardener.
42 Equivalent to the old drying chamber. There is no provision here for wet laundry, which, by this date, was being undertaken away from the hall. See discussion in Appendix A.

41.611   1 coverlet to each bed
41.612   4 old chairs

No. 55
Armo[u]ry
   41.613   30 posts with iron armory on them, and coats of mail
   41.614   1 old square chest, with armory and other things belonging

No. 56

Chamber next the Armo[u]ry
   41.615   3 large chests, 1 old ditto
   41.616   1 large next of drawers
   41.617   1 small case lin'd with green cloth
   41.618   12 Roman emperors in frames
   41.619   2 old embossed brass sconces, and some other small things

No. 57

Coach House, &c.
   41.620   Belonging to the Coach House (but now in the Great Hall) a chaise for
         one horse with harness
   41.621   In the saddle house 1 old side saddle and bridle
   41.622   Belonging to the Moat and Lay Pond,[43] 2 boats and oars &c., which are
         now in the Coach House.

Finis

---

[43] This supports a date post–1741 for creation of the second 'lay pond', which is visible in the frontispiece illustration and described in its caption.

APPENDIX A

THE DEVELOPMENT OF HELMINGHAM HALL, 1597–1741

Plates 6–9 show each elevation of Helmingham Hall as seen today from its gardens. Plate 10, adapted from a 1950s ground-floor plan drawn by J.C. Dennish, reveals the building to be complex and multi-layered, particularly on the north side of the courtyard.[1] Plate 11, a view of the present courtyard, reveals differences in building materials, window insertions, modification of wall heights and roof levels, all resulting from significant changes made in the eighteenth and nineteenth centuries.[2] Extensive modifications involved demolition and restructuring of courtyard-facing walls and the application of brick facings to large areas of the building.[3] Internally, the hall is an architectural feast, celebrating centuries of change: there are glimpses of late medieval, heavily moulded timbers; whilst vagaries in floor levels and mixtures of flooring materials within and between rooms testify to changes in scale and in use from utilitarian to residential spaces or vice versa.[4] Brass-cased door locks, marble chimney pieces and intricate plasterwork display evidence of sophisticated taste in the eighteenth century, whilst curious wall paintings on the first floor speak of work begun as early as the sixteenth century. All of this is well published.[5] What the inventories offer is an opportunity to identify the changes that took place between 1597 and 1741, and how the use of Helmingham Hall evolved in parallel with the significant elevation in status enjoyed by the Tollemache family over the same period.

Three of the four inventories describe spaces as 'new' and 'old' and these references provide a reliable signpost to change, which is modest in 1597 at a time before

---

[1] T/Hel(S)/28/1, 2. At the time of writing (2016), the www.helmingham.com website displays images and a short video sequence, both incorporating aerial views.

[2] Similar evidence of change is visible within the courtyard on all four elevations.

[3] As distinct from the 'mathematical tiles' hung on laths applied to the first floor of the south front, visible in Plate 6. Much of what appears to be solid brick on the elevation visible in Plate 11 is an applied facing of thin slips of brick, a method confirmed by a survey of the building undertaken in 1956 by Cautley & Barefoot, architects, Ipswich. T/Hel/9/5/41/1.

[4] T/Hel(S)/28/1, 2. Scrutiny of the original 1950s plan reveals that Dennish noted differences in floor levels and contradictions in the direction taken by floor and ceiling joists, both of which confirm the removal or erection of internal walls. In addition, he notes, particularly in the east range, mixtures of boarded and paved floors within the same room, which is strongly suggestive of a change from utilitarian to residential use (and vice versa). The likelihood is that part of the east range was once the brewhouse, for which the inventory evidence is discussed below.

[5] The architectural features and internal layout of Helmingham Hall were explored in detail by Arthur Oswald (1956); elements were discussed by Eric Sandon, *Suffolk Houses* (1977), and by James Bettley and Nikolaus Pevsner, *Suffolk: East* (2015). Stephen Podd confirmed that the development of the park is no less complex than that of the hall (*PSIAH* 42, 2009, pp. 38–58).

Plate 6. Helmingham Hall, south elevation. Photograph by Victor Gray, 2016

Plate 7. Helmingham Hall, north elevation. Photograph by Victor Gray, 2016

Plate 8. Helmingham Hall, west elevation. Editor's photograph

Plate 9. Helmingham Hall, east elevation. Editor's photograph

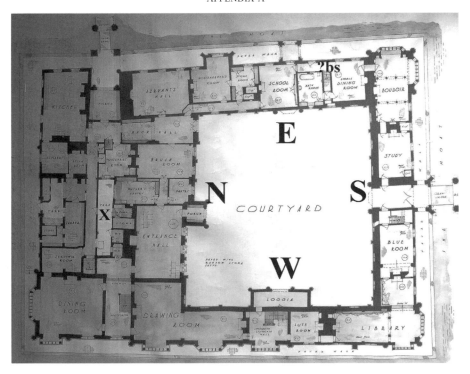

Plate 10. Ground floor plan of Helmingham Hall in the 1950s by J.C. Dennish of Ipswich. The original orientation of the plan is maintained but compass points have been added to accompany discussion in Appendix A, where a yard ('x') and a speculative site for the back stairs ('?bs') are mentioned. Helmingham Archive, T/Hel(S)/28/1, 2, reproduced by kind permission of the Lord Tollemache

Helmingham's head of household, Lionel Tollemache, was elevated to a baronetcy. The 1626 inventory, compiled by his successor, Sir Lionel Tollemache, 2nd baronet, is rich in detail and anecdotal commentary. It shows more significant building work and reveals some of the disruption associated with occupying and equipping two homes. It provides also a more expansive view of the rural household and its operation than that of 1597, as well as an unexpected insight into how the property was kept secure. The gap in time between 1626 and 1708 results in a record of two extremes: fulsome individual room descriptions in 1626 are reduced to abbreviated groupings of rooms in 1708, by which time the family has been further elevated and Helmingham Hall has become the country seat of the 3rd Earl of Dysart. However, the 1708 inventory is the first to separate the record by floor level, a detail lacking from either of the two earlier documents. No part of the house is described as 'new' in 1708 but there are notable differences since 1626 in the way in which its space is occupied and used. Three decades on, in 1741, more is described as 'new' than in any of the other inventories, marking the energetic activity of the 4th Earl of Dysart, whose programme of further improvement, both to the house and grounds, accelerated in the years immediately following the date of this inventory.

Plate 11. The courtyard of Helmingham Hall, looking north: the three tall windows to the left of the porch belong to the great hall. Photograph by Victor Gray, 2016

There are no internal floor plans before the Dennish draughts of the 1950s to provide a template on which to reconstruct earlier layouts. However, three documents from the eighteenth century support some details in each inventory. Plates 12, 13, 15 and 16 are based on a 1720 sketch plan drawn by Thomas Brereton, who was estate steward to the 3rd Earl of Dysart.[6] The source of his draught has been discussed in the introduction and is summarised in the caption to Plate 12. The footprint of the house on its moated site at this date retains features such as bridges, yards and gates that were noted in the 1626 inventory, making it possible to illustrate and analyse the frequent mentions of security in that record. Plate VI is an extract from a survey of the Helmingham Estate by Richard Tollemache, dated 1729, from which a detail is presented as Plate 14. Plate 17 is based on an unattributed drawing of Helmingham Hall and its environs from the south-east, dating post-1741 and pre-1783, a larger version of which is used as the frontispiece to this volume.[7] It shows a house whose architectural style is far removed from the one seen today, yet one in which elements of all four inventory descriptions are recognisable. To make best use of the available materials, the structure of this appendix follows the chronology of the inventories. Each section is supported by one or more of the plates summarised above.

Perambulation of the 1597 household inventory
The 1597 compiler adopted a systematic, floor-by-floor perambulation without recording floor levels or staircases. Rooms are discussed below in the order in which they are listed in the inventory but their grouping is arbitrary, designed to draw attention to features or functions that suggest or question their likely location. Numbers contained within square brackets provide unique 1597 transcription refer-

---

6   T/Hel/1/64.
7   Private collection.

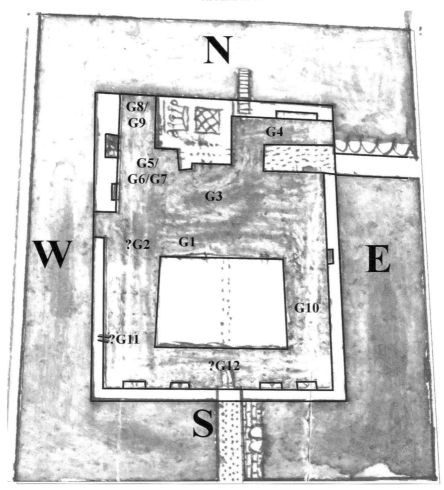

Plate 12. Speculative ground-floor plan of Helmingham Hall in 1597 superimposed on a detail of the 1720 plan by Thomas Brereton. Brereton's original (see Plate 1) has been rotated to create this plan. Orientation points and the numbers G1–G12 accompany a discussion of the route of the 1597 perambulation

ences. Plate 12 identifies ground-floor features prefixed by G where these can be located with confidence, or ?G to indicate uncertainty.

The 1597 route begins at the principal room in the house, which is the hall, and proceeds to record the contents of all rooms located at ground level, both in the main house and its offices within the confines of the moated site.

hall (G1); parlour (?G2); beer cellar; wine cellar; Smyth's storehouse (all suggested by G3)

From the hall it is likely that the compiler moved north and then west to the cellars and storehouse. The inventory mentions a new window in the hall and seats made for it in 1597 and 1598 (97.16), and refers to purchases of new linen for 'her parlour'

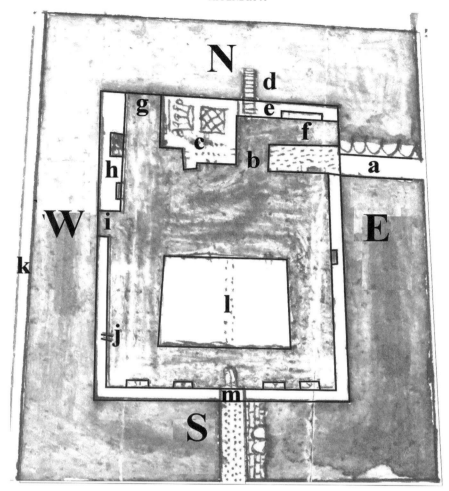

Plate 13. Speculative positions of access points and external features of Helmingham Hall named in the 1626 inventory, superimposed on a detail of the 1720 plan by Thomas Brereton (see Plate 1). Orientation points and the letters a–l accompany a discussion of the route of the 1626 perambulation

[97.1008]. Speculatively, the hall was modified at or about the time of the inventory to accommodate a new or enlarged parlour facing west, suggested by ?G2, Plate 12.

kitchen (G4)

When Helmingham Hall was built in or about 1510, the kitchen was almost certainly detached in order to reduce the risk of fire spreading into other areas of the house. The kitchen continues to occupy the cool, north-east corner of the site to this day and there is no reason to suppose that the 1597 kitchen was anywhere else. Plate 12 shows that by 1720 it was linked to the main house by a short covered passageway.

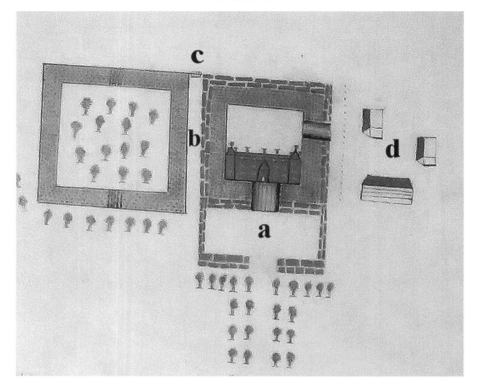

Plate 14. Detail from 1729 survey of the Helmingham Estate by Richard Tollemache (see colour Plate VI for a larger extract). The features marked a, b, c and d accompany discussion in Appendix A concerning the areas west, south and east of the hall that were not included in Thomas Brereton's plan of 1720. Helmingham Archive, reproduced by kind permission of the Lord Tollemache

More information emerges in 1626 to confirm that the passageway was secured by locked gates.

The 1597 house was dominated by the numerous functions required to keep its residents fed and cared for, summarised below. These tasks needed a small army of resident staff, ten of whom have sleeping chambers allocated in the house, with capacity for at least eight more. Individual locations for the working areas mentioned below cannot be confirmed but are suggested on Plate 12 as being within reach of the kitchen and readily accessible by staff working in the main house. The household offices, identified below, cater largely for tasks that do not require heat; where they do require heat, it is not the constant demand posed by the kitchen, suggesting that they could be sited safely within the confines of the moated site.

pastry (G5, Plate 12)

The name persists in professional catering today and relates now, as in 1597, to the making of confectionery, a range of activities described in footnote 12 to the 1597 transcription. The work demands an ambient cool temperature, an environment offered away from the kitchen on the north-facing part of the site.

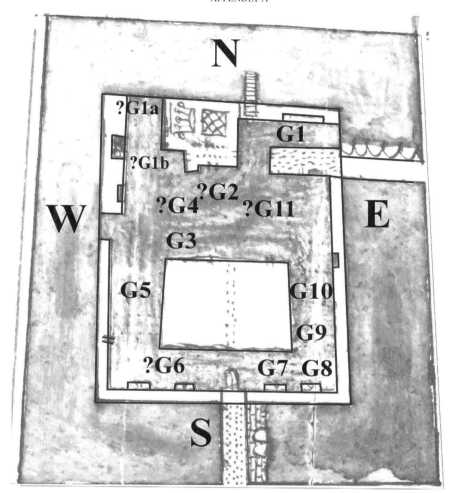

Plate 15. Speculative ground-floor layout of Helmingham Hall in 1708, superimposed on a detail of the 1720 plan by Thomas Brereton (see Plate 1). Orientation points and numbers G1–G11 accompany a discussion of the route of the 1708 perambulation

larder; husbandmen's hall; verjuice house (G6, Plate 12)

Contents of the larder (97.171–179) show it to be equipped for salting, brining and packing meats for long-term storage. The preceding stage is undertaken in the 'lard house' (see below). The siting of the husbandmen's hall, where staff would have congregated for their meals, between the larder and the verjuice house (which, because of its seasonal nature, is used in 1597 for storage of random items), seems odd. The only feature that the three spaces share is a lack of heat.

inner dairy; outward dairy; lard house; cheese chamber (G7, Plate 12)

The inner dairy and the lard house are equipped with sources of heat, as is the 'outward' (outer) dairy, a space whose contents show that it was used also as a laundry in 1597 (97.231–233). Both dairies needed access to water. The unheated

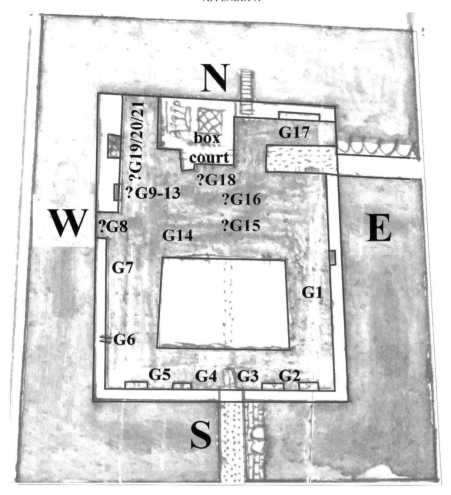

Plate 16. Speculative ground-floor layout of Helmingham Hall in 1741, superimposed on a detail of the 1720 plan by Thomas Brereton (see Plate 1). Orientation points and the numbers G1–G21 accompany a discussion of the route of the 1741 perambulation in Appendix A. Note the ornamental design based on an earl's coronet planted by the time Brereton produced his plan, a topiary feature in the area described in the 1750s as the box court

cheese chamber, dedicated to the storage of cheeses for finishing and ripening, if not on the ground floor, could have been on the first floor above the lard house. The lard house was unheated and used for the initial preparation of carcasses of meat which were then finished and stored in the larder.

Sites for the following are uncertain but, given their place in the perambulation, it is likely that they were located at the extreme north-west of the range suggested as G8/G9 on Plate 12 because the bakehouse, in particular, posed another potential fire risk.

Plate 17. Speculative guide to the layout of Helmingham Hall in 1741 based on detail from an unattributed drawing from the south-east, dating between 1741 and 1783. See caption to frontispiece. Key: A, kitchen; B, entrance gateway from east bridge separating the kitchen from C, the east range, with its prominent, off-centre bay; D, the gable end of the south range; E and I, ornamented bays at each end of the south range including F, G and H; J, roof space above the south range complete with its four gabled dormers; K, just visible, gabled dormer in the roofline of the north range, apparently at a different level from L, the adjacent roofline at higher level. The outer courtyard, surrounded by a post-and-rail fence with a gate giving access to the buildings east of the moat, was surrounded by brick walls when illustrated in 1729 by Richard Tollemache (see Plates VI and 14); M, N and O, outbuildings lying east of the moat. Based on drawing at Helmingham Hall, reproduced by kind permission of the Lord Tollemache

163

boulting house (G8/G9, Plate 12)

The bolting house is equipped not only for its primary task of sieving and grading of flour but also for the mixing of dough (97.259–276), a task that demands access to a source of potable water and proximity to the bakehouse, which comes next.

backhouse [bakehouse] (G8/G9, Plate 12)

In addition to meeting the daily bread consumption of thirty residents, the bakehouse at Helmingham was put to use as its temperature cooled for baking whole fruits and drying pastes and other confections, suggesting its proximity to the kitchen and pastry.

brewhouse (G10, Plate 12)

Probably self-contained and not interconnecting with the south range. Brewing needed heat and a ready supply of water and, like bread, there was a daily household demand for beer, confirmed by the presence of thirty hogsheads, or 1575 gallons, for its storage in the cellar (97.67). In 1597 the brewhouse was part of a two-storey building, confirmed by the phrases 'chamber over the brewhouse' and 'little chamber next to the same' (described later in the perambulation), located close to the south range of the main house.

Sites for the following are uncertain but, based on their order in the perambulation, following the brewhouse and before the compiler begins recording the first-floor rooms of the main house, they were outside the moat to the east, an area not illustrated by Brereton in his 1720 sketch. A 1729 estate plan by Richard Tollemache, a detail of which is identified at 'd' on Plate 14, indicates a group of buildings east of the moated house[8] and Plate 17, albeit two or three decades later, illustrates a group of service buildings on the same site (marked M, N and O and described in its key).

mill house

Unlike the 1626 inventory, which describes a 'millhouse chamber', there are no other clues in the 1597 inventory to suggest the extent of the millhouse.

fowls' house; inner fowls' house; yard

Chaff from the mill would have been fed to the fowls and explains their proximity to one another in the perambulation. The yard contained a grindstone and implements for maintaining the moat (97.303–305) and may well have been partially covered or enclosed to protect them from the elements.

stilling yard

The scope and scale of stilling was significant at Helmingham in 1597. Despite its description as a 'yard', this space must have been enclosed or, at the very least, roofed, in order to enclose and protect the furnace, its six stills and some of its high-status, silver-trimmed contents (97.306–314).

The move from the stilling yard to the next group of rooms confirms that the compiler has returned to the moated site to commence recording the contents of first-floor spaces, beginning with the principal room, the dining chamber. No attempt has been made to locate first-floor rooms on Plate 12.

---

8   Part of T/Hel(S)/27/4, a bound volume comprising ten plans of Helmingham estate and five of Framsden estate.

dining chamber

The contents do not include fire irons or other implements to confirm evidence of a fireplace. Otherwise, this room is well appointed with wall hangings and sumptuous textiles (see 97.330–344).

best chamber; inner chamber to the same; corner chamber; closet to the same chamber

Identifying the 'corner' is a challenge. In the 1626 inventory there is a room described as 'the corner chamber or gable end', whose location is thought, speculatively, to be on the first floor at the junction of the south and east ranges. Unlike the dining chamber, the best and corner chambers are both equipped with fireplaces in 1597.

middle chamber; two-bed chamber; green chamber; inner chamber to the same

Locating the middle chamber is a similar challenge. It and the green chamber both show evidence of a fireplace, suggesting that these are rooms of higher status than the two-bed or inner chambers, which may well have been allocated to staff.

my Master, his chamber

In 1597, no separate room was allocated to Lionel Tollemache's wife, Catherine, so this room was the shared marital chamber and was equipped with a fireplace. See the 1597 transcription for its contents, which included storage of linen (97.444–478). Given the scope of its contents and the status of its occupants, this is likely to have been one of the largest first-storey rooms in the house.

nursery; Mistress Cicely's chamber; maid's chamber

Mistress Cicely was the children's nurse and the 'maid' in this case probably served Catherine Tollemache and possibly her four daughters, explaining the proximity of these rooms both to the nursery and the master's chamber. None of the rooms appears to have a fireplace, which suggests that they were sited over unheated ground-floor service areas.

working chamber; drying chamber; soap house

Neither chamber is heated, suggesting positions over unheated ground-floor service areas. The soap house suggests a self-contained building, in this case one with a lockable door (97.564). However, its contents (97.549–563) reveal that the heating of ingredients for perfume-making and candle-making required no more than ventilation for the charcoal-heated copper chafers, so a first-floor location is feasible. The soap house is not mentioned in 1626, but in 1708 there is a 'candle chamber' mentioned on the first floor.

gallery

References to a gallery recur and evolve throughout the inventories. A notable feature of the 1597 gallery is the chest containing a horseman's armour (97.565), an item still in place there in 1626, when it is described more fully. Based on the 1626 evidence, the gallery was a corridor on the first floor of the south range.

old chamber; old man's parlour; inner chamber to the old man's parlour

Speculatively, the rooms described as 'old man's' imply not rooms for old men but rooms previously reserved for use by men. In 1597, all three were equipped to be sleeping chambers.

The rooms following question the view of a systematic first-floor record because they suggest a ground-floor location, so it seems likely that some parts of the house necessitated separate entry from ground level.

chamber going into the garden, entry, old parlour

Locating the chamber depends upon locating the garden in 1597. Most likely this refers to the substantial area contained within its own moat, and lying west of the moated house. Brereton shows this in 1720 as the moated garden and orchard (visible top right of his letter in Plate 1), and it seems unlikely that its site was else-where in 1597. A site on the west side of the house is suggested tentatively for the entry (Plate 12, ?G11), which would place the chamber going into the garden and the 'old' parlour also in the west range.

From these rooms, the compiler returns to the first floor of the south range, where the gatehouse chamber is taken to be at its centre.

gatehouse chamber; inner chamber to the same

three-bed chamber; kitchener's chamber; Mr Bell, his chamber; Lyonell Wieth, his chamber; Bayton's chamber; Butler's chamber; George Smythe, his chamber

Six of the seven sleeping chambers grouped together here are dedicated to staff. George Smythe, the household steward, kept a handgun at the ready (97.708), which suggests a room positioned strategically for hearing, and seeing off, marauders.

On the assumption that the rooms described above are on the first floor, the compiler then returns to ground-floor level, close to the central gateway.

porter's lodge

Suggested tentatively by G12 on Plate 12 because the lodge's position in 1597, east or west of the gateway, cannot be confirmed.

From the porter's lodge, the perambulation resumes at first-floor level with chambers that are almost certainly all occupied by staff, even though only one is named. All are likely to be in the east range.

cook's chamber; chamber over the brewhouse; little chamber next to the same

The descriptions confirm that the brewhouse (described earlier) was a two-storeyed structure.

From here, the compiler leaves the moated site to record one first-floor space above the stables, the site of which was almost certainly east of the moat.

stable chamber

The stable itself is not recorded, confirming that the compiler is recording only spaces containing what are considered to be household contents, whether located within or beyond the moat. Evidence from later inventories confirms that the stables were sited east of the moat and there is nothing in the 1597 inventory to oppose this view.

The compiler returns finally to the main house to record the contents of its roof space or spaces.

armoury, wardrobe, chamber next the wardrobes

The grouping of these three spaces, coupled with confirmation from the 1626 and 1708 inventories, suggests a roof space over the south range. Plate 17 shows that this space was substantial, and lit by four dormer windows (Plate 17, J). The wardrobe adjoining the armoury contained not only garments but also saddles and other high-value leather items. Counter-intuitive though this location may seem, given the laborious task of moving heavy items of clothing, saddlery, armour and weaponry up and down flights of stairs, the need for security was paramount.[9]

The roof-space descriptions conclude the inventory perambulation of the 1597 house. Clarification of some of the uncertainties noted here emerges from the 1626 inventory, when the bones of the 1597 house are recognisable, albeit modified and enlarged.

Perambulation of the 1626 household inventory

The inventories are inconsistent in the extent of what they record as the household. The 1626 inventory records 122 individual rooms or spaces, suggesting a household twice the size of that described in 1597 (and larger than those recorded in 1708 and 1741), but this is not the case, as the perambulation reveals. Every closet and sometimes even the space between rooms is noted, and the record extends to the garden on the west and numerous working areas beyond the moat to the east. The commentary below follows the route of the inventory, drawing attention to areas described as 'new' or 'old' and, wherever possible, correlating 1626 spaces with those described in 1597. Plate 13 emphasises external access points mentioned in the 1626 inventory, each of which is discussed in a separate commentary.

The 1626 household, whilst still dependent upon the numerous tasks related to maintaining and feeding its residents, shows a marked increase in private family use of the space, its contents suggesting a greater degree of leisure and pleasure than enjoyed by the family thirty years earlier. There are twenty-one potential sleeping chambers allocated to staff and twenty-six rooms, including sleeping chambers, for family occupation. The remaining seventy-five descriptions relate to working areas (indoors and out, some of them spaces to house animals) and to spaces such as closets for storage. Although the 1626 compiler shares the 1597 compiler's starting point of the hall, the route thereafter is more circuitous and complex, with an early emphasis on the high-status family rooms.

hall

Its position is suggested in Plate 12, G1, and details provided of the rooms following, as far as the parlour, confirm a layout similar to that of 1597.

halfpace between the hall and the cellar for strong beer; halfpace next the parlour door

The halfpace is a step or platform[10] and is a useful indicator of differences in floor levels; this, in turn, is evidence that the structure has been modified here, a clue that will be confirmed shortly. It is not until later in the inventory that the extent of the cellars is confirmed.

parlour

Suggested by ?G2 on plate 12, even though the space around it has been modified to accommodate the new chamber described next.

---

9 The need for security explains why the sixteenth-century parish armoury at Mendlesham church was, from the outset, housed in a room above the porch, its first-floor windows barred, reached by a narrow stone staircase and entry protected by a strong door with two locks.

10 D. Yaxley, *A Researcher's glossary* (2003), p. 96.

From this point, the compiler proceeds to explore the entire west range, beginning on the ground floor at its northern end, in close proximity to the hall and parlour.

> new chamber next the great parlour commonly called my Master's chamber; closet of the right-hand coming in at the door; next closet upon the right hand; closet upon the right hand of the chimney; closet upon the left hand of the chimney

Analysed in conjunction with evidence noted later, this chamber and its closets together comprise the ground-floor part of a new, two-storey construction with an accessible roofspace above and cellars below. The chamber allocated to Sir Lionel Tollemache is not equipped for sleeping but for reading, writing, relaxation and storage for items of personal interest. His sleeping chamber is on the first floor.

> chamber opposite to the Parlour door

Circulation within and between rooms is not always obvious from the inventories but numerous rooms appear to be interconnecting. The inference here, with a chamber opposite, is that this area of the house is broad enough to permit two rooms separated by communication space between them (see concluding comments to this appendix).

> music parlour; closet; other closet

The music parlour is a designation unique to the 1626 inventory. See footnote 22 to the 1626 transcription.

The next entry gives confirmation of a staircase, and its principal destination:

> the great stairs going to the dining chamber

The description emphasises that the dining chamber is evidently the principal room on the first floor and, for the first time, confirms a staircase. The 1741 inventory describes a 'great new staircase' on this side of the house, confirming that the west range offered opportunities for ongoing modification.

Next, the compiler records first-floor rooms presumed to be in the west range:

> chamber called My Lord's chamber; inward chamber; closet

These three spaces provide a sleeping and dressing suite (with a close stool in the closet) allocated to Sir Lionel Tollemache and are distinct from his ground-floor rooms. The 1626 accommodation, unlike that of 1597, provides separate suites for Sir Lionel and Lady Elizabeth, whose rooms are described much later in the inventory. However, some of this room's contents reside in 'the great new matted chamber' and 'the best chamber', suggesting disruption or reorganisation as a result of the new building work, perhaps.

> chamber at the great stairs' head

This, like the remaining rooms described here, is furnished to a high standard, to accommodate family and guests, rather than staff.

> dining chamber

The inventory records evidence of a fireplace (26.219–221) where none was recorded in the 1597 dining chamber; nor is there any evidence of one in 1708, and by 1741 there is no room designated specifically for dining, by then accommodated in a parlour. Was the 1626 dining chamber altered, perhaps by the removal of an internal wall to benefit from an existing fireplace in an adjoining room? The opportunity may have presented itself during construction of the new rooms mentioned earlier.

best chamber next the great chamber; inward chamber

None of the rooms so far described bears the name 'great chamber' but this probably refers to Sir Lionel's chamber, described above as 'chamber called my Lord's chamber'.

chamber at the clock stairs over against Mr Edward Tollemache's; over the clock stairs; Mr Edward's chamber

The site of the clock stairs is uncertain; Smythe's household accounts for 1587–89 confirm payments for repairs to a clock (see footnote 29 to 1626 inventory) but the space it occupied was not mentioned in the 1597 inventory. The inference is that the three rooms lie close together. In the 1708 inventory the 'clockhouse' is described as a discrete space, as though detached from the main house or accessed independently from it.

Evidence of new building work at first-floor level is confirmed in the next description.

new chamber; closet; inward chamber

This is almost certainly located above the 'new chamber next the great parlour' noted on the ground floor. Its suite of two or three interconnecting spaces, with a close stool in the closet, characterises the layout of high-status rooms (those not allocated to staff) at Helmingham Hall in 1626.

The rooms following provide two suites, named for the predominant colour of their taffeta furnishings, which suggests high-status occupancy (as do the closets equipped with close stools). It is feasible that the compiler has moved into the south range, and is moving from west to east, because these rooms are followed by the gatehouse chamber, which lies at the centre of the south range on its first floor.

crimson taffeta chamber, closet, yellow taffeta chamber, closet, inward chamber
gatehouse chamber, inward chamber

Given what follows, it is feasible that the gatehouse chamber and its inner room effectively blocked access to the remainder of the south range, probably because they extended from front to back of the building. This is suggested strongly by the description of its various window curtains and five curtain rods (26.371, 26.376), and confirmation that one window is 'nexte the inner courtyard' (Plate 13, 1) and the presence of two doors in its inner chamber (26.385 and 26.386), one of which may have given access to the staircase mentioned next.

With no mention of a staircase, the compiler climbs to the roof space (presumably still in the south range) but appears to visit only one part of it:

garret over the yellow taffeta chamber

The suggestion here is that the garret extends only over the taffeta chamber. Descriptions of other, larger roof spaces believed to lie over the south range come much later in the inventory.

Speculatively, the rooms that follow were located east of the gatehouse but it is uncertain whether they were located on the first or ground floor.

Mr Johnson's chamber; closet; Mr Riseing's chamber

The route moves now to the east range.

brewhouse chamber

Apart from a 'lock and key upon the door', no contents are recorded, but the assumption is that this room is at first-floor level in the brewhouse. The brewhouse itself is described much later in the inventory.

chamber at the stairs' foot next the Brewhouse called Seaman's chamber

It is evident that the compiler has returned to the ground floor, presumably because there was no internal access to the room visited next.

chamber under the Gatehouse called the Porter's chamber

Speculatively, this room lies on the east side of the gateway, described as the 'porter's lodge' in the 1597 inventory.

In the 1597 inventory there was some evidence that the compiler visited rooms on the first floor, descended a floor to visit the porter's lodge (the equivalent of the 1626 porter's chamber, which was equipped with a bed) and then returned to the first floor. It is not clear in 1626 whether the compiler remains on the ground floor to describe the rooms that follow, or whether these chambers are on the first floor.

chamber called Mr Robert Tollemache, his chamber; closet; inward chamber; steward's chamber; closet

The name of the next room confirms that the compiler has reached the end of a range. Speculatively, the room described lies at the junction of the south and east ranges.

corner chamber or gable end

There was a room described as a 'corner chamber' in the 1597 inventory, but whether this is one and the same corner is debatable. The phrase 'gable end' is suggestive of a first-floor room. Plate 17 depicts Helmingham Hall as it appeared between 1740 and 1760, viewed from the south-east: despite the gap of a century or more between the 1626 inventory and the drawing, features mentioned in the 1626 inventory are identifiable. The small window in the gable end of the south range (Plate 17, D) suggests a room such as the one described here.

The corner chamber described above seems to mark the beginning of rooms allocated to staff working outside the house. Speculatively, some or all of these were over the brewhouse:

entry between the corner chamber and Nunn's chamber; John Nunn's chamber

John Nunn has a chamber mentioned elsewhere (see below, referring to a building in the park which was, perhaps, used seasonally).

Baiton's chamber; husbandmen's chamber; green chamber; inward chamber

A green chamber was described in the 1597 inventory and the contents of the 1626 room are similar in that, ironically, none of them appears to be green.

The two descriptions that follow suggest a separate building which might well have been sited east of the moat with other service buildings.

chamber coming up the back stairs to go unto the hawks' mew

Speculatively, the hawks' mew lies beyond the moat, probably to the east. The contents include a 'lock and key to the stairs head door' and an assortment of broken furniture.

hawks' mew

The 1626 inventory is the only one of the four to identify the hawks' mew, although numerous payments relating to meat for the hawks were apparent from Smythe's household accounts of 1587–89, confirming that they were kept at Helmingham then. The mew would have been ventilated on at least one side and would have contained little except perches for the birds.

The route followed by the compiler from this point is unclear but the evidence offered by the first two rooms suggests a return to the first floor of the south range.

brushing gallery

A phrase unique to the 1626 inventory and taken to mean an area where outerwear and armour were brushed clean before being returned to storage. In 1597, a location for the gallery was thought to be on the first floor of the south range, with ready access to the roof space above. This speculation is borne out in 1626, since the brushing gallery also houses a chest containing horseman's armour (26.579) that was described also in 1597 (97.565) and, as the next description confirms (below) the wardrobe stairs lead directly from the brushing gallery:

corner underneath the wardrobe stairs

There is uncertainty about the corner described here: the wardrobes (and adjoining armoury) thought to occupy the roof space over the south range are not explored until later. There are also two 'new' wardrobe spaces, described later, and it is possible that this corner, equipped with a close stool, located conveniently for users of the wardrobe, and its wardrobe stairs, relate not to the old wardrobes but to rooms in the roof space of the new, two-storey addition built to the north-west of the site.

The perambulation that follows is also strongly suggestive of first-floor rooms to the north-west of the site, some of them over ground-floor service buildings that have yet to be recorded by the compiler.

My Lady's chamber

This, and the room following, signal a change from the shared marital room recorded in the 1597 inventory (see footnote 33 to 1597 transcription) and the provision of separate quarters for the master and mistress of the house.

maid's chamber next my Lady's
nursery chamber

In the 1626 inventory, the nursery chamber and the nursery are one and the same room. A comment notes that the room is sub-divided with pieces of fabric hung between the beds, one of which is 'between the bed and the wall that is next the moat', which might imply that the nursery is on the ground floor.

dairy maid's chamber at the old stair head

Where were these 'old' stairs located? And if there are new ones, where are they?

chamber between the maid's chamber and the drying chamber

drying chamber

As identified in the 1597 perambulation, this confirms that drying, finishing and storage of linen was accommodated on the first floor.

The following entries suggest that the compiler leaves the main moated site to record the contents of staff accommodation elsewhere, some of it located in the park.

groom's chamber

Logically, the groom's chamber would be located close to the horses, whose stables are thought to lie outside the moat within a group of outbuildings, as depicted later and visible in Plate 14 (1729, 'd') and surviving at the time of Plate 17 (1741, M, N, and O).

Humfereyes [*sic*] chamber

This and the following entries imply one or more detached buildings occupied by staff and located in the park, where they worked.

John Nunn's chamber in the park

middle chamber at Humferies house; garret there

John Nunn appears to have two chambers, suggesting seasonal use of the 'chamber in the park'. The descriptions before and after this imply that there was one building shared by several people with working responsibilities in the park, but John Nunn is the only named individual with a chamber allocated elsewhere.

There appears to be no logic to the perambulated route which meanders from the house to the park and back to the main house; but there are two possible reasons, both relating to inaccessibility. The spaces visited next, the armoury and the wardrobes, may have been locked and therefore inaccessible from the brushing gallery on the compiler's earlier visit. (This proved to be the case in 1708, when the compiler merely noted the fact that some roof-space areas were locked up and inaccessible). Given the imperative of security for items housed in the armoury and wardrobe, the keys may well have been held only by Sir Lionel Tollemache. At or about the time of this inventory compilation, Sir Lionel and Lady Elizabeth had lost their infant son, Francis, born in September and buried at Fakenham Magna less than a month later, on 21 October 1626. The circumstances suggest also why the date of this inventory was never completed, recorded only as 'October 1626'. A second reason for the apparently disjointed perambulation is that building work on the new and modified areas, which included a new wardrobe in the roof space, impeded access on an earlier visit. Whatever the reason, the compiler moves from the park to the roof space, and only then almost to the starting point of the perambulation, where much else had changed at ground level.

armoury

This and the adjoining 'old' wardrobe, as speculated in the 1597 house, are located in the roof space over the south range.

old wardrobe

Containing mostly superannuated items and lumber in 1626, this old space is almost certainly the wardrobe adjoining the armoury in the 1597 inventory.

new wardrobe

The perambulation from here to the next space suggests that the compiler has left the old roof space and moved to that covering the 'new' suite of chambers identified earlier.

chamber at the further end of the wardrobe

From this chamber, the compiler leaves the roof space and returns to the ground floor. Now at this level, the compiler's attention turns to the service and communication areas north of the hall, an area that in 1597 was explored at the outset of the perambulation. This reinforces the view that access to new and modified areas was limited, so that the 1626 compiler had to wait for an opportunity to complete the record, giving some indication of the obstacles involved and the time taken to compile this highly detailed inventory.

storehouse next the hall; pantry; inward pantry

All or part of this space may be what was described as 'George Smyth, his storehouse' in 1597; but now it is augmented by pantries which were not mentioned then.

new cellar

This, together with the new chambers identified earlier on the first floor (and the new wardrobe in the roof space above), confirm the provision of a newly built two-storey range with an accessible roof space and this new cellar below ground level in close proximity to the pre-existing cellars, which follow.

strong beer cellar; wine cellar

These were the 1597 cellars, but now the demand for beer has increased and its storage space is more sophisticated, allowing space and facilities for the washing of glasses (26.1038).

Unlike the 1597 inventory, the 1626 compiler's route visits the kitchen and associated offices as part of the final exploration of ground-floor working spaces.

kitchen

The kitchen's location is assumed to be unchanged since 1597.

pantry; scullery

These were not mentioned in 1597 but perhaps created by sub-division of other offices.

husbandmen's hall; verjuice house; larder; rompthe [room, space] between the old hall and the larder

The old hall is taken to mean an entrance hall rather than a replacement for the main hall and may well refer to changes that resulted from the provision of the new construction or from subdivision of these offices.

outward dairy

As in 1597, the name persists although its contents confirm that the outer dairy is in use also as a laundry, a name not adopted until 1708.

inward dairy; middle dairy

The middle dairy is a designation unique to the 1626 inventory, perhaps resulting from subdivision of the existing dairies.

cheese chamber; that which was a greasehouse, now a buttery

The newly designated buttery is identifiable as the 'lard house' in the 1597 inventory. The purpose of the buttery was to accommodate beer, wine and food and the means to serve them, suggesting that this was close to, if not part of, the main house and its cellars.

The areas described below were grouped together in the 1597 inventory, suggesting that in 1626 they continue to occupy the same sites on the north-west corner of the moated site.

still yard

Its contents (26.1245–1253) confirms that the scope and scale of distilling had not diminished since 1597.

baking house; meal house; poultry house

The meal house is described as the boulting house in 1597.

The final working space to be explored on the moated site is the brewhouse, on the ground floor of the east range, confirming that this was in a building with separate access, attached to, but not interconnecting with, the rest of the house.

brewhouse

The contents of the brewhouse in 1626 include a 'greate new worte tubb' (26.1295). There is a detailed description of how the building's water supply was engineered (see 26.1312).

fish chamber

The 1626 site of the fish chamber is uncertain and it is a designation unique to the 1626 inventory. Some herring barrels and barrels of bay salt were noted in the verjuice house in the 1597 inventory.[11]

The entries that follow are thought to lie beyond the moat, to the east. Plates 14 and 17 illustrate a group of buildings on this site which may be the successors to some of those recorded here in 1626.

mill house; mill house chamber, spaniels' kennel

The kennel is a designation unique to the 1626 inventory, being one of the several descriptions of spaces for animals and birds that add immeasurably to the view of activity and self-sufficiency at Helmingham Hall.

stable; saddle house

The contents of the 1626 saddle house refer only to a 'livery saddle'; high-quality saddles, many of them related to and suitably embellished for ceremony and mourning, were stored in the 1626 wardrobes and, as in 1597, with an eye to security as much as maintenance.

stable chamber; voance roof [roof void, garret] over the stable chamber

The inventory of working spaces expands the view of the working household considerably, and illuminates the range of resources and skills needed to support the 1626 residents of Helmingham Hall.

barn for corn; ladders short and long; coach house; coach house stable;
croft stable; husbandmen's stable; husbandmen's storehouse; work house;
slaughterhouse; cart house; puet's house; swill house; hogs troughs

Concluding entries in the 1626 inventory relate to the contents of recognisable outdoor areas, including the moat and the garden.

---

[11] See footnote 16 to the 1597 inventory.

pump house

Demand for water was high, particularly in the brewhouse, whose own contents describe how water was pumped to it from 'the back yard' (26.1312)

> inward courtyard; the back bridge yard next the dairy; back yard between the moat and the kitchen

Potential locations for these are suggested on Plate 13 and its caption, relating to access and security.

outward court

Brereton's 1720 plan does not extend south of the south moat, but a sketch of the house and its surroundings incorporated into Richard Tollemache's survey of the Helmingham estate, dated 1729,[12] clearly shows an outer courtyard. Indicated by 'a' on Plate 14, this shows an area south of the house contained within what appear to be brick walls, broken by an opening wide enough to admit horses and carriages. Plate 17, later in date, shows a post-and-rail fence (marked as 'outer courtyard') instead of the brick-wall surround.

long walk between the garden and the moat

The 1626 garden is taken to mean the extensive area of separately moated gardens lying west of Helmingham Hall, and the 'long walk' describes aptly what is now the grassed causeway, which separates the house moat from the garden moat (Plate 13, k). Its long extent is more clearly visible on Plate 14, marked as 'b', with what may be a gate or stile, marked 'c', at its northern end.

garden

moat

Glimpses of leisurely opportunities emerge from the contents, as well as the implements needed to keep the garden maintained, and confirmation that the garden is reached by a locked door (26.1526). Speculatively, this is the feature marked 'c' on Plate 14.

Less straightforward to locate are the sites of the next two entries:

pheasant yard; dovehouse

The pheasant house has a lock on its door and a sundial, suggesting a location where both could be seen and enjoyed. Doves need ready access to water, so the dovehouse was likely to have been sited close to the moat, but perhaps on the site to its east.

The 1626 inventory concludes with the following descriptions, which are associated:

stable yards; at the brick kiln

Given the large quantities of brick and tile recorded at both these sites (26. 1543–1549), it is clear that ongoing works at the 1626 house placed a high demand on the brick kiln.[13]

---

[12]   T/Hel(S)/27/4.
[13]   See also footnote 150 to the 1626 inventory for location of the brick kiln.

Access and security in the 1626 household

Anecdotal comments are a valuable feature of the 1626 household inventory. They help to explain how and where the house was accessible as well as describing the lengths taken to keep the place secure. Physical access to the house was limited by the moat but access within the site was equally limited, according to the 1626 inventory. The record confirms that all external doors and gates, and almost all internal doors, are equipped with locks, even if their keys are wanting. Each is named or includes anecdotal comments about the space to or from which it leads. There is a detailed summary of locked (or lockable) external doors in the glossary (see **lock**) including a sub-category of *locks but no keys*. Notably, numerous doors and gates missing their keys are those through which staff passed frequently, including one of the park gates (26.1003). Perhaps removals were deliberate, a way of avoiding the impediment to speedy circulation and communication in this complex building and its environs, or a way of avoiding the hand of authority, or both. Plate 13, is, like Plate 12, based on a detail from a sketch drawn by Thomas Brereton in 1720. Despite the distance in time between this plan and the inventories, the sketch is valuable, particularly in its depiction of the northern part of the site and its confirmation of recognisable access points mentioned in the 1626 inventory.

Explanation of features marked on Plate 13 (with 1626 transcription references):

a) The east bridge, principal access point for all household services and referred to throughout the 1626 inventory as the back bridge (see references below). A cobbled entrance extends from the bridge to (b).

b) A covered passageway, with gates on its east and west sides, the latter identified in the 1626 inventory as a locked gate to the back bridge yard (26.1514), the yard described below.

c) The back bridge yard. The 1626 inventory describes 'the back bridge yarde next the dayrye' as having 'one great crosse barre reaching frome the walle unto the gate' (26.1515) in addition to that mentioned above (26.1514).

d) Not a bridge but apparently a flight of steps descending to the moat. This may have been where boats were moored in 1626 (26.1536), giving access to the north side of the house without the need to cross either of the bridges on the east or south.

e) Brereton's line, visible immediately west of the steps, may have been a gate or doorway, a candidate for what the 1626 inventory records (26.1518) as a locked door to the back yard between the moat and the kitchen, suggesting this yard.

f) The kitchen, whose eastern wall extends to the edge of the site. This feature is one of three examples (see g and i below) which make an uninterrupted circuit of the building impossible.

g) This is one of three points (see also (f) and (i)) at which the 1720 structure extends to the edge of the platform. It is likely that the range includes the bakehouse, which has a lockable door (26.1254).

h) The sheltered nature of this yard makes it a candidate for what is mentioned in 26.503: 'one lock & kye unto the doore gooinge into the Apricocke yarde'. (See (i) below for speculation about the door.) Apricots would have flourished in the shelter of angles evident here, soaking up warmth not only from the sun as it moved into the west, but potentially also from heat released through the chimney flues suggested in Brereton's sketch.

i) A third point at which parts of the structure extend to the edge of the platform, the projection shown here is a candidate for what is described in the 1626 inventory as 'In the enterie betwene the corner chamber & Nunns chamber', from which the door gives access to the apricot yard (h). The projection effectively divides service buildings and staff accommodation to its north, and principal family accommodation to its south.

j) Brereton suggests a doorway at (j), not readily identifiable in the 1626 inventory, but which suggests the site of the 'enterie' described in the 1597 inventory (97.601–603) and the room described immediately before it (97.598–600) as 'the chamber going into the garden'.

k) The 1626 inventory refers to 'the long walke betwene the garden and the moate' (26.1524–1525), represented by (k) and then lists the contents of the garden itself (26.1526–1535). The long walk is recognisable now as the grass causeway separating the west moat from the separately moated gardens to the west.

l) The inner courtyard, access to which is via the south bridge, described below. Brereton's pair of dotted lines indicates the route from the gatehouse and across the courtyard to the main entrance to the house (marked now by an entrance porch, visible in Plate 11).

m) Drawbridge over the moat, commanding the main entrance to Helmingham Hall from the south. Brereton's 1720 sketch suggests a cobbled surface and the arched masonry structure of the bridge. Security of the inner courtyard (l) is confirmed in the 1626 inventory by references to a lock from the wall to the gate (26.1511) and by the separately lockable wicket gate within the main gate (26.1513).

Perambulation of the 1708 household inventory

There is a gap of eighty-two years until the next inventory, by which time the house is the country residence of the 3rd Earl of Dysart. The approach to listing and describing the contents of rooms in 1708 marks a distinct departure from the style of the two earlier inventories. Individual descriptions are used infrequently in favour of grouping rooms together. The advantage of this is that the layout can be interpreted with more confidence than before; the disadvantage is that contents are listed continuously, making it impossible in some cases to determine which room they occupy. Unlike the two earlier inventories, however, there is unequivocal confirmation of the two main floor levels as well as areas that are separate from the main house. Plate 15 illustrates identifiable ground-floor rooms and, as before, is based on Brereton's 1720 drawing, which was made only twelve years after this inventory was compiled. The decorative feature visible in the yard north of the house is a box garden, described as the 'box court', the plants forming a pattern combining an earl's coronet with elements of the Tollemache family fret. Firm evidence for this dates from 1758,[14] but its presence on Brereton's 1720 plan confirms that the plan for the topiary was laid out, if not already planted, almost forty years earlier.

In the 1708 household inventory no space is described as new, although many of the rooms recognisable from the 1626 inventory are put to new uses. The interlude of more than eighty years, coloured by an interregnum and the Restoration, results in subtle changes of emphasis: 'the hall' has become 'the great hall'; and any room previously related to use by 'husbandmen' refers to 'servants', as if to acknowledge the emergence of Helmingham in its new role as the principal rural seat of the earls of Dysart. There is a business-like tone to the inventory, and the record is almost devoid of staff roles or their personal names. The 1708 house sounds to be managed for occasional visits rather than occupied on a regular basis. The household steward is now the 'housekeeper'; and some rooms on the first floor are numbered, almost in the manner of a hotel. The inventory lacks anecdotal comments except where facts need to be stated for the record, such as a momentary lapse leading to the omission of some pieces of linen and their retrospective insertion, and confirmation that some trunks and all of the wardrobes were locked up and inaccessible to the compiler, who, unlike the 1626 compiler, made no return visit to complete the record.

The Helmingham Hall household of 1708 seems to be comparatively inactive. Notable absences include the stilling yard of 1597 and 1626. There are some 'stilled waters' in one of the cellars and a 'pewter still' listed in the kitchen, but no evidence of the 'six stills and their furnace' described in 1626. Apart from the hens and horses, animals and birds are now conspicuous by their absence: there is no hint of the hawks and doves, spaniels and pheasants, peewits and pigs housed in 1626. This may reflect a selective record, more limited even than that of 1597; but in all probability the significant resources once raised, reared and processed on site, necessary to support a large residential staff as well as the family, are no longer required. In addition, the capacity to buy services is greater than before and more appropriate for a house that is not occupied on a full-time basis. The inventory headings and route are adopted below. Identifiable features are noted on Plate 15 by the prefix G or ?G where the location is speculative. As before, no attempt has been made to locate first-floor rooms on this plan. The inventory indicates floor levels unequivocally, beginning with a heading of 'First story' (ground floor).

kitchen (G1); scullery, pastry, bakehouse and bolting room (?G1a)

The 1708 inventory is the only one of the four to commence perambulation at the kitchen. Its description of the four associated spaces suggests that all were located in close proximity and sited as suggested in 1626, west of the kitchen but not necessarily attached to it.

servants hall, store closet and passage (G2)

The passage suggests a location close to the main service artery running east–west behind the great hall (G3, discussed below) and, speculatively, at or near its east end.

great hall and staircase (G3)

The 1708 inventory is the first to describe this room as the great hall (previously described as the hall in 1597 and 1626), and to associate the staircase with it.

---

[14] T/Hel/9/5/12. An account paid to Sanders, a local carpenter, for replacing locks and undertaking repairs in the 'long pasheg [passage] leading to the box coourte' in 1758.

housekeeper's storecupboard (?G4)

The designation of housekeeper is unique to the 1708 inventory. Previously, the person with similar overall responsibility was known as the household steward. A location for the housekeeper's store is suggested close to the great hall and parlour, the latter now taking on the role of dining chamber (see below).

parlour, drawing room and two rooms over against them, etc. (G5)

Although the dining chamber remains on the first floor, the drawing room identifies a ground-floor room to which diners might withdraw, and 1708 marks its first appearance in the household inventories. The phrase 'two rooms over against them, &c.' confirms that the west range is two rooms deep. Speculatively, the parlour and drawing room face west across the moat and towards the gardens, whilst smaller rooms beside them (described as closets in the 1626 inventory) face east into the inner courtyard. The function of these east-facing rooms is confirmed by their 1708 contents, which include a looking-glass and a close stool (a portable lavatory).

A notable feature of the 1708 inventory is that, unlike its predecessors, it makes no mention of the gatehouse or a porter's lodge on the ground floor, suggesting that the role was no longer necessary, or at least not on a permanent basis. In 1741 an equivalent emerges as the 'footman's room next the courtyard'. The lack of a space denoting the gateway at ground-floor level makes other locations questionable, particularly those mentioned next.

the three rooms beyond the drawing room (?G6)

In the 1708 inventory the contents of these otherwise undistinguished spaces suggest that the rooms are used for the storage of lumber. The inventory is devoid of personal names, with the exception of Mr Bokenham, whose room is described next.

the room where Mr Bokenham lay (G7)[15]

in the next room and clossetts (G8)

There is nothing in the contents of these spaces to distinguish them except their proximity to the next room, described as next the brewhouse. They are assumed to lie east of the gatehouse.

room next the brewhouse (G9)

As in 1597 and 1626, there is clear evidence that the south range and the brewhouse are adjacent to one another.

brewhouse (G10)

The discrete heading for the 1708 brewhouse suggests that, like its predecessors in 1597 and 1626, it occupied a large part of the east range.

henhouse (site uncertain)

Despite uncertainty about the site of the 1708 henhouse, which may lie east of the moat, it seems likely that the compiler returns to the main site via the east bridge to visit the service spaces on the south side of the box garden.

laundry, cheesehouse, dairy and larder (?G1b)

The conjunction of these areas suggests that they occupied the positions identified for 1626.

---

[15] See footnote 25 to the 1708 inventory.

pantries (?G11)

In 1626 pantry was a new designation and two of them occupied space adjoining what was then the storehouse adjoining the hall. It seems logical that they occupied the same space in 1708 because their description concludes the ground-floor record and effectively brings the compiler back to a point close to the kitchen which was his starting point.

Second storey, i.e., first floor

The perambulation of first-floor rooms begins at the room sited centrally in the south range, and proceeds west. No attempt has been made to mark these on Plate 15 but some locations can be deduced where they mention rooms on the floor beneath.

Gatehouse Chamber

Black Velvet room and closets

Chamber over the room where Mr Bokenham lay (Plate 15, G7)

Red Chamber and closets

Chamber and closets over the drawing room. (G5 is suggested as the ground-floor location of the drawing room.)

The next two descriptions suggest the most important rooms in the west range, located towards its northern end, where a staircase rose from the ground floor at the complex junction of reception, service and communication areas.

dining room

Despite its designation, there appears to be no dining table in this room, which is equipped with gaming tables and chairs. The inventory shows no evidence of a fireplace. By 1741 there is no designated dining room and it is possible that the dining room of 1597 and 1626 was already in transition in 1708, particularly bearing in mind the next space to be described.

apartment my Lord lodges in

Given the comments above, the conjunction of this and the dining room suggests that they form a suite dedicated to the needs of the earl, his apartment being equipped with a bed, chairs, dressing and writing tables.

The complexity of the first-floor route is evident, as in earlier inventories, but confirmed for the first time with the mention of passages twice in the list below. A warren of first-floor rooms and communication areas emerges, as does confirmation that both the kitchen and the great hall had useable spaces above them.

passages

chambers the young ladies lay in and closets, etc.

candle chamber

chamber over the kitchen (The kitchen is G1 on Plate 15)

passages and drying room, etc.

chamber over the laundry

chamber over the dairy

passages over the pantries and chest there

rooms over the brewhouse (Plate 15, G10), woodroom, etc.

mens garrett and wardrobe over the hall, etc., the other wardrobes being locked up

There is no mention of an armoury in the 1708 inventory, although it reappears in the 1741 record. Presumably, it was inaccessible within the area described as 'the other wardrobes'. The description does, however, suggest that there was useable space above the great hall at this date. A gabled dormer window (Plate 17, K) protrudes from the visible roof over the range containing the great hall and the rooms to its east.

The next two headings are clearly separated from the 'second story' rooms, and indeed from each other in the original document, confirming that each area was accessed independently of the main house:

cellars

This is presumed to be located as suggested in 1626, with internal access near the great hall and external access from the box court.

clockhouse and rooms about it

This is confirmation of the speculative view offered by 1626 of a separately accessed clock tower, but its location remains uncertain.

The final three headings are clearly separated and almost certainly refer to the outbuildings lying east of the moat, on the site suggested by M, N and O in Plate 17.

Nothing in the millhouse except the mill, etc.

In the stables and over them

In the yards, coach house, etc

Perambulation of the 1741 inventory

Locations for ground-floor rooms discussed below are suggested on Plate 16. Thomas Brereton's sketch, which forms the basis for this plate, was made only twenty years before the date of the inventory. In addition, and for the first time in the 150-year span of the four inventories, contemporary evidence exists to illustrate an external view of the house as it was described in 1741. This, reproduced in Plate 17, is an extract from a larger sketch from the south-east, presented as the frontispiece to this volume. The drawing is undated and unattributed, but shows enough detail to enable it to be dated after 1741 and before 1783.[16] Although the 4th Earl of Dysart was actively occupied in repairing, maintaining and improving the house until at least 1766, there is no reliable evidence to confirm that its appearance was changed fundamentally until after his death in 1770.[17] Plate 17 represents one of the last views of the house described in the inventories, showing Helmingham Hall before its radical alteration in the eighteenth and nineteenth centuries and its trans-

---

[16]   See caption to frontispiece.
[17]   The evidence offered by prints on display at Helmingham Hall (private collection) is inconclusive, not only because of the wide date range but also because captions are incorrectly attributed to the elevations shown. 'West front of Helmingham Hall, 1760–1800' clearly shows the north front, with the east bridge in view. 'North front of Helmingham Hall, 1760–1800' is unquestionably a depiction of the east front, with the kitchen block visible to the right of view, detached from the rest of the building. Similarly, 'East front of Helmingham Hall, 1760–1800' is the south front, recognisable by its central two-storey bay containing the gatehouse and chamber above.

formation into the building seen today. Plate 17 is accompanied by an explanatory key (A–O) for ease of reference in the commentary below and to distinguish it from features identified in Plate 16.

The 1741 inventory provides evidence of a change of use in the east and south ranges of Helmingham Hall and consequent modification to the service buildings extending west of the kitchen on the north of the site. The east range, previously housing the brewhouse with staff accommodation above, has been modified since 1708 to form part of a suite of rooms for the personal use of the 4th Earl of Dysart. This is the 1741 inventory compiler's starting point. The use of 'new' is more frequent in this inventory than in any other, and there is evidence from the 4th earl's account book for 1729–1755 to suggest that modest works of modification at Helmingham began as early as 1729, the year after he inherited the title from his grandfather: extracts from the accounts are incorporated below where they provide evidence of payment for new work. However, as the introduction has shown, the 4th earl was, in 1741, concerned with financing the debts that continued to arise from his late father's affairs. As a consequence, his more significant works at Helmingham did not begin until after the date of this inventory, but what can be recognised here are the early stages of a systematic approach to modifying and improving the house.

Ground floor (headings refer to Plate 16)

My Lord's dressing room (G1)

Evidence discussed below suggests a site close to the south-east corner of the house. The projecting bay marked as C on Plate 17 is sited off-centre and, speculatively, this marks the point of access for the earl's private suite of rooms running south from the bay.

library and closet, exclusive of books (G2)

With the dressing room, these formed a private suite for the 4th earl, combining the functions of a dressing room with those of a study and library. Their suggested site, on the south-east corner of the house, is based on the survival of features identified by Arthur Oswald as possibly part of the 4th earl's original library, based on the fact that the room is handsomely appointed with columns whose function was to create bays for bookcases.[18] The 1741 inventory description of the room 'exclusive of books', notes six 'brass-cased locks' (41.60), some of which may have been fitted to the bookcases as well as the doors to the room and its closets. The 1708 inventory confirmed that part of the east range was occupied by the brewhouse (as it had been since 1597). Work on re-siting the brewhouse (see below) can be dated confidently to 1729/30 and, similarly, an account paid on 9 March 1729 reveals that the £21 16s. paid was the balance of a bill amounting to £65 10s. due to the widow of the late Robert Lay for joiner's work. This is a significant sum, perhaps sufficient to cover the cost of building the framework of the bookcases in the newly created library. Larger still was Henry Cheere's bill for 'three chimney pieces set up at Helmingham', in the sum of £136 19s. paid on 2 May 1739.[19]

---

[18] Oswald, Country Life, 16 August 1956. As part of the far-reaching construction of parts of the house in the nineteenth century, the library was removed to the south-west corner of the house. On Plate 10, the 1950s plan, which was modified by Oswald to illustrate his articles, this area is described as the boudoir.

[19] BPA volume 926. Equivalent to more than £12,000 in 2005, according to TNA currency converter estimate. Elegant marble chimney pieces survive in the rooms identified here.

gateway room (G3)

On the assumption that the compiler is moving clockwise through the ground floor from the south-east corner, this room is immediately east of the gatehouse. It is not until later in the inventory that a 'footman's room next the courtyard' is identified, a role and space that sound to be replacements for the porter's lodge.

Courtoy's room (G4)

Based on the premise above, this room, which has a fireplace, lies west of the gatehouse.

Tallemache's room (G5)

Richard Tollemache, the 4th earl's estate steward.[20] This room also has a fireplace. It may not have interconnected with the long drawing room, described next.

Plate 17 shows a projecting bay at each end of the south range (indicated by E and I), embellished with crow-stepped gables and finials at roof level. From the 1741 inventory, it is unclear whether or not the next room extends into the bay visible on the west (I).

long drawing room (G6)

The description of this room as 'long' suggests that it extended to the extreme south of the west range and into the ground-floor bay (I) visible on Plate 17; and its three pairs of window curtains support this (41.93). Plate 10, the 1950s ground-floor plan, indicates a change of level at the junction of the south and west wings (shown with steps annotated 'Down' into the bay of the library). These steps were, presumably, inserted as part of the nineteenth-century alterations when an internal wall was removed between the two wings to create the L-shaped library.

little stucco room (G7)

Suggestive of ornamental plasterwork, and, despite the designation of 'little', this room was probably once much larger until robbed of space to create the passage and new staircase described below. It is noticeable from Plate 10 how the fireplace dominates the room (described on the 1950s plan as the 'Lute Room') – more evidence that the room it served was once much larger.

The 1741 inventory confirms that there are two separate staircases in the west range. The 'new' is in addition to the great staircase (which was mentioned in 1626 and 1708). The proximity of the two staircases suggests an improvement to first-floor communications, perhaps reducing the number of interconnecting rooms.

passage and new staircase (?G8)

The passage was generous, capable of holding two tables, one large and one small, and two arm chairs (41.115–121). Its situation next to the old drawing room (see below) suggests a rearrangement of space to accommodate the new staircase. As suggested above, the 'little stucco room' may have become 'little' when it lost space for insertion of the passage and new staircase, described by Arthur Oswald as the 'Georgian' staircase and attributed by him to the 4th earl.[21] See footnote 11 to the 1741 transcription regarding payments made to Joshua Kirby for painting 'three

---

[20] See footnote 9 to the 1741 inventory.
[21] Oswald, *Country Life*, 16 August 1956.

new rooms and a staircase'. These rooms emerge below as a new room next to the pantry, the new billiard room and the new square room next to the nursery.

old drawing room next the parlour (?G9–13)

The 'old' drawing room has been superseded by the long drawing room but may still have functioned as a withdrawing room, since the adjoining parlour functions as a dining room in 1741 (see below).

parlour (?G9–13)

For the first time in the inventories, no room is designated as a dining room but this parlour is equipped for at least twelve diners, who could withdraw to the 'old' drawing room next to it. Accounts raised between 1729 and 1731 by a London upholsterer, Henry Heasman, some of which relate to Ham, refer to an 'Eating Parlour' at Helmingham (BPA Volume 925), confirming that the old dining room had been superseded soon after the 4th earl's accession to the title.

great staircase, upper and lower landings with passage next the parlour (?G9–13)

This staircase was identifiable in the 1626 and 1708 inventories, when it led to the first-floor dining room. The 1741 description, which lists the contents of all four areas (41.148–159), mentions tables, chairs and a large collection of pictures and maps.

The ground-floor perambulation describes two further rooms before turning east to describe the great hall. Of these, the 'second' room is fully equipped as a bed chamber.

first room next the parlour (?G9–13)

second room next the parlour (?G9–13)

great hall (G14)

The presence of '48 leather buckets' (41.188) in the great hall is a reminder of the ever-present risk of fire damage in a house heated by open fireplaces. Changes in layout emerge in the area between the great hall and the kitchen.

butler's pantry (?G15)

new room next the pantry (?G16)

Butler's pantry is a designation unique to this inventory. It and the new room may result from further changes to the room described in 1708 as the housekeeper's store cupboard. The work to create this new room may have been undertaken as early as 1729–30 in parallel with other changes discussed below (see brewhouse).

kitchen (G17)

Throughout the span of the inventories, the location of the kitchen is presumed to be unchanged (and the kitchen occupies the same area of the site today).

A number of the service buildings listed in 1708 are not mentioned in 1741, notably the scullery and pastry. One or both of these may been converted or demolished to accommodate the brewhouse. Sites are suggested cautiously on Plate 16, prefixed by (?G).

servants hall (?G18)

flour room, bakehouse (?G19/20/21)

brewhouse (?G19/20/21)

The brewhouse no longer occupies the position identified for it in 1597, 1626 and 1708 but appears now to be sited west of the kitchen with other service buildings. The brewing equipment was upgraded in March and April 1730, a decade before this inventory was compiled. Payments recorded in BPA Volume 926 include an account dated 18 March 1729 [1730] for £9 17s. 6d. paid to William Bedwell for 'three coolers and an underbeck'. On the same date James Clark received £7 9s. 0d. for himself and labourers for unspecified work and 'helping to brew'. On 29 April 1730 there is payment of £30 for 'a large guile fatt, mesh-ffat, wilsh & rudder', all significant items of brewing equipment and large enough to suggest a fundamental upgrade.[22] Working back from those dates, there is a noticeable group of payments related to building work: 17 December 1729, for lime (£17 10s. 6d), and on the same date to John Pettit for carpenters' work £46 8s. 0d.[23] These are followed by payments on 12 January 1730 for bricks and tiles (£12 19s. 0d.) and on 13 January to John Jones, 'painter' (£1 5s. 0d.).

The rooms that follow are thought to be part of the range of service buildings west of the kitchen suggested by ?G19/20/21.

backhouse and next the dairy

dairy

steward's room

dry larder

wet larder

The ground-floor perambulation ends with the cellars, not marked on Plate 16 but presumably accessible, as before, internally and externally from the box court.

small beer and ale cellar

old beer and wine cellar

First floor

On the basis that the perambulation follows the route adopted by the compiler for the ground-floor rooms, then the first rooms to be described are in the east range, presumed to begin above G1, but no attempt has been made to plot them on Plate 16.

Lady's dressing room

Lord & Lady's bedchamber

back stairs and gallery

As suggested earlier in this commentary, the east and south wings are now interconnecting. The back stairs suggest the small staircase marked as '?bs' on Plate 10, the

---

22 TNA currency converter, valid to 2005, suggests an equivalent of almost £2600.

23 TNA currency converter, valid to 2005, suggests an equivalent close to £4000. This may have covered not only the framing required to accommodate a new brewhouse but possibly also the creation of the 'new room' next to the butler's pantry and, indeed, changes needed to create the new suite of rooms for the earl, part of which originally housed the brewhouse. The payments mentioned here are all recorded in BPA Volume 926, described as 'Receipt book of the Earl of Dysart recording payments for personal, household and estate expenses at Helmingham, Ham, Charing Cross and Harrington, 1729–55'.

1950s plan, which rises from the ground floor of the east range and gives access also to rooms in the south range. The 1741 perambulation supports this, describing next the 'long gallery' with five rooms leading off it.

long gallery

Presumed to be the in the south range. The 1741 inventory is the only one that fails to designate a 'gatehouse chamber', describing five rooms only with numbers.

1st, 2nd, 3rd, 4th and 5th rooms in gallery

On the assumption that the five rooms in the gallery occupied the whole of the south range, then the next room, described as the new billiard room, was sited above the long drawing room (Plate 16, G6).[24] Players would have needed room to move around the table, which makes this long room an ideal location. It seems from the inventory that the new billiard room was not yet in use because the table (41.512) was still in the old billiard room (located a few rooms beyond) and the 'sticks &c.' (noted at 41.512) were to be found next to that in the 'closet adjoyning to the red room'.

new billiard room

little room hanged with red paper

The compiler records the clock room next; but its location is no easier to identify than it was in the earlier inventories. Its use now is mixed: 'in the closet 1 eight-day turret clock with a bell & stone dial plate' (41.498), but otherwise the room is a repository for glass and china, including '83 wine and beer glasses' (41.487) and '127 china plates' (41.492). Given that there is no first-floor dining chamber in 1741 (indeed, no designated dining chamber), the presence of these items on the first floor suggests that they were rarely used.

clock room

red room

old billiard room

From the next description it is unclear whether the staircase mentioned here rises from the 'new' staircase or the 'great' staircase, both mentioned on the ground floor of the west range.

chamber next the staircase

further chamber

new square room next the nursery

nursery

left hand of nursery

right hand of nursery

Sites for the following mention the location of their ground-floor equivalents, suggested above.

---

[24] The glossary entry for **billiards** describes the eighteenth-century game.

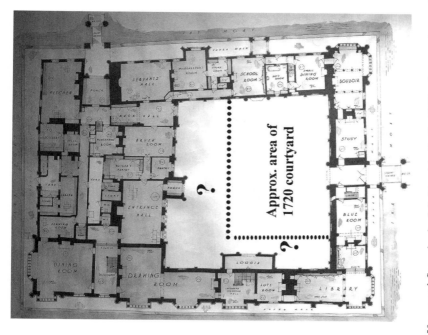

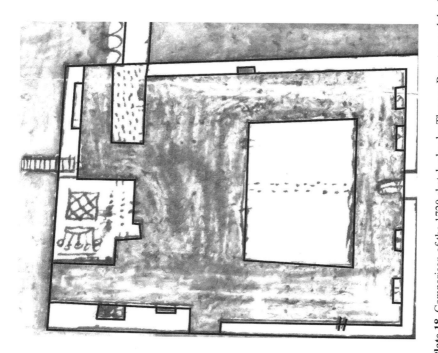

Plate 18. Comparison of the 1720 sketch plan by Thomas Brereton and the 1950s ground-floor plan by J.C. Dennish. On the 1950s plan question marks draw attention to areas which were apparently filled with structures on the Brereton plan; and the approximate area of the 1720 courtyard is indicated. Based on documents in the Helmingham Archive, T/Hel/1/64, T/Hel(S)/28/1, 2, and reproduced by kind permission of the Lord Tollemache

chamber over the backhouse:

chamber over the Steward's Room

Sites for all of the remaining rooms are uncertain, and the first may lie outside the moat.

gard[e]ner's chamber

laundry

The contents of the laundry include an iron grate but there is no evidence for a copper or any other means of heating water (41.589–596). The 1741 laundry sounds to be the equivalent of the drying room recorded in each of the three previous inventories, equipped for ironing, finishing and storage of linen, in which case its 1741 location may be on the first floor. Facilities for wet laundry are mentioned nowhere in this inventory, which may mean either that they were housed with other unrecorded services east of the moat, or that laundry was carried out elsewhere in the village and returned to the hall only for finishing.

Locations for the next two rooms are unidentifiable: logically, the first suggests the porter's lodge; but if that is the case, then it and the room described only as 'next the moat' (there is nothing to identify which of its four sides is described here) may be inaccessible from within the house. Both rooms are equipped with beds.

footman's room next the court yard

next the moat

As in 1597, the stable chamber is mentioned but not the stable. Its 1741 location is assumed to be east of the moat.

stable chamber

For the first time, there is no mention of wardrobes but the armoury and chamber next to it, which in previous inventories were described with the wardrobes, are presumed to remain in situ in the roof space over the south range.

armoury

chamber next the armoury

coach house, &c.

With the exception of the stable chamber, mentioned above, the phrase 'coach house &c' is the only suggestion of buildings located east of the moat.

Conclusion

Cumulative evidence from the four inventories confirms that, in spite of the natural limitations imposed by its moat, Helmingham Hall succeeded in accommodating the changing needs of its resident family over 150 years. The 1720 Brereton sketch plan and the 1950 Dennish ground-floor plan, presented together in Plate 18, show that the greatest area of change in the 230 years that separates them is evident on the north part of the site. This is unsurprising, since this area offered the only capacity for expansion, a process which began in 1597 and gathered pace as demand diminished for the wide range of household offices associated with the sixteenth-century house, in favour of a broader range of residential accommodation. Over time, the building developed almost to the full extent of the site on the north, and only a sliver of the original open courtyard survives (Plate 10, X).

A question that remains largely unanswered by the inventories relates to the central courtyard area as drawn by Brereton in 1720. By his own admission he did not measure the hall because his inclusion of the house in his sketch was secondary to the main purpose of his letter, which was to propose a new planting scheme for the park to the north. However, despite his caveat, numerous features of the house and its site mentioned in the inventories are identifiable from his plan. Even if his plan was unmeasured, it nonetheless illustrated details of yards, access routes, obvious projections from the main structure, as well as some window openings and external doors. Close inspection reveals also a series of dotted lines visible beneath the swirling wash of ink that Brereton used in his sketch to distinguish the main body of the house. These lines suggest the direction in which supporting timbers were laid. Plate 18 emphasises the accuracy of Brereton's sketch in his representation of the line taken by the east range, which runs parallel to the moat and, as a consequence, was not built in a straight line but at an angle, the same feature visible on the Dennish plan.

However, an obvious discrepancy between the two drawings is the area occupied by the courtyard. Given his attention to detail elsewhere, and despite his own note of caution, it seems unlikely that Brereton would have made such an error of judgement in representing what was one of the most prominent features of the site. His sketch suggests a courtyard half the size of that shown on the 1950s plan, largely because his depiction of the main body of the house north of the courtyard, and of the west range, shows both to be almost twice the depth of the same areas indicated by Dennish. A comment in the 1708 inventory offers a small piece of evidence to support a broader west range, describing rooms on the ground floor as 'parlour, drawing room & two rooms over against them, &c.', suggesting a width at that date sufficient to accommodate rooms side by side, some facing west and some facing east into the courtyard. All four inventories confirm the complexity of the building and the number of functions it had to accommodate, many of them housed in the deep area between the kitchen and the courtyard. If Brereton's plan is reliable in other respects, then it is feasible that his depiction of the 1720 courtyard is correct, suggesting that large parts of the structure on its north and west sides have been lost, whether as a result of fire damage or as a consequence of the structural remodelling undertaken in the late eighteenth and nineteenth centuries. The dotted lines and question marks superimposed on the Dennish plan surround the approximate area of the 1720 courtyard. Together, the four household inventories and Brereton's 1720 plan have made the bones of Helmingham Hall recognisable; but the extent of the 1720 structure is one of many intriguing questions about Helmingham Hall that remain to be answered.

APPENDIX B

The Tollemache family at Fakenham Magna, *c.* 1622–1665

The decision to add the material presented here was prompted by frequent mentions throughout the 1626 household inventory for Helmingham Hall of 'Fakenham', the family's shorthand for the property known as Lugdons (or Lagdownes) in the parish of Fakenham Magna, Suffolk. As outlined in the introduction, numerous Tollemache children were born, some of them buried and others married at Fakenham Magna, rather than at Helmingham (or Ham House), which suggests a commitment to, and affection for, Fakenham that warranted recognition. Accordingly, the material selected for this appendix aims to show the extent to which the Tollemaches of Helmingham and Ham were, simultaneously, the Tollemaches of Fakenham Magna from 1622 until approximately 1665. Two generations of the family are represented by these records: Sir Lionel Tollemache, 2nd baronet, who died in 1640; and his son, also Lionel, 3rd baronet and subsequently 2nd Earl of Dysart, who died in 1669.[1] The materials, presented under seven headings, conclude with comments on the circumstances surrounding the end of the Tollemache family's association with Fakenham, and reflections on its forty-year duration.

1. Survey documents of Fakenham Magna from the Helmingham Archive (1622– 1626)[2]

Fakenham Magna[3] is represented in the Helmingham archive by a collection of written surveys and plans dating from 1622 to 1626; all are filed together and the collection shares a common reference.[4] The largest survey document describes a perambulation which commences at the south end of the village near the church and proceeds northwards along the highway. Despite significant landscape changes resulting from development of the Euston estate after 1666, some features of Fakenham, as described in these seventeenth-century survey documents, are recognisable today. The highway running north–south through the village is now the A1088 between Thetford, four miles to the north, and Ixworth, two miles to the south. For the whole of its length, and in its elongated 'S' shape, the village street

1   T/Hel/1/15: The 2nd earl died in Paris on 15 January 1668 [1669]. His son-in-law, Lord Allington, who was with him at the time, wrote a letter of condolence to the Countess of Dysart on 19 January.
2   T/Hel/24/6.
3   'Fakenham' hereafter. In 1639, Charles II granted the union of the churches and livings of Euston and Fakenham Parva, on the other side of the valley from Fakenham Magna, to the Earl of Arlington. (http://www.british-history.ac.uk/cal-state-papers/domestic/chas2/1668–9/pp258–305).
4   T/Hel/24/6.

follows a course parallel with the river lying to its east, the Black Bourn, a tributary of the Little Ouse. South of the church, where road and river each form a curving bend, the Bourn brook is crossed by a secondary road diverting from the A1088 and leading south-east towards Bardwell. Land lying west of the village street, identified as common land in the survey documents, has been exploited for numerous purposes since the seventeenth century, including development of the airfield that now distinguishes RAF Honington to the south-west.

The contrasts between the landscapes at Helmingham and Fakenham are illuminated by the surveys, which describe multiple occupation of the large expanse of heath land which dominated the parish of Fakenham. The heath was worked in small strips, many of them described as 'wents'. This prominent feature, together with areas of fen and the proximity of Lugdons to the river (see Plate 19), shows Fakenham to be fundamentally different from the timber-rich clay lands around Helmingham, much of which were held by the Tollemache family and let to tenants.[5] There are sharp contrasts, too, between the houses: Plate 20, an enlarged detail from the documents, shows the brick-built house to be substantial but small in comparison with Helmingham Hall. Similarly, Plate 19 shows the whole site of Lugdons to amount to no more than an acre, its narrow plot bordered by the river at the rear and the village street at the front. A commentary follows each group of extracts to summarise what the surveys and plans have revealed about Sir Lionel Tollemache's holdings.

Extract from survey of 1622

Fakenham Magna: A survey of the whole towne beginning at the scite of the mannour. A furlong lying at ffakenham Church on the north of the said church and abutting upon the river towards the East and upon the high way leading from Ixworth to Thetford towards the west. Begin next the church and goe northward.

Thos. Rushbrook: The scite of the mannour fairly built with iij barnes and one stable, a backhouse, with orchards, gardens, hemplands lieth on the north of the Church and abutteth on the [*illeg.*] a high way towards the west and containeth iiij acres.[6]

Holofernes Cooke:[7]

---

5   There is no evidence that the acquisition of Fakenham was prompted by its potential for tenancies, although this might have been a long-term strategy in the mind of the 2nd baronet. The rental records of his successor, the 2nd Earl of Dysart, in the Helmingham archive (T/Hel/25/7) show receipts in 1647 of between £45 and £50, rising in 1649 by £20, £10 on account of 'my honourable Mother, for my Mansion House called Lagdownes, with the yards, Gardens and orchard thereunto belonging', and £10 from other small pieces of land on which his mother was paying rent. From 1651, the rental income is confined to payments from his mother, and after 1654 there is no further income from the Fakenham lands.

6   This confirms the site of Thomas Rushbrook's manor, later known as Fakenham Hall. Remnants of the manor's gate piers, including some Tudor brickwork, are visible by the Thetford–Ixworth road near the church.

7   Holofernes Cooke, who died in 1647, is described as 'gentleman' of Eriswell in his will (Suffolk probate index (Sudbury), R2/59/445; W1/104/75). His name appears also on a list of Suffolk lawyers active in 1607 in taking work from the Court of Common Pleas. (Accessed online at: aalt.law. uh.edu/Attorneys/attpages/FullAttorneyList1607.html). Eriswell is located close to the Suffolk and Cambridgeshire border, and lies some thirteen miles north-west of Fakenham, confirming that Cooke's land-holdings were dispersed. The jurisdiction of the Court of Common Pleas was confined to civil cases between subject and subject, and Cooke's knowledge of land opportunities was doubtless widened as a result.

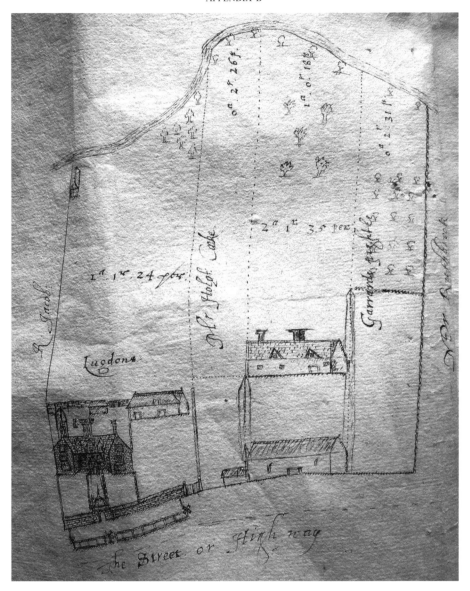

Plate 19. Plan of 'Lugdons' at Fakenham Magna, showing the proximity of the house to the river, bordering its land at the rear, and the 'street or highway', at the front. Helmingham Archive, T/Hel/24/6, reproduced by kind permission of the Lord Tollemache

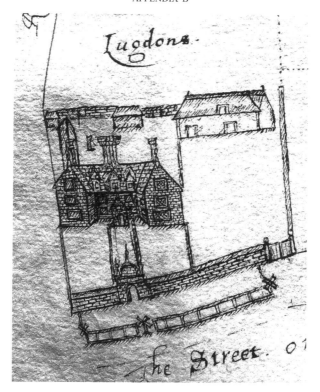

Plate 20. Enlarged detail from plan (see plate 19) of 'Lugdons' at Fakenham Magna, 1622, to accompany discussion in Appendix B. The gated entry into an outer courtyard from 'The Street' and the ornamental brick wall and gateways between it and the house are clearly visible, as are the ranges of outbuildings and water pump in the rear yard. Helmingham Archive, T/Hel/24/6, reproduced by kind permission of the Lord Tollemache

Holofernes Cooke rent late Thomas Doe[8] held by coppie of Court Rolle one pightell called Garrards next on the north and it abbutteth upon the foresaid way towards the west and upon the river towards the east and containeth j acre.

The same holdeth further one messuage with a garden to the same [pertain]ing and abbutteth with the last pightell and containeth j acre [*illeg.*]

The same holdeth lands and tenement builded with a stable thereto [north abutting at the last and containing iii roods].

Sir Lionell Tallemache knight & Baronett holdeth by coppie one tenement called Lugdons together with the close adjoyning of late Archinwald Martine[9] lying [*illeg.*] north and abutteth with the last tenement and containeth 1 acre.[10]

---

8   The surname recurs in the Suffolk probate index (Sudbury), particularly in the villages surrounding Fakenham, although there is no Thomas listed.
9   Archinwald Marten, Honington, 1639, A5/4/74, Suffolk probate index (Sudbury).
10 The area noted on the plan (Plate 19) is shown as 1a. 1r. 24 perches.

Richard Jacob: Jacob hath next in his occupacion a tenement called Matthews with the croft adjoining late Edward Rookwood and it abbutteth with the last tenement and containeth iij acres.

In summary, the survey extracts above confirm that Lugdons (or Lagdownes), the property occupied by Sir Lionel, was a bond tenement, held by copyhold, lying north of Thomas Rushbrook's manor house, from which it was separated by three other plots.

Extract from survey dated 1622

The lands sometimes Calabors, of late Ballards, now Sir Lionell Tallemache Knight and Baronet, truly bounded and measured Anno Domini 1622.

The messuage together with the yards, pightles, gardens, orchards thereto belonging, lying between the common river on the SE, the highway on the NW, the one end abutting upon the horse pool and the other upon the Great or high way and contains together with the small piece of meadow on the South side of the river. The whole amounts to ij a. ij r. xxvii p. viij dec.[11]

The features described in the above extract are illustrated on a sketch plan, reproduced as Plate 21. This has been annotated to identify features including those mentioned above.

Additional notes to the survey file confirm that further acquisitions were made in 1624, the first headed 'Landes purchased of Mr Rouse[12], Anno domini 1624, late Archinwalde Martin'. Eight small sketches are added to the text, each a small rectangle with little else to distinguish or identify them except for two, one of which is noted as abutting 'The Heath', and the other is described as being 'Calves Pightle', larger than the rest, located in the neighbouring parish of Sapiston, where it is bordered on its east by 'the way to Bardwell'. A note of the total records that the eight plots purchased of Mr Rouse in 1624 amounted to '16 acres 2 roods 33 perches 7 dec' (7 dec is 7/10ths of a perch). The next entry records 'More landes purchased of Mr Rowse Anno Dom: 1624', described as:

Lugdons Crofte wherein standeth the new barne lyeth between the landes of the rectorie of Ffakenham on the south of Mr Holofernes Cooke towards the north and abutteth upon the lands of John Barnes west, and the common street towards the east, containeth by measure: 1 a. 2 r. 30p. 7d.

Neither the description nor the extent can be recognised from the detail visible on Plate 19. Further small plots are described in a continuous text, some illustrated with small sketches barely occupying the space of a line or two of writing, but many of the sketches are unidentifiable because not all plots are named, only measured. However, several of them abut the heath, where their names are suggestive of the narrow strips associated with common land, including 'Langland went', 'Infeild went', 'Northfeild, the upper wente', 'Northfeild, the nether went', 'Overwhart went', 'Clipston went' and 'Outshifts'.

A note declares that 'The contents of the severalls compryhended in these 5 former leaves is 80 ac. 2 r. 38 perches', but addition of all the plots of land (including Lugdons) recorded in the surveys suggests that between 1622 and 1624 Sir Lionel's

---

11 The plan (Plate 21) does not indicate acreages; but 'dec' (and 'd') is used throughout the five surveys to indicate tenths of a perch.

12 Suffolk probate index (Sudbury) records a Thomas Rouse, clerk, at Ingham, 1684: A5/5131, A4/9/42.

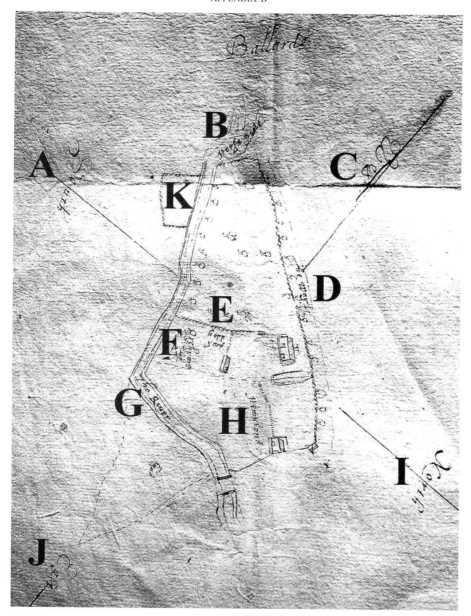

Plate 21. Plan of 'Lands of Calabors, of late Ballards', Fakenham Magna, 1622, the survey of which is transcribed in Appendix B. Key: A, south; B, horse pool; C, west; D, the highway; E, pightle; F, messuage and yards (including hop yard), gardens and orchard; G, river; H, hemplands; I, north; J, east; K, the small piece of meadow on the south side of the river. Helmingham Archive, T/Hel/24/6, reproduced by kind permission of the Lord Tollemache

acquisitions amounted to more than that, totalling 109 acres 1 rood 14 perches and 5 dec (5/10ths of a perch). He must have acquired considerably more in the years following because, at his death in 1640, his *inquisition post mortem* confirms his possession in Fakenham of two messuages, 220 acres of land, 7 acres of meadow, 20 acres of pasture and liberty of foldage for 50 animals in Fakenham Magna, Fakenham Parva, Euston, Honington and Sapiston, lately bought from Holofernes Cooke and Barbara his wife.[13] A 'platform' or sketch plan, incomplete, loose in the file, is described as 'A platforme or description of great ffakenham in the Countie of Suffolk finished in Anno Dom. 1626'. Because part of the document is missing, it is impossible to speculate as to whether it provided evidence of other lands acquired between 1624 and 1626 that would account for additional acquisitions. What the 'platform' does confirm is the dominance of common land lying west of the Thetford–Ixworth road, the major part left blank but labelled 'Common Pasture' and intersected by two paths, one of them labelled 'Bury Way'. Between Bury Way and the Thetford–Ixworth road lie six small plots of land, some of them overwritten with the legend 'Overwhart Lands', including three areas of unmeasured 'Demesne' and 'Demesne of the mannour'. Fragmentary though it is, perhaps the most significant element of this document is the date it was finished, which coincides with the date of the compilation of the Helmingham household inventory. The family was certainly settled into life at Fakenham prior to that date because their son, Lionel, was baptised there in 1624 and a further son, Francis John, in September 1625; Francis was buried at Fakenham a year later, on 21 October 1626. Between then and 1633, items were removed from Helmingham to equip Lugdons, all of which are listed below.

2. 1626–1633: removals from Helmingham Hall to Fakenham Magna, extracted from the 1626 Household Inventory for Helmingham Hall[14]

The household inventory for Helmingham Hall, begun in 1626, records items that were removed from there to Fakenham until 1633. The entries are summarised below (with their reference number from the 1626 transcription shown in brackets) to confirm the gradual process of equipping one house from the other. Some are dated; others have an identifying mark to show that they were the subject of a subsequent stock-check. Each is identified by an insertion, either as a marginal note (indicated as \ ... /), or by a note fixed into the inventory, some dating their removal to Fakenham. The compiler's uncertainties are sometimes revealed by deletions. Where these occur, the entry is enclosed within < >, to conform with the editorial method used throughout the transcriptions. Only once, when faced with an item that cannot be located at Helmingham, does the compiler admit defeat in the comment 'removed to Ffakenham or some other place'.

one otter fflewe + \sent to ffakenham/ (26.7)

This, a net designed for trapping otters, suggests that the predations of these aquatic creatures were a problem at both locations, but more so at Fakenham than at Helmingham.

---

13 TNA, C142/601/45. In 1622, Holofernes Cooke had numerous holdings in Fakenham, including plots of land and property lying adjacent to the eastern boundary of Lugdons.

14 T/Hel/9/1/1.

one bundle of things packed up in a dornex coverlitt with a peece of a coutche chair
\Thinges to be sente to ffakenham/ (26.10)

This entry adds immediacy to the record by confirming that these unidentified things were packed up and ready to go when the inventory was compiled in October 1626. It suggests the disruption that accompanies any house removal, let alone the loss of an infant child buried at Fakenham in the same month.

one peece of joyned worke like a deske to sett a booke or a lookinge glasse against it
\removed to Ffakenham or some other place/ (26.22)

The first of several examples describing an item that has multiple uses, or which the compiler found difficult to identify categorically. Given the equivocation in the commentary, it is possible that its use has changed again since the entry was first made, and the item exists but has not been recognised. See also 26.42 below.

<one other fouldinge table wth a turned pillar & a crosse foote to beare it up beinge to fasten against a wall, twoe boxes one greater & thother lesser > \Thinges appointed to be sente unto Ffakenham/ (26.42 and 26.43)

Despite the confirmation that these items have been earmarked for removal, ostensibly in 1626, both entries are deleted from the inventory at the time of a subsequent stock-check to confirm that they are no longer at Helmingham.

one inlaide chiste for wryghteings \carried to <Hellmingham> \Faknam// (26.69)

This and 26.87 below, suggest confusion at times of subsequent stock-checks.

one large blacke leather truncke locke & kye \carried to <Hellmyngham> \Faknam// (26.87).

one pewter standishe with the appurtenancs \carried to Fakenham/ (26.129)

Twoe Irishe stiched chaires with armes fringed & covers of buckram to them the one greate & the other lesser; one other hyghe chaire of irishe stitche without armes; one lowe chaire of Irishe stiche; xii highe stooles seated with Irishe stiche; iiij lowe stooles seated with Irishe stiche. All the wholl suite of Irishe stiche fringed & covered with buckram cases of [illeg.] lyned with pap[er] (26.212–216)

This large group of entries, bracketed together and related to a marginal note reading 'all this suite removed unto ffakenham' represents the largest removal of furniture. The suite came from the dining chamber at Helmingham, and provided seating for up to twenty people.

one blacke leather truncke without a locke \removed to Fakenham/ (26.253)
one darnix covringe lyned wth another old one <yt is in the gable & there are things packed up in it to sende to ffakenham> (26.493)

The deleted comment occurs within a list of items originally in 'The corner chamber and gable end' which are bracketed together and relate to a marginal note: 'All things removed'. It is apparent that this room and the space listed next, described as 'In the enterie between the corner chamber & Nunn's chamber' had been cleared of all their contents at some time after the items were packed up ready to send to Fakenham. As discussed in appendix A, the disruption was caused by building work at Helmingham Hall, and the 1626 inventory contains many examples of contents being moved from room to room.

one lowe stoole corded with blacke velvett \removed to ffakenham/ (26.563)

\A cushion of redd and blewe stuff which came out of the greene chamber sent to ffakenham/ (26.593)

one coutch chaire of stammell wth watchet lace & fringe suitable; one greate longe cushion of stammell laced & fringed wth foure greate tassells att eache corner one, <in colour> suitable, to the coutch trimminge; ij lesser <scarlett> \stammell/ cushions suitable to the coutch \trimming/ the coutch & cushions \covrd/ <\corded/> [sic] with cases of buckerum; one stammell cannopie laced & fringed wth whatchett coloured lace & fringe; the vallence iiij curteynes of stammell coloured cloathe whereof twoe greater & ij lesser wth heade peece all suitable to the topp, beinge all packed uppon a <peece of> darnix cupborde \cloathe/ (26.596–601)

The editing evident in this list of items, related to a marginal comment confirming that they were 'removed to ffakenham', characterises the pains taken to correct and refine the details of removals. The distinction between 'scarlett' and 'stammell' is something that would be known only by someone familiar with both, to whom the distinction mattered.[15] This, and the occasional use of the first person in comments about removals (examples occur below), suggests the guiding hand of Lady Elizabeth Tollemache.

one little clocke & larm [alarm] \Removed to ffakenham now Carver hathe it to mend/ (26.610)

Carver is a name that recurs in the household accounts for Helmingham in 1587–88, suggesting that although the item was sent to Fakenham, it may have returned to Helmingham for repair, perhaps by a descendant.

one olde conye haye \carried to ffakenham/ (26.705)

A net for trapping rabbits, which proliferated on the light, sandy soils of Fakenham.

<illeg.> \ij greate/ hangeinges of saie greene & red \old/ \carried to ffakenham/ (26.774)
one olde greye sumpter cloath imbroydered wth a red & yellowe cloath wth armes & with a broade lace \At Faknam/ (26.789)
one darke <sea greene> \French greene/ cloathe cloake wthout cape or lyneinge
\September 1633 App[arent]ly was brought to Faknam and afterwards as I remember, made into chaires and stooles/ (26.795)

A note inserted into the 1626 inventory (cited below) confirms that the cloak was left there originally on 7 August 1629. See 26.810 below. The 'I' is probably Lady Elizabeth Tollemache.

one brantched blacke damask gowne wth ij broade silke & goolde laces, lyned wth velvett blacke \at ffakenham/ (26.802)

The majority of items remaining in the wardrobes at Helmingham in 1626 were related to mourning, stored there for the convenience of the family when they returned to Helmingham for funeral ceremonies: but this and other items listed below at 26.808–809 confirm the need to be equipped for similar occasions at Fakenham: both are items of mourning wear.

Note pinned to folio 136:

Thinges broughte from Hellmyngham to ffakenham Auguste the 7th 1629
one blacke taffata cloake laced wth blacke purle lace and lyned wth taffita (26.808)

---

15 Both are woollen textiles and both are red in colour but **stammell** is a coarse cloth whereas **scarlet** is soft and fine. See entries for each in the glossary.

one russett taffita cloake lined wth russett taffita sarsnett (26.809)

one frenche greene cloath cloak wthout cape or lyneinge (26.810)

The 'frenche greene cloath cloak' is the item put to new uses, recalled above (26.795) and noted here in a comment added in 1633, four years later. This is one of numerous examples confirming that every item missing from Helmingham, however modest, had to be accounted for as accurately as possible.

vj cushenings of arras iii of them wth pomegranetts & thother wth a roose \packed up to be sente unto ffakenham/ (26.817)

These are venerable items, recognisable from the 1597 inventory, the designs probably embroidered by Catherine Tollemache, mother of the 2nd baronet.

iiij other great cushions of arras worke all of them wth golde \all at fakenham/ (26.818)

one smalle \long/ cushion imbroydered \now at Faknam/ (26.819)

one other \little long/ cushion case, of brantched velvet unfilled \now at Faknam/ (26.820)

one longe cushion of white taffata imbroidered [with] gingerlyne velvett & backed wth orrenge tammy & purple taffata \now at Faknam/ (26.821)

one other longe cushion of yellowe damaske imbroidered wth purple velvett, backed wth silke chamlitt <&> \in/ divers colours \now at Faknam/ (26.822)

The correction made here by the compiler, deleting '&' and replacing it with 'in', both similar sounds when 'and' is spoken casually or hastily, suggests that the details were dictated but misheard, then edited to correct the error.

Between folios 136 and 137, bound into the spine of the volume, the following note is written on one side of a tiny fragment of paper:

2 carpetts of tapestry whereof one shorter used for a cubbard cloth the other longer for a table cloth brought to Faknam the 13 of ... [missing] (26.833)

Given that other items were removed on 7 August 1629, also noted separately and pinned into the inventory (see 26.808–810 above), speculatively these were removed a week later, on 13 August 1629.

ij great peeces of birde worke \curteynes/ with ringles used in my la: chamber \now at Faknam bought thether against my daughter Allingtons lying in of her firste child/ (26.859)

This informative commentary relates to Elizabeth, daughter of Sir Lionel and Lady Elizabeth Tollemache, who married William Allington, Esq., in the parish church at Fakenham Magna on 20 February 1631. A son of the couple was baptised there on 11 April 1633, although whether or not he was the first child mentioned here is uncertain. The use of 'my daughter' in the annotation suggests, once again, the hand and direct involvement of Lady Elizabeth. It confirms also that Elizabeth Allington's first child was to be born at her parents' house, a pattern that recurs with Tollemache wives.[16] The curtains would have been drawn around the bed, or possibly used

---

[16] As discussed in the introduction to this volume, Catherine Tollemache, mother of the 2nd baronet, gave birth to (and buried) her first child at her Cromwell family home, North Elmham, Norfolk; but her second child was born at Pakenham, home of her mother-in-law, Lady Susan Spring. Lady Elizabeth Tollemache's experiences were remarkably similar: her first child, also a son, was born in 1614 in the parish of St Martin-in-the-Fields, at her Stanhope family's London home. The child, a son, died within two years and was buried at Helmingham in 1616. Her second child, Elizabeth, was

to sub-divide a large room (as they are used elsewhere at Fakenham, see below, 26.888). Primarily, this was done to provide the level of seclusion from daily life during the period of confinement, most of it spent in bed, then considered to be essential for women immediately before and after childbirth.[17]

> viij^t [8] peeces of greene & yellowe darnixe some greater & some lesser wch came out of my maisters seconde clossett upon the right hande goinge in out of the great parlr \They were brought to Faknam, as I remember, and made into curtaines to part the great parlor/ (26.888)

The compiler recalls the location of the fabric at Helmingham; but the 'I' is Lady Elizabeth.

A note pinned into the 1626 household inventory confirms numerous removals:

> Brought from Hellmingham the 1 of October 1630, 42 dishes of sillver fashion, of 7 severall sortes, ther being 6 dishes of every sorte, 10 silver fashion sausers and 9 sillver fashion round plates, of 3 severall sortes \and 1 long venison plate/ (26.1005)

This summary offers the only reference to silver (if silver-fashion is, indeed, silver) in the entire 1626 inventory. In addition to these items, the note also confirms that the following were 'brought' from Helmingham, and presumably taken to Fakenham, on the same date:

> 1 great iron trevit (26.1006)
>
> 2 \<new>/ kellers of the newer sorte, wch Harlings wife used in the dayry (26.1007)
>
> a wicker hamper wth a cover \sent to fakenham with horse bitts/ (26.1032)

Another note is pinned into the 1626 inventory to record removals seven years later:

> 2 spitts brought from Hellmingham to Faknam in December 1633, whereof j great beefe spit fitted for a trundle, and the other a square bird spit with a crancke (26.1088)

These are significant culinary items and their removal in December 1633 implies that they would be put to use at Fakenham to roast joints of beef and whole fowl for Christmas and New Year festivities.

> ij pillers whereon a table did lie, it is att fakenham the table \made a pasterie borde/ (26.1115)

The inserted comment reveals the new purpose of a table-top following its removal to Fakenham from Helmingham. The removal must have occurred earlier than 1626, when only the pillars remained at Helmingham.

The next item is not a removal, but the description confirms that cheese was being made at Helmingham and transported regularly to wherever the family was in

---

baptised in 1615 at Framsden, where her mother-in-law, Dame Catherine Tollemache, was presumably occupying the dower property, Framsden Hall. It is this child, Elizabeth, who is referred to here, confirming that she, too, will give birth to her first child at her mother's home, not at Helmingham but at Fakenham.

[17] Lucy Worsley describes the rituals surrounding childbirth for high-status women in Tudor and Stuart times (*If walls could talk: an intimate history of the home* (London, 2012), pp. 18–20). Confinement before the birth lasted for up to a month. After the birth came another month of limited activity which included 'sitting up'. The long period of confinement, by now two months or more, concluded with 'churching', a service still to be found in the Book of Common Prayer, before a return to the full demands of marital, social and domestic life.

occupation. Cheese made from the morning milk, the first milking, was considered to be superior to that made from subsequent milkings:

one little rounde hooped boxe wthout a cover to send morning milk cheese to ffak-enham or London (26.1200)

an olde hoggsheade used to putt hoppes in \sent to ffakenham/ (26.1315)

The following three entries provide more evidence of the way in which the 1626 inventory compiler pursued the whereabouts of every item belonging to the Helmingham household. Each describes a partial removal:

of elmeinge borde wch came from the brick kilne xxij \3 sent to ffakenham/ (26.1364)

ij paire of shacke traise \one sent to fakenham/ (26.1427)

5 horse collers in prt leather \one sent to fakenham/ (26.1430)

The final entry in this list of removals seems to relate to the elm boards mentioned above (26.1364) as if justifying why they were sent to Fakenham:

iij longe elmeing planks wch nowe belongeinge unto the slideinge table att ffakenham (26.1498)

This long list of removals confirms that Fakenham was not equipped at the expense of Helmingham; indeed, numerous items were modified and put to new uses at Fakenham, particularly textiles; and, with the exception of the two great spits removed in December 1633, the lack of them would have made little difference to the day-to-day operation of Helmingham Hall. Even the removal of the suite of furniture to accommodate twenty people (26.212–216) left Helmingham's dining room equipped with at least that many seats.

The mention of Elizabeth Allington's lying in for the birth of her first child is a clear sign that Fakenham, not Helmingham, was established as the focus of family life by 1631. Whether the need for a male heir and a larger family was cause or effect of the move, the 2nd baronet's family increased rapidly following the acquisition of Fakenham.[18] Three months before the birth of Bridget, who would be his last child, Sir Lionel seized an opportunity that simultaneously exploited the natural environment of Fakenham and conveyed additional status which would pass to his heirs: he obtained a swan-mark.

3. Indenture of 1634 relating to the sale and purchase of a swan mark

The otter flew removed from Helmingham in 1633 was surpassed by a more elegant water-related acquisition in 1634, when Sir Lionel Tollemache of Fakenham acquired a swan mark from Henry Bedingfe[i]ld of Oxburgh.[19] The agreement survives at Helmingham Hall and one side of the document shows a drawing of the mark, described as a 'Catheren wheele' (reproduced in Plate 22). This high-status acquisi-

---

[18] See caption to Plate III for details of the four daughters born between 1615 and 1621. Children baptised (and, in some cases, buried) at Fakenham were: Lionel (25 April 1624), Francis John (22 September 1625, buried 21 October 1626), Margaret (20 March 1627, buried 24 August 1642), Mary (8 August 1628, buried 24 August 1642), Jane (30 September 1629), Dorothy (14 December 1630, buried 1 September 1641) and Bridget 3 July 1634 (SRO(B), Fakenham parish registers, FL569).

[19] T/Hel/26/8, Indenture, sale of swan mark by Sir Henry Bedingfeild [sic] of Oxburgh [sic] to Sir Lionel Tollemache of Fakenham, 9 April 1634. The family name is, correctly, Bedingfeld but the indenture is transcribed as it was written.

Plate 22. Sketch of the Catherine wheel swan mark appended to an agreement dated 9 April 1634, by which Sir Henry Bedingfeld of Oxburgh, Norfolk, sold this mark to Sir Lionel Tollemache of Fakenham Magna, Suffolk. The agreement is transcribed here with a discussion of the statutory obligations and hereditary privileges it conveyed as part of the ancient custom of swan-keeping. Helmingham Archive, T/Hel/26/8, reproduced by kind permission of the Lord Tollemache

tion by Sir Lionel reflects the ongoing reduction in circumstances for the resolutely Catholic Bedingfeld family, who were fined almost to penury for their recusancy, experiencing brief periods of relative stability amidst others, such as sequestration of their estates in 1648, that almost destroyed them.[20] Generations of Bedingfelds had held individual swan marks and Oxburgh Hall was noted for its large area of distinctive swan pens and yards, some of them still active in 1725.[21] There, the

---

[20] Summarised by Dr Andrew Eburne in the National Trust's Conservation Plan for Oxburgh Hall, Gardens and Park, July 2006. I am indebted to the National Trust for access to this document.

[21] Swan pens are marked on the 1725 plan of the Manor of Oxborough by Wilstar (NRO, BRA 2524/2 and 3).

birds' preferred diet of aquatic vegetation, readily available in the slow-moving waters skirting the Hall's formal grounds, was augmented by regular supplies of grain. However, the agreement made with Sir Lionel, transcribed below in full, makes it clear that swans whose beaks were marked by Sir Henry's swanherd with the Catherine wheel roamed as freely as a 'pinioned' bird might roam throughout the land, but most especially in the areas once dominated by thousands of acres of undrained land offered then by the six counties named in the document.[22] Terms used in the indenture are specific: the 'white swan' defines any adult swan in full white plumage; 'eyrerers' (eyrers) are nesting birds; 'sygnetts' (cygnets) define young birds from hatching time until full-grown.[23] The custom of swan-keeping was ancient, involving responsibilities as well as rights, and a discussion follows the transcription to set Sir Lionel's important acquisition in context.

THIS INDENTURE made the Ninth day of Aprill in the Tenth yeere of the Raigne of our Soveraigne Lord Charles by the grace of God of England Scotland France and Ireland Kinge defender of the ffaith or Annoqe dom. 1634 **Betweene** the right worshipp[fu]ll Sir Henry Bedingfeild of Oxeburgh in the County of Norfolk Knight of the one pte and Sir Lyonell Tollemach of Ffakenham in the county of Suffolk \Knight and/ Baronett of the other pte **Witnesseth** that the said Sir Henry Bedingfeild for and in consideration of the some of Twenty Shillings of lawfull English mon[e]y to him in hand paid \by the said Sir Lyonell Tollemach/ before the insealinge and delivery of these presents (the receipt whereof the said Sir Henry Bedingfeild doth by these presents acknowledge and of every part thereof acquitith and dischargeth the said Sir Lyonell Tollemach his heires executors and administrators for ever by these presents) hath bargained and sold and by these presents clearly and absolutely bargaineth and selleth unto the said Sir Lyonell Tollemach his heires executors and assignes for ever All that his Marke of Swannes called the Catherine Whele and alsoe all & singular the white Swannes Eyerers and Signetts marked with the same marke beinge uppon any River or water within the County of Norfolk Suffolk Cambridge Lyncoln Huntington Northampton or elsewhere within the Realme of England and all the Right tythe possession and intereste which the said Sir Henry Bedingfeild hath or in any wise may have in and to the same Marke of Swannes with all the Swannes and Signetts of the same Marke **To have and to hold** all the said Marke of Swannes with all the Swannes and Signetts of the same Marke to the said Sir Lyonell Tollemach his heires executors and assignes for ever **In witness** whereof the p[ar]ties firste above mentioned \to these Indentures/ theire hands and seales interchangably have sett the day and yeere ffirste above written

[Signature and seal of H Bedingfeild]

Signed sealed and delivered in the presents of us [Signatures of Nicholas Timpley and Edward Drewett]

The 20s. paid by Sir Lionel was a modest amount bearing in mind that live swans sold for upwards of 10s. each, and anyone applying to a regional swanmaster to register a new swan mark paid 6s. 8d. Swan-keeping by individuals was permitted by statute and, in the medieval period, was extensive in the areas within striking distance of Fakenham, where waterlogged lands converged along the borders of

---

22 All marked swans were 'pinioned', their wings clipped to prevent them flying. The acknowledged source on all matters related to the mute swan is N.F. Ticehurst, whose extensive work as a naturalist and historian culminated in his publication of *The Mute Swan in England: its history and the ancient custom of swan-keeping* (London, 1957).

23 Ticehurst, *ibid*, pp. 120–4, which provides an extensive glossary of terms.

Cambridgeshire, Suffolk and Norfolk. Exploitation was rife until the statute of 1482 imposed strict rules governing the keeping of swans. From then, only persons in receipt of a minimum net annual income from rentals of 5 marks (£1 13s. 6d.) were eligible to apply for the right to own and mark swans. If approved, the individual paid a fee (then) of one mark (6s. 8d.) in return for the grant. The individual's mark was entered into a roll as a permanent record. There were strict regulations to be followed by the owners of swan marks, particularly adherence to the annual check and count of all birds bearing the mark, known as 'swan upping'. Norfolk Record Office holds the country's largest collection of swan rolls and other records related to swan-keeping, including five years of the manorial swan-upping records for 1667–1672 at North Elmham, formerly the home of Sir Lionel's maternal grand-parents, the Cromwells.[24] Swan-keeping, and its appeal, declined over time, due in part to the ravaging of the birds' favoured environment by extensive fen-drainage schemes which gathered pace from the mid-seveneenth century. Swans were desir-able as a bird to serve at the high-status table, notably those of religious institu-tions, whose marks proliferate in the Norfolk and Suffolk swan rolls.[25] With the dissolution of religious institutions the value of swan-keeping began to decline even further. However, once granted, a swan mark was treated as property, an asset like any other that could be bought, sold and traded and, as the indenture shows clearly, an asset that would pass to Sir Lionel's heirs for ever, but subject always to the fulfilment of their responsibilities.[26]

Swans aside, the diverse sporting opportunities offered by the west side of Suffolk, most particularly the area lying between Thetford and Newmarket, had held an enduring appeal for three generations of kings, albeit interrupted by an inter-regnum. These included the hunting of deer, the taking of game, including the trap-ping of rabbits, and, latterly, horse-racing. James I, who died in 1625, three years after Sir Lionel's acquisition of property at Fakenham, spent a considerable amount of time at Thetford, occupying a property there which he is said to have used as a hunting lodge from about 1609.[27] Charles I also spent time at Thetford, which was only four miles from Fakenham Magna. On 17 February 1636 he granted a warrant to Sir Lionel Tollemache, gentleman of the Privy Chamber, 'for preservation of his Majesty's game of hare, pheasant, partridge, and other wild fowl in Thetford and Ipswich, and within 12 miles thereof'.[28]

Sir Lionel died in September 1640. It would be his heir who would take the family forward for another quarter of a century at Fakenham and beyond. In 1648

---

[24] NRO Case 26b/26. Swan-upping accounts of North Elmham, 1667–72. By this time, the manor of North Elmham had passed from the Cromwell family. However, the swan mark, which is illustrated in the swan-upping records, is still shown as 'HC', which suggests that it was initiated by Sir Lionel's maternal grandfather, Henry, 2nd Lord Cromwell.

[25] Some of the swans might well have been for Sir Lionel's own table, as it seems they were in the past for Oxburgh Hall, whose 1598 household inventory (NRO, JER 269 55x1) describes a curiously named item in the kitchen as 'the devil's dyke dish', something large enough to hold and carry aloft to the high table a bird as large as a swan.

[26] Responsibilities were not to be taken lightly. The North Elmham swan-upping records detail the circuitous route followed by their swanherd, summoned with all others by the regional swan-master to attend on a specific day in order to undertake the annual check and count of marked swans, all of which activity was recorded. Errors, such as mis-counting swans or cygnets, had to be reported to the swan-master. Failure to report accurately, if discovered subsequently, led to the imposition of a fine.

[27] Known popularly as 'the King's House', historical sources for which are summarised online at: thetfordtowncouncil.gov.uk/history.kings-house.

[28] Calendar of State Papers Domestic: Charles I, 1635–6, ed. John Bruce (London, 1866), pp. 231–64.

Sir Lionel Tollemache, 3rd baronet, married Elizabeth Murray of Ham House, Richmond (Surrey). Following the death of her father, William, in 1655, Elizabeth inherited the title of Countess of Dysart and Sir Lionel became 2nd Earl of Dysart. Despite the capacious and urbane environs of Ham House, at least three of the Earl and Countess of Dysart's five children were born and baptised at Fakenham.[29] Between the first and last child, life was disrupted by the interregnum, a period for which there are no documentary records relating to Fakenham in the Helmingham archive.[30] However, some insight into how life resumed at the restoration of Charles II in 1660 comes from three sources. First, a parish record from Euston; next, extracts from a year of building activity recorded in the Earl of Dysart's household accounts for 1661; and finally a record of land that he leased from the Earl of Desmond, who was his neighbour at Euston, in 1662.

4. Poem inscribed in the Euston parish register, c. 1660[31]

> When traytors domineered in Saints disguise
> And Hell-gott Presbytereans made their Prize
> Off Charles the First then Churche and State were torne
> And in black stormes of Warre laye both forlorne
> Then Loyall Priests in their just rights were crost
> And then this broke more years and more was lost
> If thou art grieved cause here thou has no place
> And canst not find thy yeare and daye of Grace
> To King and Keyser render still whats due
> And curse that hell-gott Presbytyrean Crue

It is little wonder that the 2nd Earl of Dysart's household accounts open in April 1661 on a celebratory note, recording payment of £2 6s. 0d. for 'twelve bottles of sacke holding thirteen quarts for the coronation day' and 1s. 0d. 'to the man for bringing them home', and another payment of 1s. 0d. for 'gunpowder for the bonfire'. The coronation of Charles II took place at Westminster Abbey on 23 March 1661 and John Evelyn's diary entry gives a detailed account of the day in London. However, there is no doubt that the Earl of Dysart was recording retrospective payment for a celebration in Suffolk, as the title of his account book confirms: 'Volume of domestic expenditure at Helmingham or Fakenham 1661–1663', extracts from which follow.

---

[29] The Earl and Countess of Dysart had five children, Lionel, baptised at Helmingham in 1649, followed by Thomas, born in 1651, Elizabeth, baptised at Fakenham on 26 July 1659, Catherine, baptised at Fakenham in February 1662 and William, baptised at Fakenham in February 1663.

[30] There is nothing in the Helmingham Archive relating directly to domestic life during the interregnum; but E.D.H. Tollemache, *The Tollemaches of Helmingham and Ham* (Ipswich, 1949), pp. 56–8, writes of the contrast between Sir Lionel's and his wife's family circles: he cautious and keeping his own counsel, probably at Fakenham when he was not in London or abroad, she known to be a loyal and active supporter of the exiled king, exchanging letters in code with others of a similar mind. Rosemary Baird, in *Mistress of the House* (London, 2004), pp. 96–9, writes similarly about the activities of the singularly tenacious Elizabeth.

[31] Viewed and transcribed in the church of St Genevieve, Euston, register under glass.

5. Extracts from Volume 878, Buckminster Park Archive: 'Volume of domestic expenditure at Helmingham or Fakenham 1661–1663'[32]

The entries below relate only to the year beginning 20 April 1661 and are selected because they record expenditure on building works and improvements thought to relate to Fakenham. The year-long record emphasises the programme of systematic repair and renewal of the house and shows the extent to which the 2nd Earl of Dysart was an employer and purchaser of services and goods locally. Totals have been inserted below at the end of each week, but these did not form part of the original record and are defined by *italics*.

The weekly accounts beginning 20 of Aprill 1661

	£	s.	d.
two hundred of nayles			10
glew [glue]			7
a chaldron of lime		8	6
three cheese vats and a cheese bread	0	15	2
a clensing sieve	0	0	6
a fleeting dish	0	0	2
a churn	0	4	0
a churn dish	0	4	6
a washing basket	0	1	10
five bowles	0	4	3
a cheese tub	0	4	6
a keeler	0	5	0
a paire of bellowes	0	1	8
a haire line	0	2	2
two lockes and keyes	0	1	8
two hundred nayles at 8d. per hund.	0	1	4
Six hundred nayles at 6d. per hund.	0	3	6
one thousand nayles at 4d. per hund.	0	3	4
two thousand nayles at 2d. per hund.	0	3	4
two thousand nayles of another sorte	0	1	8
two tilors [tilers] for three days	0	3	8
Total	*3*	*10*	*2*

Week beginning 27 April 1661

	£	s.	d.
For a joyner		11	0
For bringing timber from Thetford		2	0
Two bushels of haire		1	4
Ocker [ochre] and whiteing			4
For timber and the carpenters wages	2	1	6
For a locke and a key		3	0
For the mason for laying chimneys and other worke	1	16	0
Total	*4*	*14*	*2*

---

[32] Extracts are reproduced here by kind permission of Sir Lyonel Tollemache.

Week beginning 4 May 1661

	£	s	d
For Sheathes[33] helping the Masons and Carpenters five days		2	6
For a playsterer [plasterer] five days		5	0
One thousand of bradds[34]		7	6
Three hundred of ten penny nayles[35]		2	6
Two hundred of eight penny nayles		1	4
Three thowsand of large tackes		3	0
Two thousand of smooth headed nayles		2	8
Six pound of spanish brown		1	6
Spanish blake [black]		1	0
Oker [ochre]			6
Siesing [sizing][36]		2	0
Blacking			9
Spanish brown		1	6
Indegoe [indigo]		2	0
Paynters oker		1	0
Two tylors a forthnight's worke		13	4
A thousand of nayles		1	8
For going over Thetford bridge with the cart severall times			10
A thousand and halfe of nayles at 2d. [per 100]		2	6
Total	*2*	*13*	*1*

Week beginning 11 May 1661

	£	s	d
For the paviers five dayes working with his man at 2s. 6d. per day		12	6
For the carpenters blanching [blanking] a chamber t[w]elve foot long sixteene foot wide	2	0	0
Foure hundred foot of irish boards at 17sh. [sic] per hundred	3	7	0
Three bunches of lasts at 2 sh. per bunch		6	0
Six paire of joints [joists?]		4	0
For three men six dayes at 5 sh. per diem	1	10	0
For the carpenter himselfe five days		10	0
For one hundred and foure foot of quarters to line the joise		12	6
For the Mason for himselfe foure days and a half		9	0
For his foure men seaven dayes and a halfe at five shill: and 4d per diem	2	0	0
An iron doore for the furnace[37]		2	6
A thousand of last [lath] nayles		1	4
Five hundred of 4d. Nayles		1	8
Five hundred of 6d. Nayles		2	6
Two hundred of 8d. Nayles		1	4
Total	*12*	*00*	*4*

---

33 Shead or Shede is a surname associated with seventeenth-century Barningham, a village close to Fakenham. The Suffolk probate index (Sudbury) lists blacksmiths and labourers there whose deaths occurred between 1682 and 1700.

34 Brad: a thin, flat, tapering nail with a lip on one side of the head (Yaxley, p. 20).

35 Ten penny nails: 10d. per hundred.

36 Sizing is the preparation of a plastered surface prior to painting or decorating and in this context is the commodity itself, the gelatinous size.

37 The furnace was probably for the wash-house, which is mentioned in the week following.

Week beginning 18 May 1661

For 200 of pavements and thirteene of brickes	3	5	2
For six pound of powles for pipeing		2	0
For Watts[38] the carpenter and his man one day		2	8
For Wellam[39] the plaisterer two dayes		2	0
For one and twenty dayes worke for the joyner and his man		19	6
For a table		10	0
foure tables		16	0
For seaven bedsteads	4	11	0
For irons for the furnace for the wash-house and a large trevett weighing seven pound and foure pound at 4d. per pound	2	9	0
Total	*12*	*17*	*4*

Week beginning 25 May 1661

For six thousand large tax (tacks)		6	0
For a thousand 3d. Nayles		1	10
For whiteing foure dozen		4	0
For blackeing one dozen		2	0
For oker one dozen		1	0
For a table in the parlour		10	0
Total	*1*	*4*	*10*

Week beginning 1 June 1661

For a brewing copper and a boyler in kitchen[40]	17	0	0
For irons and other things of Will Hawkes the smyth[41]	7	15	0
For Watts the carpenter and his man foure dayes wanting half a day		8	0
For the tylor [tiler] and his boy foure dayes		5	4
Total	*25*	*8*	*4*

Week beginning 8 June 1661

A thousand tackes		1	4
For the mason for himselfe foure dayes		8	0
For two men and two boyes fourteen dayes	2	12	0
For the paviour and his man two dayes		5	0
For Watts the carpenter one day		1	4
For the glazier repairing windows and mending		10	0
Total	*3*	*17*	*8*

---

[38] Possibly of Hopton, where the Suffolk probate index (Sudbury) has two Watts, both Thomas, who died in 1675 and 1683.

[39] Welham, Wellam, Wellham are recurrent names listed in Suffolk probate index (Sudbury) in the vicinity of Bury St Edmunds.

[40] These two items suggest a major upgrade in the brewhouse and kitchen: £17, according to TNA currency converter at 2005 values, was the equivalent of about £1300.

[41] William Hawkes, blacksmith, Great Fakenham, 1672 (R2/65/379, W1/124/122, Suffolk probate index, Sudbury).

Week beginning 22 June 1661

	£	s	d
For six hundred brickes		14	6
For the smyth William Hawkes for iron for the furnace and other things	11	15	0
For repairing windowes and making new	2	10	0
For the pavior and his man six dayes		15	0
For gravell		2	4
For one hundred of fine stroke nayles		2	0
Total	*15*	*18*	*10*

Week beginning 27 July 1661

	£	s	d
For timber and working to William Scott	19	0	0

Week beginning 10 August 1661

	£	s	d
For a man and his boy two dayes thatching the piggstye		3	0

Week beginning 11 October 1661

	£	s	d
For John Salisburie[42] for carrying fifteen load of wood and three load of tile	2	8	0
For three thousand tiles and four ? tiles	2	14	10
Total	*5*	*2*	*10*

Week beginning 18 October 1661

	£	s	d
For tables and other work to Francis Hunt the joyner	11	0	0

Week beginning 9 November 1661

	£	s	d
For the brickelayers for cleansing the well and other worke six dayes	1	0	6

Week beginning 13 December 1661

	£	s	d
For the tiler as appeareth by his bill	10	9	10
For Francis Hunt the joyner in full of all his bills	3	0	0
For Mr Burgis the glazier for windows for the stables and the cellars and leading the copper in the kitchen and other worke	3	0	0
Total	*16*	*9*	*10*

Week beginning 24 January 1662

	£	s	d
For Mr Burgis the glazier according to his aquitt		6	0

Week beginning 15 March 1662

	£	s	d
For two thousand of repairation nailes		3	6
For three bunches of hart lath		6	6
For two bush: of haire for the masons		2	0
For the Glazier as by his aquitt	1	9	7
For twentie bush: of Lime		5	0
For two hundred of sixpenny nayles		1	0

---

[42] Possibly John Salisbury, yeoman, of Great Barton, d. 1691 (R2/71/534, W1/145/91, Suffolk probate index (Sudbury)).

For one more of hart lath		2	2
For two bush: of heare for ye Masons		2	0
For two pound of glew		1	2
For one bush. of sand		1	4
Total	2	*14*	*3*

Week beginning 22 March 1662

For setting on a lock upon the granery doore at Uson [Euston]	2

Week beginning 29 March 1662

For one thousand of repairation nailes		2	2
For two bunches of laths		2	4
Total		*4*	*6*

Grand total	*138*	*8*	*10*

From the above, it is clear that the dairy, brewhouse and kitchen were the subject of significant works of repair and improvement, and in addition a new chamber measuring 12ft by 16ft was constructed. Beyond these major items (and some new furniture), the earl turned his attention to smaller repairs, including glazing the stables and cellars and cleaning out the well. In the year April 1661 to March 1662 his building works boosted the rural economy by £138 8s. 10d., approximately £10,600 at 2005 values.[43] According to the 1662 Hearth Tax Return for Fakenham, recorded on 23 October 1662, 'Sir Lyenell Tallemach hath hearths 40', making his property the largest in the parish.[44]

6. Additional payments unrelated to buildings, 1662–63

Among the less prosaic items of expenditure in the 2nd Earl's accounts, two are notable: in October 1662, Goodman Callow was paid 1s. 8d. for 'one thousand of clove gilleflowers'. Dates of payment do not necessarily correspond to time of purchase, which makes it impossible to know when these changed hands and whether they were plants or flower heads (or, indeed, whether they relate to Fakenham) although the surname recurs in contemporary wills listed in the Suffolk probate index (Sudbury), p. 93, which suggests a local connection. Known now as clove-scented pinks, the flower heads were distilled and their fragrant water use in remedies and to improve household commodities. Similarly intriguing are three payments relating to plants and flowers, all in 1663: on 22 May, 5s. 2d. was spent on 'water lilies'; on 12 June, 10s. 0d. was spent on '2 bushells of water lilies'; and 6s. 0d. for 'three thousand of roses'.[45] The roses were almost certainly for distillation to provide supplies of rose-water; but the water lilies might have been purchased as plants destined for the river bordering Sir Lionel's property, for the enjoyment

---

[43] The cost of staffing and running the house was above and beyond this and Fakenham was only one of three to be supported. By way of context, in 1664 the Earl of Dysart summarised his total outgoings for the year as £1978 6s. 2d. (roughly equivalent to £158,000 at 2005 values). The circumstances of this record are discussed below.

[44] 'The Hearth Tax Return for the Hundred of Blackbourn 1662,' transcribed by S. Colman, *PSIA* 32, 2 (1971), p. 168.

[45] BPA Volume 879.

of the swans bearing the Catherine wheel mark acquired at a bargain price by his father, and now his to enjoy.

7. Articles of agreement of 1662 relating to the acquisition of meadow land at Fakenham Magna

A modest land acquisition was made in 1662 when, on 28 January, articles between Sir Lionel and the Earl of Desmond record that Sir Lionel agreed to pay a total of £44 per annum, payable in two equal instalments, in return for leasing certain parcels of (unmeasured) land.[46] One piece of land was called Long Fen, at £18 p.a., and also 'three millers middoes [meadows] at £15 a year'. Let also were the 'Dovehouse Close and the Hard Middoe' for £11 a year. Sir Lionel agreed to 'enter all these middoes and pasture on 18 Aprill next, from thence from yeare to yeare as longe as the two partyes doe agree ... ' It was further agreed that 'Sir Lionell or his asines is to cutte & drayne all these meadoes as he shall thinke to abayte it out of his rente & that he shall have liberty to cutte fencing woode about these grounds & for no other use, and the sheepe to goe in the Dovehouse Close [and in Long Fen deleted] from Christmas till the 16th of Aprill and with free feed upon the heaths wth great cattle.'

Sir Lionel's attention to the lands he leased from the Earl of Desmond can be traced in payments he made in 1663. On 10 July, Goodman Watts's children were paid a total of 3s. for three days' work 'gathering stones for the Long Fen gate', and Goodman Hamblin's boy and maid were paid 2s. for three days doing the same work. Between then and 22 July, payment of £1 10s. 0d. was made 'to the mowers for cutting downe the Long Fen and other works', and 1s. 6d. to '3 woomen of Barnum [Barnham or Barningham] for making hay in the Long Fen'. Goodman Hamblin himself was paid 3s for three days' work there, followed by 2s. 6d. for 'his boy', and 1s. for two days' work by Goodman Hawke's maid. The largest payment relating to the Long Fen was made on 22 July to 'Goodman Watts for posts and rayles and other work'. Responsibilities did not end with the lease or the labour: on 5 February 1664, payment of 6s. 0d. was made 'For the church wardens rate for Long Fenn for a hole [whole] year'. [47]

The departure from Fakenham Magna

The family's departure from Fakenham Magna in 1665 is likely to have been prompted or hastened by the 2nd earl's failing health, which led him to live in France for the last four years of his life. The timing coincides also with two related events: the death of Sir Lionel's neighbour at Euston, George Feilding, Earl of Desmond, on 31 January 1665, and the subsequent acquisition in 1666 by Henry Bennett, Lord Arlington, of Euston Hall and some 2000 acres of land situated in Euston, Fakenham Magna, Fakenham Parva, Honington, Sapiston, and Coney Weston. As a result, Euston and its environs would be transformed, a process that began in 1671 when a grant from Charles II permitted Lord Arlington to empark. In the same year, on 25 May, Lord Arlington was granted permission to 'stop up a way from Sapiston to Thetford, through his grounds in Little Fakenham, and also

---

[46] T/Hel/26/9.
[47] BPA Volume 879.

to enclose a highway through his grounds from Blackwater to Great Fakenham, making others of equal size and convenience from the south of Little Fakenham Groves to the street of Great Fakenham'. [48] The numerous acquisitions of land made by Sir Lionel Tollemache between 1622 and 1626 suggest that he was alert to the potential of change in his own time, and perhaps hoped to consolidate and expand his Fakenham lands whenever opportunities arose; but whether he or his heir could have foreseen the extent of the sweeping changes begun by Lord Arlington in 1666 is a moot point. With advice from John Evelyn on planting and William Kent on design, Lord Arlington's vision was pursued and expanded by his son-in-law, the Duke of Grafton, with advice from Lancelot 'Capability' Brown. As a result, the parish of Fakenham Parva and its church disappeared altogether as the carefully crafted Euston Park emerged east of Fakenham Magna and the Bourn Brook; but the Tollemache family would not be there to witness the results.

Evidence for the departure comes from a record, randomly kept, entitled 'The booke of generall disbursments at Helmingham or Fakenham and Ham, 1661–5'. [49] Characteristics of the 2nd Earl of Dysart's surviving records include the duplication of details in other volumes, and a lack of detail about the property to which a payment relates. Lists of payments are interspersed with periodic summaries of income and expenditure which are not related to properties. However, several entries stand out from the 1661–65 volume to suggest that the relationship with Fakenham was coming to an end:

The whole sums received Anno domini 1664:	£1532 00s. 00d.
But the totall sums noted are charged upon this year's receipts by reason of my leaving Fakenham:	£1817 00s. 00d.

'My leaving Fakenham' may refer to the Earl of Dysart's own departure for France, apparently in the hope of finding relief from ill-health. In the event, he never returned, dying in Paris in 1669. However, the following entries from a summary later in the volume suggest that leaving Fakenham did, indeed, mean leaving it for good:

The totall disbursments of Ano. Domini 1664:	£1978 06s. 2d.
Received Ano. Domini 1664	£1817 00s. 00d.
Received more for goods sould at Fakenham	£40 05s. 00d.
Received in all:	£1857 06s. 00d.

No details were found to elaborate on the goods sold at Fakenham, but £40 5s. 0d. clearly did not make up for the shortfall between income and expenditure, even if, as the previous entries suggest, the 1664 accounts were loaded with additional expenditure that might otherwise have been spread over a longer period. A later heading states:

An account of Generall Disbursements beginning with the year 1665 from the 25 day of March. The time when my family did first remove to Ham.

---

[48] [S.P. Dom Entry Book 34, f. 94] in Calendar of State Papers Domestic, Charles II, 1671, ed. F.H. Blackburne Daniell (London, 1895), pp. 213–89, accessed via British History Online (http://www. british-history.ac.uk).

[49] BPA Volume 879.

Entries beyond that date include evidence of the protracted journey of the family from Fakenham to Ham, recorded as:

Bucknam's charges upon the way with my children:

At Newmarket	5s. 0d.
At Chesterford	7s. 0d.
At Bishops Stortford	4s. 6d.
At Hogsdone [?Hoddesdon]	6s. 0d.
At Islinton [Islington]	4s. 7d.

The family regularly divided its time between Ham, Fakenham and Helmingham, and the comment in the heading might refer to one of those regular shifts from one to the other, were it not for the following:

1665 28 March: Paide to Mr Rushbrooke his fine whereby Mr Turner is made free to enter upon the Coppiehold Lands: £10.

The extracts from the surveys presented earlier in this appendix confirm that Sir Lionel Tollemache held Lugdons as a bond tenement by copyhold, and that the lord of the manor of Fakenham Magna was Thomas Rushbrook, and the 'Mr Rushbrook' mentioned in 1665 is probably a descendant.[50] A 'fine' is the legal term for a conclusion. Turner was a surname common in the area bounded by Bury St Edmunds and Mildenhall, particularly in the seventeenth century. Scant though they are, the references cited above are some of the last that relate to expenditure relating to Fakenham (apart from 15s. for the poor of Fakenham on 1 April), leading to the conclusion that the family did relinquish Lugdons around Lady Day 1665.

The reasons suggested in the introduction for the Tollemache family's decision to acquire and occupy property at Fakenham remain speculative. There is nothing presented in this appendix to change the view that the attraction for the 2nd baronet, which can be dated to 1622, stemmed from the relationship between the Stanhope and Tollemache families, in particular the union of Bridget Stanhope and George Feilding, albeit not until 1630. Feilding, as Earl of Desmond, remained at Euston until his death in 1665, by which time he had been neighbour to both the 2nd baronet and his son, the 2nd Earl of Dysart. Frequent references to the Earl of Desmond's gardener occur in the 2nd earl's accounts. The gardener brings plants or produce on some occasions, but on others the payments may be for his occasional services, perhaps offered at times when the Earl of Desmond was away. The lease of additional land from the Earl of Desmond to the Earl of Dysart in January 1662 is one of the last clear links between the two noblemen before death claimed the Earl of Desmond in 1665, an event that was followed rapidly by sweeping changes to the estate he once occupied. It is after this sequence of events that the 2nd Earl of Dysart, by now dogged by ill-health, brought the forty-year relationship with Fakenham to a conclusion.

---

[50] Suffolk probate index (Sudbury) records a Thomas Rushbrook, gent., of Eriswell, R2/69/309; W/138/105, 1684.

GLOSSARY AND INDEX OF HOUSEHOLD GOODS

Each reference number cited in the glossary enables pinpoint retrieval of its entry in the relevant inventory, which is identified by its prefix: 97. for 1597; 26. for 1626; 08. for 1708; and 41. for 1741.

With the above in mind, collective editorial categories have been avoided as far as practicable and are adopted only for: *brewing*; *colours*; *laundry, dry*; *laundry, wet*; and *silver*, each supported by cross-references. Editorial sub-categories are shown in italics, e.g. *defined by dimensions*; *modified for other uses*.

For each entry, modern spellings are presented first, followed by variants, with cross-references provided wherever inventory spellings are alphabetically remote from modern equivalents. Where the same word has multiple definitions, the word is shown each time in **bold** (followed by its distinctive context in brackets), e.g. **salt** (commodity); **salt** (serving vessel).

Some items have eluded definition. Speculation has been kept to a minimum and, where conflicting evidence exists or the context offered by the inventories is at variance with published reference sources, all interpretations are given. In addition to the published sources historians of many persuasions were generous with their help, but final responsibility for errors, omissions and misunderstandings rests with the editor. For abbreviated references see above, p. xii.

adze, adds: carpenter's tool, short-handled, with a thin, arched blade designed for taking chips off timber, 26.1458.

alarm, clock and larm: see **clock**.

ale stool: see **beer stool**.

almain rivets, almon ryvets: see **armour**.

almonds, screw press for: almonds appear regularly in the late 16th-century recipes of Catherine Tollemache, who specified that the nuts should be ground using a pestle and mortar to create the consistency needed for her almond-paste sweetmeats such as marchpane. The 1708 inventory reveals a labour-saving alternative, 08.136.

ancient, annciente: a flag, banner or standard carried to identify the bearer, particularly when participating in military activities, 26.13. See also colours for an armour; cornet.

andiron, andyron: the front, taller, pair of ornamental uprights designed as part of the firedogs, or supporting framework, for combustible material burned in an open hearth (as distinct from a closed grate, q.v.). The name appears nowhere in the 1741 inventory. In 1626 and 1708, some descriptions include distinguishing characteristics such as dimensions and construction details. Notably, one set has cotton covers to prevent excessive tarnishing of the brass during periods when fires were not lit, 97.433, 97.596, 97.624, 26.118, 26.383; brass, 26.78, 'all but the feet', 26.243; brass knops, 08.273, 08.492; cased with brass, 08.463, with covers, 26.249; great, 26.50; high iron, 26.647; long-shanked, 26.1150; low, 26.79, 26.190, 26.334, 26.451.

See also **cobiron**.

angellica vat: see **cheese, vat**.

angelot, angelet: see **cheese**.

apparel: generic term used in the 1597 inventory to head lists of family clothing, footwear and accoutrements (including **saddles**) stored in Helmingham Hall's wardrobe. The inventory lists apparel in order of seniority of family member, beginning with Lionel Tollemache, followed by his wife, Catherine, their four daughters and two of their three sons. By 1626, items relating only to **mourning** are recorded in the wardrobes. In 1708 the wardrobes are locked up and inaccessible and are not mentioned at all in 1741. For individual items, see **breeds, coat, cloak, doublet, foot cloth, garter, girdle, gloves, gown, hanger, hat, hose, jacket, jerkin, jump, kirtle, laces, pantofles, petticoat, points, pumps, safegard, shoes, sleeves, stockings, stomacher, string, tags, vastguard**.

apple roaster, tin: although the purpose is obvious, the design is uncertain; strictly, roasting refers to cooking before an open fire, whilst baking refers to cooking in an enclosed oven, and utensils were designed to suit, 08.171.

arbour, arbor: garden structure, seat for, 26.1521.

arming: description of weapons intended for military rather than ceremonial or sporting use. See **dagger; sword**.

armour: items of armour, described also in the inventories as 'arms', are described as listed below. Some entries in the 1626 inventory include commentary on how items were deployed in their time, particularly where they are described as old or old fashioned. Footnote 52 to the 1597 inventory gives details of the background to Lionel Tollemache's preparation for active service in 1588, including the increasing payments to his armourer. The Helmingham Hall armoury housed most of its armour and weapons but some items were described as belonging to **saddles** and were stored with them in the wardrobes:

almain rivets, almon ryvets: originating in Germany (Almain) in the 15th century, lightweight, flexible armour composed of overlapping plates of steel sliding on rivets. Evidence of payments to the armourer in Smythe's 1588 household accounts for Helmingham Hall reveals that rivets for the new armour were of copper, 97.756.

armory, iron, 41.613; *unspecified*, 41.614.

coat, coats of mail, male: almost certainly synonymous with almain rivets (q.v.), 26.738, 41.613.

corslet, corselet: generic term describing both the wearer or, in the context of the Helmingham inventories, an item of defensive armour designed to protect parts of the upper body. A corslet consisted principally of a breastplate and backplate, but might also include a helmet, gorgets (protection for the throat), tassets (protection for the thighs), gauntlets and protection for the arms. Some of the inventory entries comment on obsolescence, others state merely 'complete' or identify whether the items were 'black' or 'white' (unpolished or polished steel, although Yaxley (p. 4) suggests that 'white' may refer to armour painted white). Corslets are categorised in the inventories as below, 'foot arms' meaning armour for the foot-soldier as distinct from that for the horseman:

black, complete, 97.754.

foot arms, old, 26.721, 26.722.

gauntlets, gantellet gloves, 26.720, 26.730.

white, complete, 97.755.

horseman's armour, horseman's arm[e]s: items listed below are all identified in the inventories as being components of a horseman's armour:

black, 97.565, 97.750, 97.751.

breastplate, bresteplate, of steel and stored in a bag with other items, 26.731.

headpieces and gauntlets, 26.720; **cap[pe]s for headpiece**, 26.745.

case[s], bag[ges] for, 97.752, 97.753, 26.579, 26.730, 26.731.

posts to hang armour upon, 26.749, 41.613.

arms, armes (coats of arms): taken to be those of the Tollemache family with the notable exception of silver plates engraved with 'Joyce's cote'. This refers to the arms of the Joyce family, who held Creke Hall and its lands at Helmingham until the union through marriage (in 1487) of the Joyce and Tollemache families:

embroidered, 26.291, 26.348, 26.789; **in raised work**, 08.542; **in turkey work** (hand-knotted, richly-coloured wools), 97.334, 97.357, 97.339, 97.341, 26.816; **in velvet**, 97.371, 97.618.

engraved on silver, 97.1093, 97.1094, 97.1098, 97.1105, 97.1119, 97.1120, 97.1125, 97.1132, 97.1133, 97.1142, 97.1145, 97.1146, 97.1147, 97.1148, 97.1149, 97.1153, 97.1156, 97.1161, 97.1162, 97.1163, 97.1164, 97.1165, 97.1171, 97.1172, 97.1173, 97.1174, 97.1176, 97.1179, 97.1180, 97.1181, 97.1182, 97.1186, 97.1189, 97.1190, 97.1191, 97.1195, 97.1198, 97.1209, 97.1210, 97.1212, 97.1213.

illustrated on 'the Scotch peers protest', 41.483. See also **pictures**.

escutcheons, scutchions, arms displayed on a shield or heraldic emblem, 97.31, 26.53, 08.172.

hatchment, diamond-shaped heraldic panel, 41.264.

inlaid, on coffer, 97.475; **on writing stand**, 08.521.

sentchings (?escutcheons), 26.126.

See also **cipher; genealogical rolls**.

arms, armes (armour), not the weaponry of modern parlance: see **armour**.

arras: *see* **tapestry**.

arrow: isolated references, independent of bows: **forked head, for,** 26.52; **with,** 26.52; **old,** 26.746. See also: **bow; crossbow; gaffle; longbow; slur bow**.

axe, butcher's, 26.1131.

backgammon, table, rattling box and dice for: this ancient board game for two was banned for a time by Elizabeth I but re-emerged into popularity in the 17th century, 41.177. See also **games**.

bacon grease, pot of, 26.1238. See also **grease**.

bail, baile: see **bile**.

baize, baies bay(e)s: textile produced in a range of qualities from coarse to fine, characterised by a thick woollen weft and, originally, a warp of linen but by the time of the inventories, of fine wool. The inventories show its applications to be diverse:

boothose top(p)s, 26.880.

carpet(t) (cupboard), 26.380.

gown, 97.969.

lacings and linings of, 97.873, 26.148, 26.235, 26.790, 26.814, 26.825, 26.852, 08.413.

piece, peece of, 26.826, 26.849.

seat (close stool), 08.413.

baking pan: see **pan.**

barrel, barrell (storage vessel): constructed of wooden staves held tightly in position by a series of metal hoops; identified mainly at Helmingham by their contents. (See also **bowl, cask, firkin, keeler, vat.**) The hall's vessels were maintained and replaced regularly by an itinerant cooper (Coleman, pp. 11–12):

bay salt[e], 97.191.

capers, 97.78.

churn, see **butter.**

fish, fyshe, 26.1342.

half barrel, 97.189, 08.376.

herring, 97.190, 26.1285, 26.1326 (both 'old').

lamp black, lamblack, almost pure carbon collected from the soot deposited by a burning torch; used as a pigment (Yaxley, p. 119), 08.156.

old, 26.1327.

olives, ollyve, 97.78.

unspecified, 97.188.

barrel, barrell (bar): in the 'Husbandmans Storehowse' in 1626 is 'a crosse peece of woode to winde or scrue about a roope in a paire of traices, called a barrell'. According to *Ogilvie's Imperial Dictionary* ... (ed. Annandale, London, 1855, p. 223), this use of the word derives from its ancient roots, recognisable in *bar* (W), the branch of a tree, a bar, 26.1448.

barrel, barrell (gun-barrel): see **gun.**

barrel churn: see **churn.**

barrel lock: see **lock.**

basin, bason, basson: those listed below exclude items of **silver** (q.v.):

china, blue, 08.230.

Delftware, 08.175, 08.182.

earthen, white (stoneware), 08.202.

glass (with dimensions), 08.185, 08.186.

pewter (with ewer), 26.979, 26.997, 26.998.

tea, for, 41.104, 41.161.

unspecified, 97.64, 97.110, 41.34.

See also **silver.**

basket, baskett, baskitt:

covering, to cover food en route to or when cleared from the table, 97.51, 26.1023.

chickens, to carry on a horse, 26.1341.

child's clothes (with dimensions), 08.567.

clothes, to carry in, 08.351, 08.352.

dessert (of pewter), 08.213.

'to stop hopps from running into the liquor in the cooler', 08.310. See also *brewing*.

wicker, for linen, 26.677, 26.678.

See also **skep.**

baster, basting, bastengge: utensil for basting foods with their own fat or juices to keep them moist during cooking (particularly roasting before an open fire):

> **ladle,** 26.1090; **brass,** 08.25, 41.219.

> **dropping, tin,** 08.108.

batfouling net: see **net.**

bay, bayes: see **baize.**

bay salt: see **salt** (commodity).

bearded stone jug, jugge: stoneware jug or drinking bottle with a handle, embellished externally with a bearded face. Imported mainly from Germany until the early 1700s, when comparable examples were made in England. Known also as Bartmann or Bellarmine jugs: **great,** 97.59, 97.90; **lesser,** 97.60.

bearing cloth, cloath: Yaxley (p. 10), defines this term as both a child's christening robe and a burying cloth. This item is the latter, being of black velvet, 26.825.

beaver hat, hatt: Yaxley (p. 10) distinguishes between beaver, a felted cloth, and beaver fur, used to make hats, which these are likely to be, 97.875, **old,** 26.827.

bed: a mattress in modern parlance. In the 1708 inventory, then more frequently in that of 1741, there are examples of the use of 'bed' to describe the item of furniture, but these are rare in comparison to the continued use of the word to describe a mattress. Indeed, the 1741 inventory does include references to **mattress.** 'Featherbed' is used also as a generic term in discrete lists where numbers of beds, pillows and bolsters are recorded periodically in updates to the 1597 inventory even when the filling is the lowest-quality flock. Beds were laid over a **mat** (q.v.) supported by a trellis of cords (q.v.). For both see **bedstead,** below. The 1741 inventory provides no details of fillings for beds or mattresses, but these govern the descriptions listed in the 1597, 1626 and 1708 inventories and are listed here:

> **down, doune[e], down:** used as a filling for beds (mattresses), bolsters and pillows, down describes the inner layer of the feathers of young birds. These are soft and fine, having almost no barbs, and offer high levels of warmth and insulation. Generally, items filled with down are found only in the chambers of the higher-status members of the family and household at Helmingham: 97.315, 97.316, 97.347, 97.374, 97.420, 97.499, 26.113, 26.138, 26.179, 26.230, 26.294, 26.322, 26.350, 26.552, 26.589.

> **feather, fether, feather, fether:** used as the filling for beds (mattresses, referred to throughout these inventories as featherbeds), bolsters and pillows. Feather-filled beds, in particular, had to be turned and aired regularly. Periodically, Helmingham called upon the services of the 'featherbed dryver' (Coleman, p. 13) whose task was to unstitch the covering, redistribute and/or replace the feather filling, which became clogged with perspiration over time: 97.317, 97.395, 97.414, 97.439, 97.446, 97.456, 97.481, 97.488, 97.503, 97.516, 97.573, 97.592, 97.606, 97.630, 97.648, 97.654, 97.670, 97.680, 97.687, 97.695, 97.702, 97.720, 97.728, 97.737, 97.744, 97.779, 26.169, 26.258, 26.264,

26.274, 26.312, 26.339, 26.365, 26.372, 26.388, 26.393, 26.423, 26.436, 26.449, 26.468, 26.475, 26.491, 26.508, 26.521, 26.525, 26.533, 26.551, 26.572, 26.618, 26.622, 26.628, 26.652, 26.687, 26.692, 26.712, 08.263, 08.279, 08.392, 08.405, 08.433, 08.448, 08.471, 08.507, 08.546, 08.598.

flock: a generic term for the tufts of waste material such as wool, and later cotton, used as the filling for beds (mattresses), bolsters and pillows. Flock was the lowest quality of filling, feather and down being the highest, and few examples are recorded at Helmingham: 97.326, 97.655, 97.661, 97.714, 26.321, 26.494, 26.526, 26.537, 26.540, 08.293.

straw, 08.243.

bedpan, bedpanne, pewter: as now, lavatory designed for use in a bed, 08.69. See also **bedstool**. For related items, see **chamber pot; close stool**.

bedscrews: see **bedstead**, *tools for maintaining*.

bedstead: in modern parlance, a bed; but, throughout the span of the inventories, not a composite piece of furniture. Entries in the 1597, 1626 and 1708 Helmingham inventories identify each bedstead in terms of its components; but there is less clarity in the 1741 inventory, which uses **bed** variously to mean both a **mattress** (a word used only in the 1741 inventory) and the piece of furniture now known as a bed. Isolated examples from 1741 lacking enough detail to attribute a design are listed below as **bed, *unspecified***. An editorial category of ***defined by dimensions*** acknowledges a method of description unique to the 1708 inventory, even though most of its entries add information to provide a more detailed view of how each bedstead was furnished. Bedsteads, like **beds** (q.v.), demanded periodic maintenance: details are provided in an editorial category of ***tools for maintaining***. For bed-linen see **linen**; for coverings see **blanket; bolster; counterpane; coverlet; pillow; quilt; underquilt**.

bed, *unspecified*, 41.500, 41.557, 41.569, 41.577, 41.582, 41.597, 41.603, 41.608.

bed and bedstead, description unique to the 1741 inventory, suggesting that the bedstead is in two parts but perhaps not necessarily of the same construction, 41.72, 41.82.

bedlines, bedlynes, synonymous with **cords** (q.v.), Yaxley (pp. 10–11) cites East Anglian evidence of bedlines as early as 1464. The single entry in 1597 is for spare bedlines in storage: 97.952.

bedscrews, see below: ***tools for maintaining***.

boarded, borded, definition of this description in the 1597 inventory is uncertain because then the term referred both to panelled bedsteads and to the boarded base which was an alternative to the more pliable **cords** over which the **bed** (mattress) was laid, 97.660, 97.712, 26.542.

carved, 97.370, 26.419, 26.446.

coach-head-bed, description unique to the 1741 inventory and qualified by a colour, suggesting that the coach-head incorporated a covered headboard and/or lined canopy above, made to resemble the interior of a coach. The use of 'bed' in these descriptions appears to be synonymous with the modern use of the word: **green damask**, 41.365; **red**, 41.166.

cords, cordes, co[a]rded: plaited cords were strung in a trellis fashion across a **bedstead** base to support the **mat** and **bed**. Only two cords were used, each woven in and out of holes pierced around the base: one cord was strung from top to bottom, the other from side to side. Each cord was secured with a knot after tightening. For discussion of the process of cording see ***tools for maintaining***, below. Notably in 1597 there are only some isolated **bedlines** (q.v.) kept as spares, implying that cords were considered an integral part of the bedstead at the time, 26.111, 26.113, 26.138, 26.168, 26.185, 26.234, 26.256, 26.263, 26.275, 26.295, 26.311, 26.318, 26.338, 26.347, 26.364, 26.370, 26.391, 26.392, 26.404, 26.419, 26.435, 26.447, 26.473, 26.490, 26.507, 26.520, 26.524, 26.539, 26.549, 26.555, 26.567, 26.588, 26.617, 26.621, 26.629, 26.651, 26.686, 26.692, 08.262, 08.278, 08.292, 08.540, 08.541, 08.542; ***modified for other uses***, 26.536; **girth web**: (of woven rather than plaited cords), 26.1331.

couch bed: see **couch**.

curtains *for*: most bedstead curtains were supported by rods fixed to the top of the **headpiece** and/or to the **posts**; but the 1708 inventory describes some 'tacked to the sides and feet'. The main descriptors are textiles: these are presented in modern spellings below; alternative spellings and detailed definitions of the textiles can be found elsewhere in the glossary. Frequently, inventories describe bed curtains within, or following, a detailed description of other components of the bedstead and include additional details of colour, design or embellishment:

buffin, 97.636.

camblet, blue, 41.526; yellow, 41.412.

cloth, 26.601, 08.259; **purple,** 41.82; **red, laced and fringed,** 41.569; **red, silk-lined,** 41.505; **silk-lined,** 08.447, 08.468.

damask, green, 41.395, **silk-lined, green,** 41.366, **red,** 41.166.

dimity, 08.541, 41.441; **white,** 41.400.

Eyrelonde (see **Irish cloth**), 26.315.

green and white pieces for, 41.443.

Kidderminster stuff, 08.540.

plaid, plad, lined with yellow silk, 41.544.

sarcenet, 97.401, 26.349.

satin, 26.420.

say, 97.426, 97.451, 97.579, 97.612, 26.112, 26.371, 26.448, 26.474, 26.549, 26.555, 08.283.

serge, 08.432; **paned,** 08.470.

Scots-plaid, silk lined, 08.505.

silk, 97.372, 08.403, 08.506.

stuff, blue watered, 41.597, 41.603, **flowered,** 41.72; **green,** 41.563, 41.563; **green watered,** 41.424, 41.577; **red, old,** 41.582.

taffeta, 97.353, 26.146, 26.183, 26.229, 26.292, 26.319.

unspecified, 41.66, **green,** 41.384.

worsted and linen, 08.391.

For window curtains *see* **curtains, window**.

defined by dimensions: a method of identification unique to the 1708 inventory in which height is the primary measurement. At least one of these bedsteads was high off the ground and challenging to access, judging by an item described as 'a low **bench** about 5 foot long – or a step to set by a bed side': 08.258, 08.277,

08.390, 08.402, 08.431, 08.445, 08.468, 08.469, 08.504, 08.540, 08.541, 08.542, 08.597.

field: demountable, portable, its name deriving from use in military campaigns, 97.418, 97.444, 97.628, 26.549, 41.384, 41.400; **inlaid**, 26.555; **varnished black**, 26.227.

frame of, 08.539.

half-headed: Evidence in the Helmingham inventories suggests that there may be more than one definition of this term. Yaxley (p. 12) defines half-headed as a canopy (or **tester**) that extends for only half the length of the bedstead. However, Edwards (1986, p. 50) confirms that some bedsteads had low **headpieces**, or headboards. Helmingham's 'half-headed' entries, particularly those rich with detail in the 1626 inventory, suggest headboards because they appear to be part of bedsteads of simple construction, none of them mentioning posts or testers. All are located in staff chambers or are secondary bedsteads in higher-status rooms: 08.412, 08.446, 08.635, 08.689; *with* **boarded bottom**, 26.542; **corded**, 08.292; *with* **feet and sides**, 26.497, 26.661; **livery**, 26.404; **matted and corded**, 26.311, 26.338, 26.364, 26.524, 26.536, 26.539, 26.651.

headpiece, headpeece, beds-head, head, headboard: sometimes carved but often upholstered to match the curtains and **tester** (*q.v.*) or canopy, which it supported. Early bedsteads often had low headpieces to which **posts** were fixed, one at each corner, matched by a pair of posts at the foot end of the bedstead. Between them, the four posts could support hanging curtains, with or without a cover above. Structural change came in the late Elizabethan period with the introduction of a full-height headpiece capable of supporting a **tester** which extended for the full length of the bedstead and was supported by two full-height posts at the foot end. Helmingham's inventories provide rich additional detail about headpieces, whose primary categories are listed here.

blue and yellow striped stuff, 26.364.

carved, 26.111, 26.446.

cloth: **blue linen**, 26.474; **purple**, 08.259; **red**, 08.447, 08.468; **stammell coloured**, 26.601.

damask, yellow, 97.371, 26.348, 08.469.

dimity, dimoty: **white**, 08.541.

headboard, 08.539.

inlaid, 26.419, 26.446.

Kidderminster-stuff, 08.540.

linsey-wolsey, 08.597.

painted, 26.587, 26.629.

say, red and blue, 26.257.

silk, green with coats of arms, 08.542; **yellow quilt**, 08.506.

taffeta, green, 97.352, 26.291.

velvet, black, 26.227, 08.402.

wrought, old, 26.777.

See also **half-headed**.

knob(s) for: wooden, 26.783.

livery: (in the context of these inventories, beds provided for staff) 97.693, 97.718, 26.168, 26.256, 26.404, 26.435, 26.507, 26.686, 26.672.

low: 97.452, 97.486, 26.387. See also **trundle**.

mat: a low-profile, woven mat, usually of hemp, was placed over the trellis of plaited **cords** (*q.v.*) in order to provide a flat, supportive surface for the mattress, known as the **bed** (*q.v.*) Methods of recording evolve: the 1597 inventory identifies each bed mat as an individual item, whereas the 1626 inventory is less consistent, often describing the mat in conjunction with the cords and frequently associating both with the bedstead to which they belong. References decrease notably in 1708 and by 1741, the term mattress is evident: 97.346, 97.366, 97.373, 97.392, 97.394, 97.413, 97.419, 97.438, 97.445, 97.454, 97.480, 97.487, 97.498, 97.515, 97.572, 97.591, 97.605, 97.629, 97.647, 97.653, 97.669, 97.679, 97.686, 97.694, 97.701, 97.713, 97.719, 97.727, 97.736, 97.743, 97.965, 26.111, 26.113, 26.138, 26.168, 26.185, 26.234, 26.256, 26.263, 26.275, 26.295, 26.311, 26.318, 26.338, 26.347, 26.364, 26.370, 26.387, 26.391, 26.392, 26.404, 26.419, 26.435, 26.446, 26.473, 26.490, 26.507, 26.520, 26.524, 26.536, 26.539, 26.549, 26.555, 26.567, 26.588, 26.617, 26.621, 26.629, 26.651, 26.686, 26.692, 08.278, 08.295, 08.394, 08.409, 08.435, 08.454, 08.473, 08.549.

See **mat** and **matted** for references to floor coverings.

mattress, term unique to the 1741 inventory, on occasion leaving some uncertainty about the nature of the mattress when mentioned in the same description as a **bed**. Fillings are never mentioned in 1741 but possibly a mattress is a thicker layer, or topping: 41.73, 41.83, 41.167, 41.367, 41.396, 41.413, 41.425, 41.501, 41.527, 41.545.

plain, plaine: speculatively, bedsteads of simple construction lacking posts; all are located in rooms occupied by staff: 97.646, 97.726, 97.735, 97.742.

poste[a]d, post[e]s: pairs of uprights, or posts, sometimes of the same height but sometimes taller at the head and shorter at the foot, were attached by screws to the bedstead frame. Periodically, posts had to be disassembled: for discussion see **bedstead, *tools for maintaining***. By the Elizabethan period some of Helmingham's 'posted bedsteads' may well have been earlier pieces modified. In all events, the posts provided upright support for a **canopy**, or **tester**, and/ or for **curtains** and/or a **valence** hung from a rail, or rod; but not all posted beds had these embellishments: 97.345, 97.364, 97.393, 97.412, 97.437, 97.479, 97.497, 97.571, 97.590, 97.604, 97.652, 97.668, 97.678, 97.700, 97.711, 26.111, 26.263, 26.275, 26.291, 26.318, 26.347, 26.392, 26.490, 26.567, 26.617, 26.629, 26.1330, 26.1331; **carved**, 26.370; **coloured blue**, 97.685, 26.177; **high**, 26.473, **old**, 26.621, **turned, walnut**, 26.138.

staff, staves: Edwards (1986, p. 69) explains that portable bed staves had numerous uses including providing the means by which coverings could be held in place and/or smoothed, 26.149, 26.237, 26.300, 26.332, 26.354, 26.379, 26.559, 26.593.

tent bed, a description unique to the 1741 inventory and qualified by textile and/ or colour of the tented canopy: **green damask**, 41.394; **yellow camblet**, 41.412.

tester, teaster, teastern[e]: synonymous with, but referred to rarely in the inventories, a **canopy** (see below) designed to provide a roof, or ceiling, above the bedstead and usually extending for its entire length. Editorial headings of *with* and *without valance* have been adopted but otherwise the categories adopt only the initial characteristics recorded in the inventories.

canopy, cannapie, cannopie, cannoppie:

Eyrelonde, 26.315.

satin, 97.466.

stammell, 26.600.

canopy frame, 26.584.

tester *with valance*: in the 1741 inventory the presence of a tester is inferred from descriptions of beds with curtains and valences, even though other details of the bedstead are not included:

buffin, green, 97.635.

camblet, blue, 41.526.

cloth, purple, 08.259, 41.82, **red,** 08.468.

cloth of silver & black velvet, 97.400.

cutwork, coopwork, coupwork (see **embroidery**), 97.611, 26.276.

damask, yellow, 97.371, 26.348.

flowered stuff, 41.72.

fringe, set on scolloped: (scallop shell-shaped edging forming a valence), 08.540.

gilt knobs, bells and buttons (trimmed with), 26.550.

Kidderminster stuff, blue and white, 08.540.

plaid, plad, lined with yellow silk, 41.544.

raised silk embroidery, 08.390.

say, purple, 26.177; **red,** 26.555; **watchet,** 26.447.

silk, green, 08.542; **scarlet,** 08.431; **yellow,** 08.469; **yellow quilt,** 08.506.

taffeta, crimson, 26.320; **green,** 97.352, 26.291.

tobine, ash-coloured, 26.138.

undefined, 26.549.

velvet, black, 97.578, 26.227, 08.402.

watered stuff, green, 41.424.

tester *without valence*:

bells (trimmed with), 97.450.

buckram, buckrum: from the late 16th century, coarse linen or cloth stiffened with gum (Yaxley, p.26), 97.509; red and green, 97.520.

cover [*for*], 26.139.

gilt knobs, for, 26.145; with, 26.111.

joined, joyned, 97.685, 26.520.

linen, linnin, 97.485, 97.509, 97.443.

painted, 26.629; old, 26.621.

sacking, sackin, 97.675.

satin, satten, green, 26.420.

say, red, 97.425, 97.450; **red and watchet,** 97.365, 26.257.

staining, steyning cloth (painted cloth), 26.392.

stuff, blue and yellow striped, 26.370; **old, diamond-wrought,** 26.263.

velvet, black and white, 26.474.

tools for maintaining: bedstead frameworks had to be dismantled for periodic maintenance, most particularly tightening of the bed-cords (see **cords**) and the following entries convey valuable information about the process:

cranks, iron 'to turn in the screwes', 26.783. See also **wince**, below.

mallett and wrinche (wrench) **to cord a bed**: cords (see **bedstead: cords**) sagged over time and had to be tightened periodically. Dr Charles Kightly, who was responsible for advising the Victoria & Albert Museum on their restoration of the Great Bed of Ware, commissioned the making of a wrench for this purpose, based on the design of a 16th-century original. In principle, the loose end of the cord was slotted through two holes in the wrench, which was rotated tightly against the bedframe. The cord was then knotted under tension and the wrench removed by sliding the wide end of the aperture over the knot. However, having considered the Helmingham inventory description, Dr Kightly suggests that the mallet may have been used to hammer the knot and wrench into position with the intention of leaving the wrench in place until it was hammered out again for the next re-cording (personal communications 13 and 20 August 2014): 26.794.

screws, iron, for a bedde: these secured bed-posts to the framework and had to be removed whenever the bedstead was dismantled for maintenance, 26.783.

wince: (for bed screws): a tool used to loosen and tighten the iron **screws** which secured the posts of a bedstead to its framework: 08.594. See also **cranks**, above.

trundle: low, designed to slide beneath another bed; also known as 'truckle', but not in these inventories, 97.514, 26.568, 26.574, 26.662. See also **low**, above.

valence, vallence, valance: see **tester**.

bedstool: type of **close stool** (*q.v.*) for use in a bed, 26.595. See also **bedpan**.

beer: see *brewing*.

beerstools: see *brewing*.

bee skep, bees skeps: large, upturned baskets used as beehives, 97.570.

beetle and wedges: within details of the double press (see **cheese**), wedge hammered into place by the beetle, or large mallet, 26.1210.

bell, 97.185; 08.569.

belonging to the clock, 26.273, 41.498.

great horse collar bells, 26.1469.

hand-bell for dinner, 41.259.

hanging in iron frame, 26.15.

horse collar, on, to ring in hands, 08.371.

small, 41.186.

bellows, bellowes, pair of: squeezed by its pair of handles, the bag allowed a stream of air to be emitted under pressure to encourage a fire to burn, 97.39, 97.242, 97.457, 97.563, 26.50, 26.77, 26.166, 26.191, 26.219, 26.251, 26.307, 26.335, 26.362, 26.461, 26.565, 26.615, 26.648, 26.1149, 08.223, 08.275, 08.531, 41.39, 41.59, 41.89, 41.98, 41.112, 41.127, 41.145, 41.164, 41.176, 41.359, 41.375, 41.409, 41.422, 41.456, 41.519, 41.538, 41.556.

English black jappaned, 08.426.

plain, 08.464.

small, 08.484, 08.623.

bench, bentch: a long seat, generally distinguishable from a **form** (*q.v.*) by having a back, 97.4, 97.182, 26.5, 08.441; **low** ('or a step to set by a bedside'), 08.610.

bench, bentch: a flat surface defined by its use: **boarded, for dogs to lie upon,** 26.1367; **work [for]:** 26.1472, 08.313.

bender: also known as a **gaffle** (*q.v.*), in the context of the Helmingham inventories, the mechanism for bending a **crossbow** (*q.v.*), 26.516.

See also **gaffle bow** and **slurr bow.**

bile, bail[e]: hoop or ring, often a detachable, semi-circular handle, 26.1201, 26.1205, 26.1319, 26.1323, 08.141.

See also **tree, baile.**

bill, blackbill: iron or steel blade about a foot long with one sharp edge, 97.771.

See also **halberd: bills.**

billament: habiliment or ornament; see **lace.**

billiards: rooms described in the 1741 inventory include an old and a new billiard room, although only the old one, sited on the first floor, contains its table, with a comment that its 'sticks' are stored in another room. There are numerous versions of the indoor game of billiards but all emerged from an outdoor game, popular in France, similar to croquet, involving the use of a stick (known as a mace) with which to propel balls through or around hoops or other obstacles on a table. The indoor version maintained the association with its fixed table covering of a green baize cloth to resemble grass. In 1741 the table had a bed of wood. The slate bed was not developed until the nineteenth century. Before the development of cushions and pockets the edges of the table were banked to prevent balls falling off. The mace, similar in shape to a hockey-stick, could be reversed if the head was too large for the manouevre. The word 'cue' comes from the French for tail, describing the tail-end of the stick: **billiard table lined with green cloth**, 41.512.

bin, binne, bing: container, usually of wood, sometimes with internal partitions, 97.46, 97.71, 26.1010, 26.1132, 08.92, 08.685; **wine bins**: 41.352; see also **wine.**

birdcage, byrd cage, wire, wyer, 26.958.

See also **cage.**

bird's eye, birde eyede, burd eye, birde worke: a textile, woven of linen and silk, patterned to resemble birds' eyes: **coverlet, coverlitt,** 26.407, 26.395; **curtains,** 26.859; **tester of sackin[g]** *of,* 97.675.

bits and bosses for horses: bridle parts, 26.90, 26.933, 26.934.

black: when used to describe weapons, e.g. **bills, blackbills,** or **armour** (q.v.), black identifies the material as iron or unpolished steel.

black moores, blackamoores: bulrushes in full bloom (Halliwell, p. 180), mentioned in the needlework design of a cushion, 97.791.

blackbill: see **bill.**

blackjack, blacke jacke: leather jug, tarred on the outside.

great, 97.58, 26.1025.

leather jack, 08.108.

lesser, 97.60, 26.1025.

old, little, 26.711.

blade, blad: describes 'a pair of great blads to wind silk or crewel'. Halliwell (p. 182) cites Richard Huloet's work of 1552 (Abecedarium Anglo-Latinum): 'Huloet has "blades or yarn wyndles, an instrument of huswyfery'; 26.761.

blanket, blancket, blankitt: *described occasionally as one, most frequently as pairs. Variant spellings and definitions of textiles can be found elsewhere in the glossary:*

fustian, 97.323, 97.350, 26.232; **old**, 26.847.

grey, 26.495.

Irish, 26.113, 26.451, 26.553.

lined (with pieces of hanging), 08.395.

linsey-wolsey, 97.663.

old, 26.265.

russett, 26.437.

Spanish, Spanish woollen, 26.142, 26.181, 26.297, 26.324, 26.352, 26.374, 26.557.

unspecified, 97.322, 97.441, 97.594, 97.650, 26.394, 26.572, 26.622, 26.623, 08.266, 08.281, 08.408, 08.436, 08.511, 08.550, 08.601, 41.74, 41.84, 41.168, 41.368, 41.385, 41.397, 41.401, 41.414, 41.426, 41.502, 41.528, 41.546, 41.558, 41.564, 41.570, 41.578, 41.583, 41.598, 41.604, 41.609.

woollen, 97.368, 97.377, 97.398, 97.416, 97.423, 97.448, 97.462, 97.483, 97.489, 97.506, 97.518, 97.576, 97.609, 97.633, 97.656, 97.658, 97.664, 97.672, 97.682, 97.689, 97.697, 97.704, 97.715, 97.721, 97.729, 97.738, 97.746, 97.782, 97.783, 26.170, 26.340, 26.366, 26.389, 26.406, 26.424, 26.653, 26.688; new, 26.259, 26.313; white, 26.279, 26.469, 26.476, 26.492, 26.509, 26.522, 26.527, 26.533, 26.538, 26.541, 26.591, 26.619, 26.631, 26.694, 26.713.

blindles, blindells, pair of: speculatively, blinkers for horses, 26.1362, 26.1387.

blood, bludd: only the 1626 inventory describes the contents of the slaughterhouse: **bowl 'in the ground'**, 26.1490; **pail,** 26.1489.

boar, boore, male swine, reared and slaughtered on site: grease: earthenware pots of 'grease', including boar's, are stored in the cool and airy cheese chamber, 26.1238; sty, stye, 26.1506, 26.1508. See also grease; hog; lard.

board, boord(e), bord(e): generally, a flat, wooden surface; the word was used commonly to describe a portable **table**, and was a component of the early **cupboard**; but references listed here are specific in ascribing a purpose and exclude the use of the word within items described as 'boarded':

bakehouse, in, 97.268.

box, used as, 26.613.

bread, *for* (after it is withdrawn from the oven), 26.1256.

brick and tile (described as having come from the brick kiln, whose site and output are discussed in footnote 150 to the 1626 inventory), 26.1358.

cheese (to lay cheeses on), 97.196, 97.254, 26.1236.

chopping, 97.250.

climbing, klimeing: described as having come from the brick kiln, as are the **brick and tile boards** (*q.v.*), these would have been laid on a roof structure to facilitate access for repair and/or for tile-laying, 26.1364.

copper, to lay over (to form a lid over the boiling vessel), 26.1292, 08.300.

cover for pheasant's meat tub, 26.1539.

dresser, 97.113, 26.1057.

fowl, foul (describes a perch in a fowl-coop), 26.1281.

half-inch boards, '12 foot apeece', which were 'lent by the Bailive' for Catchpole's wedding, 26.1365.

joined together, 97.692.

moulding, molding, mulding (rolling out and forming doughs and pastry), 97.163, 97.267, 26.1103, 26.1255.

ovis (eaves), 26.1502.

pastry, pasterie (describes an item reused to create a pastry board), 26.1115.

peewit's, puet's house, to cover (describes a boarded roof), 26.1502.

old, owd, 26.505, 26.668.

scalding, 26.1058.

shop-board, tailor's, shoppborde, tailers: shop counter or display and serving table, in this case in use previously by a tailor, 26.500.

square, and stone to press linen: e.g. 26.1017. See also *laundry, wet*.

stilling yard, in, 97.306.

trestles, on, 97.723.

valance, vallans, 08.539.

See also **table**.

board cloth, cloath, clothes: (generic term occurring only in 1597 summaries of **linen** napery, describing coverings laid on a **board** in use as a **table**; but *see* also **cupboard cloth** and **tablecloth**):

damask, long, 97.1088.

diaper, 97.1072, 97.1077.

'for her parlour', 97.1008.

hall, 97.1013, 97.1020, 97.1040,

holland, 97.1061, **short**, 97.1063, 97.1064.

parlour (describes sources, including 'ouer home-made yearn'), 97.1017.

boat: for use on the moat, 26.1536, 41.622; for use on the lay pond (referring to the fish pond in the ley), 41.622; **Dutch, in glass frame**, speculatively, a model, since the phrase 'in a glass frame' is distinct from descriptions of glazed and framed pictures, 41.2. See also **oars**.

bodkin, bodkinge: in the context of the inventories, a small **dagger** (*q.v.*), 97.43.

boiler, boyler: large pot or cauldron for boiling or stewing:

brasen, 97.116.

brass, 26.1059, 41.239; **copper**, 41.239; **great (for boiling dogs' meat)**, 26.1060.

small, in iron frame, 08.12.

stewing, old, with cover, 08.37.

tin, 08.12.

used as kettle for scalding milk bowls, 26.1142.

bolster, boulster: designed as a single cushion or pillow to fit the width of a bed. Rarely, the inventories describe also the textile of the containing cover (see **tick**). Down was the highest-quality filling, feather the next and flock the lowest. Not all fillings are recorded in the three earlier inventories and none at all in 1741 (see *unspecified*, below). Descriptions of some chambers reveal a combination of fillings, including flock beds provided with feather bolsters and featherbeds equipped with flock bolsters. See **bed** for definitions of **down, feather** and **flock**.

> **down, doune**, 97.318, 97.348, 97.375, 97.421, 97.440, 97.447, 97.501, 97.607, 26.140, 26.230, 26.294, 26.323, 26.350, 26.449, 26.556, 26.589.

> **feather, fether**, 97.319, 97.655, 97.670, 97.720, 97.728, 97.737, 26.113, 26.169, 26.180, 26.258, 26.264, 26.277, 26.312, 26.339, 26.365, 26.372, 26.388, 26.393, 26.423, 26.436, 26.468, 26.475, 26.491, 26.508, 26.521, 26.525, 26.533, 26.537, 26.551, 26.572, 26.618, 26.622, 26.630, 26.652, 26.687, 26.693, 26.712, 08.393, 08.434, 08.449, 08.547.

> **flock, flock, flocke**, 97.327, 97.655, 97.714, 26.494, 26.508, 26.526, 26.534, 26.540, 08.294.

> *unspecified*, 97.367, 97.688, 97.703, 97.745, 97.396, 97.415, 97.458, 97.482, 97.505, 97.517, 97.574, 97.593, 97.631, 97.649, 97.662, 97.681, 97.696, 97.780, 08.264, 08.280, 08.406, 08.474, 08.508, 08.599, 41.64, 41.76, 41.85, 41.170, 41.386, 41.399, 41.402, 41.416, 41.426, 41.504, 41.530, 41.548, 41.559, 41.566, 41.572, 41.580, 41.585, 41.600, 41.605, 41.610.

See also **pillow**.

bolting, boulting, bulting: to bolt is to sift or sieve, and at Helmingham in 1597 there was a designated 'Bulting house' (renamed 'Meale howse' in 1626, 'Bolting roome' in 1708 and 'Flower (flour) Room' in 1741) in which flour, stone-ground in the Millhouse, was graded through sieves and mixed with water in 'minging' or mixing troughs to create dough for baking in the adjacent bakehouse:

> **hutch**, chest, usually on legs, 97.258, 26.1268, 08.91; **tub, tubbs, great**, 97.260.
> See also **bultelle; flour; mill; minging; sieve**.

bond, bonde: in the context of these inventories, describes a removeable band or hoop, with or without ears or handles, for attachment to various utensils, 26.1319, 26.1320, 26.1321, 26.1322.

books, shelves for: the designation of a room as the 'Library' at Helmingham appears for the first time in the 1741 inventory, where it is discussed in footnote 7. However, there is valuable documentary evidence of book storage in the 1626 inventory, described as 'one joyned frame wth foure shelves to sett books upon', 26.102.

boord, boorde, borde: see **board**.

bottle, the inventories define bottles by their material, purpose or contents:

> **beer, hogshead beer**, 08.660; **strong beer**, 08.659. See also *brewing*.

> **cases for, with,** in context, the cased bottles contained items related to personal washing and grooming: 41.32.

> **earthen**: earthenware, 26.947. See also **stone**, below.

> **empty**, 08.662.

glass, great, 26.1052; **high square**, 08.174; **leather-covered**, 97.76, 26.946; **round 'like those they keep leeches in'**, 08.174; **wicker, wicker-covered**, 97.77, 26.947, 26.1053.

leather, 08.109.

oil, 97.87.

pint, 08.663; **'with some sort of stilled [*distilled*] waters'**, 08.664.

stone (stoneware): **vinegar**, 26.1228. See also **earthen,** above.

verjuice, 26.1227.

vinegar, 97.140, 26.947, 26.1228.

water, 08.384.

wine, wyne: **claret**, 08.661; **stor[r]ing**, 26.1054.

wooden, 26.1028.

boules: see **bowls**.

boulting: see **bolting**.

boutelle: see **bultelle**.

bow: rack, pins and hooks to bend a bow to put on a string, 26.515.

See also **crossbow; gaffle; longbow; slur bow**.

bowl, bowle, boule, boulle: for high-status bowls listed with the family's plate, see **silver**. References below are to bowls with specific uses:

blood (in the slaughterhouse), 26.1489.

butter, 97.206.

cleansing (milk), 97.208.

cold meat, for, 08.358.

flour, 26.1272.

kneading, 08.85.

milk, 97.201, 97.203, 26.1181.

minging (mixing), 97.261.

whey, 97.204.

'wooden handle', 08.36.

See also **silver**.

bowls, bowles, boules, bouls: **pairs of,** for the game of bowls, **flat**, 97.41, 26.706; 26.952, 26.443.

box, the inventories reveal a variety of containers described as boxes, identified primarily by their materials and/or contents:

board used for box, 26.613.

boarded, long, narrow, 26.718.

close-stool, cedar, 08.248, 08.462; **covered with Kidderminster stuff**, 08.527.

deal, deale, 26.659, 08.142, 08.593, 08.596, 41.323, 41.465.

dice, for gaming tables: 08.500, 08.591. See also **rattling**.

dredging, drudgeing: to hold the flour to be 'dredged' or sprinkled on to roast meat before its final basting, allowing it to brown but not burn, 08.35, 41.313.

greater, 26.43.

lead, for ointment (for horses), 26.1390.

leather, black, 26.45; **black leather pattent box,** speculatively, as this is stored with assorted outdoor items, a box to hold pattens, clog-like overshoes worn to protect footwear from mud: 26.90.

lesser, 26.43.

little, with drawer, 26.760.

old, 26.643.

oval, ovall, gilded, 26.72.

partitions, with, 08.115; **deal,** 08.593.

pepper, 97.142, 41.312.

powder, 41.29.

pricks (sharp-pointed instruments), 26.1099.

rattling, for backgammon dice: 41.177. See also above, **dice.**

round with '7 hollow leads to put coloures in for a lymner', describes an artist's paintbox: 26.1337. See also **limn; pictures.**

round-hooped without cover 'to send morning milk cheese to ffakenham or London', 26.1200. See also **cheese.**

salt, 97.139, 26.1080, 26.1260, 41.315.

soap, soope, 97.556.

spice, tin, 41.268.

square, 26.628; **gilded and painted;** 26.70; **little,** 41.22; **painted,** 26.71.

stand for ['**things to sett boxes or trunks upon'**], 08.582.

sugar, suger, of engraved silver, 97.1145, 97.1171, 97.1209.

table leaves, *for storage of,* 26.1.

unspecified, 26.90, 26.109.

wainscot, waykneskott (of), 97.40, 08.142.

weights, box of, 26.56.

with lock and key, 97.477, 97.495.

wooden, for red lead, 26.956.

writing, wryting[s], for, 26.44.

See also **touch-box.**

brake, bracke for bread: Halliwell (p. 205) offers sixteen definitions for 'brake', one of which is a baker's kneading trough, which suits the context, 26.1257.

branched, brantched: term describing figured textiles, the pattern resulting from a method of weaving that gave permanent effects with the potential for the item to be reversible. Kerridge (pp. 48–9), discusses a wide-ranging terminology. For examples, see **damask** and **velvet.**

brand, sheeps (for marking sheep), 26.1443.

See also **marking irons.**

brass: Yaxley (p. 21) explains that 'modern brass is an alloy of copper and zinc in the proportion 2:1. However, as the word "bronze" only came into use *c.*1730 for the alloy of copper and tin in the proportion 9:1, many references to "brass" before then must mean "bronze", particularly if the object is a cooking pot'. *Passim.*

brazell, brazil: brazil wood, having a red colour and renowned for its durability; traditionally used to make bows for stringed musical instruments. The 1626 inventory describes a **leading staff** of brazil, tipped with silver and furnished with a buckram cover, 26.67.

bread, breade (baked goods): the inventories identify specific utensils and containers for the bread baked in Helmingham's 'Backhouse' (bakehouse):

bin, with partition, 97.46.

board, borde for, used when removed from baking oven: 26.1256.

brack, brake for, baker's kneading trough: 26.1257.

grate, closed cupboard with a grating, or lattice front: 97.137, 26.955, 26.1079.

kape, a keep, safe, or small closed cupboard: 26.1020.

rasp, rasper, to scrape breadcrumbs from a loaf: 08.377, 41.277.

skepp, wicker, to carry bread in, 26.1261.

bread, breed (lid): see **cheese**.

breadths, breads, breds, bredes, bredths, breeds: in the Helmingham inventories both **hangings** and **sheets** are quantified in this way. Yaxley (p. 22) explains that, governed by statute, the breadth of cloth varied over time, and cites a range from 54 to 63 inches in the 16th century. Lengths, where noted, are measured in yards, feet and inches and recorded to the quarter-inch. See also **ell**.

breastplate, brest(e)plat(e): defined by *OED* as an item of body armour; the inventories mention this item in association with others, some 'belonging' to saddles: 97.877, 26.731 26.916, 26.917, 26.918, 26.920, 26.922.

breeds of black velvet: in context, although these may be **breadths,** their presence in the 1597 Wardrobe suggests that they may be hat brims, an alternative definition offered by Halliwell (p. 209), 97.906.

brewing: an editorial category drawing together those items related to ale and beer in Helmingham's four inventories, each of which confirms that the household's brewhouse produced quantities of beer (ale with hops added to allow longer keeping) for storage in the hall's numerous cellars, which were extended over the period of these inventories.

ale stool, ale-stoole: two X-shaped pieces of wood joined together to form a cradle support for barrels or casks, 08.375, 08.648, 41.340, 41.350, 41, 353.

See also **beer stools**, below.

beer glasses, 26.1026, 08.387.

beer[e] stools, stales, stalls, synonymous with **ale stools** (q. v. above), 97.68, 26.1040, 26.1044, 26.1241, 26.1308.

bottles of beer, 08.659, **of 'hogshead beer'**, 08.660.

broad bin, great, with two lids, 97.71.

cock: brass, brassing, 26.1037, 08.655; **water**, 26.1311. For examples other than in the brewhouse or cellars see entry for **cock**.

cooler, 97.276, 26.1297, 08.302 (with dimensions), **large (3)**, 41.282.

copper: large boiling vessel, 97.272, 26.1292 (of brass), 08.299 (with dimensions), **large, with iron door to furnace and copper cock**, 41.278. For an example used other than in brewing see entry for **copper**.

cover(s), kovre(s), 97.284; **boarded, for the copper**, 08.300.

cowl, coul(e): a large tub with two upstanding ears through which the **cowlstaff** was passed, enabling the tub to be lifted by two men. This process is described clearly in the 1626 entries for this item and **cowl-staff**, below, 97.280, 26.1299, 41.339, 41.348.

staffe, staves, see **cowl**, above, for description, 26.1301, 41.339.

For cowls in use other than in brewing, see within alphabetical entries for **milk** and **swill**.

dale, dalle: conduit or soakaway, clarified by each entry, 26.1298; **short**, 26.1299, 26.1312.

filtering, filtring stone, *OED* says 'any porous stone through which water is filtered', although the earliest quotation offered is from 1821; the only mention of this item is in the 1741 inventory and perhaps it was used in the brewhouse to filter water being pumped in from the moat: 41.338. See also **pump**.

firkin, old, for hops, 26.1306.

funnel, funnell, tunnell, 97.70, 26.1307, 41.349.

gatherer, gatherrer, uncertain; but given its location, this could be what *OED* (citing 1874) and twenty years earlier Ogilvie's *Imperial Dictionary* ... (ed. Annandale, London, 1855, p. 369) describe as a 'gathering-hoop', used by coopers for drawing in the ends of the staves of a barrel or cask to allow the permanent hoop to be slipped on: 26.1300.

gyle, guile: describes **wort** (the infusion of malt and water) fermenting in the brewing process. See **vat** and **yield** below.

hogshead: both a measure (63 wine gallons) and the name of its container, 97.67, 97.278, 26.1309, 41.343, 41.347, 41.353; **half hogshead**, 41.347.

hogshead stand, 41.342.

hop sieve, 41.284.

hop skepp(s), baskets, 26.1305.

jet(t): a spout, nozzle or tap, 97.282, 26.1298.

keeler(s), kellar(s): broad, shallow, hooped wooden vessels, 97.69, 97.279, 26.1310; **beer**, 41.345, **latch** (to catch drips), 26.1039, 26.1047; **to wash glasses in**, 26.1038.

mash: malt and hot water, together forming **wort**, which, as it ferments, is known as **gyle**. For the vessels involved in each process, see **tub** and **vat** below.

pail, payles, 97.287; **with iron hoops**, 41.265.

penne staffe: Yaxley (p. 151) offers nothing specific to this context but defines 'penn' as a gun-barrel, deriving from its resemblance to a quill-like pipe. Given the description in the 1626 inventory of the 'penn staffe, stuke and underbeck', whose combined purpose was to drain wort from the 'great mash fat', a pipe or the staff or stick associated with it seems likely, 26.1293.

praytree: speculatively, the upright part, or housing of, the 'pray' or lever, through which water was pumped, 26.1036, 26.1312.

See **pump**, below, for specific details of how the water supply for brewing was engineered. See also alphabetical entry elsewhere in the glossary for **tree**.

prongs, iron, 41.285.

pump, *with* lead cistern, 08.657; **leaden**, 41.337; **from the moat**, 41.279; **from the under-deck**, 41.27; **with praytree and cistern in the 'newe seller'**,

26.1036; **with praytree and dale** (conduit) **to bring water from back yard to brewhouse**, 26.1312.

shovel, sholve, 97.283.

step ladders, 41.286.

stuke: Halliwell (p. 811) provides a definition in stook, 'a sort of stile beneath which water is discharged'. This one lies beneath the mash vat in 1626 but its position in 1597 is not defined, 97.286, 26.1293.

tap staff, tapp staffe, 26.1168; see **wiltch**, below, with which this item is listed.

tilter, mechanism for tilting a barrel: 26.1041, 26.1045, 41.351.

trough, 97.281, 08.305. 08.306, 08.307 (with dimensions), 41.283.

tub, tubb, 97.277, 41.344; **brewing, large**, 41.281; **large, and under-deck**, 41.280; **wort tub**, 26.1295, 08.304 (with dimensions).

tunnell: see **funnel**.

under-beck, underbecke, under deck: Halliwell (p. 900) defines under-deck as 'the low broad tub into which the wort runs from the mash-tub', this being the precise location of the item as described in the 1626 and 1741 inventories: 26.1293, 41.279, 41.280.

vat, fatt: the vessels in which each stage of brewing took place; for definitions of **gyle, mash** and **wort,** see alphabetical entries elsewhere within *brewing*.

gyle, guile, great, 26.1294. See also *yield*, below.

mash, mashe, mashing, meesh, 97.273, 26.1293, 08.301 (with dimensions); **stirrer(s) for**, 26.1296, 08.309.

working, 08.303 (with dimensions).

wort, worte, 97.274.

yield, yeild, the term appears only in the 1597 inventory and is taken to be synonymous with **gyle** (*q.v.*), a term not used then, 97.275. See also **tub,** above.

wilch, wiltch, wicker: Halliwell (p. 931) defines this as a strainer, to capture sediment, 26.1168.

wort, worte: the infusion of malt and water. See **vat** above.

brick, bricks: fired at, and recorded in, the estate's brick kiln (discussed in footnote 150 to the 1626 inventory), 26.1543, 26.1547.

brine tub, bryne tubb: a wooden tub of sufficient proportions to allow the immersion of raw foodstuffs, particularly joints of pork, in brine, a strong solution of salt and water, prior to storage for use as a cured meat, particularly bacon, 97.174, 26.1126. See also **salt; souse**.

britches, worn under **drawers** (*q.v.*): 26.848.

broad stitch: see **needlework**.

brush, brushes: with one exception (*unspecified*), the inventories identify the purpose or characteristics of each brush:

bristle with wooden handle, 26.221.

clothes, with yellow mohair (moiré) top, 08.490.

cobweb, copwebb, new, 26.785.

hand, 41.27.

hard, round, 08.163.

hearth, harth, the word 'hearth' is used only in the 1708 inventory to define these brushes but not in 1741; however, the context is clear in the 1741 inventory where the brush is part of a suite of fireside tools: 08.222, 08.427, 08.483, 41.39, 41.59, 41.70, 41.89, 41.98, 41.112, 41.127, 41.145, 41.176, 41.359, 41.375, 41.392, 41.409, 41.456, 41.538, 41.556.

Indian, for hangings, Yaxley (p. 109) explains that Indian may not mean from India but from China, India, Japan or the Middle East: 08.429.

lists, of, lists are narrow strips of cloth; in this context, the strips are bound together and attached to a handle to create a brush that was less abrasive than rushes or bristle: 26.824.

unspecified, 97.917.

buckets, leather: given the quantity (48) and material, these were almost certainly kept ready for fire-fighting in what was called the great hall by 1741, filled with sand or water from the moat. Leather buckets were prone to split and were water-proofed with a pitch lining: 41.188.

bucking, buck(e)ing: see *laundry*.

buckram, buckrum, buckerum: from the late 16th century, a coarse linen or cloth stiffened with gum and, as some entries reveal, lined with paper for additional stiffening when used to protect furniture:

bag (for harness), 26.922.

cases, covers for furniture, 97.331, 26.159, 26.160, 26.161, 26.162, 26.163, 26.188, 26.198, 26.199, 26.200, 26.202, 26.206, 26.212, 26.245, 26.599; **lined with paper**, 26.211, 26.216, 26.244.

cover for a leading staff (*q.v.*), 26.67

lining for, footcloth, 26.831, 26.832; **'honnces' (?harness)**, 26.829.

piece of: used as packing material, 26.815; **to cover saddle**, 26.915.

screen, 97.621, 26.108.

tester, 97.509, 97.520, 26.139, 26.227.

buff, buffe: see **leather**.

buffin, buffon: textile: narrow, fine cloth (originally from wool of the Angora goat) used for garments, upholstery and furnishings:

chair, 97.402, 26.454.

curtains (bedstead), 97.636.

petticoat (*q.v.*), 97.928, 97.932, 97.936.

stool, 97.26.

tester and valance, 97.635.

bullet bag, bullett bagge: see **gun**.

bultelle, boutelle: uncertain: Halliwell (p. 218) says that 'bultle' is bran, and these items are noted in the 'Bultinge [Bolting] House' in 1597 and the 'Meal howse' in 1626, where they are described as 'one finer thother coarrser', which suggests a type of sieve or sifter, 97.264, 26.1274. See also **bolting**.

bulting: see **bolting**.

burd eye: see **bird's eye**.

bureau: two examples appear only in the 1741 inventory, reflecting the rise in popularity of bureaux in the late 17th and 18th centuries. One of the Helmingham examples is described clearly, combining shelves for books, protected by glazed doors, with a writing surface and storage below; but the other is listed only as 'bureau' with no additional details. Edwards (p. 123) explains that the bureau has never been clearly defined, and that names such as bureau, secretaire, escritoire and scrutore were applied to a wide variety of designs and can be confusing; this is evident in one of the Helmingham examples, the **scrutore** being only part of the walnut bureau, and referring to its writing surface, 41.1, 41.404.

bushel, bushell, bushill: in context, a vessel with the capacity to hold a bushel (a measurement of volume: 4 pecks or 8 gallons), 26.1399, 26.1404, 08.624; **half-bushel measure**, 08.693.

butt: large wooden tubs listed in the cellars, probably for **wine** (*q.v.*), 08.649.

butter: as with **cheese, cream, maw, milk** and **whey** (*q.v.*), the inventories specify utensils and equipment strictly in relation to their role in butter-making:

> **barrel churn**: a small, cradle-mounted barrel laid on its side so that the cream inside could be agitated by rotation to form butter. Yaxley (p. 43) describes several means of operation: the barrel churn could be 'mounted on gimbals on a stand which was swung to and fro, or end over end, or had paddles operated by a cranked handle'. The sole example is recorded in the 1626 inventory as made in 1617, 26.1179.
>
> **bowl, boul(e)**, 97.206.
>
> **churn with 2 winches**, 41.293.
>
> **keeler, kellar, killer**: broad, shallow, straight-sided, hooped wooden vessel, 97.205, 26.1183, 08.344, 41.292.
>
> **scraper of bone**, 08.212.
>
> See also **dairy**.

buttons: inventory entries to decorative buttons and associated trimmings offer considerably more detail than offered by the editorial summaries below.

> **bone**, 26.800.
>
> **gold**, 97.948, 97.862, 97.889, 97.909, 97.969; **gold and silver**, 97.800.
>
> *saddles, on*, 97.877.
>
> *upholstery, on*, 26.447, 26.550.

cabinet, cabbinett: cabinets could be large, with glazed doors for display of decorative items above, and a closed cupboard beneath; or small, supported on a trestle with lockable doors which opened to reveal drawers for documents or small items of value, 26.85; **walnuttree**, 41.373, **large**, 41.172, **small**, 41.172.

caffa: textile used as a furnishing material. Caffa might be a figured satin with a silk warp and a linen weft; a woollen velvet, e.g. a worsted pile on a linen ground, or a version known as Genoa velvet, which was made in silk: **chair**, 97.335; **stools**, 97.331.

cage: for quail (*q.v.*), 97.229. See also **birdcage**.

cake pan: see **pan, cake**.

cake print, carved: consigned to storage in the Old Wardrobe by 1626, this would have been a decorative wooden stamp applied to confectionery, a technique described in some of Catherine Tollemache's recipes for fruit pastes (known also as cakes), on which the imprint would appear in relief, 26.766.

calf, calves: mentioned in relation to slaughterhouse equipment and the extraction of rennet (*see* **maw**), 26.1215, 26.1488.

calico, callico: light cotton fabric imported from India: **tablecloths**, 08.682; **table cover, flowered**, 41.105, 41.161; **window curtains**, 08.524, 08.525, 08.477.

caliver: see **gun**.

callasina: Uncertain: speculatively, related to a placename, suggesting an imported gown, perhaps from Castille, or the word may be a variant of **castilliano**, a cloth also imported originally from Castille but produced in England by the time of the 1597 inventory, which contains the sole reference, 97.919.

callin barrels: see **gun**.

camblet, chamblet, chamlitt: fine cloth, made in the 16th and 17th centuries from the long hair of the angora goat (Yaxley, p. 31):

bedstead curtains, blue, 41.526; yellow, 41.412.

chair cover, gold, embroidered, 26.202.

counterpanes, blue, 41.526; **yellow**, 41.412.

cushion backing, silk, 26.822.

hangings, wall, yellow, 41.412.

kirtle lining, gold, 97.895.

tent-bed, 41.412.

tester, blue, 41.526.

window curtains, blue, 41.533; **yellow**, 41.412.

Narrow camblets of worsted are known as **buffin** (*q.v.*).

camel-hair, cammell heare growgraine: **doublet and hose of**, 97.809. See also **grosgrain**.

candle[s]: there is no inventory evidence of candle-making at Helmingham after 1597. However, in all four inventories there are numerous entries describing candle-related items:

candleplate: Speculatively, the item is synonymous with a chamber stick, the 'plate' being the lipped base (to catch drips) bearing a socket into which a candle is inserted, 97.285, 97.659, 97.667, 26.657; **brass[e][ing]**, 97.5, 26.8, 26.23, 26.136, 26.966, 26.1095, 26.1340, 08.146, **iron, yron**, 97.111, 26.270, 26.442, 26.545.

candlestick[s], 97.62, 97.504; **brass**, 97.92; 08.67; 08.334; **broken**, 26.942; **hand, brass**: 41.226, **old**, 97.112; **pewter**, 97.549, 26.976; **stand, brass**, 41,226, **wire, wyer**, 26.1232.

chest [for], 26.1049, 26.1225.

coffer [for], 97.542.

hutches, 41.322.

iron, 41.226, **hand**, 41.25.

snuffers: **brass[e], pair**, 26.51; **iron**, 41.24.

socket [for], 26.1031.

stand for, japanned, 41.516; **mahogany**, 41.516; **old**, 41.88.

standers and, 26.1372.

See also **sconce, torch[es]**.

cane: Edwards (p. 202) confirms that rattan cane for seated furniture was imported into England from the Malay Peninsula through the East India Company in the late 17th century. By 1747, however, caning had fallen from favour. The 1708 inventory lists the only examples recorded at Helmingham, items which may well have migrated from Ham House, where suites of cane-seated chairs were listed in a 1728 inventory (*Ham House*, pp. 465–8): **chairs**, 08.220, 08.555, 08.607; **child's chair**, 08.538, 08.585.

canister: 41.28, 41.471.

canopy: see **bedstead, canopy**.

canvas, canvis, canvise, kanvis: textile, woven originally from hemp (*Cannabis sativa*), and also from flax (*Linum usitatissimum*) to produce a strong, unbleached cloth with a wide variety of applications at Helmingham Hall:

> **case for a cocking net** (*q.v.*), 26.703.
>
> **chair bottom**, 26.41.
>
> **doublet, dublet**, 97.808, 97.941, 97.942.
>
> **lining** *for*: **honnces (?harness)**, 26.829; **tapestry**, 26.224, 26.791. See also **koord**.

capon: domestic cock castrated for fattening and eating: **grease, pot of**, 26.1238; **tray for mixing capon's meat (feed)**, 26.1286.

capteyne: captain; see **leading staff [for]**.

carbine, carbyne: see **gun**.

carpet (table covering): in the 1597 inventory this refers to a thick, tapestry-like covering for a table or other flat surface, including that described as a 'cupboard'; by 1626; carpets are specified also as **wall hangings**; and in 1708 the word is used in both contexts, and, for the first time, to describe a floor covering (see below). Catherine Tollemache's household miscellany includes a set of needle-work instructions for creating a table carpet of 20 feet in length (Coleman, p. 94). Dimensions are provided for each carpet in the 1708 inventory, confirming that several tables were of considerable size. In 1741, descriptions refer to protective 'covers' (*see* **table, cover for**), invariably of green cloth.

> **cloth, of**, 26.458, 26.1014, 08.420, 08.421.
>
> **cupboard**, 26.303, 26.380, 26.833.
>
> **dornex, of**, 97.526.
>
> **table**, 97.32, 97.338, 97.339, 97.340, 97.784, 97.961, 26.115, 26.247, 26.304, 26.833, 08.420, 08.452.
>
> **turkey-work** (?table carpet), 26.49, 26.203, 26.793, 08.629.
>
> See also **carpet frame; board cloth; tablecloth**.

carpet (floor covering): there are few examples in this context, 08.467, 41.360, **large**, 41.94. See also **mat, matte, matted** for other floor coverings.

carpet frame: frame designed to hold a large piece of carpet needlework (wool stitched through canvas) while work was in progress, 97.956, 26.667, 26.682 (containing a piece of needlework in progress). See also needlework frame.

cart, carte: the 1626 inventory provides descriptions of carts and associated items for draught-horses beyond that conveyed by the categories summarised here, 08.697.

> **boarded both sides**, 26.1492, **open**, 26.1492.

cradle rave: see **raves**, below.

foorestoole pillar, iron, old: uncertain, but see **pillar for raves**, below, 26.1325.

hoops, hoopes for cart naves: a nave is the centre block of a wheel-hub, 26.1467.

iron wheels, 26.1492.

ladders: ladder-like framework projecting from the front of a cart, 26.1492.

raves, raves, cradle rave, pillar for rave: Halliwell (p. 670) defines 'raves' as 'additions to a waggon without which it is not considered complete. The raves or shelvings are two frames of wood which are laid on the top of the waggon in such a way as to meet in the middle, and projecting on all sides beyond the body of the vehicle, enable it to carry a larger load.' All entries including reference to cart raves are included here, 26.1325, 26.1439, 26.1440.

ropes, roopes, 26.1425.

saddle, saddles: for cart-horses, 26.1422.

saddle tree, trees: upright supports on which to hang saddles, 26.1449.

strake, strakes: iron rim of a cart wheel, 26.1453.

stuff[e]: in this context, the word describes grease destined to lubricate carts, especially their wheels. The presence of a firkin filled with cart stuff in the 1597 lard house supports this, 97.248. See also **grease**.

case, small, cloth-lined, 41.617.

case for a sword hilt: this phrase is used only in the 1626 inventory for an item of leather lined with cotton: 26.931. See also **scabbard**.

case for a wash ball, container for personal washing soap: 41.33.

casement curtain: see **curtains, window**.

cask, caske, kaske: wooden storage vessel: 26.1416; **cheese cask**, 97.256; **wine, wyne cask (old)**, 26.1055. See also **wine**.

cast: see **gun: pistol**.

castilliano: see **callasina**.

casting net, casteing nett: Given the context in 1597 and the description of the weights for an old casting net described in the 1626 fish chamber, this looks to be one and the same item, a net for dredging fish, perhaps from the moat, 97.10; **leads of**, 26.1346.

ceil, seeling[e]: in the context of the inventories, wooden panelling, also used in the construction of furniture, 26.5, 26.9; see also wainscot.

celestial globe: not the globe itself, but described as 'draught of part of the celestiall globe': 08.576. See also globes.

chafer, chaffer: a container for combustible materials such as wicker, charcoal or coals placed beneath a **chafing dish**. However, in the case of slow-burning perfumes designed to counteract odours, the chafer alone would be used: 97.121; **brass**, 26.702, 26.968; **copper**, 97.551.

chafing dish, chafeing, chaffing, chaffyne dishe, dyshe: dish placed above a **chafer** and designed to maintain the temperature of cooked food: **brasen**, 97.93; **brass**, 26.967, **iron**, 97.130, 41.453; **silver**, 97.1172; 97.1210.

chain, chaine, chayne: on doors, with locks, 26.1368; **with hook**, 26.1446; **with plough**, 26.1456, 26.1457, 26.149; **with rope to lead a horse to water**, 26.1389.

chair, chaire, chayer, chayre: chairs at Helmingham Hall are identified by age, construction, size, material, and, where upholstered, the fabric, colour and design of the seats and/or backs. The categories listed below provide only the initial descriptive words and phrases in an attempt to convey the meticulous attention to detail evident throughout the inventories. Some chairs listed in the 1597 inventory emerge as 'old', 'old-fashioned' and/or ' broken' in the 1626 inventory, but are put to use in staff chambers. By 1708, chairs are described frequently in sets; and cane makes its first appearance. In 1741, leather is mentioned often and the Windsor chair is listed for the only time:

arm, armed, arm'd, with arms, 26.212, 26.897, 08.397, 08.561, 08.691, 41.80, 41.116, 41.166, 41.477, 41.514, 41.567; **carved and inlaid**, 08.398.

backed, 26.302.

bed, 26.244.

> **cane**, 08.220, 08.555, 08.608.

child's, children's, 97.27, 97.603, 26.642 ('verie old'), 41.553; **cane**, 08.585; **carved, cane backed and seated**, 08.538.

cloth, 41.506, 41.568, 41.574.

couch, coutche, 26.41, 26.596; **piece of**, 26.10.

covered, 08.270, 08.275, 41.92; **great**, 26.159, 26.188, 26.201, 26.202, 26.206, 26.242, 26.328, 26.358.

damask, 08.250, 41.11, 41.65, 41.160, 41.166, 41.355, 41.366, 41.514, 41.522.

easy, great, 41.366.

elbow, elboe, 08.249, 08.251, 08.269, 08.271, 08.414.

embroidered, 97.385, 97.527, 26.454.

high, 26.159, 26.208, 26.213.

joined, 97.22, 97.469, 97.583, 97.619, 97.641, 97.951, 26.427; **seated and backed with**: embroidered caffa, 97.335; **yellow satin**, 97.336; **satin of bridges**, 97.618; **seated with leather**, 97.21.

leather, lether, 08.32, 08.323, 08.368, 08.620, 41.108, 41.135, 41.389, 41.405, 41.420.

leather-backed, 26.38; **and seated, great**, 26.121.

little, seated and backed with, turkey work, 97.334, 26.39; **crimson satin**, 26.200.

low, covered, 26.160, 26.243; **black leather**, 26.222.

old, 08.289, 04.592, 41.612; **broken, leather**, 08.95; **elbow**, 08.288; **with leather seat**, 26.569. See also **turned; wainscott**.

old-fashioned, 26.122; **wooden**, 26.410.

seated with: fine turkey work, 08.415; **tent stitch**, 26.245.

seated and backed with: buffin, buffon, 97.402; **cloth**, 08.457, 08.480; **clouded silk**, 08.514; **coarse turkey work**, 08.416; **Scotch plaid**, 08.513; **tuftaffeta**, 97.429; **velvet**, 97.337, 97.354, 08.495.

turned, 97.470, 97.584, 97.620, 97.674, 97.691, 97.707, 97.732, 97.951, 26.529; **broken**, 26.428, 26.570; **great**, 26.116; **old**, 26.763; **with hoop of needlework**, 97.24.

unspecified, 41.87, 41.125, 41.309, 41.425, 41.587, 41.601.

velvet, 41.464, 41.515.

walnut, walnuttree, 41.534.

wainscot(t), 26.455, 26.479; **great**, 26.562, **old**, 26.896, 26.1357.

wicker, 41.568.

Windsor: both *OED* and Edwards (p. 319) cite 1724 as the earliest date when a Windsor chair was mentioned in correspondence: Lord Percival, writing of his 1724 visit to Hall Barn in Buckinghamshire, reported that his wife was carried into the gardens 'in a Windsor chair like those at Versailles'. The chair is an all-wooden seat in which the bow and spindles of the back and legs are dowelled into the seat and the stretchers into the legs. The appearance of six Windsor chairs in the great hall at Helmingham suggests that they were in use for dining. If so, this was at a date well before their significant production (centred on High Wycombe) and rise in popularity for use other than outdoors. However, they were apparently used indoors in taverns and inns and perhaps the set in the great hall was intended to convey the spirit of conviviality, especially bearing in mind the presence in the same room of a picture described in 1708 as a cookshop and in 1741 as a large kitchen piece: 41.180.

without seats, 08.608.

wooden, 08.298.

chaise for one horse, with harness: a light travelling carriage more usually drawn by a pair of horses. This one is mentioned in the 1741 coach house inventory with a note that although it belongs there, it is currently in the great hall: 41.620.

chalk, chalke, mallet to beat with, 26.1114.

chamber: refers generally to a room, irrespective of floor level. Defined throughout the inventories by occupant or purpose and discussed in the footnotes.

chamber pot, pott: small metal or earthenware receptacle, equipped with a handle, used as a lavatory, particularly at night-time, and stored usually beneath the bedstead. However, the inventories show that only sleeping chambers occupied by members of the family, or those used by guests, were equipped with a pot. Anyone else would have been expected to leave the building to relieve themselves. Few are mentioned in the 1708 inventory and in 1741 none at all are listed, although **close stools** are listed in both: 97.110, 97.363, 97.389, 97.411, 97.436, 97.463, 97.496, 97.550, 97.587, 97.625, 97.645, 26.150, 26.193, 26.236, 26.301, 26.333, 26.355, 26.378, 26.434, 26.560, 26.593; **earthen, white**, 08.203; **pewter, to be exchanged** (*q.v.*), 08.68.

See also **close stool; bedstool**.

chamblet, chamlitt: see **camblet**.

changeable: used to describe fabrics whose colours and textures appeared to change when seen in different lights: **taffeta, purple and green**, 26.229, 26.235.

charger: large plate, platter or flat dish, usually for serving food, a term redundant beyond the 1597 inventory when these utensils were described by their size relative to one another, 97.94, 97.160.

chariot, chariott: a private carriage. Yaxley (p. 39) says they were four-wheeled until the 18th century and then usually two-wheeled. The 1708 inventory lists one, but only the top or cover for one appears in the 1626 inventory: **lined with grey cloth**, 08.701; **fore-glass for**, 08.499; **top or cover for**, 26.902. See also **chaise; coach**.

chayer, chayre: see **chair**.

checkerwork: pattern formed by alternating colours or textiles: **coverlet of**, 26.425.

cheese: as with **butter, cream, maw, milk** and **whey** (*q.v.*), the inventories specify utensils and equipment specific to cheese-making, both in the dairies and cheese chamber, where cheese was ripened and stored:

  board, boorde: flat surface either for working or, especially in the cheese chamber, for storage of ripening cheeses. Nine are recorded there in 1626, described as being on eleven trestles, 97.196, 97.254, 26.1236.

  box: 'one little rounde hooped boxe w[i]thout a cover to send morning milk cheese to ffakenham or London', 26.1200.

  bread, breed(e): lid or cover for a cheese vat, of sufficient weight to act as a **press** for softer cheeses, sometimes carved with a motif (see **printing** below):

  great: the 1626 inventory describes one of these as 'printed now turned playne', 26.1189; **not fit for use**, 26.1190.

  plain, playne, 97.212.

  printing: carved with a pattern, providing a decorative imprint on the surface of the cheese, 97.211, 26.1187.

  small, smaller: there are nine of these in 1597 but only four in 1626; these may well have been for the smaller angelot cheeses (see **angelot**, above), 97.213, 26.1188.

  unspecified, 08.343, 41.296.

  cask[e]: recorded in the cheese chamber; speculatively for the storage of soft cheeses in brine, 97.256.

  cleansing bowl, clensing boule: related to the cleanser, or sieve, through which milk was strained before being warmed, 97.208.

  curd colanders, curde cullenders, earthen, 26.1206.

  fat: see **vat**, below.

  powdering tub, pouldering tubb: powdering is salting, an essential part of the cheese-making process, 26.1223. See also **salting**, below.

  press: screw-operated; this was the alternative to pressing with a **bread**, allowing more downward pressure to be exerted and more liquid to be expelled, resulting in a harder cheese. The inventory entry for the new double cheese press in 1626 includes details of its mechanism, described in 1708 as 'with two screws'.

  double, 97.194; **new**, 26.1210.

  with two screws, 08.339.

  unspecified, 41.297.

  salt, saulte, saulting: items related to the process of adding salt to cheese are not specified in the 1597 inventory, but the 1626 and 1708 inventories are specific:

  cowl, coule, old, for, 26.1209.

  firkin, ferkin with white salt, 26.1219.

  tray for, 08.341, **great**, 26.1211; **leaden**, 41.298.

  See also **powdering tub**, above, and **souse tub**, below.

  souse tub, sowse tubbes: brine tubs kept in the cheese chamber for regular washing of the rinds of **angelot** cheeses during ripening. 97.257, 26.1223.

tongs, cheese, 41.304. See also **milk: tongs**.

tray: **old, to put fennel seed in**: the location of this 'old' item in the 1626 dairy may be inconsequential; but speculatively, fennell seeds were used to sweeten rennet (see **maw**), 26.1237.

tub: Yaxley (p. 41) defines this as 'flattish wooden tub in which curds and whey were separated by curdling with rennet'. The 1626 inventory reference is oblique, referring to a stool on which 'to stande the cheese tubbe' but not identifying the tub itself. However, both 1597 and 1626 inventories refer to a milk tub and the 1708 lists a milk tray, either of which might have served the purpose (see **milk**), 26.1222, 41.294.

vat, fat(t): vessel, usually lined cheesecloth or muslin, into which the curds were placed after separation from the whey (see **tub**). The 1597 inventory records a total of twenty vats, giving an indication of the scale of the hall's cheese production at the time, listed either by purpose or condition:

angellica: in context, a variant spelling of **angelot**, since there is no obvious connection with the angelica plant related to a vat in the dairy, 26.1186.

angelot, angelet: angelot is a soft cheese whose surface demanded regular washing with salted water during ripening (*Larousse Gastronomique*, London, 2009, pp. 20 and 225). Importantly, in the context of their location in the Cheese Chamber, the 'sowse tubbes' (see above) contain brine and their presence in the designated space for cheese-ripening at Helmingham in 1597 confirms the household's sophisticated approach to cheese-making: 97.218.

copper, 97.210, 41.278 (with furnace and copper cock).

great, 97.209, 26.1184 (including some past use).

smaller, 26.1185 (including some full of holes in the bottom).

unspecified, 08.342, 41.296.

For equipment specific to other dairy tasks, see **butter, cream, maw, milk** and **whey**.

chess: **gaming tables and men for**, 26.57. See also **backgammon; goose game; tables, gaming**.

chest, chist: one of the most common storage containers (with **trunks**), particularly in the 1597 inventory, where items of household linen were described in terms of the chest in which they were stored and its location in the house. High-value items, including the finest-quality linen, were under lock and key and were located in the chambers of heads of household or senior members of the resident staff:

bound, cased, with iron, 97.492, 97.533, 97.731, 41.62, see also **with lock and key**.

candle, 26.1049, see also **with lock and key**.

cypress, 08.552.

defined by dimensions, 08.486, 08.603, 08.605.

great, 97.950, 26.625; 26.768; **dansk[e]** (*q.v.*) 26.603; **for ashes**, 26.1250, **wooden**, 26.676; **wooden like a church chest**, 26.269; see also **with lock and key**.

large, 08.135, 08.535; **long**, 41.520; **long square**, 41.508; containing **musical instruments**, 08.640.

linen, *containing*, 41.428, 41.444.

long, 97.535; see also **with lock and key**.

mahogany, 41.61.

oats, for, 26.1401; see also **with lock and key**.

old, 97.47, 97.731, 97.540, 97.706, 97.748, 97.962, 97.963, 26.412 ('old fashioned'), 26.439, 26.502, 26.664, 26.752, 26.900, 26.1110, 26.1314, 26.134, 41.575, 41.615.

saddles, for, 26.1383.

ship's, 97.539.

spice[rye], 26.1108.

square, old, *containing* armour, 41.614.

undefined, 08.641.

with lock and/or key, 97.538 ; **bound with iron**, 97.471, 97.472; **with padlock**, 97.531; **candle**, 26.1225; **dansk, inlaid**, 97.617; **flat, black leather**, 97.474; **great**, 97.616, 26.580, 26.883; **inlaid**, 26.83; **joined**, 97.537; **leather with three drawers**, 97.473; **long**, 97.512, 97.536, 26.940; **oats, [for]**, 26.1382; **plain**, 97.513; **trunk chest**, 97.566, 26.939. See also **coffer** and **trunk**.

without a bottom, 08.536.

writings, for (wryghteings), inlaid, 26.69.

chest of drawers, mentioned for the first time in the 1741 inventory: 41.549, **walnuttree**, having a leafe to let down like a table: 41.532.

chevron, chevern: a decorative motif: **blue, on table napkins**, 97.1069.

See also **diaper; linen**.

chicking: chicken.

child, children, a nursery is listed in each of the four inventories, but items designed for children are limited to the following:

case for a child's knife, fork and spoon, 08.522.

chair, chayer, 97.27, 97.603, 26.642, 08.538, 08.585, 41.553.

clothes basket, 08.567 (with dimensions).

going cart: a framework on wheels designed to support a child learning to walk; *OED*'s earliest citation dates from 1649: 08.588.

chimney, chimnye: because chimneys and their flues were an integral part of the hall's structure, they are mentioned only in references to decorative and utilitarian items as listed below:

carved pieces of an oval moulding for, 08.646.

chimney end, Turkey work carpet on, 08.466.

chimney piece:

escutcheons of arms in, 26.53.

long picture framed for, 26.290.

map, framed for, 26.153; **on**, 26.248.

tapestry [on], 26.152.

verdures, verders (designs of living, green plant materials), 26.376.

chimney stock: the back of a grate (Halliwell, p. 809), 26.1334.

fire dog in, 26.16.

printed iron to set at, 26.1334.

trammels in: hangers for pots, 26.1071.

wainscot, to set before in Summer: a screen, 26.26.

wainscot cupboard for, 26.646.

china: prior to the development of English porcelain manufacture from the mid–18th century, china was imported. The large numbers of items recorded in the 1741 inventory reflect the increasing availability of English-made items:

basin, bason, blue, 08.230.

coffee cups, blue and white, 41.103.

dishes, 41.201, 41.493.

enamelled coffee and tea cups, saucers, teapot etc., 41.161.

inkstand, 41.31.

plates (127), 41.492.

punch bowl, large, 41.494.

tea cups and saucers, basin etc., 41.104.

tea dish, green, 08.231.

teapot, tea-pott, brown, with gilded handle, 08.229.

chipping knife, 97.56.

chist: see **chest**.

chocolate, chocolet, chocalat: like coffee and tea, a beverage that increased in popularity from the late 17th century onwards. Chocolate was imported into England as 'nibs': these were created by roasting and crushing the beans and mixing them into a paste with water. These nibs had to be scraped into sweetened milk and boiled rapidly, then the mixture frothed with an instrument called a *molenillo* or *molinet*, of which the **mill**, below, is a version. The mill had to be rolled vigorously between the hands until an emulsion formed, and an aperture in the lid of the chocolate pot (sometimes concealed beneath a removeable finial) allowed for its insertion and removal: **mill**, 08.158, 41.210; **pot, copper**, 41.210; **1-pint**, 08.157.

chopping block, 97.173, 26.1094, 26.1125, 26.1220, 08.356, 41.330.

chopping board, boord, 97.250.

chopping knife, 97.136.

churn: see **milk**. See also **butter: barrel churn**.

cider bag, cydar bagg: of hair, for straining the juice from apple pulp, 08.173.

cipher, cypher: described on pewter items engraved with coronets of the earls of Dysart: **dishes**, 08.57; **plates**, 08.56. See also **arms** (coats of arms).

cipris: see **Cyprus**.

cistern, sesterne, sisterne: associated generally, but not exclusively, with the storage of water:

copper, 41.208.

japanned (lacquered), 41.49.

lead, leadeing, leaden, 26.1036, 26.1510, 08.657.

marble, white, 08.218 (with dimensions), 41.133.

wood, in the ground, for hogs meat, 26.1504.

cittern, sittern: wire-stringed musical instrument here referred to in an oblique reference: **cases for, with locks but no keys**, 26.131. For other musical instruments see **harpsichord, lute, organ, spinet, virginals**.

clapper for napkins: see *laundry, dry*.

claws: **gilded, for bed feet**, 08.487.

cleansing, clensing: see **cheese: cleansing bowl**.

cleaver, clever, clyver: hook or broad knife for chopping, 97.134; **to chop hawks' meat**, 26.577; **with wooden handle**, 26.1231.

climbing boards: see **boards**.

climbing hook, climbinge hooke, clymeinge hookes: for climbing trees; both references locate these hooks in the chambers of men involved with park-keeping at Helmingham, John Nunn and 'Humfery': **one**, 26.518; **pair of**, 26.708.

cloak, cloake, cloke: protective outer garment, often hooded, worn by both sexes. Inventory descriptions include details of linings, bindings, fasteners and trims. Recycling is exemplified in the editorial category *modified for other uses*, where the French green cloth cloak recorded in 1597 has been used, the compiler says, 'as I remember' to cover chairs and stools at the Fakenham property. Definitions of unfamiliar textiles can be found elsewhere in the glossary:

bag, bagge to carry in, 26.779.

cloth, cloath: **black**, 97.872, 26.800, 26.801, 26.811, 26.814; **black cloth capes for**, 26.863; **French green, grene**, 97.865, 26.810; **purple**, 97.909; **Valentia blue, blew**, 97.866.

lining, lyning: described individually, making reference to the cloak from which it was removed: **silk shag, shagge**, 26.803; **taffeta, taffata, taffatie**, 26.796, 26.797.

modified for other uses, 26.795.

mourning, morning, 97.874, 97.938.

riding, 97.873.

satin, satten: **white**, 97.910.

taffeta, taffatie, taffety, taffaty, taffita, 97.863: **black**, 26.804, 26.805, 26.808, 26.813; **plain black**, 97.864; **black tuft taffeta, furred**, 97.912; **russett**, 26.809; **white**, 97.911.

velvet: **black**, 97.859, 26.812; **Dutch black**, 97.860.

See also **apparel**.

clobe: see **globe**.

clock: the contents of a 'clockhowse', the area 'at the toppe of the howse' for a great clock, are identified first in the 1626 inventory (but see there footnote 29, which suggests an earlier clock) and describe a clock mechanism operated by lines and weights; by 1708 this clock has a pendulum, a feature whose appearance in England is dated by Edwards (p. 81) to 1658. In 1741 the instrument in the closet of the clock room is described in more detail, and clocks in the Earl of Dysart's dressing room are described with their movements and the names of their eminent makers, but no details of their cases.

clock, 26.272, 08.665.

and larm (alarm), the 1626 inventory describes a 'little clocke and larm' to be mended: 26.610.

pendulum, 08.665.

pendulum clock by Gray: Benjamin Gray (1676–1764) was appointed Watchmaker in Ordinary to George II in 1742, the year before compilation of the Helmingham inventory. For the latter part of his working life he was in partnership with his son-in-law, Francois Justin Vulliamy (*ODNB*). Gray made both bracket and longcase clocks but no details of the Helmingham case are provided: 41.7.

spring: describes a spring-driven clock, probably for a table, 08.219.

spring clock by Graham: following his apprenticeship to Henry Aske, George Graham (1673–1751), began to work for Thomas Tompion in 1696. In Tompion's last years he took Graham on as his partner. Graham was master of the Clockmakers' Company in 1722 and a member of the Royal Society. He made significant contributions to the development of horology (*ODNB*): 41.6.

turret, eight-day, with bell and stone dial plate: 41.498.

close stool, cloose, closse stool(l)e: portable lavatory, reserved only for the highest-status members of the household, consisting of a pan, a removable form of **chamber pot**, enclosed within a wooden box whose surround formed a seat, the whole closed by a lid which was sometimes upholstered. The inventories reveal that by 1708 some of these were elegant pieces of furniture. It is noticeable that there are fewer in 1741 than in any of the three earlier inventories. 97.544, 97.568, 97.883, 26.255, 26.309, 26.363, 26.583, 41.361, 41.410; **cedar, with velvet seat**, 08.527; **covered with Kidderminster stuff**: 08.527; **little**, 41.562; **locking, cedar**, 08.462; **mahogany**: 41.48, **old**, 26.336, 26.430, **old, decayed**, 26.770; **old, without pan**, 26.669; **pan for**, 97.561; **old pans for**, 26.771, 26.1339; **round**, 41.541.

See also **bedstool**; **chamber pot**; **urinal**.

cloth: in the context of these inventories, a term used broadly to describe items made of woven cloth, whatever its constituents (linen, wool and mixtures of these and other materials). References occur frequently in descriptions of apparel, household table linens and furnishing textiles, not all of which define the type of cloth; but for specific items see **linen**.

cloth of gold: there are numerous deletions of cloth of gold, particularly in the 1626 inventory, in favour of **cloth of silver** (*q.v.*). The identity of the metallic thread would have been judged by its colour, and tarnishing would have made it difficult to distinguish between the two. The art of producing cloth woven, or interwoven, with either gold or silver thread is associated with Venice, where vellum was gilded and cut into strips which were wound around silk or hempen threads. In the mid–15th century, Augsburg and Nuremberg developed the art of drawing gold-plaited silver bars into wire. The wires could then be flattened and interwoven with silk yarns dyed in rich colours like crimson and purple. Until the 17th century tissues of cloth of gold and of silver, or **cloth of tissue** (*q.v.*) were imported into England from Italy, France and Flanders and appear not to have been produced here in any quantity. By 1638 the manufacture was already well established in London, having developed rapidly there around the expertise of immigrant Milanese producers after about 1611 (Kerridge, pp. 127–8): **collar for a doublet**, 26.866.

cushion cloth, cushions of, 97.794; **of gold arras**, 97.791, 26.818.

forms seated with, 97.330, 26.198.

See also **embroidery: gold**.

cloth of silver: see **cloth of gold** for definition of the manufacturing process and the amendment of the two terms in the 1626 inventory. Items identified as cloth of silver are: **piece, peece of**, 26.838; **stools, stooles corded with**, 26.208. See also **embroidery: silver**.

cloth of tissue: tissue is from the obsolete French verb *titre*, to weave. From the 18th century, 'tissue' was applied to both rich or fine, delicate, gauzy fabrics; but from the 13th until the 18th centuries the term was associated with rich fabrics incorporating metal threads, particularly of gold or silver, often formed as raised loops. The phrase cloth of tissue emphasises the richness of such materials woven together:

cushion of, in crimson and gold, 97.788. See also **cushion**.

embroidered with, 97.787. See also **embroidery**.

clothing: see **apparel** for categories.

clouded: a term used only in the 1708 inventory, describing, in each case, the textile used in seat coverings. *OED* cites 'clouded stockings' in 1682 and 'clouded silks' in 1796, almost ninety years after the Helmingham inventory, defining 'clouded' as having cloud-like markings. Variant spellings and definitions of unfamiliar terms can be found elsewhere in the glossary:

linsey-woolsey, 08.577.

say, sey, 08.271.

silk, 08.514.

stuff, 08.571.

clyver: see **cleaver**.

coach, coatch: alluded to in the record of associated items but conspicuous by its absence from the coach-house, where only an old, four-wheeled one is recorded in 1626 and where there is a **chariot** (*q.v.*) in 1708. Note that although references here are as presented in the inventories, it is possible that some coaches are couches; uncertainties are indicated with *?couch*:

draft for, 'when the horse goeth lengthwise', 26.1494; **drafts for, pair of**, 26.1481.

honnces (*?harness*) **for coach horses**, 26.829; **backs of**, 26.1379.

old, 26.1412; 26.665 (*?couch*); **old coach bed**, 26.1396 (*?couch*).

pales (*?couch*), 26.1397.

sawn pieces for, 26.1403.

See also **chaise; chariot; and couch**.

coal, cole, coole[s]: in addition to some information revealed in the entries for **grate**, the 1626 and 1708 inventories confirm those fires reliant upon coal, which is a word not mentioned in any context in the 1597 inventory. The brass pans, noted as old in 1626, are described as being for 'cooles or ashes', suggesting the distinction between collecting the residue of burnt fuel: clinker (spent coal), and ash (from wood): **brass pan for (old)**, 26.754, 26.1251; **rake for**, 26.1262, 08.314.

coard(es): see **bedstead: cord**s. See also **koord**.

coat, coote, cote: outer garment: **black velvet**, 97.867; **green, grene damask** (silk damask), 97.944; **horseman's, of black velvet**, 97.862, 26.807; **of red cloth**, 26.828.

coat, coats of mail, male: identified only in the 1626 inventory, these are almost certainly synonymous with the almain rivets (*q.v.*) listed in 1597, 26.738. See also armour.

coatch: see **coach.**

cobiron, cobbiron, cobyron: a type of **andiron** (*q.v.*) embellished by a cob, or knob, at the top of the each front vertical support and capable of being equipped with hooks to support horizontal spit-rods:

brasen, 97.37.

brass, 26.65; **knobbed with**, 26.164, 26.306.

low, 97.14, 26.127, 26.564.

one, 26.6, **great**, 26.904.

pair of, 97.388, 97.409, 97.453, 97.586, 97.644, 26.361, 26.614, 08.4, 08.286, 08.619, 08.326, 08.443, 41.256; **large**, 08.127, 41.185, 41.227.

small, 41.227.

three, 26.481.

two, one higher than the other, 08.297.

unspecified: 41.37, 41.56, 41.70, 41.81, 41.89, 41.112, 41.113, 41.127, 41.145, 41.164, 41.176, 41.359, 41.375, 41.392, 41.409, 41.422, 41.456, 41.468, 41.519, 41.538, 41.556.

See also **andiron**.

cobweb brush, copwebb brushe, new, 26.785. See also **brush**.

cock: for cocks fitted in Helmingham's brewhouse and cellars, see *brewing*: **cock** elsewhere in the glossary. Those listed below relate to locations elsewhere in the hall and its environs: **brass, brassinge**, 26.1100; **water**, 26.1151, 26.1247, 26.1516.

cocking, cockinge: in the context of these inventories, 'cocking' refers to catching and shooting birds (synonymous with **fowling**, *q.v.*); all the items are recorded in 'Humferies Chamber' in 1626, together with numerous tools associated with his task of maintaining the park and grounds: **cloth**, 26.704; **net, with a canvas case**, 26.703; **piece** (gun), 26.700. See also **fowling**; **net**.

coffee: the popularity of coffee as a beverage in England increased exponentially in the latter part of the 17th century. Consumption spread to high-status households and is reflected in the range of purpose-designed items listed in the 1741 inventory: **cups, blue and white china**, 41.103; **and saucers, sawcers, enamelled china** 41.161; **mill,** presumably for grinding coffee beans, 41.263; **pot, copper**, 41.210.

coffer, cofer: storage box, associated particularly with items of value, including cash and spices; apparently more in use at Helmingham in 1597 than at any other time, 97.82; **candle**, 97.542; **flat, leather-covered**, 97.511; **great, for spice**, 97.522; **joined**, 26.86; **lock for (no key)**, 26.1002; **old**, 26.531. See also **chest** and **trunk**.

colander, cullender: open, dish-shaped vessel pierced with holes and used for draining excess liquid from raw or cooked ingredients. Defined in the inventories by their material:

brass, 26.973, 08.102.

earthen: (**curd colanders**, see also **cheese**) 26.1206.

pewter, 97.161, 97.558, 26.996, 41.266.

tin, old, 08.145.

cole: see **coal**.

collar, coller, for a horse, 08.704, 26.1356; **leather, in p[a]rt**, 26.1430. *for* **mill-horse**, 97.290.

colours: mentioned in all four inventories; those of 1597 and 1626, in particular, are rich in descriptive detail and use explicit words and phrases to describe the colours of textiles used in clothing and household furnishings, often including the word colour for the avoidance of doubt, particularly where a colour and a textile bear the same name. The list below is selective and recurrent colours are noted only as *passim*. Definitions and references are provided for those which are unfamiliar. Combinations of colours, some of which are included below, are frequent, either where they are woven together, pieced together or when embellishment is applied (see **embroidery** for examples):

ash, ashe: taken to be a silver-grey, 97.804, 97.805, 97.892, 97.918, 97.969, 97.845 (lining of), 26.138, 26.148, 26.156, 26.836.

black: *passim*. See also **soot**.

bloom-coloured: taken to be pinkish, 08.447.

blue: *passim*. See **watchet, Valentia blue**.

brown: rarely mentioned, and where this colour is stated, it results from the item's natural material (sacking, napkins of hemp and a brown china teapot) rather than from a dye, 97.816, 97.1067, 08.992.

buff: resembling **buff** (Fr. *buffe*), a stout oxhide leather, whitish-yellow in colour, 08.252.

carnation, cornation: pinkish-orange, salmon pink, the colour of the gloves worn by Catherine Tollemache in her portrait (Plate I), 97.822, 97.899, 97.928, 97.932, 97.936.

changeable taffeta of purple and green: similar to watered surfaces, achieved through a weave in which colours appear to change in changing light, 26.229, 26.235.

chestnut: reddish-brown, probably based on the colour of the fruit of the sweet chestnut, which was long-established in England by the time of the 1597 inventory, 97.903.

clay: taken to be grey with a yellowish-brown tinge, darker than **ash**, 97.811.

clouded: uncertain, thought to be a design of cloud-like markings rather than a colour, represented in the inventories by: **silk**, 08.514; **stuff**, 08.571.

copper gold: taken to be a burnished orange-brown, 97.340.

corket red(d): uncertain, possibly deriving from 'cork' as defined in *Ogilvie's Imperial Dictionary* ... (ed. Annandale, London, 1855, p 589), which says that 'cork, kork' is: 'the name given in the Highands of Scotland to a lichen, *Lecanora tartarea (see* CUDBEAR*)*, from which a domestic crimson or purple dye is made. It is with this that home-made tartans are dyed.' However, *OED* offers documentary evidence for the etymology of cudbear no earlier than 18th century. The word appears nowhere else in the inventories and in the absence of any convicing evidence to the contrary it might be a mangled variant of 'cockerel', reminiscent of a cock's comb, 97.808.

crimson, cremson: familiar as a purplish-red, but included to emphasise the subtle distinctions of red in the inventories (see **corket red** and **scarlet)**, 97.787, 97.788, 97.877, 26.200, 26.825, 26.905, 26.906, 26.917, 08.248, 08.397, 08.495, 08.496, 08.497, 08.562, 08.563; **flowered crimson**: (speculatively, figured, the flowers worked into the weave), 08.515, 08.516.

deroy-coloured, deroy[e]: not to be confused with duroy, which is a type of woven cloth (Kerridge, p. 62), deroy is a bright tawny (orange-brown) colour, known also as 'king's colour' or 'colour de-roy', a variant of Fr. *de roi*: 26.878, 26.880.

diverse colours, divers coloures, checkerwork of: an effect, evidence of the motif formed by the use of multiple colours. The colours are not specified here, nor where the phrase 'diverse colours' is used in other entries, 26.425.

duck's meat, duckes meat: taken to be the purplish-red of raw duck flesh, 97.841.

filbert, filbierd, filbird: taken to be brown, resembling the nut, filbert, 97.806, 97.824.

flame: taken to be bright orange-red and recognisably different from red or scarlet, 97.831, 97.840.

French green, grene: the inclusion of 'French' suggests a green recognisably different from other shades, 97.865, 26.795, 26.810.

gingerline, gyngerline: a pale red-orange colour: *OED* cites 1611 as the earliest use of gingerline, and an etymology of 'apparently a perversion (after ginger) of Italian *giuggiolino* of similar meaning; a transferred use of *giuggiolino*, gingili', 26.821.

gold: see **cloth of gold**.

green: *passim*. See **French green, popinjay green, sea green, seawater green**.

grey: mentioned only once, 08.701.

hare- (heaire-) coloured: suggests the brown shades of a hare's coat rather than a colour related vaguely to 'hair', 97.894.

horseflesh: entered but deleted and replaced with 'tawny', suggesting some confusion, and the word was never used again, 26.797.

mouse-dun(n): used only in the 1626 inventory, this suggests a grey-brown colour, 26.874, 26.876.

olive, oliefe: the word appears only in 1597, 97.902.

orange, orrenge-coloured: a unique mention of this colour, combined with **watchet** (*q.v.*) to form the silk stitching on a Spanish leather 'post-pillion', or saddle, suggests that the orange colour is distinguishable from **orange tawny** (see below), 26.935.

orange tawny, orrenge, orreinge, orring, orringe taun(e)y(e): a brownish-orange colour, possibly synonymous with **tawny** (*q.v.*), but there may be a distinction between the two hues, 97.844, 26.148, 26.156, 26.730, 26.731, 26.821, 26.851. See also **orange-coloured**, above.

peach: taken to be the colour of peach flesh, likely to be more orange in hue than the pinkish-orange **carnation**, above, 97.908, 97.913.

popinjay green, popinejaye greene, popping jaye grene: the green colour of a parrot, 97.832, 26.857.

printed velvet, black: an effect achieved through weaving, 26.801.

purple, 97.371, 97.796, 97.871, 97.909, 26.799, 41.82.

See also **changeable taffeta** for examples of purple and green.

red: *passim*. See **corket red, crimson, scarlet, stammell**.

reddish: a distinction used only once, 26.908.

russet(t): potential for confusion arises here because the word means both a coarse woollen cloth of grey or reddish-brown, as well as the colour itself. However, where colour is indicated in the inventories, a number of repetitive deletions and insertions of 'black', particularly in the 1626 inventory, imply that russett was of a hue so deep that it could be mistaken for black, 97.807, 97.815, 97.817, 97.873, 97.889, 26.74, 26.804, 26.805, 26.806, 26.809, 26.909, 26.912.

rust-coloured, 26.865.

sand: taken to mean a pale gold or light yellowish-brown, 97.834, 97.920.

scarlet, scarlett: as with **russet** and **stammell**, there is potential for confusion between the smooth, soft, woollen cloth usually dyed in this colour, and the colour itself, notably mentioned only in the 1708 inventory, a date which may be significant in terms of readiness of supply: Yaxley (p. 180) says that until the 18th century, the dye relied upon kermes, the pregnant female of the insect *coccus ilicis*; but thereafter 'kermes mineral' was antimony trisulphide: 08.249, 08.431, 08.432, 08.632.

Scotch plaid, Scotts-plad, plad: plaid is a twilled woollen cloth with a checked or tartan pattern. Its earliest appearance at Helmingham is in 1708, doubtless following the taste for it at Ham House, the family's principal residence as earls of Dysart after 1648, exemplified by bed hangings of plaid listed in the 1655 inventory (*Ham House*, pp. 434–6): 08.502, 08.505, 08.513, 41.544.

sea green, seagreene, sea gr(e)ene: possibly synonymous with **seawater green** but presented separately here because references suggest a distinction between the two, 97.829, 97.830, 97.969; 26.458; **dark**, 26.795 (deleted and replaced with 'french grene').

seawater green, grene, sea water grene: possibly synonymous with **sea green** (*q.v.*), but references suggest a distinction between the two, 97.907, 97.925, 97.926, 97.930, 97.934.

silver: see **cloth of silver**.

sky, mohair, 08.632.

soot: see **yellow and,** below.

stammell: the red colour of a coarse woollen cloth of the same name (*q.v.*). Reference to the colour appears only once, in the 1626 inventory: 26.601.

tawney, tawny, tauney, tauny, taunye: a brownish-orange colour. Tawny and **orange-tawny** (*q.v.*) may be synonymous or may confirm a distinction between the two hues, 97.857, 26.825 (deleted and replaced with crimson), 26.826, 26.837, 26.843 ('**tauny diamond velvett**'); 26.861 ('or redd'), 26.923; **and popinjay green**, 26.857; **with gold**, 26.908. See also **orange tawny**.

Valentia blew (cloth): uncertain: this may refer to the colour Valencia blue and/ or to the cloth itself, 97.866.

watchet, w(h)atchett: pale blue colour, 97.821, 97.914, 26.447, 26.448, 26.600; **and green**, 97.826; **and tawny**, 26.635; **and yellow**, 97.827.

white, *passim*, but see below for combination with other colours.

whit[e] and: black, 26.281; **green**, 97.825; **red(d)**, 26.183, 08.540; **with crimson**, 97.897; **and yellow**, 97.828; **with silver**, 97.910, 97.919.

whitish, 08.259.

yellow, *passim*, but see below for combination with other colours.

yellow, yealow, yelloe, and: green and blue, 26.367; **and purple**, 26.348, **with purple, blue and yellow)**, 08.469; **and soot(e)**, 26.113; **with silver**, 97.819, 26.358, 26.840; **with watchet(t)**, 26.359; **white and green (with black)**, 08.402; **with black, blue and white**, 08.506; **yellow purple**, 97.372.

colours, coloures for an armour: essential to identify the bearer in military action in the days preceding recognisable uniforms, entries in the inventories describe flags with the same purpose as **ancient** (*q.v.*) and **cornet** (*q.v.*). The 1626 inventory is fulsome in its description, 26.858.

colours of lead, coloures of lead: lead paints, ground on a purpose-designed stone, recorded in 1626, 26.1336.

comb, combe: French curriscombe and maine combe: for grooming a horse, 26.1380; **tow, towe**: used to remove debris from beaten hemp or flax, 97.252.

coney, cunnye hayes: nets designed for catching rabbits, 97.11.

cooler: see *brewing*: **cooler**.

cooling pen, koulinge peene: listed only in the 1626 Bakehouse, this suggests a 'pen' or containing space in which bread is allowed to cool after removal from the bake-oven, 26.1265.

coop, coope (fowl, poultry coop, relative sizes and details of construction are included in the 1626 references), 97.292, 26.1277, 26.1278, 26.1279, 26.1281, 26.1282, 26.1283, 26.1284, 08.317; **spade for cleaning**, 26.1289.

cope work, coope work: see **embroidery**.

copper (large boiling vessel), not necessarily made of copper but the name has persisted into modern times): 08.338 (with capacity), 41.241, 41.287. See also **brewing: copper**.

copper (the material), *passim*; the material is mentioned throughout the inventories but most frequently in the 1741 inventory for a wide range of culinary utensils and implements, one of which is a 'copper kitchen with furniture'. See **kitchen**.

corded *with*: term used widely throughout the inventories; can mean tied or fastened with cords but alternative contexts suggest backings (of cushions or their covers, for example) and the description of a furrowed or striped textile: *passim*.

cords: see **bedstead: cords**. See also **koord**.

cork or gnomon: 26.54. See also **gnomon**.

corn-screen, skreen: form of sieve for winnowing, separating chaff and other debris from grain, 08.688; see also **fan; screen**.

cornet: flag or standard, bearing the colours of a troop of horse: **of black and white damask**, 97.870; see also **colours for an armour; and ancient**.

staff: pole that supports the cornet, 97.7; see also **leading staff**.

corselet, corslet: see **armour**.

cotton, coton: given the uses described in the 1626 and 1708 inventories, items listed below could be of true cotton (imported) and/or of cottoned woollen cloth produced in England, describing a finish achieved by raising a soft, fluffy nap and then shearing to an even surface:

bag for saddle items, 26.923.

cases for armour, 26.579, 26.730, 26.731.

covers for andirons, 26.249.

fringe, 08.540.

lining: for saddle, 26.907, 26.908; **for sword case**, 26.931.

pieces of, 26.850.

window curtain(s) of, 26.128, 26.289.

couch, coutch, coutche: an item of furniture that took the form either of a chair, constructed to allow its extension, or a fixed day-bed. It is possible that some entries of **coach** (*q.v.*) are phonetic presentations of **couch**; uncertainties are indicated with *?couch*:

bed, pieces of, 26.948.

chair, 26.41, 26.596, **piece of**, 26.10.

damask, blue, 41.64; **red**, 41.160

frame, 26.63.

leather, 41.43.

long, 08.515.

old, 26.665 (*?couch*).

old coach bed, 26.1396 (*?couch*).

pales (*?couch*), 26.1397.

screws of iron belonging to, 26.948.

tabby (tobine?), **large red**, 41.91.

unspecified, 41.513.

velvet, black, 41.473.

coule: see **cowl**.

coulestaff: see **cowl-staff**.

coulter: see **plough**.

counter table: flat surface similar to a shop counter, 97.955.

square table 'or a counter', 26.886.

counterpane, counterpain, counterpoint(e): punctured quilt, stitched through both layers. The root of the word emerges from the O. Fr. *culte-pointe, coulte-pointe, coute-pointe*. Variant spellings and definitions of unfamiliar terms can be found elsewhere in the glossary:

camblet, blue, 41.526; **yellow**, 41.412.

cloth, laced with silk, 08.259, 08.447.

damask, green, 41.366, 41.395; **red**, 41.166.

dimity, 08.667.

flowered, 41.427.

Kidderminster stuff, 08.540.

taffeta, lined with baize, 26.148, 26.235; **lined with Jane fustian,** 26.299, 26.325.

See also **coverlet.**

couplings for hounds: 41.52.

covering, coveringe baskets: used to cover food, particularly when cleared from a table using a **voider** (*q.v.*). 97.51, 26.1023.

coverlet, coverlete, coverlett, cov'rlet: coverlit, cov'rlitt, cov'ring, Yaxley (p. 54) confirms that coverlit has at its root the French *couvre lit* (bed cover). Variant spellings and definitions of unfamiliar terms can be found elsewhere in the glossary:

arras, 97.351.

bird's eye, 26.395, 26.407, 26.624.

carpet, 41.599, 41.605.

checkerwork of diverse colours, 26.425.

cloth, red, 97.683, 97.705, 97.716, 97.730, 97.739.

dornix, 97.378, 97.484, 97.490, 97.508, 97.595, 97.610, 97.781, 97.717, 97.722, 97.747, 97.781, 26.10, 26.113, 26.171, 26.367, 26.654.

hangings used for, 08.602.

linsey-wolsey, 08.437, 08.479.

lists, 97.665, 26.438, 26.470, 26.492, 26.510, 26.523, 26.528, 26.533, 26.538, 26.541, 26.572, 26.620, 26.622, 26.624, 26.689, 26.695, 26.714.

old, 41.584, **tapestry,** 97.699, 97.740; **very old,** 26.496.

striped, 41.579.

wool, wollen, 97.651, 97.417, 97.442, 97.449, 97.464, 97.519, 97.577, 97.634, 97.651, 97.658, 97.673, 97.690, 97.698, 26.558, 26.632; **'wrought with birdes and buckes',** 97.424; **'wrought with buckes',** 97.399.

numerical summary of, 97.324.

unspecified, 97.369, 26.260, 26.341, 26.390, 26.477, 26.633, 26.634, 26.635, 26.788, 08.296, 08.396, 41.401, 41.565, 41.611.

See also **counterpane.**

cowl, cowle, coul(e): a large tub with two upstanding ears through which the **cowl-staff** was passed, enabling the tub to be lifted by two people. See entries listed in *brewing*; **milk; swill.**

crabs, crabbes, trough to stamp in: unripe crab apples were used to create **verjuice** (*q.v.*): for culinary use 26.1475.

cradle, wicker, 97.966, 26.765 (old); **quilt for,** 26.823. See also **child.**

crank, cranke: a handle or lever used to operate a rotating mechanism, each of which is identified in the inventories:

iron, for grindstone, 97.303.

iron, to turn in bedscrews, 26.783. See also **bedscrews; bedstead:** *tools for maintaining.*

for spits, crankes for speets, 97.169. See also **spit.**

cream: as with **butter, cheese, maw, milk** and **whey** (*q.v.*), the inventories specify common utensils and equipment strictly in relation to their purpose when used in the dairy, where the following are specific to cream:

cups, in the dairy, probably for measuring cream, 41.302.

firkin, ferkin (*q.v.*), 97.214, 26.1192.

crewell: worsted yarn of two threads (two-ply) for tapestry and embroidery, or the cloth woven from it, 97.425, 97.611, 97.635, 97.881, 26.163; **twisterers with iron wheels for,** 26.762.

crewett: see **cruet.**

crib, cribb, 41.562.

crook, crooke: iron, with a handle, 26.1485.

crossbow[e]: bow designed to shoot short feathered bolts or short arrows (quarrels).

arrows [*for*]: 26.517.

bolts for, 26.517.

broken, 08.154.

case[s] [*for*], 26.90; **in a case,** 26.516.

steel, 08.153.

See also **bow; gaffle; longbow; slur bow.**

cruet, crewett, 08.200, 08.235, 08.385; **glass: vinegar, vyneger,** 26.1026.

crupper, croopers, crop, crope, croper: the leather strap buckled to the back of a saddle and passing under the horse's tail, 26.748, 26.918, 26.919, 26.920, 26.922. See also **dock.**

cuirass, quirace, quirace lace: defined by *OED* as part of a breastplate, the 1597 examples are both described with numerous items belonging to saddles: 97.877, 97.881.

cullender: colander (*q.v.*).

cunney, see **coney.**

cup, cuppe, for cups listed discretely as part of the family's plate, see **silver.** No material or purpose is ascribed to the 'deep' cups listed in the 1626 dairy:

and saucer, for tea, 41.104, 41.161.

coffee, blue and white china, 41.103; **enamelled china,** 41.161.

deep, 26.1218.

pewter: half-pinte, 08.63.

See also **cream; silver.**

cupboard, cubboard, cub[b]o[o]rd[e], cupboord: an item of wooden furniture whose design is determined by its function. Some incorporate storage above or below, with or without doors which may or may not be lockable. Livery cupboards incorporate a flat surface for serving food if they are listed in dining rooms (similar to a sideboard); but when listed in chambers they relate to the storage or presentation of clothes or other items related to dressing. 'Press cupboard' appears only in the 1708 inventory, although 'press' (for linen) appears in 1597. Based on their locations, the 1708 press cupboards are for storage, and the contents may well be linen. Prior to this date, Helmingham's extensive stock of bed- and table-linen was stored in chests and trunks:

cushen cloth, uncertain, but probably refers to a storage cupboard for supplies of cushion cloth (canvas) 97.468.

deal, 41.602.

little, 97.523, 97.491.

livery, 97.3, 97.329, 97.358, 97.383, 97.404, 97.432, 97.614, 97.638.

long, 97.19.

old, 41.272; **oaken**, 41.306.

press, 08.134, 08.366, 08.559; **with 3 small cupboards on top**, 08.574.

table, 08.554.

with lock and key, 97.45, 97.80, 97.162.

cupboard cloth: cover for the flat surface of a **cupboard**. Variant spellings and definitions of unfamiliar terms can be found elsewhere in the glossary:

arras, 97.582.

cloth, blue, 26.562; **green**, 97.405, 97.639, 97.33, 26.187.

damask, 97.1084, 97.1089.

diaper, 97.1073, 97.1080.

dornex, 26.601; **copper gold of diverse colours,** 97.340; **black and white,** 97.615, 97.428; **blue and green,** 97.478.

flaxen, 97.1066.

green, embroidered with velvet, 97.382, 26.239.

holland, 97.1062.

linen, 97.1016.

livery, green, 26.860.

tapestry, 97.785, 26.833.

turkey work, 26.158, 26.331, 26.357; **with arms,** 97.357; **of slips,** 26.240.

unspecified, 97.1052.

See also **board cloth; colours; embroidery;** *linen.*

curtain, partition: textile used as a room-divider: **dornex,** 26.644; **tapestry,** 26.97.

curtain, curteyne, curteys, window: window coverings were comparatively rare items in gentry households during the late Elizabethan period, as the 1597 inventory confirms. Numbers increase in 1626 but few are recorded in the 1708 inventory, although dimensions are provided for some of the curtains listed. In 1741 window curtains are often accompanied by a matching valance, and these are in the same textile and colour as the bedstead curtains and valance. Variant spellings and definitions of unfamiliar terms can be found elsewhere in the glossary:

calico, white, 08.524, 08.525, **white striped**, 08.477.

camblet, blue, 41.533; **yellow**, 41.412.

casement curtain, 26.466.

cloth, green, 41.573.

cotton, green, 26.128, 26.289.

damask, green, 41.356, 41.366, 41.387, 41.395; **red,** 41.160, 41.166; **yellow,** 41.467.

dornix, 26.445; **green and yellow,** 26.60.

Eyrelonde, 26.548.

flowered stuff, 41.72.

linsey-woolsey, speckled green, 08.423.

muslin, 08.670; **striped**, 08.633.

old, 41.86.

say, green, 26.155, 26.176, 26.217 (noted as 'hanging open'), 26.226, 26.327, 26.345, 26.608 (noted as 'great'); **old**, 08.260; **red**, 97.451; **red and green**, 97.406; **yellow**, 08.543.

serge, red, 08.455.

stuff, green, 41.567, **red**, 41.507.

tabby, red, 41.93.

unspecified, 41.66; **red and green**, 26.416; **white**, 41.554.

verdures, 26.96, 26.376.

watered stuff, blue, 41.12, 41.523; **green**, 41.424, 41.508; **red**, 41.136.

window cloth: of arras, 97.344; **dornex, black and white**, 97.428; **old**, 97.391; **say, blue and yellow**, 97.585.

See also **tapestry: window pieces**. For bed curtains see **bedstead: curtains**.

curtain rod, curteyne rodd: generally an iron rod or pole, sometimes described with its 'ringles' (rings). No mention is made in the 1597 inventory of how window curtains are supported, but of those recorded in the 1626 and 1708 inventories most describe their rod and rings (see **curtain, window** above).

cushion, cushen, cushenings: portable cushions (as distinct from fixed upholstery) used with all forms of seating, whether in windows, on backless benches and forms or chairs and couches. Descriptions rarely reveal details of fillings but are eloquent about decorative cases, or covers. With the obvious exception of *unspecified*, the sub-categories below offer abbreviated descriptions of detailed entries. Variant spellings and definitions of unfamiliar terms can be found elsewhere in the glossary:

arras, 26.817 (see also **tapestry**, below).

gold, worked with black moores (*bulrushes*) 97.791.

worked with gold, 26.818.

cloth of gold, 97.794.

cloth of tissue, crimson and gold, 97.788.

coupwork, blue and yellow, 97.430.

cushion case, unfilled, of branched velvet, 26.820.

damask, embroidered: crimson, with cloth of tissue, 97.787; **yellow, with purple velvet**, 26.822.

embroidered, small long *[sic]*, 26.819.

feather, old, corded with twill, 26.637.

Irish stitch and ash-coloured taffeta, 26.156.

mockadoe, embroidered with black velvet and blue twist, 97.789.

needlework with slips of silke of diverse colours, 97.786.

satin of bridges, old, 97.403, **green**, 97.642.

stammell, laced and fringed, 26.597, 26.598.

stuff, red and blue, 26.562, 26.593.

taffeta, white, embroidered with gingerline velvet, 26.821.

tapestry, 97.35, 97.677; **wrought with: lilies, roses and violets**, 97.792, 26.817; **pomegranates**, 97.793, 26.817.

Turkey or Morocco: implies imported, rather than of 'turkey work' (*q.v.*), 08.566.

turkey work, 97.34, 26.204, 08.373, 08.428, 08.442, 08.517, 08.609.

with (*coats of*) **arms**, 97.341, 26.816.

unspecified, 97.461, 97.528.

velvet: black, embroidered with silk slips, 26.246; **crimson, with tassells**, 26.205.

cushion cloth, cushinge, quoshion cloathe: a **canvas** used widely as a furnishing fabric, usually embellished with **needlework**. The material was used also as a culinary strainer, most particularly for hot fruit pulp destined to create jelly-like confections (Coleman, pp. 19–20). Similar to a plain holland (linen cloth), cushion cloth is closely woven, although the number of holes per inch can vary. The close weave means that when in culinary use, cushion cloth would offer the slow straining capability of a modern jelly bag, whose purpose is to ensure that the resulting liquor is as clear as possible:

cupboard: uncertain, probably where supplies of cushion cloth were stored, 97.468.

cushion cover, 97.794.

form (made of), 97.359.

stool (made of), 97.384, 97.431, 26.241, 26.305, 26.360.

cut, cutt: term used in the 1597 inventory, in particular, to describe the art of revealing one layer of textile beneath another, the top layer being cut or slashed and a small portion of the underlying layer, usually, but not exclusively, in a contrasting colour or texture. The lower layer, sometimes referred to as 'pane' (panel) was either pulled through or made visible through the cut, or slash. Entries have been abbreviated below using *and* to summarise items having two colours or textiles; but inventory descriptions often include details of construction and/or other embellishments. Variant spellings and definitions, where appropriate, can be found elsewhere in the glossary:

chair: yellow satin *and* silver, 97.336.

doublet: ash taffeta, striped, 97.804; **filbert taffeta**, 97.806; **purple satin**, 26.799.

doublet and hose: black satin, 97.802, 26.798; **black taffeta**, 97.803.

kirtle: black satin, 97.893; **black velvet *and* gold camblet**, 97.895; **hare satin**, 97.894; **white satin *and* crimson**, 97.897.

sleeves: black velvet *and* lawn, 97.904.

vastguard: ash satin, 97.892; **black satin, printed**, 97.891.

See also **pinked**.

cwart: quart, 26.945.

Cypress, cipris: Yaxley (p. 61) defines this as a term applied to several varieties of cloth, but particularly to a light transparent black cloth originally made in Cyprus, but in England from the late 16th century, and used as a kerchief and in mourning; sometimes cloth of gold, or satin. Lawson (2013, p. 576) writes that it resembles cobweb lawn or crepe. Inventory references, recorded only in 1597, reveal other colours: **garters**: **black**, 97.838; **green**, 97.839; **hat**: **black silk**, 97.843; **lined with black silk**, 97.842.

dagg: see **gun**.

dagger, daggard: a short-handled, bladed weapon, 97.767, 26.737, 26.881; gilt, gilt handled, 97.847, 26.881; silvered, 97.846. See also bodkin.

dairy: spaces described as 'dairy' are discussed in Appendix A. Because the 1597 and 1626 inventories are specific about the purpose of items listed in the Helmingham dairies, entries referring to butter, cheese, cream, maw, milk and whey are here indexed individually.

Damascene, damasked: metal, particularly steel, incised with designs filled with silver and gold: pair of spurs, 97.852.

damask (silk): the inventory references listed below identify items made of silk damask. (For items of household linen known as **damask** and **diaper**, see **linen**.) Damask is a rich silk cloth figured with elaborate designs and figures, often multi-coloured, produced originally in Damascus but imitated widely, particularly in Italy, throughout the Middle Ages, from where most silk damasks were imported into England until the 16th century at least. Examples from the inventories are diverse, and are summarised below. Alternative spellings and definitions of unfamiliar terms can be found elsewhere in the glossary:

bearing cloth: crimson, *with* black velvet, 26.825.

bed-head, curtains, counterpane, top and **valence: green**, 41.366, 41.395; **red**, 41.166.

chair: scarlet, 08.249, **blue**, 08.251, 41.11, 41.65, 41.522; **green**, 41.355, 41.366; **red**, 41.160; **chair covers, blue**, 08.631.

coat, green, 97.944.

colours for an armour: (speculatively the same item as the earlier **cornet**, below), **black and white with a red cross**, 26.858.

cornet (flag), **black and white**, 97.870.

couch, blue, 41.64; **red**, 41.160.

cushion: crimson *with* cloth of tissue, 97.787, 97.788; **yellow *with* purple velvet**, 26.822.

gown, ash, 97.918; **black, branched (figured)**, 26.802; **green**, 97.924.

hangings: green, 41.387; **red**: 41.129, 41.160; **yellow**: 41.467; **scarlet with sky mohair**, 08.632.

petticoat: seawater green *with* black velvet, 97.907.

stool: hare-coloured, 08.579.

table carpet, red silk, 08.452 (with dimensions).

tent-bed, green, 41.394.

tester: ash-coloured, 97.578; **white *with* black velvet**, 26.474; **yellow *with* purple velvet**, 97.371, 26.348, 08.469.

window curtains, green: 41.356, 41.387; and **valence: red**, 41.160; **yellow**: 41.467.

dansk, danske: Danish, identifies chests in these inventories. The term may be used to describe Baltic oak or deal (*OED*; Yaxley, p. 63).

darnix, darnex[e]: see **dornix**.

deal, deale deall: Yaxley (p. 64) defines this as 'sawn board not less than 9 inches broad and not more than 3 inches thick', historically applied mostly to fir or pine imported from northern Germany and the Baltic area:

box, 08.596; **with 12 partitions,** 08.593; **without a cover,** 26.659, **old,** 08.142.

doors '2 of them painted white', 08.255.

dresser, 41.189.

ladder with deal stiles, 26.1410.

plank, planck fastened to wall to write upon, 26.399.

shelf, shelves, 26.401, 26.543.

deer suet: see suet.

Delftware, Delfware: tin-glazed earthenware, originating in Delft, but English examples include the Malling jug, Kent, dating from 1550. The 1708 inventory is the only one to use this description for Helmingham's household pottery, some of which is defined also by size and some offering details of design:

basons, 08.175, 08.182.

dishes, 08.176, 08.177, 08.178.

plates, 08.180, 08.181; **'pritty',** 08.179.

tea dishes, similar in shape to a deep saucer, precursor of the tea cup, 08.183.

See also **china; tea**.

deroy: see **colour**.

desk: in the 16th and 17th centuries, a desk supported on legs as a free-standing item of furniture, or may consist only of a box, but is defined by its usually sloping top designed for reading or writing: **'joyned work',** 26.22; **reading,** 41.45; **writing,** 26.99, 41.41, 41.78. See also **reading stand; writing stand**.

dessert basket (pewter), 08.213.

dial, diall, sun-dyall: detailed references in the 1626 inventory describe the components of sundials, listing pieces of brass for dials and gnomons; some are in the process of being constructed, others in place, some indoors, some outdoors:

in the ffeasant yard, 26.1538 (on a post).

in the parlour: 'in the window next the Courtyard', 26.54.

in my ladies [sic] chamber, 26.609.

in the long walke between the garden and the moate, 26.1525.

small brass sun-dyall, 08.558.

dice boxes, 08.500. See also **box, rattling; table: games, gaming**.

dies, dice, for backgammon, 41.177.

dimity, dimoty: stout, figured or striped cloth of cotton and wool mix: **bedstead curtains,** 41.441; **white,** 08.541; **counterpanes,** 08.667; **covers for beds,** 41.441.

dish, dyshe: for dishes listed discretely in the family's collection of plate, see **silver**.

boiled meat, boile, boyle meat dishes (pewter), 26.981, 26.993, 26.994, 26.1230.

broad verged, 97.153.

Delftware (*q.v.*), 08.176, 08.177, 08.178.

great, 97.97, 97.154.

middle, 97.98, 97.155.

'**molten with vergis**' (tarnished through contact with verjuice), 26.994.

pewter: **butter**, 26.1230 **lesser**, 26.1230, **salad, sallet**, 26.1230.

salad, sallet, 97.100, 26.985.

small, 97.99, 97.156.

See also **chafing dish, churn dish, fleeting dish, trafeing dish**; see also **silver**.

dock, docks for light horses: the crupper of a saddle or harness, 26.748. See also **crupper**.

dog, dogges, dog irons, firedogs: in an open hearth, the iron framework of support for logs. Halliwell (p. 60) explains that the word was at one time synonymous with andiron, which explains why the 1597 inventory does not refer to dogs, only to **andirons** (*q.v.*) and **cobirons** (*q.v.*). **one**, 26.16; **pair of**, 26.78, 08.221, 08.528, 08.556; **with brass knops**, 08.424; **iron**, 41.250. See also **andiron; chimney; cobiron; fire; grate**.

dog-wheel, dogges wheele: confirmation that in 1708 a dog, confined in a caged wheel, was used to operate the treadwheel that rotated the roasting spit before the kitchen fire: 08.7. See also **spit**.

dornix, darnix[e], dornex (sometimes presented as dornicks, but not in these inventories): fabric of wool, linen, silk or mixture, originating in Doornijk (Tournai, Belgium); by the 15th century, manufactured in Norwich (Yaxley, p. 68). Identified by its purpose and, often, colour in both 1597 and 1626, but not mentioned in 1708:

carpet (cover for a table or similar flat surface), 97.340, 97.526.

coverlet, cov[e]rlitt, cov[e]ring[e] (**bed**), 97.378, 97.484, 97.490, 97.508, 97.595, 97.610, 97.717, 97.722, 97.747, 97.781, 26.10, 26.113, 26.171, 26.280, 26.367, 26.493, 26.654.

cupboard cloth, cloath, 97.340, 97.478, 97.615, **piece of**, 26.601.

curtains, curteyn[e]s (window), 26.60, 26.445.

hangings (wall), 97.427, 97.613, 26.59, 26.154, 26.281, 26.445.

piece, peece[s], 26.485, 26.773, **double, dubble**, 26.636, **made into curtains**, 26.888, 26.890.

doublet, dublet, dublit: close-fitting upper body garment, with or without sleeves. Variant spellings and definitions of unfamiliar items can be found elsewhere in the glossary:

and hose: black satin, 97.799, 97.801, 97.802, 26.798, **black taffeta**, 97.803, **camel-hair grosgrain**, 97.809; **canvas, 'corket red' with velvet hose**, 97.808; **sacking, brown**, 97.816; **serge, black**, 97.937.

ash, striped and cut, 97.804.

black satin, pinked, 97.797.

canvas, tuft, 97.941; **white**, 97.942.

filbert taffeta, cut, 97.806.

fustian, clay colour, 97.811, **white**, 97.810.

satin, green, 97.813, **purple, cut**, 26.799; **white**, 97.795.

dough, dowe: **keeler**, 41.274; **scrape(r)**, 26.1275, 08.83.

down, doune: see **bed** for definition of down filling.

261

drag, dragge: a drag-net, or length of netting drawn into a pocket and pulled through the water to catch fish, 97.8.

draught, draughts, draft (horse): **for a coach 'when the horse goeth lengthwise'**, 26.1494; **pair of, for a coach**, 26.1481. See also **coach**.

draught (drawing): **part of a celestial globe**, 08.576; **small, in oak frames**, 08.565. See also **limn; pictures**.

drawers: **one pair of green and olive coloured, 'to weare over britches'**, 26.848.

drawing line: part of a draw net, used for catching coarse fish, 97.12.

dredging, drudgeing box: pierced with holes to enable flour to be dredged or sprinkled onto roast meat before its final basting, allowing it to brown but not burn, 08.35.

dreeping: dripping (*q.v.*).

dresser: the dresser as a composite piece of furniture, incorporating spaces for display, preparation, serving and storage, appears first in the 1708 inventory. The word 'dress' is related to the preparation and presentation of food and a dresser board describes a flat surface, but it is clear that by 1741 the dresser had become as valuable for its storage capacity as for its useable surfaces:

bords, 97.113, 26.1057.

deal, 41.189; **with 6 drawers**, 41.486; **large, with 12 drawers**, 41.589; **new, with 3 drawers**, 41.200.

large, 41.260.

on trestles, 08.639 (with dimensions).

unspecified, 08.29 ('one with a drawer'); 08.93, 08.100, 08.355.

dressing glass: unique to the 1741 inventory, where they are positioned on square mahogany tables in bedchambers or dressing rooms (a designation also unique to this inventory): 41.5, 41.173, 41.354, 41.403. See also **looking glass**.

drinking bottle, bottell: **'in form of a dagg** (pistol)', 97.57.

dripping, dreeping pan, panne: open pan placed beneath the revolving **spit** (*q.v.*) to catch juices from a piece of roasting meat, 97.120, 08.16, 41.244 (and stand for). See also **latch pan**.

drugge wheele, bound with iron: (drug: to pull along or drag) 26.1493.

drying (of laundry): see *laundry, dry*.

drying irons: consigned to storage in the storehouse next the hall, two pairs of drying irons whose purpose the 1626 inventory describes clearly. Cakes, in context, could be pastes made of fruit and sugar, or breads and biscuits made with or without flour, examples of all of which were recorded by Catherine Tollemache, whose recipes specified lengthy periods of drying, sometimes extending to days, in gentle heat (Coleman, *passim*): **broad, for cakes**, 26.960; **round, for herbs for medicine**, 26.960.

dublit, dublitt: see **doublet**.

dudfen, dudfin: a cart-horse bridle, 08.703; **halters for**, 26.1428.

dumb waiter, mahogany, no other details are provided, but generally at this date (1741) a dumb waiter consisted of a central pole supporting two or more tiers from which diners or drinkers could help themselves without the need for a waiter to attend them. The earliest record of a dumb waiter in correspondence appears to date to 1727, when Lord Bristol purchased one from Robert Leigh, a cabinet-maker (Edwards, p. 227): 41.134. See also **waiter, small**.

dung crome: a long-shafted tool, with its tines bent at 90°, for moving dung, 26.1438; **iron for**, 26.1329.

Dutch boat: the description says this is 'in a glass frame' which suggests a model, not a picture, 41.2. See also Plate 4.

dyeing, dying pan, panne: see *laundry, wet*.

ear, eare: handle on a utensil or container, *passim*. See also **plough eare**.

earthenware, earthen, earth: unglazed pottery, stoneware, most listed in working spaces and used for storage, 97.178, 97.249, 26.947, 26.1133, 26.1206, 26.1238, 08.110, 08.147, 08.148, 08.202, 08.203; **jar with sweetmeats**, 41.201.

egg slice: an item recognisable today as the flat, slotted implement to slide under eggs cooked in a frying pan or similar, 08.26. See also fish slice.

eightsquare, describes octagonal-shaped items:

stand, with **leather cover,** 08.520.

table, 26.604, 08.519; **half of a folding table,** 08.636.

walnut, walnuttree stand, 08.482.

writing stand inlaid with Tollemache arms, 08.521.

See also **foursquare; threesquare.**

ell: unit of length, an English ell being 45 inches. The 1708 inventory, the only one to use the term, refers to curtains of 'ell wide serge of five foot bredths', 08.432.

elm, elmeing timber: four pieces of sawn, 26.1477; **square table** [*of*]: not square but rectangular, as the dimensions reveal, 08.320. See also **foursquare; three-square; three long planks (now belonging to a sliding table),** 26.1498.

embroidery, embroidered, embroder(ed), imbroder(y)(ed), imbroyder(ed): at the time of the three earlier inventories, embroidery embraced a range of techniques used to describe embellishment, some stitched or worked directly onto the surface of an item made of woven textile or needlework, some achieved through the application of ready-made pieces, particularly embroidered panels such as 'slips' (see below). Definitions and specific references to the techniques, designs or components of embroidery are given priority below (with brackets to enclose summary of the item embellished). Some embroidered items listed in 1597 can be detected in 1626, particularly when referred to as old or worn. By 1741, the word appears nowhere in the inventory. Spellings of items and textiles have been modernised below; variants and definitions can be found elsewhere in the glossary:

arms *(coat of)*: (on green taffeta tester etc.), 26.291.

cloth of silver and yellow twist: (on tester of red say), 97.425.

cloth of tissue: (on crimson damask cushion cover), 97.787.

cloth, red and yellow *(coat of)* **arms:** (on old grey sumpter cloth), 26.789.

cope work, coope work: speculatively a variant of cutwork, designs created by pulling threads or otherwise forming holes to reveal the textile beneath: (on tester and valence), 26.276; **blue and yellow** (cushions), 97.430; **red and yellow** (on tester and valence), 97.611.

embroidered: (chair back), 97.527; (chair, white taffeta-covered), 26.201; (cushion, small long [*sic*]), 26.819; (girdles, black), 26.871; (quilt), 08.411; (Scotch saddles, crimson velvet), 26.905 (black velvet tester etc.), 08.402.

gold: (on mouse-dun velvet hangers), 26.876; (on satin girdle and hangers), 26.867; broad gold silk lace (on/for great tawny velvet saddle), 26.907, 26.923.

silk: black (on cloth-of-gold girdle and hangers), 26.870; **of diverse colours** (on white caffa-covered chair), 97.335; **raised** (on tester etc.), 08.390.

silver: (on mouse-dun velvet hangers), 26.874; (on black satin doublet and hose): **droppings with black silk and silver galloon lace** 26.798; and **silk of diverse colours** (on green taffeta tester etc.), 97.352; (on girdle and hangers, velvet-lined), 26.869.

slips, slip[p]s: small panels of plant-based designs (which are themselves pieces of embroidery) applied as embellishments to textiles or needlework items (on black velvet-covered chair): 26.242; (on turkey-work carpets), 26.203.

silk slips: (on black velvet-covered long window cushions), 26.246; (on purple say tester etc.), 26.177; (on black velvet tester etc.), 26.227; (on turkey-work cupboard cloth), 26.240; **of diverse colours:** (on green-velvet backed needlework cushion), 97.786.

velvet, black: (on black foot cloth), 26.831; (on crimson bearing cloth), 26.825; (on crimson chair), 97.402; (on red buffin-covered stool), 97.26; (on red cloth-covered chair and stools), 97.385; (on crimson satin-covered chair and stools), 26.200; in flowers (on buffin-covered chair), 26.454; **and blue twist** (on mockadoe and black tuftaffeta cushions), 97.789; and **twist of silver** (on sea-green petticoat), 97.908.

velvet, blue: (on crimson satin-covered chair), 97.337, 26.206.

velvet, crimson, arms (coat of arms embroidered on green satin-covered chair), 97.618.

velvet of diverse colours: (on green cupboard cloth), 97.382, 26.239.

velvet, gingerline, 26.821 (on white taffeta cushions, backed with orange tammy and purple velvet).

velvet, purple: (on gold camblet-covered chair), 26.202; (on long cushion of yellow damask), 26.822; **arms** (on yellow damask tester etc.), 97.37, 26.348.

velvet, watchet: (on straw-coloured taffeta-covered stools), 97.332; (on yellow satin-covered stools), 26.359.

English fire locks: see **gun.**

escutcheon, escucheon, eskutcheon: see **arms** (coats of arms).

Europe: old map of, 08.284. See also **globe; map; pictures.**

ewer, eawer: lidded jug: **old,** 26.998; **pewter,** 26.979.

See also **silver.**

Eyrelonde: Ireland; the term is reserved in these inventories to describe **hangings** (*q.v.*). See also **Irish.**

false leather: see **scabbard, false leather.**

fan, ffann, fanne: form of sieve for winnowing, separating grain from chaff and other debris, 97.291, 26.1361, 26.1399, 26.1404. See also **corn-screen; screen.**

fat: used throughout the four inventories for **vat.** See **brewing; cheese.**

feasant, ffeasant: see **pheasant.**

featherbed, fetherbed: see **bed**.

felloe, fellowe: outer rim of a wheel, 26.1493.

fence: sword or foil used in fencing: **old**, 97.768.

f[f]ender, literally, fend-iron, a protective and often decorative low frame bordering the hearth. Lindsay, in *Iron and Brass Implements of the English House* (1964, p. 17), asserts that fenders became an essential safety device only when the fire was raised, either in a loose or fixed grate. The 1708 and 1741 inventories confirm this with descriptions of other protective elements associated with a raised fire: 08.3, 41.252, 41.320, 41.456, 41.556, 41.593.

fennell seed, ffennell seede, old tray for: although its location in the 1626 cheese chamber may be coincidental, there is evidence that fennel seed was used to sweeten and improve the storage capabilities of rennet, although this comes from an 1844 treatise on the chemistry of food (by James Finlay Weir Johnston, accessed via archive.org: https/archive.org/details/lecturesonapp.lijohngoog). Yaxley (p. 41) cites Leonard Mascall (d. 1589), who suggests various forms of acidic vegetable matter, such as the juice of the 'blessed thistle', as a coagulant alternative to **rennet** (*q.v.*): 26.1237.

ferret, firritt, hutch for, 26.1519.

field bedstead: see **bedstead**.

fill bells: see **thilbells**.

firbelowed: see **furbelowed**.

fire, ffire, fyre, items prefixed with fire or where the context is clearly related to maintaining and cleaning out fires:

> **fork, forke**: long 2- or 3-pronged fork for manipulating logs on a fire, 97.86, 97.127, 26.6, 26.16, 26.1074, 08.315, 08.327.

> **iron to lay, set before**: **great long**, 26.1333; **when it is raked up**: speculatively, a form of protective screen to prevent ash spreading beyond the hearth, 26.24.

> **pan, pane, panne,** Yaxley (p. 79) defines a fire pan as 'small shovel on long handle for removing ashes; flat pan for carrying fire': 97.386, 97.410, 97.434, 97.459, 97.588, 97.622, 97.640, 26.50, 26.65, 26.118, 26.250, 26.306, 26.310, 26.361, 26.432, 26.483, 26.1447, 41.38, 41.58, 41.70, 41.81, 41.89, 41.98, 41.112, 41.127, 41.145, 41.164, 41.176, 41.255, 41.320, 41.359, 41.375, 41.392, 41.409, 41.422, 41.456, 41.468, 41.479, 41.484, 41.519, 41.538, 41.556.

> **poker,** 08.9, 41.98, 41.255, 41.320, 41.593.

> **shovel, shovell, sholve,** 26.165, 26.191, 26.220, 26.285, 26.334, 26.383, 26.460, 126.564, 26.614, 26.1149, 08.9, 08.224, 08.493, 08.530, 41.593.

> **sifter,** 08.9.

> **tongs,** 26.191, 26.220, 26.250, 26.285, 26.306, 26.334, 26.383, 26.432, 26.460, 26.564, 26.614, 26.1149, 08.493, 41.39, 41.57, 41.70, 41.81, 41.89, 41.112, 41.145, 41.164, 41.176, 41.255, 41.320, 41.359, 41.375, 41.392, 41.409, 41.422, 41.456, 41.479, 41.519, 41.538, 41.556, 41.593.

firkin, ferkin, ferkyn: a cask, the capacity of which varied with its use. Yaxley (p. 79) cites: ale or beer: 9 gallons; wine: 84 gallons; butter 64 lb gross, 56 lb nett but advises that variations existed. Those listed below refer to their intended contents:

cart stuff(e) (*q.v.*), 97.248.

cream, 97.214.

flour, flower, 08.81.

maw (*q.v.*), 97.215.

new, 26.1242.

oatmeal, ote meal, 97.216.

old, with white salt, 26.1219.

firritt: see **ferret**.

fish, fishe, fyshe:

barrells 'sometimes used to carrie fishe in', 26.1342.

box, lead-lined, 'to water fishe in', 26.1501.

kettle, copper, 41.205; see also **stew pan, fish**.

slice, round brass, 'nigh 16 inches wide', 08.103.

stewing, stueing pan for, and cover, 08.19; **round brass**, 08.101.

flagon, flaggon: jug-like vessel with a narrow mouth: **copper, large and small**, 41.209; **pewter, 'each holding about a gallon'**, 08.61; **great**, 26.974.

flask[e], container for liquid: **empty**, 08.658.

flask[e], container for gunpowder: **old**, 97.776; see also **gun**.

flaxen: see **linen**.

flaying, fleaing: the stripping or skinning of animals: the 1626 slaughterhouse records a **'puntche to undersett a beast when it is a fleainge'**, 26.1484.

fleet, flete: see **milk**.

flesh fork: see **fork**.

flesh, fleshe hook: hook capable of suspending a carcass of meat, 26.1004.

flew: a fishing net, either a drag-net or fixed net. 97.9, 26.1347; **otter flew**: a net for trapping otters, often set in the vicinity of fish-ponds because of the otter's predatory behaviour (Butcher, *Rigged for River and Sea*, 2008, p. 135). This one was sent to Fakenham, where the Stour flowed through the grounds of Sir Lionel's property, Lugdons, 26.7. See also **drag; drawing lines; net**.

flock: see **bed, flock**.

flour, flower, fflower, ground in the on-site **horsemill**:

bin, bingg, 08.92.

bowl, bowle, 26.1272.

hutch, 41.273.

keeler, killer, 97.167, 26.1258.

tub, 41.269.

See also **bolting; bultelle; minging; mill**.

foot cloth, cloath: can mean a floor-mat; but in the context offered by each inventory, these are ornamented velvet cloths designed to hang to the ground on each side of a horse for use at funerals, for example: 97.868, 26.832; **new**, 26.831.

footstool: see **stool**.

footwear: see: **boots; shoes; pantofles; pumps; slippers**. See also **apparel**.

fork, forke: long-handled forks for culinary use (flesh forks) are recorded in all four inventories, but the table-fork was not in common use in England until after 1611. In *Taste: the story of Britain through its Cooking*, Colquhoun (2007, p. 134) recounts how the implement was previously regarded with suspicion. It does not appear in the Helmingham inventories until 1708; quantities were considerable by 1741:

beef, beefe: long-handled, two- or three-pronged fork for handling meat during cooking, 97.128, 26.1091; referred to in 1708 as a flesh fork, see below.

case for a child's knife, fork and spoon, 08.522.

flesh: serving the same purpose as the beef fork, above. 08.27, 41.221.

hafted (all table forks) **black**, 41.316; **ivory**, 41.197; **white**, 08.379.

See also **fire: fork; pitchfork**.

form[e]: a backless bench providing multiple seating, usually for dining; but some forms are recorded in working areas, where their purpose was utilitarian, if not always specified in descriptions:

arbour, for: in the 'outewarde courte', a garden area beyond the moat (marked as 'a' on Plate 14). This is described fully as 'formes with feet for benches in the arbour', the backs presumably being part of the arbour structure, 26.1521.

cushion cloth, cushen cloth (canvas), 97.359.

four-footed, 26.1013, 26.1105, 26.1154, 26.1374.

joined, joyned, 97.601, 26.18; **seated with 'Candish his stuff' being cloth of gold**, see footnote 30 to 1597 inventory for discussion of Thomas Cavendish, 97.330.

little, 97.724, 26.544.

long, 97.181, 26.501, 26.1116, 08.31, 08.98.

low, 26.658, 26.1138, 26.1303.

old, with feet, 26.1288.

old-fashioned, 26.35, 26.117.

saddles, for, 26.899.

seated with cloth of gold, 26.198. See also **joined**, above.

short, 97.183, 26.1042, 26.1086.

stool (forme stoole), 26.1155.

unspecified, 97.2, 97.20, 97.227, 97.269, 26.4, 26.1176.

walnut, wallnuttree, 26.36; **'bought since this inventory was made'**, 97.16. See also **bench**.

foursquare: A term used only in the 1708 inventory to define an item of rectangular shape: **pans, panns for cakes**, 08.207; **voider, voyder**, 08.137. See also **eightsquare***;* **threesquare**.

fowling piece, foulinge peece: a firearm whose purpose is described unequivocally in the 1626 inventory as 'to shoot haukes meate', 26.698. See also **cocking; net**.

frail, fruit fraile: a rush basket used for packing fruit, 26.963.

frame: a term used generally throughout the inventories for frameworks of wood or iron with numerous purposes, but one notable example describes an early form of storage for **books** (*q.v.*).

freeing: frying, see **pan, frying**.

french lock: see **gun**.

fringe, fring, fringed, *passim*; a term describing the way in which items as diverse as furnishing textiles, clothing and saddlery are trimmed, edged or bordered. The inventories are inconsistent in describing the materials and colours of the fringes. At least some of the fringe was woven at Helmingham Hall on a special loom called a **lucet** (*q.v.*). See also **gimp** and **thrums.**

frying, freeing: see **pan, frying**.

fuddling glasses: definition uncertain, but probably glasses in which to mix liquids before drinking, 08.590.

funnel, tunnel, 97.70; **tin, old**, 08.144; **with iron spouts**, 26.1307; **wooden**, 08.653.

furbelowed, firbelowed, ffirbelowed: term used only in the 1708 inventory to describe items of glassware and baking pans with flounced or fluted edges, 08.176, 08.189, 08.211.

furnace (below the **still**, *q.v.*), 26.1245, 26.1247; in the brewhouse (see ***brewing***): 41.278.

fustian, fusten, ffustin, fustine: describes different types of cloth ranging from coarse cotton and linen to weaves of linen and silk. Fustians were manufactured in such a way as to produce what Kerridge (p. 50) describes as 'an unbroken succession in all directions of alternating short and long loops, the combination of which gave rise to two levels of pile, which might then be cut to give the appearance of almost hemispherical clusters'. No references appear in the 1708 inventory. Spellings below have been modernised; variant spellings can be found in cross-references for items listed elsewhere in the glossary:

blankets, 97.323, 97.350, 26.232, 26.847.

doublet, 97.810, 97.811.

jean, jane fusten, jane fustine: heavy twilled cotton cloth, originally from Genoa (known also as Genoa fustian): **lining of**, 26.299, 26.325.

tick, ticking, 26.322, 26.350.

gaffle, according to Halliwell (p. 388), a gaffle is 'that part of the crossbow that is used in bending it': **bow with nuts and benders**, 26.516; **pair of**, 08.155. See also **bow; crossbow; longbow; slur bow**.

gallipot, gallie pote, gallypot[t], unlidded, straight-sided storage pot, usually of earthenware. Although commonly associated with apothecaries, Catherine Tollemache's recipes (Coleman, pp. 16–17, 74, 97) specify gallipots for the storage of fruit preserves and conserves. Once filled, the pots were sealed with paper or bladder covers. *OED* suggests that the name derived from the galleys on which supplies of glazed earthenware pots were carried from the Mediterranean. Some of the earliest English delftware makers, potters active from the mid- to late–16th century, described themselves as 'gallipot makers'. Mentioned only in the 1597 inventory, where either contents or embellishments are described: **capers**, 97.79; **tipped and footed, futted, with silver**, 97.1177, 97.1214.

galloon: galowne, see **lace**.

games: revealed mainly through references to **table, games, gaming,** and also to **men, tablemen,** there is evidence that at different periods of time **backgammon, chess, draughts** and **goose** were played at Helmingham. By 1741 two rooms were allocated to **billiards.**

garden, gardiner: the 1626 inventory is the only one to list the contents of the garden (not including plants), although a pair of shears makes an appearance in a group of working spaces mentioned in 1708. The list below includes also items indicated on Plate 14 as (a) 'outwarde courte' and (b) 'the longe walke betwene the garden and the moate', since all are related to enjoyment of the outside areas leading to the garden, which is an area secured by (c) a locked door:

arbour, 26.1521.

bench, bentch to sitt upon with a backe, 26.1535; see also **arbour**, above.

dial (sundial) on a turned post, 26.1525.

hoe, howe, 26.1529.

ladder 'for the gardiners use', 26.1411. See also **ladder**.

lock and key, locke and kye, to the door, 26.1526.

pruning knife, pruneinge knyfe for, 26.1338.

rake, iron, 26.1528.

roller, stone, 26.1522, 26.1533; wooden, 26.1523, 26.1524.

scythe, sithe, new, to mowe the walkes, 26.1532.

shears, sheires, sheers, pair of garden, 26.1530, 08.349.

spade, 26.1527.

water pots, potts, one greater, one lesser, 26.1534.

garters: tied below the knee to secure hose or stockings. The 1597 inventory includes a discrete list of garters belonging to the apparel of Lionel Tollemache, listed below in modern spellings: **Cyprus** (*q.v.*), **black**, 97.838, **green**, 97.839; **duck's meat colour**, 97.841; **French, of flame colour**, 97.840.

gauntlets: see **armour**.

genealogical rolls, in cases: 41.496.

gilt, gilded, guilt: discrete lists of plate in the 1597 inventory, updated in 1604 and 1608 (with anecdotal notes of items purchased in 1609), discern between items of silver and silver gilt, 'double' gilt and parcel gilt. Gilt was applied as a thin layer of gold on a silver base. For all items, see **silver**.

gimp: a twist of silk with cord or wire running through it, used especially as trimming; mentioned only in the 1708 inventory, 08.469, 08.562, 08.563, 08.570. See also **fringe**.

gingerline, gingerlyne: pale red-orange colour. See also **colours**.

girdle: a belt, often described as a 'pair' with their matching 'hangers' which, in context, are not short swords as defined by, e.g. Yaxley (p. 98), but the means by which they might be secured to the girdle in a decorative casing or cover, often of sumptuous materials. The editorial category of ***unspecified*** includes girdles for which no material or colour is described.

black, embroidered with black silk, velvet-lined, 26.871.

for bullet bags, 26.732.

unspecified, 97.943.

velvet, old, 97.960.

with matching hangers:

    black silk on cloth of gold, velvet-lined, 26.870.

    embroidered with silver, velvet-lined, 26.869.

gold, embroidered on satin, velvet-lined, 26.867.

laced with gold twist, laid with leather, 26.868.

needlework, silver and gold, velvet-lined, 97.844.

silver, lined with ash-coloured velvet, 97.845.

See also **hangers**.

girth web, webbe: material more commonly associated with horses, this reference is offered in the description of the **cord** 'sometimes' used for a bedstead as an alternative to the commonly used plaited ropes, 26.1331.

glass, glasses: not in common use at the table in any form in gentry households until the 17th century, a fact confirmed by the evidence of the Helmingham inventories. The majority of 1708 references include the dimensions of glassware:

basin, bason, 08.185, 08.186.

beer, 26.1026, 08.387, 41.487.

bottle, covered with leather, 97.76, 26.946; **great**, 26.1052; **high square 'like they keep leeches in'**, 08.174 (see also **high**, below); **wicker**, 97.77.

covers for, 08.234.

cruet, cruett, crewett, 08.200, 08.235; **vinegar, vyneger crewetts**, 26.1026.

decanters, 41.491.

dish, 08.187, flat, 08.188, **furbelowed, firbelowed** (flounced edges), 08.189.

doors, mentioned in the description of a walnut bureau, 41.1.

frame, mentioned in the description of a 'Dutch boat', probably a glass cover, 41.2.

fuddling glasses, uncertain, but probably for mixing liquids before drinking, 08.590.

glasses (unspecified, but with dimensions), 08.191.

high, to keep leeches in, 08.240 (see also **bottle**, above).

jars, jarrs, 41.328.

jelly, for, 08.193, 08.194, 08.195, 41.457.

keeler, to wash glasses in, 26.1038.

little, 08.199.

mugs, muggs, flowered, 41.490.

rummer, a large drinking glass, 08.233, 41.488.

salts, 41.325.

salver, 08.196; **sweetmeat glass fit for salver**, 08.198.

saucer, sawcer (for serving cold sauce) 08.190, 41.489.

shelves to set glasses upon, 26.1249.

sweetmeats, to keep in, 08.192.

syllabub (*q.v.*), **whip sillybub**, 08.201.

tumblers, tumbler glass, 08.197, 08.232.

urinal, 41.40.

water, 41.488; **large**, 08.386.

wine, 26.1026, 08.388, 41.326, 41.487; **high narrow**, 08.237, **'the same shape but flourished'**, 08.238; **small**, 08.236.

See also **dressing glass; looking glass**.

globe, clobe, celestial(l), draught of part of, 08.576.

globes, pair, with leather cases: 41.44.

gloves, pairs of: it was common for the insides of leather gloves to be sweetened with perfume, sometimes prior to sale but often a task undertaken at home in high-status households, primarily to counteract the residual odours of the tanning process: **plain, playne, sweet**, 97.836; **tanned, tande sheep's leather, lether**, 97.837. See also **hawk: glove; armour: gauntlets**.

gnomon: rod or pin on a sundial that shows the time by the direction of its shadow; **brass**, 26.54. See also **dial**.

going cart: see **child**.

gold, goolde, goulde: used sparingly as adornments and sumptuous trimmings for clothing or household goods and as a thin layer of gilt on items of plate at Helmingham Hall; but the allusion to the currency of gold is evident in the specialist scales and box of weights recorded in 1626: '**to waighe outlandishe goolde**', 26.56. See also **buttons; cloth of gold; embroidery; fringe**.

goose game, a newly created game, barely six months old when it was recorded in the 1597 inventory (see footnote 4), 97.30.

gotch: a large, big-bellied pitcher: **stone, two-quart**, 08.382.

gown: comprised the outer part of a lady's dress; it might consist only of a sleeveless bodice and skirt under which other garments were visible; or the sleeves and stomacher (bodice) might be integral. For other elements of ladies' wear recorded at Helmingham, see: **kirtle, petticoat, safegard, sleeves, stomacher, vastguard**. The 1597 inventory records apparel separately for individual members of the family, providing full descriptions of the gowns of Catherine Tollemache and her four daughters, then aged between 8 and 14. The archives hold also a letter written to Catherine in 1605 by her London dressmaker, Roger Jones, who had despatched to Helmingham a trunk full of modish gowns designed for her and her daughters' approval, describing colours and designs of gowns in detail (Coleman, pp. 132–3). Spellings below have been modernised. Variant spellings and definitions of unfamiliar terms can be found elsewhere in the glossary:

callasina, white, with parchment lace of silver, 97.919.

cloth: of silk russet, with gold buttons and lace, 97.889; **old, sand colour, with hanging sleeves, bound with silver lace**, 97.920.

damask, ash colour, with hanging sleeves, bound with parchment lace of silver, 97.918; **green, laid with silver lace**, 97.924.

French say, green, bound with lace of seawater green silk and silver, 97.925, 97.929, 97.933.

mourning gown, 97.921, 97.927, 97.931, 97.935; **with kirtle and stomacher**, 97.890.

tuft taffeta: bound with curled gold lace, 97.887; **old, black and purple**, 97.888.

velvet, black: old, 97.886; **plain, bound with black lace**, 97.885; **with hanging sleeves**, 97.884.

See also **kirtle, petticoat, safegard, sleeves, stomacher, vastguard**.

grate (bread grate): a closed cupboard, with a grate or lattice front, in which to store bread, 97.137, **with cover**, 26.955; **the cover wanting**, 26.1079.

grate (fire grate): in common with other features integral to the structure of the building, hearths are not recorded in the household inventories. However, grates for confining combustible material were considered portable. Between 1597 and 1708, the solid brick or stone base of a hearth supported a metal dog-grate (see **dog; andiron; cobiron**), a framework that allowed logs to be supported above the hearth. This arrangement permitted better air-flow, encouraging the fire to burn. However, during the span of the inventories the increased use of coal demanded more confinement, and grates became increasingly complex. The 1708 inventory reflects their sophistication, describing grates by their form and identifying their individual components:

bar, barr: iron bars that span the base of the grate to support combustible material, 08.1; see also **forebar**.

cheeks: a pair of brick or iron side-pieces, one positioned either side of the interior of the grate, set from its back to its front; Yaxley (p. 40) asserts that the cheeks were to retain a coal fire, 08.2.

forebar[r]: describes the bars positioned at the front of the grate, one above the other, to retain combustible material piled vertically, 08.1.

iron, with bars and cheeks, 41.253, 41.320, 41.593.

long [grate]: not defined by measurement, but by the quantity of **forebars** (5) and **bars** (2) which served to support and retain the combustible material, 08.1. For related items, see **andiron; cobiron; chimney; dog; dog-wheel; fire; furnace; spit**.

grater, large, 41.223; **sugar**, 41.317.

grease: in the context of these inventories, animal fats collected and rendered on site (in the 1597 'lard house', for example, or as described in 1626, a now-modified room 'that wch was the greasehowse'). The resulting 'grease' was then packed into earthenware containers which, if the contents were destined for culinary use, were stored in cool spaces with a reliable air-flow, such as the cheese chamber, where these can be found: **bacon**, 26.1238; **boar's, boores**, 26.1238; **capon**, 26.1238.

See also **cart: stuff**.

grese, three-leaved, speculatively, in the manner of a clover leaf, mentioned as a design on a silver-gilt cup, 'new bought' in 1608, 97.1189.

gridirons, griddirons, gridyrons: iron grid, sometimes equipped with legs and/or a handle, for cooking (grilling) before an open fire, 97.143, 08.33, 41.243, 41.319. See also **roast iron**.

grindstone, grinding stone: operated by hand, as distinct from those found in the millhouse, 97.303, 26.1253.

stone to grinde coloures of lead upon, 26.1336. See also **limn; pictures**.

See also **millstone; quern**.

grosgrain, grograinte, growgraine: Kerridge (1985, p. 54) defines grosgrain yarns as 'large, rounded twists'; the inventory identifies cloths made from these yarns:

camel-hair, cammell heare, doublet of, 97.809.

silk, hangers of, 26.872.

guilt: see gilt.

gun, gunne: the majority of firearms at Helmingham are identified by name or by their firing mechanism, the minority by their material or form. Their accoutrements are listed here also:

barrel, callin: speculatively, the 'two olde callin barrels' listed in the 1597 armoury are the barrels of guns no longer in use, 97.774.

brass-barrelled, 08.626.

bullet bag, bullett bagge: entries confirm that some bullets remain stored in their bags, and others identify the girdle, or hanger, the belt by which bags were hung from the waist, 26.732, 26.733.

caliver, light musket or harquebus, fired without a rest, capable of firing ball, shot or arrows, 26.725; see also **touch-box** below.

carbine, carbyne, firearm, a short musket, taking its name from the carabin who carried it (Yaxley, p. 33). Halliwell (p. 231) writes that *carabins* were 'a sort of light cavalry from Spain, first mentioned about the year 1559. They were perhaps so called from their carabines, or muskets.' Helmingham's carbines are identified by their intended user, their design and/or the items that accompanied them: **for horsemen, with powder flask**, 26.723; **with inlaid stock, french lock and powder flask**, 26.724.

case, 41.53; **pistol case**, 41.466.

dagg, heavy pistol or handgun, 26.728.

flask, powder flask, for gunpowder, 26.723, 26.724, 26.725, 26.727; **horn**, 41.54; **leather**, 41.51; **old**: 97.776.

guns, unspecified, 41.482, 41.508 (stored with sundry unrelated items in a chest).

handgun, 97.708, 26.90.

long, 08.627.

matchlock: describes the method of ignition of a gun and, in the reference cited below, idenfies the weapon as being 'old, with match locks'. Match was a length of either slow- or quick-burning cord which, when lit, led fire to the gunpowder. Smythe's household accounts for 1587–89 record regular purchases of gunpowder and match, 26.734.

musket rest: this item, notable for being 'tippt with silver', describes the Y-shaped rest pushed into the ground in order to allow time for the slow-burning cord, match or matchlock to ignite the powder, 26.68.

petronell[e]: by the late 16th century, defines a short carbine or long pistol fired with the butt on the chest (L. *pectus*, chest, and see Yaxley, p. 152, for earlier definitions). Some petronells at Helmingham are cased; others are stored with their accompanying moulds (for making the shot). Entries include details of firelock mechanism, design or embellishment of the stock, 97.757, 97.758, 26.726, 26.727, 26.729.

pistol, pistale, pistall, pistell: handgun, identified variously by component materials, embellishments, method of firing, whether or not they are cased and/or accompanied by moulds for making shot or flasks to hold gunpowder:

brasing [brass], 97.759.

cast [of]: two, but not necessarily matched (Halliwell, p. 234): 97.761, 97.762. **with fire cocks and pair of moulds,** 97.760.

unspecified: 41.50; four pistols, held with a long gun and a brass-barrelled gun in the chamber over the dairy, 08.627.

touch-box: for carrying or priming touch-powder, here for a caliver (*q.v.*) 26.725.

hacksaw, haggesawe: saw for cutting metal, 26.1450.

hake, haik: adjustable hook, incorporating a ratchet, on which to hang pot-hooks or S-hooks which, in turn, supported cooking pots suspended above an open fire, 26.1148, 41.249, 41.318; **old**, 26.1318. See also **hale**; **pot hook**.

halberd, halbard, halbert, halburd, holberd: a battle-axe with blade and spike. These weapons were retained even when old or broken, 97.770, 41.508; **bills,** 26.739; **head** [*of*], 26.413. See also **bill.**

hale, haile, hayle: pot hook, 08.6, 08.325; see also **hake; pot hook.**

halfpace, half pace: a step up or down, a change in level. A description unique to the 1626 inventory, where it is used in the headings to describe adjacent spaces in the house. See footnote 5 to 1626 inventory.

half rounds: clay roof-capping tiles fired in the on-site **brick kiln** (*q.v.*), but a supply (with no estimate of how many) is kept to hand in the stable yard in 1626 for current building work, 26.1546. See also **bricks; pavements; roof tiles; square tiles**.

halter: rope or leather strap with which to lead or tie-up horses: **dudfen**: (for cart-horse bridles) 26.1428; **open**, 26.1429.

hammer, 26.1465, 08.239; see also **mallet**.

hamper: Yaxley (p. 97) advises that in medieval times this was a large box, case or trunk, and from *c.* 1600, a wicker basket, 97.83, 26.90, 26.891, 26.942; with **covers, lids**, 26.757, 26.885; **great**, 97.543; **old**, 97.778, 26.684, 26.1264; **wicker**, 26.1032.

handboard: a tea-tray, 41.101. See also **teaboard**.

handsaw, hande sawe: small-toothed saw that could be used with one hand, 26.1459.

hanger: in context, these are not the short swords known as hangers, but the means by which they might be contained in a decorative casing or cover, often of sumptuous materials. All are recorded in pairs and some entries note to whom they had been given. References here are for those listed individually, but see **girdle**: *with hangers*, which describes them with the matching belt from which they were suspended. Spellings below have been modernised; definitions of colours and textiles can be found elsewhere in the glossary:

gold, velvet-lined, 26.875, 26.876.

silk grosgrain, velvet-lined, 26.872.

Spanish leather, 26.873.

velvet, mouse-dun (colour), embroidered with silver, 26.874.

hangings: wall hangings, usually described in multiples or noted as 'hanged around' a room. Mainly of thick, woven textiles such as tapestry, whilst decorative, hangings offered a measure of protection against the damp and cold inherent in a late-medieval, moated house. Comparison of inventory entries not only reveals detail of colour and design but also confirms those hangings that survive in position between 1597 and 1626. With the exception of 'old' and reused hangings, the 1708 inventory provides dimensions. Descriptions distinguish between wall hangings and **wall coverings** (q.v.), confirming that both were portable. Variant spellings and definitions of unfamiliar terms can be found elsewhere in the glossary:

arras, 97.36, 97.342, 97.343, 97.356, 97.381, 26.48.

camblet, yellow, 41.412.

cloth, 97.637.

damask, green, 41.366, 41.387; **red,** 41.160, 41.166; **red silk,** 41.129; **scarlet, with sky mohair,** 08.632; **yellow,** 41.467.

dornix, 97.427, 97.613, 97.676, 26.59, 26.175, 26.281, 26.445.

of Eyrelonde (Ireland), 26.548.

flowery, 08.389.

old, 08.647.

say, 97.407, 97.580, 26.114, 26.774.

Scotch-plaid, 08.502.

tabby (tobine), white, 41.129.

tapestry, 26.151, 26.224, 26.288, 26.326, 26.344, 26.377, 26.791, 26.792 (or carpets), 08.401, 08.430, 08.444, 08.465, 08.494, 08.503, 08.630, 41.454, 41.517, 41.524, 41.540.

turkey-work carpet hanging over the chimney, 08.466.

used for coverlets, 08.602.

verdures, 26.96, 26.376.

See also **tapestry; wall coverings**.

harp: not the musical instrument but an engraving 'like one' on brass, 26.965.

harpsichord, harpsicorde: stored in a garret in 1708, 08.643. For other musical instruments, see **cittern; lute; organ; spinet, virginals**.

hat, hatt, 97.945; **beaver, with gold band,** 97.875; **black,** 97.939; **black beaver, old,** 26.827; **black felt,** 97.842; **coloured,** 97.916, 97.940.

bands, bonds *for,* 26.864. See also **breeds**.

hatchet, hatchett: small axe, described with an accompanying hook, presumably held in one hand to secure a piece of growing timber, for example, which was cut with the hatchet held in the other hand, 26.710, 26.1464.

hauser rope: Halliwell (p. 438) says 'hause' is the neck or throat, in this case describing a rope for a horse, 26.1432.

hawk, hauk, hawk: hawk mews are described only in the 1626 inventory (see footnote 48 to the 1626 inventory), but entries in Smythe's 1587–89 household accounts recording the purchase of meat for the hawks confirm that they had long been kept at Helmingham, doubtless providing a valuable service in hunting vermin (and possibly for sport):

cleaver, clevver to chop hawks' meat, 26.577.

glove: long, strong gauntlet worn by a hawker to protect against the sharp talons of a hawk being supported on the outstretched arm, 97.4.

hawking bag, bagg, 97.849.

perch, pearke, 97.13.

wrynettes to take young hawkes in: nets or traps in which to capture or hold young hawks, 26.513.

hay, haye, cutting spade for, 26.1463.

hayes, cunnye hayes, conye hay: net for trapping coney (rabbits), 97.11.

hayle: see **hale**.

hazel lath, hazle lathe: **bunch of**, 26.1473; see also **lath**.

headpiece, headpeece (protective helmet): **cap[pe]s for**: 26.745. See also **armour**.

headpiece (bedhead, headboard): see **bedstead: headpiece.**

heads: taxidermy: **buck**, 26.17; **stag, stagg**, 26.17.

headstall, headestalle: part of the bridle or halter that goes round a horse's head; most described in detail with associated items as 'belonging to' specific saddles, 97.877, 26.916, 26.917, 26.919, 26.920, 26.921. 26.922.

heare, heaire: hare-coloured. See **colour.**

hearing, hearinge (hair): the references below relate to fine sieves and strainers made of hair. See also *laundry, dry* for details of **hearing lines** for linen.

    milk cleanse, clense: sieve through which to strain milk, 26.1136, 26.1229.

    temes: sieve through which to strain milk, 97.222.

    yeast cleanse: sieve for cleaning yeast, 26.1259.

hearing, hearinge: **herring** (*q.v.*).

hearth and back, iron, a phrase used only in the 1741 inventory, by which time it is likely that coal was used more commonly than wood for fires throughout the house: 41.36, 41.55, 41.70, 41.112, 41.113, 41.127, 41.145, 41.164, 41.176, 41.359, 41.375, 41.392, 41.409, 41.422, 41.479, 41.518, 41.538. For related items see **andiron; bellows; coal; cobiron; dog; chimney; fire; furnace; grate**.

hearth brush, harth brush: brushes for cleaning a hearth are mentioned frequently (see **brush: hearth**), although only so named in 1708: 08.222, 08.427, 08.483.

hemp, hempen, hemping: Items described as **hempen** were woven from the fibres of hemp. See **linen.**

hengell, jemmer hengell: hengell is a simple pin hinge (Yaxley, p. 102); Halliwell (p. 483) defines 'jemewde' as 'joined with hinges': 26.1454.

herring, hearing, hearinge: **old barrels for**, 26.1285.

high stove: see **stove.**

hoe, howe: see **garden.**

hog, hogge: pigs kept at the hall, their accommodation and items related to their slaughter, are mentioned only in the 1626 inventory; but details in all four records refer to the lard house and/or larder:

    cistern, sestern, wooden, for hogs meat, 26.1504.

    hoggescoate (pigsty), 26.1506.

    sty, 26.1506, 26.1508.

    troughs, 26.1506.

    See also **salt** (commodity)**; grease; lard**.

Hogarth, prints by, see **pictures, prints**.

hogshead: in the context of the inventories, a container, a coopered barrel, capable of containing 63 wine gallons or 52½ Imperial gallons. Where contents are not specified, the location is listed below:

cellars: the inventory does not specify whether or not these hogsheads are full, recording 30 in 1597 but only 17 in 1708. In 1626, 33 are noted in the **brewhouse**, listed below, some of which have their previous locations recorded, 97.67, 08.650.

brewhouse, 97.278, 26.1309.

claret wine, 97.73.

empty, 97.74.

hogshead beer: a term used only in the 1708 inventory to identify some of its bottled beer, 08.660; see also **brewing**.

old, to put hops in, 26.1315.

re-used for: **meal tubs**, 26.1271; **oats**, 26.1401.

verjuice: 'nigh full', 26.1118; *in vergis house*, 97.187; *in foule's house*, 97.294.

holberd: see **halberd**.

holland, hollond: the textile known as a holland is **linen**, both coarse and fine; but the 1626 inventory refers to a 'hollond wool twilte' (see **quilt**), suggesting either that this is a quilt imported from Holland, or perhaps with a holland (linen) base worked in wool. With this exception see **linen**.

honnces for coach horses, speculatively, phonetic presentation of harness, 26.829.

hood: item of apparel, usually part of another garment, 97.909; **black, mourning, mourneing**, 26.834; **pennystone** (*q.v.*), 26.879.

hoop, hoope(s): references to 'hooped', referring to the iron hoops in place on coopered items, are excluded; but those to detached hoops are included here. The most significant reference below is to parts of a chair which may have been used in a hothouse: the hoops described in this entry are consigned to the storage in the old wardrobe in 1626, along with other superannuated items. Speculatively, the description of this 'olde thinge with hoops' as 'sometimes a chaire' could be a case of mistaken identity. If of metal, these hoops could have been designed to fit around the necks of heavy planters. Pots containing tender plants had to be lifted in and out of stove- or hot-houses, or even unheated protective houses, as the season demanded. Planters came in two versions: clay pots with integral handles, one either side, or metal-hooped wooden tubs, with a similar pair of handles. An illustration of 1676 shows both versions (see Richard Mabey (ed.), *The Gardeners Labyrinth*, 1988, p. 54). A series of hooped planters are clearly visible in the background. In the foreground a clay pot is being lifted by two men, one in front of the pot and one behind. Each man stands between a pair of long poles, one slotted through each handle from front to back, which enables the pot to be lifted and its heavy weight to be spread. Although this is a highly speculative definition, the very particular wording of the 'olde thinge' suggests that the hoops may well have been designed for such a task, though whether there was ever a 'whotthouse or stove' at Helmingham is a moot point and begs more investigation:

ex wort tub, 26.1316.

for cart naves (rims), 26.1467.

from a chair in a hothouse, 26.767.

of needlework (on chair), 97.24.

wooden, 26.685.

hoose: see **hose**.

hops: see **brewing**.

horn, horning: made of animal horn: **drinking, for horse**, 26.1391; **flask (gunpowder)**, 97.757, 97.759; **hunter's, 'tipt with silver'**, 97.957.

horseman's armour: see **armour**.

horseman's staves, given their location (in the hall, not the armoury), these are probably the remnants of obsolete shafted weapons such as **bill** or **pike** (*q.v.*), particularly since several are incomplete or broken by 1626, 26.14, 26.743.

horsemill: see **mill**.

hose, hoose: term applied both to hosiery and, up to the 17th century, to breeches, which are most evident when described with matching **doublet** (*q.v.*). References below are for pairs of hose listed individually and, with the exception of boothose, all appear to describe breeches, the entries revealing that most are of elaborate design, embellished with silk, gold or silver **lace** (*q.v.*). Spellings below have been modernised. See also **stockings.**

boothose: worn between fine **hose** and boots to prevent chafing:

kersey, sand colour, 97.834.

knitted, green, 97.835.

linen, tops laid with lace, 26.862, 26.854.

tops: deroy coloured, 26.880; **laid with silver lace**, 97.947.

cloth, 97.812.

satin, black, 97.818, 97.798.

velvet: ash-coloured, 97.805; **purple**, 97.796; **russett**, 97.807, 97.815, 97.817.

hothouse, whotthouse or stove: a solitary and oblique reference to 'one olde thinge wth **hoopes** [see **hoops,** above, for discussion] sometimes a chaire to sitt in a stove or whotthouse', 26.767.

howe: see **hoe**.

huckaback, hock-a-back, huckoback: see **linen**.

hutch: deep chest, usually on legs. See **bolting; minging.**

imbroider(ed): see **embroidery**.

Indian brush for hangings: speculatively, a soft brush of angora goat hairs, 08.429.

inkstand, china, 41.31; see also **standish.**

intermesses: in context, and referred to only in the 1708 inventory, these describe pewter plates or dishes of 'about 12½ inches', probably for the service or presentation of an intermediate course in an extensive meal, 08.48.

iron: *passim*: mentioned throughout the inventories as the material or component of diverse items. However, for specific uses of the term see **andiron; cobiron; dog; drying; fire; grid; marking; rack; roast.** See also *laundry, dry*.

Irish: so-called because the wool was imported from Ireland, woven items described as 'Irish' were produced in England: **blanket**, 26.113, 26.451, 26.553; **rug**, 97.325, 97.465. See also **Eyrelonde.**

Irish, Irishe stitch: describes the design of a variety of needlework used for furnishings at Helmingham Hall. A later (1753) definition, by which time it was considered to be out of fashion, was: 'Retiring shades … gradate or go off by degrees' (Yaxley, p. 110). The presence of a dedicated hand-loom to produce 'Irish' suggests that it was still considered desirable at Helmingham in 1626:

chair, 26.159, 26.160, 26.188, 26.212, 26.213, 26.214, 26.215.

cushion, 26.156.

hand loom 'to work Irish on', 26.759.

stool, 26.161, 26.162, 26.163, 26.189, 26.216.

Italy, old map of, 08.244. See also **draught; globe; map**.

jack, old iron: in the kitchen, speculatively part of an earlier spit mechanism, 08.10.

jacket, jackett: black satin, 26.806.

jane fusten, jane fustine: see **fustian.**

japan, jappanned, Yaxley (p. 111) advises that documents rarely distinguish between genuine and substitute work, but confirms that 'genuine oriental lacquer work became popular in the late 17th century but was expensive'. A European substitute known as 'japanning' was achieved with layers of shellac polished with tripoli powder. At Helmingham, the term occurs only in the 1708 and 1741 inventories to describe the following:

bellows, black, English japanned, 08.426.

cistern, 41.49.

lock, 41.202, 41.472, 41.543.

square stand, red, with ledges around the top, 08.419.

stands for candles, 41.516.

tea table and handboard (tray): 41.101.

tea table, japanned and gilt: 41.161.

voider, eightsquare (octagonal), 08.138; **foursquare** (rectangular), 08.137.

jar, jarr, earthen, 41.334, 41.201 **(with sweetmeats); glass,** 41.328; **stone,** 41.327.

javelin, javeling: light spear with steel or iron point fixed to a long shaft: 97.772, 26.12, 26.740, 26.741; **head of,** 26.961; **rakes** (speculatively, racks for javelins), 26.1350.

jemmer hengell: see **hengell.**

jerkin: close-fitting, short coat or jacket: **cloth of gold,** 97.800. See also **jacket.**

jet, jett: see *brewing.*

joined, jointed, joyned, joynted: describes furniture constructed with joints and made by a joiner; generally more sophisticated in construction than carpentry: *passim.*

jump, jumpe: in the context of the 1597 inventory, a short coat of black velvet belonging to Lionel Tollemache, 97.861.

kanvis: see **canvas.**

kape: see **keep.**

kask: see **cask.**

keeler, kellar, keller, killer, a wide, shallow, unlidded wooden tub or bowl: **stand**, 41.290; **wash**, 41.289.See also **butter; maw; sifting; washing; whey.**

keep, keepe, kape: a safe, or small closed cupboard, 97.81; **for bread,** 26.1020; **joined**, 97.500; **lock but no key,** 26.938; **old**, 41.311, 41.462.

kelne, kiln: see **brick kiln**.

kennel: contents of the 'spanyells kennell': **benches for the dogs to lie upon**, 26.1367; **lock and key on the door**, 26.1366.

kersey, carsey: coarse cloth woven of long wool: **boot hose of**, 97.834.

kettle: vessel for boiling. Entries reveal details about the means of lifting and also offer comparative sizes. Tea kettles heated by spirit lamps first appear in the 1741 inventory, as does a fish kettle. See also **boiler**.

band, bond for, 26.1319, 26.1322.

belonging to high stove, 08.165. See also **stove**.

binding for, 26.1323.

brass, 97.117, 97.230, 26.1061, 26.1143, 26.1201.

copper, 26.1144.

fish, copper, 41.206.

great, 'called a boiler to skald milke bowles in', 26.1142.

holding about: **1½ pails full**, 08.359; **2 pails full**, 08.347; **3 or 4 pails full**, 08.328.

large, for dogs' meat, 08.346.

old, 08.13.

tea, copper, 41.211; **lamp for**, 41.211, 41.228.

key: see **lock**.

Kidderminster, Kid(d)ermister: the term describes items of, or covered with, Kidderminster stuff, a furnishing fabric of wool with two cloths woven together so that the item is reversible: **counterpane**, 08.540; **close stool box**, 08.527; **bedstead curtains, head, tester**, 08.540.

killer: keeler (*q.v.*).

Kirby's Survey of Suffolk, in black frame, John Kirby's survey was undertaken between 1732 and 1734, with maps and his roadbook, *The Suffolk Traveller*, published thereafter. 41.471. See also **pictures; maps; plans**.

kirtle, curtell, curtle: in the context of the 1597 inventory, the kirtle is a skirt or outer **petticoat** (*q.v.*) worn by women, sometimes described with matching items. Spellings below have been modernised; variants and definitions of unfamiliar items can be found elsewhere in the glossary:

carnation, laid with silver lace, 97.899.

cloth of silver, 97.896.

mourning, with gown and stomacher, 97.890.

satin: black, cut, old, 97.893; **hare colour, with stomacher, cut**, 97.894; **white, cut upon crimson, with sleeves of the same**, 97.897.

velvet, black: cut, lined with gold camblet, 97.895; **old, laid with gold lace**, 97.898.

kitchen, listed in the 1741 inventory of the kitchen and nowhere else as '1 copper kitchen and furniture'. This is not the large boiling vessel known as a copper, which is described elsewhere in the 1741 list of kitchen contents, nor is it a more portable boiler made of copper, also mentioned elsewhere in the kitchen. Based on *OED* definitions, it could be a Dutch oven or a tea urn. There are no other clues in the inventory description to suggest what the 'copper kitchen and furniture' includes, but the inference is clear that this was a composite item: 41.224.

kneading: utensils for kneading dough, a term used only in the 1708 inventory: **bowl**, 08.85; **keeler**, 08.89.

knife, knyfe, knives, knyves (culinary and domestic): in the 1597 inventory knives were listed only as household items, one for use in the garden but most involved in food preparation. Knives used at table were considered the property of individuals and therefore not listed in household inventories. The table fork was unknown at Helmingham in 1597, so the knife and spoon were the only utensils in use. Rules of use were strict: food taken with a knife from a communal plate was transferred to the diner's plate, where it was cut if necessary and eaten either from the same knife or with a spoon. However, it was considered unacceptable to return to the communal serving plate with any utensil that had been placed in the diner's mouth. By 1741 knives and forks for use when dining appear in the inventory:

basket *for*, 41.197.

black hafted (29) and forks (50), 41.316.

case for child's knife, fork and spoon, 08.522.

cases for, with covers, 26.1029.

chipping, 97.56.

chopping, 97.251, 97.136, 41.331, **iron**, 41.215.

dress souse, to: (in this context, ears and feet of animals, preserved in brine), 26.1226.

ivory-hafted, and forks, 41.197.

oyster knives in a case, 26.1030.

prun[e]ing[e] for a garden, 26.1338.

scrape trenchers, to, 26.1021.

shredding, shreading, 97.135, 26.1078, 08.337.

tray, copper, 41.212.

voider, voyder (generally, clearing, removing food), 97.54.

white hafted, 08.378 (see also **black hafted**, above; **fork**).

knife (weapon): **in scabbard**, 97.251, 26.74; **shoulder**, 26.516.

koord: occurs in description of the canvas lining for a piece of tapestry which has been removed to storage; uncertain but probably refers to an edging or binding: 26.791.

koulinge peene: see **cooling pen**.

kovre: cover.

lace: Yaxley (p. 118) explains that prior to 1563 lace-making in England relied upon looping and knotting threads, referred to as needlelace or needlepoint lace, woven from any combination of linen, jersey, worsted, silk or hair. Bone, bobbin or pillow lace was formed on a pillow, using bone bobbins, introduced by immigrants from Mechlin and Lille after 1563. Loom lace was introduced by Flemish immigrants in the reign of Elizabeth I, one of its early centres of production being Norwich. One of the medieval documents collated by Catherine Tollemache and known as her *Secrets* (Griffiths and Edwards, 2001, pp. 77–94) includes a lengthy treatise on the step-by-step making of a variety of laces. The document begins by explaining movements of the threads using the fingers on each hand and allocates to each method the code letters of A, B, C and D. These letters are then used throughout the rest of the instructions which cover borders, bows, broad laces, open laces, thin laces and many more. In the context of these inventories, lace is referred to primarily by type and/or colour. Editorial categories are used below to separate the three applications of lace.

lace on items of apparel:

black, 97.885; 26.811, 26.839; **broad**, 26.801; **purle**, 26.808; **tufted**, 26.805.

black silk, 26.862; 97.863, 97.872, 97.798, 97.818; 97.862; **broad**, 97.799; 97.860.

broad, 26.880.

curled, 97.801.

galowne, galloon, black and silver: (**galowne lace** is a narrow, close-woven ribbon or braid of silk, gold or silver thread), 26.798, 26.865.26.798.

gold, 97.889, 97.892, 97.946, 97.898, 26.868, 26.807, 97.805; **broad**, 26.854; 97.865, 26.802; **curled**, 97.802; 97.887; **and silk**, 26.799; **old (and buttons)**, 97.948; **and silver**, 97.866.

green, 26.879.

parchment lace: Kerridge (p. 24) defines 'parchmentry' as the name given to the production of narrow-wares, or 'parchments', braids created on a narrow loom, and says that the words were anglicisations of *passement* and *passementerie*. Alternatively, Lawson (p. 582) says that parchment 'was at the core' of the braid known as parchment lace, which may allude to the Venetian technique of winding gold or silver threads around vellum: **of gold**, 97.892; **of silver**, 97.918, 97.919.

silk, plain, 97.867; **russet, broad**, 26.812; **and gold**, 97.815; **seawater green and silver**, 97.925, 97.929, 97.933; **white**, 97.911.

silver, 97.947; 97.861; 97.836; 97.920, 97.924, 97.750; **broad**, 97.910; 97.899; **and gold**, 97.807, 97.871, 26.806.

small, 26.800.

white, 26.828.

lace on furnishings (item summarised in brackets):

billament (habiliment or ornament), **velvet**, 97.868.

black velvet: (foot cloth), 26.832.

blue silk: (bedstead curtains, valance and counterpane), 08.447; (chair), 08.457.

broad: (sumpter cloth), 26.789.

broad black russett (bunches of), 26.856.

orange tawny and ash: (bedstead curtains and counterpane), 26.146; (window cushions), 26.156.

rust-coloured galloon: (bunch), 26.865.

stammel: (couch chair), 26.597.

tawney and popinjay green (bunches), 26.857.

watchet: (bedstead canopy), 26.600; (chair), 26.596.

whitish silk: (bedstead curtains), 08.259; (chair), 08.269, 08.270.

lace on saddles etc.

black silk, 26.908.

gold, 26.907, 26.923.

tufts, 26.905.

yellow, 26.829.

ladder, lather: entries reveal where ladders are stored and where they are in use, and describe them by length relative to one another, 26.1405, 26.1407, 26.1408, 26.1409, 26.1410, 26.1411 (for the gardener's use; see also **garden**). See also **step ladder**.

lamp black, lamblack: almost pure carbon collected from the soot deposited by a burning torch; used as a pigment (Yaxley, p. 119), 08.156.

landscape: see **pictures**.

lantern, lanterne, lanthorn[e]: portable lamp, particularly for outdoor use, carried by a top handle, lit from within by oil (fish, vegetable or whale) and fitted with transparent panels. 'Lanthorn' derives from the use of horn for the panels prior to the use of glass: 97.221, 97.554, 41.30; **glass, large**, 41.181; **glass with mahogany frame**: 41.117, 41.157, 41.382; **sconces for**, 41.35.

lard: melted and clarified pork fat which, when cold and solidified, was used for a wide range of culinary purposes, including pastry-making, frying and basting food. The process of preparing lard was a function of the 1597 Lard House, whilst the end product was stored and used in the Larder, which is where these items are recorded:

pot, potte, of earth[enware], 97.178; **tub, tubbe**, 97.175. See also **hog; grease**.

larm: alarm; see **clock**.

latch keeler, killer: identified in the new and the strong beer cellars, where they were used to catch drips of beer, 26.1039, 26.1047. See also *brewing*.

latch pan, brass, a dripping pan, placed beneath meat to catch the fat and cooking juices, 26.1068. See also **dripping pan**.

lath, lathe, bunches of: kept at hand in the 'workhowse', these were narrow strips of wood to be used in building work, either as a base on which to apply plaster, or as supports for roofing materials: **hazel, hazle**, 26.1473; **sap, sapp**, 26.1473.

lather: see **ladder**.

lavure stave: horseman's staff, 97.6.

laundry, an editorial category adopted in order to identify and separate items related to *dry* and *wet* tasks. References to items used in the *wet* tasks can be detected only in the first three inventories, of which that of 1708 is the first to define a room or space as a laundry, grouping it with the dairy, cheesehouse and larder. There is strong evidence that its location was the same as in 1597 and 1626, when laundry tasks appear to have taken place in what was described persistently as the outer dairy. The picture changes in 1741, when the laundry describes the functions of what was described in the three earlier inventories as the drying room (or 'Drying Chamber'), whose contents are described below, under *laundry, dry*. Evidence of wet laundry tasks, or contents related to them, was not identified in the 1741 inventory, confirming that, by then, the task was undertaken outside the confines of the hall and returned to the household for starching, ironing and airing in the designated laundry.

laundry, dry:

board and square stone, to press linen: included here but 'press' here may be related to squeezing excess water from linen, rather than the process of pressing dry linen: 26.1017.

box iron, shield-shaped or oblong smoothing iron with a hollow base into which a pre-heated cast-iron heater of the same shape would be inserted: 41.310.

clapper for napkins: uncertain, speculatively, an early version of a mangle for drawing (or clapping) the fabric of napkins tightly between rollers or flat pieces of wood or metal to smooth them: 08.331.

copper saucepan for starch, 41.594.

frying pan, recorded in the 1597 drying chamber this item was almost certainly pre-heated by filling with embers or coals and used for smoothing: 97.541.

hearing, hearinge lines, lightweight lines made of hair, on which to hang and dry linen: 26.683, 26.1173, 26.1252.

ironing cloth, 41.596.

irons, 08.330; **smoothing irons**, 41.595.

linen horse, horss to hang linen upon, stand or support for drying or airing linen: 08.329, 41.590.

linen press, for dry linen, which may have incorporated a screw press in the upper cupboard or it may have been a screw press without a cupboard surround, particularly at the earliest date: 97.569, 26.679.

marking irons 'for L and T', listed in the 1708 inventory in the rooms grouped together as 'laundry, dairy, cheesehouse and larder', but their proximity to the clothes baskets suggests that they may be for marking linen with the initials of Lionel Tollemache: 08.350.

smoothing table, 97.530.

suffering press to dry linen on, 'suffering', designed to bear, or support, damp linen (unlike a **linen press** enclosed in a cupboard) and similar to, if not synonymous with, the **horse** described above: 26.680.

laundry, wet:

block, on which laundry was beaten, although evidence of a beetle or similar beating implement is lacking throughout the inventories: 26.1172; **on four feet**, 08.322.

board and square stone, to press linen, speculatively, in this context, 'press' is related to squeezing excess water from linen, rather than the process of pressing dry linen. 26.1017.

bucking, buck(e)ing, generally a bucking tub (or keeler) is a washtub; but specifically the tub in which soiled linen was soaked in lye, the alkalised solution of ashes and water which leached out dirt:

keeler, killer, 26.1162.

tub, tubb, 97.233; **great**, 26.1159; **large**, 08.340; **lesser**, 26.1160.

dyeing, dying pan, panne, reserved for mixing coloured dyes; most would have been used to colour fabrics, but Catherine Tollemache's recipes specify 'dyers waters' to colour plants (Coleman, pp. 39–41): 97.231.

rinsing, rinseing tubs, 26.1161.

washing keeler, 97.147, 97.236, **on four feet**, 26.1163.

washing tub, tubb, 97.232.

lawn: a fine linen (and later cotton) fabric used in apparel and for culinary tasks: **sieve, scieve**, 08.84, 08.143; **sleeves, drawn out for**, 97.904.

lead, leading: diverse uses of lead are identified, most particularly in the 1626 inventory, including home-ground colours (lead paints):

box 'with vjj hollowe leads to putt colours in for a lymner': (a paintbox for an artist), 26.1337. See also **limn; pictures**.

chest, lined with ('for watering fish in'), 26.1501; see also **fish**.

cistern, sesterne, 26.1036, 26.1510, 08.657.

clock, weights for, 08.665.

flew (*q.v.*) with leads and corks, 26.1347.

mould, 'to run sheet leade in', 26.1324.

net, casting (weights) **from**, 26.1346.

ointment, lead box and cover for, 26.1390.

pans, for water (for pheasants), 26.1540.

pipe, pieces of, 26.1335, 08.587.

plate of, 26.109 (?for limning).

pump, 26.1509.

red, box for, 26.956.

stills, 26.1245.

stone, to grind colours of, 26.1336.

weights, 97.106, 97.177, 26.950, 26.1129, 08.361, 08.362, 08.363, 08.364; see also **scales**.

leading staff, staves: given that both examples are embellished with gilt or silver and tassels, and one is for a captain, these are versions of the **cornet staff** (*q.v.*), designed to support the flag or cornet identifying the military bearer when leading his troop of horse, 26.66, 26.67.

leaf: see table.

leather, lether: the 1587–89 household accounts confirm that cattle hides were sold periodically to local tanners and the funds added back to the household account (Coleman, pp. 26–7). However, many of the leather items identified in the inventories attest to the import of luxury goods. Spellings below have been modernised:

bags full of feathers, 08.586.

blackjack, jack, 08.108.

bottle, 08.109.

box, 26.45, 26.90.

buff, buffe, a stout bovine leather (from Fr. *buffe*), whitish-yellow in colour, whose surface was buffed, or abraded, during the tanning process. Yaxley (p. 26) notes that jerkins and soldiers' clothes were made from it, and comments that one side was smooth, treated with oil, the other rough. Items of buff, like others manufactured from animal skins, were stored in Helmingham Hall's wardrobe in 1597 because, like outer garments, they demanded regular maintenance. In 1626 they had migrated to the armoury and, in the case of three of the saddles, were considered to be old and consigned to the roof void over the stable chamber. The 1708 inventory provides the first use of the word to describe a **colour** (*q.v.*), but identifies no items made of buff leather:

privy doublet, privie dublet: an upper body garment worn beneath a jerkin, 97.869.

saddle: **great buffe**, 26.747, 26.913; **other, corded with buff**, 97.881; **old**, 26.1402; **steel, corded with buff**, 97.880.

case for a sword hilt, 26.931.

chair, seated/backed with, 97.21, 26.38, 26.121, 26.222, 26.569, 08.32, 08.95, 08.368, 08.323, 08.620.

chest, 97.472, 97.473, 97.474, 97.492.

coffer, covered with, 97.511.

collar (horse), 26.1356, **part leather**, 26.1430.

cushion, 08.272.

girdle and hangers, 26.868; see also **hangers** below.

glass bottle, covered with, 97.76, 26.946.

gloves, 97.836; **of tanned sheep's leather**, 97.837; See also **gloves**.

hangers, Spanish, 26.873.

pantofles, Spanish, 97.857.

postpillion, 26.935.

pumps, Spanish, 97.858.

saddle, 26.909, 26.911, 26.912, **cover**, 97.876, 26.906, 26.907, 26.908, 26.910, 26.912; **furniture (for)**, 97.879; **Spanish**, 97.878.

scabbard, 26.929; **false leather**, 26.930.

shoes, Spanish, 97.854, 97.855.

stand, eightsquare, cover for, 08.520.

stirrup, stirropp, stirope leathers, 97.879, 26.909, 26.1384.

stool, 08.324, 08.369, 08.578.

suite (headstall, reins, breastplate and cropper), 26.922.

trunk, 26.87, 26.89, 26.253, 26.602, 26.641, 26.655.

leech, leeches, bottle to keep in: bloodsucking parasite used in the medical proce-dure of bleeding, and mentioned only in the 1708 inventory by virtue of the distinctive glass bottles in which leeches were kept, 08.174, 08.240. See also **glass**.

leed: lid. *Passim.*

leved: leaved, as in 'leved grese' (three-leaved); see **grese**.

limn, lyminge, lymner: to limn is to illuminate, to paint in colours; descriptions in the 1626 inventory reveal the activities of a 'lymner' at Helmingham Hall:

box: the equivalent of a paintbox, described as 'a round box with a cover with vjj hollow leades to put colours in for a lymner', 26.1337.

cloth, large piece of: 'whereon pte of a picture is begun to be limned', 26.125.

wooden frame: 'to sett a picture upon when yt is a lyminge', 26.108.

See also **draught; pictures**.

linen, lynnen: in the context of these inventories, the term is used in both specific and generic descriptions. Discrete inventories headed 'Linen', dated 1604 to 1609, were incorporated into the 1597 inventory. They detail the qualities, numbers and whereabouts of specific items of bedlinen and napery. Linen is woven from the fibrous stems of flax, and descriptive inventory terms distinguish between the qualities (**diaper, damask, holland** and **flaxen**). Lists of linen include also lower-quality **hempen** or **hemping**, woven from the fibres of hemp. All references to **sheets** in the 1597 inventory include detailed measurements. Comments in the lists of linen include dates of purchase, from whom items were purchased or by whom made, and the date if made or altered at the hall. The 1626 inventory is silent on household linen, recording only that there is a trunk of it, locked up, and by inference inaccessible because 'My Lady holds the key'. At this time the family was living more often at Fakenham than at Helmingham and would have taken their household linens with them. The 1708 inventory also notes a locked trunk, but does provide an abbreviated summary of accessible linen, as does the 1741 inventory. The 18th-century lists of linen include **calico, dimity** and **muslin** (*q.v.*). Throughout the inventories, the word 'linen' is used also as a generic term when referring to **cloth**. See also **hose, boothose**. Items whose linen types or qualities are not identified by any of these terms are included below, with summary details, as ***unspecified***.

damask: Yaxley (p. 62) offers distinct definitions of the linen known as damask: figured fabric combining linen warps and worsted (woollen yarn) wefts, the development and production of which was centred on Norwich from about 1584. Attributions here are speculative but are distinct from the 'diaper' damasks identified below:

cloth, carving, 97.1085, 97.1090; **cupboard,** 97.1084, 97.1089; **large,** 41.432; **long,** 97.1083, 97.1088; **small,** 41.432.

napkin, 97.982, 97.1087, 41.433.

tablecloth, 97.980.

towel, 97.1086, 08.668.

diaper, diapir, diapur: dyaper: a twilled linen, richly figured in its weaving so that the play of light on the surface emphasises its design, particularly when used for table linen. Its name comes from the diamond-shaped design figured into the weave. Considered to be damask of the highest quality:

cloth, board, 97.1077, **cupboard,** 97.1073, 97.1080; **fine,** 41.434; **long,** 97.1072; **table,** 08.671.

napkin, 97.974, 97.1079, 97.1082, 08.669, 08.672, 41.435.

towel, 97.972; 97.1059, 97.1074, 97.1078, 97.1081, 08.673, 41.459.

See also **damask, silk**.

flaxen: **cloths, cupboard,** 97.1066; **sheets,** 97.1039, 41.430.

hemp, hempen, hemping, hempeing cloth: lower-quality items of napery and bedlinen, some entries commenting on their condition and some confirming their designation for staff use:

cloth: **carving,** 97.1051, **cupboard,** 97.1052, **dresser,** 97.1058; **husbandmen's,** 97.1057; **square,** 97.1050, **table,** 97.1056.

napkin, 97.976, 97.978, 97.1054.

rubbers, 97.1055.

sheets, 97.1036; **coarse,** 97.1047; **new,** 97.1048.

towel, 97.975, 97.979, 97.1053.

holland, hollond: the linen textile known as a holland is produced as **coarse** (described in the inventory as 'somewhat courser', 'ordinary' or 'plain') and **fine**. Where there is doubt, items have been included under ***unspecified***:

coarse, somewhat courser: sheets, 97.1005–1007 inclusive.

fine finer: **cloth**: **board**, 97.1061, 97.1064; **sheets**, 97.989–1003 inclusive, 97.1026.

ordinary: **sheets**, 97.1031.

unspecified: **cloth**: **carving**, 97.1065; **cupboard**, 97.1062, **long**, 41.437; **short board**, 97.1063; **napkins**, 97.1067, **coarse**, 41.438, **long**, 41.436; **pillowbeer** (pillowcase), 97.971, 97.1032, 41.440, 41.442; **sheets**, 97.970, 97.1019 (includes price per yard), 41.429; **old**, 97.1033; **tablecloths, little**, 41.439.

See also **quilt** for an item of 'holland wool'.

huckaback, hock-a-back, huckoback: Yaxley (p. 107) defines this as 'thick linen cloth of northern English manufacture, with alternative weft [horizontal] threads raised to provide a rough surface'.

napkins, 08.675; **tablecloths,** 08.674, 41.445.

Irish cloth, sheets, 41.431.

linen, unspecified:

breakfast cloths, 41.446.

cloth: **board**, 97.1008, 97.1013, 97.1017 'of Cropton and our home-made yarn', 97.1020, 97.1034, 97.1040; **carving**, 97.1060; **cupboard**, 97.1016; **dresser**, 97.1071, 97.1021; **square**, 97.1009; 97.1010; **table, hall**, 08.681; **long**, 97.1014; **short**, 97.1015.

napkin, 97.987; **brown**, 97.1068; **wrought with a blue chevron**, 97.1069.

pillowbeer, pillowbier (pillowcase), 97.983, 97.985, 97.986, 97.1029, 97.1034, 08.677.

sheets, 97.1023, 97.1024, 97.983 'such as I lye in'; **better sort for servants**, 41.449; **finer**, 97.1025, **old**, 97.1037, 97.1041, **ordinary**, 97.1028, 41.448; **other**, 97.1045; **servingmen's**, 97.1044, 'made in the year 1596', 97.1045; **overworn**, 97.1042.

tablecloths, 41.447.

towel, 97.981; 97.1070, 97.1018, 08.678, 41.447; **oyster**, 97.1011; **round**, 08.679.

wallets, a cloth bag for carrying food, for example: 08.680.

linsey-wolsey, linsey woolsey, linsey woolsea, linsie wolsie, lynsiye: cloth with a linen warp and a woollen weft.

blanket, 97.663.

chair, 08.577.

coverlet, 08.437.

curtains, bed, 08.597.

curtains, window, 08.423.

hanging, 26.114 (deleted and replaced with 'say').

wall coverings, 08.479.

livery, liverie, liv[e]rye: multiple definitions, but when used in conjunction with items of furniture the inventory context dictates the purpose. Livery **cupboards** and **tables** are associated generally with dressing. A livery **bedstead**, on the other hand, is provided for staff. The term does not occur in any form in the 1741 inventory.

lock: considered a portable item and listed throughout the inventories, whether fixed to doors or household goods. The reference is frequent but details are too specific to warrant an entry of *passim* except in the case of unnamed internal doors (because many rooms have more than one door). Meticulous attention to detail in the 1597 and 1626 inventories includes items of furniture and/or doors equipped with locks but lacking keys. Keys are not mentioned at all in the 1741 inventory, where the material of the lock is used to describe it more frequently than details of its function or position. In all four inventories, where items or rooms are locked and inaccessible to the compiler, this fact was noted, sometimes with details of who held the key. Locked household goods are invariably high status, some of them 'new', or they store high-value items such as linen and spices. Editorial categories are in *italics*:

> **brass-cased,** a description unique to the 1741 inventory, which does not distinguish on what these locks are found; where there are multiples, some may be fitted to doors and others to items within the room: 41.60, 41.71, 41.99, 41.114, 41.121, 41.128, 41.147, 41.165, 41.178, 41.187, 41.376, 41.380, 41.393, 41.411, 41.423, 41.480, 41.485, 41.521, 41.525, 41.539, **old brass**, 41.458.
>
> *external doors*: **back yard**, 26.28; **back yard between moat and kitchen**, 26.1518; **back bridge yard, gate to**, 26.1514; **bakehouse**, 26.1254; **brewhouse**, 26.1291; **[?]buttery (formerly greasehouse)**, 26.1239; **[?]cheese chamber**, 26.1235; **coach house stable**, 26.1415; **corn barn**, 26.1406; **dovehouse**, 26.1541; **'enterie' leading to apricot yard**, 26.503; **fish chamber**, 26.1526; **garden**, 26.1313; **house**, 26.1001; **larder[?]**, 26.1122; **leading to still yard**, 26.1035; **between old hall and larder [?]**; 26.1136; **inner courtyard (wall to gate)**, 26.1511 (wicket gate in), 26.1513; **inner dairy**, 26.1174; **meal house**, 26.1267; **middle dairy: (new lock)**, 26.1208; **millhouse**, 26.1351; **outer dairy**, 26.1139; **peewits', puets house**, 26.1499; **pheasants' yard (spring lock)**, 26.1537; **poultry [fowl] house**, 97.302, 26.1276; **saddlehouse**, 26.1381; **scullery[?]**, 26.1109; **slaughterhouse**, 26.1482; **soap house**, 97.564; **spaniels' kennel**, 26.1366; **stable**, 26.1368; **husbandman's stable**, 26.1420; **storehouse, husbandman's**, 26.1434; **vergis (verjuice) house**, 26.1121; **workhouse (lock broken)**, 26.1471. See also Appendix A for discussion of access and security.
>
> *fixed to household goods*: **barrel**, 26.1001; **box**, 97.477, 97.495; **cabinet with drawers**, 26.85; **chest**, 97.471, 97.472, 97.473, 97.474, 97.512, 97.513, 97.531, 97.536, 97.537, 97.538, 97.566, 97.616, 97.617, 26.83, 26.579, 26.1225; **coffer**, 97.475, 97.511, 26.86; **close stool box**, 08.462; **cupboard**, 97.162, 97.491, **with multiple locks**, 97.45, 97.80, 26.937; **cupboard table**, 26.606; **oat chest**, 26.1382; **drawers containing silver**, 41.191; **spice cupboard**, 26.1102; **table**, 26.61; **trunk**, 97.476, 97.494, 97.510, 97.521, 97.524, 97.532, 97.534, 97.566, 26.87, 26.88, 26.89; **wine bins**, 41.352; **writing box**, 26.44.
>
> *internal doors*, *passim*.

iron, 41.199, 41.267, 41.499, 41.510.

japanned, 41.202, 41.472, 41.543.

locked, locked up: **chest**, 26.580; **closet**, 41.481; **trunk containing horseman's armour**, 97.565, 26.579; **trunk of linen**, 08.683; **trunks**, 26.579, 26.884; **virginals**, 26.123.

locks but no keys: **bin**, 26.1010; **chest (trunk-fashioned)**, 26.939; **coffer**, 26.1002; **croft stable**, 26.1418; **cupboard**, 26.1000; **keep**, 26.938; **lute and cittern cases**, 26.131; **chests**, 26.883, *internal doors*, 26.166, 26.337, 26.343, 26.385, 26.386; **plate lock**, 08.592; **park gates**, 26.1003; **pump house**, 26.1508; **stock lock**, 26.1328, 26.1462; **swill house**, 26.1503; **trunks**, 26.884.

plate lock, Yaxley (p. 125) defines this a a lock in which the works pivot on an iron plate: 08.131, 08.227, 08.228, 08.501, 08.532.

spring lock, *OED* cites the use of this phrase from 1485 and gives an example from 1602, defining the item as 'a common form of lock in which a spring presses the bolt outwards, thus rendering it self-locking except when secured by a catch'. The sole example secures the Steward's Chamber in 1626: 26.488.

stock lock, Yaxley (p. 125) defines this as a lock contained in a stock, or wooden block, secured to the inside of the door: 08.38, 08.96, 08.117, 08.215.

longbow, 97.626. See also **bow; crossbow; gaffle; slur bow**.

looking glass, the manufacture of glass for use in mirrors was uncommon until the early 17th century, earlier versions being made of metal; and in 1620 the importation of looking glasses was forbidden (Edwards, pp. 309–10): **in walnut frame**, 08.247; **stand for**, 26.22; **table looking glass, in frame**, 08.523, 08.557. See also **dressing glass**.

loom, hand: see also **lucet,** below.

Irish, to work on: speculatively, this refers to Irish stitch, which refers to a design created by graduating colours, 26.759.

thrums (q.v.) **or fringe** (*q.v.*), to work: both terms relate to the weaving of narrow braids, or edgings, so this hand loom would have been similar to (if not the same as) the lucet described below, 26.758.

lucet(te), lucit: a small, hand-held device on which to weave narrow braid, 08.580.

lute: cases for, 26.131. For other musical instruments, see **cittern; harpsichord; organ; spinet; virginals**.

mallet, mallett, 08.654; **wooden: to beat brick and chalk**, 26.1114. See also **bedstead,** *tools for maintaining*.

malt, mault, there is no evidence for a malthouse, nor is the process apparent from descriptions of the brewhouse in any of the inventories. The items below relate to grinding and then brewing with malted barley:

stones for, confirmation in the 1626 inventory that the millhouse had two sets of grinding stones, one reserved for malted barley: 26.1354.

thing to stir malt with: for use in the mashing vat, 08.309.

manger: a feeding trough for horses or cattle, 26.1369, 26.1417, 26.1419, 26.1421.

mantletree: consigned to storage in an area of the roof void in 1708, this item occurs in one of two consecutive references to **mouldings** (*q.v.*); speculatively it refers to the supporting structure of a mantlepiece, in this case 7ft 9in long, 08.645.

map, maps: the 1626 and 1741 inventories identify and describe maps on display, noting some framed and others on rolls or rollers:

England, on rolls, 41.197.

Europe (old map of), 08.284.

Italy (old map of), 08.244.

Kirby's Survey of Suffolk, in black frame, 41.471.

Scotland, part of, 08.285.

screen covered with, 41.537

Suffolk, in oaken frame, 08.611.

undefined, 26.47, 26.153, 26.248, 41.156; **large, on rollers,** 41.119; **on rolls,** 41.151.

with the heads of the Kings of England, on rolls, 41.154.

world, framed, large, 26.46.

See also **globe; plans; pictures.**

marble, white: dimensions are noted for each item: cistern, oval, 08.218; **mortar,** 08.139; **table,** 08.217; **unpolished pieces of pavement,** 08.291.

marking irons 'for L and T'. See *laundry, dry.*

mash, meesh, mesh: hot water added to malt creates mash, the first stage of **brewing.**

mat, matte, matted: notwithstanding the frequent references to **bedstead: mat** (*q.v.*), when the 1626 inventory refers to a chamber or **romph[e], rompht** (*q.v.*) being matted, often recorded as the final item in the room's inventory, it indicates the presence of floor coverings. No floor coverings of any kind can be detected in the 1597 inventory. Their existence was considered important enough in 1626 for a room to be noted as 'the greate newe matted chamber' (see footnote 24 to the 1626 inventory). Unless specified otherwise, floor mats (like bed mats) were made of woven hemp: 26.94, 26.103, 26.167, 26.192, 26.252, 26.308, 26.384, 26.471; **long matt,** 41.383; **Portugall platt:** refers to the plaiting or weaving method of the mat, 08.241 (with dimensions); **rush mat** (with dimensions), 08.242. See also **carpet, floor.**

match, matchlock: see **gun.**

maund: see **seed-mande.**

maw, mawe(s): rennet is a word that appears nowhere in the four inventories but is curdled milk found in the **maw,** or stomach, of an unweaned or **wennell** (see below) calf. The acid in the curdled extract was added to fresh milk to facilitate the cheese-making process. The acidulous juices of some plant material offered an alternative: Yaxley (p. 41) cites Leonard Mascall (d. 1589) listing alternatives such as 'the flowers of a wild thistle, or the seede of the blessed thistle, or the juice of a figge tree, or the leaves and hoarines which groweth at the small end of the artichokes, or ginger … or the blacke mutable thistle'. There is no evidence for this at Helmingham, but see **cheese: old tray for fennel seed** for discussion. As with **butter, cheese, cream, milk** and **whey** (*q.v.*), the inventories specify common utensils and equipment strictly in relation to their purpose when used in the dairy, the items below relating to maw or wennell:

firkin, ferkin (cask), 97.215.

pot, potte, a container designated for maw: 97.224.

wennell calves mawe keeler, a wennell calf is a suckling calf and this keeler (shallow, straight-sided, hooped vessel) is used to collect its maw, or stomach, from which curdled milk (rennet) was obtained: 26.1215.

meadow rake, 26.697; **and rake heads,** 26.1349.

medicine, medicyne: there is only one direct use of the word, occurring in the 1626 inventory description of **drying irons** (*q.v.*). See also **leeches.**

meesh: see **mash.**

men, table men: gaming pieces referred to in descriptions of the **table** (*q.v.*) on which the game was played, some of which identify the number of pieces, but the name of the game (chess) is mentioned only once, 26.57. See also **goose game.**

mew, mewe(s): see **hawk.**

milk, milke, milking: As with **butter, cheese, cream, maw** and **whey** (*q.v.*), the inventories record the majority of utensils and equipment strictly in relation to their purpose when used in the dairy. The following are specific to milk:

bowl, boule: 69 milk bowls are revealed by the three 1597 references; by 1626, there are 24, only 15 of which are useable, 97.201, 97.203, 26.1181; **new, of the tray fashion,** 97.226.

cleanse, clense: unlike the cleansing bowl, below, this was a fine hair sieve: **new,** 26.1229; **old,** 26.1136; see also **sieve.**

cleansing bowl, clensing boule: a dish pierced with holes to act as a sieve for straining milk to capture fine hairs and other foreign bodies, synonymous with **trap dish,** below, 97.208.

cowl, cowle: a large but shallow tub with two upstanding ears (open handles) through which a rod (cowl-staff) was passed to enable carriage of the cowl by two people, 97.199, 97.234, 26.1177.

fleeting dish, fleetinge: fleeting is the process of skimming cream from milk, 26.1196.

keeler, kellar, killer: a wide, shallow, straight-sided, coopered wooden tub or bowl in which milk was allowed to cool, 97.207, 26.1182, 26.1183, 41.300.

kettle called a boiler to scald milk bowls in, 26.1142.

pails, milking, 26.1216; **with iron hoops,** 41.295.

pan, pans, 97.225; **brass: broad,** 26.1180.

pots, earthen, 41.301.

sieve, milk, 41.303; see also above, **cleanse.**

tongs: tongs resembling an X-shaped trellis stretched above a vessel to allow sieves etc. to drain. 97.220, 26.1195.

trap dish, trafeinge dishe: the information describing the purpose of this item: 'to clense milke wthall', confirms that 'trafe' is synonymous with trap, and both are synonymous with the cleansing bowl, described above, 26.1208.

tray, 08.345, 41.299.

tub, tubbe, 97.198; **lately renewed,** 26.1214.

mill, millstones: at Helmingham the millhouse was equipped with two pairs of grindstones (at first-floor level) connected to a vertical shaft. One pair was for grinding flour, the other for malt to be used in brewing. On the floor below, a horse was attached to the shaft, which it rotated by walking in a continuous circular route. With the help of gearing, the shaft rotated the stones on the floor above. The 1708 inventory offers no details, recording only that there is 'nothing in the mill house except the mill etc.', and there is no mention in the 1741 inventory. See footnote 24 to the 1597 inventory for a summary of evidence for the use of domestic mills.

horse mill: complete, 26.1352; **with two pairs of stones**, 97.288.

stones, millstonn: **for hard corn**, 26.1353; **for malt, mault** (with hoppers etc.), 26.1354; **pieces of, broken**, 26.1359; **worn**, 97.289.

See also **malt; quern; meal hutch; scuppett**.

minging, mingeinge: mixing (mingling), especially dough: **bowl, boule**, 97.261; **hutch, deep plank**, 26.1268; **trough**, 97.259. See also **bolting**.

mockadoe, mackadow: in context, this is a silk textile with a resemblance to **damask**, whose entry it replaced here, 97.789.

mohair, mohair: definitions include the long wool of the Angora goat; and a perversion of the word *moiré*, describing grosgrain (*q.v.*), yarns woven to create a watered effect, which is the most likely definition of the top of a clothes brush recorded in 1708, 08.490.

molding: see **moulding**.

mole, mowle: **spring trap for catching**, 26.1451.

morning: see **mourning**.

morning milk: the first milking of the day was considered to produce the finest cheese. According to the 1626 inventory, Helmingham clearly reserved this for the family, describing a little round hooped box without a cover in which 'morning milk cheese' was transported from Helmingham to Fakenham or London, 26.1200.

Morocco: in the 1708 inventory, a description of cushions (see **cushion**) 'of Turkey, or Morocco', suggests that these items were imported, rather than embroidered with needlework in richly coloured wools known as '**Turkey work**' (*q.v.*). However, at this date, the two terms might have been used synonymously.

mortar: bowl-shaped vessel in which to pound ingredients with a pestle (*q.v.*). The two are invariably described together in the inventories (see **pestle: and mortar**).

moulding: consigned to storage in an area of the roof void in 1708. This term occurs in two consecutive references: **carved for an oval panel over a chimney**, 08.646; **for a mantletree**: speculatively the term refers to the supporting structure of a mantlepiece, in this case 7ft 9in long, 08.645.

moulding board, molding, mouldinge borde, mulding boord: flat surface or table on which bread dough or pastes were worked and moulded. In 1597 and 1626 some are recorded in the bakehouse and some in the 'Pastery', a cool area separate from the kitchen where all forms of paste (flour-based and fruit and sugar combinations) were created. By 1708, the task is probably undertaken in both areas on a **dresser** (*q.v.*), 97.163, 97.267, 26.1103, 26.1255.

mourning, morneing, mourneing, mourner, morning: items of black apparel for adults and children and other items related to horses, all specified for mourners and mourning, are identified in the 1597 inventory. It is noticeable that almost all of the items recorded in the 1626 wardrobe at Helmingham are black, suggesting that whilst the family kept their other apparel with them at Fakenham and Ham, a supply of mourning clothes were kept at the hall in readiness for funerals of senior members of the family at St Mary's church:

cloak, 97.874, 97.938.

gown, 97.890, 97.921, 97.927, 97.931, 97.935.

headstall, reins, crop, breastplate and cloth being 'part of the furniture for', 26.920.

hood, 26.834.

musical instruments, 08.640, not defined; see also **cittern**; **harpsichord**; **lute**; **organ**; **spinet**; **virginals**.

musket rest: see **gun**.

muslin, muslyn: by the Early Modern period, the term referred to a fine, thin cotton fabric, imported from India until its manufacture began in England in the closing years of the 17th century. There is no evidence of its use at Helmingham prior to the record offered by the 1708 inventory: **window curtains**, 08.633, 08.670.

mustard pot: 41.314.

mustard quearns: see **quearns**.

nails, nayles: yellow, synonymous with brass, each mentioned in descriptions of upholstery, 26.38, 26.121, 08.457, 08.459, 08.480.

neats tree: see **tree**.

ne[e]dlework[e]: defines work stitched directly onto canvas, as distinct from woven textiles (including tapestry), and **embroidery** (*q.v.*), which denotes decorative motifs applied to the surface of both woven textiles and needlework:

> **bed, bedd**: stored in a chest and taken to be a framework or support to hold a piece of needlework in progress, 97.1091.
>
> See also **frame**, below, and **carpet frame**.
>
> **broad stitch, stiche**: inserted in the 1626 inventory to replace the deletion of 'tent stitch' and the only appearance of this phrase. 'Broad' may be a variant, or phonetic, spelling of 'bred' or 'braid'. Levey, in *The Hardwick Hall Embroideries* (2007, p. 272), explains that bred, or braid, stitch would have resembled a braid or plait, and could be achieved by various means: 26.608.
>
> **frame**: to hold a piece of needlework in progress, 26.666.
>
> See also **bed**, above, and **carpet frame**.
>
> **low stool** (of, covered with), 26.40, 26.329.
>
> **scallop shells, skallupp shilles** (design on the seat of a low stool), 97.25.
>
> **tent stitch, tente stiche** (seated with): also known as *petit-point*, tent stitch is worked across two intersecting canvas threads, 26.245, 26.608.

net, nettes: for trapping birds and fish:

> **bat fowling, batfouling**: designed for the nocturnal catching of roosting birds. Yaxley (p. 9) says that bat fowling nets had two forms: 'either shaped like a large tennis-racket with a head approx 5 feet long by 3 feet wide, on a handle (17th century), or a semicircle of wood, hinged in the middle and held at either end of the semicircle with a loose net forming a pouch', 97.186.
>
> **casting** (for fish), 97.10; **leads of old,** 26.1346.
>
> **cocking** (for birds), 26.703.
>
> **partridge, partradge,** 97.42.
>
> **quail, quails,** 26.90.
>
> **wrynettes:** 'to take young hawkes in', 26.513.

See also **drag; drawing line; flew.**

oars: 41.622; see also **boat.**

oat, oate, ote, oate meale: oats were fed to the horses; Smythe's 1587–89 house-hold accounts reveal regular purchases of oatmeal and the inventory descriptions suggest that some of it was used for feeding fowl and some in the dairy. Items specifically used for oats are listed below:

bin, bing, 08.685.

chest, 26.1382, 26.1401.

firkin, 97.216, 26.1194.

sieve, seeve, 26.1385, 41.271.

tub, tubbe, 97.296.

oil, oyl cloth for the floor: Yaxley (p. 141) explains that canvas oilcloths, coated with a mixture of paint and oxidised linseed oil and decorated in simple patterns, were in use from the 1720s. The Helmingham example is in the parlour: 41.146.

ointment, oyntment: **lead box for**: (for horses) 26.1390.

oliefe: olive (**colour**, *q.v.*).

olives, ollyves: **barrel of**, 97.78.

organ: the 'musique parlour', a designation unique to the 1626 inventory, includes a **small treble organ**, 26.124.

For other musical instruments, see cittern, harpsichord, lute, spinet, virginals.

otter flew: see flew.

oven lid, iron, ovens were integral but lids were portable: 41.248 (kitchen), 41.276 (bakehouse).

ovis: eaves; see **board: ovis.**

owd: old.

oyster(s): copious quantities were purchased by the household steward in 1587–89 (Coleman, pp. 30–3) and the inventories confirm purpose-made items related to handling and eating them: **knives for, in case,** 26.1030; **table folding, for,** 26.21; **towels,** 97.1011.

pale, paling, paelinge: fencing, particularly around the park, which was also gated and locked in 1626 (see **lock**). The item recorded is one in which the household's ownership is challenged: **paling wimble**: augur used to form the hole for a fence-post, 26.709.

pan, pann, panne: the inventories are inconsistent in their record of pans with a culinary purpose. The 1708 inventory contains a detailed list of 'pannes for cakes'. References below include any pan for which there is a distinctive descrip-tion, including the material from which it is made. Bottoms and covers (lids are associated with **pots**, *q.v.*) are recorded separately, confirming that both are interchangeable:

baking, 97.144; **copper**, 41.207.

boiling, boyeling, brass, 08.166; **broad**, 26.972, 26.1204; **cover for**, 26.969; **little**: 1205; **middle**, 26.1203; **old**, 97.165.

brass, large, 41.216.

cake pan, pannes for cakes, the 1708 inventory is the only one to specify pans for baking cakes, describing them by shape, size or material:

bottom for, 08.79.

foursquare (rectangular), 08.207.

oval, 08.206.

frying, freeing, 26.1224 (see also *laundry, dry*); **brass**, 08.348.

dripping, dreeping: **dripping**: open pan placed beneath the revolving **spit** (*q.v.*) to catch juices from a piece of roasting meat, 97.120, 08.16; see also **latchpan,** below.

latchpan, brass: dripping pan to catch fat and juices from roasting meat, 26.1068. See also **dripping**, above.

pasty, 08.161.

pattepans, pattypans, for baking numerous small cakes in one pan. The separate entries for bottoms (whose numbers do not always match the quantities of pans) confirm that the bases were removeable and that some were interchangeable:

of brass, 08.76; **bottoms for**, 08.76.

firbelowed (having a fluted edge) **without a bottom**, 08.211.

oval, 08.209, 08.210.

of tin, 08.77; **bottoms for**, 08.77.

unspecified, 41.230 (25 items).

round, 13 inches wide, with a bottom, 08.78.

small round taper, 08.204.

straight, round (with straight sides), 08.205.

threesquare (triangular), 08.208.

preserving, large, deep pan designed to boil ingredients, particularly fruit, with added sugar for preserve-making: **flat saucepan for**, 08.21; **of about 3 pints**, 08.367.

pudding, usually a deep pan designed for boiling puddings, but here listed in the 1597 dairy: 97.219.

sauce pan, a pan in which to cook sauces, 08.20, 08.106, 08.168; **brass**, 41.204, **copper**, 41.204. **flat (or preserving pan)**, 08.21.

stew pans, brass, 41.203, **copper**, 41.203.

stew [stue] fish pan, brass, round, 08.101.

See also **bedpan; dyeing pan; firepan; lead (water); milk; warming pan**.

pantofle(s), pantaffels, pantafles, pantoufle(s): footwear, backless, with a low heel: **velvet, black**, 97.856, 97.915. See also **Spanish**.

parchment lace: see **lace**.

particon, particion: see **partition**.

partisan, partisine: long shaft with a spear-shaped tip, a foot-soldier's weapon developed in the 15th century (see Yaxley, pp. 148–9 for variations in design and use), 97.769.

partition, particon, particion: mentioned in descriptions of divisions within hencoops and items of furniture etc., but see **curtain, partition** for clear descriptions of textiles used as room-dividers.

partradge: **partridge**: see **net**.

pattepan, pattypan: see **pan**.

pavements: clay floor tiles, fired in the nearby **brick kiln** (*q.v.*), 26.1549. See also **marble**.

payle: see **pail**.

pearke: perch. See **hawk**.

peck, pecke: a measure of capacity (two gallons or a quarter of a bushel) and, in this case, vessels that held it, or a proportion of it, 26.1399, 08.693.

 half-peck, 26.1385, 26.1399. See also **bushel**.

peel, peele, peal: flat, spade-like implement on a long handle, designed to slide food, particularly bread or pastry, in and out of hot ovens: **and rake**, 41.276; **iron, yron**, 97.129, 97.270, 26.1262, 08.74; **wooden**, 26.1104; **pie, pye**, 08.75.

peewit, puet: peewits (lapwings) were kept in captivity to provide a source of meat for household consumption. Their 'howse' is described only in the 1626 inventory (see footnote 136 to the 1626 inventory). Smythe's 1587–89 household accounts confirm that peewits were being kept and fed then (Coleman, p. 34).

pendulum clock, see **clock**.

penny-stone: defined by Halliwell (p. 615) as 'a kind of coarse woollen cloth': **hood for a horseman's headpiece**, 26.879.

pepper box, pepper was purchased regularly in large quantities at Helmingham in 1587–89 and used for both culinary and medicinal purposes: 97.142, 41.312.

pestell and morter, the pestle is a club-shaped instrument designed for pounding ingredients in a bowl-shaped mortar. Although invariably described together in the inventories, pestles and mortars of different materials are noted, and some were specified in Catherine Tollemache's recipes for use together, notably a wooden pestle to pound ingredients in a marble or alabaster mortar:

 brasen, 97.559.

 brass (mortar), 26.1092, 08.72 **(and pestle)**, 41.246.

 iron (pestle), 26.1092, 08.72.

 marble, 41.247 (and wooden pestles), **white**, 08.139 (with dimensions).

 material unspecified, 97.310; great, 97.529.

 wood, 97.138, 26.1093; two pestles, 26.1093; pestle, 08.140.

petronell[e]: see **gun**.

petticoat, petticoot, pettiecote, pettycoot, petty coot: an undergarment designed to be visible when worn as a layer immediately below a **gown**. Spellings below are modernised. Definitions of textiles and unfamiliar colours can be found elsewhere in the glossary: **buffen, carnation and white striped**, 97.928, 97.932, 97.936; **damask, seawater green, embroidered**, 97.908; **peach colour**, 97.908.

pewter, silvery-grey alloy of lead and tin in the proportion of 4:1 by weight (**Yaxley,** p. 152), *passim*.

pheasant, f[f]easant yard: see footnote 147 to the 1626 inventory.

picadill, picadilly, pickeadillie(s): a type of high collar or ruff (*Ogilvie's Imperial Dictionary ...* ed. Annandale, London, 1855, pp. 437–8): **white satin,** 26.877.

pick[e], pike, pyke: infantry weapon with pointed steel or iron head on a long wooden shaft, 97.773, 26.742; staff (staves), 26.744.

picture[s]: throughout the three earlier inventories, 'picture' identifies all forms of art. In 1741, items listed as drawings, portraits, prints and miniatures are sometimes described only by how many there are, or by the detail of their frames, or whether or not they are 'with glasses':

brasen, from grave stone, 97.775; **long brass,** 26.753.

cookshop, 08.118; see also below, **kitchen piece.**

dog, 26.135.

drawings, framed, with glass, 41.17.

Dutch landscapes, 41.377.

Dutch plan of Zurich, framed, 41.381.

frame(s), in: 4 young ladies, hand-in-hand, 08.121; **'ceesars heads'** (with dimensions; see also **Roman emperors**): 08.124; **full-length,** 41.183; **full-length of gentleman and lady in mourning,** 08.119; **hawk and birds,** 41.15, **head, in oval frame, carved and gilded,** 08.488; **heads, lesser,** 08.126; **heads, other,** 08.125; **horse,** 41.16; **landscape,** 41.14, 41,67; **long, for chimney-piece,** 26.290; **on horseback,** 41.183, **small, smaller,** 26.462, 26.611, 26.932, 41.183; **to the knees,** 08.122; **to the waist,** 08.123, 08.489; *unspecified*, **over chimney:** 41.69; **woman's,** 26.104; **20** (20 pictures contained within one frame), 26.10; **young gentleman, full length,** 08.120.

fruit piece, 41.478.

historical pieces, 41.183.

King Charles the first and his two sons, 08.170.

Kirby's Survey of Suffolk, framed, 41.471.

kitchen piece, large, painted, 41.182; listed in the great hall in 1741, this is almost certainly the **cookshop** picture listed above.

miniature, framed, 41.13, 41.109, 41.163, 41.175, 41.421; **'of my Lord** *[4th Earl of Dysart]* **on copper',** 41.407. See also **portraits.**

pastoral piece, large, 41.184.

perspective views of cities, 41.120, 41.378, 41.381; **and maps, plans and views,** 41.156.

plans of Ham House, 5, framed, 41.381.

portrait, framed, 41.13, 41.68, 41.109, 41.118, 41.126, 41.139, 41.163; 41.183, 41.184, 41.374, 41.391, 41.421, 41.478, 41.535; **'of my Lord** [4th Earl of Dysart]', 41.174; **'of my Lord on copper':** 41.96; **oval,** 41.162, 41.452; *unspecified*, 41.148; see also above, **miniature.**

prints, 36, 41.18; **'of the cartoons', 8,** 41.110; **'concerning Charles the 1st',** 41.555; **of Don Quixote, 22,** 41.141; **Dutch, 8, French, 8,** 41.364; **of Hogarth's 'Harlot's Progress',** 41.111; **of Hogarth's 'Rake's Progress', 8,** 41.143; **hunting,** 41.356; **Italian, 20,** 41.97, 14, 41.408; **mezzo tinto of the Emperor of Germany,** 41.149; **other, 18,** 41.120; **other by Hogarth** 41.143; **portrait prints,** 41.153; **'the Scotch peers protest, &c. with their coats of arms',** 41.483; **of the Virgin Mary,** 41.150; **small,** 41.362, **40 small,** 41.469; *unspecified*, 41.363, 41.379.

prospects of the city and great church of Milan, 9, 41.152.

Roman emperors, 12, 41.618; See above, **frames [in], 'ceesars heads'.**

views and plan of Greenwich Hospital, 41.155.

unspecified: 26.612, 41.69.

See also **draught; limn; maps; plans.**

pie plate: for serving pies, 97.104, 97.159. See also **platter.**

pigeon: mentioned only in the 1626 inventory in the dovehouse, where it is clear from the existence of tables for their meat that the pigeons were being fed. Traditionally sited close to water so that the birds could drink freely, Helmingham's dovehouse is likely to have stood close to the moat: 26.1542.

pillow: with the exception of the cushion pad, all are pillows for bedsteads. See bed for definitions of down and feather fillings:

cushion (describes a pad for a cushion), 97.794.

down, downe, doune, 97.320, 97.349, 97.376, 97.397, 97.422, 97.608, 26.113, 26.141, 26.179, 26.231, 26.278, 26.294, 26.323, 26.351, 26.373, 26.450, 26.552, 26.557, 26.590.

feather, fether, 97.321, 26.405, 26.450, 26.475, 26.521, 26.552, 26.557; fine, 26.278.

large, 08.600.

unspecified, 97.460, 97.507, 97.575, 97.632, 97.671, 26.587, 08.265, 08.407, 08.450, 08.475, 08.509, 08.548, 41.76, 41.85, 41.171, 41.370, 41.399, 41.402, 41.417, 41.426, 41.504, 41.530, 41.548, 41.559.

pillowbeer: pillowcase: see **linen.**

pinked, pincked: pinking refers to a method of cutting along an edge of material to prevent fraying; but refers also to the piercing of small holes in material to form a pattern. Given the context, either is possible:

doublet, satin, 97.797; **lining, taffeta,** 26.796, 26.797, 26.813. See also **cut.**

pin, pinne: generally, a fixing, but one which allows an item to be removed readily, as in the case of the shelves and tables, both of which were considered portable:

iron, 26.515, 26.546, 26.1210.

shelf upon, 26.627, 26.887.

table fixed to wall with, 26.514, 26.639.

tile, 26.1470.

pipkin: small or medium-sized three-legged pot, either of earthenware or metal, 97.166.

pistol, pistale, pistall, pistell: see **gun.**

pitcher: large jug or ewer equipped with lip or spout: **one gallon,** 08.149; **three-pint,** 08.150.

pitchfork: two-pronged fork with a long shaft, designed for pitching hay, straw etc., 26.1375, 26.1520, 08.687; **long,** 26.1348.

plaid, plad, Scotch-plaid, Sco(t)ts-plad: plaid is a twilled woollen cloth with a checked or tartan pattern:

chair seats and backs covered with, 08.513.

curtains, 08.505 (with dimensions).

curtains and valance: 41.544.

hangings, 08.502 (with dimensions).

plan, plans: of Greenwich Hospital (and views of), 41.155; **of Ham House,** 41.381; **Suffolk Estate, on rolls,** 41.144; **of various places (and perspective views),** 41.156; **Dutch plan of Zurich,** 41.381; see also **maps; pictures.**

plancher: floor, platform, 26.155.

plank, planck(e): generally, describes a piece of timber used as a flat surface. See also **board, table.**

plate, utensil, described previously as platters, and then probably made of metal, china plates first appear in large numbers in the 1741 inventory, as do the purpose-made racks and basket for them. Not all plates are defined by their material in 1741:

basket, copper, 41.231.

best, 41.236.

china, 41.201, 41.492 (127 plates).

ordinary, 41.236.

rack, 41.258, **double iron,** 41.196.

soup plates, soop-plates, 41.235.

plate, generic term used to head discrete, updated lists of silver and silver-gilt items in the 1597 inventory. See **silver.**

platter: term used in the 1597 inventory to describe a plate or dish identified by shape or size; large quantities are recorded in the 1597 household steward's store-house, from where they would have been supplied for plating up and delivery to the dining table. Those recorded in the 1597 kitchen are fewer in number but distinguished by their shape or greater capacity:

broad verged, 97.151.

deep, 97.150.

fleet, old, 97.152.

great, new, 97.95; **old,** 97.107.

middle, 97.96, 97.108.

pewter, not fit for use, 41.238.

See also **charger; dish; Delftware; intermesses; pie plate; plate; silver; trencher.**

plough, ploughe, components of which are referred to only in the 1626 inventory:

bearing chain, bearinge chayne, 26.1457.

chain, great, 26.1456.

coulter, vertical blade to cut through the soil: 26.1435.

ear, eare, of several fashions, the plough ear was a mechanism at the front of the plough beam, consisting of a hook that could be latched on at different heights. This would alter the line of draught through the plough chains: 26.1444.

foot chaines 'that gooeth next the ploughes eare', 26.1457. See also above, **ear.**

old, 26.1480; **with 'iron eare and foote chaine',** 26.1497.

share, horizontal blade to cut the soil and transfer it to the mouldboard, where the soil was turned after cutting, 26.1435.

traces, traysses for a horse, now in use in the millhouse, 26.1431.

300

points and tags: point (or arming point) is a tie or fastening on an item of apparel and tag is an ornament attached to it, often of silver, and sometimes 'wanting' (missing). Summarised descriptions below offer modern spellings:

black silk and silver points, 26.798; **with silver tags**, 97.813.

yellow silk, silver tags, 97.819, 26.840.

poker: see fire.

pole to smooth a bed, 08.491.

See also **bedstead: staff, stave**.

pomegranate, pomegranet(t), pumgranet: a fruit imported to from Spain during the span of the inventories, but with a history of culinary and medical use dating back to ancient times. Characterised by its abundance of small, pulpy, coral-coloured seeds, the fruit was represented frequently in stylised form in architecture and the arts throughout the Renaissance. In images of Elizabeth I, the pomegranate represents, variously, chastity, fecundity and everlasting life. At Helmingham it appears in cushion and border designs, 97.793, 26.203, 26.817.

pomell [pummell]: in context, this is an ornamental knob, gilt or inlaid, terminating the hilt or handle of a sword, 26.882.

poniard, punniarde: short sword: **inlaid with gilt, in black velvet scabbard** (sheath), 26.73.

porringer: small bowl or cup, usually with two handles, mentioned only in the 1597 inventory, 97.103, 97.157. See also **silver** for porringers forming part of the family's collection of plate.

portmanteau, port mantue: case or bag, especially for carrying clothes on horse-back: 97.958.

portrait: see **picture[s]**.

Portugall platt: plaited floor-covering: see **mat, matted**.

posnet: long-handled cooking pot, of small to medium size, with three feet, 97.119.

post-pillion, poste-pillion: a cushioned pad placed behind the saddle for a second rider, 26.935, 26.1386. See also **saddle**.

pot, potte: used variously to describe a container or cooking vessel made of various materials. Most 1708 references add approximate capacities. References below exclude pots in the family's collection of plate (*see* **silver**):

brass, 97.309; **great**, 97.118, 97.545, 26.1062; **middle**, 97.546, 26.1063; **lesser**, 97.547; **little**, 26.1064.

earthenware, earthen, 26.1133, 08.110, 08.148.

pewter: great, 97.88.

pint pot, 08.62.

stew pot, copper, 41.205.

stoneware: stone: 'typt with silver and gilt', 97.313; **'typt with silver'**, 97.314.

See also **lard; maw; copper; posnet; pottage; skillet; wine**.

pot-hook, pott hookes: a toothed bar hung vertically in the chimney, its teeth capable of supporting a ratcheted hook known as a **hake** (*q.v.*) from which to suspend a cooking pot; described usually in pairs, 97.126, 26.1065, 08.8; see also **hale**.

potion piece: see **silver**.

pottage: the 1708 inventory contains the only specific reference to what is considered by culinary historians to have been part of the diet of every rank of society since medieval times. Pottage described, broadly, a thickened soup or stew which might contain almost any combination of ingredients of which one would be grain (including bread) or pulses. The 1708 inventory refers to: **plates of 'old pewter'**, 08.54; **pots of brass**, 08.11.

potted meat, oval pots for, 08.184.

pottinger, pottenger: small bowl or cup for soup or similar, **pewter**, 26.986.

praytree: water pumps were operated by a 'pray' or lever (Moor, *Suffolk Words and Phrases,* 1970, p. 292); **tree** (*q.v.*) describes a robust upright support, 26.1036; **long iron**, 26.1509.

preserving pane: see **pan**.

press, presse, generic description for an item of furniture generally combining a cupboard top with shelves or drawers below; however, the inventories reveal distinguishing features and purposes as follows:

    cupboard, 08.134, 08.366, 08.559, **with 3 small cupboards on top of it**, 08.574.

    [with] drawers for wrightings (documents), 26.82.

    linen: this may have incorporated a screw press in the upper cupboard or it may have been a screw press without a cupboard surround, particularly at the earliest date, 97.569, 26.679. See also *laundry, dry*.

press: see **cheese**.

press, screw, for almonds, 08.136. See also **almond**.

prickle, wicker basket (Halliwell, p. 645), in this case full of empty flasks in one of the cellars, 08.658.

pricks: sharp-pointed instruments, 26.1099.

printing bread: see **cheese**.

pritty: probably 'pretty', ornamented, refers here to plates, 08.179.

pudding bags: of cushion cloth (canvas) or muslin, used to wrap puddings for boiling, 26.1234.

puet: see peewit.

pumell: see **pomell**.

pumgranet: see **pomegranate**.

pump, pumpe, water, see *brewing*.

pump, pumpe, footwear, see **leather**.

punch bowl: 41.324; **large china bowl**, 41.494; **silver ladle for**: 41.191.

punniarde: see **poniard**.

purle lace: twisted thread of gold and silver wire, 26.808; see also *lace on apparel*.

quail, kept at Helmingham for domestic consumption: **cage**, 97.229; **nets**, 26.90.

quearns, querns, mustard: a pair of hand-operated grinding stones for mustard seeds, the lower one stationery, the upper one revolving, 97.132, 26.1076, 08.99; **bottom stone for**, 26.1120; **old pair**, 97.193, 26.1317. See also **millstones**.

quilt, twilt[e], stuffed bed-covering. 'Twilt' is used exclusively in the 1597 and 1626 inventories, 'quilt' only in 1708 and 1741:

    flowered, 41.75, 41.415, 41.503, 41.529, 41.547, 41.571.

green, 41.384.

hollond, hollande wool *[sic]*, holland is a type of **linen** (q.v), 26.144, 26.296; **old**, 26.853; **white**, 26.592, 41.169, 41.369, 41.398.

silk: embroidered, 08.411; **green**, 08.413; **red**, 08.476 (with dimensions); **yellow**, 08.506, 08.512 (with dimensions).

underquilt, 08.453, 08.510.

white, 97.379; **wool cradle**, 26.823.

quirace, quirace lace: see **cuirass**.

racks, rack irons, spit racks: iron uprights on feet, placed at either side of a hearth, to support a **spit** (*q.v.*), 97.122, 26.1069, 08.5; **top end of**, 26.1455.

raines: see **reins**.

rake: a wide, toothed head on a long-handled shaft, an implement designed for dragging, whose uses are specified in the inventories:

coal, 08.314; **of iron**, 26.1262.

garden, of iron, 26.1528.

meadow, 26.697, 26.1349; **heads for**, 26.1349.

moat, 97.305.

rapier, rapire: small sword used only in thrusting, 97.766, 26.73, 26.735.

black, 97.848.

gilded hilt, 97.764.

silvered, 97.846.

raynes: see **reins**.

reading desk, mahogany: numerous designs existed in the 18th century, some in the form of a lectern (suggested by the **reading stand**, below), others in the form of tables with adjustable stands to accommodate a book: 41.45. See also **desk**.

reading stand, large, mahogany: suggests a lectern, or item of similar design, 41.474.

reaynes: see **reins**.

redgwithes: see **ridgewith**.

reflector, wooden, definition uncertain, but the context suggests a screen to be used in front of a fire: 41.257.

reins, raines, raynes, reaynes: mentioned only in descriptions of multiple, matching items, such as those 'belonging to' headstalls and saddles: 97.877, 26.916, 26.919, 26.920, 26.922.

rennet: although the word appears nowhere in the inventories, those for 1597 and 1626 refer specifically to utensils for collecting and holding **maw** (*q.v.*), this being the stomach of an unweaned calf from which rennett (curdled milk) is extracted.

ridgewith, redgwithes: Yaxley (p. 172) defines a ridgewith as 'ridgeband, the part of a harness of a draught-horse running across the back', 26.1492.

ringles: curtain rings, mentioned with **bed curtains** and window curtains (see **curtains, window**).

rinsing, rinseing: see *laundry, wet.*

roast iron, roste, rostinge, rostyron: an iron plate or grid irons on which to roast (or grill) small joints of meat before the open fire, 97.243, 26.1082, 26.1146.
See also **gridiron**.

roller, rowler: garden roller:
   stone and iron with wooden frame, 26.1522, 26.1533.
   wooden, with cross iron (crossbar), 26.1523, 26.1524.
   See also **garden**.

rolling pin, rowling pinn, 08.80.

romph, romphe, rompth, rompthe: Yaxley (p. 174) offers 'rumthes' for 'rooms'. Used only in the 1626 inventory, the term describes the floor of a room, area or space between rooms, most usually matted with floor coverings, 26.94, 26.103, 26.252.

rope, roope: explanations in the 1626 inventory describe the following uses:
   (with) eyes and cowl staves: to lift beer barrels, see **cowl-staff**.
   hemp, across a chamber: (on which numerous items were hung), 26.782.
   See also **womb rope**.

rostyron: see **roast iron**.

rubber, to rub[b]e with: the implements and/or cloths for cleaning surfaces (rubbing, dusting, buffing, polishing): **linen**, 97.1055; **'thing made for to rubbe the parlour'**, 26.27.

rug, rugg, rugge: not a floor covering but a thick woollen cloth, and in these references used as a bed covering:
   blue, 26.452.
   crimson, 26.325.
   green, 26.143, 26.182, 26.298, 08.282; **Irish**, 97.325, 97.465.
   red, 26.375.
   white, 26.233.
   yellow, 26.314, 26.353, 08.551.

rummer: see **glass**.

runlet, rundlet(t), runlitt: in the context of the inventories, a small barrel; the word also refers to a measure of capacity (18½ wine gallons, or 18 after 1700; 15 Imperial gallons), 97.295, 97.308, 26.1243; **vinegar**, 08.568.

rush mat, 08.242.

russett: refers to a coarse woollen cloth of grey or reddish-brown colour: **blanket**, 26.437; **lace, bunches of broad black**, 26.856; **scabbard**, 26.74. See also **colours**.

sack, sacking, sackin (coarse hemp or flax cloth): **bolster ticking made of**: 26.693; **piece(s) of**: 26.781, 26.925; **pillow cases made of**: 26.780.

sack, sacking, sackin: (mixture of linen and silk woven to produce cloth used for upholstery and clothing): 97.675, 97.905.

saddle: listed frequently with items belonging to it, some of which were intended to adorn the horse and some the rider. The 1597 inventory notes saddles only in the wardrobe, where they are maintained and stored with items of apparel and leather. As noted under **mourning**, the 1626 inventory reveals that items of apparel remaining at Helmingham after the family acquired, and largely removed themselves to, the Fakenham property, relate to the ceremonial solemnity of funerals and mourning; the same can be said of some of the 1626 saddles and their associated furniture, whether stated explicitly or not, particularly when black, or embellished with black velvet:

black velvet: furniture belonging to, 26.924.

buff: **great**, 26.747, 26.913; **corded with buff**, 97.881; **old**, 26.1402; **steel, corded with buff**, 97.880.

cart-horses, for, 26.1422.

chest (for), 26.1383.

leather, 26.909, 26.911, 26.912, **cover**, 97.876, 26.906, 26.907, 26.908, 26.910, 26.912; **furniture (for)**, 97.879; **Spanish**, 97.878.

livery, with stirrups, stirrup leathers and old bridle, 26.1384.

scotch, 26.905, 26.910.

tawny velvet, furniture belonging to, 26.923.

woman's, furniture for, 26.919.

safegard: an outer skirt or petticoat worn to protect clothing from soiling, 97.909. See also **vastguard,** with which this is believed to be synonymous.

salamander, a flat metal plate on a long handle, heated and used to brown foods: 41.255.

saller, seller, cellar: see salt.

salt (commodity): Helmingham's household accounts for 1587–89 confirm that salt was purchased as 'black' and 'bay', the latter being of higher quality than the former. Some of the copious quantities of fresh fish purchased by the household were salted for long-term storage in the fish chamber; salt was essential, too, in the curing of meat and the making of bread and cheese.

bay salt: **barrel of**, 97.191; **tub of**, 97.192.

box: lidded wooden box in which to store salt and keep it dry so that it was readily available for use, 97.139, 26.1080, 26.1260.

powdering: salting, strewing with salt: **round tubs with covers**, 08.354.

salting tray, trey, 08.341, 41.329; **great, for cheese**, 26.1211; **leaden**, 41.298.

salting trough, trowgh: open trough or tub capable of accommodating large joints of meat for salting, 97.171; **long**, 08.353.

tub, large, 08.71.

See also **brine; cheese; souse**.

salt (serving vessel): **pewter**: **with covers**, 97.105; **celler, saller**, 26.977; **stub, great**, 26.978. See also **silver** for salts forming part of the family's collection of plate.

salver: **glass**, 08.196, **sweetmeat dish to fit**, 08.198; **old pewter**, 08.51, 08.52.

sarcenet, sarsinet, sarsnet(t), sasenet: very fine soft silk cloth.

curtains (bed), **black and white**, 97.401, **yellow**, 26.349.

lining (including sarcenet 'drawn out' through cuts in an upper layer of a garment), 26.227, **filbert**, 97.902, **russett**, 26.809, **seawater green**, 97.903 **white**, 97.922, 97.923, 26.835.

satin, sattan, satten: cloth resulting from a weaving method described by Kerridge (pp. 46–7) as 'cloths in which the warp predominates over and almost completely covers the weft. Each weft thread intersects the warp once and once only in each repeat, so that the face of the cloth has an extraordinary smoothness that can be enhanced further by pressing'. Unfamiliar items are defined elsewhere in the glossary:

canopy (bed), 97.466.

chair (coverings), 97.336, 26.200, 26.358.

cloak, 97.910, 26.800.

cushion, 26.205.

doublet, 97.795, 97.797, 97.813, 26.799, **collar for**, 26.866.

doublet and hose, 97.799, 97.801, 97.802, 26.798.

embroidery, 97.337, 26.206.

girdle and hangers, 26.867.

hose, 97.798, 97.818.

jacket, 26.806.

kirtle, 97.893, 97.894, 97.897.

picadillies, 26.877.

stool, 26.359, 08.562.

tester, valance and curtains (bed), 26.420.

vastguard: speculatively, synonymous with **safegard** (*q.v.*), an outer skirt or petticoat worn to protect clothing from soiling, 97.891, 97.892.

satin of bridges [Bruges]: a satin mixture of silk and linen, originally from Bruges: **chair (coverings)**, 97.618; **cushion of**, 97.403, 97.642; **pillow** (cushion), 97.794.

sauce, sawce, boat, brass, 41.229.

sauce pan, pann: see **pan**.

saucers, sausers: containers for serving sauce. The large numbers recorded in the 1597 inventory suggest that one may have been provided per diner, 97.64, 97.101, 97.102, 97.158; **glass**, 08.190 (with dimensions), 41.489; **pewter**, 26.980, 26.991, 08.66. See also **cups and; silver (silver fashion)**.

saw: see **hacksaw; handsaw**.

say, sey: cloth of fine texture, Yaxley (p. 179) says originally woven of linen but of wool or wool mixture by the 16th century. Kerridge (p. 6) defines the manufacturing process for all says, describing it as a 'distinct two-and-two twill with a single weft and a warp twisted from two or three threads'.

chair, clouded, 08.271.

cloths, window, 97.585.

coverings, wall, speckled, 08.257, 08.276.

curtains, bed, 97.426, 97.451, 97.579, 97.612, 08.283.

curtain, window, 97.406, 08.260, 08.543.

cushion, 97.787.

French, gown of, 97.925, 97.929, 97.933.

hangings, wall, 97.580, 26.114.

pieces of, 97.380, 97.390.

tester, 97.365, 97.425, 97.450.

scabbard, scabberd[e]: protective sheath to house a bladed weapon, 26.735, 26.736, 26.737; **false leather:** speculatively, oilcloth, canvas treated with oil, which was used in the 17th century for clothing (*OED*), 26.930; **leather,** 26.929; **russett** (*q.v.*), 26.74; **velvet,** 26.75, 26.926 26.927, 26.928; see also **case for a sword hilt.**

scalding board, scaldeynge borde: probably used in the preparation of animal carcasses, which were placed on the board and scalded with hot water: 97.115, 26.1058.

scales, scales and their weights are described variously in the four inventories; all related items are listed below:

iron balance without beam, 26.1437.

iron beams and wooden scales, 41.336.

brass weights, 41.336.

lead weights, 97.106, 97.177, 26.950, 26.1129, 08.361, 08.362, 08.363, 08.364, 41.336.

scales: brass, 08.114; **for 'outlandishe goolde' [and box of weights],** 26.56; **wooden,** 26.957, **with beams,** 26.1130, 08.360.

scallop, scol[l]op[ed], skallupp, skollope shills: a design motif based on the shape of a scallop shell:

cup, silver-gilt, 97.1195.

fringe (instead of valance), 08.540.

stool, needlework on, 97.25.

valance, 08.283, 08.505.

scarlet, scarlett: a smooth, soft, woollen cloth usually dyed in this **colour,** for which Yaxley (p. 180) says that the dye relied upon kermes, the pregnant female of the insect *coccus ilicis;* but that 'kermes mineral', used in the 18th century, was antimony trisulphide: 08.249, 08.431, 08.432, 08.632.

scieve: see **sieve.**

sconce: generally, a candlestick, either fitted with a screen and handle for carrying, or a bracket candlestick fitted to a wall: **brass,** 08.28, 08.169, 08.333, 41.23, 41.35, 41.195; **old embossed,** 41.619, **oval,** 08.128; **tin,** 08.370, 41.217.

scopett, scuppett: narrow shovel with edges turned up (Yaxley, p. 181).

corn (feed), for, 26.1395.

iron, 26.93, 26.1461.

meal[e], 26.1355, 08.90.

old, 26.1460.

wooden, 26.1376.

Scotch peers protest, title of a print, 41.483. See also **pictures.**

Scotch-plaid, Sco(t)ts-plad, plad: see **plaid.**

Scotland, part, map of, 08.285.

screen, skreen[e] (item of furniture): notably lacking from the 1708 inventory, the framed, footed and folding screens described in the two earlier inventories, and in that of 1741, were used variously to protect delicate faces from the heat of an open fire, for privacy, and to ward off draughts,

firescreen, 41.358; **Indian,** 41.123, 41.138; **printed** 41.95, 41.107.

screen, 97.621, 26.25, 26.107, 26.582, 26.764; **covered with maps,** 41.537. **leather, gilt and painted:** 41.122, 41.137, **old,** 41.455.

screen, skreen, corn-skreen (form of sieve): for winnowing, separating chaff and other debris from grain, 26.1393, 26.1398, 08.688. See also fan.

screw-press for almonds, see **almonds.**

screws for bedposts: see **bedstead,** *tools for maintaining.*

scrutore: variant of escritoire, the writing surface forming part of a **bureau,** 41.1.

scuppett: see **scopett.**

scythe, sithe, sythe: to mow the walks, 26.699, 26.1532; **staff,** 26.699. See also **garden.**

seales skynne: sealskin, mentioned as the covering of a trunk, 97.476, 26.88.

seed-mande, maund: a maund is a large basket with handles, 08.625.

seeling: see **ceil.**

seeve: see **sieve.**

serge, searge: Yaxley (p. 184) says 'woollen fabric, little different from say': **curtains, bed,** 08.470, 08.432; **curtains, window,** 08.455; **doublet and hose,** 97.937.

sesterne: see **cistern.**

settle: wooden bench, usually with arms and a high back. In this case, joined to the wall, 26.3.

shack trace: see **traice.**

shag, shagg(ed), worsted cloth or silk with velvet nap on one side: **cloak lining,** 97.859, 26.803, 26.814; **piece of,** 26.849.

shave: spokeshave, carpenter's and wheelwright's drawknife consisting of a straight blade sharpened on one edge, with a handle at either end at right angles to the blade, and used by drawing towards the person (Yaxley, p. 186): 26.1459.

shears, sheers, sheires, garden, 26.530, 08.349. See also **garden.**

sheep, sheepe(s): brand, 26.1443; **iron, to hang,** 26.1488; **gloves of tanned sheeps' leather,** 97.837.

sheets: see **linen.**

shelf, shelves: considered portable, otherwise they would have been excluded from the inventories; sometimes described with their supporting 'pins' (fixings). *Passim.* See also **books.**

shoe iron: 41.26.

shoes: see **Spanish.** See also **leather** for footwear specified by type.

shopboard, tailor's (tailers shoppborde): a re-used shop-counter or display table, noted as having been removed from the corner chamber in 1626, 26.500. See also counter.

shovel (fire): see **fire.**

shredding, shreading knife: see **knife.**

shutter, shutt (for window), 26.532.

sieve, scieve, seeve, sive, 97.262, 26.1394, 08.694.
 cleansing (for straining milk), 26.1169.
 lawn, of, 08.84, 08.143.

meal, for, 26.1273.

oats, for, 26.1385.

See also **cleanse; sifter; sifting keeler**.

sifter: in the context of the 1708 inventory, a sieve to separate solid debris from ash when cleaning out a fire, 08.9.

sifting keeler, sifteinge killer: for sifting large quantities of meal or flour, 26.1269, 08.87.

silk, silke: with the exception of silk stockings in 1597 (97.820–824), silk emerges as a component of many other textiles in use at the hall including **bird's eye, caffa, chamlett, cloth of gold, damask (silk), cloth of silver, sarcenet, satin, tobine, velvet**. The majority of references refer to narrow-wares such as braids, fringes and laces, and are mentioned frequently as linings. *Passim*.

sillibub: see **syllabub**.

silver: the 1597 inventory identifies and, in some cases, provides provenance for individual items of family plate; it also includes updated lists for 1604 and 1608 and annotates individual items purchased in 1609. Items are described as gilt, double gilt or parcel (partial) gilt, the gilt being applied as a thin layer over a silver base. Design details are included frequently, summarised briefly below. The 1626 inventory offers no more than a broad description of a collection of silver-fashion dishes and plates removed to the Fakenham property and refers to silver-fashioned pewter, for which see **pewter**. In 1708 only two inventory entries mention silver, but locked cupboards, inaccessible to the compiler, may have held plate. The 1741 inventory describes three locked drawers, one of which contains salts and a punch ladle. Provenance is recorded in the case of some items, discussed in footnotes 87–96 to the 1597 inventory.

basin, bason, bassin, and ewer, eawer, 97.1095.

    double gilt, engraved with arms, 97.1093, 97.1119.

    parcel gilt, engraved with arms, 97.1094, 97.1120, 97.1146, 97.1179.

    plain, engraved with arms, 97.1147, 97.1180; **round,** 97.1148, 97.1181.

    See also **basin** and **ewer** elsewhere in the glossary.

bowl, boule, boulle:

    cream, 97.1160, 97.1196.

    double gilt, with cover, given by the Queen, 97.1155, 97.1188.

    gilt, with cover, 97.1100, 97.1129, 97.1192.

    parcel gilt (silver gilt), broad, 97.1099, 97.1127, 97.1156.

    silver, 97.1102, 97.1128, **broad,** 97.1101, 97.1131; **plain,** 97.1158, 97.1159, 97.1193, 97.1194.

    of unspecified plate, 97.1103, 97.1104, 97.1130.

    See also **bowl** elsewhere in the glossary.

candlestick, 97.62. See also **candlestick** elsewhere in the glossary.

cup, cupe, cuppe: drinking cup, usually for wine:

    double gilt, guilt, 97.1153, **in fashion of a nutt,** 97.1122; **in fashion of a peare,** 97.1123; **great high standing,** 97.1121; **high standing,** 97.1150, 97.1151, 97.1156, 97.1189, 97.1190, 97.1191, 97.1195, **standing, with**

covers, 97.1096, 97.1186 **and a man in the top**, 97.1183, 97.1184, **and a man holding the stalk**, 97.1185.

gilt, guilt: with cover and a man in the top hunting the stalk, 97.1152.

dish, dyshe:

chafing (*q.v.*), **chaffyne, engraved with arms**, 97.1172, 97.1210.

of silver fashion of 7 severall sorts, 26.1005.

See also **chafing dish** and **dish**.

pieces, bought in Ao 1609; no detail is offered of the ten pieces of 'v severall stiles': 97.1216.

plate, plat, platt:

engraved with Joyce's cote (see **arms:** coats of arms), 97.1174, 97.1211.

fruit, 97.1113, **engraved with arms**, 97.1142.

See also **plate; platter** elsewhere in the glossary.

porringer, 97.1112, 97.1144; **with cover:** 97.1175, 97.1212.

See also **porringer** elsewhere in the glossary.

pot, potte: gilt, double, dubble: with cover, 97.1153; **with cover and ears**, 97.1098, 97.1125, **and man upon the top**, 97.1126, 97.1186; **high standing, engraved with arms**, 97.1149, 97.1182. See also **pot** elsewhere in the glossary.

potion piece, peece: definition uncertain: this item of silver, recorded in the 1597 inventory, has only one 'eare', or handle and is recognisable in periodic updates of plate, 97.1111, 97.1143; **engraved with arms**, 97.1176, 97.1213.

punch ladle, *OED* cites 1600 as the earliest reference to a punch-pot and offers other 17th-century references to the drink made with a mixture of alcoholic or non-alcoholic ingredients including spices and sugar. There is no specific mention of a punch bowl in the 1741 inventory: 41.191.

salt, sault: lidded container for salt; an item of importance on the dining table and some of whose richly detailed descriptions are summarised only briefly below. Simple and elaborate shapes, including square, bell, nut and pear, and designs incorporating a man, sometimes climbing up a stalk, were popular motifs in the 16th and early 17th centuries:

broad, plain, 97.1217.

cover, with, 97.1108, **plain**, 97.1203.

double gilt, 97.1107; **bell: double**, 97.1165; **given by Quene Elizabeth**, 97.1161, 97.1197; **little**, 97.1110, 97.1134, 97.1201, 97.1202; **high: engraved with arms**, 97.1162; **with cover**, 97.1133, 97.1200; **round**, 97.1164; **square**, 97.1106; **with cover, engraved with arms, a man in the top**, 97.1132, 97.1163, 97.1199; **with cover, engraved with arms**, 97.1105, 97.1198.

gilt, 97.1109; **with cover**, 97.1136, **round**, 97.1135.

unspecified, 41.191.

salt cellar, seller, 08.380. See also **salt** elsewhere in the glossary.

spoon, spone: only the 1597 inventory, with its discrete lists of plate and their updates, records silver spoons in detail, revealing large numbers. None is mentioned in 1626 and few in 1708:

apostle, appostle, ap(p)ostelles, 97.1115, 97.1140, 97.1170, 97.1208.

double gilt, 97.1114; **engraved with 'L & T',** 97.1166, 97.1204; **great, with knops,** 97.1137.

plain, playne, 97.1117, 97.1139, 97.1169, 97.1207.

with knopp(e)s, 97.1116.

with gilt knops, 97.1138, 97.1168, 97.1206; **engraved with L & T,** 97.1167, 97.1205.

sugar spoon: the presence of silver spoons dedicated to sugar, and a silver sugar box (see below) complete with its own spoon, confirm that the status of sugar as a luxury item was reflected when it was served at table in 1597. Smythe's household accounts reveal it to be an expensive commodity purchased mainly in large, cone-shaped loaves, varying in weight, and costing 1s. 5d. per pound in 1588, although prices fluctuated (see Coleman, pp. 36–7). For service at table with a spoon, sugar would first have to be cut or shaved from such loaves and then pounded to a suitable fineness using a pestle and mortar, 97.1178, 97.1215.

unspecified design, 97.1118, 97.1141, 08.381.

sugar box, engraved with arms, 97.1145, 97.1171; **with spoon,** 97.1209.

tankard, tankerd: no tankards of any material other than silver-gilt are mentioned in the 1597 inventory, and none of any description in 1626 or 1708: **double gilt with cover,** 97.1097, 97.1154, 97.1187 **and ears,** 97.1124.

See also **embroidery: silver.**

sithe: see **scythe.**

sittern: see **cittern.**

skallupp: see **scallop.**

skep, skepp(e): deep wicker basket put to a variety of uses at the hall:

bee: when used open side down, a bee skep was an early form of beehive, 97.570.

bread, to carry in, 26.1261.

hops, hopps, 26.1305.

meal, to carry in, 26.1261.

muck, 26.1290.

soiled linen, for, 26.663.

unspecified, 97.265.

skewers, iron, and 3 lark spits, 41.218.

skillet, skellet[t]: describes both a small pan with integral short legs, a handle, and a pot that sits within a framework of legs and handle, 97.552, 26.1070.

brass, in a frame, 26.1224.

copper, 41.213.

gallon, 08.104.

pint, 08.18; **three-pint,** 08.105.

quart, 08.17.

with iron frame, 26.970.

skimmer, skommer: long-handled, slotted spoon for removing surface scum or fat from liquids, 97.131.

brass, 26.971, 26.1089, 26.1145 (with wooden handle), 41.216.

skollope: see **scallop**.

skreen(e): see **screen**.

sled, slead: sledge for transporting goods and implements, 08.699.

sleeves: apparel, particularly for ladies, was composed of individual elements; in the 1597 inventory, sleeves are described often with other items of apparel, particularly **gown, kirtle, stomacher** and **vastguard** (*q.v.*); however, those listed below are discrete references. Entries reveal rich additional detail, particularly where sleeves consist of two layers, one textile drawn through cuts in the other. See footnote 54 to the 1597 inventory for details of correspondence between Catherine Tollemache and her London tailor in 1609, with regard to sleeves:

    taffeta, seawater green, 97.926, 97.930, **white, drawn**, 97.923.

    vardingall (farthingale: refers to padded hoops to build out sleeves at the junction with the shoulder), 97.901.

    velvet, black, cut, 97.904.

slip[p]s: the reference below is the only one unrelated to **embroidery** (*q.v.*), and describes a plant-based design on silver. The term relates to a slip, or cutting, as it does in the embroidery designs described elsewhere: **rose slips**: describes the decorative motif on a silver cup, 97.1191.

slur bow, slurr bow and bender: Halliwell (p. 760) defines a slur-bow as 'a kind of bow, probably one furnished with a barrel, through a slit in which the string slided [*sic*] when the trigger was pulled'. 26.708. See also **bow; crossbow; gaffle; longbow**.

smoothing: see *laundry*.

snaffle, snarfle: see **horse**.

snuffers, described as a pair, and used to extinguish candles: **iron**, 41.24.

souse, sowse: (brine), see **cheese: angelot**.

souse, sowse: (generic term for the ears, feet etc. of cattle or pigs which were trimmed and stored subsequently in brine): **barrow to lay neats sowses upon**: (cattle parts) 26.1491; **knife to dress**, 26.1226; **tub, tubb, now used for pouldering** (salting), 26.1223.

spade: cutting, for hay, 26.1463; **garden**, 26.1527; **iron, with wooden handle**, 26.1289; **old**, 26.1460.

spaniel, spanyell's kennel (contents of) 26.1366, 26.1367.

Spanish: items listed below appear elsewhere in the glossary, but the term 'Spanish' appears often enough to warrant a separate entry. Despite the conflict, in which the Tollemache family was actively involved in 1588, the adjectival use of 'Spanish' occurs in the 1597 inventory, persists in 1626 and refers to fine, high-quality goods. The term does not occur in the 1708 or 1741 inventories:

    blankets: always recorded in pairs, and located only in high-status sleeping chambers at the hall, 'Spanish blankets' were fine, soft, fleecy blankets or rugs produced in England from the mid–16th century, first using fine, soft wool imported from Spain but later woven with English wool: 26.142, 26.181, 26.297, 26.324, 26.352, 26.374, 26.557.

    hangers, pair of: (for weapons) 26.873.

pantofles, pantoufles, pantafles, tawny leather: type of backless footwear, 97.857.

pad[d] saddle, leather, 97.878.

post[e]-pillion, 26.935: a pillion was a light saddle; post-pillion suggests a cushioned saddle for a second rider.

pumps: footwear with a low heel, sometimes worn for dancing, 97.858.

shoes, shooes, leather, new, 97.854; **old,** 97.855.

speckled: term used only in the 1708 inventory and refers to the appearance: **linsey-woolsey (woolsea), green and yellow,** 08.597; **say, sey,** 08.257; **stuff,** 08.561.

spice, spicerye: Smythe's household accounts for 1587–89 record the periodic purchase of cinnamon, cloves, ginger, nutmeg and pepper (purchased by the pound or half-pound) and a quarter of an ounce of saffron. Secure storage of spices is reflected in the inventories, entries revealing details of the removal back and forth between spaces of one of the spice chests and its eventual relegation to a candle chest: **box, tin,** 41.268; **chest for,** 26.1108, **with lock and key,** 26.1225; **great coffer for,** 97.522; **locks and keys** (to a cupboard in the wall), 26.1102.

spinet, spinnet, keyboard instrument, similar to a harpsichord, 41.476. For other musical instruments, see **cittern; harpsichord; lute; organ; virginals.**

spirket, spurket, spurkit[te]: metal hook, peg or candle spike (known also as a pr[y]iket[te], but not in these inventories): **brass,** 26.106; **iron,** 97.179, 26.20, 26.55, 26.76; **turned wooden,** 26.962.

spit, speet, spitt: horizontal iron rod designed to revolve in front of an open fire and support roasting meat. Spiked holders gripped the meat to ensure that it revolved evenly with the motion of the rod. References below reveal that different types of spit were used to suit the meat or fowl being cooked, and were turned by numerous methods. Annotations in the 1626 inventory reveal also that spits were removed from Helmingham to Fakenham in December 1633:

beef spit, 26.1088.

bird spit (square) with a crank, 26.1088.

chain(e)s, 08.39.

crank(e)s for, 97.169, **to turn,** 26.1067.

dog's wheel: occupied by a dog whose pedalling movement rotated the wheel connected to the spit, 08.7.

iron, large, 41.242.

lark, larke, and iron skewers, 41.218.

rack, top end of, 26.1455.

short, 08.332.

smoke jack and chain for, 41.254.

spit, speet, 97.124, 08.14, **with trundles for the wheel,** 26.1066.

turnspit, turnspeet wheele, 97.141; **and lines,** 26.1081; **piece of iron for,** 26.1087.

See also **jack.**

spoon: before the introduction of the table **fork,** spoons and blunt knives were the utensils commonly used for dining. Of those, knives were the personal property of a diner and therefore mentioned rarely in the inventories. Only the 1597 inventory, with its discrete lists of plate and their updates, records spoons in detail, revealing large numbers (see **silver**). None is mentioned in 1626 or 1741 and only one in 1708, **child's, case for,** 08.522. See also **silver.**

spring clock: see **clock.**

spring lock: see **lock.**

spurket: see **spirkit.**

square tiles: 'square' often translates as rectangular in these inventories (based on the evidence provided by detailed dimensions recorded in 1708, in particular); these may be roof tiles, fired in the **brick kiln** (*q.v.*) but a supply, not counted, is to hand in the stable yard in 1626 for current building work, together with **bricks, half rounds** and **pavements** (*q.v.*), 26.1544.

squeare: square.

stammell: by the late 16th century, a coarse woollen cloth produced in Norfolk, usually dyed red, and also refers to the **colour** (*q.v.*). Yaxley (p. 200) suggests that the name was a variant of **stamin**. Not to be confused with **stammet** (*q.v.*): **canopy (bed),** 26.600; **couch chair,** 26.596; **curtains, bed,** 26.601; **cushion,** 26.597, 26.598.

stammet, stammett, tammy, tamiye: not to be confused with **stammell** (*q.v.*), stammet, also known as **estamet** or, more frequently in these inventories, **tammy,** was the name given to the glazed cloths made from stammet or tammy yarn which had been shrunk and smoothed by scouring (Kerridge, pp. 53–4). Corrections to entries in the 1626 inventory reveal that stammett was frequently confused with other textiles with a surface sheen such as buffin and satin: **chair,** 26.454; **cushion linings,** 26.246; **lists** (*q.v.*) **bundle of,** 26.889; **tester, valence and curtains (bed),** 26.420.

stand, stands: term unique to the 1741 inventory and sometimes describing small pieces of furniture: **candle,** 41.516; **old,** 41.88; **for chest,** 41.62; **mahogany,** 41.8, 41.46, 41.102, **large reading,** 41.474; **japanned, for candles:** 41.516; **octagon stand tables, old,** 41.161; **small:** 41.508.

standish[e]: a stand for pens and ink: **pewter,** 26.129. See also **inkstand.**

step ladder, 41.286; **old:** 41.47; see also **ladder.**

still: distillation vessel. Distillation was undertaken on a large scale at Helmingham Hall in 1597 and 1626. See footnote 27 to the 1597 inventory for details.

> **brassinge bottom of, old,** 26.1340.
>
> **leaden stills over furnace,** 26.1245.
>
> **pewter,** 08.214.
>
> **pewter covers for,** 26.1246.
>
> **still pans, panns,** 97.557.
>
> **stilled waters (distilled), pint bottles for,** 08.664.
>
> **stills with their furniture,** 97.311.
>
> *unspecified,* 41.453.

stirrups and stirrup leathers, stirope(s), stirripps, 97.881, 97.882, 26.747, 26.913, 26.914 (without leathers), 26.1384; **copper,** 97.878; **French,** 26.909.

stockings: see also **colours** for definitions of unfamiliar terms:

> **silk, black,** 97.820; **carnation,** 97.822; **filbert,** 97.824; **green,** 97.823; **watchet,** 97.821.

worsted, black, 97.833; **flame**, 97.831, **popinjay green**, 97.832.

worsted in mixed colours; watchet *and* **green**, 97.826; **yellow**, 97.827; **white** *and* **green**, 97.825; **sea green**, 97.829; **yellow**, 97.828.

See also **hose**.

stomacher, stummacher: covering for the chest. Mentioned only in the 1597 inventory of Catherine Tollemache's apparel, and invariably included in descriptions of other matching items:

kirtle, hare-colour satin and, 97.894.

mourning gown, kirtle and, 97.890.

sleeves: green taffeta and 97.922, **olive-colour taffeta** *and*, 97.902; **chestnut-colour** and, 97.903; **white tuft sacking** and, 97.905.

vastguard, black satin, sleeves *and*, 97.891.

stone, stonne: utensils or vessels made of stoneware or earthenware, referred to also as **earth, earthen**: *passim*.

stone: grinding stone (*q.v.*). See also **millstones; querns**.

stools, stolles: described primarily by their relative heights, numerous stools at Helmingham are sets covered with matching cushions, whether fixed or loose, and forming part of a suite with other furniture in a room. Although the **chair** was becoming more common from about 1600, backless seating such as stools and **forms** maintained their popularity, particularly for dining, for at least three centuries more. The 'four-footed' stools recorded in the 1626 inventory are all found in working areas and staff chambers, the term implying that these are simply constructed stools without cushions. The editorial category of 'cover for' is included to draw attention to an illuminating example of textile recycling, part of which included covers for chairs and stools:

backed, 08.562.

buffet[t], 08.399.

cloth, 41.551.

cover for, 26.795.

cross-framed, 08.516.

cushion cloth (canvas), 97.384, 97.431, 26.241, 26.305, 26.360.

defined by colour: 41.10, 41.451.

defined by dimensions, 08.578.

embroidered, imbrodred in velvet, 97.385.

fo[u]lding, with stuffed seat, 08.417.

foot[e]stool[e], 26.163, 26.209, 26.218, 26.244.

four-footed, 26.268, 26.716, 26.1113, 26.1304.

high[e], 26.161, 26.210, 26.215, 26.216, 08.485.

joined, joyned, joynt, of joyner's work, 97.23, 97.331, 97.602, 26.37, 26.100, 26.283, 26.382, 26.409, 26.429, 26.456, 26.486, 08.272, 08.461, 08.692, 41.308.

leather, 08.324, 08.369, 41.581.

lesser form(e), 26.1155.

little, 97.55, 26.200, 26.207, 08.621.

long[e] (in working areas), 97.247, 26.1226, 26.1244.

longish [upholstered], 08.497.

low[e], 97.355, 26.40, 26.162, 26.189, 26.199, 26.211, 26.244, 26.302, 26.328, 26.329, 26.359, 26.511, 26.563, 26.608.

low[e] joi[y]ned, 97.25, 97.26, 97.332, 97.333.

old, 08.94, 41.606.

old-fashioned, 26.134, 26.262, 26.316, 26.342, 26.368, 26.381, 26.512.

plain, playne wooden, 26.681.

square, 08.252, 08.458, 08.459, 08.496, 08.563, 08.570, 08.571, 08.579, 08.606, 41.198, 41.388, 41.495, 41.552; **high square**, 08.485.

used as a supporting stand or surface in working areas, 26.750, 26.1156, 26.1167, 26.1176, 26.1222, 26.1302.

velvet: 41.9, 41.42, 41.406, 41.551.

without seat, 08.608.

See also **bedstool; beerstool; close stool**.

stove: this refers also to a **hothouse,** or greenhouse; but in culinary terms, before the word was applied generally to a cooker, or cooking range, a stove referred to two distinct devices, both heated by charcoal. One was partially enclosed, similar in design and portability to a lantern, and used for protracted, gentle drying (over a period of days in some cases) of foodstuffs such as sweetmeats and fruit pastes. Some dough mixtures for biscuits were also dried before baking (*bis cuit* means twice baked), as demonstrated in Catherine Tollemache's late-16th-century recipes (Coleman, pp. 110–11). The other stove was the equivalent of a hotplate or series of hotplates, useful for preparing soups, sauces or other foods for which the direct heat of an open fire was too intense. Contemporary illustrations show them to be integral to their kitchens and vented through flues; but inclusion in the 1708 and 1741 inventories confirms Helmingham's culinary stoves to be portable:

high, 08.164.

iron, and back, 41.98.

kettle belonging to high stove, 08.165.

stands, iron, for the stoves, 41.245.

strainer, brass, large, 41.214.

strake: see **cart**.

string: in context, part of the hanging support for weapons or their accoutrements, worn around, or descending from, the waist:

for a dagger:

of black silk, 97.851.

with tassels of silver, 97.850.

for a pistol and flask, of crimson silk, 97.759.

stuff: textile, a worsted (woven) cloth of long wool; although some of the references below may be examples of the more liberal use of the word:

clouded, 08.571.

cushion, 26.562, 26.593, 26.898.

green-coloured, 26.122.

orange tawny, 26.851.

petticoat, 97.928.

silk, 26.199.

speckled, 08.561.

tester of, 26.263, 26.370.

stuke: see *brewing*.

suet, suyett: the solid fat surrounding animal loins and kidneys, reserved for culinary and household uses. Catherine Tollemache's recipes specify 'sheep suyett' for soap-making (Coleman, p. 126):

> **deer suet, dere suett, cakes of:** Yaxley (p. 64) says deer suet was used for greasing (armour, for example). Whether or not the deer were from Helmingham's own park at this date is a moot point, 26.1199.

> **pot for**, 26.1191.

Suffolk, map of, 08.611.

suitable [to], suyt[e]able: matching, in colour, design or material, especially in descriptions of furniture and furnishings. *Passim.*

sumpter cloth: a sumpter is a saddle-bag or pack, and this the cloth beneath it, 26.789.

sundial: see **dial**.

swill cowl (coule) and cowl-staff (coulestaff), 26.1164. See **cowl** for definition.

sword: bladed weapon defined variously in the inventory entries, all but one of which provide detail of design, purpose or size, 97.765.

> **arming** (for military use), 97.763.

> **cross[e] hilts** (with cross-shaped handles), 26.736.

> **short**, 26.74.

> **with pomell**, an ornamental knob terminating the hilt, 26.882.

syllabub, sillibub: a drink or confection based on milk or cream curdled by the admixture of wine, cider or other acid, and often sweetened and flavoured. Despite *OED* references from 1537, the word does not appear in the household inventories until 1708: **whip sillibub glasses**, 08.201; **white pot for, with cover**, 08.151.

table, taboll: tables are identified more closely at Helmingham than any other category of furniture. Whilst many are single pieces of furniture, some equipped with leaves to extend their size, others, particularly those listed in working areas, comprise a top or board supported on trestles. This arrangement offered portability and the option to construct a table to the size needed, and was in common use for tables until the late medieval period. The categories listed below present only the initial descriptive words or phrases in an attempt to convey the meticulous attention to the detail evident throughout the inventories. There are two editorial groupings: *modified for other uses*, unique to the recycling of tables described in 1626; and *defined by dimensions*, a method of primary description unique to the 1708 inventory. Unfamiliar terms listed below are defined elsewhere in the glossary.

> **backgammon, back-gammon**, 41.177; see also below, **games, gaming**.

> **billiard, billard**: 41.152; see also **billiards**.

cedar, little, 08.133.

counter, 97.955.

cupboard/with cupboard, 26.606, 26.640, 08.554, 08.575.

defined by dimensions, 08.267, 08.367, 08.615, 08.617, 08.637, 08.638.

double-leafed, 08.533, 08.616; see also long, with double leaf.

eight-square: (octagonal) 26.604, 08.519.

elm, square, 08.320.

fastened to wall, 26.514, 26.1012, 26.1248.

fir, on trestles, 26.267.

folding: cross-frame for, 08.254; for oysters, 26.21; half [of], 08.636; square, 26.33; with folding leaves, 26.32; with pillar to fix against wall, 26.42.

frame, 08.634.

frame with drawing leaves, 26.2, 26.31, 26.196.

games, gaming: backgammon, with rattling box and 3 dies, 41.177; goose, 97.30; pair for chess, inlaid with bone, 26.57; pair, with men, 26.64, 26.951, 08.498, 08.500.

inlaid, fine, 41.130, large, 41.90.

japanned, japan'd: and gilt tea, 41.161, square tea and handboard, 41.101.

joined, joyned, jointed, 97.49, 26.1012.

joint stool table, 08.321.

lifting up, partitions under, 08.253.

little, 97.72, 97.525, 26.464.

livery, 97.467, 97.581, 26.84, 26.115, 26.186, 26.238, 26.282, 26.426, 26.457, 26.478, 26.480, 26.561, 26.605, 08.618.

long, 97.1, 97.17, 97.180, 26.1, 08.97, 41.591; on frame, 26.639; fixed to wall, 26.639; high square, 41.469; on trestles, 97.567, 26.578, 26.671; on trusses, 41.261; with double leaf, 08.97; with drawing leaves, 26.30, 26.1; with leaves to turn up, 26.656.

mahogany: card, 41.100; night, 41.371; oval, 41.115; round, 41.63, 41.357; square, 41.131, 41.158, 41.357; with drawer, 41.4, 41.173, 41.372, 41.418, 41.475, 41.531.

marble, white, 08.217, on carved frame, 41.132.

modified for new uses, 26.787, 26.1115, 26.1170, 26.1498.

oak, oaken, 08.418, 08.439, 08.451, 08.460, 08.518, 08.560; high, 08.422, 08.604; little, 08.564; long, 41.179; oval, 41.159; small, 41.390; with three leaves, 08.318.

octagon stand tables, old, 41.161.

old, 26.530, with a drawer, 41.606.

old-fashioned, 08.690.

oval, 08.130, 08.216, 41.79.

pairs of, 97.29. See also tables, games.

pigeons meat, for, 26.1542.

pillars, on, 26.1140.

short framed, 97.598.

slideboard: this term occurs only in the 1626 inventory where it was deleted and replaced by 'with drawing leaves', 26.1.

smoothing, 97.530. See **smoothing** for details of the ironing process.

square, 97.18, 97.328, 26.247, 26.304, 26.639, 08.287, 08.534, 41.77, 41.275, 41.450, 41.550, 41.586; **large**, 41.307, **little**, 26.941; **old, with drawer**, 41.262; **or a counter**, 26.886; **small**, 41.419; **walnut, inlaid, on triangular foot**, 26.604; **with drawer**, 41.354, 41.403, 41.450; **with frame**, 26.98, 26.408; **with lock**, 26.61.

trestles, on, 97.733, 26.893, 08.612; **ash, leaf on**, 08.319; **plan(c)k used as**, 97.50, 26.396, 26.672; **short**, 97.710.

wainscot: of three heights, 08.440.

walnut, with drawer, 08.245, 08.481.

See also **board**.

table, cover *for*: in the 1597, 1626 and 1708 inventories, protective covers for tables and other flat surfaces, or boards, were described as a carpet; but in 1741 this has given way to the cover; **flowered callicoe**, 41.105, 41.161; **green cloth**: 41.41, 41.90, 41.100, 41.130.

table men: gaming pieces where the game is not specified, 26.64, 26.951, 08.498, 08.500. See also **chess**; **table: gaming**.

table rings: At periods when large numbers of dishes were presented on a table at the same time, circular table rings with hollow supports helped to save space by lifting some dishes and fitting others around the base of the table ring, which was narrower than the dish it supported. Some rings were reversible because they were 'waisted', with the top and bottom halves of different circumferences, but from the inventory descriptions it is not possible to confirm the shapes here. Commonly of silver (and known also as dish-rings but not in these inventories), the 1626 inventory describes them as 'wicker'; given that there are extensive and updated lists of silver in the 1597 inventory, none of which contains table rings, it is highly probable that the 1597 rings, defined only by quantity, were also of wicker. This attribute makes both Helmingham references important evidence of early design: *defined by quantity*, 97.53; **pewter**, 41.237; **wicker**, 26.1016.

taffeta, taffata, taffatie, taffaty, taffatye: thin, plain-woven cloth, stiffened with extra weft threads (including silk in the medieval period). By the 16th century it incorporated linen and other materials, and it appears extensively throughout the 1597 and 1626 inventories to describe apparel and household furnishings. In the 1626 inventory rooms are named 'crimson taffeta chamber and yellow taffeta chamber', although the textiles descibed in the latter are of silk damask. There is no mention of taffeta in the 1708 or 1741 inventories.

chair, white, 26.201.

cloak, 97.863, **black**, 97.864, 26.804, 26.805, 26.808; **russet**, 26.809; **white**, 97.911.

counterpane, ash colour, 26.148; **changeable, of purple and green**, 26.235; **crimson**, 26.325; **green**, 26.299.

curtains, bedstead, 97.353; **ash colour**, 26.146; **changeable, of purple and green**, 26.229; **crimson**, 26.319; **green**, 26.292; **white and red**, 26.183.

cushion, ash colour, 26.156; **white, backed with purple**, 26.821.

doublet: ash colour, 97.804, **filbert colour**, 97.806.

doublet and hose, black, 97.803.

linings: of **cloak, black**, 26.813; **horse flesh** or **tawny colour**, 26.796; of **doublet: tawny**, 26.837; **white**, 26.835; of **horseman's coat, yellow**, 97.862, 26.807; **jacket, black**, 26.806.

pieces of, black, 26.796.

rug, 26.325.

sleeves: seawater green, 97.926, 97.930, 97.934, **white**, 97.923.

sleeves and stomacher: green, 97.922, **olive colour**, 97.902.

stools, straw colour, 97.332.

tester *etc.*, **crimson**, 26.320, **green**, 97.352, 26.291.

See also **tuftaffeta**.

tags, tagg(es): see **points and tags**.

tammy, tameye, tamiye, tamy, tamye: see **stammet**.

tankard, tankerd: see **silver**.

tap staff, tapp staffe and wicker wiltch: see **brewing**.

tapestry, tapistry, tapstrey: arras and verdure are included in this category, all describing decorative textiles, the design of which is achieved through the weaving process. However, the word is used widely in the inventories and in some instances descriptions suggest that items may be of **turkey work** (not woven but **needlework**, stitched in wool on canvas and intended to resemble tapestry), suggesting the strong resemblance between the two and the inherent difficulty of distinguishing between them. Definitions of items listed can be found elsewhere in the glossary:

    arras: the name originating from the town of Arras in north-east France, which became famous for the manufacture of tapestries rich with figures and scenes. Both decorative and functional, arras hangings offered some protection against the inevitable cold, damp and draughts of a late-Tudor moated house. The term does not appear in the 1708 inventory, which refers only to **tapestry** (*q.v.*).

    coverlet, 97.351.

    cupboard cloth, 97.582.

    cushions, cushenings, 97.791, 26.817, 26.818.

    hangings, 97.36, 97.342, 97.343, 97.356, 97.381.

    window cloth, 97.344.

tapestry:

    carpet, table, 97.784, 26.833.

    chair (of **fine turkey work**), 08.415.

    coverlet, old, 97.699, 97.740.

    cupboard cloth, 97.785, 26.833.

    cushions, 97.792, 97.793.

    hangings (wall), 26.48, 26.151, 26.224, 26.288, 26.326, 26.344, 26.377, 26.791, 26.792 (or carpets), 08.401, 08.430, 08.444, 08.465, 08.494, 08.503, 08.630.

    room lined with, 41.509.

window pieces, peeces, 26.225, 26.288.

verdure, verders: tapestries with designs based on green, living plant materials: **hangings**, 26.96, 26.376; **window pieces**, 26.96.

See also **needlework; turkey-work**.

tawny, orange tawny: see **colours**.

tea, the beverage was unknown in England until circa 1650–55 and by the 18th century had become fashionable in those households where its high cost could be borne. The 1741 inventory reflects the range of goods related to the making, serving and taking of tea, including sets of matching china:

basin, bason, 41.104, **enamelled china**, 41.161.

cream pot, 41.161, **and sugar dish**, 41.104.

cups and saucers, 41.104.

dish: predating the use of cups, tea was drunk from a saucer-like dish, 08.183.

kettles and lamp, 41.211.

lamp for tea kettle, 41.228.

pot(t), 08.229, 41.104, 41.161.

saucers, sawcers, 41.161.

table, Japanned, and gilt, 41.161, **and handboard**, 41.101.

teaboard: a term unique to the 1741 inventory, and describes a tea-tray: **mahogany**, 41.20. See also **handboard**.

telescopes: *OED* cites references to the telescope from 1619, but its only appearance in inventories dates to the time of the 4th Earl of Dysart, who had two of them in his dressing room (see Plate 4): 41.3.

tent stitch: embroidery in which the stitches were worked across intersections of the threads of woven cloth; also called petit-point, but not in the 1626 inventory, which is the only one of the four to mention tent stitch: **chair, seated with**, 26.245; **stool, covered with**, 26.607 (deleted and replaced with '**broad stitch**', *q.v.*).

tester: see **bedstead**.

textiles: woven fabrics, numerous examples of which emerge from the inventories and are presented in glossary entries for: **baize, bird's eye, buckram, buffin, caffa, calico, callasina, camblet, canvas, cloth, cloth of gold, cloth of silver, cloth of tissue, cotton, cushion cloth, damask, dimity, dornix, fustian, grosgrain, kersey, Kidderminster stuff, lace, lawn, linen, linsey-woolsey, mockadoe, mohair, muslin, penny-stone, plaid, russet, sacking, sarcenet, satin, Satin of Bridges, say, serge, stammell, stammet, stuff, taffeta, tobine, tuftaffeta, Turkey, twill, velvet, wool.** See also **tapestry, embroidery, needlework**.

thilbells, fill bells: Yaxley (p. 216) cites Halliwell: 'the chain-tugs to the collar of a cart-horse, by which he [*the cart horse*] draws', 26.1426.

threesquare: triangular; this term appears only in the 1708 inventory: **cake pans**, 08.208.

thrum, thrumes: mentioned only once throughout the inventories, and, given the context, the second of seven definitions of 'thrum' offered by Halliwell (p. 871) is most appropriate, describing the material used in the hand loom described below as 'the extremity of a weaver's warp, often about nine inches long, which cannot be woven. Generally, a small thread, **hand loom [for] thrumes or fringe,** 26.758. See also **loom.**

tick, ticking, tike: the word defines a specific type of linen cloth in 1708, but earlier references use the term as the generic description for the stitched cover of a pillow or bolster, as distinct from the removable, outer **pillowbeer**, or pillowcase. Textile definitions can be found in alphabetical entries elsewhere in the glossary:

fustian, fusten, 26.322, 26.350.

'made of an old sack', 26.693.

'old flock bed tike', 26.776.

ticking, chair seat of, 08.397.

tile, tiles: the 1626 inventory includes the brick kiln, considered part of the household because it supplied bricks (*q.v.*) and tiles for the house and its outbuildings. In addition to the contents of the brick kiln, supplies (not enumerated) of bricks and tiles were to hand in the stable yard in quantities beyond counting. The tiles recorded at both sites are listed below:

half-round, 26.1546.

pavements, 26.1549.

roof, 26.1545.

square: uncertain, 26.1544.

tiles, 26.1548.

tilter: see **brewing.**

timber, great chains to draw, 26.1452.

tin: metal utensils specified only in the 1708 inventory:

apple roaster, 08.171.

boilers, of which two are in iron frames, 08.12.

colander, cullender, old, 08.145.

cover, covers: for pewter dishes, 08.22; **old, for dishes,** 08.112.

dropping baster, 08.108.

funnel, tunnel: old, 08.144.

pasty pan, small, 08.161.

pattepans and bottoms, 08.77.

sconce, 08.370.

watering pots, old, 08.162.

to be exchanged: *passim*: a recurrent phrase referring to a wide range of items, often metal or precious metal, to be disposed of and replaced. Comments added to the 1597 inventory of plate remark on items that have resulted from exchanges.

tobine, tobyne: a stout twilled silk:

pieces of, 26.836; **tester and valence,** 26.138; **window cushions,** 26.246.

tongs, mentioned with culinary items, 41.220: see also **fire; milk.**

torch, torche: holder for an open, burning light of tow or other combustible material soaked in oil or tallow. 97.84. See also **lantern.**

touch-box: receptacle for lighted tinder, carried to ignite the firearm known as a **caliver** (*q.v.*).

tow comb, towe combe: sometimes known as a heckle, a piece of wood set with several rows of sharp teeth through which beaten hemp or flax would be drawn to remove unwanted, short or useless fibres and pieces of stem (Yaxley, p. 220). In the 1597 inventory of the lard house yarn reels were listed as the next item. The combination of tow comb and yarn reels suggests that the fibres and fat were combined here to make the lights for torches (see **torch**), 97.252.

trace, traices, traise, traysses: the rope or leather straps connecting a draught animal to the load it is pulling; usually listed in pairs:

collar and, 97.290, 26.1356.

hand, 26.1423; **other new pair without seals**, 26.1424.

pairs of, 08.702.

plough whereof one used at the mill, 26.1431.

shack, shacke: (shack is fallen corn), 26.1427.

silver, with saddle, 26.906.

trafeinge dishe: see **milk.**

traices, traise: see **trace.**

trammel, tramwell: chimney iron from which to hang cooking pots, 97.123, 97.239, 26.1071.

trap, trapp: animal trap: **great iron**, 26.701; **great, with a spring**, 26.949; **moles, mowles, to catch**, 26.1451.

tray, trey, 97.168, 97.195, 97.226, 26.1211, 26.1237, 26.1286, 26.1500, 08.341, 08.345, 41.21; **mahogany**, 41.192. See also **cheese; knife; milk; salt.**

traysses: see **trace.**

tree: describes a robust upright support: **baile trees to support partitions**, 26.1371; **cart saddle**, 26.1449; **neats**: to support an animal carcass, 26.1098, 26.1488. See also **mantletree; praytree; whipple-tree.**

trencher: from Fr. *trancher*, to cut. A flat or slightly dished slab, round or square, on which to cut and serve food. In medieval times, trenchers were created from thick slices of bread, capable of holding food; doubtless this gave rise to the phrase 'a good trencherman' because the plate, as well as its contents, could be eaten; the shape was retained in trenchers of wood and other materials. Their continued popularity is confirmed by the cumulative record of many dozens in both 1597 and 1626, when some were described as new. By 1708, only nine are recorded:

fruit trencher, 97.66, 26.954.

hall, now in the dairy, 26.1018.

knife to scrape with, 26.1021.

new, 26.953.

unspecified, 97.63.

wooden square, 08.152.

trestle, tressell: Mentioned frequently as a portable support for boards, tables and planks: *passim.*

trivet, trevet(t): support, usually three-legged, for a cooking pot, placed before an open fire, 97.125, 97.238, 26.1147; **great**, 26.1072; **great iron**, 26.1006; **iron**, 26.1263, 41.251; **small**, 26.1073; **triangle**, 08.15, 08.113.

trunk, truncke: in 1597 trunks and chests provided the majority of storage for items of high value, such as spices and linen, and most were fitted with locks and keys. Those distinguished by their coverings or contents are summarised separately below, as are those from the 1708 inventory offering dimensions: 97.494, 97.510, 97.521, 97.524, 97.532, 97.534, 97.566, 97.946, 97.949, 97.964, 26.87, 26.89, 26.253, 26.412, 26.502, 26.579, 26.602, 26.626, 26.641, 26.655, 26.641, 26.675, 26.884, 26.901, 26.939, 08.400, 08.537, 08.642.

great, with linen that my lady keep the key herself, 26.674.

leather, great, 41.460; **small red**, 41.463.

linen, locked up, 08.683.

locked, contains black horseman's armour, 97.565, 26.579.

sealskin covered, 97.476, 26.88.

stand for, 08.582.

with dimensions, 08.572, 08.573, 08.581, 08.583, 08.584, 08.613.

wooden, with nets in, 08.614.

See also **chest; coffer**.

tub, mahogany: 41.19.

tuftaffeta, tuft taffaty: a velours with tufts of silk, or of yarn in which silk was mingled (Yaxley, p. 224). Mentioned only in the 1597 inventory:

bedstead canopy, 97.466.

chair seated with, 97.429.

cloak, 97.912.

cushions, 97.789.

gown, 97.887, 97.888.

vastguard, 97.900.

See also **taffeta**.

tumbler glass: see glass.

tumbril, tumberelle, tumbrell: two-wheeled cart, 26.1413, 08.698.

tunnel: funnel (*q.v.*).

Turkey 'or Morocco': Turkey, as distinct from **turkey-work** (see below) defines goods, principally hand-knotted **carpets**, in rich colours and patterns, imported from Turkey and the Levant, as the inventory description makes clear: **cushions**, 08.566.

turkey-work, turky, turkye worke: distinguishes English items of needlework on canvas in hand-knotted, richly coloured wools which resembled those imported from Turkey and other Levantine countries. Inventory comments note those items for which the completed work resembled **tapestry** (*q.v.*), and individual entries comment on designs including coats of arms and plants:

carpet (table covering), 97.32, 97.338, 97.339, 26.49, 26.203, 26.247, 26.303, 26.304, 26.793.

carpet (hanging), 08.466, 08.629 (uncertain, may be floor coverings).

carpet, under the bed, 08.467.

chair, seated and/or backed with, 97.334, 26.39, 08.415, 08.416.

cupboard cloth, 97.357, 26.158, 26.240, 26.331, 26.357.

cushion, 97.34, 97.341, 26.204, 26.816, 08.373, 08.428, 08.442, 08.517, 08.609.

pieces of, 26.792.

See also **Turkey or Morocco; tapestry.**

turnspit: see **spit**.

twill: in context, the item below refers to the cloth, 'corded' meaning backed or covered. Kerridge (p. 23) notes that numerous 'twillweavers were at work making mixed linen and hempen twills' in centres within a 10-mile radius of Helmingham, including Ipswich, Waldringfield, Parham, Hacheston and Earl Soham: **cushion, corded with**, 26.637.

twilte: see **quilt**.

twisterers with iron wheels for silk or crewell, describing a machine to twist threads destined for use in embroidery or needlework, 26.762.

underquilt: See **quilt**.

urinal, glass: 41.40.

valence, valance, vallans: in modern parlance, a pelmet. See **bedstead**.

Valentia blew cloth, cloak of: this may refer to a blue **colour** and/or to the cloth itself, 97.866.

vardingall: variant of farthingale, but applied in the 1597 inventory to descriptions of sleeves. Generally, farthingale is defined as the hooped support provided beneath items of ladies' apparel, designed to exaggerate and hold in place the flare or span of a skirt. Farthingale sleeves, speculatively, are either designated for wear with items supported by such a hoop (although none is identified), or are themselves hooped, 97.901. See also **sleeves**.

vastguard, vastgard: mentioned only in the 1597 inventory as a heading with curtles and sleeves. Speculatively, synonymous with **safegard** (*q.v.*), an outer skirt or petticoat designed to protect clothing from soiling, particularly when riding: **ash colour satin**, 97.892; **black satin, with stomacher and sleeves**, 97.891; **black tuft taffeta, old**, 97.900; See also **safegard**.

velvet, vellvett, velvett, velvette, velvit, velvitt: textile with a dense, smooth, short-piled surface, originally of silk. Inventory entries reveal several deletions of the word in favour of other silk-based textiles to which it bore a similarity. The 1626 inventory of the wardrobe shows items of black velvet maintained at Helmingham for funerals (see **mourning**), whilst the 1708 inventory describes the contents of a 'Black Velvett room'. Velvet appears extensively in all four inventories, used substantially and as an embellishment (**embroidery**), summarised below by item:

bearing cloth, 26.825.

bedstead tester *etc.*, 97.371, 97.400, 97.578, 26.227, 26.348, 26.474, 08.402, 08.469.

breeds, 97.906.

chair, 97.337, 97.354, 97.402, 97.618, 26.75, 26.206, 26.208, 26.242, 26.243, 26.302, 26.328, 08.397, 08.414, 08.495, 41.116, 41.464, 41.515.

cloak, 97.859, 97.860, 26.812.

close stool box, 08.248.

coat, 97.862, 97.867.

crop *etc.*, 26.918.

couch, 08.515, 41.473.

cupboard cloth, 97.382, 26.239.

cushion, 97.786, 97.787, 97.789, 26.205, 26.246, 26.820, 26.821, 26.822.

foot cloth, 26.831, 26.832.

girdle, 97.960.

gown, 97.884, 97.885, 97.886.

hangers, 26.874.

headstall *etc.*, 26.916, 26.919.

horseman's armour, 97.750.

hose, 97.796, 97.805, 97.807, 97.808, 97.815, 97.817.

jumper, 97.861.

kirtle, 97.895, 97.898, 97.899.

lace, 97.868.

lining(s), 97.865, 97.842, 97.845, 97.842, 26.800, 26.801, 26.802, 26.867, 26.869, 26.870, 26.871, 26.872, 26.875.

pantofles, 97.856, 97.915.

petticoat, 97.907, 97.908.

piece(s) of, 26.842, 26.843.

saddle *etc.*, 97.876, 97.878, 26.778, 26.905, 26.906, 26.907, 26.908, 26.911, 26.916, 26.923, 26.924.

scabbard, 97.43, 26.73, 26.75, 26.926, 26.927, 26.928.

sleeves, 97.904.

slippers, 26.845.

stool, 97.26, 97.332, 97.355, 97.385, 26.209, 26.210, 26.211, 26.302, 26.328, 26.359, 26.563, 08.252, 08.496, 08.497, 08.516, 08.562, 08.563, 41.9, 41.42, 41.406, 41.551.

table carpet, 08.452.

See also **branched**.

verdure, verders: see **tapestry**.

verjuice, verges, vergis, verjuice: juice extracted from unripe crab-apples (and sometimes grapes, although there is no evidence in the inventories), for culinary use:

bottle, 26.1227.

hogshead, 97.294, 26.1118 ('nigh full'), 26.1309.

stall, 26.1118.

strainer, wooden, 26.1476.

troughs, 97.298; **to stamp crab (crab apples) in**: (there is no evidence of a press or other means of extracting the juice), 26.1475.

virginals, virginal(l)es: referred to as a pair (set) of virginals, an early stringed instrument comprising one string, one jack and one quill per note. The keyboard and action were contained within a square, lidded box which had to be supported on a table: **old pair of**, 97.599; **made like a harp**, 26.895; **pair of**, 97.28; **locked**

up, 26.123. For other musical instruments, see **cittern, harpsichord, lute, organ, spinet**.

voider, voyder: a basket, vessel or tray used to carry or, more usually, to clear away food, and related utensils for scraping or clearing food from plates etc., 97.65, 26.992; **eightsquare (octagonal) japanned**, 08.138; **foursquare (square or rectangular) japanned**, 08.137; **knife**, 97.54, 26.1027; **wicker**, 08.374.

wagon, waggon, 08.696.

wainscot, waynscot[t], waynskott, weyn[e]scott : a word used to describe both furniture and panelling constructed of good-quality oak board and plank from the Baltic countries. Yaxley (p. 231) adds that wainscot from Russia, Germany and Scandinavia was often imported into Britain through Holland. 97.15, 97.40, 26.9, 26.26, 26.455, 26.479, 26.562, 26.582, 26.646, 26.896, 26.1357, 08.142, 08.256, 08.440. See also **ceil; chair; press; table**.

waiter, small, suggests a small tray, this one holding condiments and their vessels, but could be similar in design to a **dumb waiter**, 41.19.

wall-coverings: only the 1708 inventory reveals that the walls of some chambers are covered with textiles. Unlike tapestries, these coverings are not described as hangings. Areas of a room excluded from coverings are described, too: usually they are chimney-breasts, where textiles would be liable to heat damage or would create a fire risk; and the area behind high bedsteads, where they would have been invisible. However, given that the inventory records only portable goods, the coverings must have been removable, probably stretched over light-weight framed panels fixed to the walls: **speckled green linsey-woolsey**, 08.479; **speckled say**, 08.257, 08.276; **tapestry**, 08.430. See also **hangings; tapestry**.

wallet, walletts: see **linen**.

walnut, wallnutte, wallnuttree: walnut timber used in furniture-making. The **forms** listed in 1597 were important enough to warrant a commentary on their dates of purchase, which were since the inventory was made. The 1626 inventory identifies a drawleaf **table** with a 'Dutch frame of wallnuttree': Edwards (pp. 364–5) offers a range of evidence to confirm that walnut and its products were imported as demand increased, and identifies 17th-century English walnut plantations raised profitably for the purpose:

bedstead, 26.138.

forms, joined, 97.16, 26.36.

looking glass, frame of, 08.247.

stands, pair of, 08.246.

table, 26.32, 26.604, 08.245.

warming-pan, warmeing pann: long-handled pan, pre-heated and used to warm a bed, 26.772; **brass**, 08.589, **with wooden handle**, 08.335; **copper**, 41.222.

washing, washeing: see *laundry, wet*.

watchet: a pale blue colour. See also *colours*.

watering pots: see **garden**.

weather glass: Sotheby's records the sale in Amsterdam (27–29 April 2010, sale 2857, lot 572) of a Netherlandish weather glass 'Donderglass', described as 'probably Liege, 18th century', and illustrates a pear-shaped glass, embellished with stippling, suspended by a glass loop. The Helmingham item, described in the 1708 inventory as '1 brass sconce and 1 old weather glass', is taken to be an early version of a barometer, 08.169.

weights, waights, weits: see **scales**; see also **clock**.

wennell, see **maw**.

whalebone, whales bone: the material of a rod, whose purpose is not described, 26.80.

whey, whaie: watery liquid residue remaining when acidulated milk forms curds. As with **butter, cheese, cream, maw** and **milk**, the inventories specify common utensils and equipment strictly in relation to their purpose when used in the dairy: **bowl, boule**, 97.204; **keeler, killer**, 97.235, 26.1135, 26.1215.

whipple-tree: Halliwell (p. 928) says: 'The bar on which the traces of a dragging horse are hooked, and by which he draws his load', 26.1446.

white: when used to describe **armour** (*q.v.*) white identifies the material as polished steel. However, Yaxley (p. 4) surmises that the term may refer also to armour painted white. See also **black**.

wicker: basketware woven from willow stems, with a wide variety of uses at the hall:

bottle of glass (cover for), 97.77; **bottles**, 26.947, 26.1053.

bread, to carry in, 26.1261.

chair, 41.568.

cradle of, 97.966; **old**, 26.765.

hamper with a cover, 26.1032.

linen basket, 26.677, 26.678.

meal, to carry in, 26.1261.

screen (to protect from heat of a fire), 26.25, 26.764.

skep for soiled linen, 26.663.

table rings, 26.1016. See also **table rings** elsewhere in the glossary.

thing to stand up in the mashing vat, 08.308.

voider (*q.v.*), 08.374.

wiltch, 26.1168.

See also **bee skep; skep**.

wig block, 41.607.

wilch, wiltch: see *brewing*.

wimble: an augur. See **pale**.

wince: see **bedstead**, *tools for maintaining*.

window cloth: see **curtain, window**.

wine, wyne: each inventory confirms supplies of wine. By 1626 there is a dedicated wine cellar. The household accounts of 1587–89 record regular purchases of claret, sack and white wine (Coleman, pp. 36–7), not all of it destined for drinking: Catherine Tollemache used claret to add colour to her 'paste of hippes of the colour of corall' (Coleman, p. 102); contributors to her household miscellany specified it by the pint as an ingredient in medicines (Coleman, pp. 51–5):

bin, bing, wine, the three wine bins are recorded as 'lock'd up', so it is likely that they contained quantities of wine in bottles: 41.352.

bottle(s): great glass, 26.1052; **wicker**, 26.1053.

butt: large wooden tub speculatively for wine but could be for beer, 08.649.

cask, 26.1055.

claret, clarrett, bottles with, 08.661; **hogshead of**, 97.73.

glass, 26.1026, 08.388; **high narrow**, 08.237 (*and*) **flourished**, 08.238; **small**, 08.236.

pipes, in this context, a measure, usually of wine, of 126 gallons, and the name of its container, a butt, or large barrel: 41.346, 41.353; **with iron hoops**, 41.341.

pot, pott: (for serving wine): **pewter**, 97.89, 26.975.

stall, stalle, 26.1051.

storing (storringe) wine bottles, 26.1054.

See also **silver: cup**.

wool, wo[o]llen, wolling: *passim.*

womb rope, wombroopes: belly-rope or girth for a horse, 26.1492.

world, large maps of, 26.46. See also **globe; map**.

worren: worn, as in showing signs of wear. *Passim.*

wrightenges, wrightings, wryghteings, wrytings: writings, documents, referred to in the context of items of furniture related to them. See **desk; writing stand**.

wrinch: see **bedstead, tools for maintaining**.

writing desk: 41.78; **mahogany**, 41.41.

writing stand, eightsquare (octagonal), **inlaid with Tollemache arms**, 08.521. See also **desk; writing desk**.

wrynettes: trapping nets, described in the 1626 inventory as 'vj wrynettes to take young hawkes in': 26.513. See also **hawk(s)**.

BIBLIOGRAPHY

MANUSCRIPT SOURCES

Archives of the Tollemache family, Helmingham Hall
LJ I/15, Catherine Tollemache's receipts for pastery, confectionary, etc.
T/Hel/1/1, Letter from Lady Susan Spring to her son, Lionel Tollemache, 10 August 1588
T/Hel/1/5, Letter from Roger Jones to Catherine Tollemache, 20 December 1605
T/Hel/1/64, Letter from Thomas Brereton to the Earl of Dysart, 1720
T/Hel(S)/2/2, Letters patent creating Lionel Tollemache a baronet, 22 May, 9 Jas. I (1611)
T/Hel(S)/3/116, Will of Catherine Tollemache, 19 March 1621
T/Hel/9/1/1, Household inventories for Helmingham Hall, 1597 and 1626
T/Hel(S)/9/1/1, An inventory of the goods and furniture, etc., in and about Helmingham Hall, 1741
T/Hel(S)/9/1/5, Inventory of household goods and furniture at Helmingham, 1707/8 [January 1708]
T/Hel(S)/9/1/6, An account of linen at Helmingham Hall at my Lord's coming July the 6th 1742
T/Hel/9/1/7, Account of linen which came from Harrington, January 1708
T/Hel/9/1/8, Account of linen at Helmingham 9 December 1750 (?1742)
T/Hel/9/1/9, Account of linen 1759 which came from Harrington or Woodhey in the year 1741
T/Hel/9/2/1, Library catalogue, Helmingham Hall, 1762
T/Hel/9/5/33, Memorandum of agreement between the Earl of Dysart and William Dimmock, gardener, 7 April, 1766
T/Hel/10/8, Catherine Tollemache's recipes
T/Hel/21/1, 1612–19 accounts of Lionel Tollemache, 2nd baronet
T/Hel/22/5, Indenture: Lionel Tollemache, Earl of Dysart, and Richard Burchett of London, shipwright, 31 May 1708
T/Hel/24/6, The lands of Sir Lionel Tolmach, Baronet in Fakenham, surveyed in the year 1622, accompanied by small plans: also a survey of the whole town beginning at the site of the manor
T/Hel(S)/27/4, Plans of the Helmingham and Framsden estates of the Earl of Dysart, by Richard Tollemache, surveyor, in 1729
T/Hel/26/8, Indenture, sale of swan mark by Sir Henry Bedingfeld of Oxburgh to Sir Lionel Tollemache of Fakenham, 9 April 1634
T/Hel(S)/28/1, 2, Floor plans of Helmingham Hall by J.C. Dennish, 1950s
T/Hel/123/9, Mortgage, 15 March 1709
T/Hel/123/15, 16, Lease and release, 4, 5 March 1741

Bodleian Library, Oxford
Ashmole MS, 1504

City of Westminster Archives Centre
St Martin-in-the-Fields parish register, 19 January 1551–31 October 1619

Norfolk Record Office, Norwich
BRA 2524/2 and 3, Map of the manor of Oxborough belonging to Sir Henry Beding-feld by I.I. de Wilstar, 1725
FC 306/1, Norfolk swan roll, *c.* 1500 [photographic copy of MC2044, which is not presented to searchers]
HMN6/258–290 770X2, Papers on Norfolk swan rolls
JER 269 55x1, Inventory taken at Costessey Hall, Norfolk, 1590, bound with inventory taken at Oxburgh Hall, 27 November 1598
NCR Case 26b/26, Swan-upping accounts of North Elmham, 1667–72

Suffolk Record Office, Bury St Edmunds
FL614/4, Pakenham parish register: baptisms 1562–1812
FL569, Fakenham Magna parish registers: baptisms 1562–1812; marriages 1566–1980; burials 1559–1811

Suffolk Record Office, Ipswich
FB42, Framsden parish register
FB46/D1/I, Helmingham parish register
HD 1538/134/8, Letters Patent of Queen Elizabeth I, 2 April 1586, granting licence to Sir William Springe, wife Susan and Lionel Tallemache, esq. to alienate to Leonard Caston, gent., and John Badshawe, manors of Bentley Hall, Framsden, etc.
HD 1538/228/1–19 (19), Indenture: Dame Katherine Tallemache to her son, Lionel, 2nd Baronet, 1613
HD 1538/253/151, 16 November 1592, Letters Patent of Queen Elizabeth I, appointing Lionel Tollemache as sheriff of Suffolk.
HD 1538/253/155, Indenture: Lionel Tollemache and Robert Jermyn, 1575
HD 1538/253/165, George Smythe's household accounts for Lionel Tollemache, 1587–89

The National Archives, Kew
C142 Chancery: Inquisitions post mortem [IPM], Series II, and other inquisitions, Henry VII to Charles I:
C142/162, IPM of Lionel Tollemache 'the Elder', 1571–72
C142/175, IPM of Lionel Tollemache, 1575–76
C142/327, IPM of Sir Lionel Tollemache, 19 January, 10 Jas. I (1612–13)
C142/601/45, IPM of Sir Lionel Tollemache, 2nd Baronet, d. 1640/1
PROB 11 Prerogative Court of Canterbury and related probate jurisdictions: will registers:
PROB 11/54, Will of Lionel Tollemache 'the Elder', 1571
PROB 11/57, Will of Lionel Tollemache, 1576
PROB 11/80, Will of Henry, Lord Cromwell, 1592
PROB 11/120, Will of Sir Lionel Tollemache, Baronet, 1613
PROB/11/137, Will of John, Lord Stanhope, Baron of Harrington, 1621
PROB 11/329/54, Will of Sir Lyonell Tollemache of Helmingham, 1669
PROB 11/613/273, Will of The Honorable Lyonel Earl of Dysart of Harrington, Northamptonshire (1727)

PROB 11/702, Will of the Dowager Countess of Dysart, 13 May 1740

Tollemache family papers in the Buckminster Park Archive, Buckminster, Leicestershire

Vol. 873, Symon Neale his accompt to the honorable Lyonell Tollemache, 8 September 1653–8 September 1656

Vol. 878, Volume of domestic expenditure at Helmingham or Fakenham, 1661–1663

Vol. 879, The booke of generall disbursments at Helmingham or Fakenham and Ham, 1661–5

Vol. 884, The Booke of Domestick Expences at Helmingham or Fakenham and Ham, 1661–5

Vol. 896, A booke containing the weekely expence of such provitions as are laide in in grosse in the house at Helmingham or Fakenham, 1663–4

Vol. 897, Household accounts at Helmingham or Fakenham, 1671 and 1678–83

Vol. 926, Receipt book of the Earl of Dysart recording payments for personal, household and estate expenses at Helmingham, Ham House, Charing Cross and Harrington, 1729–55

PRINTED SOURCES

Allen, M.E. (ed.), *Wills of the Archdeaconry of Suffolk 1627–1628*, SRS 58 (2015)

Annandale, C. See *Ogilvie.*

Anon., *Larousse Gastronomique* (London, 2009)

Anon., *The history of the Spanish armada, which had been preparing three years for the invasion and conquest of England, ... containing the truest and most particular lists*, Eighteenth-Century Collections Online Print (London, 1759)

Arnold, Janet, *Queen Elizabeth's Wardrobe Unlock'd* (Leeds, 1988)

Bailey, M., *Medieval Suffolk* (Woodbridge, 2007)

Baird, Rosemary, *Mistress of the House* (London, 2004)

Barker, N., *Two East Anglian Picture Books: a Facsimile of the Helmingham Herbal and Bestiary and Bodleian MS Ashmole 1504*, The Roxburghe Club (1988)

Best, M.R. (ed.), *The English Housewife* (Montreal, 1986)

Bettley, J., and Pevsner, N., *Suffolk, East: the Buildings of England* (London, 2015)

Blair, C. (ed.), *The History of Silver* (London, 1987)

Blatchly, J., *East Anglian Ex Libris* (Reading, 2008)

Blatchly, J., 'Coats of arms tell own stories', *East Anglian Daily Times*, Saturday 12 June, 2010

Booth, D.T.N., *Warwickshire Watermills* (Smethwick, 1978)

Boothman, L. and Hyde Parker, Sir Richard, *Savage Fortune: an Aristocratic Family in the Early Seventeenth Century*, SRS 49 (2006)

Boynton, L., *The Elizabethan Militia 1558–1638* (Newton Abbot, 1971)

Brears, P., *Food and Cooking in 17th-Century Britain – History and Recipes* (London, 1985)

Brears, P., *Tudor Cookery, Recipes and History* (London, 2003)

Brears, P., *Stuart Cookery, Recipes and History* (London, 2004)

Brigden, R., *Ploughs and Ploughing* (Princes Risborough, 2002)

Butcher, D., *Rigged for River and Sea* (Hull, 2008)

Carmichael, W.L., *Callaway Textile Dictionary*, 1st edition (La Grange, Georgia, 1947)

Cokayne, G.E., *Complete Baronetage* (Stroud, 1983)

Colquhoun, K., *Taste: the Story of Britain through its Cooking* (London, 2007)

Coleman, M., *Fruitful Endeavours: the 16th-Century Household Secrets of Catherine Tollemache at Helmingham Hall* (Andover, 2012)

Cooper, T., *Elizabeth I and Her People* (London, 2014)

Day, I., *Perfumery with Herbs* (London, 1979)

Dennison, M., 'Under lock and key', *Country Life*, 27 April 2016, pp. 88–9

Dovey, Z., *An Elizabethan Progress* (Stroud, 1996)

Eburne, A., *Conservation Plan for Oxburgh Hall, Gardens and Park, Oxborough, Norfolk* (July 2006)

Edwards, R. (ed)., *The Dictionary of English Furniture*, revised edition, 3 volumes (Woodbridge, 1986)

Emmison, F.G., *Tudor Food and Pastimes* (London, 1964)

Emmison, F.G., *Tudor Secretary: Sir William Petre at Court and Home* (London, 1961)

Evans, N., *The East Anglian Linen Industry: Rural Industry and Local Economy, 1500–1850* (Aldershot, 1985)

Evans, N., 'Housekeeping in 1605', *Suffolk Review*, Volume 4, No. 4, pp. 164–6

Gage, J., *The History and Antiquities of Hengrave in Suffolk* (London, 1822)

Garner, E.H. and Archer, M., *English Delftware* (London, 1972)

Gentle, R. and Field, R., *English Domestic Brass, 1610–1800* (London, 1975)

Griffiths, Jeremy and Edwards, A.S.G., *The Tollemache Book of Secrets*, The Roxburghe Club (2001)

Grimwade, M.E. (compiler), Serjeant, W.R. and R.K. (eds), *Index of the Probate Records of the Court of the Archdeacon of Sudbury, 1354–1700*, Volume I: A–K, Volume II: L–Z, British Record Society (1984)

Halliwell, J.O., *Dictionary of Archaisms and Provincialisms*, 2 volumes (London, 1872)

Hardyment, C., *Home Comfort: a History of Domestic Arrangements* (London, 1992)

Hardyment, C., *Behind the Scenes: Domestic Arrangements in Historic Houses* (London, 1997)

Harris, J., 'The Prideaux collection of topographical drawings', *Architectural History*, Volume 7, 1964, pp. 17; 19–21; 23–9; 41–108

Hartley, D., *Food in England* (London, 2012)

Harvey, J., *Early Gardening Catalogues* (Chichester, 1972)

Harvey, J., *Early Nurserymen* (Chichester, 1974)

Harvey, J., *Mediaeval Craftsmen* (London, 1975)

Henderson, P., *The Tudor House and Garden* (New Haven and London, 2005)

Hobhouse, P., *Plants in Garden History* (London, 2004)

Hole, C., *The English Housewife in the 17th Century* (London, 1953)

Jourdain, M., *English Decoration and Furniture of the Early Renaissance, 1500–1650* (London, 1924)

Kerridge, E., *Textile Manufactures in Early Modern England* (Manchester, 1985)

Lamb, P., *Royal Cookery: or, the complete court-cook containing the choicest receipts in all the particular branches of cookery now in use in the Queen's palaces, to which are added bills of fare for every season in the year.* Eighteenth-Century Collections Online Print (no date)

Laroche, R., 'Catherine Tollemache's library', *Notes and Queries*, June 2006, pp. 157–8.

Lawson, J.A., *The Elizabethan New Year's Gift Exchanges 1559–1603* (Oxford, 2013)

Legge, A.J., *The Ancient Register of North Elmham, 1538–1631* (East Runton, 2008)

Levey, S.M., *Elizabethan Treasures: The Hardwick Hall Textiles* (London, 1999)

Levey, S.M., *The Hardwick Hall Embroideries: a Catalogue* (London, 2007)

Lindsay, S., *Iron and Brass Implements of the English House* (London, 1964)

MacCulloch, D., *Suffolk and the Tudors: Politics and Religion in an English County 1500–1600* (Oxford, 1986)

Mabey, R., *The Gardener's Labyrinth, Thomas Hill: the first English Gardening Book* (Oxford, 1987)

Mercer, H.C., *Ancient Carpenters' Tools* (Mineaola, New York, 2000)

Montgomery, Florence M., *Textiles in America 1650–1870* (New York, 2007)

Moor, E., *Suffolk Words and Phrases* (1823, reprinted Newton Abbot, 1970)

Moxon, J., *Mechanick Exercises: or the Doctrine of Handy-Works* (1703 edition, reprinted Dedham, Mass., USA, 2009)

Murdoch, T. (ed.), *Noble Households: Eighteenth-Century Inventories of Great English Houses: a Tribute to John Cornforth* (Cambridge, 2006)

Ogilvie's Imperial Dictionary of the English Language, new edition edited by C. Annandale, 4 volumes (London, 1855)

Oswald, A., 'Helmingham Hall, Suffolk ' (parts I–V), *Country Life* 1956: 9 August, pp. 282–5; 16 August, pp. 332–5; 23 August, pp. 378–81; 27 September, pp. 656–9; 4 October, pp. 712–15

Ozell, J., *M. Misson's Memoirs and Observations in his Travels over England, written originally in French and translated by Mr Ozell* (London, 1719)

Paston-Williams, S., *The Art of Dining* (London, 1993)

Paston-Williams, S., *A Book of Historical Recipes* (London, 1995)

Payne Collier, J., *Household Books of John, Duke of Norfolk and Thomas, Earl of Surrey, temp. 1481–1490*, The Roxburghe Club, 1844

Peachey, S. (ed.), *Murrell's Two Books of Cookery and Carving* (Bristol, 1993)

Peachey, S., *Cooking Techniques and Equipment 1580–1660*, 2 volumes (Bristol, 1994)

Podd, S., 'Helmingham Park – a complex development', *PSIAH*, 42 (2009), pp. 38–58

Rackham, O., *Trees and Woodland in the British Landscape* (London, 1993)

Reed, M.A. (ed.), *The Ipswich Probate Inventories, 1583–1631*, SRS, 22, 1979

Rogers, J.E. Thorold, *A History of the Agriculture and Prices in England from the Year after the Oxford Parliament (1259) to the Commencement of the Continental War (1793)*, Volume VI, 1583–1702 (Oxford, 1887)

Roundell, Mrs C., 'The Tollemaches of Bentley; the Tollemaches of Helmingham; Helmingham Hall', *PSIA* 12 (1904), pp. 97–128

Rowell, C. (ed.), *Ham House: 400 years of Collecting and Patronage* (New Haven, 2013)

Sambrook, P.A., and Brears, P., *The Country House Kitchen 1650–1900* (Stroud, 2010)

Sandon, E., *Suffolk Houses* (Woodbridge, 1977)

Saunders, J.B., *Mozley and Whiteley's Law Dictionary*, 8th edition (London, 1970)

Scott, S.D., 'Anthony Viscount Montague's Book of Orders and Rules 1595', *Sussex Archaeological Collections* 7, 1854, pp. 173–212

Shaw, W. A. (ed.), *The Knights of England*, Volume 2 (London, 1906)

Smith, A. (consultant ed.), *The Country Life International Dictionary of Clocks* (New York, 1979)

Spring, J., 'The medical recipe book of the Spring family', *Suffolk Review*, 38, 2002, pp. 1–14

Starkey, D. (ed.), *The Inventory of Henry VIII: The Transcript*, Volume 1 (London, 1998)

Steer, F.W., 'The inventory of Arthur Coke of Bramfield, 1629', *PSIA* 25 (1951), pp. 264–87

Stuart, R., *The Dairy 1580–1660* (Bristol, 2000)

Swynfen Jervis, S., *British and Irish Inventories* (Furniture History Society, 2010)

Synge, L., *Antique Needlework* (Poole, 1982)

Thornton, P. and Tomlin, M. (eds), 'The furnishing and decoration of Ham House', *Furniture History* 16, 1980

Ticehurst, N.F., *The Mute Swan in England: its History and the Ancient Custom of Swan-Keeping* (London, 1957)

Tollemache, E.D.H., *The Tollemaches of Helmingham and Ham* (Ipswich, 1949)

Whittle, Jane and Griffiths, Elizabeth, *Consumption and Gender in the Early Seventeenth-Century Household* (Oxford, 2013)

Wilson, A.C. (ed.), *The Country House Kitchen Garden 1600–1950* (Stroud, 2003)

Wilson, A.C. (ed.), *Banquetting Stuffe* (Edinburgh, 1991)

Wilson, D., *Moated Sites* (Princes Risborough, 1985)

Woolgar, C.M., *Household Accounts from Medieval England* (Part I), Records of Social and Economic History, new series, 17 (London, 1992)

Worsley, L., *If Walls Could Talk: an Intimate History of the Home* (London, 2011)

Wyllie, B., *Sheffield Plate* (London, 1913)

Yaxley, D., *A Researcher's Glossary of Words found in Historical Documents of East Anglia* (Dereham, 2003)

Young, F. (ed.), *Rookwood Family Papers, 1606–1761*, SRS 59 (2016)

WEB RESOURCES

Calendar of State Papers Domestic, Charles II, 1671, edited by F.H. Blackburne Daniell (London, 1895), pp. 213–89, accessed via British History Online: http://www.british-history.ac.uk

Nancy Cox and Karin Dannehl, *Dictionary of Traded Goods and Commodities 1550–1820* (Wolverhampton, 2007), online database accessed via British History Online: http://www.british-history.ac.uk

Oxford Dictionary of National Biography Online

Oxford English Dictionary Online

James Finlay Weir Johnston, *Lectures on the Applications of Chemistry and Geology to Agriculture*, 1844, accessed via archive.org: https://archive.org/details/lecturesonapp.li00johngoog

INDEX OF PEOPLE AND PLACES

Allington, Elizabeth (née Tollemache) 81, 199, 201
Allington, William, later Lord Allington 81, 190 n.1, 199
Arlington, 1st Earl of *see* Bennett, Henry

Bai[gh]ton, Bayton 66, 170
Baldry, Andrew 144–5 n.35
Balls 57, 93
BARDWELL 191, 194
Barnes, John 194
BARNHAM 211
BARNINGHAM 211, 207 n.33
Bedingfeld, Sir Henry 201–3
Bedwell, William 185
Bell, Mr 25, 166
Bennett, Henry, 1st Earl of Arlington 211–12
BENTLEY xxii n.43
BETHLEM HOSPITAL xxvii, 57–8 n.30
Bokenham, Anthony 117, 122, 179, 180
Bokenham, Bridget *see* Prideaux
Brereton, Thomas xxi Plate 1, xxxi, xxxiii, 157, 158 Plate 12, 159 Plate 13, 160 Plate 14, 161 Plate 15, 162 Plate 16, 164–6, 175–8, 181, 187–9
Brown, Lancelot ('Capability') 212
Buckenham, linen weavers 37, 37–8 n.79
Bullok, William 35
Burgis the glazier 209
BURY ST EDMUNDS xvi, xxiii, 196, 208 n.39, 213

CALABORS, Fakenham Magna 194, 195 Plate 21
Callow, Goodman 210
CAMBRIDGESHIRE 204
Carteret, Grace *see* Tollemache
Carver 71, 75, 198
Catchpo[o]le xx, 101
Cautley & Barefoot 153 n.3
Cavendish, Henrietta *see* Tollemache
Cavendish, Thomas 15

Charles I, King 114, 150, 203–5
Charles II, King 48 n.14, 190 n.3, 205, 211
Cheere, Henry xxxvi
Cicely, Mistress 19, 165
Clark, James 185
Coke, Arthur xx
COLDHAM HALL xix
Cooke, Holofernes 191, 193–4, 196
Cromwell, Catherine *see* Tollemache
Cromwell, Edward, 3rd Baron Cromwell of Oakham (d. 1607) xxiv, 41, 43 n.96
Cromwell, Henry, 2nd Baron Cromwell of Oakham (d. 1592) xxiii, 33 n.57, 42 n.92, 204 n.24
Cromwell, Mary (née Paulet) wife of Henry, 2nd Lord Cromwell (d. 1592) 33 n.57, 42 n.91, n.92
Cromwell, Thomas, Baron Cromwell of Oakham, Earl of Essex (d. 1540) xxiii

Dennish, J.C. 153, 156 Plate 10, 157, 187 Plate 18, 188–9
Desmond, Earl of *see* Feilding, George
Doe, Thomas 193
Downing 103
Dysart, Countess of *see* Tollemache, Elizabeth
Dysart, Countess of *see* Tollemache, Grace née Carteret
Dysart, Countess of see Tollemache, Grace née Wilbraham
Dysart, 1st Earl of *see* Murray, William
Dysart, 2nd Earl of *see* Tollemache, Sir Lionel [d. 1669]
Dysart, 3rd Earl of *see* Tollemache, Sir Lionel [d. 1728]
Dysart, 4th Earl of *see* Tollemache, Sir Lionel [d. 1770]

Eburne, Dr Andrew 202
Elizabeth I, Queen xvi, xviii, xxiii, 28, 42, 44, 216, 281, 301, 310

ERISWELL 191
EUSTON xxviii, 117, 190, 196, 205,
210–13
Evelyn, John 117, 205, 212

FAKENHAM MAGNA [FAKENHAM]
xvi-xviii, xx, xxv, xxvi-viii, 46–7,
51, 55–7, 65–6, 68, 69 n.50, 70, 71,
73 n.56, 74, 77, 78 n.72, 79–81, 87
n.87, 88, 90 Plate 3, 92, 95, 99, 101,
103 n.132, n.133, 104, 106, 172,
190–213, 230, 241, 245, 266, 287,
293, 305, 309, 313
FAKENHAM PARVA [LITTLE FAKEN-
HAM] 190, 212
Feilding, Bridget (née Stanhope) xxviii, 213
Feilding, George, later Earl of Desmond (d.
1669) xxviii, 205, 211, 213
Fitzroy, Henry, 1st Duke of Grafton 212
FRAMSDEN xxii, xxiv, xxvi, xxvii, 103
n.129, 164 n.8
Frenchman, the 82

George II, King 199–200 n.16, 246
Grafton, 1st Duke of see Fitzroy
Graham, George 132, 246
Gray, Benjamin 132, 246
Gray, Victor 145, 154 Plates 6 and 7, 157
Plate 11
GREAT BARTON 209 n.42

HAM HOUSE, Richmond, Surrey xii,
xvi–ii, xix, xxiv, xxviii, xxxii–v,
134–5 n.3, 145, 184, 185, 190, 205,
212–13, 237, 251, 293, 298, 300
Hamblin, Goodman 211
HARRINGTON, Northamptonshire xvi,
xvii, xxv, xxvi, xxxii, xxxiv, 185
Harvy, Thomas xxvii n.75
Hawkes, William 209
Heasman, Henry 184
HELMINGHAM
brick kiln 101 n.121, 108 n.149, 109
n.150
church xxvi n.72, xxxiv, xxxv, 20, 63
n.37, 117 n.25
Creke Hall 43 n.94, 216
estate xxx, 103 n.129, 107 n.144, 117,
129, 135, 137, 157, 160 Plate 14,
164, 175, 183, 300

gardens and grounds of Hall, xxxvi, 103
n.131, 162 Plate 16, 23, 51 n.22,
108, 151, 166, 167, 174, 175,
176–7, 179, 181, 188–9, 215, 232,
260, 267, 269, 277, 283, 289, 304,
308, 327
manors of xxx, xxxiv, 38 n.80
moats xxi, xxii, xxxvi, 13, 107, 108, 141,
152, 163 Plate 17, 164, 166, 170,
174–5
parish 325
park xxi, xxxi Plate 1, xxxii, xxxiii,
xxxvi, 65, 68 n.45, 74 n.59, 60, 61,
75 n.63, n.64, 104 n.134, 109 n.150,
153 n.5, 170, 172, 176, 189, 245,
248, 290, 295
HELMINGHAM HALL, rooms and
working spaces
apartment 'my Lord lodges in' 124, 180
apricot yard 65, 176, 177
armoury 22 n.40, 27–8, 69 n.49,
75–6, 113, 166–7, 171–2, 181, 188,
215–16
backhouse. bakehouse 12, 97, 164, 185,
188, 231
barn for corn 102, 174
billiard room 147, 148, 184, 186, 225
black velvet room 26, 55, 121–2, 180,
325
Bokenham's room 117, 122, 179, 180
bolting, boulting bulting house, see also
flour room and also meal house
11–12, 97, 178, 228, 234
brewhouse 12, 27, 62, 98–9, 107, 118–19,
129, 141, 153 n.4, 164, 166, 170,
174–5, 179, 181, 182, 184–5
butler's pantry 139, 184, 185 n.23
buttery 5–6, 15 n.29, 88 n.91, 96, 173
cart house 106, 174
cellars 6, 89, 143, 158, 164, 167, 173,
181, 185
chamber [excludes closets to and inner
rooms to], bakehouse, over 150,
188
Balls' 57 n.18
Bayton's 25, 66, 166, 170
Bell's (Mr) 25, 166
best 15–16, 55–6, 165, 169
butler's 26, 166
candle 21 n.39, 127, 165

Cicely's (Mistress) 19, 165
cook's 27, 166
corner (or gable end) 16, 65, 60 n.32,
   170, 177
crimson taffeta 59–60, 169
dairymaid's 72, 171
dining chamber, dining room 51 n.23,
   54–5, 124, 130 n.43, 137 n.13, 165,
   168–9, 180, 184
drying 21, 73, 128, 151 n.42, 165, 171,
   180, 188, 283
fish 99–100, 174
gardener's 151, 188
going into garden 23, 51, 166, 177
great 52, 169
green 17–18, 67–8, 165, 170
groom's 73, 172
Humfery's 74–5, 172
husbandmen's 26, 66–7, 170
Johnson's (Mr) 61–2, 169
kitchen, over 127, 180
kitchener's 25, 166
Lady's 69–71, 171
laundry, over 128, 180
Lord's 52–3, 168
Lord's and Lady's 144, 185
maid's 20, 71–2
Master's 18–19, 48–50
middle 17, 165
new 48, 58–9, 149
Nunn's 65, 74
pantries, over 128
red, hang'd with red paper, red room
   122
Riseing's (Mr) 62, 169
Seaman's 62, 170
Smith, Smythe's (George) 26, 166
steward's 64, 170
three-bed 24, 166
Tollemache, Mr Edward's 57–8, 169
Tollemache, Mr Robert's 63–4, 170
two-bed 17, 165
working 20, 165
Wyeth's (Lionel) 25, 166
yellow taffeta 60, 169
young ladies 126–7, 180
cheesehouse, cheese chamber 11, 96,
   119–20, 161–2, 173, 179
clock-house, -room, -stairs, -tower 57–8,
   130, 148, 169, 181, 186

coach house 103, 131, 152, 174, 181, 188
court[yard], *see also* yard 47 n.10, 48
   n.14, 61, 89 n.93, 107, 157 Plate
   11, 153, 162 Plate 16, 163 Plate 17,
   175, 177, 187 Plate 18, 188–9
Courtoy's room 135, 183
dairy 9–11, 93–6, 101, 119–20, 128, 142,
   161–2, 173, 179–80, 185
dovehouse 108, 175, 299
drawing room, long drawing room 115,
   117, 123, 136, 137, 179, 183, 184,
   189
dressing room 132, 133 Plate 5, 144, 168,
   182, 185
entry, the 65, 166, 170
flour room, *see also* boulting house *and*
   meal house 141, 185
footman's room, *see also* porter's lodge
   151, 179, 183, 188
fowlhouse, hen-house, poultry house 13,
   97, 119, 164, 174
gallery, brushing gallery, long gallery 22,
   69, 144–7, 165, 171–2, 185–6
garret 61, 75, 102, 129, 169, 172, 174,
   181
gatehouse, gatehouse chamber 24, 60,
   63, 120, 166, 169, 170, 179, 180,
   183, 186
greasehouse, *see also* lard house 96, 173
hall, great hall xxiv, xxix, 3, 45–6, 113,
   138, 157 Plate 11, 158–9, 167, 178,
   180–1, 184
hawks' mew 69, 170–1
hogs' troughs 106, 174
housekeeper's store 113, 142 n.30, 179,
   184
Humfery's house 75, 172
husbandmen's hall 9, 92, 161
husbandmen's storehouse 104, 174
kitchen 7, 89–92, 110–111, 139–141,
   159, 163 Plate 17, 173, 176, 178,
   180, 184
larder, dry, wet 9, 92, 119, 143, 161, 173,
   185
lard house, *see also* greasehouse 11, 96
   n.109, 161–2, 173
laundry 10 n.18, 93 n.104, 119, 128 n.39,
   161, 179, 188
library 50 n.19, 134, 182, 183
little stucco room 136, 183

meal house, *see also* boulting house *and see also* flour room 97, 174
mill, millhouse, millhouse chamber 13, 100, 101, 131, 164, 174, 181, 292
music parlour 51, 168
nursery 71–2, 149–50, 165, 171, 186
old man's parlour 22–3, 165
pantry, pantries 87, 88, 120, 128, 173, 180, 184
parlour, great parlour 22–3, 36 n.72, 50, 115, 137–8, 158, 165, 166–8, 179, 184, 189
pastry 8, 14 n.27, 91, 112, 160, 184
peewit's, puet's house 106, 174
pheasant yard 108, 175
porter's lodge, chamber, *see also* footman's room 26–7, 63, 166, 170, 179, 183, 188
pump house 107, 175
roof 34 n.63, 69 n.49, 78 n.72, 103 n.129, 149 n.108, 163 Plate 17, 166–7, 168, 169, 171–3
saddle house 102, 152, 174
scullery 91, 112, 173, 178, 184
servants' hall 112, 141, 178, 185
slaughterhouse 105–6, 174
soap house 21, 127 n.37, 165
spaniels' kennel 101, 174
square room, new 149, 186
stable, stable chamber 27, 102, 151, 166, 172, 174, 181, 188
stairs, staircase 51, 53, 62, 69, 72, 76 n.71, 88 n.90, 113, 136–7, 144, 149, 156 Plate 10, 168–171, 178, 180, 184–6
still, stilling yard 14, 21 n.39, 96–7, 164, 174
steward's room, storehouse 6 n.10, 64, 142
storehouse, store closet 112, 173, 178
swill house 106, 174
verjuice house 9, 92, 161, 173
wardrobe xx, 28–34, 55 n.26, 69, 76–85, 166–7, 171–3, 178, 181, 188
woodroom 129, 181
work house 105, 174
yard, *see also* courtyard 13, 46, 107–8, 131, 159 Plate 13, 164, 175–6, 181
HENGRAVE 14 n.27

HONINGTON 193 n.9, 196, 211
HOPTON 208 n.38
Humfery 74–5, 83, 172, 245, 248
Hunt, Francis 209

INGHAM 194
IPSWICH xxii n.43, xxxi n.72, xxvii n.74, xxviii, xxx, 35, 136, 145, 153, 156 Plate 10, 204, 325
IXWORTH 190, 191, 196

Jacob, Richard 194
James I, King xvi, xxiv, 43 n.93, 43 n.96, 204
Jermyn, Robert, later Sir Robert xxiii
Jermyn, Susan, *see* Spring
Johnson, Mr 61, 169
Jones, John 185
Jones, Roger 28–9 n.54, 271
Joyce family 43, 44, 216, 310

Kent, William 212
KETTLEBURGH 62
Kirby and Company 144–5 n.35
Kirby, John 136 n.11, 147, 280, 291, 298
Kirby, Joshua 136 n.11, 139 n.19, 144–5 n.35, 183

Lacy 105
Lane, Dorothy *see* Tollemache
Lauderdale, John, 2nd Earl, later 1st Duke of *see* Maitland
Lawson, Jane A. xviii n.24
Lay, Robert 182
LONDON xvi, xvii n.19, 67, 95, 199 n.16, 205
LOPHAM, NORTH 37–8 n.79
LOPHAM, SOUTH 37–8, n.79
LUGDONS, LAGDOWNES, Fakenham Magna xvi, 190–1, 193–4, 196, 213, 266

Maitland, John, 2nd Earl, later 1st Duke of Lauderdale xvii n.15, xix n.29, xxix
Martin[e], Archinwald 193
MENDLESHAM 167 n.9
MILDENHALL 213
MONK SOHAM 38 n.80
Moore, Edmund 74 n.60

Morris, Mr 128
Moxon, Joseph 48 n.14
Murray, Elizabeth, Countess of Dysart *see* Tollemache
Murray, William, 1st Earl of Dysart (d. 1655) xvi

NEWMARKET 204
NORTH ELMHAM, Norfolk xxiii, 199 n.16, 204
NORFOLK RECORD OFFICE 204
NORWICH CATHEDRAL 117 n.25
Nunn, John 65, 68, 74, 172, 177, 197, 245
Nunn, William 80

OXBOROUGH, Norfolk 202
OXBURGH HALL 201–2, 204 n.25
Ozell, John 113 n.9

PAKENHAM xxiii, 199 n.16
PARIS, France 190 n.1, 212
Partridge, Affabel 41 n.92
Paulet, Mary *see* Cromwell
PECKFORTON CASTLE, Cheshire xvii n.21
Peirson 82
Pettit, John 185
Podd, Stephen 13 n.24, 74 n.59, n.60, 153 n.5
Prideaux, Bridget (née Bokenham) 117 n.25
Prideaux, Edmund 117 n.25
Prideaux, Humphrey 117 n.25

Riseing, Mr 62, 169
Rookwood, Edward 194
Rookwood, Elizabeth xix
Rouse, Thomas 191, 194, 213
Rushbrook, Thomas 194

Salisburie, Salisbury, John 209
Sanders, [carpenter] 178 n.14
SAPISTON 194, 196, 211
Scott, Scote, William 209
Seaman 62, 68, 170
Shead[e], Sheath[e] 207 n.33
Sherwode 68
Smythe, George 57 n.29, 64 n.38, 53 n.71, 105 n.135, 106 n.136, 166, 169, 171, 215, 273, 275, 295, 297, 311, 313
Spring, Bridget *see* Wingfield

Spring, Lady Susan (formerly Tollemache née Jermyn) xxii, xxiii, 42 n.91, 199 n.16
Spring, Sir William xxiii, 40 n.87, n.88
Stanhope, Bridget *see* Feilding
Stanhope, Charles, 2nd Baron of Harrington, Northamptonshire xvii
Stanhope, Elizabeth *see* Tollemache
Stanhope, John, 1st Baron Stanhope of Harrington [d. 1621] xvi, xxv, xxvi
Stanhope, Sir Michael [d. 1621] xxvi, xxviii
Swynfen Jervis, Simon xi, xix

THETFORD, Norfolk xvi, 190–1, 196, 204, 206–7, 211
Ticehurst, N.F. 203 n.22, n.23
TILBURY CAMP, Essex xxiii, 6 n.9, 22 n.40, 27–8, n.52
Tollemache, Anne (b. 1589) 33, 59
Tollemache, Anne (b. 1619) Plate III, xvii n.75
Tollemache, Lady Catherine (née Cromwell) (?1557–1621) Plate I, xxi, xxii-iii, xxvi, xxviii, 14, 28 n.54, 33 n.57, 40–41, n.88, 57 n.30, 144–5 n.35, 165, 199, 214–15, 235, 237, 249, 262, 268, 271, 281, 284, 299, 312, 315–17, 328
Tollemache, Catherine (b. 1586) 33 n.58
Tollemache, Dorothy (née Lane) 63
Tollemache, Edward (b. 1596) xxii, xxiv, xxvii, 34 n.62, 41–3, 57, 63 n.37, 169
Tollemache, Elizabeth (b. 1615) Plate III
Tollemache, Elizabeth (b. 1621), *see* Allington
Tollemache, Elizabeth (née Murray), Countess of Dysart (d. 1698) xvii n.15
Tollemache, Elizabeth (née Stanhope) (d. 1643) xvi, xxv, xxvi, 18, 69 n.50, 70 n.51, 113 n.10, 172, 199 n.16
Tollemache, Elizabeth *see* Allington
Tollemache, Grace (née Carteret) (1713–1755) xxxii, xxxiii
Tollemache, Grace (née Wilbraham) (d. 1740) xvii, xxxiii
Tollemache, Henrietta née Cavendish (d. 1718), xxx
Tollemache, John (d. in infancy, 1581) xxiii
Tollemache, John, 1st baron xvii n.21, xxvii n.75

Tollemache, Katherine (b. 1617), Plate III

Tollemache, Sir Lionel, 1st baronet (d. 1612) xv, xvi, xx n.35, xxii-v, 3 n.2, 5 n.5, 6 n.9, 18 n.33, 19 n.34, 22 n.40, 23 n.44, 27 n.52, 28 n.56, 33 n.56, 40 n.87, 41 n.90, 43 n.93, 144–5 n.35, 156, 165, 215, 269, 279

Tollemache, Sir Lionel, 2nd baronet (d. 1640) Plate II, xvi, xxiv, xxv, xxvi, xxvii 113 n.10, xxviii, 40 n.87, n.89, 42–3, 47 n.12, 48 n.16, 49 n.17, 52 n.24, 57 n.30, 69 n.50, 81 n.79, 83 n.81, 113 n.10, n.11, 156, 168–9, 172, 190–1, 193–4, 199 n.201–4, 212–13, 266

Tollemache, Sir Lionel, 3rd baronet, 2nd Earl of Dysart (d. 1669) Plate III, xvi, xxviii, xxix, 190, 196, 205, 210, 211–13.

Tollemache, Sir Lionel, 4th baronet and 3rd Earl of Dysart (d. 1727) Plate IV, xvii, xxix, xxxiii, 111 n.14, 156, 284

Tollemache, Sir Lionel, 5th baronet and 4th Earl of Dysart (d. 1770) Plate V, xvii, xxxii, 15, 156

Tollemache, Lionel, Lord Huntingtower (d. 1712) xvii, xxx, xxxiii

Tollemache, Mary (1585–1667) 33 n.57

Tollemache, Richard Plate VI, 107 n.144, 135 n.9, 157, 160 Plate 14, 163 Plate 17, 164, 175, 183

Tollemache, Robert (b. 1592) xxiv, 34, 63, 93 n.106, 170

Tollemache, Susan (b. 1583) xxiii, xxxiii n.49, n.50, xxvi, 33, 33 n.56

Tollemache, Susan (b. 1621) Plate III, xxvii n.75

Tollemache, Susan (née Jermyn) see Spring

Tollemache, Timothy, 5th baron (b. 1939) xv

Tompion, Thomas 246

Turner 213

Vulliamy, Francois Justin 246

Watts, Goodman 211

Watts, Thomas 208

Wel[l]ham, Wellam 208

Wilbraham, Grace see Tollemache

William, King 117 n.25

Wilstar, I.I. de 202 n.21

Winchester, Marquess of 40–41, n.88

Winchester, Marquis of 57 n.33

Wingfield, Bridget (née Spring) 40–41 n.88

Wingfield, Sir Robert 40, 43 n.95

WOODHEY, Cheshire xvii

Worsley, Lucy 200 n.17

Wyeth, Wieth, Lionel 25 n.47, 38

THE SUFFOLK RECORDS SOCIETY

For over sixty years, the Suffolk Records Society has added to the knowledge of Suffolk's history by issuing an annual volume of previously unpublished manuscripts, each throwing light on some new aspect of the history of the county.

Covering 700 years and embracing letters, diaries, maps, accounts and other archives, many of them previously little known or neglected, these books have together made a major contribution to historical studies.

At the heart of this achievement lie the Society's members, all of whom share a passion for Suffolk and its history and whose support, subscriptions and donations make possible the opening up of the landscape of historical research in the area.

In exchange for this tangible support, members receive a new volume each year at a considerable saving on the retail price at which the books are then offered for sale.

Members are also welcomed to the launch of the new volume, held each year in a different and appropriate setting within the county and giving them a chance to meet and listen to some of the leading historians in their fields talking about their latest work.

For anyone with a love of history, a desire to build a library on Suffolk themes at modest cost and a wish to see historical research continue to thrive and bring new sources to the public eye in decades to come, a subscription to the Suffolk Records Society is the ideal way to make a contribution and join the company of those who give Suffolk history a future.

THE CHARTERS SERIES

To supplement the annual volumes and serve the need of medieval historians, the Charters Series was launched in 1979 with the challenge of publishing the transcribed texts of all the surviving monastic charters for the county. Since that date, nineteen volumes have been published as an occasional series, the latest in 2011.

The Charter Series is financed by a separate annual subscription leading to receipt of each volume on publication.

CURRENT PROJECTS

Volumes approved by the council of the Society for future publication include *Crown Pleas of the Suffolk Eyre of 1240,* edited by Eric Gallagher, *The Woodbridge Troop of the Suffolk Yeomanry, 1794–1818,* edited by Margaret Thomas, *Loes and Wilford Old Poor Law Records*, edited by John Shaw, and *Monks Eleigh Manorial Documents*, edited by Vivienne Aldous; and in the Charters Series, *The Charters of the Priory of St Peter and St Paul, Ipswich*, edited by David Allen, *Bury St Edmunds Town Charters*, edited by Vivien Brown, and *Rumburgh Priory Charters*, edited by Nicholas Karn. The order in which these and other volumes appear in print will depend on the dates of completion of editorial work.

MEMBERSHIP

Membership enquiries should be addressed to Mrs Tanya Christian, 8 Orchid Way, Needham Market, IP6 8JQ; e-mail: suffolkrecordssociety@gmail.com

The Suffolk Records Society is a registered charity, No. 1084279.